GAY RELIGION

GAY RELIGION

EDITED BY
SCOTT THUMMA
AND EDWARD R. GRAY

ALTAMIRA PRESS
A Division of Rowman & Littlefield Publishers, Inc.
Walnut Creek • Lanham • New York • Toronto • Oxford

ALTAMIRA PRESS
A division of Rowman & Littlefield Publishers, Inc.
1630 North Main Street, #367
Walnut Creek, CA 94596
www.altamirapress.com

Rowman & Littlefield Publishers, Inc.
A wholly owned subsidiary of The Rowman & Littlefield Publishing Group, Inc.
4501 Forbes Boulevard, Suite 200
Lanham, MD 20706

PO Box 317
Oxford
OX2 9RU, UK

British Library Cataloguing in Publication Information Available

Library of Congress Cataloging-in-Publication Data

Gay religion / edited by Scott Thumma and Edward R. Gray.
    p. cm.
    Includes bibliographical references and index.
    ISBN 0-7591-0325-9 (hardcover : alk. paper) — ISBN 0-7591-0326-7 (pbk. : alk. paper)
    1. Gays—Religious life—United States. 2. Homosexuality—Religious aspects. I. Thumma, Scott, 1957- II. Gray, Edward R., 1958-

    BL625.9.G39G39 2005
    200'.86'64—dc22

2004007018

Printed in the United States of America

⊗™ The paper used in this publication meets the minimum requirements of American National Standard for Information Sciences—Permanence of Paper for Printed Library Materials, ANSI/NISO Z39.48–1992.

CONTENTS

Foreword

WILLIAM McKINNEY AND MARY A. TOLBERT

AY RELIGION MARKS A WATERSHED in the study of lesbian, gay, bisexual,
and transgender (LGBT) religious experience in contemporary American
society. Rather than understanding the relationship between LGBT people and religion as a problem to be debated, which so much other literature seems
to assume, this volume recognizes the richly diverse religious experiences of gay
people as a new and as yet unmapped resource in the history of American religious expression. Gay religion, as discussed in this volume, is a cross section of the
cornucopia of modern American spirituality. Like other religious people in
the United States, gay men, lesbians, bisexuals, and transgendered people seek sol-
ace for their souls in a dazzling array of institutional religions and noninstitu-
tional spiritual practices. For some, erotic experience itself becomes the golden
pathway to spiritual awakening and expression, much like the spiritual pilgrimage
of some of the saints of early and medieval Christianity.

By emphasizing the diversity and richness of gay religious experience, this volume challenges the current public discourse around religion and LGBT people.
Despite popular opinion, gay people are not foreign to religious communities,
even quite conservative or fundamentalist religious communities. LGBT people
are and have been active members and leaders of widely diverse communities of
faith for decades, indeed centuries. Perhaps because the rhetoric of some conservative religious groups has vilified gay people so loudly, many Americans believe
that gay people stand outside of religious life entirely or are, perhaps, actively antireligious. While that view might possibly describe some LGBT people who have
rightly identified conservative religious groups as the primary obstacle to civil and
social justice for gay people, there are many others, whose voices are heard in this
volume, who reject the narrowness and exclusive theology of conservatives yet still

embrace the beliefs and practices of those religious traditions. For them, the fight with conservative Christians is not only political and social, it is also theological and biblical. Even when contemporary fundamentalist groups have attempted to shut the door against their openly gay members, those members have insisted on opening windows of communication and continuing identification with their conservative religious homes. As this volume clearly witnesses, gay people can truly be found everywhere in American religion. From Christian fundamentalism to mainline denominations to New Age religious practices, gay people, like many others in American culture today, are experimenting with the great variety of religious forms available to them.

Gay Religion is more than a sophisticated mapping of the presence of LGBT persons in religious organizations; it is also a reminder of the inherent adaptability of religious forms in the American experience. We see that as self-identified gay people come out and insist on full participation in existing religious institutions, many of those institutions show a remarkable ability to adapt and change in the light of the new voices in their midst. In much the same way, the religious marketplace itself changes as new religious communities emerge. In what may be the most provocative and controversial argument in this book, the authors suggest that gay people are also redefining the meaning of being religious in popular culture.

Gay Religion is an important contribution not only to the growing field of LGBT or queer studies but also to the sociological and ethnographic study of religion. As America and other nations become more religiously diverse and new spiritualities emerge within, alongside, and outside established faith communities, understanding the dynamics of religious change becomes critically important. This volume provides new vistas for analyzing those dynamics across a wide spectrum of religious institutions and spiritual practices.

It may be that society will someday look back and wonder why a book like this was needed; that is, why gay religious practices would need to be singled out and lifted up from American religious practices generally. While we hope the day will come when all people achieve the full equality in religious communities that we believe gay people enjoy in the eyes of God, we suspect the unique spiritual experience of the LGBT community is often unacknowledged and perhaps even unknown to many contemporary religious people in the wider world. This volume begins to fill that important political, educational, and spiritual gap. We certainly cannot know the future, but this important book is an excellent guide to the present.

Introduction

EDWARD R. GRAY AND SCOTT THUMMA

SELDOM DOES A DAY PASS that the news services do not contain a story high-lighting debates over the place of gay and lesbian believers in American re-ligious life. Whether these stories discuss the viability of homosexuality as a Christian lifestyle, one church's acceptance of gays and lesbians as clergy or bish-ops, or the protests of a gay rights group at a major denominational gathering, it seems that the nation's press and the public's attention are captivated by accounts of conflict between religious entities and gay men, lesbians, bisexual, and trans-gender individuals (LGBT). Yet within this media attention, one is hard pressed to find positive stories of gay religious life or tales of organizations harmoniously merging homosexuality and religion. Yet these stories abound. Supportive religious groups have flourished, though underreported in the media, from the beginning of the gay rights movement in the 1960s.

Likewise, in the academic arena, researchers and scholars have spent consider-able effort on the necessary tasks of apologetics and the construction of a gay or queer theology or on the historical examination of the debates and conflicts around religion and homosexuality. Within the fields of sociology of religion and contemporary religious studies very little attention has been paid to identifying and exploring the supportive gay religious organizational alternatives being cre-ated. This absence of a significant body of analytical and ethnographic research on gay religious organizations and expressions is not meant as a critique. Gay re-ligion is a relatively new area of spiritual expression. As such it has required con-siderable effort on the more pressing tasks of theological definition and ideological clarification than charting and accounting for the organizational de-velopments. Nevertheless, now that the definitional effort is well underway, schol-arly attention should be turned not just toward the difficulties of establishing a positive gay religious presence in existing institutional forms but also toward the examination of new and inventive forms of religious expression created in support of the diverse gay spiritual life in America.

The essays chosen for inclusion in this volume are meant to contribute to a broadening of our understanding of gay and lesbian religious practice and expression in North America at the beginning of the twenty-first century. As a whole, they paint a much richer and more nuanced portrait of what gay and lesbian groups and individuals are doing to express their religious and spiritual needs, desires, and sensibilities. These essays by social scientists and scholars of religion are compelling examples of (a) revitalization of traditional religious expressions, (b) emergence of new religious communities, and (c) spiritual originality found in new, popularly available alternative choices. Each essay promotes an appreciation of the enduring patterns and innovative impulses in North American religious life. The emergence of a gay and gay-friendly spiritual sphere is explored in these vivid essays from the perspective of particular denominational traditions, sectarian or subaltern groups, or popular culture.

Gay religion in America has been, to date, overshadowed by controversial theological debate within nearly all traditions. This volume is not part of that debate. Instead, it is an attempt to situate gay religion within an explicit theoretical framework. This framework recognizes continuity and innovation on the part of religious groups and individuals as paradigmatically American—even among a group variously persecuted or silenced by religious institutions. This volume, then, is a report on constructive institutional forms of gay religious life as found in denominational groups, subaltern communities, and broader cultural expressions. Likewise, this reporting is not presented as wholly unique but rather is placed within the context of the unfolding story of religious innovation in North America.

The collection aims to highlight particular institutionalized examples of gay spiritual practice rather than attempt a comprehensive or all-inclusive examination of LGBT religiosity. At the same time, we have selected essays that place the phenomena deliberately within and across the American religious narrative. The authors of each of these essays take for granted that some gays are religious and some religious people are gay. This is not ideology, but description. There is nothing new in that statement, except that it is now openly acknowledged by nearly everyone. What is importantly new for scholars of religion—and others—is the availability of a wide range of religious choices for lesbians, gays, bisexual, and transgender persons over the last thirty years (as this volume will bear out). That gay and lesbian persons can now experience the freedom of choice of religious expression in a way like never before—in spite of lingering homophobia and heterosexist privilege in religion—is noteworthy. Placing this development in a wider understanding of religion in America is an important and necessary task. (See the final chapter by Marie Griffith.)

That these supportive gay religious structures have emerged should not be surprising. American religion has always been the expression of groups (Warner 1994). What is interesting about these religious phenomena is the conflicted place lesbians and gay men have in religious traditions. Many still hold a deep alliance to these traditions and struggle to create a place of their own within these institutions. Other lesbians, gay men, bisexuals, and transgenders follow a more sectarian impulse. This leads to the creation of what we call subaltern communities of faith. Still others pursue new forms of spiritual practice outside easily recognized religious structures in popular culture.

Each of these options—revitalizing a tradition, creating a new faith, or finding spiritual fulfillment through popular culture—is a work of commitment. Following a spiritual discipline, being "religious," or even simply being "spiritual" requires making a choice. No longer is faith simply "received," (although some passive reception is still at work). Gay persons—along with everyone else—must find their own way and work out their own salvation with "fear and trembling." Whether gay men and lesbians begin the search near or far from a tradition, today they face a variety of choices from which to construct religious and spiritual beliefs and practices. The countless new choices that have emerged, including innovations such as e-religions, further demonstrate the complexity of modernity's range of spiritual options. Cyber-versions of established religions are now available at our fingertips to be examined, advocated, and embraced. (Brasher 2001)

The detachment of the realm of spirituality from the realm of organized religion, seen in the acceptability of being "spiritual but not religious," offers yet another avenue whereby someone can become a person of faith. Faced with this smorgasbord of faith traditions, gay men, lesbians, and other sexual minority persons must intentionally decide how to be religious, what balance of continuity and innovation they want, when, from whom, and for what ends.

Religious choice is complex and multifaceted for all of us, and even more so for those who are lesbian, gay, bisexual, and transgender seekers or believers. Contributing to the complexity of religious expression by gay persons are the organizational, theological, and cultural constraints placed upon them as nonheterosexual persons. Forty years into the gay rights movement and only a handful of religious groups are unconditionally accepting of gays and lesbians as both full members and potential clergy. However, as this volume demonstrates, gays and lesbians face no lack of options. The possibilities for gay-supportive worship are plentiful, even beyond the cases we examine (see the appendix for a more extensive listing of supportive groups). And while the choices open to these persons of faith may appear to some as if they are strange or exotic, these religious alternatives—this collection shows—are instances of established, enduring patterns of continuity and innovation in North American religious life.

No one religious expression, form, or media fits all heterosexual persons. No one would challenge that. Too often, however, the choices for gay persons have been understood as very bleak: to sit more or less quietly in a tolerant religious group, quit organized religion altogether, or embrace a faith practice that is exclusively homosexual. Previous scholarship has continued to reinforce this (we believe false) framework. Creating one's own medium of religious expression is an American specialty, regardless of sexual orientation. Moreover, establishing innovative practices—and persuading others to adapt them—has an equally American pedigree (Stark 1985: 359). The explorations of gay religion described within this volume show how gays and lesbian are—unsurprisingly, we think—part of a continuing American religious tradition of innovation and continuity.

The plurality of forms and expressions of religion and spirituality for gays represents an innovative turn of both ideological transformation and organizational revitalization. Over the last few decades, exemplary charismatic individuals, and also groups of ordinary believers, have worked to create distinctive gay/lesbian spaces in the religious landscape of the United States. Each of these innovations is distinctively gay but also thoroughly religious. The membership of Dignity, Integrity, and other denominational groups have reached thousands and impacted the polity of nearly all the major religious traditions. Likewise, leaders within the Universal Fellowship of Metropolitan Community Churches have worked to establish the organization as a national denomination. Today, congregations of this predominantly gay denomination have become flagship institutions, alongside the gay bar, of a proud gay community in North American cities. Still other persons create new media of spiritual expression drawing on local culture such as The Gospel Hour, Atlanta's popular drag performance of gospel music.

This volume's essays are reports from these new spiritual precincts. The sometimes daring, always fascinating, and never wholly predictable homesteading of new spiritual expressions is not foreign to the American religious landscape, however. One need only look at the internal revitalization efforts within national denominations based on the restructuring as well as mergers and schisms of earlier clusters of congregations to identify the malleable nature of denominational heritage groups. Likewise, an even cursory investigation of the highly successful homegrown religion the Church of Jesus Christ of Latter-day Saints demonstrates the vitality of sectarian innovation at work. Finally, many recent reports from the field describe a large percentage of Americans as having become deinstitutionalized, eclectic consumers of religious ideas. Whether drawing on New Age practices, nature spirituality, or dozens of other available religious options, there is strong evidence of an increasing trend toward individualistic and generalized cultural expressions of spirituality.

The new gay and lesbian religious expressions described in this volume, like their earlier predecessors on the religious landscape, can be better understood as duplicative of patterns long established in U.S. religion. They parallel the American commitment to denominational life, but also the innovative sectarian impulse as well as a more detached culturally based spirituality (see Stark and Bainbridge 1987; Roof 1993).

This volume brings together various ethnographic and ethnographically-inspired writings on the lived religious expressions of gays and lesbians. Each is a distinct, stand-alone, descriptive exploration of spiritual practices. These accounts are not meant to encompass the whole of LGBT religious life in the United States. Nor are they offered as voyeuristic or exhibitionist renderings of novelty. Rather these accounts demonstrate the depth and breadth of gay religion and spirituality in society today.

The contributors to this volume are as diverse as the phenomena they describe. While all are interested in religious practice, their disciplinary backgrounds encompass sociology, anthropology, history, psychology, and religious studies. They include gay men, lesbians, straight men, and straight women. Their writings are richly descriptive, theoretically informed accounts of both the novel and ordinary religious places gays and lesbians have created. Some of the essays focus more directly on the expressive practices of a group; others delve deeply into stories of individual belief; and a few reflect on ritualized public events or behaviors.

These accounts, taken as a whole, situate gay religion within the larger religious economy of North America. Likewise, the essays demonstrate both enduring patterns and innovative impulses in American religion from the perspective of gay men, lesbians, and other sexual minorities.

These contributions are arranged to reflect the coeditors' typology for understanding gay religion. This typology is neither a self-identification of the persons, groups, or activities reported, nor a selection made by the authors in each case. The volume's typology is a heuristic device for locating the groups and activities reported. This schema is intended to identify gay religion as part of a larger American economy that defines religious tradition within denominational organizations and subaltern communities, and through explicit and implicit expressions of "the religious" in popular culture. This interpretative framework is embedded in a perception of American religion as a dynamic of both innovation and continuity. Following this typology, the volume's contributions are organized into three sections: denominational heritage groups; subaltern communities; and popular culture.

Members of denominational heritage groups hold an allegiance to a particular religious tradition and give priority to this heritage over identification with their sexual orientation. They create gay space in the tradition or seek revitalization within a specific religious denomination or national organization.

Subaltern groups, like those in denominational traditions, are primarily religious organizations. However, they privilege gay identity over preexisting religious tradition. These groups expressly seek a spirituality and organizational form that flows from the gay experience rather than from traditional belief and practices.

Popular culture is not religion at all—at least not explicitly. These events and performances and other popularly available cultural activities do not privilege religious traditions or organizations. Nonetheless, our researchers demonstrate how certain forms of popular culture provide gay persons with new media of individual (if also shared) spiritual expression.

Some contemporary expressions of gay religion are firmly entrenched in traditional religious institutions as they attempt to carve their own spiritual niches. Several efforts are entrepreneurial and pioneering impulses toward the creation of new institutional traditions. Others represent more recent inclinations toward cultural modification and individualistic spiritual practices. Taken together these adaptive changes demonstrate the complexity of religious innovation and revitalization within LGBT religious life as well as the plurality of choice of spiritual practice outside "official" religious structures available to gay and lesbian persons in North America.

A short interpretative essay introduces each section. These introductions attempt to say something synthetic about each of the three areas of gay religion and also briefly summarize the essays that follow. This dialogue between innovation and continuity, new and old paradigms, cultural reproduction and cultural creativity, homogeneity and heterogeneity continues in R. Marie Griffith's concluding essay. As a historian of American religion, Griffith raises challenges to the imposition of categories she sees our typology inadvertently doing. Her chapter, likewise, initiates several productive conversations—about the state of gay studies and its relationship with religious studies, about the use of categories to normalize understandings of sexuality, and other such issues—that we believe this collection of essays will indeed help shape.

DENOMINATIONAL HERITAGE EXPRESSIONS

I

WHEN ONE THINKS OF THE CONTINUITY of religious traditions in the United States, the institutional reality of the denomination comes immediately to mind. The denomination is the quintessential organizational form in American religion.[1]

Although congregations, as voluntary groupings of like-minded individuals, are the local and most immediate expression of faith in the country, they seldom have the organizational complexity to ensure longevity and the perpetuation of a distinctive religious tradition. Denominations, on the other hand, are large-scale collections of congregations under a common name and unified purpose, at least ideally, banded together to do what individual churches cannot accomplish alone.

In addition to being a network of local faith communities, denominations contain bureaucratic layers of committees, departments, managers, and offices of authority to accomplish these larger objectives. Tasks such as operating global missions, performing publishing duties, providing insurance and pensions, setting educational requirements for clergy, and, of course, creating laws that maintain denominational identity boundaries are the usual duties of these national organizations. In short, denominations are the organizational keepers of religious continuity in America.

However, denominations are more than just bureaucratic fortresses; they also symbolize a culture that comprises distinctive theological doctrines, worship rituals, and even an identity that shapes a way of being religious in our society. While there is considerable debate over the extent to which these cultural forms are still salient in the modern world, there is ample evidence that they do still exist (Ammerman 2000).

More than mere names or labels, denominational identifiers are intertwined with status, values, norms, and traditions at a deep personal level for many individuals.

Being Catholic, Lutheran, Baptist, or Pentecostal implies volumes theologically, culturally, and socially, both for those inside and outside the church. These identities draw boundaries not just between cultural traditions but also between forms of ritual practice. More than that, however, these denominational marks provide the substance out of which an individual's religious identity, character, and thought patterns are crafted. Religious life for many Americans is embedded in this denominational identification.

It is fair to say, although little evidence exists to prove it, that the majority of lesbians and gays who are organizationally religious worship within congregations affiliated with national denominational institutions. Likewise, it seems reasonable to assume that the vast majority of LGBT religious persons grew up relating to one of the twenty largest denominations or religious groups, as did more than three-quarters of all Americans. Furthermore, the personal stories in nearly every chapter of this section attest to the deeply ingrained denominational loyalties present. Many of those interviewed expressed the attitude that, even in the face of rejection and theological condemnation, they couldn't think of themselves as anything other than a believer in the denominational tradition in which they were raised.

Given this enduring and deeply imbedded denominational character of American religion, it should come as no surprise that most of the earliest gay religious organizational efforts arose out of mainstream denominations including the Roman Catholic Church, the Episcopal Church, and the Evangelical Lutheran Church of America. Groups such as Dignity (discussed by Primiano in this volume), Integrity, Lutherans Concerned, and others (see appendix) were established in the late 1960s through the mid-1970s in an effort to provide a gay presence and yet create an inclusive space within their particular religious tradition. These organizations often functioned independent of their corresponding denominations, but sought to support LGBT believers, educate the larger denomination, and push for policies that allowed for the full inclusion of gay members.

Even with the considerable heterogeneity of spiritual expression among gays and lesbians in America, much of their religious activity continues to happen within denominational traditions. Unfortunately, the accounts of this activity generally focus on tense national debates and controversial decisions rather than on the progressive strides made in moving these religious organizations toward greater openness and inclusivity. The efforts of these denominationally aligned groups have been pastoral and personally transformative for individuals to be sure, but the groups' existence also characterizes how the large national organizations change and adapt from within through individual actions of revitalization and renewal.

Leonard Primiano, in his exploration of the changes that have taken place in the Dignity chapter of Philadelphia, shows how the group functioned in the lives of individuals to keep them within a Catholic tradition that rejected them. Over time the Dignity chapter became a religious community, a sacred space for them, and eventually could even be viewed as having developed into a gay ethnic Catholic parish.

The challenging perspectives and messages broadcast by these groups brought pressure to bear on the formal theologies and organizational forms of the denominations. In some cases, these groups gained official recognition and voice within their denominations. Organizational units of these denominations such as the United Church of Christ Coalition for LGBT Concerns, Friends for Lesbian and Gay Concerns (Quaker), and the Unitarian Universalist's Office of Lesbian, Gay, Bisexual, and Transgender Concerns all play a prominent role in shaping denominational culture and attitudes from within the official structures.

A number of these religious traditions have had little difficulty incorporating LGBT members into their communities. Groups, such as those just discussed as well as Reform Judaism, the Buddhist tradition, and the Santería religion (see Shokeid's, Cadge's, and Vidal-Ortiz's articles in this volume) have embraced LGBT persons as official and full participants. It is important to note, however, that even within these groups some level of tension with the traditions, especially around issues of marriage and gender norms, is still evident.

Moshe Shokeid, in a chapter entitled "Why Join a Gay Synagogue" from his 1995 work, *A Gay Synagogue in New York,* describes the reasons that members gave for being part of a gay synagogue in New York City. Although Reform Judaism officially has been very receptive of gays and lesbians, the members of Congregation Beth Simchat Torah constantly spoke of their congregation as "home" and experienced an acceptance there that was missing in other Reform congregations.

Wendy Cadge argues in her essay "Lesbian, Gay, and Bisexual Buddhist Practitioners" that in Buddhist practice generally and in local temples she studied very little was made of an individual's sexuality. Although LGBT Buddhists had formed various support groups, a distinct LGBT orientation has played a minor role in Buddhist spiritual practices.

Within the Santería spiritual tradition, Salvador Vidal-Ortiz's chapter entitled "Sexuality and Gender in Santería: LGBT identities at the Crossroads of Santería Religion" shows considerable evidence of a LGBT presence in the religion. His research explores the prominent role gay males in particular have taken in the religion and how, in so doing, they have begun to transform aspects of religious practice from within.

There are other denominations, however, where LGBT support and caucus groups have met considerably more resistance from their religious traditions. As a result of this, within many of these denominations with members having diverse theological perspectives (such as the Presbyterian Church, USA; the United

Methodist Church; and the American Baptist Church), an alternative strategy of incorporation into the tradition can be seen at work. Organizations have formed parallel structures to the denominations in which networks of supportive congregations, parachurch groups, and ministers who have declared themselves "reconciling" or "open and affirming" of full inclusion of LGBT members are sustained.

Wendy Cadge describes two such "reconciling" congregations in her second contribution to this volume titled "Reconciling Congregations Bridging Gay and Straight Communities." One of the congregations she highlights was already quite open to having gays and lesbians in its midst when it decided to vote to become "reconciling." The decision for this group was a natural affirmation of what it already was. The second church she studied took on the task of exploring what it might mean to be "open and affirming" (O&A) as an exercise in identity construction, an effort that stretched over many months. It eventually concluded this process by making the decision to be O&A as an affirmation of what it wanted to become.

These congregationally-based efforts at LGBT inclusion within denominational traditions could be seen as an alternative approach to effect innovation, at a more local level, within a national structure that officially rejects full participation. Although outside official structures, this alternative strategy has, nevertheless, had a profound effect on national denominational dynamics. The exploration of this approach identifies an important truth: that national denominational change is often the result of efforts by individuals or congregations as much as it is by denominational bureaucrats or national convention pronouncements.

Additionally, there are certain traditions within the American religious scene that outright reject any inclusion of LGBT religion within their midst. A large percentage of denominations and religious groups in the country fall within more conservative Evangelical and Fundamentalist theological approaches. For these traditions, yet another strategy of supportive organization has arisen to sustain members of the tradition who want to remain "within the fold." These groups are primarily affective and educational networks made up of individuals who desire to stay within the tradition but want a gay-supportive perspective of their faith tradition. Members of these groups often suffer considerably from the tension with their local congregation and the larger denomination.

In this volume's essay, "No Longer an Oxymoron: Integrating Gay and Lesbian Seventh Day Adventists," René Drumm writes about one such group. She described the difficulties that Seventh-day Adventist gays and lesbians have in struggling with their faith tradition. She goes on to outline a process by which certain Adventist members draw on gay-supportive persons, groups, and resources to finally reconcile their faith and sexuality while remaining within the denomination.

In "Gay Evangelicals: Negotiating a Religious Identity," Scott Thumma traces a similar process for conservative Southern Evangelicals but from the perspective of a supportive organization and its leadership's efforts to provide a context in which this reconciliation could take place. He argues that these denominationally related groups play an important role in helping to create a plausible gay evangelical identity for individuals while also functioning as a mediating structure between an intransient denominational position and the need on the part of believers to remain within that tradition.

Richley Crapo's contribution to the volume, "Latter-day Saint Gay, Lesbian, Bisexual and Transgendered Spirituality," portrays the multiple difficulties faced by LGBT Latter-day Saints in their dealings with the Mormon Church because of both its theology and its emphasis on heterosexual marriage. These support groups may be the only positive rendering of the faith these LGBT members receive.

While not overly influential in effecting change within their larger denominational traditions, these groups do offer innovative twists on the theological perspective of their traditions while also presenting alternative options for living a life of faith within those denominations.

Another organizational entity exists within this theologically conservative strain of Christianity that must be taken into account in a discussion of gay religion in America. This is the movement among various Baptist, Pentecostal, and nondenominational churches to provide a path out of "the gay lifestyle." The primary purpose of such "reparative therapy" groups is to assist individuals to change their sexual thinking, behavior, and, perhaps, orientation. The national network of these semi-independent local ex-gay ministries is called Exodus International and has a sizable presence within the Evangelical Protestant world.

Christy Ponticelli, in her chapter "Shades of Grey or Back to Nature," takes the reader into the ex-gay world from the perspective of the national Exodus organization and a small local support group. Her exploration of what happens within one such group highlights the ambiguity of both the message and the resulting transformation. She argues that it is this ambiguity that makes this an appealing, but often temporary, option for certain gay and lesbian conservative Christians.

Taken together, these essays remind us that national religious organizations and traditions of our society are composed of more than just their official pronouncements and majority opinions. Within any social organization there are divergent perspectives and undercurrents of belief and practice, at odds perhaps with the sanctioned majority view, that deserve the attention of sociologists and historians.

The articles within this denominational heritage section offer considerable evidence that gays and lesbians haven't wholly abandoned the traditional denominational organizations that function as the foundation of the American religious landscape. Rather, these contributions show that certain LGBT persons have expended considerable effort to remain a part of the religious traditions in which they grew up. This seldom comes without personal cost to the individuals. It also often requires the creation of new organizational realities within or parallel to these denominations. However, the efforts of these denominational prophets are not in vain, for in their efforts to create a place within their traditions, they have introduced into the various denominational systems innovations both in structure and in theology that will eventually have profound implications.

Note

1. While the term "denomination" tends to be used to denote Protestant Christian groups, it is being used here in a more generic manner to identify all national religious organizations and traditions including the American Catholic Church. The argument has been made that even religions such as Judaism, Hinduism, and Islam, when in the American context, develop denomination-like structures and functions (Swatos 1998). For additional material on denominations see William Swatos 1998; Bryan Wilson 1959; or David Martin 1962.

The Gay God of the City
The Emergence of the Gay and Lesbian Ethnic Parish

LEONARD NORMAN PRIMIANO

> *We attempt I guess in our worship life to, I hate to say it this way, to function as a parish. We celebrate all the holidays. We try to do it in a meaningful religious kind of way. We don't do off the wall things just to be seen or heard. We try to provide the meaningful experience [realizing] that, although it's in the parish, most gays and lesbians are not comfortable [there]. And because of the real lack of a relationship are not terribly interested in going there for it.*

—THE PRESIDENT OF DIGNITY/PHILADELPHIA, 1988

D URING THE CLOSING DECADES of the twentieth century, lesbian, gay, bisexual, and transgender (LGBT) Roman Catholics in the United States desiring to practice their religion faced a series of complex choices regarding their ecclesial, liturgical, and parish lives. Should they remain members of the traditional parishes where they have always been present, some actively serving on parish councils and liturgy committees, though not publicly expressing themselves as gay or lesbian? Should they seek out the gay Roman Catholic affinity group called "Dignity," which began in 1969 in California (Roche 1995) and gradually spread across the country, often but not always meeting on institutional Church property? Should they engage in binary religious affiliations with both religious communities? Dignity, the "national lay movement of lesbian, gay, bisexual, and transgender [Roman] Catholics, their families and their friends" (Helminiak 1996), has played a significant part in the history of post–Vatican II American Catholicism as one of the most influential of the LGBT religious affinity groups in the United States.[1] Dignity's regional chapters provide not simply counseling services, but also extensive spiritual, educational, and social goals for its members. Members of Dignity retain their traditional Catholic faith and practice and work for the transformation of the Church's sexual morality from one that excludes homosexuals and homosexual sexual activity to a sexual ethic that accounts for what they feel is the reality of the experiences of their lives.

This article concerns the contribution of Dignity chapters to the various configurations of gay and lesbian Catholic congregationalism in America in the last three decades. More specifically, I want to address the conceptualization by some Dignity members within the urban context of Philadelphia, Pennsylvania, that their chapter is a parish, in fact a "gay ethnic parish." Such concepts, I argue, are useful emic models befitting the character of the culture of Catholic Philadelphia, the form that this chapter of Dignity has taken during almost thirty years of development, and the creative negotiations of the tradition by these vernacular Catholics. This historical ethnography is drawn from research on the members of the Dignity chapter in Philadelphia where I have been permitted to do fieldwork for more than fifteen years, from 1986 to 2002 (Primiano 1993a; 1993b; 2001), but concentrates on the developments and ideas of members from the late 1980s.

For those readers unfamiliar with Catholicism, its history in America, and relevant terminology, it is necessary to begin this discussion by explaining what a parish—and especially what an "ethnic" or "national" parish—is and how such congregational entities still mark Catholic life in the city of Philadelphia. A parish itself is a defined community of Catholics established within the specific geographic boundaries of a diocese. The pastoral care of the parish is the responsibility of a priest called its "pastor." The pastor who is to collaborate in his duties with "parishioners and ministers" (McBrien 1995: 963) is appointed by the diocesan bishop. Historically, priests always led parishes, but in contemporary America priest shortages have resulted in nonclerical administrators of parishes.[2] Unlike Protestant Christians, parish membership within institutional Catholicism is not meant to be the decision of a Catholic individual or family. The Church essentially preassigns Catholics to membership in the parish closest to their place of residence.[3]

To meet particular pastoral obligations, a diocesan bishop may request and appoint members of a religious order or congregation to administer a parish. It is, therefore, possible if warranted that "diocesan bishops . . . organize parishes non-territorially, in accordance with special religious or sociocultural needs, like rite, nationality, or language" (McBrien 1995: 958). Such a practice was the case in the late nineteenth and early twentieth centuries in the United States.[4] Specific "ethnic" or "national" parishes were developed at this time in response to the tremendous influx of non-English-speaking European immigrants in cities like Philadelphia, New York, and Chicago with churches built within the ethnic neighborhoods themselves to serve these local communities directly (Dolan 1985: 195–218; Morris 1997: 123–32). Italian-speaking religious orders such as the Scalabrini Fathers, for example, were asked to staff parishes with a majority of ethnic Italian parishioners. This practice was also the case with Polish, Ukrainian, Lithuanian, and other immigrant parishes.[5] This strategy had, in fact, been used earlier in the century in the Midwest with the growth of the German and French Catholic populations in both urban and more rural contexts.

Immigrants were flooded with ethnic expressions at such churches, from hearing relevant sections of daily masses said in their native European language to a constellation of culture-specific paraliturgical and social activities. Don Brophy, reflecting in the Jesuit periodical, *America*, on the Catholic tradition of nonterritorial parishes based on language and ethnic origin, notes that "the church [in nineteenth- and early twentieth-century America] . . . recognized that religious experience is mediated through culture and that people should have opportunities to encounter God in ways that are culturally meaningful to them" (Brophy 2001: 13).[6] As ethnic neighborhoods and their Catholic populations started to disperse after the Second World War,[7] families and individuals were permitted to retain their parish affiliation because of their ethnic heritage even though they no longer resided in the geographical area served by that particular church. While this tradition has waned because of decreasing European immigrant membership base, it remains intact for now in older ethnic parishes in cities like Philadelphia.[8]

Dignity/Philadelphia was a Catholic congregation with a potentially large cultural and regional membership base, but no institutional church sponsorship. It had no church-appointed pastor or chaplain. In Philadelphia, it was never permitted to hold its services in a Catholic sanctuary. Basing its objections on past moral perspectives on natural law as well as scriptural passages and interpretations, the Roman Catholic Church teaches that homosexual orientation is morally neutral but homosexual activity is morally wrong (Boswell 1980: 91–117; Harvey 1987: 95–117; Jordan 2000: 26–37). The homosexual orientation, therefore, is not considered intrinsically bad or evil, and the individual is not necessarily responsible for it. Homosexual behavior, however, is always judged objectively wrong, but responsibility for such actions might be lessened because of circumstances that take away one's freedom. The pastoral "solution" of the Roman Catholic Church to the issue of homosexuality is for the individual to develop self-control through the practice of celibacy. An active homosexual genital lifestyle is totally unacceptable in the view of institutional Roman Catholicism.[9]

Since it is impossible for a "gay and lesbian" parish to exist with institutional sanction, my description is ostensibly, like the pairing of the terms "gay" and "lesbian" with "Catholic," an oxymoron (Primiano 1993b: 89). But anyone who knows Catholics and is familiar with Catholic culture is well aware that the tradition, like many other religions, bears witness to a significant homosexual membership, so that while these series of terms and ideas seem contradictory in the ideal, in reality they are not.[10] All that is necessary is for one to maintain a flexible notion of parish as a congregation of a church, but in this case "apart from and alongside" (Yoder 1990: 80) a diocese and under the charge of not priests or ministers but a concerned laity. In the formation of a congregational setting that would attract people not only from the gay neighborhood of Center City in Philadelphia, but from various parts of the city as well, Dignity Philadelphians drew from the model of an ethnic parish with which they were quite familiar.

In 1986, the tenuous affiliation between Dignity and institutional Catholicism was severed by the Vatican "Letter to the Bishops of the Catholic Church on the Pastoral Care of Homosexual Persons" promulgated on 31 October by the Congregation for the Doctrine of the Faith headed by Joseph Cardinal Ratzinger. This Vatican missive was a direct response to the existence of Dignity in the United States, and ironically was anything but pastoral for it led to Dignity chapters being ordered by bishops to leave Catholic parishes.[11] Undaunted, Dignity activities continued, often within the confines of friendly Protestant sanctuaries. While Dignity/USA membership declined after the proclamation of the Vatican letter in 1986 from 5,000 to 3,800 in the beginning of the 1990s (*National Catholic Reporter*, 16 August 1991), the organization continued to attract new members (to make up for those it lost) and the attention of the news media allowed it additional venues for its message of openness to full Christian acceptance of a gay sexual life. From the mid-1980s to 2000, Dignity/Philadelphia kept a consistent membership of between 200 and 250 individuals. In the opening years of the new millennium, Dignity had 2,500 dues-paying members nationally, and the Philadelphia chapter had 170–200 members.

In an age when many individual Catholics viewed the tradition's practices and culture as irrelevant and easy to abandon, these gay and lesbian Catholics felt it was necessary, deserved, and desirable to retain their affiliation. "We are the Church" was a common battle cry heard during confrontations with the Catholic hierarchy. These were Catholics, and they would not allow anyone, especially the functionaries of institutional Catholicism, to tell them they were not. Ironically, these functionaries in the priesthood and Catholic hierarchy were often cited by Dignity members as being homosexual themselves, and sexually active as well. Dignity members viewed this situation as the ultimate hypocrisy because these priests, for the sake of their careers, would neither publicly admit their orientation nor support other homosexuals in their quest for understanding, toleration, and legitimacy. The institutional hierarchy of the church was in the uneasy position of knowing that members of the church's ordained priesthood were supporting Dignity chapters who were in sympathy with these believers and who possibly were gay themselves.

The 1986 Ratzinger letter spoke of the homosexual orientation as being "ordered toward an *intrinsic* moral evil and thus the inclination itself must be seen as an objective disorder" (emphasis added, Congregation for the Doctrine of the Faith 1988: 2). Indeed, if there was something *intrinsic* to many Dignity members, it was their Catholicism. Their Catholicism was an innate part of who they were as human beings. "Catholicism," my consultant Jeffrey remarked, "is in my blood."[12] There existed in them a strong cultural attachment to Roman Catholicism, as well as a strong spiritual commitment to the Catholic faith as it is personally interpreted. Those having been born and raised as Catholics felt that Catholicism was, as Father Jake, their former chaplain, noted to me, their "birthright" and their "roots." "I am a *Roman* Catholic," he said, "I believe what I was brought up to believe." Dignity was Debra's "Catholic community," and her religion she described as "cradle Catholicism." As Greg noted, "I grew up in this church. I love the church for whatever abstract reasons." John also spoke of being born into Catholicism: "In my personal case, it's the tradition I grew up in, my family is all Catholic, my friends are all Catholic. And although I disagree with a lot of what they say, somebody has to stay in and say something." When I asked John, who later became a president of the Dignity/Philadelphia chapter, to characterize the membership of Dignity, he explained:

> The majority of its members are from the Catholic tradition, and still consider themselves members of the Catholic family, and we reserve the right to remain in that family and respectfully, but purposefully, disagree with teachings on sexual ethics and morality. The majority of people who go there really do subscribe to most of the theological principles and are more steeped in the tradition, involved in it.

Dignity, I noted during the course of my fieldwork, would be referred to by members as "Church" with a capital "C," meaning a part of the larger Catholic tradition, but also as "church," with a small "c," meaning their local place of worship. "Oh, that's across the street from church," individuals would say, meaning across from the Episcopal St. Luke and the Epiphany where Dignity ran its Mass and weekly social hour. "Look at the information table at church," one member would say to another. Given its opportunities for both spiritual and social expressions, Dignity assumed for many of its members the status of their church or "parish," be it the city's first gay ethnic parish. While the chapter's officers were uneasy to declare that publicly, such a designation and structure was what they knew best. As the president of Dignity declared in a radio interview in March 1986: "We attempt I guess in our worship life to, I hate to say it this way, to function as a parish. . . ."[13] Still, this former officer of the chapter, as well as former Philadelphia archdiocesan seminarian, told me that he knew that St. Peter Claver Catholic

Church, about six blocks from St. Luke and the Epiphany Episcopal Church, "is geographically my parish church, but Dignity is really my parish church." The archdiocese had, in fact, closed St. Peter Claver Church as a fully functioning parish in June 1985, still allowing Mass in its sanctuary on Sundays. "Of course," the archdiocese "would never send their people to Dignity for Mass. They are sent to St. John the Evangelist." His statement that "St. Peter Claver has as many people at their Sunday Masses as Dignity on Thirteenth Street" caused me to consider the effect that Dignity had on the Sunday attendance of area Catholic parishes. One could speculate that if the gay congregation of Dignity (which in the 1980s could number more than 200) had been allowed to operate out of St. Peter Claver, that parish perhaps would have remained open and been more robust and financially sound in the eyes of the archdiocese.[14]

Dignity/Philadelphia still holds its weekly liturgies on Sunday evenings at 7:00 p.m. in the basement of the Episcopal Church of St. Luke and the Epiphany in Center City Philadelphia, as it did in the late 1980s when I did intensive interviews with Dignity members. They moved to this location from another Episcopal Church property in 1986.[15] The group, founded in 1973, has continuously advertised its presence in the local gay and lesbian newspaper. Its Masses are well known among the gay community and providing that weekly liturgy has been the major service offered to members and visitors. Dignity made possible a gay-lesbian-bisexual-transgender-affirming Catholic liturgical context. For individuals "there for Mass," Dignity represented a meaningful weekly liturgy they desired to attend. Its services, therefore, were the only occasion for them to fulfill the Sunday Mass obligation and keep a connection to any organized religion. If it was not for Dignity, they might not have had any relationship to a religious group at all, and certainly they would not maintain any formal connection to Roman Catholicism. This Mass, however, was not necessarily the first of the day for some Dignity members.[16]

Individuals also used Dignity as a supplement to their Sunday religious activities. For these people, the Dignity Mass was their second Mass of the day, and usually also their second reception of the Eucharist for the day. They fully supported the organization's cause, but they still desired the connection to a recognized Catholic parish. At an after-Mass dinner to which I was invited (2 November 1986) at a nearby restaurant known to cater to gay clientele, I took special note of a conversation between three consultants, in which one asked the others if they kept up contacts with old family parishes or if they went to Catholic churches near where they lived in the city. "I go to church here. Dignity is my church," was one response. "Yes, I only go to Dignity, not my parish church," said the other. "Really?" the questioner replied. He was quite surprised that they did not retain an affiliation to a parish, as he did. He often attended Mass twice on

Sundays. Considering the position of the church today on a number of issues including the homosexual question, he told me, "I wouldn't be a Catholic except for the fact that I was raised as one." Those who attended regularly knew that some others viewed a visit to Dignity more as a social occasion than a strictly spiritual one. They took this all in stride. I noted during the 2 November 1986 meal how remarkable it was that so many gay people would go to Mass at 7:00 on a Sunday evening when so many of their peers were going to bars or engaging in athletic activities, such as the gay volleyball league. I was told, "Some go to check out the new meat. Others come regularly. You can tell who they are. [Still many people] are really there for Mass."

As one of the men that I had dinner with later explained to me (14 December 1986), he had actually tried many different Christian services, but he was never as satisfied with them as he was with the Catholic service. "It's in my blood," he said, "and I have explained it to people that way. I guess I really wouldn't go to church anymore, if it weren't for Dignity." Of course, since the liturgy began at 7:00 p.m., and the Sabbath traditionally lasted from sunset to sunset, it did not fulfill the Sunday obligation in the technical sense set forth by the institutional Catholic Church, nor were its priests technically allowed to say its Masses without the permission of the local bishop. The ordinary, that is the bishop of the diocese, had not given them faculties to say Mass or preach in Philadelphia. In fact, John Cardinal Krol, then the archbishop of the city, ordered Philadelphia dioc. san priests not to say Mass for Dignity at all. The chapter, therefore, depended on unique clerical resources: Philadelphia priests who belonged to religious orders that were less fearful of the cardinal's direct wrath on their priestly placements and overall careers; priests from other dioceses who were imported to the city to preside at Dignity's Sunday liturgy; and priests who had broken with the hierarchy and now lived in the city. For this reason, Dignity/Philadelphia's priest presiders included parish and religious order priests, as well as men who were on personal sabbaticals from the priesthood and active ministry.[17] As far as Dignity members were concerned, the powers bestowed at priestly ordination were all the legitimacy Dignity's priests needed. What also gave the liturgical acts of these priests further credibility to this community of Catholics beyond the approval of any local bishop was the personal courage and determination they showed to minister to gay and lesbian people against the wishes of the hierarchy.

While the great majority of those present at Dignity's Masses were the products of traditional Catholic families and diocesan schools in the Philadelphia and Southern New Jersey area, there were also non-Catholic Christians in attendance, as well as some Jewish visitors.[18] One Jewish man not only attended the Mass, but he sang the hymns and knew the words to the prayers, reciting the Sanctus, Agnus Dei, and Our Father along with the congregation. He did not attend every week, but he was more than a casual visitor, though he was not a dues-paying Dignity member. He did not receive communion, but other non-Catholics certainly did.[19] After his day of work with his own congregation, a United Church of Christ minister would secretly come to the Dignity Mass. He noted that he was "liberal in politics and conservative in theology," preaching strict Reformed theology in his sermons. He did not like what he called the "wishy-washy theology" of the gay denomination, the Universal Fellowship of Metropolitan Community Churches (UFMCC),[20] which he had attended in Philadelphia. He felt that because the Metropolitan Community Church tried to please many gay Protestant constituents, their overall theology was weak and undefined, and he specifically gave their sacramental theology as an example. "I don't agree with the Catholics altogether, but at least this organization always presents a single [orthodox] view of theology, Church, and sacraments." He was not as attracted to Roman Catholic moral theology. He did feel a sense of community at Dignity. "They don't ask questions. There's a good feeling here." He enjoyed the fellowship of these gay Christians and was hopeful of developing a possible romantic relationship.

Dignity, like any social group, had its ephemeral elements who my consultant Don had identified as "drop-ins" and "tourists." Travelers, people looking to make contacts, friends, and other floaters became a part of the landscape of Dignity's weekly services. In some way, Dignity's Masses were the gay Catholic equivalent of the services in the great Catholic cathedrals of Europe during the tourist season when visitors to the town, usually Catholic, stop in to experience or simply see these spiritual or social gatherings or to connect with the group. Several such floaters attended Dignity Masses. Such individuals, of course, did not establish doctrine or theological responses to the institutional church. They were sampling Dignity as religious or social cruisers who wandered through the chapter's Sunday services trying to make some connection, but who had no significant role in defining the content of the group or its direction. These individuals were not a part of the community, as much as they were an aspect of the environment of Dignity. Granted not all gay visitors cared for their experience at Dignity. One young man characterized the cruising nature of the social hour after Sunday Mass as nothing but a "meat market." This man approached me after a public lecture I had given on Dignity and stated his opinions. He told me of the less than favorable impression that he felt from Dignity in the half dozen times he had gone to Mass there.

The quality of Dignity as a small faith community challenging oppressive church teachings and leadership was described by my consultant, Jeffrey, as "like the early Christians hiding away there, celebrating their own beliefs" (8 February 1987). Such a position actually stimulated some individuals to be more active in a religious organization than they normally would. One man I spoke to (22 June

1986), for example, was making money for Dignity's treasury by selling lavender T-shirts and buttons with Dignity/Philadelphia's logo for people to wear during the New York City Gay Pride Weekend in June 1986. Carrying the shirts in a shopping bag, we conversed as he and a friend walked down Thirteenth Street after the Mass. Periodically, they hugged men they knew, tried to sell them shirts, or simply talked openly about which men they thought were attractive. Between the Dignity Mass concluding and the many gay bars in the area, the street become so filled with gay men by 8:15 on a Sunday evening that they felt quite comfortable engaging in such actions. It was against this backdrop that we conversed about institutional Catholicism in Philadelphia. This man complained to me that John Cardinal Krol would not attend a recent ecumenical prayer service for people with AIDS, though the archdiocese did send a representative. "Every Catholic diocese in America had at least an outreach for AIDS victims and Philadelphia is the only one which doesn't because of Krol, that twisted little bitch." I replied that he certainly was involved in Dignity. "Yes," he answered, "as a regular Catholic, I didn't do much of anything. Now as a gay Catholic, I'm doing everything . . . selling T-shirts, saying rosaries in public, everything."

Though aware of their adverse relationship with the institutional hierarchy of the church, Roman Catholic members of Dignity/Philadelphia managed to combine the seeming contradiction of their active homosexual lifestyles with an active commitment to the Roman Catholic faith.[21] This negotiation of Catholicism can be perceived through three distinctive understandings of their ethnicity. Dignity members were ethnic Catholics by way of nationality; they were ethnically Catholic by their common association and knowledge of the American Catholic tradition; and they were sexually ethnic Catholics by way of their self-identified lives as gay, lesbian, bisexual, or transgender people.

Dignity members represented diverse ethnic Catholic backgrounds as descendants of the nineteenth- and early-twentieth-century immigrations from Europe (such as Irish, German, Italian, and Polish). Those traditions remained with them and, as my consultant John acknowledged to me, their Catholicism was tied to such ethnicity. It could also be said that the depth of cultural sharing they experienced went beyond specific nationalistic commonalities to the level of being "ethnically Catholic" in America. That is, like many contemporary United States Catholics, their Catholicism rather than their particular ethnic heritage was their specific point of cultural reference.[22] Catholic beliefs, ideas, values, and sensibilities constituted an essential part of their personal identities. They felt a strong attachment to and acceptance of the basic liturgical, theological, sacramental, even ecclesiastical elements of the Catholic tradition. These individuals, many of whom were between thirty and fifty years of age, had experienced both the unquestioning legalism of pre-Vatican II American Catholicism communicated to them during their Catholic parochial school education (or Catholic religious instruction, CCD or Confraternity of Christian Doctrine classes) and the unbinding of such strictures in the years following Vatican II (that is, post-1965).

The connection to Catholic culture for Dignity members naturally extended beyond institutional dogmas, hierarchical activities, and authoritative texts to the social, individual, customary, and material experiences and expressions of the religion of American Catholics. These Catholics shared a cultural knowledge that included everything from pre-Vatican II references to holy cards, pagan babies, limbo, mortal sin, St. Christopher medals, burgeoning parochial schools, and the wearing of white at first Holy Communion to post-Vatican II emphases on liturgies in the vernacular, Bible reading, nuns without habits, priests being called by their first names, the placement of Holy Communion in the hand, and the option to drink consecrated wine directly from a chalice. Some essentials of Philadelphia's Catholic culture that remained for Dignity members included bingo, tales of altar boy service, block collection, and conservative church prelates. Through ethnic, family, customary, and educational associations, Dignity Catholics easily related to each other through the culture of American Catholicism, a familiarity of worldview, shared experience, and personal beliefs.[23]

The culture of Catholicism had an intense effect on the lives of these Dignity members as it had on many Catholics, but what remained unique about these individuals was their expression of their Catholicism in light of their sexual lives and relationship to gay and lesbian culture. The gayness of Dignity was an element that even the casual observer of one of its liturgies would notice immediately, perhaps even before noticing how Catholic Dignity was. Dignity as a social entity represented a synthesis of Catholic and gay sensibilities. The cohesive element at Dignity, what attracted its ecumenical congregation, people unaffiliated with any religion, and Catholics of every description from radically separatist to liberal reformist to conservative traditionalists, was the gayness of the community.

Unlike the churches filled by the ethnic European forbearers of these men and women, Dignity was not based on nationalistic ties. Nor did concerns of hierarchy inspire the creation of Dignity; rather, these congregations emerged from the desires of these faithful Catholics to live as sexually active gays and lesbians. Many Dignity Philadelphia members saw themselves not only as a "culture," but, reflecting their experience of living in a city of ethnic neighborhoods, they conceived of themselves as a separate ethnicity. With issues of sexual orientation central to their conception of their ethnic parish, their sexual ethnicity transcended any nationalistic character or association they might have experienced. This ethnicity, as they defined it, was not constructed, contingent, or fluid; it was a salient feature of their humanity, unifying them through a common biological predisposition (Primiano 1993b: 90). All the members of Dignity I conversed with or interviewed explained that they were born "congenitally gay." Furthermore, and crucial to understanding their spirituality as Dignity Catholics, they understood this biological reality to be a creation of God. Dignity members would never deny that "gayness" could be traced as a historical construct or a product of culture, but their religious beliefs cemented their feeling for being "born gay" to their perception that God creates all things for a specific purpose. As Jackie, a convert to Roman Catholicism, succinctly explained: "I guess I do think that God created me as gay. I see my being gay as an expression of God's will . . . whether he created it in the womb or before my conception." And to take this point to its theological conclusion, John asked the question: "If God created us gay, did he really create us gay and not expect us to be loving human beings in the full potential that we have . . . no God would create you to be not loving."

A feeling of community was built atop an edifice of Catholic and sexual familiarity at Dignity. This intentional community forged a sense of belonging, which many of these Catholics had not felt from a religious group since they personally recognized their homosexuality. Some of these individuals had left their parishes because they felt no support there for themselves as homosexual persons. As Stephen said, "I don't believe that the Catholic Church includes me when they say family. . . . And just the way the Church looks on gay people which is the way most society looks on gay people, at best pitiful and at worst as criminals and degenerates." Dignity was for many members their last resort as practicing Roman Catholics. This was what John admitted: "If it wasn't for Dignity, I'd probably be Episcopalian or Quaker or something. . . . If it wasn't for that I probably would not have this outlet to get in touch with the spiritual side of my being which helps me." Dignity members felt relief upon finding an organization that supported the integration of their homosexuality and their Catholicism while also being a center for meeting people outside of the social context of the gay bars. Jeffrey recalled: "Here was this thing you'd grown up with, you've been Catholic for twenty-odd years and all of a sudden you don't feel like you belong to it anymore. Then you find this group of people who are saying it's okay to be Catholic, it's okay to be gay, come and celebrate with us, and it really felt good."

Nevertheless, the intrinsically Catholic appeal of Dignity extended to the membership's recognition of the chapter not as a Catholic club or even as a movement within the Church but as a parish. Dignity/Philadelphia represented a new configuration of the American Catholic urban parish. Speaking broadly about parishes in his historical assessment of American Catholic congregations in the northeast United States, Joseph Casino comments that the parish community "has been and will be, a mirror and an example to a constantly changing American society" (1987: 101). Beginning in 1969, gay and lesbian Roman Catholics began to have that mirror publicly reflect their sexuality. Indeed, the organization of Dignity chapters by laity and clergy exemplified a changed America where new freedoms were sought by American Catholics for the expression of their sexual natures.[24] Dignity was the Roman Catholic connection to Philadelphia's gay and lesbian community with members recognizing it as the parish of the city's gay and lesbian Catholics. Many of these individuals had become depressed during the last half of the 1980s with what they considered the complete lack of pastoral consideration given to gay people suffering from AIDS in the archdiocese. In the midst of AIDS decimating their community, their church, as an institution, although having tremendous influence and resources, did not actively assist those who were suffering. Dignity suffered along with those afflicted, yet as a community it grew in strength and solidarity both as a reaction to and result of this rejection. For at Dignity, there were actual priests giving homilies that said there was nothing wrong or shameful about being gay and even that gay love and gay sex was a normal, natural part of God's creation. These priests spoke openly of issues relating to gays and lesbians. In this time when AIDS was striking down so many of their friends and even themselves, this was a Catholic organization that openly mourned for the dead, prayed for the ill, and publicly acknowledged the suffering and ravages caused by the mysterious disease. The clergy did this (for the most part) without prompting feelings of guilt and rejection but by accentuating pride and acceptance.

Whether acting as supplement or the sole source of Catholic contact, Dignity assumed as much of a parish role as it could for a lay organization. In the 1980s, there may have been no children running down the aisles, babies crying, wedding banns being read, or a choice of Sunday liturgies (and it was a Mass said in a Protestant church basement), but Dignity as it existed was the worshipping and social community for many of its members. The textures of parish liturgical life were found there: the Sunday Mass, the priest, the homily, the collection basket, and that most essential element, the Eucharist. These elements were very Catholic in character. The makings of a social life were there as well: dances, socials, and the after-Mass gathering. These markers were less specifically Catholic for it was quite easy to belong to a Catholic parish in late twentieth-century America and have little contact with other parishioners. While Dignity lacked many of the traditional services of a parish, it took on this role for those gays and lesbians who had either done without one in their lives or wished to supplement the church they normally attended. These were the people who referred to it not as "Dignity the special interest organization," "my community," or "Dignity the base community," in the words of contemporary liberation theology, but simply as they would the parishes of their youth, as "church." Davis, a chapter officer, did not "see Dignity as a parish, but it is serving the parish need for me personally." He longed for the day that the liturgical responsibilities of Dignity could be assumed by a "local parish" and Dignity would become "social, a support group." As Loretta perceived it, Philadelphia's Dignity chapter quite naturally took on some of the qualities of the city's conservative Catholic life:

> But Philadelphia, again, you can't take the city out of the organization. I always thought that one of the reasons Philadelphia's Dignity chapter thrived was because the city was so Catholic, that people transferred the allegiance they felt for their parish into another organization, and also because there is an adversarial position that exists with the archdiocese. And that can be a very strengthening factor to an organization, and that shouldn't be overlooked.

Dignity officials, for fear of antagonizing the Philadelphia archdiocese, were, as already noted, careful not to refer to the organization as a parish or, for that matter, the city's gay parish. Such hesitation represented a glaring example of ambiguity and irony for an organization that by its very existence challenged the church and its authority, but which also by its very existence desired to be in union with that institution and the power it was wielding to repress them. Stephen, a Dignity officer, voiced the contradiction stated by many of Dignity's administrators as they represented Dignity as a temporary pressure group within the Roman Catholic Church, while actually relating to it as his parish:

> Dignity is a group of Catholics, I never say a Catholic group, working within the gay/lesbian community. We have roots here that go back. . . .We hold weekly Mass. We do much that a regular parish does. If it looks like a duck and walks like a duck. . . .We look and act and breathe like a parish. We are a temporary pressure group, but we work as an ethnic parish for gay and lesbian people. That's a distinction that I have to make.

As noted, one of Dignity's positive characteristics was the openness of its Catholic community to welcome all segments of the gay and lesbian community, and matching this attitude was its willingness to make changes in certain liturgical rules to not alienate the diverse congregation. The priests of Dignity for their part would acknowledge both the Catholic and the ecumenical or community-wide appeal of these services by making their prayers and homilies acknowledge the more religiously diversified audience. They also actively cooperated with other Philadelphia gay religious groups by having their ministers or rabbis preach or attend the Mass on special occasions. The chapter took no particular measures to enforce the Catholic Church's rule that only Roman Catholics receive the Eucharist. In fact, non-Catholics were permitted to be lectors at these Masses, as well as Eucharistic ministers, that is, they assisted with the distribution of the consecrated bread and wine or grape juice, as well as consumed the remaining uneaten elements.[25] This was not to say that everyone agreed with this decision, especially those more traditionally minded Catholics in the chapter who worked to maintain church rubrics at Dignity, though these individuals were also quite aware that the organization and its liturgy were completely illicit in the eyes of the institutional Roman Catholic Church.

As evidenced from the after-Mass announcements, Dignity as a social organization sponsored everything from seasonal dances and parties to book discussions and sales.[26] Dignity's Education Committee sponsored CPR training. Members could go jogging with each other. They met and dated people from Dignity. They had dinner and visited the bars with friends from the chapter. It was not their only social outlet, but it sought to provide some social occasions and certainly manifested an atmosphere of local community, especially for many gay and lesbian Catholics in the Philadelphia area. I, in fact, was frequently told that Dignity in the 1980s was the largest meeting place for gay men in Philadelphia outside of a bar situation. One informant told me: "I would venture to guess that a third of the gay population has been to a Dignity service in Philadelphia." He also added: "Although it's been billed as the largest gathering of gay men and women outside of the bars, it is still a very small circle. It is a very small community and people tend to know other people's business, and that at times can be very uncomfortable for people. . . ."

Dignity thrived by offering social, support, and advocate services to whoever was interested, but its major focus remained its spiritual component. Members could have their confessions heard at Dignity; they could have their spiritual director at Dignity; they went to Sunday Mass at Dignity and, if desired, Mass on holy days of obligation at the chapter's Eleventh Street headquarters, Dignity House; they had their throats blessed at Mass on St. Blaise Day; they attended midnight Christmas Mass there; they received blessed palms from Dignity on Palm Sunday; they went on retreats sponsored and organized by the chapter; they went to AIDS memorial services there; they were sent special Christmas and Easter envelopes for their holiday donations to Dignity; they were lectors or Eucharistic ministers there; they sang or played an instrument in the music ministry; and they could even convert to Roman Catholicism through Dignity. It should be noted that people were not married[27] or buried through Dignity, and converts, if they felt it necessary to have institutional recognition of their conversion, would have to ask a friendly priest to place their names on a parish record somewhere in the city. Other opportunities provided by Dignity included trips to Lourdes under the sponsorship of Dignity New York and even a visit to the Vatican during a European tour organized by Dignity/USA. More importantly from the perspective of social outreach to their own community, Dignity's Christmas Eve midnight Mass (10:00 p.m.) and social hour made sure that members who lived alone or had no family were not forgotten during this time of celebration.

In any parish context, some members only participate in its spiritual or social life and leave committee work and active participation in decision making to a small group of interested individuals. Dignity was no different. When it came time to nominate officers to run the chapter, there were actually few people willing to commit to the responsibility and time commitment such office demanded. A core of interested individuals who sat on its committees and became its officers basically ran the organization.[28] In fact, in 1986 these officers ran unopposed for their positions due to a lack of names for nomination. In a letter in the May 1986 issue of the chapter newsletter, *The Independence*, a chapter officer rebuked the membership for their lack of active interest. Like a pastor reminding his parishioners about their responsibility in maintaining the activities of and contributions to the parish, treasurer Mark Ratkus in his "Officer's Message" solicited more support:

> Do I assume that Dignity will always be around? I pose this question to myself and to each of you because the vitality and longevity of our Chapter depends on my and your personal response to it. . . . At first glance, the state of our Chapter appears to be superior. However, other considerations about our Chapter temper my optimism. For example, it was difficult recently to elicit willing nominees for Chapter offices and all offices were uncontested. Also, while our weekly offerings have held steady, this is because some members are extremely generous—the implication is that some donate little or nothing. Further, I hear some very active members express the sentiments of "burn-out" or the occasional feeling that their efforts are being taken for granted. How then can we build on Dignity's accomplishments and be confident about the future? Paul speaking to the Church at Ephesus reminds us as well: "Your mind must be renewed by a spiritual revolution, so that you can put on the new self that has been created in God's way" (4:23–24). An increase in our *active* community and its membership would extend our ministry of promoting God's way in a truly revolutionary manner. So let's put on our "new selves." Let's stop feeling free to contribute and begin to feel obligated to do so. Let's not just assume that "Dignity will always be around." Let's make sure that it is! (vol. 13, no. 5: 1–2)

The "Officer's Message" for April 1986 had also posed a series of questions attempting to promote more active participation by the membership. The executive secretary, Kevin Davies, succinctly summarized his perspective on the purpose of Dignity:

> Do you want Dignity to continue as a viable force in the community? Do you enjoy attending Dignity's mass and social hour? Do you appreciate the alternatives Dignity provides in meeting people? Are you able to relate more to the scriptures, teachings and priests by attending Dignity? Do you find the people at Dignity a basically friendly group? Do you want Dignity to continue to grow? Do you want to help Dignity help yourself? Do you feel better about yourself after attending Dignity? Do you think Dignity will be here in ten years? five years? next year? (vol. 13, no. 4: 1)

The questions asked in these 1986 statements can be answered now. Dignity has persevered both attacks by the institutional Catholic Church and indifference and even scorn by members of the LGBT community. Dignity still exists though most of the men present in the mid-1980s Masses and social hours that I attended have moved on: to spiritual but not institutionally religious lives; to relationships with other more accepting Christian denominations; to Catholic parishes with more accepting pastors and congregations; and to the afterlife after battling HIV, AIDS, and, with Dignity now almost thirty years old, to natural causes of death. For many individuals, Dignity was a stopping off point for a few weeks, a few months, a few years in their journey to affirm their feelings about their sexual orientation. A core group of about fifteen members remain from the days of my most intensive fieldwork, and Dignity, resembling the fluidity of leadership of an archdiocesan parish, has had several generations of leaders and supporters.

And is Dignity still observed by my original consultants as an ethnic parish? Just as when I first did my interviews in 1987, the assessments are both affirmative and negative in 2002.[29] Two particularly helpful responses illuminate how Dignity members view themselves and the chapter they developed. Loretta, who was not actively involved in the chapter in 1987 but continues her membership and yearly contributions for its support, reflects positively about its work in Philadelphia. When she attends Dignity Masses a few times a year, she is now struck by Dignity's history and tradition. She conceives of it not so much as an "ethnic" parish, but as a "parish":

> There is squabbling within Dignity in Philadelphia. Yet, there is always the sense that you could go there week after week after week. The way you would to your parish with its own sense of traditions. . . . And when you enter the worship space now, the first thing you notice are a series of banners with the names of the people [Dignity members] who are deceased. [That is] very, very powerful. So there you are worshipping with people you may have known for years. Some of whom you do not know. . . . You also have the sense of the past. That so clearly right smack in front of you. Almost like you're in a church that has crypts, like down in [Old] St. Mary's where you walk through the crypts to get into the church. It's a very Philadelphia development. . . . Again . . . every Dignity chapter takes on the character of the city in which it is located. . . . Dignity to me right now feels very much like a [Philadelphia] parish.

Stephen remembered telling me that Dignity was his parish, describing it as a gay ethnic parish. Noting that the chapter is now graying and has difficulty attracting young people, he feels quite satisfied with what Dignity/Philadelphia has accomplished, especially for many individuals dealing with their homosexuality and the experience of "coming out." While not wanting to describe Dignity as an ethnic parish, he could not help but return to familiar conceptualizations:

It is politically incorrect then and now for me to say that Dignity is a gay ethnic parish because we really are a support group for gay people within the Catholic Church. . . . I know Dignity/Philadelphia has grown up as a gay ethnic parish. . . . I think out of necessity have become a gay ethnic parish. It's not what we were there for, and it's not what we are supposed to be. . . . Yes, I still think we are. . . . It is not Dignity's mission to form a parallel church. It is to work with the hierarchy and with the people in the Church to diversify themselves to get rid of their homophobia, to get rid of their sexism. We are to teach them by our lives. We believe the spirit is diverse. We believe the Holy Spirit wants this. We are going to work through the Holy Spirit with our church. . . . We're not supposed to be a gay ethnic parish, but we've grown into one.

Dignity liturgies were and continue to be self-reflective occasions of performance, celebration, and tension expressing the vernacular union of Catholic and gay culture, and serving as a refuge for Catholic and non-Catholic gays and lesbians that sought a spiritual safe haven. The liturgies displayed a mixture of individual and group expressions of Catholic and gay orientation, identity, alienation, and contestation. In this sense, the Dignity Mass was as much a statement to the non-gay world, including fellow Catholics, that gay people had a religious dimension to their culture as it was to the antireligious elements within the gay community that a spiritual life is not antithetical to the gay experience. It was this intense commitment to a strong spiritual environment that made these Masses appealing to gay people of all religious backgrounds. For those individuals interested in a Catholicism that was open to all marginalized peoples, Dignity was a new embodiment of religious community, one that combined traditional elements with a revolutionary and accepting sexual theology. Dignity was a place where a constellation of ethnicities could be expressed in a unique context of American vernacular Catholicism.

As demeaned, disdained, and rejected as they were by the institutional Church throughout the 1980s, many gay and lesbian Catholics refused to leave their tradition. Dignity members reflected the study of Catholic beliefs, practices, and values published by Gallup and Castelli examining data from 1965 to 1986. This source states that as much as Catholics felt alienated and dissented from the institution, they would not depart from it or break "their sense of ownership of the Church" (1987: 43). Borrowing from Debra Campbell's assessment of the laity in the age of aggiornamento: "Somewhere in the midst of the fragmented American laity, among the professional ecclesial ministers, . . . the alienated women," the patronized and demeaned "of the local parish," and the alienated and rejected gays and lesbians "lurks invincible the spirit of the American laity" (Campbell 1990: 280).

The twentieth-century American Catholic Church was notable for the crucial role it played "in molding the world of its communicants. At no point before or since have the connections between the Church and its members been as dense; at no point the Catholic culture so cohesive" (McGreevy 1996: 5). Dignity members in the 1980s were very much products of that cohesive Catholic culture. These Catholics at this time desired the Church, to accept, embrace, and absorb them and their uniqueness as gay and lesbians. They turned to an ecclesiastical form they knew, the parish, to model their community. By the new millennium, Dignity/Philadelphia developed additional parish services: Mass booklets and inclusive language hymnals; liturgies in their large worship space on holy days of obligation; ceremonies of marital union; anointing of the sick; and baptisms of children. Like suburban parishes growing with young families, the children of same-sexed couples on some evenings run between the chairs and fall asleep on the shoulders of their parents. Dignity's population may not be robust, but it certainly reflects the developing priorities of the LGBT community.

Robert Orsi's 1999 edited volume, *Gods of the City*, presents a useful tableaux of religious communities and expressions that have populated the spiritual and physical spaces of urban America from Italian Catholics to Japanese Presbyterians and from African-based Caribbean religions to members of the Salvation Army. He writes of these various religious communities sharing the space of the city that "in the intersection of different cultures on the urban landscape, new and interesting cultural forms have taken shape" (1999: 281). More typically gay, lesbian, bisexual, and transgender members of these traditions simply existed within these religious communities, worshipping "alongside" but afraid to express themselves in any public way. Empowered by the sexual revolution and the gay liberation movement of the 1960s, the gay God of the city emerged to take a public place in churches and synagogues, congregations that could have closed without gay presence and support. This empowerment also caused new religious forms to emerge, spiritual sites created by gay and lesbian people for themselves in the core of urban America. Dignity became such a religious space for LGBT Roman Catholics. Just as "sacred spaces in particular city neighborhoods serve as centers of national and international religious affiliation" (Orsi 1999: 53), Dignity's existence opens up this statement to include the recognition of sacred contexts as centers of sexual affiliation. It is vitally significant to the history and culture of American religion to recognize how these believers have populated, negotiated, and created religious spaces as well as their own vernacular religious lives (Primiano 1995).

With consistent parish closings in cities like Philadelphia, New York City, Chicago, and Detroit since the late 1980s and 1990s,[30] the emergence of new Roman Catholic worshiping communities within these same U.S. metropolitan areas is a significant reminder that a practicing population of Catholics does indeed remain in urban contexts. Since Vatican II (1962–1965), a greater sense of independence by Catholics has led a growing percentage of them to be more discriminating about their parish membership and search out a parish community suited to their needs and interests (Morris 1997: 299–300; Brophy 2001). For example, if they prefer a conservative or progressive pastor and the style of management, leadership, or spirituality such a man expresses, they may travel a great distance from their homes on Sundays and even during the week just to be a parishioner (see Wilkes 2001). Many pastors in twenty-first-century America accept the reality of such fluid parish affiliations and are often pleased to be attracting new parishioners even at the expense of another parish. "Magnet churches draw members from territorial churches that lack personality or a distinct culture" (Brophy 2001: 12). In Philadelphia, Dignity, in fact, is such a magnet church as it continues to draw Catholics back to the city from the suburbs for its services and activities.[31] These Catholics, the progeny of the immigrants of a century or more ago, are not welcomed in the churches built by their ethnic forbearers, yet still seek out the religion of their childhood. They have created in response their own unconventional churches, their own vernacular parishes. The God of the Catholic immigrants has been transformed into their sexually inclusive God, the gay God of the city.

Notes

I would like to thank the members of Dignity/Philadelphia for their time, assistance, and candor during my work. The staff of the Cabrini College Library have been invaluable aids to my research including Sherry Becht, Rosemarie DeMaio, Alan Silverman, and Anne Schwelm. Kathleen Malone O'Connor, Deborah Ann Bailey, Justin Falciani, Ron Karstetter, Leo A. Murray, S.J., Michael L. Murray, Steven F. Reynolds, and Lourdes Barretto were all enormously helpful. Drafts were carefully read by John DiMucci, Kathleen M. Joyce, Nancy L. Watterson, and my colleague at Cabrini College, Charlie McCormick.

1. When I write Dignity/Philadelphia, I am referring to the local chapter. When I write Dignity, Inc., Dignity USA Incorporated, or Dignity/USA, I am referring to the national organization with administrative offices headquartered in Washington, D.C., but not the D.C. chapter. My use of "Dignity" usually refers to the Philadelphia chapter, but the context of the sentence tells the reader if I am using the name to refer to Dignity in a more general sense as an organization.

2. See Harris (1999) for a brief description of the priest shortage.

3. Brophy (2001: 13) discusses this point from the perspective of Second Vatican Council documents and the 1983 Code of Canon Law.

4. McGreevy makes the point that "from the Council of Trent [1545–1563] . . . onward, canon law stressed that the parish served all of the souls living within its boundaries,"

and that occasionally there was a need for national parishes to serve the people of a "distinct national or racial character" (1996: 11). He provides useful references to the history of the parish and national parish concept, especially Ciesluk (1944) and Mickells (1950).

5. The issue of using language to preserve the faith and customs of a particular immigrant group of Catholics to America was a controversial issue in nineteenth-century Catholicism, especially among the German settlers to the United States. Conservative bishops feared that the Americanization of their German-speaking parishes would destroy the cohesiveness of their Catholic communities, while more progressive bishops saw the need for American Catholics to blend into Protestant America as necessary for the Church to thrive, soothe anti-Catholic suspicions, and perhaps attract converts to the faith of Rome (See Dolan 1985: 169, 297–303).

6. Brophy adds that the practice of maintaining ethnic parishes continues today, but at this time it serves the interests of the large population of Catholic immigrants who have arrived since the mid-1960s. "Fully 10 percent of American parishes are nonterritorial ethnic communities for Chicanos, Dominicans, Vietnamese and similar groups" (2001: 13).

7. See, for example, Orsi's account of Italian Harlem (1985: 69–74). McGreevy also writes of the debates over retaining national parishes over "territorial" parishes in the postwar period (1996: 82–84).

8. For example, in the case of five remaining Polish ethnic parishes, as long as one parent is of direct Polish heritage, membership in the congregation, as well as a place in the parish school, is permitted no matter the distance the parish is from the individual's home.

9. See Harvey (1967; 1979) who succinctly states the view of the Church in two *New Catholic Encyclopedia* articles considering theological, biblical, psychological, and pastoral perspectives, as well as in his book (1987). Smith and Dilenno (1979) also present the Church's position. Other useful personal, historical, theological, legal, psychological, moral studies, and reflections on homosexuality and the Roman Catholic tradition that examine the Church's moral position include Bailey (1955); Batchelor, ed. (1980); Boswell (1980; 1994); Gramick, ed. (1983); Nugent, ed. (1983); McNeill (1976; 1988a; 1988b; 1995; 1998); Task Force on Gay/Lesbian Issues, San Francisco (1986); Gramick and Furey, eds. (1988); Holtz (1991); Nugent and Gramick (1992; 1995); Goss (1993); Smith (1994); Genovesi (1994); Coleman (1995); Sullivan (1996); Comstock (1996); Peddicord (1996); Twiss (1998); Hanigan (1998); Curran (1998); Farley (1998); Stoltz (1998); Jordan (1997; 2000). For specifically lesbian perspectives, see Heyward (1984); Zanotti, ed. (1986); Hunt (1991). For specific references to Dignity, see Solitano (1994); Wagner, et al. (1994); Helminiak (1996, 1998); Stone (1998).

10. See Jordan (2000) for a critical commentary on homosexuality in modern Catholicism.

11. The specific occasion for Dignity chapters being asked to leave Catholic parishes was the passing of a resolution in the House of Delegates at the Dignity/USA 1987 national convention in Bal Harbour, Florida, a suburb of Miami, changing the ambiguous nature of a key passage of their Statement of Position and Purpose to define more clearly

the agenda of Dignity concerning the physical expression of gay and lesbian sexuality. The Miami or Bal Harbour Resolution added a significant second sentence to section 2:

We believe that gay men and lesbian women can express their sexuality in a manner that is consonant with Christ's teaching. *We believe that we can express our sexuality physically in a unitive manner that is loving, life giving and life affirming.* We believe that all sexuality should be exercised in an ethically responsible and unselfish way. (emphasis added)

12. These men and women were not so much "informants," a term used in contemporary ethnography to refer to those individuals who supplied information during fieldwork, but "consultants" to this task, a term that emphasizes the development of knowledge through a process of mutual respect between individual members of a community and a fieldworker (See, for example, Lawless 1988, 1992, 1993; Lassiter 2000, 2001; Hinson 2000). I use "consultant" throughout this article to refer to the many people who shared the stories of their Catholic lives with me.

13. This quotation is from a 30 March 1986 Easter Sunday interview on the University of Pennsylvania's FM radio program *Gay Dreams* with the current chapter president and a female member of Dignity.

14. See Vincent F. A. Golphin, ("Black Catholics Angry about Closing of Parish," *National Catholic Reporter*, 9 May 9 1986: 24) for specific details concerning the closing of St. Peter Claver.

15. Begun as a Home Liturgy Group meeting in a member's apartment, the chapter held liturgies for six months in St. Rita of Cascia Church on South Broad Street in 1974. This was its only time for meeting in an archdiocesan property.

16. Similarly, at this time the Episcopal gay and lesbian affinity group known as Integrity and the Lutheran group Lutheran's Concerned met in Philadelphia on days and times other than Sunday (usually in the evening and not every week), allowing its members to worship within Episcopal congregations on Sunday mornings.

17. In the 1990s, heterosexual men who left the priesthood to marry, especially members of an organization called CORPUS (the Association for an Inclusive Preisthood), also presided at Dignity liturgies.

18. I would estimate that 20 percent of the individuals in attendance at Dignity Masses during the late 1980s and early 1990s were not Roman Catholic.

19. A Catholic friend of this man saw his participation in this way: "Buddy is saying the Agnus Dei and the Our Father, he's Jewish, it's hilarious. . . . But there's a commonality of us all, he was a part of the community and worshipping the same God that we all believe in but at our service. Right now he's living with an ex-Catholic who doesn't go to Dignity." I sat next to this man at one of the Masses. He told me that, while he was not considering converting to Roman Catholicism, he liked the atmosphere and solidarity of these liturgical occasions.

20. As Wilcox (2000: 15) explains: "The UFMCC is the denominational organization, headquartered in Los Angeles, to which each individual Metropolitan Community Church (MCC) belongs."

21. While non-Catholics also participated in Dignity's Masses and held memberships in the organization, this study emphasizes the Catholic majority.

22. See Fish's differentiation between "ethnic Catholic" and "ethnically Catholic" (1982: 86).

23. See Santino's reflections (1982) on the culture of American Catholicism from the folkloristic perspective, and Primiano (1999) on the culture of American Catholic material culture.

24. Casino also notes that "there never was anything that could be called the 'typical' parish" (1987: 10). Each congregation was unique because of the ethnic community, the leadership, the local concerns, and the individual personalities of the Catholics that constituted it. Dignity/Philadelphia exemplifies that uniqueness. It is unique from other Catholic institutionally sponsored congregations, as well as unique from other metropolitan Dignity chapters. For example, I have suggested in the past that Dignity/Philadelphia is unique in the way women negatively experience the chapter (1993a, b). My fieldwork in the 1980s and 1990s with Dignity chapters in New York City, Boston, and Atlanta, and what I was told anecdotally about other chapters, painted a more positive portrait of Dignity and women's response and acceptance than in Philadelphia.

25. Several members of the liturgical committee felt no problem with a change such as the practice of having non-Catholic Eucharistic ministers. Stephen explained to me:

> To me personally, it's not such a big issue. . . . I believe it's the Liturgy Committee policy that as long as you believe that it's the body and blood, it's okay, you can be a Eucharistic minister. That's the general consensus of the community after tons of arguments. At one time, they didn't want non-Catholic readers for the same reason. As long as you have the reverence for the body and blood of Christ, and in my mind even if you thought it was just symbolic, but you still had the reverence or symbolism of what was going on, I don't have a problem with that. . . .

26. One book that received much discussion was *Lesbian Nuns: Breaking Silence* (Curb and Manahan 1985), quite controversial upon its initial publication. See Gramick's opinion article (1985) on the publication of the book.

27. As of 1986–1987, Dignity/Philadelphia to my knowledge did not engage in formal Rites of Union for its members who requested them.

28. The chapter business meetings were the time when the general assembly of the membership was to convene for the purpose of deciding on the business of Dignity/Philadelphia. While the steering committee was powerful in that it made important decisions affecting the entire chapter, such as the use of both wine and grape juice at the weekly Mass, the general assembly of the membership did retain the ability to rescind or amend a prior action of the committee. Still, though the quarterly business meetings were open to anyone and conducted after the weekly social hour, they were rarely well attended. The first one I attended in 16 February 1986 only attracted seventeen people. Opening and closing with a prayer, officers of the various committees each made reports, and the entire meeting was run using parliamentary procedure. Among the topics discussed were the recent implementation of the use of grape juice along with wine in the Mass; the groups allowed to meet in the chapter's headquarters, Dignity House (such as an Alcoholics Anonymous or a transsexual support group); the liability insurance that the chapter paid on

the property; and plans for the celebration of the chapter's thirteenth anniversary Mass and celebration in the last weekend in April. The chapter at this time was fiscally sound with no debts and even a certificate of deposit in a local bank.

29. In the summer of 2002, I went back to find the thirteen individuals who had served as the key consultants of my original study. A microcosm of the Dignity member-ship, I discovered that in the intervening years three had died of AIDS or AIDS-related diseases; two had left Dignity completely (one of these individuals had left the Catholic Church and one presently did church work for the archdiocese of Philadelphia); two had left the state; three still belonged to the chapter but infrequently attended its liturgies; and three remained active in the chapter.

30. See the following newspaper articles: "Landmark Catholic Churches Closing" (*The Washington Post*, 27 December 1987); "Detroit Prelate Backs Plan to Close 43 Churches" (*The Los Angeles Times*, 15 October 1988); James Risen, "Day Bittersweet for Detroit's Aging Parishes" (*The Los Angeles Times*, 25 December 1988); Bob Secter, "Chicago Archdiocese to Shut 31 Parishes, Many Schools in Sweeping Cost-Cutting" (*The Los Angeles Times*, 22 January 1990); "Talks of More Church Closings Provokes Ire in Philadel-phia" (*National Catholic Reporter*, 3 July 1998); Teresa Malcolm, "Parish Closings Predicted" (*National Catholic Reporter*, 1998).

31. Such actions are similar to their heterosexual suburban counterparts who return to progressive inner-city parishes (such as St. Vincent de Paul Church in the Germantown section of Philadelphia) in this age of transient Catholics searching for a satisfying parish experience and being attracted to a magnet parish. See also the description of Holy Trin-ity Church in Washington, D.C., in Naughton (1996).

A parallel development in the fifteen years since the 1986 Ratzinger letter has been the migration of many gay and lesbian Catholics from their local parishes and even from Dig-nity itself to urban "gay-friendly" Roman Catholic parishes. Usually staffed by religious orders not diocesan priests (i.e., Jesuits or Franciscans, not priests under direct obedience to the local prelate), here sympathetic pastors openly sponsored AIDS ministries and other programs under the mission of the church's necessary ministry to homosexuals.

The movement toward these parish settings where Catholicism for gays seems an ac-cepting place may have more to do with internal gender and liturgical politics of Dignity congregations than the sexual politics of the institutional church. For example, the Dig-nity chapter that is the focus of my study, Dignity/Philadelphia, has had a problem at-tracting and retaining lesbian members (Primiano 1993a, b). The chapter has engaged in discussions and changes in liturgical practices that have given women a greater role in such functions as reading scripture, preaching, and representing the congregation at the altar. These changes have angered more traditionally minded men who searched for a parish that is both accepting of gays and liturgically traditional. The Society Hill parish of Old St. Joseph's began an outreach to gay and lesbian Catholics in 1990 and for many individuals fulfills their present needs. Some of these individuals have migrated from Dignity.

Reconciling Congregations Bridging Gay and Straight Communities[1]

2

WENDY CADGE

D RIVING THROUGH THE CENTER of Baltimore, a newcomer might do a double take as she passes a large gray stone church with a gay pride banner hanging over the front door. "Praising God, Seeking Justice," reads the banner with a gay pride rainbow flag at its center. The newcomer might be puzzled. A church with a gay pride banner out front? Is it a gay church? Maybe one of the all gay Metropolitan Community churches?[2] If this person sees that it is a United Methodist church, she might be more confused. Newspaper coverage in the past several years has reported on the debates about homosexuality taking place in the United Methodist denomination.[3] Is this church involved in those debates? Is the church even United Methodist anymore?

St. John's United Methodist Church located on the corner of Twenty-seventh and St. Paul Streets in Baltimore, Maryland, is a Reconciling Congregation or one that publicly welcomes all people, regardless of their sexual orientation, into the life of its congregation. It is one of more than 175 United Methodist congregations across the nation that decided, since 1984, to declare themselves Reconciling Congregations.[4] While all do not have rainbow flags hanging over their front doors, all are sending important messages to their communities: gay, lesbian, and bisexual people should be welcomed completely into the life of the church.[5] At a time when the United Methodist denomination officially says that homosexuality is "incompatible with Christian teachings," St. John's and other Reconciling Congregations across the country disagree.

Mainline Protestant denominations in the United States have been thinking, talking, and arguing about homosexuality for more than thirty years (Cadge 2002).[6] National governing bodies in the United Methodist, Presbyterian, Evangelical Lutheran, and American Baptist Churches currently maintain that homosexuality is "biblically . . . a departure from the heterosexual structure of God's Creation," "a sin," and "incompatible with Christian teaching."[7] While these denominations do not bar gay and lesbian people from their congregations or denominations, their policies have created the impression among gay, lesbian, and bisexual people that they are not welcome there. Beginning in the mid-1980s, congregations that disagreed with these denominational statements said so, publicly, forming networks of like-minded congregations in their denominations and across denominations in the process. These Reconciling Congregations in the United Methodist Church and More Light, Welcoming and Affirming, Reconciling in Christ, and Open and Affirming congregations in the Presbyterian, American Baptist, Evangelical Lutheran, and United Church of Christ, respectively, are forming a welcoming church movement across the country in the process.[8]

This chapter briefly describes the history of United Methodist debates about homosexuality before focusing on how two United Methodist congregations became Reconciling Congregations and both gay and straight people found support and community there. By welcoming gay, lesbian, bisexual, and straight people into worship together, Reconciling Congregations serve as a bridge between gay and straight communities, often changing the way straight people think about homosexuality and gay people think about the church in the process. Like at St. John's United Methodist Church in Baltimore, gay, lesbian, bisexual, and straight people in the two congregations described here worship together and come to know each other as people. An older woman in one of these congregations described to me how her thinking about homosexuality changed as her congregation considered becoming Reconciling. "The homosexual people in the congregation are healthy people raising children," she told me. "When you love people, you want to be supportive of what they need and you learn." By shifting questions from homosexuality as a concept to questions about homosexual people sitting at the other end of the pew, Reconciling and other welcoming congregations personalize the issue and play a vital role in bridging gay and straight communities in the United States.

History

Like in the other mainline Protestant denominations, the United Methodist Church has been thinking and talking about homosexuality since the early 1970s (Udis-Kessler 2002; Moon 2001; Wood 2000). The denomination made its first statement about homosexuality in 1972 saying that it considers the practice of homosexuality "incompatible with Christian teachings." While this statement has been challenged at General Conferences since 1972, the statement remains, a bit qualified, in the 2000 *Book of Discipline* (the official summary of current denominational policy):

> Homosexual persons no less than heterosexual persons are individuals of sacred worth. All persons need the ministry and guidance of the church in their struggles for human fulfillment, as well as the spiritual and emotional care of a fellowship that enables reconciling relationships with God, with others, and with self. Although we do not condone the practice of homosexuality and consider this practice incompatible with Christian teaching, we affirm that God's grace is available to all. We implore families and churches not to reject or condemn their lesbian and gay members and friends. We commit ourselves to be in ministry for and with all persons (2000 *Discipline*, 161G).

The question of whether gay and lesbian people can be ordained in the United Methodist Church was addressed indirectly at the 1976 and 1980 General Conferences and then directly at the 1984 General Conference when the answer was clearly stated: no. At the 1984 General Conference, a proposal calling for the "commitment of clergy to 'fidelity in marriage and celibacy in singleness'" was adopted, thus outlawing people engaged in homosexual relationships from being ordained since gay men and lesbians cannot be married. The *Book of Discipline* currently states:

> While persons set apart by the Church for ordained ministry are subject to all the frailties of the human condition and the pressures of society, they are required to maintain the highest standards of holy living in the world. Since the practice of homosexuality is incompatible with Christian teaching, self-avowed practicing homosexuals are not to be accepted as candidates, ordained as ministers, or appointed to serve in The United Methodist Church (2000 *Discipline*, 304.3).

A "self-avowed practicing homosexual" is further defined as a person who "openly acknowledges to a bishop, district superintendent, district committee of ordained ministry, board of ordained ministry, or clergy session" that she or he is a "practicing homosexual."

In recent years, the denomination has also been involved in highly publicized court cases about whether gay men and lesbians can be married by United Methodist clergy in church buildings. Before 1996, some United Methodist clergy were quietly conducting holy unions or other marriage-like ceremonies for gay men and lesbians across the country. Other clergy and lay people disagreed with this practice and at the 1996 General Conference delegates voted to add the following sentence to the *Social Principles of the United Methodist Church*, "Ceremonies that celebrate homosexual unions shall not be conducted by our ministers and shall not be conducted in our churches" (quoted in Wood 2000). This policy was challenged by

UMC pastor Jimmy Creech who in 1997 preformed a ceremony of union for a lesbian couple inside his church building. A year later a United Methodist Church court found Creech not guilty of violating denominational policy on a technical issue, the extent to which policy was binding to local congregations. The implications of the policy were quickly clarified.[9] Several years later, Creech officiated at covenant service for two gay men and at the church trial that resulted was found guilty and was stripped of his ordination in the United Methodist Church.[10] Presently, the *Book of Discipline* clearly states, "Ceremonies that celebrate homosexual unions shall not be conducted by our ministers and shall not be conducted in our churches" (2000 *Discipline*, 332.6).

Debates about homosexuality in national denominational meetings have been accompanied by significant grassroots activity around the issue, despite the fact that the denomination voted in 1976 not to provide funds for any groups that supported homosexuality.[11] The first group of gay men and lesbians came together under the name "Gay United Methodists" in 1975 to "insist that our lives and loving are gifts of God, not rebellion against the divine will."[12] The group later changed their name to Affirmation and has been present at every General Conference since 1976.

In the early 1980s, members of Affirmation began to discuss starting a program through which local churches could show their support for gay and lesbian people. Affirmation members Mark Bowman, D. J. Porter, and Perry Wiggins began to develop a plan. Rev. Robert Davidson, a minister at West Park Presbyterian Church in New York City, wrote a statement of conscience in 1978 that said that congregations who disagreed with statements or actions their denominations made around homosexuality should say so, publicly, and welcome gay men and lesbians into their congregations. This led to the More Light program in the Presbyterian Church, which was a model for the Reconciling Congregation program. Discussions at Affirmation meetings in 1982 about the need for reconciliation between the United Methodist Church and gay men and lesbians led to the name "Reconciling Churches" and later "Reconciling Congregations." At an Affirmation meeting in September of 1983, a plan for the Reconciling Churches or Reconciling Congregation program was presented that closely resembles how the program operates today.[13]

In 1984, Mark Bowman and Beth Richardson volunteered to serve as co-coordinators of the Reconciling Congregation program and began to put together a brochure about how to become a Reconciling Congregation. At the United Methodist General Conference in June, the denomination decided that gay and lesbian people could not be ordained. The morning after the vote, Affirmation members gathered outside of the Civic Center in Baltimore where the meeting was being held and passed out information inviting congregations to become Reconciling Congregations as a way of voicing their opposition to policies adopted by the United Methodist Church that do not welcome gay men and lesbians into all aspects of church life. Within one month, two congregations had decided to become Reconciling Congregations and by the end of the year nine congregations had joined the program.

To become a Reconciling Congregation, congregations were invited to go through a process of study and reflection about the church and homosexuality and then to vote as a congregation about joining the program. Congregations have joined steadily since 1984 as evident in figure 2.1.

As more congregations joined and the Reconciling Congregation program grew in the following years, its goals were threefold. First, the program wanted to "strengthen local churches by helping them consider justice and ministry issues arising from the involvement of gay men and lesbians." Second, they wanted to "support local churches willing to be visible servants in ministry to and with gay and lesbian United Methodists." And finally, the program aimed to "identify local churches where all persons, including gay, lesbian, and bisexual persons, are welcomed as full participants in the Body of Christ."[14] Mark Bowman has explained that the program's main emphases were to shift the focus of discussion away from morality and toward ministry. Morality questions focus on what the Bible says about homosexuality and about whether individuals can be both gay and Christian. Ministry questions emphasize the question, "Can you be a Christian and exclude people from your church?"[15]

In 2000, the Reconciling Congregation program changed its name to the Reconciling Ministries Network because it included campus ministries and other

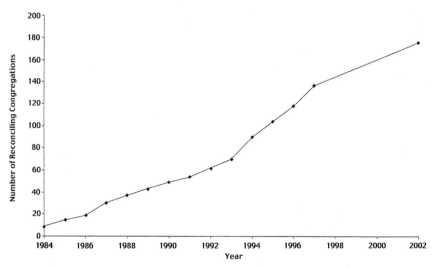

Fig. 2.1.   Number of Reconciling Congregations 1984–2002.
Source: http://www.mnetwork.org/thistory.html

reconciling groups in addition to individual congregations. The Reconciling Ministries Network is a "national grassroots organization that exists to enable full participation of people of all sexual orientations and gender identities in the life of the United Methodist Church, both in policy and practice."[16] The program provides materials for congregations that are considering becoming Reconciling, including a Bible study called "Claiming the Promise" that was designed to put same-sex love in a broader biblical context. It also provides support to current Reconciling Congregations and continues to lobby the denomination to change its official positions about homosexuality. As of June 2002, the Reconciling Ministries Network included 176 Reconciling Congregations, 25 Reconciling Campus ministries, numerous other reconciling groups, and 17,000 individual Reconciling United Methodists.[17]

Two Reconciling Congregations

The remainder of this chapter describes how two particular congregations, one on the West Coast and one on the East Coast of the United States, decided to become Reconciling Congregations and have acted on that commitment since they made it. These descriptions are based on three months of participant observation, a review of historical materials, and interviews with members and the ministers at each congregation conducted in the summer and fall of 1996. The real names of the churches and ministers are used here, though the names of church members have been changed to protect their privacy. Bethany United Methodist Church in San Francisco was one of the first United Methodist churches to become a Reconciling Congregation. The First United Methodist Church of Germantown (FUMCOG) in Philadelphia joined later and the process through which it became a Reconciling Congregation is fairly representative of how most churches go through this process.

Bethany United Methodist Church, located on the edge of the gay Castro District in San Francisco, was founded in 1965 through the merger of two other United Methodist churches in the area. When this research was conducted in 1996 the church had about one hundred members and sixty to seventy people in worship on Sunday mornings. About half were straight and half were gay, lesbian, or bisexual. Bethany became a Reconciling Congregation in 1984. When the Reconciling Congregation program began in 1984, Rev. Karen Oliveto, the minister, told me that the church "looked around and said, 'well we're already doing all of this . . . let's proclaim it.'" A longtime member of the congregation and chairman of the administrative board proposed that the congregation become Reconciling and the proposal was accepted without a congregational vote. "The major struggle that the church needs to be engaged in, at least in America," this church member told me, "is the struggle to become a Reconciling Congregation. . . . I mean the gay community has been struggling in one way or another for a long time and the church has not been involved for the most part. My feeling is that we will be able to get a more humanitarian view towards what humanity is once the church gets involved. . . ."

When Bethany decided to become a Reconciling Congregation, it already had many gay members. Part of the reason, members told me, that the congregation became Reconciling without a vote was because they had been involved in AIDS work for many years. A former church organist was one of the first people in the Bay Area to be diagnosed with AIDS and to die from the disease. Having been through the trauma of AIDS as a congregation, one member told me, made becoming a Reconciling Congregation not such a major issue.

Bethany's status as a Reconciling Congregation is clear from the advertisement the church has placed in the yellow pages, the gay pride flags that hang inside and outside of church buildings, and the symbol of the Reconciling Congregation program that is on many church publications. Gay pride beads are available in a basket at the back of the sanctuary and some people wear them during worship. Once a year the congregation has a Reconciling Sunday and it supports the national ministries of the Reconciling Congregation Network in many ways. To make clear their welcome to gay, lesbian, bisexual, and transgendered people, the congregation has been active in gay pride parades and in a street fair that takes place every year in the Castro District in San Francisco. These activities are a way to do outreach, one member told me. They are a way "to do some healing in the gay, lesbian, bisexual, transgendered community . . . as a way to say we are a religious community and we are not going to beat you up." The congregation has remained very involved in AIDS work and numerous community organizations meet in church buildings every week.

Church members say the congregation has changed some since it became a Reconciling Congregation and has taken in new members, both gay and straight. This mix of gay and straight members was important to everyone. "The gay members are really clear," Karen Oliveto, the pastor, explained to me, "that they don't want this to be another Metropolitan Community Church. They don't want this to be an all-gay church. The straight members really enjoy and are committed to gay and lesbian issues and being part of and having gays and lesbians influence their lives. Parents like having their children know the full diversity of the human community." An older straight church member told me that the Reconciling Congregation program as been "good for the church. . . . The mix is good. I hope it doesn't get one sided. The older people have been very accepting of gays and lesbians in the church and love them—realizing that they probably had a relative who was gay but didn't dare say so in the past." In addition to including people with many different sexual orientations, the church includes members from many racial backgrounds.

Among its gay and lesbian members, Bethany United Methodist Church has attracted a disproportionate number of people who were trained in the ministry. Glenn Jones, for example, was raised in a United Methodist church in the Midwest. He completed a master's degree in lay ministry in the 1970s but left the church shortly thereafter because his lover was not interested in religion and he thought Christians were operating in ignorance about homosexuality. He became involved in the Metropolitan Community Church some years later saying that because he was not comfortable with the bar scene, it was his greatest outlet into the gay and lesbian community. He found the Metropolitan Community Church, however, to be a bit too fundamentalist. Twenty-five years after he left the United Methodist Church, Glenn returned. A difficult roommate situation led him to look for a more "life affirming kind of experience," and on Christmas Eve in 1995, Glenn attended Bethany both because it was a United Methodist church and because it was close to his home. He had visited Bethany on the two previous Easter Sundays, but it was not until his visit on Christmas Eve 1995 that he learned about the movement to fully welcome gay, lesbian, bisexual, and transgendered people into individual congregations and the United Methodist denomination more generally. Glenn became involved in Bethany over the next few months, he told me, because he needed "that personal self love" and because he believed "the resistance to gay and lesbian civil rights, the bedrock resistance to it, is in religion and Christianity" making the church "central to the next stage of gay and lesbian civil rights." Glenn believes in a God "who cares very much about our lives and will be in our lives if we just ask," and in scripture that does not condemn gays and lesbians at base level. He said, "That notion [of scriptural condemnation] needs to be dispelled and can be dispelled if the people in power in the churches take a different position." Since getting involved in Bethany, Glenn has been a prayer leader and has organized people to march in the gay pride parade in San Francisco.

Like Glenn, Susan Jones and Mark Adams, two other Bethany members, were trained in the ministry. Susan actually pastored a church for several years in the early 1980s. She left the ministry in the mid-1980s when the denomination was making the decision that gay and lesbian clergy could not be ordained ministers and has moved between jobs in other denominations and non-church jobs since that time. She has been involved in Bethany since the early 1980s. Mark Adams, another Bethany member, was ordained as a United Methodist minister and remained closeted for more than fifteen years, coming out just before he was ready to retire. "I would have been fired if I said anything earlier," Mark told me. Known and respected throughout the area, Adams believes his coming out influenced people's attitudes. "They [the church] needed to glean that we weren't so different from other people. They needed to get over reading, seeing, and thinking about the really raunchy aspects of homosexuality—which are the same as those for heterosexuality. They need to see that our career and family goals are the same—there is a need for substantial families among us." Since it became a Reconciling Congregation in 1984, Bethany United Methodist Church in San Francisco has been a leader in efforts to include people of all sexual orientations in its congregation and the United Methodist Church more broadly.

Unlike Bethany, the First United Methodist Church of Germantown (FUMCOG), located in the Germantown area of Philadelphia, went through a lengthy process of discussion and debate before declaring itself a Reconciling Congregation in 1990. While there is no "typical" Reconciling Congregation, the majority have stories more like FUMCOG's than like Bethany's. The process by which FUMCOG became a Reconciling Congregation was centered on education followed by a congregational vote. It was slow and difficult at times, though gay and straight members of the congregation both report benefiting from it.

Founded in the eighteenth century, the congregation at FUMCOG has a history of involvement in social justice issues and is committed to ministering in its urban location. The congregation was involved in the civil rights movement and more recently was involved in issues related to race, immigration, homelessness, and the Sanctuary Church movement that supported Central American refugees. When this research was conducted in 1996 there were five to six hundred people on the active rolls of the church and several hundred in worship on Sundays. Whites and African-Americans were both involved with the congregation, which was mostly straight but included a few gay and lesbian members. Unlike Bethany, which was led by one minister, FUMCOG was led by Theodore Loder, the senior pastor, and several associates in 1996 when this research was conducted.

FUMCOG began the process of becoming a Reconciling Congregation when Rev. Loder approached the Social Concerns Committee with the idea. Believing that the issues surrounding gay and lesbian rights in the churches are justice issues, he asked the congregation to consider becoming a Reconciling Congregation. At first a group of people, almost all of whom were gay or lesbian or straight with personal reasons for interest, came together and began to discuss the issue. The senior pastor and members of the administrative board quickly realized that a more representative sample of the congregation was needed in order for the congregation to formally consider the topic of homosexuality and suggested that a task force be appointed to talk about homosexuality and the possibility of becoming a Reconciling Congregation. The pastor and administrative board thought a more diverse group was needed for several reasons. First, they wanted to show that gay and lesbian people as well as those with personal reasons for interest in the issue were not alone in the struggle. Second, with such a large congregation the group had to be diverse enough that most church members would know and trust a committee member to facilitate comfortable communication if they had questions or concerns. And third, the process needed the credibility provided by a diverse group. Some of the people in the initial group were part of the task force that was appointed and others formed a separate group that did much of the legwork as the congregation discussed the issue of homosexuality over the next two years. Before the task force could begin its formal work, however, they had to reconcile themselves to working together. In these early conversations, gay and lesbian members of the task force were upset that their initial group was not trusted and straight members of the task force were concerned that people might conclude, based on their involvement, that they were gay or lesbian.

For the next two years, the task force led the congregation in study and discussion about homosexuality. The senior pastor preached about the issue early in the process, and the congregation's approach to the issue was faith based, with a deep concern about what God and the Bible had to say about homosexuality. Members of the congregation studied biblical passages, read medical reports, thought about the arguments made by theologians, and heard from several gay and lesbian people about their experiences. The task force also staffed a table on Sundays after worship, distributed literature at the weekly coffee hour, wrote articles for the church newsletter, and held classes about homosexuality as part of the adult Sunday school curriculum. Informal discussions were also held in people's homes. Child psychologists and experts from Parents and Friends of Lesbians and Gays (PFLAG) spoke at the church and several gay and lesbian people who were involved in the congregation but had not been out as lesbian or gay in a very public way also spoke. These personal narratives were particularly important, one member told me, "When people had to put a face to the concept [of homosexuality] things changed. 'Wait, this is someone I have known all my life.'" Throughout the process, the task force members worked to "encourage an environment where people could freely express their feelings," although this was sometimes difficult because people's feelings and opinions were strong.

At the end of the two years, the task force submitted a report to the administrative board and the administrative board then voted unanimously to allow the congregation at large to vote. A Sunday was designated and when the vote was taken five people dissented and the rest were in favor of becoming a Reconciling Congregation. A Reconciling Statement was adopted, the central portion of which reads,

> In becoming a Reconciling Congregation, we affirm the full participation of gay men and lesbian women in our church community and in the Church at large in-

cluding recognition of the gifts and graces they may bring to the ordained ministry in local congregations.

This statement is reflected in the litany recited at the reception of new members. In addition to the litany, a service is held once a year to celebrate the congregation's commitment to the Reconciling Congregation program and funds are sent to the national office. As a result of becoming a Reconciling Congregation, the congregation decided to establish a permanent Religion and Sexuality Committee to think about sexuality more broadly. In the period when this research was conducted, the committee had held workshops, screened videos, and hosted informal conversations on a number of topics related to sexuality.

Like at Bethany, both gay and straight people attend FUMCOG, although, unlike at Bethany, the majority of people at FUMCOG are straight. Many of the gay and lesbian people at the church have visited or attended the Metropolitan Community Church but do not like the segregation and want to be in sexually mixed environments. According to Ann Marie Donohue, a staff associate at the church, gay people come to FUMCOG for the worship, to be together with other people, and to know they will be included without needing to make a personally public statement. "People are here and are who they are with their partners and children sharing in the ordinariness of life," Ann Marie told me. "Lesbian couples with children are a family and they want to be at church without having to be an anomaly and provide explanation."

While a few people reported being frustrated that FUMCOG has not been more vocal around gay and lesbian issues, many others spoke strongly about how the church's decision to become a Reconciling Congregation influenced their lives and experiences at the church. Karen Atkinson, a lesbian in her forties, first came to FUMCOG in the early 1980s to attend a funeral for a gay couple who had died within a few weeks of each other. She was surprised and impressed with how the minister spoke of them as a couple but at the time was still angry with the church and not ready to return. Karen was raised in an Episcopal family in which the love of God was instilled in her early in life. As a young adult she received a perfect attendance award for thirteen years of church participation and after graduating from college earned a master's degree in theology. Karen told me that she understood she was a lesbian when she was twenty-two, and that by the time she left seminary was a "gay, angry, feminist person" who did not think she would ever find a church where she would be happy. It was not until her ten-year seminary reunion that she realized she wanted to go back to church and the United Methodist congregation where she had attended her friends' funeral was the only one in the area where she felt welcomed.

When Karen and her partner Kathy visited FUMCOG with the intention of getting involved, the congregation was just voting to becoming a Reconciling Congregation. Karen and Kathy found the congregation's public commitment refreshing and welcoming.

> We just came to FUMCOG at the right time. Talk about the grace of God or whatever you want to call it. What an absolute joy it is to be accepted by a community of faith as a lesbian couple. We have begun to understand more fully who we are and have expanded our faith and spirituality in a wonderful community in which to grow, learn, and question. . . . I feel like a whole person.

Doris Beadsly, a married, straight, twenty-year member of FUMCOG spoke about her experiences with FUMCOG's decision to become a Reconciling Congregation very differently.

> I never had the opportunity to meet people of different sexual orientations before FUMCOG began to discuss the issue and I was surprised to see that gay and lesbian people in our community all seemed so normal. I didn't know much [about homosexuality] and when people revealed their sexual orientations in our community in conversations and discussions in which it felt appropriate, I realized there is nothing flagrant in how they seem. They are individuals. They are just people with different talents as they become known to us: one is good in drama, another is gifted in social work. You get to know them. They are good people. They don't stand out in any way as being eccentric. Some individuals I like more than others, that's how it is with all people, but overall I care about them as people and would do anything to help them maintain the relationships that are important to them. The homosexual people in the congregation are healthy people raising children. When you love people, you want to be supportive of what they need and you learn.

She went on to say,

> I always thought sexual orientation was some kind of a choice. Now I know if they chose, I think they would choose to be heterosexual because it's so much easier. And who's to say they shouldn't be homosexual. I used to think about homosexuality as an illness. I had an uncle like that, I realize now, I didn't know when I was a child. To seek for what they need to be healthy people, they [homosexuals] get condemned. People just can't help it. That's how they're attracted and they're happy if they find someone who thinks about them in that way.

When asked about the process through which FUMCOG became a Reconciling Congregation, Doris told me that,

> The pastor paved the way to becoming a Reconciling Congregation with remarks that were helpful. Initially we had to learn to hold judgment. We were approach-

ing this from the Christian orientation, and we are all here together and need for-giveness for something. The central message of love and the news of the Gospel are more important than the interpretation of any single verse. We need to read scripture with our minds. The message of love was the key. I attended an adult academy session about sexuality and we occasionally talked about it in church. There were meetings in which we discussed homosexuality. At one, an older man with gray hair spoke up in favor of gay and lesbian people and I think that was important, to see support between generations. For people who have trouble with this, it helps to have older white male support. It's very hard to maintain prejudice when you really know people. It's easier to think about "them" as "them" when they are marching in parades.

As a result of what she learned at church, Doris describes her thinking as changed.

My husband and I now try to make comments when people say something prej-udiced. We find now that as sweeping statements are made we are more aware. We can say, "We find at our church people who aren't like that." We can counteract stereotypes and quote what gay and lesbian people at church have said. Our con-gregation is a warm one; you don't want them [homosexuals] to have to hide. You just don't want people that you care about to be mistreated. You want them to be able to raise their children. The peopleness of people becomes so important. The rest seems like details.

Conclusion

Bethany United Methodist Church in San Francisco, the First United Methodist Church of Germantown in Philadelphia, and other United Methodist Reconcil-ing Congregations across the country are publicly welcoming people of all sexual orientations fully into the lives of their churches. While the United Methodist de-nomination continues to debate homosexuality, these congregations are acting out their commitment to full inclusion for all people on a day-to-day basis. As the sto-ries people at Bethany and FUMCOG told me about their involvement in these congregations reveal, fully inclusive churches are centrally important to gay, les-bian, bisexual, transgender, and straight people in the United States today. Gay and lesbian people were relieved to find congregations outside of the all-gay Met-ropolitan Community Church where they could be who they are without fearing condemnation or exclusion. Straight people, like Doris Beadsly quoted above, learned a great deal about homosexuality as their congregations became Reconcil-ing Congregations and found themselves thinking about the issue in a new way.

While it is easy for the work of welcoming congregations to be overshadowed by national debate and the very real conflict and controversy that has developed around homosexuality in some congregations, it is important not to overlook the ways these congregations are ministering both to gay and to straight people.[18] The experiences of gay and straight people at Bethany and FUMCOG show that through the process of becoming a Reconciling Congregation, United Methodist and other mainline Protestant congregations bridge gay and straight communities in ways not possible in other social sectors.

Notes

1. This chapter is based closely on Wendy Cadge "God's Rainbow Families of Faith: Reconciling Congregations Bridging Gay and Straight Communities," Honors Thesis, Swarthmore College, Department of Sociology and Anthropology, 1997. I use "gay" here as a shorthand way to refer to gay, lesbian, bisexual, and transgender people. I use the terms homosexual and gay, lesbian, and bisexual interchangeably throughout this paper.

2. The Metropolitan Community Church was founded in Los Angeles in 1968 by Rev. Troy D. Perry to address the religious needs of gay, lesbian, bisexual, and transgender people. For a discussion of its history, see Wilson 1995; Perry 1990; and http://www.ufmcc.com/. For a more sociological analysis, see Warner 1995.

3. Corrie Cutrer, "Eight UMC Pastors Quiet Denomination," *Christianity Today* 44, no. 13 (13 November 13 2000); "Methodists Protest Church Policy on Gays," *Christian Century* 117, no. 22 (August 2–9 2000); "Debate over Same-Sex Marriage Splits a United Methodist Church Near Atlanta," *New York Times* (24 June, 1999); Gustav Niebuhr, "68 Clerics Face Judgment over a Same Sex Union," *New York Times* (11 June 1999).

4. This number is current as of June 2002. http://www.rmnetwork.org/whoarewe.phtml

5. Welcoming congregation programs in the mainline Protestant denominations all include gay men and lesbians. Most include bisexual people and fewer include transgender people.

6. By "mainline Protestant" here I refer to the six largest mainline Protestant denominations in the United States: the United Methodist Church, the Presbyterian Church (USA), the Episcopal Church, the Evangelical Lutheran Church in America, the United Church of Christ, and the American Baptist Churches (Wuthnow and Evans 2002).

7. "Sex, Marriage, and the Family," Lutheran Church in America Fifth Biennial Convention Social Statement, 1970; "Sexuality and the Human Community," United Presbyterian Church 182nd General Assembly, 1970: 468–470, 888; "Addition to Social Principles," United Methodist Church General Conference, 1972; "Resolution on Homosexuality," American Baptist General Board, October 1992.

8. Tangible elements of this network include the *Open Hands* magazine published since 1985 and national welcoming church conferences held regularly.

9. Judicial Council Special Session, D-833, August 1998.

10. http://www.umaffirm.org/cornews/creech57.html

11. That restriction remains. The 2000 *Book of Discipline* states that "no board, agency, committee, commission, or council shall give United Methodist funds to any gay caucus

or group, or otherwise use such funds to promote the acceptance of homosexuality. The council shall have the right to stop such expenditures." 806.9

12. http://www.umaffirm.org/afhistory.html

13. "A Brief Chronological History of the Reconciling Congregation Movement," http://www.rmnetwork.org/history.phtml

14. "How to Become a Reconciling Congregation," Resource Paper 2, May 1994.

15. Mark Bowman, telephone interview, 9 December 1998.

16. http://www.rmnetwork.org/whoarewe.phtml

17. http://www.rmnetwork.org/whoarewe.phtml

18. For evidence of this debate in congregations, see Hartman 1996.

No Longer an Oxymoron   3
Integrating Gay and Lesbian
Seventh-day Adventist Identities

RENÉ DRUMM

I am still a quite conservative Adventist. The Adventist lifestyle is something that works for me and something that I worked out with God on my knees after many hours of prayer and studying and tearful contemplation. The same goes for my homosexuality. I have peace in my heart that God accepts me as I am. Being the omnipotent God that He is, He knew I was going to be gay long before I was a gleam in my Dad's eye. Now I see my homosexuality as a blessing. It took a long time to get there—34 years, but now I've made it.

This is a story about people who were brought up in the Seventh-day Adventist (SDA) church and who, in the process of growing up, discovered that they were gay or lesbian.[1] Since the SDA church condemns homosexual behavior, the two different personas held by gay and lesbian members of the church were in automatic conflict. This essay documents the pain and struggle of people who are an integral part of a system that rejects who they are, their personhood, their being. The lived experience of these individuals may parallel common struggles of other persons who are rejected by religious systems. It is, however, a unique struggle to grow up gay or lesbian in the highly sectarian Seventh-day Adventist Church. For many such believers, being Christian means being an Adventist; therefore, to integrate their sexual and religious identities they must find distinctively Adventist ways of legitimating their sexual orientation. Their integration must come about from within an Adventist system that denies the possibility of being gay and Christian if they are to reconcile their Adventist Christian faith with their sexuality. This, then, is a story that illustrates personal resilience and triumph through the struggle for sexual and Seventh-day Adventist identity integration.

For Seventh-day Adventist Christians, what does it mean to be "brought up in the church?" It usually means having at least one Seventh-day Adventist parent. People who are raised in the church probably attended some Adventist-affiliated school and regularly participated in church activities. Growing up in the SDA church also means holding some basic Evangelical Christian beliefs such as that the Bible is the inspired word of God, that Christ came to earth as God/man to die for the sins of humanity, and that there is a heaven where saints who believe in Jesus will live forever.

Being brought up in this distinctive religious tradition also includes adhering to quite distinctive religious beliefs and practices that set Seventh-day Adventists apart from other Evangelical Christians. As their name implies, Seventh-day Adventists observe the Seventh-day (Saturday) as the divinely sanctioned day of worship. They hold that Jesus will come to earth again to save the living faithful. They also believe that those who have "fallen asleep" (died) in Jesus will be resurrected and taken to heaven (rather than going to heaven soon after death). The personal practices of Seventh-day Adventists promote a holistic religious and cultural identity of human life, in addition to the more spiritual aspects. For example, in the Adventist church, there are beliefs about eating (the lacto-ovo vegetarian diet is preferred), drinking (no alcohol), being entertained (no dancing, going to a movie theater is discouraged), dress (no jewelry), and of course, sexual behavior (no premarital sex and no sex with same-sex partners).

Adventists have interpreted scripture to support these distinctive beliefs and have outlined the beliefs in a book called *Seventh-day Adventists Believe . . . 27: A Biblical Exposition of Fundamental Doctrines* (Ministerial Association 1988). Altogether, this group's unique theological position creates a distinct cultural–religious reality that melds these religious convictions with members' personal identities.

Given these doctrines, growing up Adventist also means growing up believing in the inherent sinfulness of homosexual behavior. Adventists believe that homosexual desires are temptations that the Devil uses to separate a person from God. Within this reality, an Adventist gay or lesbian person is an oxymoron. The two cannot exist harmoniously together.

Despite formidable theological obstacles, including the teaching that persons are condemned to hell for being attracted to the same sex, SDAs still do come to identify as gay or lesbian Adventists. What processes do persons go through to arrive at this identity integration? What happens to the person's faith and Adventist identity as a result of this integration? Many of the Adventist gay and lesbian persons I interviewed appear to go through three basic phases of identity negotiation as they deal with their religious beliefs and their sexual orientation. These phases include a period of struggle and turmoil, a striving toward self-acceptance, and a survivalist stance coming about through decision making and redefinition.

The portraits of these courageous believers struggling to redefine themselves as gay and lesbian Adventists come from interviews I conducted with fifty-seven people. These stories were shared in an in-depth interview process and through written autobiographies from gay and lesbian (current and former) Adventists. I also obtained further information by posting questions to members of KinNet, an Internet group offering support to gay, lesbian, transgender, and bisexual Adventists. The interviews varied in length according to how much the person wanted to share or the time available. The shortest interviews lasted about an hour while the longest one was six hours. Although I talked to both men and women, more men than women participated. I spoke only to adults over eighteen years of age. The youngest person I interviewed was twenty-one and the oldest was seventy-three. In terms of ethnic and cultural diversity, most were Caucasian, although a few were from Asian, African American, and Hispanic cultural backgrounds. There is also some international diversity, including one person from Australia and two Canadians. All those interviewed had graduated from high school. More than half had completed college, eight received master's degrees, two graduated from medical school, and three earned doctoral degrees. All of the names I share are pseudonyms to protect people's privacy unless they specifically requested otherwise.

Growing Up Adventist

I often began my interviews with the question, "How did you become an Adventist?" The following response by Marvin typifies just how deeply ingrained the Adventist identity is in the people to whom I spoke. The responses to this question, much like Marvin's, indicate the Adventist religious identity involved more than just beliefs to be held or a group to which one belongs.

> To answer the question of how I became an Adventist, I'd have to say that I don't know what else I could have been. I was born in an Adventist hospital (on the Sabbath, no less), to SDA parents who had graduated from SDA schools, sent there by their SDA parents. I went only to SDA churches and my parents socialized almost exclusively with SDAs. My aunts and uncles were SDAs. One set were missionary doctors, another uncle was an academy Bible teacher. My mother's father had been a missionary to Japan.

Since I too grew up in an Adventist home, I was prepared to hear of typical patterns of Seventh-day Adventist families. Indeed, most of the people I talked to described a typical Adventist upbringing that included practicing family worship, following a vegetarian diet, keeping the Sabbath, and performing other traditions promoted by the church. In contrast to some of the early research on families in which gay children were raised (Pattison and Pattison 1980), nearly all those interviewed related that they had come from a close-knit family. As Donald affirmed, "I come from a very loving and caring family. We are very close to this day. I call them all the time and assure them that I love them. They do the same."

Most of the people I talked to attended a church-affiliated school for at least some portion of their education. One of the gay men I interviewed commented, "The greatest influence on my development as an Adventist was probably the fact that I attended SDA schools from first grade through a master's degree."

This combination of being raised in Adventist homes and attending Adventist schools created a powerful mechanism of enculturation into Adventist teachings and traditions. Most people accepted the Adventist religion and belief system in its entirety. Nathan described this enculturation process.

> I went to boarding school for academy and an Adventist college a few hours away after I graduated. I had a good experience. My teachers were great. I really never questioned the Adventist beliefs having grown up in the environment.

This pattern of uncontested acceptance of the social and theological environment led to similar paths for many of the people I talked to, beginning with struggle and turmoil over their gay or lesbian sexual orientation.

Struggle and Turmoil

The norm of heterosexuality was especially strong among the people I interviewed. These persons predominantly believed that they were heterosexual until they could no longer deny the reality that something else was going on with them. Generally, the response to this evidence was resistance. These gay and lesbian Adventists devised multiple ways to not be lesbian or gay. My dissertation study (Drumm 1998) details the lengths to which these Seventh-day Adventists went in order to resist becoming gay or lesbian. The efforts included denial, religious participation, psychotherapeutic work, social involvement, and the ultimate effort, attempted suicide.

During this initial phase, these persons engaged in a profound struggle to try to understand not only their sexuality, but also what it meant in terms of their religious beliefs. The emotional and spiritual pain that the participants experienced is reflected in the numerous strategies they used to resist homosexuality.

Denial—An Effort in Pretend

While denial is a typical response in understanding oneself as gay or lesbian (Troiden 1984), gay and lesbian Adventists employed this protective mechanism extensively. Some participants remained in denial even in the face of strong evidence. For example, Nan, who had been in a same-sex relationship for two years recalled, "Although we were lovers in every sense of the word, we had both been raised in such strict homophobic religions that we never admitted we were lesbians. We told ourselves we were two people who fell in love with each other and both just happened to be female." In another case, Charles, who was an Adventist minister and had been heterosexually married for ten years, was arrested for same-sex solicitation in a public place. After the arrest, he still was not able to see himself as gay. He recalled his thoughts after his disclosure to his wife about the arrest, "I told my wife what had happened [about my same-sex encounters] and we both thought it was a phase."

The people I interviewed often connected their denial with religion or God. John, a former student missionary remembered, "I never claimed or owned being gay. It was just always an unnamed troubling temptation that I battled with." A daughter of a prominent Adventist administrator who was in college at the time reported, "My first reaction [to realizing my homosexuality] was screaming inside, 'No! God, No! I'd rather die.'" For these individuals, since homosexuality was seen as a moral issue and a sinful condition, it was something to be resisted as other temptations and sins.

Religious Efforts

In the midst of their struggles, these persons turned to tools from their upbringing to attempt to change their sexual orientation. All of those I interviewed prayed to have their homosexual desires taken away. Joanne recalled her intense religious efforts: "I spent entire nights agonizing in prayer with God. Begging Him, 'Please Lord! Please! Don't let me be gay!' I found myself praying, 'Please Lord, let this cup pass from me but your will be done.'"

Adventists believe that God, through the Bible, promises help in times of need. Adventists are taught to claim these promises, that is, believe that God's help will come to them if they ask. Sue, a lesbian engineer who grew up in a missionary family, remembered her efforts to rely on God's help. "I resolutely decided I could overcome this, with God's help. It was sin and all sin could be overcome through Christ. I began looking for Bible texts to admonish myself. I'd look for promises of overcoming and ask friends to pray for me."

These prayers often came in the form of "laying on of hands." This is a religious ritual where Adventist ministers and elders of the church pray for the person who needs "healing" while gathered in a group and physically touching the individual being prayed for. Alan recalled his experience with the prayer ritual, "Soon after my first affair I was filled with guilt. So the next morning I said to him [my partner], 'You can't stay here. This is wrong.' He left and I got into the religion thing again. People prayed for me with laying on of hands."

When trying to resist homosexuality, some lesbian and gay Adventists would immerse themselves in religious activities hoping that the homosexual tendencies would lessen. Nathan, a pastor's son, described his efforts. "I did a lot of praying. I got involved with church activities like leading song service and youth activities, helping out with Pathfinders, and leading Sabbath School."

Psychotherapeutic Efforts

About one-third of the people I talked to sought professional help including traditional talk therapy, aversion therapy, and even residential treatment in an attempt to change of their sexual orientations. In each case, these efforts failed. These failures support existing literature that documents the difficulties that are typically encountered in attempts to change sexual orientation (Friedman and Downey 1994). Richard's comments attest to this difficulty, "I prayed, fasted, wept, had aversion therapy, but God would not make women sexually attractive to me or take away my fascination with men."

In some cases, failure to change was not the only problem associated with treatment. One of the persons I talked to was sexually abused while attending a church-affiliated "change ministry" program. This ministry was operated by a "reformed homosexual" who was also a former SDA minister (Lawson 1987). The director of this program made sexual advances toward this person almost immediately after he committed himself to residential treatment. He described being abused by the director from his first weekend at the center until he left more than a year later. Subsequent interviews with former residents revealed widespread sexual abuse among the counselees (Lawson 1987).

Social Efforts

Another way these gay and lesbian Adventist believers tried to resist their homosexual desires was to pursue a heterosexual relationship and get married. Most, but not all, of these persons knew by the time of their marriage that they were gay or lesbian, however, they hoped that marriage would change their orientations. Nan remembered the futility of her heterosexual marriage,

> I guess I allowed myself to fall in love with the idea that this guy loved and cared for me. When he asked me to marry him, I was thirty-two years old and figured this was God's answer to my prayers. After all, we were taught that if we asked God to take away unnatural desires He would do so.

An Effort Not "To Be"—Suicide Attempts

Research indicates a higher rate of suicidal thoughts and suicide attempts among sexual minority adolescents than among their heterosexual peers (Russell and

Joyner 2001). It is not surprising, therefore, that about one-fourth of those I talked to also attempted suicide in a final desperate effort to rid themselves of their homosexuality. Jason recalled, "I thought that suicide would be the best solution to my problem [being gay]. Death seemed like the only option. Death appeared to hold everything I wanted from life and which life couldn't give me—everlasting peace and permanent freedom from homosexuality."

Coming Out Adventist

After spending some time in denial and finally coming out to oneself, many of the people I talked to came out to others including their family. Because Adventist religious beliefs prohibit homosexuality, nearly everyone I interviewed experienced some form of rejection if they came out to family members. The rejection by family members varied from mild distancing behavior to a total disowning of the person. Nathan, an Adventist pastor's son, recalled the painful night he came out to his parents. "My dad took it hard. At one point he came into my bedroom and said, 'If your mother and I would have known about this, she would have had an abortion.'"

Most Adventists parents tried to convince their lesbian and gay children how "wrong" homosexuality was. While some did not reject outright their son or daughter, they did explicitly reject an essential part of them, their sexuality. Carol recalled a confrontation with her parents about her sexual orientation. "When my parents became aware of my homosexual involvement they sat me down. They read from the Bible and told me about how homosexuals are going to hell, and they tried to get me out of it."

Some parents took an optimistic approach that their son or daughter would eventually change his or her mind. Mark remembered his mother's reaction after he came out to her, "I did come out to my mother, who is praying for me. She hasn't turned her back on me. She's hoping that I'll see the light, that I will come to her way of thinking, that it [homosexual behavior] is a sin."

While most gay and lesbian Adventists experienced rejection on some level, there was often an eventual reconciliation over time. Some families came to accept the gay or lesbian family member, however, only if that person's gay or lesbian identity was downplayed. In some cases, the same-sex partners of gay or lesbian family members were treated as nonexistent. In other cases, families accepted the family member and treated his or her partner as an "in-law." Richard, who came out to his family later in life, reflected on this gradual acceptance.

> I think that my family's acceptance of me is related to when I chose to tell them about my sexuality. I was able to come out to them after I was comfortable with myself and could be positive and tell them that I felt that God was using me.

When my partner came along, not many years later, they liked him and liked what they saw of us together. There was a very touching moment one morning when we were visiting them when Dad and Mum drew us together and Dad made a little speech saying how much they liked him and welcomed him into the family.

Striving Toward Self-Acceptance

Lesbian and gay Seventh-day Adventists developed and used a variety of strategies to come to a self-acceptance of their sexual orientation. This acceptance occurred in spite of family and religious socialization that prohibited homosexual behavior. It appeared as though the participants needed to come to some type of resignation that their sexual orientation was not going to change before moving on to self-acceptance. After putting time, effort, and financial resources into attempting to change, these individuals eventually realized that change was not going to happen to them in the time they allowed for it, with the resources they were able and willing to devote. Joanne attested to a long struggle leading up to the point where she finally came to this resolution.

> I've prayed, memorized scripture, fasted, changed my diet, been anointed, prayed for the Lord to "cast out the demon of homosexuality" from me, been in counseling— all in the attempt to eradicate this sexual orientation from my heart and mind. I've suppressed my desires and longings to express love, all with the one goal of living a life of holiness, in obedience to God's commands and His ideal for my life. I've spoken with SDA gays and lesbians who have grown up in the SDA church, who are in committed, loving relationships, and have tried to convince them of the "error of their ways." After nearly twenty-five years of praying for God to change me, to take these desires away, to give me the strength to "live a life of purity," my sexual orientation was as strong as ever.

The efforts these interviewees made in coming to self-acceptance involved both social and religious tools. The social efforts focused on developing new role models, while the religious efforts centered on activities such as reexamining scriptures for new interpretations, seeing God in a new way, or believing that God had given a sign of blessing. For these persons, it appeared that in order to understand and accept their sexual orientation, some "reckoning" had to occur around religious beliefs.

Developing New Role Models

Finding new role models proved to be an important strategy in helping gay and lesbian Adventists move toward self-acceptance. All those I interviewed searched for other people to help them understand how they, as Christians brought up in families whose religious beliefs prohibit homosexual behavior, could be gay or lesbian. In addition, they sought information from others about how they might integrate these apparently conflicting selves. Generally, the role models that were sought out were other Adventists, rather than individuals from the larger gay or religious communities.

One way that gay and lesbian Adventists found supportive role models was through SDA Kinship International, an organization that offers networking and support for lesbian, gay, bisexual, and transgender Adventists. Kinship originated in the early 1970s when a gay Adventist placed a notice in the classified section of *The Advocate* (a national gay newsmagazine). Thirty-seven former Adventists responded from all areas of the United States and Canada. In 1976, two men placed an ad for a meeting in Palm Desert, California, which launched SDA Kinship International. The organization, incorporated in 1981, now has a board of fifteen officers and ten regional coordinators. Kinship's website notes that the "current list of members and friends includes well over a thousand people in 16 countries" (SDA Kinship International 2001). SDA Kinship sponsors activities such as chapter meetings, socials, retreats, picnics, potluck dinners, workshops, worship, recreation, and an annual camp meeting. Every two months Kinship publishes a newsletter, the *SDA Kinship Connection*, and sponsors an online computer group, KinNet.

In 1987, the General Conference of Seventh-day Adventists filed an unsuccessful lawsuit against SDA Kinship for "breach of trademark" (Lawson 1992). The church did not want Kinship using the Seventh-day Adventist name because it might give the impression that the church endorsed Kinship's activities. The case was argued in the federal court in Los Angeles in February 1991. In its verdict, the court rejected the General Conference case and Kinship was allowed to continue using the full name: Seventh-day Adventist Kinship, International (Lawson 1992).

Kinship provides assistance and support to its members through reading materials, personal dialogue, and professional referrals. The organization attempts to address the problems of Adventist parents and families of gays, lesbians, bisexuals, and transgender individuals. It also provides specialized support for those touched directly or indirectly by AIDS (SDA Kinship International 2001). For nearly all of the participants in this study, Kinship played a part in connecting them to new role models.

> I got the number for Kinship, called and talked to Linda. She suggested I go to California over spring break to meet some Kinship members. I went and met two women and their partners. I felt for the first time that I had met my own kind. We were soul mates. We talked and talked and talked. I learned so much about lesbian

language, literature, books, and tapes, the culture. Another couple showed me a different side of the culture. We went to a gay play that was really raunchy. By the time I left California, I realized that there was lot of good and a lot of bad in the lesbian culture and I would need to sift through it (Sue).

Through Kinship, Sue had her first introduction to gay culture. Part of that introduction felt familiar to her, like a puzzle piece of her had been missing all of her life and had finally been found. On the other hand, the part of gay culture that didn't mesh with Adventist values left her feeling uncomfortable and wary.

For Adam, his guard was up before joining Kinship. He remembered his first meeting as rather neutral. In contrast to Sue, Adam recalled this encounter with Kinship as significant, although not the life-changing experience she had. In spite of these lukewarm feelings about the group itself, Adam has maintained his connection to Kinship since that first meeting.

> After I heard about Kinship, I made contact with a member and went to my first meeting. Although I can't say that the meeting was an incredibly wonderful experience, it was good to meet other gay Adventists, and I was sufficiently impressed to join Kinship. I have been a member ever since.

Kinship has created a place where gay and lesbian Adventists can belong. This is a new experience for many of these persons. It is a place they can ask questions about the issues that trouble them most. For Nan, she was able to learn about how other gay and lesbian Adventists interpret scripture and traditional Adventist writing about sexual orientation. She related, "I learned of Kinship through the *Gayellow Pages*. It was a great relief to realize [from Kinship contacts] that nowhere in the Bible or the Spirit of Prophecy is there a mention—let alone a condemnation—of homosexuality as one's natural orientation."

George is currently a nonpracticing Adventist, but is very involved in Kinship. He sees the organization as an important ministry. He knows the loneliness and isolation that being gay and Adventist can bring to one's life and wants to be part of helping other gay Adventists find peace about who they are.

> I want to share with gay men and women as I have been so powerfully blessed. I see the ongoing need for mentoring, giving, and role modeling as a gay man, for it helps all concerned, and it is a two-way street. Within the organization of Kinship, I feel blessed to have so many wonderful role models.

Some Adventist gays and lesbians have also found new role models through KinNet. KinNet is an Internet discussion group initiated by members of Kinship. Peter attested to the importance of KinNet. "Being the computer nerd that I am, I had never heard of any gay SDAs until I was surfing the net on my own and

found KinNet." Tammy had an even more dramatic reaction upon finding Kin-
Net,

> Soon after we got our computer and were connected to the Internet, I started surf-
> ing and found KinNet. I couldn't believe it! I screamed out to my partner, "Oh,
> my God! There are gay Adventists." I contacted them right away and they have
> been like family to me.

In some cases, KinNet is the gay or lesbian believer's only connection to Adventism and an Adventist community. Craig, a very "out" third-generation Adventist
illustrates the importance of these electronic ties to the faith.

> There was a time in my life when I could not see myself as anything else but an
> Adventist. I was proud of that label. It was as much a part of me as my brown
> hair and blue eyes. Today, I see it fading in my rearview mirror as I go down the
> highway. Were it not for KinNet, I am sorry to say, I wouldn't care about it any-
> more.

For some KinNet members, the network provides the kind of support they
need in order to feel understood and to gain a deeper understanding of their own
lives. Leon, a former Adventist pastor remarked, "I have some supportive friends
here in [this city], though no one who understands both what it means to be an
SDA and what it means to be gay. That's why I've found KinNet a blessing this
past week."

The presence of these extra-congregational support structures doesn't mean
that congregational support is completely absent. A few of those I talked to did
find Adventist role models and supportive persons among church members in
their congregations. One male recalls,

> I became friends with one of the teachers at the church school when I was in col-
> lege. He was single and ten years older than me. After a while I felt I could trust
> him and unburdened myself completely, telling him all about my sexual life. He
> was understanding and told me he felt the same way. It was such a relief to be able
> to talk about things with someone who understood and didn't reject me, plus he
> was the first real gay Adventist I knew.

Given the sectarian nature of the Seventh-day Adventist faith, the act of finding another Adventist who is also gay or lesbian is very important in the process
of reconciling these identities. Adventists implicitly tend to discount other religious paths, even Evangelical Christian ones. Either you are an Adventist or you
become nonreligious. There are a few persons who convert to other religions, but
not very many. For example, of those I interviewed, one person had converted to
Catholicism and one to Judaism. This theological stance makes it all that much

more important to find role models and support groups, even a virtual one, from within the Adventist tradition.

Gay and Lesbian Community

One might think that the larger gay and lesbian community might also provide supportive ties, but this was not the case with those to whom I talked. Very few persons developed important role model relationships within the larger gay and lesbian community. Mel, a closeted male who seldom attends church, remarked, "I can't seem to fit into the general gay society. The reason I joined Kinship is I'm looking for friends who are like me, or those who can at least understand what I'm dealing with."

Adventists sometimes tend to perceive non-Adventists as very different than themselves. Part of Adventist theology includes being "in" the world, but not "of" the world. That is, the value of separateness is stressed, which often translates as "stay away from non-Adventists" unless you're trying to evangelize them. Tom described his resistance to the large gay community this way,

> I have very limited contact with the larger gay community. I belonged to a listserve for married gay men, but felt culturally uncomfortable, probably in many ways because I am so culturally Adventist. So I dropped out of that. I have attended a gay codependency anonymous group, but rarely do so anymore because I also feel very culturally uncomfortable there.

Carol, too, found her Adventist norms and values kept her apart from a more secular gay community, "The gay community offers so much in things I don't relate to like 'new age,' drugs, and alcohol. I also see a lot of codependency in the gay community. There's lots of bad out there. On those issues, I'm not with the gay community."

Another illustration of Adventist gay and lesbians being uncomfortable with the larger gay and lesbian community is reactions from people about frequenting gay bars. Although bars are one of the best-known gay meeting places, the gay and lesbian Adventists I interviewed seldom go there. Adam remembered his first adventure to a gay bar,

> I knew of one gay bar in the local area, so I proceeded to go there one Wednesday evening. As a lifelong Adventist, and as someone who had not more than one or two swallows of any alcoholic beverage, a bar was not a particularly comfortable place for me. I ordered a 7-UP, sat at a table, and mostly just looked around.

Ted, who left the church many years ago, still does not frequent gay bars. "I have quit going to bars, dancing, and that kind of thing since I tend to see those places now as 'meat-racks' and good only for cruising."

Religious Efforts Toward Self-Acceptance

Almost 90 percent of the participants in this study reported that they needed to achieve a new understanding of certain biblical passages in order to come to self-acceptance. The Bible itself is important to this group of people. Even if they were right with themselves, they needed to find ways to be right with the biblical texts that people associate with homosexuality. Having role models who had struggled with and reconciled being gay and being a Christian did not eliminate their need to seek biblical understanding for themselves. Nathan shared his struggle over "getting right" with the text: "I really had a hard time with what I believed the Bible was saying against homosexuality. I loved my faith and didn't want to give that up. I knew my homosexual feelings were very strong and so were my Christian beliefs."

The Adventist church teaches that the Bible condemns homosexuality. Most participants had never questioned traditional Adventist interpretations of the Bible passages that refer to homosexuality. Not until they faced the issue of homosexuality for themselves, did the persons I interviewed reconsider the Bible texts used by the church to denounce homosexuality. During this review, these persons, like Joanne, did not rely on traditional Adventist interpretations of the Bible texts.

I began a real sincere prayer and study campaign, desiring to know only the truth in regards to homosexuality and the scripture. I was willing to accept whatever direction God would lead. Having spent my entire life on the side of believing homosexual behavior was a sin, I was still most comfortable with that belief. I spent weeks, and months, in prayer and study. And over that time, my picture of those few scriptural texts that are used to condemn homosexuals began to change. I had a friend who took me to an MCC (Metropolitan Community Church) and I went to hear a study. The title was "Homosexuality in the Bible" and it made me look at Bible texts differently, especially those particular texts [that refer to homosexuality]. I realized that I could be gay and Christian.

For about half of the lesbian and gay Adventists in this sample, their view of God's nature (as more loving and accepting) or their view of God's commandments about homosexuality altered in relation to their acceptance of their homosexuality. This change came about as they began to see God as more accepting of homosexuality than they previously believed. Comments by Marvin and Mitch describe this process.

I felt that I couldn't be a Christian and gay at the same time. I felt that God wasn't interested in or concerned about what I did or how I did it. I was gay and therefore cast out of His presence. Now I've come to believe that the truth is that God is love, that he offers mercy, comfort, healing, and salvation to all who believe—gay, straight, black, white, fat, thin.

As I grow in my Adventist walk, I find God to be more open-minded. More and more I'm tending to believe it [homosexuality] may be okay as long as it's done in the proper way, a monogamous way, consenting and caring.

While many participants developed this new view of God through their interactions with new role models, books also served as the catalyst to help persons like Joanne get a new picture of how God relates to gay and lesbian persons.

I read a book entitled *Healing Grace* by David Seamands. It helped to change my entire picture of God, from demanding of perfection for acceptance and salvation, to loving me simply because I was His child, and offering me salvation through grace alone.

For some lesbian and gay Adventists, coming to a self-acceptance of their homosexuality required a "sign" of God's approval. Adventists teach that God has given signs to people, as exemplified in the Bible, as to what course to pursue in life. Those persons I interviewed grew up believing in looking for signs from God. Therefore, this action became a tool or way to help them accept their homosexuality. When something happened that confirmed their gay Adventist status, they saw this as a sign or message from Heaven. Sue remembered her first experience with feeling what she interpreted as God's approval.

Spring break we went to Maine skiing and spent the whole week being together. I experienced what it was like to live with a woman, cooking, skiing, and making love, with no fear. It kept going through my head, "God, is this what we were supposed to be doing?" We were making love one morning and all of a sudden a beam of sunlight came in and touched both of us and an immediate realization hit me that it was right.

Joanne, too, related a similar sign she perceived coming to her through a dream.

I had a dream that woke me with the horrible screams of a woman echoing in my mind. The dream was an image of me fighting with myself. As I thought about the dream, I was overwhelmed with the message that the dream carried from God. "Stop fighting with yourself Joanne! Stop worrying about trying to change! Just give it all up to me. Trust me. I'll take care of it all."

Four gay and lesbian Adventists in this sample received a message from someone they saw as an authority figure in the church. This message helped them accept their homosexual identities. Jim recalled talking to his pastor, who said,

Jim, some people's lives seem to go smooth, but yours seems to go up and down. Although you don't appreciate the ups and downs now, you'll come to appreciate them and the way God made you later in life. Some of you guys don't fit the normal mold just like my Ed [his son].

Jim remembered this conversation as significantly influencing his ability to accept his homosexuality. Irene, a woman I interviewed went to an Adventist college president for answers about her sexual orientation. "I went to see him and I told him 'This is who I am [lesbian],' and I asked him, 'What does this mean?' He pulled out books that explained Bible texts with the real Hebrew meaning. I took it from there."

From that interaction, Irene received the clear message that she could be both an Adventist and a lesbian. "It was like the whirlwind inside me stopped and I was able to meld my spiritual and sexual identities."

Surviving Through Redefinition

The Adventists described in this essay are survivors. These lesbian and gay Adventists found ways to come to some level of self-acceptance in the face of rejection from not only society, but from the church they loved and beliefs and practices they followed. The data suggests three basic ways that gay and lesbian Adventists redefined who they were and made decisions about church membership in order to integrate their religious heritage and their sexual orientation. These ways included leaving the church, remaining celibate and staying in the church, and staying in the church while affirming their gay or lesbian sexual orientation.

Approximately one-third of the people I talked to chose to leave the church. The majority of study participants who left the church did so simply because they no longer believed the church doctrines. Some persons who left the church still believed the church doctrines, but realized that they could not conform to the expectations of the church (celibacy) and decided to leave. A third reason that individuals left the church was that they felt wronged by the church. In general, these people believed most of the Adventist doctrines, but did not attend church because of the church's stance on homosexuality. This group of people felt that the church had rejected them and, in return, they rejected the church.

A small number of the people I interviewed decided to remain celibate. This choice allowed participants to stay members of the church while acknowledging to themselves that their sexual orientation would not change. Most people making this choice remained closeted. Gays and lesbians who practice celibacy can hold church membership in good standing since the church's objection is focused on homosexual behavior rather than orientation. The problem with celibacy is that it requires the person to live a life without the hope of a life partner. This approach sometimes led to cycles of abstinence followed by periods of promiscuity in those I interviewed. In follow-up communication a few years after my initial study, Ernest, who describes himself as an accomplished musician and remains closeted in his church, shared his experience with that cycle,

> Of course this "revolving door" [celibacy followed by promiscuity] could not revolve forever. I found myself being absolutely, totally celibate. It was, like in AA, one day at a time thing. One day at a time stretched somehow into about seven years. Then I "fell off the wagon." Of course I threw the baby out with the bath water and went back to my life of promiscuity. But I continued to read my Bible and pray. After a while, I realized that unbridled promiscuity is not a happy thing. Right now, I know that total celibacy is possible but it may not be healthy for *my* body. Promiscuous sex, sexual activity without love and commitment can often exasperate feelings of loneliness and lead to a revolving door, a vicious cycle of unproductive, unhappy behavior.

While celibacy may work for some individuals, it is unclear how effective it is as a long-term strategy to reconcile religious convictions and sexual orientation. More research is needed in this area to understand the role of celibacy in the life of a Christian gay or lesbian person.

Integrating Gay and Lesbian with Adventist Affiliation

The majority of participants integrated their religious heritage with their sexual orientation by coming to believe that they could remain Adventists and have a same-sex life partner. Participants emphasized monogamy and commitment in the heterosexual tradition as part of this choice.

About 60 percent of the lesbian and gay Adventists I interviewed had fully integrated their sexual orientation with their Adventist lifestyle and church membership. These persons were fairly open regarding their sexual orientation and their Seventh-day Adventist affiliation. In general, study participants who integrated gay or lesbian orientation with church membership were either in a committed same-sex relationship or were looking for a life partner.

What is it that keeps some gay and lesbian SDA openly in the church? While there is not one clear reason, the persons I interviewed shared a variety of reasons they choose to stay.

> The simplest reasons [for staying] are ones of inertia—I like staying with what I know. Also I far prefer Evangelical worship and Bible study to the Roman Catholic liturgy and theological training in which I was raised. But, to the point, why stay as a gay man? I have a deep love for the Bible, to the point that I read it in Greek and Hebrew, own numerous scholarly commentaries, and regularly publish in technical journals. The Adventist Church more than any other I have encountered takes the Scriptures seriously, and expects the laity to understand what

they believe and why. Early Adventism took apart every church doctrine and examined it thoroughly, accepting or discarding in accordance with their study of the Bible, not tradition. That method resonates with me. Time will tell how long I can last in a hostile environment. But, I am more than my sexual orientation, and those other parts of me do belong in this church.

Erin, an out-of-the-closet lesbian, reflected on how her identity remains Seventh-day Adventist although she disagrees with church doctrine,

> I have [accepted] all of this [Adventist] culture into my whole self. I am an individual and although I follow some of the eating habits there is more of the culture in me than I sometimes care to speak about. But don't try to get me to give up my church membership. I am an Adventist although I reject most of what is acceptance and belief.

This personal attachment to the Adventist church and the significance of being a member is reflected in the comments by Carolyn, a health-care professional who is a fourth-generation Adventist. "I don't like the idea [of not having] any attachment to this church, that I know how lost I would feel if I suddenly were not a card-carrying SDA. I do not like the wave of despair that sweeps over me when I dare to imagine that scenario."

These responses reflect cultural, social, and theological reasons that gay and lesbian Adventists remain in the church. These individuals do not see the church as "perfect." Most persons who spoke of their attachment to the church also had some criticisms, but nonetheless, they did not want to be "kicked out" of the church or have their membership taken from them. As Erin said, "I am still a member but have had to fight for that as a principle. I have moved onward but never to another church. At 73, I still may and I am thinking about the UU [Unitarian Universalists]."

When it worked out for gay and lesbian Adventists to stay in their churches without having their membership withdrawn, it seemed as if several conditions came together. The conditions that facilitated people to more successful integration of their lesbian or gay identity with their church affiliation included having an accepting church congregation, a job that would not be in jeopardy if sexual orientation became known, and an accepting family.

The condition that appeared mandatory for a fully integrated identity was having an accepting local church congregation. Without an accepting church congregation, the person's church membership was often withdrawn. Ellie, who just came out at age forty-four reflected:

> I once went to a church a long time ago in Missouri, and I was being torn between telling the pastor then about my sexuality. I then found out his sister and

daughter were lesbians. He was so open, and kind about this subject that he didn't condemn them, or chastise me about my choice of friends.

Carol had been away from the church for some time when she found KinNet and Kinship and realized that going back to church was an option. Carol, who is in a committed relationship, shared about her relationship with the church:

> My involvement with the church has been less than average in the last six years. It's not because I don't believe—I do—but I was limited because of how I thought the church may perceive me. But lately I've found a refuge in the church. When I go to prayer meeting, my partner comes with me. The pastor said that if the gay fellowship in his church increases, he would be more than happy. People in this church are warm and accepting, or at least not mean. So, I've started to go back to church more and try to teach my partner who is not an Adventist any more.

The congregations that were open to gay and lesbian members were often led by pastors who understood that sexual orientation was not a choice. Pastors with gay affirming attitudes befriended these gay and lesbian Adventists and welcomed them to their congregations.

Another important condition for integrating a lesbian or gay orientation with Adventist affiliation was for the person to hold a job in which sexual orientation was not an issue. None of these participants were in position where their employment would be jeopardized by coming out publicly. Most participants in this category were self-employed or worked for non-church related organizations. Brandon, an Adventist physician, reported, "I came out to my boss [an Adventist] and she said, 'I don't see it [your sexuality] as an issue.' Then she told the president of the company, and the president said the same thing."

Having an accepting family was another condition facilitating the integration of gay or lesbian identity and church affiliation. While the majority of families in this sample initially had difficulty accepting a gay or lesbian member, over time they did accept the gay or lesbian family member. Nathan shared, "Now I feel loved by my family. I understand that they had to have a 'coming out' period of about three years. Since my father is an Adventist pastor, it was important for me to be accepted by him before I could go back to church."

When gay and lesbian Adventists decide to not go to church, they often will still identify themselves as Adventist and make efforts to stay connected with other Adventists in ways such as the following comments from Barbara reflect.

> People [come back to Adventism because they] miss the culture of it. It is like a family to many, and who wants to be without support of the family that raised them or accepted them at some point. I do not know what solution there is to that

problem except perhaps to find some new culture of acceptance elsewhere, which for me right now is Kinship.

Conclusion

Seventh-day Adventist lesbians and gay men share a heritage that is more than a set of religious beliefs. Adventism is a way of life. It is a culture, an identity. From this study, it appears that when personal identities collide, a painful struggle ensues. It also seems true that through the struggle, a new definition of self emerges. People survive the redefinition process and come to a more vivid understanding of their beliefs, the types of behaviors they can and will tolerate, and a sharper picture of what defines their personhood in an Adventist way. More than anything else, it appears that what this group of people wants is recognition that it is possible simply to be Adventist and gay or lesbian.

> Despite the church's official opinion, there are two things I've always been—always will be—a Seventh-day Adventist and a lesbian. God doesn't expect me to try to be something I'm not, or say I can't be something I believe in.

Note

1. All of the participants in this study were at some time doctrinally Adventists, believing that the Bible condemns homosexual behavior. Because of this belief, the participants engaged in a series of less than successful efforts to change and not "be" gay. As a result, some participants chose to leave the church or remain celibate as a way to reconcile their sexual orientation with religious beliefs. However, most participants eventually came to redefine what it means to be Adventist and gay or lesbian through involvement with other Adventist gays and lesbians.

Negotiating a Religious Identity
The Case of the Gay Evangelical

4

SCOTT THUMMA

*I am a born-again Christian and sought help through prayer and the church,
but I am still gay. Could it be possible God accepts me as I am? (letter to
Good News)*

*Such disbelief is no surprise when a person's spiritual roots are grounded
in a heritage that quite rightly emphasizes the Bible as the Word of God
written, and not just a random collection of outdated writings. So when
confronted with traditional cultural bound interpretations of supposed antigay passages, the Bible honoring gay is thrown into a whirlwind of spiritual
confusion. It's a joy, then, to share with these people that they can indeed
reconcile born-again faith with their lifestyle.*

A LEADER OF GOOD NEWS IN THE NEWSLETTER[1]

FOR MANY EVANGELICAL CHRISTIANS, a homosexual lifestyle and a conservative religious identity are simply incompatible. According to a majority of
conservative Christians, there is no such thing as a gay Christian or a biblical
justification for such a lifestyle.[2] Yet, for members of one gay evangelical group, this
option is not only a possibility, it is also a reality and an imperative. This group,
called Good News, formed specifically for the purpose of helping persons reconcile
their gay lifestyle with their evangelical religious identity. This task, while threatening for those with a traditional evangelical religious identity, nevertheless is seen as
one that must be attempted. Members accomplish this change through identity negotiation and socialization. In other words, they negotiate the traditional religious
identity, in very selective areas, through interaction with Good News. Members are
reconciled to their gayness, but still retain their evangelical religious identity.

Religious identity change has been characterized primarily in traditional con-version language as a "radical reorganization of identity, meaning, life" (Travisano 1970: 594) or as an abandonment of one religious identity for a new and different one (Kilbourne and Richardson 1989). This is the case because few re-searchers examine less dramatic identity changes that occur within a particular re-ligious tradition, commonly known as "alternations" (Travizano 1970). Through an analysis of the interaction between Good News, its members, and a traditional evangelical identity, a complex and subtle process of identity negotiation comes to light.

Accommodation of discrepant identities does not always result in an either/or decision that destroys one of the identities. Rather, identity negotiation can be construed as a process in which much of these identities remain intact. Members of Good News come to accept themselves as gay Christians without giving up their evangelical identity. Certain aspects of members' evangelical religious iden-tity are revised to incorporate incongruous, but perceived as essential, characteris-tics of their sexual identity into their total self-concept. For these persons, their core identity becomes a gay evangelical Christian one.

A Socialization Process of Identity Negotiation

Identity negotiation can best be understood as a facet of adult socialization. The symbolic interactionist perspective (Mead 1934; Goffman 1959; Garfinkel 1967; Berger and Luckmann 1967) offers a description of the dynamics involved in socialization. It is through the interaction of self and society that meaning sys-tems are created and sustained. Both self-concept, "what one thinks one is like" (Troiden 1984), and identity, the content of the self-concept in relation to a so-cial situation (Gecas 1982), arise from this interaction. Socialization is the process by which the self internalizes social meanings, reinterprets them, and, in turn, re-sponds back upon society. As such, socialization can be viewed as the continual formation of self-concept over time (Gecas 1986). From this perspective, identity negotiation, whether religious or sexual, is a part of the natural process in which people engage to create a more stable and coherent self-concept (Becker 1963; Straus 1976; Gecas 1982). Conversion, from this point of view, is identity nego-tiation that involves a complete change in the "core identity construct" (Staples and Mauss 1987).

Often one's self-concept becomes organized around a central or "core iden-tity" construct (Hart and Richardson 1981; Gecas 1981), which gives some unity or consistence to the other identities of the person. The stability of the core iden-tity (or *master* status in Becker 1963) resides in the interplay between one's con-tinual experience of the world, the relative meaning assigned to such experiences,

the plausibility of these meaning systems for ordering existence, and one's interaction with a significant "reference group" (Loftand 1969). This is not to imply
that all persons' self-concepts are directed by a strong core identity. Neither does
this assume that all people strive to maintain complete self-consistency. Most people live with a great deal of inconsistency in their lives. The tendency to develop
a strong core identity, however, is intrinsic to certain societal roles or contexts.
John Hart and Diane Richardson (1981) have found that gays often organize their
self-identity around their sexual identity. This is also very common for persons
who hold stigmatized identities (Goffman 1963). The ideologies and practices of
many religious groups encourage a self-concept organized around one's religious
identity (Ammerman 1987; Peshkin 1986). A particular view of the world becomes the sacred canopy that makes sense of all other experiences. The more a
person is encapsulated and indoctrinated in a religious perspective the less likely
he or she is to change (Gecas 1981; Greil and Rudy 1984a).

Identity Dissonance as Motivational Mechanism

A discussion of socialization is incomplete, however, without an examination of
the question of motivation (Gecas 1986). In symbolic interactionist writings the
question of motivation has often been deferred to discussion of "motives," "le-
gitimations," and "accounts," especially in terms similar to Mills's (1940), and
Scott and Lyman's (1968) usages. The concept of motive is akin to attribution
theory; both offer linguistic justifications for a particular act or pattern of behavior. Motives are the professed reasons or accounts of motivations or impetus for
change. This facet of socialization is essential; however, it does not address the internal mechanisms for change.

   One way to approach the question of motivation is by considering what those
who sought Good News had in common. In a majority of conversion studies this
has been a problem. After-the-fact accounts about members' lives prior to conversion have been seen as colored by ritualized biographical reconstruction (Greil and
Rudy 1984b; Snow and Phillips 1980). The present study, however, closely examined letters written to the group prior to ideological contact in order to evalu-
ate the identity and motivation of those seeking interaction with Good News.

   According to these observations, at first encounter with this organization 74
percent of potential members expressed a strong desire to resolve the felt tension
between being a conservative Christian and having homosexual feelings. This tension can be understood best in terms of cognitive dissonance theory (Festinger
1957; Prus 1984), which states that an amount of internal dissonance may be
produced by holding two inconsistent cognitive elements. These need not be log-
ically incongruent, nor do they necessarily require resolution. The motivational

force of cognitive dissonance arises when the person perceives the inconsistency intolerable, and thus seeks dissonance reduction in some form.

Generalizing the dynamics of cognitive dissonance may be useful in interpreting the condition of two incongruent identities being held by the same person. While many persons may hold incongruent identities in a workable tension, these identities seldom both function as organizing "core identities" of the self-concept. Those persons who contact Good News perceive both identities as crucial to their self-concept. The identities, as originally construed, are mutually exclusive; however, they are also considered too important to surrender. This dissonance between the identities functions as a motive for change, or dissonance reduction, only if the person perceives this state as problematic. For most of those who came to Good News, the dissonance between their gay and evangelical identities was intolerable and had to be resolved.

Religious Identity Revision

Many facets of religious identity revision have been explored by those studying conversion. Much of this work focuses on the acceptance of a new religious identity (Kilbourne and Richardson 1989) or a shift from one identity to another (Greeley 1981). Often this change in identity is perceived to be an either/or alternative. The result is radical conversion or a segmented, compartmentalized self-concept. Using a socialization model, however, the individual variations within a particular religious identity become evident because the focus is on the dynamics of the social interaction. Religious identity revision can be equated with any other kind of socialization; it simply involves a different organizational context (Greil and Rudy 1984b). The interaction between the social group and the active individual provides the crucial content and context for change.

There has been a movement in recent years to frame conversion in terms of a socialization process (Long and Hadden 1983; Machalek and Snow 1985; Kilbourne and Richardson 1989). This has enabled theorists to tie religious identity change to a larger body of literature on human development. This perspective frames the convert as actively engaged in the search for meaning and fulfillment. It makes possible a greater appreciation of the dialectical relationship between the individual and the group. The social group is still seen as having a formative function, but it is no longer perceived as the only force in socialization. It remains a source for social meaning and, at the same time, limits the contents of one's identity through group forms and the availability of role models. But conversion, and any identity change, becomes better understood as a product of negotiation between the individual and the social context (Straus 1976). While social interaction and involvement with others is necessary for the validation and maintenance of a revised identity, the individual is seen as the active agent.

A Description of Good News as the Context for Change

Good News is a parachurch evangelical organization whose national office and primary group are in Atlanta. The group meets every two weeks in a local gay center. Attendance varies, but averages about eight people. The core group consists of four persons, all white males, as are the majority of other members. Occasionally, there are a few white females or black males. The average age of those who attend is thirty-five years. In addition to this group, there are four affiliate groups in cities throughout the South and Midwest. At any time, there are hundreds of individuals, living in isolated small towns around the country, who have contact with the group through correspondence. Good News publishes a quarterly newsletter that is distributed to approximately four hundred people. The group has corresponded with more than 1,300 people in its nine years of operation.

The study of Good News took place in 1984 and 1985. The data were collected through participant observation of twenty meetings. In-depth personal interviews were conducted with seven members of Good News. Along with this, an intensive study was made of the voluminous correspondence, all issues of the newsletter, and the group's published literature. The descriptive statistics in this article are derived from the author's rough estimate of observations, plus a content analysis of group correspondence.

Good News has been meeting since 1977 under the leadership of three cofounders. Following the lead of "liberal" Christians, they have embraced a cultural interpretation of the scriptures. They continue, however, to assert forcefully their evangelical heritage and maintain many of the characteristic traditional evangelical beliefs and practices. The group officially operates with a threefold mission of dialogue with the "straight" church, enrichment for gay believers, and service to the entire homosexual community. Actually, their central task is to offer members a way, both experientially and cognitively, to reconcile a conservative Christian faith and a homosexual identity. This task is the focus of this chapter.

In this context, "membership" should be understood not as joining the group structure, but as accepting its ideology and worldview concerning the negotiation of a gay Christian identity. Evangelizing the good news of this cognitive adjustment, by which one could be both gay and a conservative Christian, occupied most of the group's energy. Because of this emphasis, rather than physical recruitment to the group itself, membership continued to decline in the years after this study ended. In 1987 the group officially disbanded. Along with an emphasis on believing over belonging, other factors that contributed to the group's demise included two founding members redirecting their energies to AIDS work and three other core members relocating and becoming more active in their local congregations. During the time this study took place, however, Good News still offered both cognitive structures and some experiential contexts by which members could reconstruct their self-concept.

Good News's mission is unified around a vision that reflects this goal of identity revision. Good News "is a family of believers who strive to forge bridges of biblical faith which serve, not oppress, lesbian and gay lifestyles." After a brief look at those who seek out Good News, this chapter focuses on how these bridges are forged or the identities of the evangelical faith and the gay lifestyle are reconciled.

The Family of Believers

According to the letters Good News receives, most persons (74 percent) who seek out the group are in the midst of an identity crisis.[3] This struggle arises from being a conservative Christian and having homosexual feelings. The tension, guilt, and confusion that result from an attempt to hold these incongruous identities together become too great for these persons. They feel as if they can no longer remain in the tension between desiring to be "good" conservative Christians and having "sinful," and specifically condemned, feelings of homosexual attraction. One person wrote to the group, "I will not and cannot disregard my faith (nor my sexual orientation). I often find myself compromising my beliefs. The Lord is disappointed with me." Another writer stated, "I have abstained from sexual involvement with others for three years because of my fear of breaking God's law. I miss the close fellowship of a lover, but I'm scared that I will go to hell if I do. I'm so lonely." A third quote from a letter to Good News clearly exemplifies this identity dissonance.

> I can remember dying inside one Sunday listening to my minister tell me and his congregation that "those queers were going to fry in Hell for the choice they made." I thought I knew Christ then. So if it seemed to be God's will for me to not be homosexual, then I'd do something about it. I prayed about it but nothing happened.

All those who come to Good News place significant value and meaning upon the conservative evangelical identity. One of the leaders made this clear in his statement: "I left the Metropolitan Community Church because I felt that they were putting gay before God. . . . They just weren't evangelical enough for me." Members' religious faith is a very important aspect of who they are. As one said, "It is through my Christian faith that I am able to define myself and know who I am." It is the core identity for most of them.

For many, their religious affiliation symbolizes a grounding in a history, membership in a tradition, and stability in a social order. An overwhelming majority of those who contact Good News (94 percent) were reared in religious families and attended conservative evangelical churches in denominations such as Baptist, Missouri Synod Lutheran, Church of Christ, and Assemblies of God. Sixty-eight percent grew up in the South or Midwest in rural areas or small towns. They were all oriented to look to religion in solving their problems and in giving meaning to their lives.

Two primary characteristics of the evangelical tradition are the doctrine of the inerrancy of scripture and a traditional moral conservatism (Hunter 1983). Both result in the creation of a very difficult atmosphere for a Christian struggling with homosexual feelings. The Bible literally states, "Thou shall not lie with a man as with a woman; it is abomination" (Lev. 18:22). Homosexuality has been a sin throughout the history of Christianity (Boswell 1980; McNeill 1976).

According to both researchers and interviews with Good News members, homosexuality is still strongly condemned in the evangelical denominations of Christianity. Hunter reports 88.7 percent of evangelicals thought homosexuality was an "immoral behavior" (1983: 85); Ammerman found 98 percent of Southern Baptists surveyed indicated that it was not a viable Christian lifestyle (1985). Roof and McKinney report that conservative Protestants were the least likely religious group in America either to affirm the civil rights of gays or to view homosexuality as morally acceptable (1987: 192, 212). For a conservative Christian, this reality presents both a theological and a social barrier to being an evangelical gay Christian.

Such a reality is clearly evident in that most members report experiencing tremendous rejection from family and friends. As one letter writer put it, "I came out to my family and they kicked me out of the house." Another actively attending member related, "I told my best friends, this Christian couple from my church, and now they won't talk to me." The social ostracism that accompanies the homosexual stigma, especially in a small town or rural area, had taken its toll on those who contacted Good News.

Every person expressed feelings of "being different from the other kids" since early childhood, seeing themselves as social outcasts. Almost every person said he or she felt or experienced rejection from a church congregation because of his or her homosexual desires. An active member recounted his experience, "I heard more and more sermons condemning homosexuality. Knowing that if I was ever found out, I might be thrown out of the church. I was in such a confused state." About 40 percent had some experience with a gay community, but very few, only 8 percent, had continual contact or exposure with a local group of gays. All of those in contact with Good News stated they desperately wanted to resolve the perceived tension between being a homosexual and an evangelical Christian. One letter writer stated, "I love God, but how can I deny my own feelings? Why should I have to sacrifice myself either to God or to the Devil because of my feelings?" They were actively seeking resolution of the tension when they responded to Good News's advertisements, "Gay and Christian, is it possible?"

Many expressed anxiety, despair, and the feeling that they had come to "the end of the rope." Religious acceptance by God, a community, and a heritage were perceived as a potential way to relieve the sense of alienation and rejection. This was often expressed as a desire to serve the Lord and become *"good,* whole" Christians, while hoping to live out authentically what they perceived to be their God-given sexuality.

Good News's Agenda—Assuring the Proper Motivations

The leaders of Good News are well aware of the situations of those who contact them. They focus the group's efforts directly on the biblical and social condemnation of homosexuality. The structure of the organization is to help members change this negative perception into a positive self-concept. A number of specifically designed tasks are intended to promote identity revision. The leadership presents these as separate and logical steps; however, within the group they take place simultaneously and are inseparable.

The written responses to those who asked for help illuminated the proposed pattern of progression. Most response letters from the core members began with counseling and the assurance that it was possible to reconcile being gay and evangelical. Next they offered their testimony, information (biblical and scientific) about how it was possible, and a list of books to read for more information. The third part of the letter often consisted of encouraging the person to seek supportive fellowship or come to Atlanta to visit the group. Finally, there was a discussion of possible pitfalls and spiritual ways of maintaining the gay Christian identity. Interviews and interaction with the group highlighted the fact that members followed this pattern intellectually, but in practice observed interactions and identity negotiation were not nearly so easily or sequentially perceived.

Good News understands its first task to be one of convincing potential members that it is permissible to alter their religious beliefs. In an initial encounter potential members must literally be counseled and assured that they will not be condemned to Hell if they tamper with traditionally "sacred" doctrines. Reinterpreting the scripture is to be viewed as a legitimate undertaking that does not destroy the validity and efficacy of the scriptures. As one of the leaders put it, "They have to realize that the house doesn't fall down if one of the bricks was out of place." This instruction can be clearly seen in the comment from a corresponding affiliate member. "The two books you sent me broke the barrier of guilt, fear, and anxiety my homosexuality had falsely imposed. The teaching I had been taught were men's fears, condemnations, and opinions spoken in God's name. They were social condemnations *not God's.*"

Once a person accepts the challenge to question doctrines and a literal interpretation of scripture, the focus then turns to one's motives for change. Although personal motivation is an absolute necessity, the "proper" framing of that motivation must be taught. The motive for challenging traditional beliefs must be spiritually grounded; it must be seen as a spiritual quest.

Good News casts the change in terms of sanctification or "growth in wisdom and perfection of the Christian life." Tension between sexuality and religiosity is understood as "an ungodly dualism between the body and the spirit." Problems resulting from a literal interpretation of scripture are redefined as issues of "cultural relativity." The choice then becomes either expressing one's God-given, unchangeable sexuality or being bound by "men's fears and opinions spoken in God's name." Once members tentatively accept this ideological perspective, "it is God's will for us to be gay and Christian," they can begin internalizing the perspective. The only correct action is to "follow God's plan for your life." In response, a potential member often asks, "How can I know for sure that what you say is God's will?"

Teaching God's Will

The second task of Good News is to present the doctrines that support the proposed identity revision. Included in this instruction are new ways to understand the identity dissonance and the issues in question. Good News often asserts that "you must know the truth and the truth will set you free." This means that the more one learns about the "correct" doctrines, the easier it is to accept the new identity. This teaching has a twofold purpose. First, the teaching must denigrate the former position by identifying the faulty reasoning and incorrect learning from which it arose. Then, the instruction must provide information to replace the former thoughts about self-identity, redefine the supportive meaning system, and prescribe the direction of future action.

Good News must teach its members the "proper" interpretation of the scriptures and, at the same time, the acceptability of the gay lifestyle. It goes about this first task by employing a historical–critical hermeneutic. This principle of interpretation reduces the condemnation of specific passages by calling into question their relevance for a modern world. One of the lenders affirmed this in a talk during a meeting. He stated, "I would still say that I believe in the infallibility of the scriptures, but what I would mean by that is certainly a lot different. I'm more liberal in the culture-related things but conservative in theology. My theology hasn't changed much."

They then offer an elaborate exegesis of these passages to show that the Greek words translated as "homosexual" are either indefinable or refer to pederasty. A third method they use is to emphasize biblical principles, such as love and acceptance of all persons, to counter the discriminatory attitudes of the church toward gays. Another of the leaders announced to the audience at a homecoming, "The bottom line—the top line—is that God loves people, all people. That to me is the basic message of the Bible."

A final theological method used to affirm the gay lifestyle is focusing on the image of God as creator. Psalms such as 139, "For you have created my innermost parts," and 100, "It is he that hath made us and not we ourselves," are often quoted. The reasoning of this creationist argument is, "Since God made me the way I am, why shouldn't I express my sexuality?" The group also relies on scientific literature to show that homosexuality is an orientation and is, therefore, immutable.[4] In this regard, the question is heard, "Why would God ask me to change something I can't?"

The primary modes of teaching are lessons presented at meetings; special guest speakers; recommended readings of supportive books, such as *Is the Homosexual My Neighbor?* by Scanzoni and Mollenkott (1978); written correspondence; and interaction with appropriate role models. These teachings offer alternative cognitive categories that support the proposed identity revisions. In doing this, Good News hopes to ensure the acceptance of the revised identity by providing a complementary meaning system to support the new identity.

Embodying the New Identity

Once the cognitive structures that support the revised identity have been presented, a third task is begun. Good News attempts to facilitate integration of the new gay Christian identity. This is undertaken in two primary ways: through evangelistic activities and through social interactions. There are a multitude of activities that need to be done for Good News to remain an organization. Members are put to work on such tasks as counseling and corresponding with newer members, writing and mailing newsletters, and planning and organizing social activities. As the newsletter challenged, "If God is using Good News to bless you and challenge you, won't you give so that others who are in despair may hear the gospel of God's love and concern for them." They are also encouraged to become involved in overt gay activities such as participating in gay rights rallies and AIDS benefits, visiting gay clubs (often to witness), and volunteering at various gay service organizations. Again the newsletter made this aspect evident, "*so* who will take the Word of Salvation and daily victorious living in Jesus Christ into the gay community?" In addition to these activities, Good News holds prayer meetings, Bible studies, spiritual retreats, homecomings, and potluck fellowship dinners. All these are open and receptive to guests and visitors.

The group also intentionally promotes evangelism to "heterosexual" congregations. Pastors of local churches are often asked to speak at biweekly meetings. Members are strongly encouraged to attend "straight" churches within a member's denominational tradition. One of the group leaders made this clear during an interview.

> I consciously chose to be a member of a predominately non-gay congregation because I believe in the concept of the family of faith, the community of faith. Christians who are gay cannot afford the luxury of isolation. We have to be willing to risk the pain, the alienation, the separation, if we are to achieve any semblance of dialogue.

According to the group's bylaws, officers and board members are required to attend straight churches as witnesses of God's redemption and grace to all people, including gays. This is also done as a sign of the group's commitment to the unity of the body of Christ.

In many ways the social activities that Good News sponsors replicate the evangelical heritage of members. Most of the social events are reminiscent of conservative church activities, such as "group dates," Bible retreats, and homecomings, which are the annual revivalistic gatherings for marginal and out-of-town members. All of these events help legitimate the new identity. Through positive interaction with others, members begin to internalize the gay evangelical identity and integrate it into their self-concept. One member expressed this in a letter, "The Mollenkott weekend retreat was quite an experience for me. That weekend was the first time in a very long time that I actually felt accepted, that I felt I belonged."

The leadership encourages those who contact Good News by letter to find a gay community or fellowship and subscribe to gay magazines, including the group's newsletter. Good News offers an opportunity for acceptance by other persons in a positive social context. They recommend that out-of-town members visit the Atlanta group, or one of the affiliate groups, and even, if possible, move to a larger town that has a gay church or fellowship in it. The group structures allow members to experiment with the tentative identity through service, community involvement, and participation in activities that parallel the evangelical Christian ones from which they would be excluded as gays. Finally, these social activities, and the acceptance gained from interaction with other group members, strengthen the process of socialization into the new identity. One member made this clear in an interview. "I decided to visit Good News. There I found, along with a wonderful group of people, a place where I could feel free to be myself and to profess my faith in Jesus Christ." This interaction promotes the assurance that the decision to accept the revised identity is a correct one.

Maintaining the New Identity

The fourth and final task for Good News is to help strengthen and maintain the newly revised identity. Community and group support are correlated strongly with continued commitment to the gay Christian identity. Many members find that acceptance by other Christians is all they need to solidify the identity revisions. However, the group uses a number of other techniques to facilitate this change. One of these methods involves negating and devaluing the former identity. Members come to regard their previous situation as a hindrance to becoming "whole" Christians. This is expressed in the statement by one of the long-time members.

> By accepting [my sexual orientation] I was able to move spiritually. I don't live a double life now. I can't change, and I don't want to change. When you are able to accept yourself and know that God accepts you and made you, you're able to go on and live a more productive and more happy life.

A second technique is to present the current gay Christian identity as part of an oppressed minority, thus seeing outside, "unenlightened," groups as hostile and misguided. "Being different" is strengthened further by the creation of an "elitist" group identity. Both conservative denominations and certain secular gay groups are viewed as opposing the truthfulness of Good News's position. The former errs in not accepting gays in the Christian fellowship. The latter is at fault for devaluing Christian involvement in the gay community. Another approach the group uses is to infuse many of the morals of the evangelical lifestyle into the gay lifestyle. Good News states that sexual expression and relationships are to be guided by biblical principles, not by wanton desires. Ideally, one should engage in sexual activity only in a committed relationship.

A fifth way to strengthen the revised identity is to compensate for the felt losses in religious orthodoxy. This is done by encouraging increases in orthopraxy. Good News offers its members many traditional evangelical activities, as noted previously. They place a strong emphasis on individual piety and outward religiosity, to such an extent that it hints of "works righteousness."

In terms of beliefs, Good News also promotes a strict adherence to all "significant" orthodox doctrines, such as the divinity of Christ, his virgin birth and bodily resurrection, the absolute necessity of personal salvation, and the belief that the Bible is the inspired word of God, correctly interpreted. One group leader made this very clear during one meeting. "A Christian can still have a high view of scripture, humanity, sin, and salvation, and yet find nothing in homosexuality incompatible with being a Christian."

They assure any inquiring person that they strongly adhere to every point of the statement of faith of the National Association of Evangelicals. Good News's statement of faith begins,

> The members of Good News profess their individual and corporate faith in the basic Biblical Truths of the full authority of Scripture, a personal commitment to Jesus Christ as Savior and Lord of Life, and the urgency of Sharing the Gospel message in both word and deed.

Finally, since Good News frames the change as a spiritual journey, the rewards of maintaining a revised self-identity are presented as primarily spiritual in nature. One out-of-town member expressed the truth of this claim, "I cannot express the spiritual release of standing clean before the Lord." The love and confirmation of worth from other Christians toward those who previously had been ostracized by the church becomes an act of redemption and forgiveness.

The group's acceptance is understood as a sign of God's approval and blessing. As one of the leaders commented, "God loves us and stays with us, forever offering forgiveness, healing, and wholeness. We live and move and have our being—including our sexual being—within the sphere of God's love." The biblical mandate of sanctification and the assurance of eternal "rewards" for a faithful Christian operate as implicit mechanisms of commitment to the new gay Christian identity.

The Individual as an Active Negotiator

Much of this discussion of the process of negotiating a gay evangelical identity has focused on the group dynamics promoting change. This was intentional; Good News presents a model into which its members are socialized. A central premise of the concept of socialization is that individuals are brought to conform to the expectations and ideals of the group through internalization and social learning. As Long and Hadden state, "the special character of the process is defined by what members *do to* novices" (1983: 5). But to view this process only as one-sided, or the novice as passively receptive, is inadequate.

Very few people who contact Good News actually end up carbon copies of the leadership. They negotiate with the group as much as the group negotiates its "identity ideal" with the evangelism tradition. Persons come to the group with varying degrees of commitment to Christianity, of openness to homosexuality, and of willingness to change. Different levels of motivation drastically influence how one responds to the identity revisions suggested by Good News. This is seen most clearly in the diverse ways the new identity is embodied. A few persons wholeheartedly accept both the new identity and the group, becoming core members (roughly 5 percent). More often people seek out Good News to resolve the identity dissonance; once the dissonance is resolved or reduced, they disappear (almost 65 percent). Sometimes a person accepts the identity and continues to maintain a surface relationship or affiliate membership with the group for occasional support and fellowship (25 percent). A small percentage (5 percent), upon hearing the message of Good News, reject it and quickly sever their connections with the group.

The Gay Evangelical

Persons who have successfully internalized a gay evangelical identity very likely may appear different from the way they were when they first sought out Good News. In most cases members accept their homosexuality and become open about their lifestyle. At that same time, they forcefully affirm their evangelical heritage. In most cases, these gay evangelicals are more pious and orthodox than they were prior to their encounter with Good News. Members certainly hold more moralistic views on sexuality and relationships than are found in the general secular gay population (Bell and Weinberg 1978). Most members report an increase in personal piety, including more Bible reading and daily devotions, a systematic study of the scriptures and of their evangelical heritage, and a greater amount of time spent in prayer and meditation. They explain these changes as resulting from feeling accepted by God.

At the same time, however, these members are no longer traditional evangelical Christians according to doctrinal beliefs. They do not believe in the inerrancy of the Bible. They are less affected by the moral proscriptions against drinking, dancing, sex outside of marriage, and, most of all, homosexuality. The leadership and some of the members align politically with the left on issues of war, poverty, individual rights, abortion, and foreign policies. Members almost inevitably become somewhat more tolerant of the rights of others such as blacks and women. Many members fit nicely with Hunter's description of the "young Evangelicals" (1983: 111). They are no longer traditional evangelicals, but in many ways they know themselves to be more authentic as gay evangelicals.

Conclusion

Except for the hermit or the isolated sect, identity negotiation appears to be unavoidable in the modern world. This is true for members of Good News, especially in light of their struggle with homosexual feelings. The gay community ideology asserts that a homosexual orientation is immutable and an essential part of a gay person's nature. This presents a difficult problem for those who seek out Good News. They feel they must remain faithful to their evangelical heritage and doctrinal beliefs—doctrines that explicitly forbid homosexuality. These persons have struggled with this core identity dissonance for years before arriving at a point where something has to be done. Yet few have any idea of how to reduce this dissonance and still remain authentic to their sexuality and religious identity.

The only possible solution they find to be viable for them is one that maintains both identities. This solution demands a negotiated settlement between the dual core identities. Some amount of accommodation is necessary. The identity negotiation requires that these Christians accept a historical critical approach to the Bible, but it does not change them into liberal Christians. The negotiated identity allows them to accept their homosexuality, while not requiring that they deny their faith. Socialization into Good News's ideology alters, but does not eradicate, members' evangelical religious identity. Good News offers a unique brand of identity negotiation. It presents an opportunity to "have one's cake and eat it too."

Through interaction with the group, members construct a gay evangelical Christian identity as an alternative to their previous dissonant religious and sexual identities. In hundreds of people who have come into contact with Good News, a change of self-concept becomes both the impetus and result of the integration of a strengthened gay identity with an accommodated evangelical Christian religious identity. Neither identity is radically compromised; rather, both are combined to create the new core identity and self-concept of a gay evangelical Christian.

Although this is a unique situation, it does raise the question of whether this same process occurs in diverse religious situations or conversion events. In conceptualizing religious identity change or conversion as an either/or proposition, researchers may be overlooking the subtlety of the individual's identity negotiation. Likewise, in ambitious efforts to show the rampant conservative religious accommodation to modernity, we may be missing those who successfully negotiate both a core evangelical worldview and very modem aspects of culture. The example that members of Good News offer us suggests that social scientists should take a closer look at what is going on in the socialization dynamics of religious accommodation to the modern world.

Notes

Reprinted with permission from *Sociological Analysis* 52 (Winter 1991): 333–47.

I. All the quotes used in this without specific references are taken from Thumma (1987) and other field notes from this study.

2. See the research findings in Hunter (1983:85), Ammerman (1985), and Roof and McKinney (1987: 192, 212). There are a few evangelical groups that do not hold this perspective; see Blair (1977), or a special issue of *The Other Side* (Olson 1984) devoted to exploring the question of homosexuality and Christianity.

3. The rest of those who contacted Good News did so for support, for fellowship, or for an opportunity to work in a Christian ministry.

4. The conceptualization of homosexual identity used throughout this chapter is the one offered by Good News. This understanding is common to many gay groups, and certain scientists; see Bell and Weinberg (1978). There is a debate presently between researchers who see homosexuality from an "essentialist" perspective and those who hold a social constructionist view. See Diane Richardson (1984) or David Greenberg (1988).

Why Join a Gay Synagogue? 5

MOSHE SHOKEID

THE FOLLOWING ESSAY is a somewhat abbreviated chapter from my ethnography *A Gay Synagogue in New York*.[1] For a year during 1989–1990 and in later shorter visits to New York, I carried on anthropological research at Congregation Beth Simchat Torah (CBST), the largest gay congregation in the United States. First initiated in February 1973, a membership of nearly one thousand male and female congregants in recent years proves its great success and continuing development as a major social and cultural institution for gays and lesbians in New York.

In my own observation of CBST I found a group of men and women, among whom were doctors, lawyers, computer programmers, academics, medical technicians, rabbis, teachers, social workers, administrators, librarians, business people, cab drivers, real estate investors, and artists. Not only were they varied professionally but they were diverse both in their Jewish experience and in their motivation for joining CBST. As I became better acquainted with them and listened to their stories, patterns began to emerge—some more clear-cut than others—in the paths that drew them to CBST and motivated them to remain there.

A Return to Roots

I joined CBST in 1983 when I first moved to New York. I had minimized my connection with Judaism shortly after coming out; the term "lesbian Jew" felt like an oxymoron. The shul gave me back my Judaism and allowed me to integrate two very important parts of myself. Our *Brit Ahavah* [commitment ceremony], which occurred at CBST in 1988, completed this integration and allowed us to be out with family and co-workers as both lesbians and Jews.

(Naomi, quoted in *Synagogue News*, February 1993)

Naomi's succinct account outlines a pattern common to a number of CBST members. About two-thirds of those with whom I became acquainted had been involved in their youth in synagogue life. Many among them later went through an often painful stage of being unable to reconcile their sexual orientation with the Judaism of their parents' synagogue community. Dissociating themselves from that synagogue frequently constituted a major step in the complex social and psychological process of coming out.

Joseph's story of his sudden alienation from his family's synagogue is a dramatic example of that process. At fifteen Joseph already knew that he was different from other boys: "I kissed girls, but wasn't into that. I felt I was misleading them. When I was called 'sissy' at school, I knew they were right."

On Yom Kippur, the day of fasting and atonement, he was reading the English translation of the confessional prayer *Al Chet* ("The sins we have committed") and was shocked: "I knew it was me the terrible words were condemning." The next year he joined his family as usual for the Rosh Hashanah service at their Orthodox synagogue. But ten days later, when the family was ready to leave for the *Kol Nidre* service that begins Yom Kippur, Joseph refused to go, and despite his parents' anger and pleading, could not be budged from his sudden resistance. Nor would he explain his refusal—as he did years later: "I decided I couldn't be associated with a religion which defines me as a sinner!" From that day on, despite the gratifying experiences he had enjoyed for many years as a youth, he cut himself off from the synagogue entirely, except for a few visits on the festive holidays of *Sukkot* and *Simchat Torah*.

At twenty-nine, Joseph was still living at home with his parents. If the subject of homosexuality came up, during a television program, for example, he would leave the room feigning indifference. He was lonely, having avoided relationships, except for a few short sexual liaisons, mainly with non-Jews, and had discovered he was too inhibited by his Jewish upbringing to be comfortable with a Gentile mate.

He had heard about CBST when he attended college in Greenwich Village, and had been curious about it, but hesitated to go, expecting to find "a bunch of old gossips." Finally, in 1978, fourteen years after his break with his family's synagogue, he ventured there for the first time. Right away he felt comfortable. He recognized two young men he had seen at an Israeli folk dance class but never spoken to. He volunteered for one of the synagogue's committees and soon met someone with whom he established his first long-term relationship. Joseph then found the courage to come out to his parents. A few years later he was elected to the synagogue's board of trustees.

About ten years older than Joseph, Edward—the classicist—told a similar story. In his youth he had entertained the possibility of a rabbinical career, but later abruptly divorced himself from Judaism:

Since I felt my gay identity and my Jewish identity to be antithetical, I stopped all my involvement in Jewish life; I simply did a flip-flop. Before that I had been practicing my Judaism and avoiding my sexuality; afterwards I began to practice my sexuality and to avoid my Jewish life. The choice seemed automatic at the time; I was only nineteen and I tended to see things in black and white.

Edward told me it was five years before he realized how much he missed his Jewish heritage. During that period his friends were mainly non-Jews, and even his Jewish friends were not, in his words, "Jewish Jews." But in 1974, when he saw the advertisement for a gay synagogue, he was immediately intrigued—but hesitant: "I was afraid it would be a mockery of a synagogue." Edward continued: "After a month of wavering I finally went there one Friday night and was pleasantly surprised to find that the synagogue was not a farce but a group of men and women who were committed to Jewish life." He soon became involved in CBST's religious affairs and was instrumental in moving it away from innovation and toward a more traditional style.

Leon, a past board chair, related a story almost identical to Edward's. Before college he had been very active in his synagogue's youth activities, but at age twenty-three he concluded he could not be anything but gay. He stopped the futile attempts to date women, left his parents' home, and went to find out what gay life in New York could offer. Being a joiner, he became active in gay organizations, which took the place of his synagogue participation. "This was now my life." In a Greenwich Village bar he met someone who told him about a gay synagogue that had been formed. He was amused: "A bunch of faggots, what do they know?"

Later that year, 1974, Leon felt a need to attend Yom Kippur services, a tradition he had stopped altogether since his parents' death a few years earlier. In the evening he went to *Kol Nidre* at a New York college but was not taken with the service. The next day he decided to attend *Yizkor*, the memorial service, at the gay synagogue and see what it was all about. He entered the church hall just as the Torah scroll was being carried among the congregants. "I kissed it with my *tallis* [prayer shawl] and felt immediately at home, as if I had gone there all my life." Leon attributed the warm atmosphere that engulfed him largely to Aaron who was leading the congregation at that time. "He spoke English with a lilting Yiddish inflection. It was a familiar sort of *yiddishkeit*, and I felt so much at home. I was back at my father's and grandfather's Orthodox synagogue." Leon soon joined a new committee, which enabled him to enter the synagogue's inner circle and ultimately become board chair of CBST.

Many, like Leon, who went on to become active in the synagogue's leadership, described a similar experience of breaking away from a deep involvement with Jewish life and later returning to it through CBST. This separation typically followed an internal transformation that led them to feel an incongruity between their sexuality and the morality of their synagogue society. This process often occurred in their late teens or early twenties, before they actually experienced the social pressures that conflict was due to produce. But while the departure from their family's synagogue was a culmination of an emotional and intellectual crisis, joining CBST, many years later, seemed a most natural thing to them: they were connecting their present life with their past experience. The most difficult part of that step was, in fact, relieving their doubts about the likelihood of a gay synagogue being authentically "Jewish." Once they had done so they were not deterred by the synagogue's style, which was not necessarily the same as their parents' synagogue. Instead, they soon started to influence its workings, bringing it closer to what they had known. "I am going back to where I was always happy as a young boy," Nathan put it.

Those whose path to CBST followed this pattern of religious alienation and return typically came from traditional—Orthodox, or at least Conservative—backgrounds, and an overwhelming number were male. Naomi's description of her journey, which introduced this section, was not common to the women I met. Women, by and large, did not report feeling a theological conflict between sexual identity and Judaism as many males had.

A Search for Spirituality

Describing two new members of the board, Leon explained that their attraction to CBST was not for cultural reasons—as his own had been—or social, but "it is the spiritual experience which is important to them."

They were among a group of congregants for whom early memories were far less important in their attraction to the synagogue. While the "Jewishness" of CBST obviously facilitated their taking the initial step in joining, this seemed to be a secondary factor in its appeal. Rather, these women and men joined the synagogue because it offered them the spirituality they were looking for at a particular time in their lives. "I come here for the spiritual experience," "in order to cultivate my soul," "I am a spiritual person" were the explanations offered.

A CBST newcomer in his early thirties, a successful and sociable salesman, told me that until recently he had been busy accommodating his sexual identity, but now he felt a need to deal with his spiritual identity. Although he had not attended synagogue since his bar mitzvah twenty years before, for the last three months he felt an urge to recite the Shema prayer before going to bed. Another man in his early thirties explained that he had little previous experience in Jewish life and felt a need to make up for that gap: "The synagogue fulfills my spiritual needs."

When he joined the synagogue eight years previously, Arnold was at a time of emotional distress. He shared his feelings with an educated, gay Puerto Rican friend from work who, more deeply involved in New York gay life, knew of the synagogue. Recognizing Arnold's spiritual void, he took him to CBST for his first visit. A few months later Arnold came back on his own and fell in love with the place he often called "our home." He volunteered for the unenviable housekeeping chores and helped prepare the weekly kiddush and holiday dinners. (Arnold was not the only one who discovered CBST, or was encouraged to join, through the information and advice of non-Jews).

Ron, a social worker, told a similar story, but one that begins in Los Angeles. Coming from a nonaffiliated family, he had no religious education and no particular bonds with Jewish life. A friend at work, who was a member of Los Angeles's gay synagogue, sensed a loneliness in him—in spite of Ron's involvement in many gay organizations—and thought he might find something at the synagogue that he lacked. Ron attended a service: "I was hooked." It started as a gratifying social experience, but Ron quickly developed a growing interest in Judaism. A few years later, on a visit to New York, he attended a service at CBST and struck up a friendship with Jack, one of the congregants most qualified in Jewish ritual and liturgy. After moving to New York, Ron joined CBST and became active in its religious affairs. For members like Ron, Jewishness was an acquired element in their life. As Jack put it: "Ron went to the synagogue without any intention of joining, but he discovered something he didn't know he was missing. Suddenly he felt good being Jewish, he felt that part which was hidden."

A Social Search

A very different group of congregants were drawn to the synagogue as a congenial place for sociability. They were neither nostalgic about their early religious experiences nor searching for spirituality. Many often confessed to being bored during the service and frequently arrived late, though in time for the social hour that followed. For them the synagogue ambience and membership compared favorably to bars and other gay meeting places. As one explained:

> You have a comfortable opportunity to meet people and feel safe. You know much more about what kind of people you associate with here. They look good. . . . The caliber of the people you meet here is far superior to that in other places. In the community center, for example, you might meet a hundred unemployed artists.

Jay told me that having returned to the United States after ten years in Israel, he joined CBST because it was a good place to renew his social life in New York. In his mid-thirties, attractive, self-confident, humorous, and affluent, he was very popular at the synagogue and sometimes did volunteer work. "You know," he told me, "many people come not because they are religious; they show up in order to see new faces and meet old friends." But he admitted the synagogue's appeal had gradually diminished for him, as it often did for those whose principal motivation was similarly social: "Somebody suggests that we go out for dinner on Friday and end up at the synagogue. But when it gets late, you think: why disrupt a pleasant evening if you don't really want to go there?" On other occasions when he had no other plans for a Friday evening, he went to CBST to take advantage of the social hour. "I love the company of Jews."

For another congregant, a rabbi, the social attraction of CBST evolved over time. After a few years of occasional visits to the synagogue, he developed a network of close friends, about ten men and women who would meet after Friday services at a nearby restaurant. His attendance become more regular in anticipation of these get-togethers: "For the first time in my life I have a group of buddies. I feel close to them and I can call on them when I am in need." Although the majority of members drawn to CBST for social reasons were not active in the synagogue and only attended irregularly, there were a few notable exceptions who became an integral part of its operation.

An unusual case was a man in his mid-fifties who had joined the synagogue fifteen years prior, right after coming out. He saw it as a natural place to start his social life, although he had been only "a two-evening Jew," attending services solely on the High Holidays. Since joining CBST, as he put it, "I have become a fifty-four evening Jew. I love that synagogue for its comfortable environment." But his involvement remained strictly social. He took upon himself the job of welcoming newcomers to the synagogue: every Friday evening he sat at a small table by the entrance, offering information, name tags, and yarmulkes; remaining there through most of the service. And, though he subsequently expanded his involvement in the gay world and became active in other organizations, he has maintained his self-appointed role at CBST. He has obviously enjoyed meeting hesitant first-timers and helping them overcome their uneasiness, and although he has sometimes been accused of pestering the young and innocent, his dedicated attendance seemed indispensable to the smooth and safe running of the Friday night service.

Another veteran congregant, Harry, often repeated the story of his path to the synagogue. His Gentile lover used to express a preference for Jewish partners. When the two separated after a few years together, his lover's ideal of the perfect mate had fixed in *his* mind, and he too decided to look for a Jewish lover. Where better than at CBST? On his first Friday visit he met the man with whom he has shared his life for the last fourteen years. He joined the synagogue and has contributed his artistic talent to its decoration ever since. His continuing affection for CBST has also kept his lover there even though he would, otherwise, have preferred a more Orthodox environment.

A Late Step Toward "Self-Acceptance"

Another group of congregants were those for whom coming to terms with their homosexuality was a longer, more difficult, and more painful course. These men and women often described their joining CBST as the culmination of a process of personal reintegration, of merging their two identities—Jewish and gay. But unlike the first group with whom they bear some resemblance, they were alienated not so much from the religion of their childhood as from their sexual identity. Among them were those who both came out and joined CBST at an older age, who were married before they acknowledged their homosexuality, or were prevented by other emotional or social factors from a break with the norms and expectations of heterosexual society.

A man in his late forties who visited the synagogue irregularly told me his story:

> I come from an Orthodox background. All my friends gradually married nice Jewish girls and had nice Jewish kids. I remained the only one unmarried, and I knew I could not marry: I hated women. But everybody was expecting me to get married. "A twenty-eight year old boy and still single?" I felt I wasn't a mensch. They made me feel like some sort of fairy. So I left the synagogue. When I found CBST I felt immediately, "Here I belong!" Here I am a mensch, although I'll never marry and won't have any children. Here I don't need to pretend I am not what I am—although I leave the lipstick at home.

Isaac's road to the synagogue was more complicated. He had joined CBST at forty-eight, the year before I met him, right after coming out to his wife and their two teenage children. He had known at a young age that he was attracted to men, but when he confided this to his father at twenty-five, the reaction was devastating: "It is better to die than live the life of a homosexual!"

Chastised, Isaac suppressed his sexual inclination and got married. Professional success and child rearing covered over the unhappiness of his marriage. In an attempt to fill their spiritual void, his wife joined a secular Jewish circle while he joined a Reconstructionist synagogue. There he became friends with Ron and Jack, an obviously gay couple, and came out to them. He explained that for many years he had suppressed the urge for male company, except for a few fleeting experiences during troubled times in his life, but the need had become too difficult to deny any longer. Ron and Jack invited him to attend services at CBST, which he did occasionally when his wife was out of town. Finally, fearing that he might experience an emotional breakdown, he came out to his wife.

Although her shock and hurt made him sometimes regret his decision, he explained that it was not an announcement about his sexual needs but a declaration "of my identity and that of my community." And in spite of the difficulties he experienced since coming out, Isaac was happy because, as he said, "I am now true to myself." For Isaac membership in CBST was a major symbol of his new existential position, a place to "validate my identity in the company of people who share it with me."

Bill first arrived in the synagogue shortly before I left New York in the winter of 1991. Now in his early thirties, he told me that as a teenager, without any family urging or even encouragement, he had chosen to enroll in a yeshiva, but when he discovered his "sinful" predilection, he distanced himself from his religion. At the same time, however, he could not reconcile with his homosexuality. He wanted to change, but could not, a predicament his family was unable to understand.

Bill went on to explain that for the last five years he had been closeted in cultural and social isolation. He was only involved with work and had no social life except for a lover with whom he had little in common, not sharing education, religion, occupation, or cultural interests. He accepted this limiting arrangement because it conformed to his family's and his own expectations of the life of a stigmatized homosexual. Gradually, however, Bill came to realize that he need not stay in this self-inflicted isolation, and was in the process of separating from his lover when he first arrived at CBST. A few weeks after we met Bill officially joined the synagogue and volunteered to work in the kitchen. As another congregant observed, Bill's affiliating with CBST was part of a process of self-acceptance: not only did it mark a return to his love for Judaism, but it was also a step toward his open participation in gay life. (When I returned to the synagogue on a visit nine months later, Bill was living with a young man he had met at CBST).

Simon's story reflects the crucial role of the synagogue in the life history of a gay man who later greatly influenced its development. From a young age Simon was attracted to Judaism and Jewish life, but circumstances denied its expression. His parents were too busy and uninterested in Judaism; in later years his wife preferred a Christmas tree to synagogue life. His separation from his wife was part of a gradual process during which he acknowledged and reconciled with what he described as his homosexual "proclivity."

In May 1973 he cut out an ad for a gay synagogue from the *Village Voice* and kept it in his jacket pocket until October, when he finally decided to go and see. "It was wonderful," he discovered. For so many years he had hungered for a synagogue, and now at last it was waiting for him. What he called "my two fantasies" materialized at once: his attraction to Judaism and his attraction to men. Lacking a serious background in Judaism, he became a diligent student, gradually improving his command of Hebrew and his knowledge of Jewish ritual and liturgy. He soon became a dominant figure in religious affairs, leading services during the High Holidays and being instrumental in compiling CBST's first full-fledged prayer book (*Siddur*), which has served the synagogue for many years.

Social Comfort and Inclusion

For a number of congregants, their motivation for joining CBST could be characterized as a desire for social comfort and inclusion. Many of the women were counted among this group. For those coming from Orthodox backgrounds, where women were seated in the synagogue balcony separate from men and denied any ritual role, or from some Conservative backgrounds, where until recently they were proscribed from rabbinical and cantorial roles and not counted in the minyan, full participation in ritual and leadership roles was liberating. Annette spoke of the women like herself who joined CBST in its early years:

> A large segment of women who were raised in traditional synagogues, and were given some education, soon discovered there was no place for them in the structure that existed. Once they matured there was no room for them to grow. They had to step back and leave it all to the men. These women, when they came to CBST, were freed. Whatever happened, they learned to live with it, because there was room for them to participate. It was a great step!

Women found themselves included symbolically as well. Jill reminisced:

> I became a member of CBST in September 1979. I had attended services a few times prior to that date, but that night was the first time I had seen the new *Siddur*, which had recently been degenderized. It was the first time I remember feeling totally a part of a Jewish worship service—there was not one jarring or exclusionary note that said I didn't belong. I remember how urgently I wanted to buy a copy of that prayer book, and how eventually I was directed to Larry, who told me it wasn't for sale and then simply gave me a copy! That night I gave him a donation and filled out a membership form, and I've been an active member ever since. This is where I learned to pray, to lead services, and to integrate Judaism into all of my life (*Synagogue News*, February 1993).

CBST, of course, was not alone in offering these opportunities to women. The Reform movement first ordained female rabbis in 1972 and various privileges in ritual were gradually allowed to women in many Conservative synagogues. Degenderized texts are not exclusive to CBST; the Havurah movement in particular was influential in that direction.[2] Those from traditional backgrounds, however, may not have felt at home with these services. But more than that, there was a wider dimension to social comfort, one not unique to women.

Many left mainstream synagogues because they felt out of tune there, and could not fit into the social fabric. This is perhaps not surprising given the central position into which the traditional family has evolved in the American synagogue and given the synagogue's promotion of the ethos of marriage and procreation. In an Orthodox synagogue, for instance, an unmarried man is easily identified since he is not entitled to wear a tallith.

Women cited their discomfort among the sisterhood of the unmarried, with whom they did not share the same expectations for the future. Jill described her unease whenever she and her lover arrived at a mainstream synagogue. Invariably, someone would approach the young women and try to fix them up with "suitable" dates. After they showed no interest, they were then totally ignored. Naomi spoke of her unsuccessful search for a synagogue when her father passed away and, again, after she lost her mother. Only when she found CBST was she in a place in which she was comfortable enough to at last say Kaddish for her parents: "In order to be spiritual you have to lose yourself. And you can't do it if you are uncomfortable or afraid you might do something which would disturb other people."

Dov, a longtime member, argued that a gay couple would feel uncomfortable even in a Reform synagogue because "the fact that they have to state their tolerance is almost intolerant. Here at least they are not uncomfortable." Jane, a member who felt a social ease at CBST despite a lack of close friends there, concluded: "This is my identity, you are comfortable in the company of people who understand you."

Finally, one might also ascribe to inclusivity the quite rare service attendance of a CBST member I met. He knew no one in the synagogue and had no social expectations He was also rather out of touch with it, inquiring: "Isn't this an Orthodox synagogue?" But CBST's open-door, no-questions-asked ethos allowed him to experience a Jewish environment whenever he felt the need, without having to explain himself.

Why Do They Stay On?

Up to this point I have described the various reasons offered by individual congregants for their initial attraction to CBST. A related but perhaps different question is, What is it that sustains their membership? What, if any, is its continuing meaning in their lives?

In his study of a gay evangelical church, Thumma observed that many sought out the church to resolve an identity crisis but "once the dissonance is resolved or reduced, they disappear"(1991: 344).[3] While the continuity of membership at CBST argues against the application of this principle, it is nevertheless true that just as their arrival at CBST often represented a personal evolution in religious and sexual identity, for many congregants this process did not cease at the door. For some, like former board chairs Morris and Norman, joining the synagogue and becoming active in its administration strengthened their gay identity and led them to become active in secular gay organizations. For others, like Simon and Ron, joining CBST encouraged them to a depth of religious education and synagogue involvement that they had not hitherto known and that they expressed through CBST. For still others, particularly those for whom joining CBST marked a return to synagogue life, a deepening religious commitment eventually—sometime years later—led them to find expression in other synagogues.

Nathan, one of the editors of the *Siddur* and active for many years at CBST, went on to join a modern Orthodox synagogue as well. He then attended services at CBST infrequently, mainly to be with his friends there. Nathan spoke of participation at CBST as a transitional stage during which people secure their Jewish and gay identities.

After returning from several years in Israel, Daniel, first editor of *Synagogue News*, and his lover became more observant and joined a modern Orthodox synagogue. Although Daniel complained that the CBST service was "too loose, lacks structure and is too remote from tradition," they continued to attend occasionally: "It is still home; it feels like an old sweater." The couple later became active in promoting an alternative, once-monthly, traditional service at CBST.

Edward, whose return to synagogue life was chronicled earlier, became more Orthodox and, in addition to CBST, joined a mainstream synagogue whose services he attended Saturday mornings. But though often sarcastic about CBST's religious style, he remained loyal to the place which first brought him back to Judaism. When the suggestion was made that CBST move its Yom Kippur service to a large hall in the Javits Center to accommodate all those wishing to attend, Edward vehemently objected: "Isn't this our home? You don't drive people out of their home on Yom Kippur."

Even among those for whom a search for greater orthodoxy was not a consideration, attitudes and practices evolved, and often so did the basis of their attachment to the synagogue. Over the years a number of active members joined other congregations, maintaining a dual affiliation with CBST: Martin, board chair, was an openly gay member of a Conservative synagogue, though his first loyalty was to CBST; Naomi and Simon both joined a Havurah group whose members were drawn mainly from CBST; others joined Reform congregations welcoming gays and lesbians.

Though they explored other congregations, such as the Reconstructionist one in which they met Isaac, Jack, the chair of the Religious Committee, and his lover Ron retained their allegiance to CBST, which had offered Ron an opportunity to discover his ethnic heritage and enabled Jack to return to a Judaism, from which he had been alienated, in the typical pattern. But the "wonderful" feeling Jack experienced upon arriving at CBST, of being able to pray again and meet other gays with whom he could talk, had gradually eroded. Jack felt he could now separate the needs of his gay and Jewish identities. He explained that if he and Ron were to move to another city and find a congenial gay society there, they wouldn't need to look for a gay synagogue. Instead, Jack believed, they could satisfy their religious needs in a mainstream one.

Referring to CBST members whose attendance had become infrequent, Jack argued—echoing Thumma—that once they had become reconciled to their identity as gay Jews they could be content without regular attendance at a gay synagogue: "Then it is enough to visit CBST once a year and feel it is still there." Jack also felt that the rote nature of the service militated against regular attendance. He explained that this was not a problem for the Orthodox, for whom prayer was a way of life, but difficult for others to cope with. He concluded that though many leave, others stay on because it is a society they want to be close to. A common thread running through all of these varied personal evolutions is a desire to maintain some connection with CBST, however attenuated. "It is wonderful there are these oases of Jewish space," Ben declared. "We are more than accidental friends. We are . . . more than other congregations. There is something special to our connection."

Family, home, community—often used interchangeably—were frequently spoken of by congregants to explain their depth of feeling for the synagogue and often invoked by service leaders and drashah (sermon) speakers. A woman who moved away from New York after a two-year membership sponsored a Kiddush, a post-service refreshment, to honor the synagogue that "was my family." Explaining the decision to renovate the sanctuary, a board member insisted: "This is our home!" Rebecca, a synagogue member for sixteen years, described the meaning of home:

> What CBST has become is my family—my home, a place where I will always be taken in. . . . My life continues to change, but the one thing I know in my heart is that regardless of what happens in my life, I can go to CBST any Friday night and find a group of gay and lesbian Jews with whom I can say Shema Yisrael (*Synagogue News*, February 1993).

Jill, a fourteen-year member, ended her comment, quoted previously, about the feeling of inclusion she had experienced at CBST:

> CBST is more than my synagogue, its members more than friends—it is my home, my extended family. It is where I go to share my joys and where I turn for comfort and consolation in times of sadness.

There were others, however, for whom this metaphor was no longer valid. A congregant who only rarely came to the synagogue commented that when it was small there was a "family feeling," but when the synagogue expanded he "got lost." Another veteran member opined that it was relevant only for those actively involved in CBST committees and able to "transcend its many groups." Simon, on one occasion, complained that the idea of CBST as family was a "myth" held onto by lonely people separated from their families. He cited his own recent absence from services for several weeks due to illness: no one had called to find out what had happened to him.

If, for many, this analogy was a strongly held metaphor and, for others, a myth, in death it sometimes took on almost literal meaning. Simon himself related the story of an older, indigent, socially isolated man, a rather pathetic figure, who attended services at the synagogue. When he died it was learned that he had appointed Norman to see to his possessions and arrange his funeral. In fulfilling that request Norman stinted neither time nor money; members of the congregation offered donations to cover the expenses and the isolated congregant was buried in a cemetery close to CBST's most beloved members. His request was deemed a test of CBST's ethos of family.

The synagogue increasingly faced these tests as AIDS introduced untimely death into its community. Martin, board chair during my observations, speaking of a congregant whose family refused to attend his funeral, declared that "we, his family, have been with him." When Lenny, who had described CBST as "my second family and home," died suddenly, his "first family" only begrudgingly attended his funeral. But as Martin observed: "Our extended family was all there. Lenny had been as lonely as the rest of us, but here in our synagogue we find our shared community."

However, death was not the only occasion for CBST to express its family ethos. Isaac, whose late self-acceptance was recounted above, voiced amazement at the Rosh Hashanah lunch he attended, which so contradicted the image he had held for many years of gays as lonely people. Other holiday dinners were often spoken of with enthusiasm—although the food was rarely more than barely edible. When Paul addressed a holiday dinner group of more than one hundred congregants, he referred to them as "our extended family," and reported that other congregations, both gay and nongay, were now imitating CBST's model of communal meals.

Early in my stay at CBST two congregants proposed the initiation of a monthly Friday evening meal, a Shabbat dinner, before the service. Jack, who subsequently made a report to the Religious Committee on one of these more intimate dinners, commented: "This is not a CBST dinner, but a family affair."

Synagogue or Community Center?

In exploring the congregants' motives for joining CBST and CBST's evolving significance, the reasons that emerge are, doubtless, not mutually exclusive. Naomi, for example, felt both theologically alienated from Judaism by her homosexuality as well as socially uncomfortable and unable to fulfill her quest for spirituality. Categorizing congregants' motives risks not only making arbitrary distinctions but generalizing across what are significant differences. The imageries and constructs of a synagogue to which congregants sought to return, for instance, were frequently widely variant. A new arrival at CBST complained about the responsive readings—a staple at Reform and Conservative, but not Orthodox services—which reminded him of a church service. For him the individual praying alone, the "davenen experience," was the essence of a Jewish service. Not only did the congregants' experiences of Judaism differ in kind but also in amount. For many members regular attendance at only holiday services was the fulfillment of their religious commitment, a pattern common—if not thought exemplary—among Reform and Conservative congregations. Joel complained that on Passover and Kol Nidre "you suddenly discover a big crowd of strangers."

Thus far the varied reasons for joining CBST and the meaning that it has for its members—why join and why remain—have been explored principally in terms of their implications for the individual congregants themselves. But from the institutional point of view its members' motivations bear on the question of the kind of institution it is, and what it should be. In broadest form, two institutional models of American Judaism seemed to emerge in the ongoing discourse at CBST: the synagogue (vaguely associated with Orthodox congregations and Conservative congregations of various shades) and the community center (associated mainly with the Reform, Conservative, and Reconstructionist movements). Veteran congregants, particularly those in leadership positions, tended to interpret CBST in terms of the first model. Larry and Leon commented:

> In New York there is no need for our synagogue to be a community center. People come here in order to daven. We are not a *beth knesset* ["assembly place," the standard Hebrew term for a synagogue] but a *beth tefillah* ["prayer place," a term mainly used in poetic presentations].

Larry admitted, however, that in the early days "we were more social, we were close-knit," although he did not regret that loss. He assumed that the other gay synagogues, being smaller, were more socially active. For others the answer was less monolithic than for Larry or Leon. As Daniel, the first editor of *Synagogue News*, posed it: "The question is whom do we address first, a social or a religious community?" Expressing a common view, a CBST regular declared: "The synagogue provides for various needs of different people."

In a Yom Kippur talk to the congregation, Martin spoke to the issue of CBST's identity, seeing it as a combination of a community center and a *shtiebl.*[4]

He pointed to CBST's uniqueness: unlike other synagogues it is not organized according to a shared theology, class, or neighborhood. Considering the varied needs and metonymies of its diverse congregation, he declared: "The shared sexual orientation is the cement which unites us."

Notes

Reprinted with permission from *A Gay Synagogue in New York.*

1. Moshe Shokeid. 1995 (2002). *A Gay Synagogue in New York.* Columbia University Press augmented edition with a new epilogue, University of Pennsylvania Press.

2. The Havurah congregations are a movement of small, informal, home-based prayer groups that dated from the founding of the first of these in 1968. See, for example, Riv-Ellen Prell (1989), *Prayer and Community: The Havurah In American Judaism.* Detroit: Wayne State University Press.

3. See Scott Thumma. 1991.

4. *Shtiebl* is the term for a synagogue in Hasidic parlance, literally meaning "a small room," where the congregants had no formal leadership. They formed an intimate small group dedicated to prayers in a much more austere atmosphere than that of the regular synagogue.

Latter-day Saint Lesbian, Gay, Bisexual, and Transgendered Spirituality

6

RICHLEY H. CRAPO

HERE IS DIVERSITY WITHIN EVERY RELIGION, but not all religions formally recognize or accept the diversity that is found within them. The ideologies of different religious traditions differ in their acknowledgment and acceptance of diversity of practice and belief. The Church of Jesus Christ of Latter-day Saints (LDS), whose members are widely known as Mormons, exemplifies a religion in which unanimity of belief and practice is idealized.

The Problem of Social Identity within Mormonism
The Mormon emphasis of uniformity within the faith results in the experience of pressure on members to suppress any characteristic that sets them apart, religiously or socially, from their fellow Mormons. This contributes to the strong pressure to remain "closeted" and results in social isolation for lesbian, gay, bisexual, and transgendered (LGBT) members who desire to continue their participation in Mormon religious life. This isolation can be self-imposed out of fear of rejection. Church leaders who commonly counsel persons not to discuss their LGBT identities with other members can also formally impose isolation on LGBT members.

The importance of "feeling at home" within a supportive social network is a powerful force in Mormonism that goes beyond the simple desire to have a friendly place of worship. In some ways, the Mormon heritage has the same qualities that ethnic groups have in defining one's social identity (see Drumm's discussion of Seventh-day Adventists in this volume for a similar dynamic). For instance, as I have reported elsewhere, as one excommunicated gay Mormon claimed,

> Neither [members nor nonmembers] understand that being a Mormon is just as much a part of who I am as is being gay. It is not just the Gospel. It isn't just the Mormon doctrine and principles. It's part of the fabric, which is made up of my

memories—both happy and not so happy. It influences how I look upon others, how I perceive the world around me. It is one hell of a big chunk of my young life. How could I just throw it all away? I can't! And I do not want to either.

Or as another put the same idea, "This is probably one of the most commonly asked questions I get, mostly from the LDS, 'How can you be Mormon, if you're gay?' For some reason church members just do not get that being Mormon goes beyond which church roster one's name appears on."

Or, as another person related, "Being a Mormon is no more voluntary than being a man, or being gay."

According to Phillips (1993: 94) the effect of the Mormon emphasis on so-cial conformity "for most celibate gay Mormons is that they live solitary, lonely lives with few social outings." This is true both within their religious community as well as outside it. Phillips cites a case that dramatizes this social isolation and loneliness with the example of a gay male member who volunteered at a homeless shelter not because he cared about the work, but, as he put it, "because it gives me someone to talk to. They're about the only ones who don't judge me" (1993: 94). He told of another gay man who drove around the streets at night looking for hitchhikers, just to have someone to talk to; and a third person who described the local talk radio station as his "best friend" (1993: 94).

Transgendered and transsexual (TS) Mormons experience similar isolation and pressures not to express one's distinctive sexual identity as well. One excom-municated transsexual woman described her experience this way:

> I did see my Bishop. He read out the provision of the Bishop's Manual. As a lawyer, I can understand when a second-class status is imposed. And by then I had seen what had happened to other TS along the way—thrown out from the church.

She further explained this pressure as alienation and isolation.

> Amongst my friends I found continued acceptance, even if they did not understand—and how could they when I could not. The pressure of alienation from others was intense, leading to three suicide attempts, all serious. But I made it, finally, to my operation in Montreal last year. Now all my ID is changed and I am a woman—legally, fully and completely. And I have found out what the word "happy" really means. But I am no longer a member of the church—and that is a sad commentary on what the church policy has done in respect of those like me and others.

Another transgendered Mormon male described his experience as a kind of ambivalent supportiveness.

Church-wise, most people are "helpful" in that they are quick to refer me to LDS social services—to "straighten me out".... Definitely I can attest to this fact: Church leaders (and members) outside Utah are much more truly helpful, and willing to support me (though they certainly would rather I not have such a thing to deal with, and certainly would rather I not choose transitioning).

Although this person's bishop is supportive, that support is only within limits: "My bishop at home has stated he will support me all the way should [karyotype testing demonstrate that] I have some anomaly to support my decision to transition. Otherwise, we shall start talking options."

The Religious Issue of Sexual Morality for LGBT Members

In addition to a generic emphasis on social conformity, the LDS denomination also is among those denominations that have specific teachings against homosexual behavior. Homosexual behavior is regarded as "serious sin." Even the thoughts and feelings associated with homosexual attraction "should be resisted and redirected" (Oaks 1995: 9). According to the *Church Handbook of Instructions*, the official policy manual provided to ecclesiastical leaders, members who have homosexual thoughts or feelings or who engage in homosexual behavior should resist such thoughts and feelings and remain chaste. Bishops may recommend psychological counseling as an aid to such efforts. Persistent homosexual behavior by either males or females, particularly by adults and especially by males who hold ecclesiastical office, is grounds for excommunication.

In a few wards (the LDS term for congregations), notably those in the coastal cities of the United States that have attracted large numbers of LGBT persons, bishops have adopted a more pastorally supportive approach to issues of same-sex sexuality. These bishops have treated violations of LDS rules of chastity outside marriage among gay, lesbian, bisexual, and transgender members as temporary lapses that do not warrant excommunication so long as the individual demonstrates sufficient contrition and expresses a continued desire to follow LDS precepts of sexual morality. In some cases, individual bishops may pursue a "don't ask, don't tell" policy such as that reported to me by one gay male who is active in the church.

The way I do it is to be firmly convinced the Church is wrong on this point, and I know that from personal revelation. Having served in bishoprics, mission, etc., I know that the church is run by well-meaning and sincere amateurs who do their best but are human. That also helps. I attend church regularly in my small inner-city branch .... The branch president "knows" [that I am sexually active] but I have stood firm that I will participate as much as I am allowed without answering questions about my personal sex life. I know I can't get into the temple without answering such questions, so I don't ask for a recommend. The result, sadly, is that I'm there every week with about forty other people and I have yet been asked to say a prayer, speak, teach, or pass the sacrament. Still, I have the gospel, the scriptures, and my prayers. Some day it may change. Maybe not. I am content either way in God's love and the warmth of his arms around me.

However, many bishops in most other places often take a stricter stand on homosexual transgressions than this, so the fear of excommunication can make it difficult for gay, lesbian, and bisexual members to communicate openly with their pastors. Similarly, although having a transgendered identity need not involve any violation of LDS rules that govern sexual behavior, some bishops have treated the simple assertion of a transgendered identity as grounds for excommunication, although several transgendered persons suggested to me that younger transgendered persons seem to be experiencing less rejection by their ecclesiastical leaders than has been true in the past.

LDS Concepts of the Afterlife as an Issue for LGBT Members

LGBT Mormons experience powerful social and theological pressures to suppress any open expression of their sexual identities. Their failure to do so not only places their social relationships as members of their local congregations at risk, but can also be perceived as a challenge to LDS theology at the deepest level.

Particular LDS beliefs and practices around heterosexual marriage pose special challenges for LGBT members of the LDS religion. Heterosexual marriage occupies a central place in the LDS community and its theology. "The family is ordained of God. Marriage between man and woman is essential to His eternal plan" (The First Presidency and the Council of the Twelve 1995). Among the most sacred LDS ordinances is that which is commonly referred to as "temple marriages." These marital "sealings" between men and women are believed to make the marital bond valid for eternity. The afterlife is conceptualized in terms of the relationships between such sealed (heterosexual) couples and their descendants through an unbroken chain of children and ancestors who have been similarly sealed to their spouses. Being sealed in a heterosexual marriage is considered to be a prerequisite to a person's attaining the "highest level of exaltation" in the next life. In these teachings, the LDS religion makes an explicit tie between heterosexuality and the afterlife that is absent in most other Christian denominations.

These distinctively LDS teachings about eternal heterosexual marriages as the highest reward in the afterlife pose a special question for LGBT Mormons about what their sexual identities will be in the next life. Since the LDS church has not explicitly addressed the question of the status of LGBT persons in the next life, individual LGBT persons sometimes try to work out their own theological ideas. For instance, one gay male who is strongly committed to LDS religious beliefs told me that fulfillment in a committed, loving same-sex relationship was so important to him that he would be satisfied if in the next life he and his partner could simply become "ministering angels," an LDS phrase that implies a somewhat lower next-life status than that which will be held by eternally married heterosexual couples. Others compartmentalize their spiritual lives by distinguishing between the LDS religion and the LDS church. For instance, a gay male who was active in LDS worship services explained this distinction between the church and the gospel to me.

> I believe that everybody has a different understanding of Mormonism. I do have a testimony of the restored gospel of Jesus Christ, but I also cannot deny the fact that I am gay. In my reconciliation, I have learned to make a separation between the Church and the gospel. I still sustain the brethren of the Church as apostles, prophets, seers, and revelators. But I don't believe that every whim that comes out of their mouths should be exercised into every individual's personal life. . . . My personal experiences have revealed to me that the Brethren are misguided on the issue of homosexuality. And perhaps other things too. The Lord has personally affirmed to me that these teachings are not right for *me*. In a most convincing way, He has told me to be true to myself. In that regards, I search for a companion to share the joys of life with.

The Politics of Marriage and LGBT Members

In addition to the social pressure to not be different, the religious prohibition of homosexuality in this life, and the theological centrality of heterosexual relationships in the next life, the LDS church has also involved itself actively in the political issue of the legal definition of marriage as an exclusively heterosexual institution. For instance, the church has actively lobbied against same-sex marriage in Hawaii and in several states in favor of so-called Defense of Marriage (DOMA) laws that restrict the recognition of marriage to heterosexual marriages (Crapo 1997a, 1997b). This adds a political dimension to the social and religious issues that LGBT Mormons must confront when working through their relationship with their church.

The very existence of bisexual Mormons is unacknowledged in church publications or sermons by top ecclesiastical leaders. Since, like heterosexual members, they experience attraction to members of the other sex, they are simply expected to conform to the church's norms of chastity before marriage and to find a compatible spouse who is not of their own sex. Thus, bisexual members are not treated as having any particular pastoral needs. Bisexual members have similar difficulty finding a support network outside the church itself. There are, at this time, no bisexual-support organizations for bisexual Mormons, although similar support groups whose members are primarily LDS gay or lesbian individuals typically welcome such persons.

Transgendered Mormons are a somewhat distinct case in that sexual behavior is not in and of itself the central identity issue that defines such individuals. Nevertheless, transgendered Mormons are confronted by the same pressures of conforming to the clear social expectations of Mormonism and many of the same religious and political issues. For instance, although transsexual surgery does not violate the LDS expectation of chastity before marriage, it is apparently perceived as an implicit challenge to the LDS belief that "gender is an essential characteristic of individual premortal, mortal, and eternal identity and purpose" (The First Presidency and the Council of the Twelve 1995). Thus it is specifically listed as among those transgressions for which official action against an individual's church membership "may be necessary" (Intellectual Reserve 1998: 95). The instructions regarding surgery are that "Church leaders counsel against elective transsexual operations. If a member is contemplating such an operation, a presiding officer should inform him of this counsel and advise him that the operation may be cause for formal Church discipline" (Intellectual Reserve 1998: 95).

Similarly, the intent to undergo transsexual surgery can be a hindrance to joining the LDS religion: "Persons who are considering an elective transsexual operation should not be baptized. Persons who have already undergone an elective transsexual operation may be baptized if they are otherwise found worthy in an interview with the mission president or a priesthood leader he assigns. Such persons may not receive the priesthood or a temple recommend" (Intellectual Reserve 1998: 26).

Challenges Faced by LGBT Mormons

A theology in which such heterosexual-family ideals are so central poses clear challenges to any person who was reared in a Mormon family and then finds that his or her sexual identity is that of a LGBT person. First, such individuals are very likely to be concerned about the possibility of rejection by both their families and their ecclesiastical leaders should they "come out." The pressure on individuals to keep issues of personal sexual identity hidden is strong. For instance, Phillips (1993) interviewed seventy-one homosexual Mormon males and found that most had not told their parents about their sexual orientation. Similarly, Benson (2001), who interviewed homosexual Mormon males about the coming-out process, found that "[t]he most common reason [for not coming out to their parents] was fear of parents' reaction. Another obstacle to disclosure for these individuals was guilt about adding to parents' emotional distress or wanting to protect their parents from painful emotions" (p. 26). Benson further found that LDS homosexual males who did come out to their families did so at a later age than is typical of non-LDS gays.

Coming out to ecclesiastical leaders is complicated by the fact that the LDS ecclesiastical organization is built on a lay ministry rather than a professional one. Thus, bishops and stake (another LDS term for a congregation) presidents have no formal theological or pastoral training. Each lay minister is given a copy of the *Church Handbook of Instructions* (Intellectual Reserve 1998). This handbook is concerned with matters of policy that are relevant to carrying out the organizational work each minister has been requested to perform. The publication, however, does not attempt to outline LDS theology or provide instruction on the skills of pastoral ministry to congregants. Thus, bishops and stake presidents must rely on their personal intuitions about how to respond to LGBT individuals and on their personal interpretations of the limited policy material regarding such issues as applying church discipline to nonconforming members. For this reason, the response of LDS bishops and stake presidents who are approached by LGBT members can vary tremendously from one ward or stake to another.

Awareness that the response of their ecclesiastical leaders is highly unpredictable and often unsupportive is a frequently mentioned concern of LGBT Mormons. They often respond to this situation by not seeking pastoral counseling at all because of their fear of possible loss of membership. One interviewee, who now describes himself as a "personally spiritual but organizationally unaffiliated" gay man, described his own previous "discord" about his relationship with the church.

> I was afraid about how the church would react and afraid about the loss of social structure and terribly depressed about marriage problems I was having, like my infidelity, because I was trying to follow the church's teachings by being a father and husband, but I kept getting involved with men.

This individual eventually resolved his cognitive dissonance by no longer participating in either Mormon or non-Mormon worship services and leaving his heterosexual marriage relationship.

Nevertheless, remaining closeted does not eliminate the dissonance LGBT Mormons experience between their religious and sexual identities. One gay man described how on one Sunday, he was sitting in the choir at the front of his ward's chapel when "this guy I had slept with the previous night came in and sat down

in the congregation!" Experiences such as this, he explained, were personally embarrassing because they challenged his previous compartmentalization of his spiritual and sexual lives and forced him to deal with a sense of hypocrisy in his
participation in the religious life of his congregation. The majority of LGBT
Mormons I interviewed described the dissonance they have experienced as primarily internal and psychological rather than as a matter of social awkwardness. Interviewees spoke about the depression and sense of loneliness they had to cope
with as closeted participants in LDS life rather than discussing embarrassing or
otherwise difficult social situations.

The most common resolution to the conflict between the religious and sexual identities of LGBT Mormons appears to be varying degrees of eventual disengagement from the church. One gay man explained that the lack of anyone to
turn to within the church for support led him to depression and the contemplation of suicide. He "opted to survive," however, and found a support network in the gay community and a spiritual home in the local Metropolitan
Community Church instead of continuing a closeted life among other Mormons. A lesbian interviewee, who now participates in the Episcopal church, explained her own feelings of lacking a support network in a Mormon setting this
way: "The LDS church is extremely patriarchal, and our mission in life is to get
married, have babies, and give up having a career, but we're not just brainless
baby machines."

In principle, the LDS doctrine does not distinguish among persons based on
their personal, subjectively perceived sexual identities. For instance, rather than
recognizing kinds of persons based on differences in sexual orientation, the church
regards differences in erotic or affective attraction simply as matters of the kinds
of "temptations" different individuals may experience. Thus, the spontaneous experience of a "same-sex attraction" to another person is not regarded as sin any
more than an unbidden heterosexual "temptation" would be. It is only behavior—
acting on "homosexual feelings" that is held to be sin.

This does not imply, however, that sexual orientation itself is a religious non-
issue. In practice, the LDS worldview does not allow for the existence of gay, lesbian, or bisexual persons. Church leaders carefully avoid the use of the term
"sexual orientation" or terms such as "gay," "lesbian," or "bisexual" as kinds of human identities. Instead, they speak only of individuals being "troubled" by "experiencing same-sex temptations." In replacing the noun phrase, "sexual
orientation," with various verb phrases, such as "being same-sex attracted," LDS
theological discourse delegitimizes sexual orientation as the basis for a person's social identity within the religious setting. One may be an LDS lawyer or an LDS
Democrat or Republican, but one may not, in the accepted language of Mormonism, be a "gay, lesbian, or bisexual Mormon."

From the viewpoint of church leaders, persons who designate themselves by one of these terms are, by the very act of self-labeling, placing themselves outside the LDS system of thought that acknowledges only "persons who experience same-sex attraction." Thus, there is no form of pastoral counseling that is aimed at dealing with the cognitive dissonance resulting from experiencing oneself as being both LDS and gay, lesbian, or bisexual. Instead, such individuals are simply counseled not to act on their temptations. They may also be referred to LDS Family Services where therapists are expected to help such persons conform their behavior to the LDS ideal of chastity outside heterosexual marriage. These therapists assist members in attempting to alter their self-perception away from "being" gay, lesbian, or bisexual persons.

The primary church document concerning homosexuality for therapists employed by LDS Family Services (LDS Social Services 1995) discusses homosexuality and lesbianism within a gender-identity learning model. This document portrays homosexual and lesbian relationships as the result of inadequate identification with the same-sex parent, poor peer relations, unhealthy sexual attitudes, early homosexual experiences, or sexual abuse. It recommends a form of "reparative" therapy intended to facilitate patients' acquisition of those gender roles that the church views as appropriate for relationships between men and women. Gay, lesbian, or bisexual members report that their own acceptance of this viewpoint can be a source of tremendous inner turmoil. For instance, several male interviewees said that as adolescents they had prayed repeatedly and to no avail for God to take away their sexual attraction to other males. When this did not work they chose to serve the church as missionaries in the hope that by demonstrating their dedication to their religion, God would surely change them so that they would no longer feel a sexual attraction to other men. When, after a year or more of missionary service, these men found themselves unchanged, they were devastated to the point of becoming suicidal.

Carving Out Niches within the Fold

Despite the powerful cognitive dissonance experienced by LGBT persons whose religious identity is LDS, some individuals chose to remain active participants in the LDS religion. The religious identification can be powerful. As one gay male whose ancestors were pioneer Mormon settlers of Utah Territory told me, "I can no more choose not to be Mormon than I can choose not to be male or homosexual." A. D. Lach, a spokesman for Affirmation, a support group for LDS LGBT persons, quotes one gay Mormon man as having said, "I am a Mormon, from a long line of Mormons, yet, I am also a homosexual. I have come to realize that I cannot cease being either. Thus, happiness depends upon my ability to reconcile these two facets of my nature" (Lach 1989). In his study of LDS gays, Phillips noted that his sample included persons who "choose to live celibate lives, attempt to change their sexual orientation, or marry heterosexually in order to maintain favor with the Mormon church" (1993: vi).

LGBT members recognize that living in full conformity to the outward trappings of Mormonism is an effort that involves compromising one's psychological identity. One fully conforming gay male explained, "The woman that I will marry will not fulfill my sexual desires entirely, but will feed me what I need from her. Together we will strive to be a 'whole.' And it will be enough to help me endure to the end." Another gay member states the conflict between practical reality and religious ideals more directly. "I am twenty-five, LDS with a rock solid testimony and planning on a life of celibacy to honor my Temple covenants. But to be realistic being alone is very hard if not impossible, but it is worth a try, and it is what I feel Heavenly Father wants me to do."

Seeking pastoral support for the problems that attend the effort to follow an LDS lifestyle can also lead to other complications. For instance, one of the gay men I spoke to is a fully committed believer in the LDS religion and the authority of his church. Since the LDS church has long been a major supporter of scouting, part of his Mormon life experience included a strong personal attachment to scouting and its ideals. As an adult, he continued to find great personal fulfillment in helping boys to progress through the scouting program. After confiding in his bishop about his commitment to remain true to the standards of the church without acting on his sexual feelings about other adult males, the higher ecclesiastical leader whom his bishop consulted, apparently believing that being gay is synonymous with being a pedophile, insisted that he no longer be permitted to play a role as an adult leader in the church's scouting program.

As noted previously, those who tell their bishops of their commitment to sexual inactivity are often counseled to remain quiet about their sexual orientation and share it with other members only on a "need to know" basis. This attitude perpetuates the social isolation of LGBT members within their religious community. According to Phillips, the result "for most celibate gay Mormons is that they live solitary, lonely lives with few social outings" (1993: 94). According to at least half of those persons I interviewed, this isolation exacerbates the problems of depression, fear of rejection, and even suicidal concerns.

Most Mormon LGBT persons who remain active in the church elect to stay closeted. Although a few choose to confide in their bishops, doing so can be problematic. The personal attitude of individual bishops may result in harsher treatment than is actually justified by the standard policy guidelines issued to each local leader. For instance, one transgendered woman reported that her bishop insisted on holding a "Disciplinary Council" because she had undergone surgery for her condition. He insisted that this was mandatory, but when she showed him that the relevant policy statement of the church was merely that church discipline "may" be required in such cases, his response was simply, "It doesn't matter. I decide." The eventual outcome was excommunication. A transsexual man explained that his bishop required him to undergo karyotype testing and took the position that he would support him only if there was evidence of chromosomal abnormality to legitimate his choice to transition from female to male. Nevertheless, even if the testing supported his case, current church policy precludes his being ordained to the LDS lay priesthood, an ordination that is required for full participation in various church activities, including marriage, which is an otherwise universal expectation for all male members.

In recent years a number of support organizations have come into being that welcome LGBT Mormons or their families as members. These groups include some that are LGBT affirmative in their views and others that have the goal of helping LGBT Mormons who wish to adhere to the strict sexual norms of their church. There are currently six primary organizations. Four of these, Affirmation, Q-Saints, Family Fellowship, and Gamofites, support an integration of the Mormon faith with LGBT sexual expression. The other two, Evergreen International and Disciples2, offer direction for members attempting to follow church teaching. Although none operate within the official structure of the LDS church, these groups offer a supportive environment for LGBT Mormons who choose to remain in the church. Each of these groups has a significant presence on the Web.

The first of these, Affirmation, is a denominational heritage group. Its goal is to serve the needs of gays, lesbians, bisexual LDS, and their supportive family and friends through social and educational activities. It has local chapters throughout the world and also hosts an Internet "chapter-at-large" on its website at www .affirmation.org. The mission of Affirmation, as stated on the site, is:

> to provide gay and lesbian Mormons and former Mormons with opportunities to make their own choices by helping them deal with issues regarding sexual orientation, spirituality, and the Church of Jesus Christ of Latter-day Saints. Since Affirmation actively supports the right of LGBT persons to find self-acceptance and fulfillment in who they are, the organization participates in LGBT-rights events and lobbies for a more LGBT-accepting position by the LDS church and educates its members and the public about homophobic characteristics of the church.

Affirmation also sponsors an electronic mailing list (Q-Saints) of interest to gay and lesbian Mormons. Most, but not all, regular contributors are men. The threads on Q-Saints include topics such as the rejection of "gay conversion" therapy by mainstream psychology and opposition to the "reparative therapy" approach of groups like Evergreen International. The conversations on the list also address problems concerning lack of support for gay and lesbian members within the church, concerns about the church's political involvement in legislative attempts to restrict legal marriage to heterosexual couples, homophobia both in and out of the church, research about sexual orientation, and issues about family relations and parenting for gay and lesbian individuals in heterosexual marriages.

Given the centrality and importance of the family within Mormonism, two of these support groups focus on familial matters. Family Fellowship is an organization for LGBT Mormons and their families. Its focus is on fostering supportive family relationships for LGBT Mormons. It hosts local groups and maintains an Internet site at http://www.ldsfamilyfellowship.org/index.htm. It also hosts annual public conferences, which act as forums for presentations on various facets of homosexuality. Recent conferences have included presentations on research concerning sexual orientation, homophobia, issues regarding relations between LGBT members and the LDS church, the politics of same-sex marriage, the impact of exclusionary policy of the Boy Scouts of America on LGBT Mormons, and personal accounts of individual LGBT members concerning their relationships with their families and the LDS church.

According to their literature,

> Family Fellowship is a volunteer service organization, a diverse collection of Mormon families engaged in the cause of strengthening families with homosexual members. We share our witness that gay and lesbian Mormons can be great blessings in the lives of their families, and that families can be great blessings in the lives of their gay and lesbian members. We strive to become more understanding and appreciative of each other while staying out of society's debate over homosexuality. We seek to put behind us all attitudes which are antifamily, which threaten loving relationships, and which drive family members apart.

The other family-oriented support group, Gamofites, is an organization for gay Mormon fathers and their partners. It describes itself as "men united in the joys and challenges of being fathers, gay, and Mormon. We are dedicated to fostering and supporting the needs and individual growth of members in an environment of confidentiality, trust, and unconditional love." This group hosts a website at http://www.gamofites.org/ and holds weekend retreats that focus on creating community through fellowship activities such as enjoying great food, laughing with old and new friends, sharing experiences, and growing personally. These weekends also include educational efforts through engaging in lively discussions directed by invited guests or by Gamofites members. Partners of members are welcome whether or not they are fathers or from Mormon backgrounds. Although it is not a religious organization, many members view this fellowship as a source of spiritual fellowship.

Two other support groups function closer to the official position of the LDS church authorities. Evergreen International is a support group for LDS persons who are uncomfortable with the idea of being gay or lesbian. Although not formally affiliated with the LDS church, its primary mission is to help its members resist gay and lesbian orientation. The website of Evergreen International is www.ldsfamilyfellowship.org.

Likewise, the web and email support group, Disciples 2, is for gay and lesbian Mormons who choose to maintain their affiliation with Mormonism and desire to live within the church's teaching on homosexuality. Their website is www. springsofwater.com/desert/disciples2. The mission of this group, as noted on their website, is as follows:

> The goal of Disciples is to provide a place of mutual support for those who have chosen or may someday choose to be in harmony with our Heavenly Father and His law as set forth by modern-day prophets and apostles. These are obeying the laws of the Lord, including the law of chastity. The purpose of these lists is to be a place of safety and comfort, as each of us grow toward our goal of exaltation and obedience to the principles and ordinances of the Gospel of Jesus Christ. We hold no means of cure or change as the only option for our lives, yet we hold dear to our hearts the desire to remain clean and pure as we move closer to freedom from this conflict known as same-sex attraction.

Finding Support Outside the Church

Most of LGBT persons of LDS background whom I have interviewed have resolved the conflict between their personal identities and their LDS religious heritage by disengaging with the LDS church. Sometimes their disengagement has been the result of their having been either "disfellowshipped" or excommunicated by their ecclesiastical leaders. Disfellowshipped persons retain their membership in the church but are restricted in terms of the level of their participation in the religious practices of the church. Others have voluntarily disengaged in ways that vary from retaining their membership but no longer attending services regularly or at all to severing their ties with the church by requesting that their names be removed from its roles.

The transition out of Mormonism is not an easy one, since many experience their LDS background not simply in denominational terms but as a matter of cultural identity. As one disaffiliated gay male put it, "It's more than a church, it's a culture." Another, who is currently unaffiliated with any denomination, put it this way: "You can take me out of the church, but you can't take the culture out of me." Disaffiliation is sometimes associated with unresolved anger. One disaffiliated gay male, a young man of about twenty-five years of age, told me,

I am . . . angry at and deeply disturbed by the Church for the untold suffering and destruction it has precipitated in the lives of so many of my gay brothers and sisters. I don't apologize for those feelings. I believe in my heart that the Church is deeply mistaken concerning its attitude and policies toward homosexuality. I still have a testimony of the gospel and resent having to attempt to find another outlet for my spiritual feelings (Crapo 1998).

Another person, a bisexual man, reported a similar sentiment,

I thought when I was younger that I was bisexual, that I could *choose* the only option the church gave me of heterosexual monogamy. Maybe I just wanted to believe it. I certainly believed that when I went to the temple before my mission, and I believed it when I married. But in the intimacy of a shared life, I couldn't sustain it. I'm still married, I'm still at home and am trying to do so until June when our younger daughter graduates. This last year brought me disfellowshipment, passage through depression, thoughts of suicide, therapy, and a new sense of self and peace on the inside. I'm going to be alright. And both God and the Spirit never left me. I am looking for a new spiritual home (Crapo 1998).

The modal pattern among those LGBT persons who have fully disaffiliated themselves from the LDS religion appears to be one of shifting towards agnosticism or atheism rather than of seeking out another denomination with a LGBT-friendly theology. Those LGBT persons with whom I have spoken in the course of my research on various LGBT issues are more likely to describe their current religious status to be agnostic or atheist rather than even "personally spiritual but not organizationally religious." Nevertheless, some do maintain a private spirituality or migrate to other denominations. For instance, among LGBT student members of Pride Alliance, a student organization at my own university, several of the lesbian members have become affiliated with the local Episcopal church, which they perceive as both accepting of gay and lesbian members and of their own feminist values. Several gay male members have found a community of spiritual support in the local Metropolitan Community Church, and a few currently participate in meetings of the Unitarian Universalist Church.

Conclusion

The centrality of doctrines and practices concerning heterosexual marriage and families makes it unlikely that the LDS church will undergo significant theological changes with respect to its expectation that LGBT persons must conform their behavior to the gender and sexual norms of the church. Although the possibility exists that the church might reassess its understanding of sexual identity in ways that would be more accepting of transgendered person's self-perception without directly challenging doctrines or practices concerning the eternal nature of the heterosexual family, the existence of transgendered persons appears to be even less acknowledged or addressed in LDS literature than are homosexual and lesbian members. The church remains similarly silent on issues concerning bisexual members. However according to the LGBT persons I have interviewed, church policy and practice regarding LGBT members does appear to be undergoing some change as church leaders become increasingly aware of the existence of LGBT members whose pastoral needs have not been previously addressed.

Even within this reality, LGBT Mormons find a place, often times contested, within the Church of Jesus Christ of Latter-day Saints. The recent appearance of electronic and face-to-face networks of support do not alleviate the ostracism LGBT Mormons find within the denomination; however, these groups may make the choice of remaining within the faith a bit more tolerable.

Sexuality and Gender in Santería 7
LGBT Identities at the Crossroads of Santería Religious Practices and Beliefs

SALVADOR VIDAL-ORTIZ[1]

I am inside a house basement transformed into a sanctuary for the divinities of the "way of the saints," or *Santería*. This *bembé* (festivity) is remarkable; several people have been possessed by deities, in celebration of a new initiate's *tambor* (drumming). It will be months before people stop talking about such presence of deities, which will make the initiate, as well as his *padrinos* ([m] godfather; [f] god-mother), proud. A thin, dark-skinned man in his late twenties has been possessed by a female *Orisha*, whose name is *Ochún*. At this moment in particular, it is not the young man who is in front of me, showering me with hugs and caring gestures to my head and shoulders, but *Ochún* (Núñez 1992). I recognize the difference in presentation, as well as gesture and voice pitch, between him and her. (T)his body has been rearticulated through a very different set of movements: a paced presence, a playful game of seduction with what seems to be a scarf, and an undoubtedly distinct look in the eyes. A male teenager has been asked to follow *Ochún* with a plate carrying honey, as this amorous *orisha* (Moreno Vega 2000) greets and shares her energy with the present. She pauses every fifteen minutes or so and licks a lit-tle honey from the plate, before personally encountering another follower or on-looker at the sacred site. *Ochún* will be here for about ninety minutes, blessing us all with her presence.

Only an hour before this possession, I had been intrigued by the appearance of a strong gay presence at this ritual in the Bronx. I am at the initiation of Wal-ter (a participants' pseudonym) on an early summer day in New York City. I esti-mate that about a third of men at this particular *tambor* are "gay," either by assuming their gendered presentation or behavior—which includes flirtation with other men—or by their self-disclosure. The initiate, as in other initiations I've heard of, and witnessed, is also of a homosexual sexual identity.

This chapter is an attempt to shed light on the many responses to lesbian, gay, bisexual, and transgender (LGBT) members in churches and places of worship in the United States as sexual minorities at a crossroads in contemporary religion. Specifically, I focus on the identity, participation, and reception of LGBT members in Santería, an Afro-Cuban religion. This research is the result of a pilot project conducted in preparation for a larger dissertation study focusing on gender and sexuality within Santería in the northeastern United States. I illustrate the negotiations of sexual identity by LGBT *Santeros* who are actively shaping the course of the religion while analyzing Santería as a religious setting that appears to offer space for LGBT participation.

Santería—along with other Latin American and Caribbean religions (*Macumba, Candomblé, Espiritismo, Vodou,* even *Curanderismo*)—involves beliefs in ritual focused on communication and interaction with ancestors, spirits, or various deities. The origins of Santería's more contemporary form, which utilizes Africa's Yoruba religion as a referent, involve migration patterns from Cuba to New York, New Jersey, Florida, other states, and Puerto Rico. As a result, international migration and internal migration within the United States are patterns essential to the practice of the religion. Thus, because it is not limited to North American, religious, or language borders (given its Yoruba, Spanish, and English languages), Santería defies many boundaries.

The study of LGBT people in Santería requires admitting that other elements—besides sexual orientation and gender identity—come into play. Understanding, for example, Santería in the "North American" context (as proposed in this book) requires recognition of the "Latin Americanization" of the United States, while noting that the racialization (Omi and Winant 1986) of "Latinos" in this country continuously frames such ethnic groups as a (racial) "other." For instance, Rodríguez (2000) has noted how Latinos reject traditional ideas of race as merely phenotype in the United States; this research might elucidate newer meanings to the context of race as currently understood in this country. I am here referring not to the skin color aspects of race, but to the construction of "Latino" as more of a racial category than an ethnic one (and that the impact of Latino immigration has forced the United States to have a more complex analysis of race than that of black and white).

The acknowledgment of Santería as a religion adds to the popular recognition that "Americans" (henceforth "United Staters") have never been more religious than they are now (Mizruchi 2001). Santería also complicates very recent findings that the number of United Staters with no religious preference has doubled (Hout and Fischer 2002). Although Santería is often not conceptualized as a religion, its members are habitually understood as engaging in multiple religious and spiritual practices (Brandon 1983). U.S. Santería practitioners alone have been estimated at one million (Harper 2000)—with cities like Hialeah, Florida, having about 100,000 worshippers, and New York and Tampa following closely (Kennedy 2000)—while three million people are Santería followers in Cuba. It makes sense to further estimate that a small, yet perhaps significant portion of these practitioners, in the United States and abroad, are LGBT-identified.

Recent autobiographical fiction such as Angel Lozada's *La Patografía* (1998), written from an Islander Puerto Rican perspective, and Emanuel Xavier's *Christ-Like* (1999), developed from the perspective of a New York Puerto Rican and Ecuadorian gay man, represent the practice of *Espiritismo* and Santería by gay-identified men. Like those novels, many of the Santeros' accounts in this chapter recognize the possibilities of participating as a sexual being in Santería, attracted to people of the same sex, yet not necessarily circumscribing to a very rigid, Americanized, "gay rights" faction. (This is a challenge to recent gay rights movement organizations, and to the sexuality and homosexuality scholarship that thrives on such fixed categorizations.) Unlike cultural writings, there has been little published scholarship on the participation, reception, and identification of LGBTs in Santería in the United States. This chapter directly addresses this void. Specifically, I illustrate how "gay" identities are understood in Santería and, in turn, how individuals often labeled as "gay" are interpellated by such identity in their process of resisting, reconstructing, and renaming altogether their experience. Throughout, I utilize "gay" to represent LGBT identities as understood by practitioners, or as the most common identity label utilized by them. (Gay narratives were privileged in these accounts, both as stories told by gay men about gay men, or by everyone as they spoke of "gay" as a central category in these discussions.) While utilizing this narrative, they both contested and reified its use. Thus in this context, the term "gay" has to be read as both a critique of organizing categories of identity as well as a representation of sexual minority status. As it will become clear, there are movements, or rather slippages, away from and toward "gay" identities.

Due primarily to space limitations, this chapter does not attempt to illustrate the history of Santería, much less a history of the participation of LGBTs in the religion. It also avoids debates on the various conceptualizations of Santería as a religion, the syncretism controversies surrounding the religion, and even homosexuality and Santería outside the United States. Finally, the chapter is not charged with the difficulty of addressing the accusations often made of the religion as an exploitative business, questions on religion and space (particularly on urban spaces), animal sacrifice controversies, and thick descriptions of the general rituals undertaken in the religion. I chose to engage with the aspects of reception and resistance from the LGBT participants, as well as the overall Santería structure of practice in New York City.

Santería or La Regla de Ocha: *The Way of the Saints*

Practitioners of Santería participate within a structure of rituals for their deities and under the direction of *padrinos* and *madrinas*. Deities are instrumental in facilitating a formation of community. Indeed, their presence is not thought to be an act for the benefit of the individual mounted, but for the benefit of all present. *Orishas* (or deities) come and participate in the activities, contributing with their charms, personalities, even funny or possessive behavior. The *Orishas* are also known as *Santos*, and they "maintain the universe and its operations" (Flores 1990: 47). Central to the religion is the appreciation, veneration, and dialogue with the *Orishas* (Cornelius 1991). The *Orishas* are an extension of *Olódumare*—the supreme being of the Yoruba and Lukumí religions and peoples who, in trinity with *Olofi* and *Olorun*, "have authority over the rest (of the *Orishas*) but are not the object of direct adoration or worship" (Barnet 1997: 79–80). There are 401 *Orishas* (Moreno Vega 2000) that people venerate in their practice of the religion. Santería, given its African origins and like other African religions (Boyer 2001), does not rest on worshiping a single or central deity, but several.

The *padrinos* and *madrinas* are responsible for guiding and directing the new initiates, especially during their first year of formal entrance to Santería as practitioners, or who are called in the religion a *Yabó*. *Yabós* are mandated to wear white clothing for a full year and seven days after their initiation. Every year after that, on the day of the *asentado* (or the one seated upon by an *Orisha*), the *Santero* sets up an altar at home to celebrate his or her initiation or *cumpleaños* (birthday). The religion has positions or responsibilities that certain people assume, such as that of the highest priest, the *Babalawo*, and people with expertise on all Santería ceremonies, an *Oriaté* (Brandon 1983). These positions or roles within the practice have been solidified at times for individuals of specific sexual orientations: for instance, heterosexual men are the only ones allowed to play the *Bata* drums, as well as to be initiated as *Babalawos*, while women (of all sexual orientations) and gay or bisexual men are not. Part of the analytic challenge for the study of the religion is to understand the possibilities and limitations of such a structure in its practice. *Espiritismo* and *Palo* (*Palo Monte* and *Palo Mayombe* are two main sects of the *Palo* tradition in Cuba, derived from those who came from the Congo) are at times collapsed within the discussion of Santería, recognizing the similarities in ritual and belief system among these religious practices in settings like New York (Brown 1999).

The chapter is divided into three main sections. After a methodological discussion and an introduction of the participants, I discuss the negotiation of identities, first framed in relationship to community and newer family configurations, and then by looking at how those identity negotiations take place.

The chapter concludes with recommendations for work on the interplay of gender and sexuality in studying the participation of LGBT individuals in Santería.

Methodology and Participants

I present accounts of nine Santeros interviewed in New York City about the participation of LGBTs in the religion. I also refer to some field notes from field and participant observations. Interviews took place between the summer of 2001 and the spring of 2002, and lasted between one and a half to three hours; ethnographic observations started in the summer of 2000. All names have been altered; a few sentences give a brief description of the subjects' lives at the moment of the interview.

Julio is a gay man in his late twenties, of Puerto Rican/European descent, currently working for the government as an information specialist. He is a practitioner, not yet initiated, and has significant background in Santería from his parents. Julio is soft-spoken, and has vast knowledge of the academic writings on the religion. He is the only participant who cross-dressed in the past, mostly for performances at clubs, and loosely identified as transgender.

Walter is a gay Puerto Rican man in his thrities, currently pursuing a graduate degree, a writer and an avid practitioner whose experience with Santería is also linked to his earlier exposure to *Espiritismo* and Catholicism. His head "was claimed" (chosen) by *Oya*, a female *Orisha*, the deity of lightning. Energetic and vibrant, Walter has taken me to some of the religious activities and has pushed me into learning more about the way of the Saints.

Ramiro is a gay Cuban, in his sixties who became initiated in Santería in 1959 in Cuba and continues to practice the religion. He left Cuba in 1980, and has since lived in various U.S. cities before settling in New York. He was raised Catholic. *Obatala* (the father of all *Orishas*) claimed his head when he lived in Cuba. Ramiro does not participate in Santería activities as often as in the past, but he remains connected to a network of practitioners.

Myrna is a lesbian from Puerto Rico, in her thirties who has her own business and also conducts readings or officiates as a *madrina*. She has been in the religion for almost twenty years. Her head was claimed by *Changó (or Shangó)*, a male deity, the *Orisha* of storm, thunder, and lightning. Myrna spoke to me candidly about the drawbacks of the religion, as well as its blessings.

Amaury is a young Asian man who speaks Spanish fluently and has been involved in Santería for several years, although he has not been initiated. He was raised in a Buddhist tradition. He has completed an undergraduate education and works for the educational system in New York. Amaury is a highly reflexive practitioner, and has taught me about local Santería's challenges of bringing newcomers, especially of other ethnic and racial groups.

José is a gay Mexican man in his thirties who works part time at a *Bodega*. His head was claimed by the male warrior *Elleguá* (the messenger of all the *Orishas*, the first and last to be honored in every ceremony performed) a few years ago. José has much knowledge of the religion; he has continued the work of his *madrina* after her recent death.

Mike is the only self-identified bisexual man I interviewed. A man in his late thirties or early forties, Mike is of European descent and born in the Northeast. He is a *Babalawo* and a *Palero* (one that practices *Palo*). Having divorced his wife several years ago, he has not had sexual activities with other men since his initiation in *Palo*.

Bebo was born in Puerto Rico and has lived in the United States for about two decades. A raised Catholic and later an Atheist, Bebo, now in his late thirties, is the head of a company that employs several staff and travels constantly. His head was claimed by *Ochún* (or *Oshún*), a female deity full of love, who brings money, fertility, and sweetness.

Petra is a Puerto Rican heterosexual woman in her late thirties, currently completing graduate work. I met Petra as a *Yabó*. She has children and is very involved in the practice of Santería. Petra's interview was one of the most illuminating ones of this project, both in terms of her capacity to express ideas as well as her observations of Santería's negotiation of sexuality and gender.

Excerpts from interviews conducted in Spanish are presented in their original form and translated in the following paragraph. I do this in order to reveal how the translation most often loses some of the nuances of the original text (often not simply rearticulating, but reinventing such reality). This presentation also assists me in the analysis and write-up of the chapter, as reading the text in the original language brings me to the moment and the circumstances of the interview. Of course only some readers will be able to appreciate and make such comparison. I share with you, those of you who can comprehend this text, the pleasure of the lisps, the use of the double *r*, the dancing of its intonation, so that this is not simply an analytic exercise, but an emotive and reflexive one (see Guzmán 1997 for a related explanation). Thus, this decision, like many decisions on how to manage the data social scientists collect in research, is one that has political ramifications.

Karen McCarthy Brown (2001), author of *Mama Lola: A Vodou Priestess in Brooklyn* (1991), reveals the problems of the often accepted view of "giving voice" to participants, as her encounter with Mama Lola after the book's publication revealed the situatedness of the *character* portrayed in the written version. As much as I "locate" the experiences of the participants, this process is still within a reductionist approach that creates specific, generic accounts of Santería practices.

The critique of "epistemological bias" Brown refers to (citing Judith Butler's *Gender Trouble*) is central to my and other social scientists' positioning ourselves vis à vis the participants we attempt to "understand." My understanding of this process undoubtedly recognizes that the presentation of their voices is a reduction of their experience; particularly in a setting in which their religion, sexual orientation, and race, ethnic, and national markers are often seen as marginal. Like Mama Lola, the generous participants of this study have changed—moreover, their experiences are so rich that it is impossible to create a fair portrayal in a few pages. I act as a medium, but unlike the participants, I do not enact the richness of the details of the experience of being possessed nor do I provide comprehensive accounts of the participants' lives outside of the context of Santería practices, which would lessen this objectifying of the textual provision of their experience.

A way of reducing the impact of many of these research limitations (from the encapsulation of a person's life into several excerpts to the relationship between "informants" and "researchers") was to bring the ethnography with me—wherever I went. By discussing my research project everywhere, at all sites where the occasion arose, I had a unique opportunity to make that very same moment become an opportunity to discuss Santería with potential participants. (This was especially important in settings where Latinos and Santeros are marginal or, at best, token participants, such as "gay" establishments and neighborhoods.) I also attended many Santería-related events and spent some time with *Yabós*—who were very noticeable because they were fully dressed in white—in public settings, either conducting interviews, or "hanging out." Instead of attending closed spaces where practitioners worshiped, I brought the practice, in as much as I could, into the open. This made my learning process and knowledge of Santería much more open to scrutiny, but it also allowed us to engage in conversations, as opposed to the fixed interview on the *other*. These conversations and interactions also informed my thinking in the presentation and analysis of the narratives shared by me in the following sections.

Family, Community, and Sexuality: Mapping the Participation of LGBTs

Much of the study on Santería requires a discussion regarding the community that Santeros form through their system of beliefs because Santería's rituals are communal and initiations and ritual organize *Santero* communities (Núñez 1992; Roberts 1999). As Julio said: "there is no way anybody can practice Santería properly by yourself. . . it takes a number of people to hold an initiation, you can't do it by yourself." Certain elements in the division of activities in Santería reveal a hierarchy of gender/sexual orientation with assigned roles in the religion that is more and more questioned by some of its members. At times, however, there is a practical aspect to dividing chores by population. Moreover, this specialization requires that people from various segments of the community come together, for the completion of a ritual, a celebration, or an initiation. There are ways in which gender and sexuality, in particular, influence the development and sustaining of a community. The impact AIDS had between *padrinos* and *ahijados* (godchildren) could have broken these ties, but it did not, as Walter said,

> Yo sí se de muchos padrinos que han cuidao' a muchos ahijados de SIDA, mi madrina fue una . . . esa red ha estado ahí . . . Ahora también hubo ahijados que cuidaron padrinos . . . no son casos aislados, todo lo que yo he oído discutir, eso siempre fue cuidarles, tu no puedes dejar a tu ahijado o tu padrino. . . . Yo todavía nunca he visto que hubiese un rechazo, y si lo hubiera habido, hubiera sido, no bien visto por nadie, esos valores no han sido promovidos, por ejemplo el rechazar a alguien con SIDA, pa' empezar, en el SIDA está San Lázaro, y en el SIDA, en cualquier enfermo está *Obatalá*—o sea tu no puedes, se te puede dar una revirada, tu no quieres a ninguno de esos dos en contra tuya: a San Lázaro por que es el dios de la enfermedad y a *Obatalá* por que es el dios que más nosotros respetamos, por que es el más poderoso.

> I do know of a number of grandparents that took care of godsons with AIDS, my godmother was one… that network has been there. . . . There were also godchildren that took care of godparents . . . these are not isolated cases, all I've heard discussed, you can't leave your godson or godparent. . . . I've never seen rejection, and if it has happened, it is not seen with good eyes by nobody, those values are not promoted, for example to reject somebody with AIDS, to begin with, *San Lázaro* is in AIDS, and in AIDS—in any ill person, there is *Obatalá*—so you cannot, they can come back to you, you do not want none of these two against you: *San Lázaro* because he is the god of illness, and *Obatalá* because he is the god we respect the most, because he is the most powerful of all.

Hence, people living with AIDS and other illnesses, as well as gay and transgender people—some of whom Walter repeatedly mentioned had AIDS and died of it in the 1980s and 1990s—could not be turned down or denied participation in Santería. Unlike people from many Christian denominations who turned their backs on people living with AIDS, as they had done with gay men before AIDS, Santería's norms discourage people from this kind of rejection. His discussion also reveals how, in different circumstances, either the godparent or the *ahijado/a* took care of each other—which complicated the view that it is often the *ahijado/a* who has to "serve" the godparent. Roberts (1999), for example, illustrates how there is reciprocity between *ahijado* and *padrino/madrina* as part of a network structure or community. The impact of AIDS triggered a reform of Santería's lineage-driven relations. Taking care of an *abijado* meant that notions of power in the lineage used were transformed; such an event also reveals a non-static set of religious practices. Godparent and godchild relations can be structured in opposition, and directives can be imposed through lineage or other means—such as in the case of gender— but historical events partially reshaped godparent/godchildren interactions. This excerpt also illustrates how there is an extension of Santería's beliefs in the formation of new families—new because of their non-nuclear composition and their non-blood related ties. It also meant that sexuality was not going to be an interfering factor in the practice of the religion by sexual minorities, a point expanded in the following discussion.

Nongay Spaces of Ritual: National and Sexual Identities

In a place like New York City, Santería offers the possibility of "gay" houses, as well as houses where people of all sexual orientations converge. (A house is a lineage of initiates, or a *línea de santo,* led by a godparent. This is one of the most "genuine characteristics" of the religion—Barnet 1997: 81.) Several participants discussed their perception that "gay-specific" Santería houses were not significant to them. Amaury said: "I've heard about [that]. . . . I don't really think that's healthy . . . like a gay shop, it's very superficial. . . . Being gay is natural, but wanting to shut everyone else out is not . . . ultimately is about family, so [they] are missing the whole point." Difference is not necessarily marked by the community, and gays can be Santeros within a specific house. In assuming homogeneity within a particular house as beneficial, I asked other participants about houses where many or mostly gay people met, or houses organized by gays. I, too, made the assumption that gayness would operate in a way akin to an ethnic identity (Epstein 1987). But Bebo challenged that view,

> Para mí la cuestión fascinante es en ese tipo de ritual, es, no se trata solamente de la cantidad de personas gay que estén practicando, sino como esas personas se tienen que reagrupar y repensarse a sí mismo, en cuanto a lo que es respeto, en cuanto a lo que es aceptación, en un espacio como ese. Hace como un mes atrás, se hizo un santo en mi familia. Entonces el Oriaté que vino a oficiar, era un gran maricón jovencito tremendo, que él llegó allí entró con todo su esplendor, y aquel espacio que estaba lleno, pues de nuestra gente, que tal vez en el diario vivir no se ven confrontados con tener que escuchar, respetar, y verdaderamente colaborar con una persona como él, se vieron obligados, y no solamente obligados, vieron el placer de tener que colaborar de esa manera. Entonces esos espacios yo los encuentro más ricos que cuando voy a casas donde todo el mundo es gay, por que ahí se da otra dinámica, ahí se da otro tipo de reafirmación, se da otro tipo de continuidad. . . .

For me, what's fascinating in these rituals is not only the quantity of gays that practice, but how these folks have to regroup and rethink one's self, with regards to what is respect, with regards to what is acceptance, in a space like that. About a month ago, there was a *Santo* in my family, the *Oriaté* who came (to act as priest) was this great *maricón* (loosely translated as sissy, faggot—will be illustrated later) so huge; he arrived there and came in with all his splendor, and that space that was full of our people, that maybe in their everyday life do not have to be con- fronted with having to listen to, respect, and truly collaborate with a person like him, they were obligated to, and not just obligated, they saw the pleasure to have to collaborate with him in that way. So those spaces I find richer that when I go to a house where everyone is gay, because there emerges another dynamic, there the reaffirmation is of another kind, and there's another kind of continuity. . . .

I was reminded that there is a tension and, alternatively, a "communication of difference" that takes place in Santería (Roberts 1999), where sexual orientation does not supersede the belief, although it is not negated either. Practitioners of all sexual orientations, according to this account, seem to derive pleasure from their sharing of a space, from communicating with each other, given that this is not something that they may experience everyday. Spaces of worship thus become rich sites for complicating the relationship between "self"—defined either as "gay" or "straight"—and "other." This is a crucial element: that ethnic identity, or national pride, or the choosing of a house based on its spiritual benefits was never oppo- sitional to collegiality and similarity based on sexual orientation—and that many gay Santeros choose to participate in the religion in varied spaces while not tak- ing their sexuality, and social organization based on sexual orientation, for granted in these circles. Other values seem to be more significant to gay Santeros apart from the sexual orientation of the people in the house: the lineage of the *padrino* and *madrina*, their *costumbres*, or ways of being. Many godchildren discussed their need to make their godparents proud, by wearing ironed clothes or looking im- peccable for an event.

At times, nationality was a point of contention among members of the houses—mainly on the part of the Puerto Ricans toward Cubans (the two pre- dominant groups of Latinos in Santería). Walter made this point when saying "*Mis casas son sumamente Latinas, nosotros hablamos Español, comemos comida Puertorriqueña—hay mucho Boricua—son muy pocos los Cubanos que yo conozco.*" (My houses are very Latino, we speak Spanish, eat Puerto Rican food—there are lots of Boricuas—I know very few Cubans.) Myrna stated that Cubans thought lesbians were too aggressive, and gay men where passive, which gave gay men more space in the religion than lesbians. Thus lesbians are not as central to the religion, in Myrna's view, in big part due to their aggressiveness and lack of submission, as interpreted by Cubans. Although there is little evidence from my research to suggest that nationality plays a big role in separating Cubans and Puerto Ricans, the network of practitioners in a given region seems to be closed off enough to organize some of these houses by nationality (this is a topic that needs more attention in future studies). Yet it is important to note that nationality might be a factor in managing the participation of LGBT individuals (again, further research is needed).

Differences occurred not just at the national identity level, but also in terms of U.S. racial or ethnic categories. I have participated in events where most participants were Latinos, with very few African-American practitioners (Afro-Latino practitioners participated in most events I attended), but the practice of Santería by African-Americans is common in New York's metropolitan area. Like other identity boundary settings where identities are negotiated in relationship to space, history, and culture, Santería has provided a space of contention over who is "truly" a *Santero*, or of where Santería, or its earlier *Yoruba* or *Orisha* versions, "truly" come from—and which one constitutes a "pure" religious form. This gets displayed as pride derived from membership in a particular national group, as illustrated previously, but also by racial or ethnic group, or by continent where a practitioner was raised. Even though some sort of tension exists, Myrna talked about going to *bembés* where the majority of folks were African-American, and participating in them.

The managing of these differences within Santería overflows when complicated with aspects of gender and sexuality. Myrna's previous excerpt merged the national with sexuality when discussing her perception of Cubans' tolerance of lesbians. Indeed, there are differences between the take on Santería's view on homosexuality by region or by nationality. Walter notes differences between Puerto Rican practitioners, as opposed to United Staters,

[Deberías hablar con] este Santero en particular, es Americano, habla con él—aunque su visión es un poco mas militante, y mas Americana dentro de la Santería, y yo creo que él, él no ha conocido la Santería de la manera Puertorriqueña, que es muchísimo mas tolerante, yo diría que de las más tolerantes. . . .

[You should talk to] this Santero in particular, he is American, talk to him—although his view is more militant, and more American within Santería, and I think that he has not known the Santería in its Puerto Rican form, which is much more tolerant, I would say that one of the most tolerant. . . .

Of particular importance in this excerpt is Walter's separation of *Puertorriqueñidad*, a sense of Puerto Rican identity, versus the "American view" embodied in this man, which tends to be "militant" when it comes to attacking and discussing homophobia in the Santero community (ironic choice of words, as since the nineteenth century Puerto Rico has experienced a militarized relationship with the United States). But this quote also says that there is an implicit distinction between an American view of gay, *American* view, and a Puerto Rican one, which might define queerness in very different ways than the United States (as generalizing as these statements are, these postures merit attention for their strong opposition to each other). Further, I see a distinction between a prescribed gay identity that stands in American terms and a homosexual identity that can be compatible with *Puertorriqueñidad*.

That gay Santeros distance themselves from gayness in the context of Santería should not be read as evidence of internalized homophobia. Indeed, reading my informants' discussions in this way reveals our lack of appreciation for ways of managing gender and sexuality that insist in their centrality for the construction of community without subscribing to the chant: "we are here, we are queer, get used to it." The following discussion offers another view, one based on identity negotiation within Santería practices.

Community and the Suspension of Gay Identities

The relationship between the *Oriaté* and the practitioners and new initiates also creates a congregation, and disrespectful interactions affect its sustenance. Hence, denunciations of Santeros' abuse of their power—for example, by sexualizing interactions with newcomers—have taken place. Several participants alluded to their role and their obligation to respect the position and authority they were given within the religion. Myrna discussed with me her resistance to present herself as a lesbian in Santería, yet she is never in the closet. Her account is one of the most powerful in these interviews. She said,

> Yo bromeo, soy la persona que más bromeo, pero cuando yo estoy en mi posición de ahora como *Santera*, yo soy *Santera*, no soy lesbiana—ni soy *straight* ni soy gay. A la gente que viene a mi casa yo les digo, yo soy *Santera* y soy lesbiana, pero soy seria; tu me vas a tratar y me vas a respetar como ser humano.

> I joke, I will be the first one to do so, but when I am in my position as I am right now, of a *Santera*, I am a *Santera*, I am not lesbian—neither am I straight nor gay. To the people that come to my house I tell them, I am *Santera* and I am a lesbian, but I am serious; you will treat me and respect me like a human being.

Myrna exemplifies one of the most salient aspects that transpired in many interviews. While simultaneously being "out," and recognizing that their participation was necessary as "queer" Santeros, many participants would go out of their way to express something similar to Myrna's posture. Bebo shared with me a similar account: "*Cuando llega el momento de tirar esos caracoles, cuando hay que sentarse en una estera, cuando llega el momento de divinación, o de tirar cocos, eso son grandes ligas, ahí lo demás se tiene que echar a un lado y la persona pues tiene que lidiar. . . . Tú estás como mensajero de tu Santo. . . ."* ("When it is time to throw those cowry shells, or time to sit on an *estera* [a woven grass mat where certain readings take place], to do a divination, or coconut readings, that's really big league, everything else is put aside, and the person has to deal . . . you are a messenger of your deity. . . .") Myrna and Bebo present the side of the priest. A priest is fully valued as a powerful being, and part of what makes a priest a "really good one"—as some mentioned—seems to be to make that distinction Myrna outlined for me. This act of simultaneously avoiding a gay category while enforcing their gay presence can be seen in accounts of lay practitioners; for instance, José made it clear that he never presented himself as anything but gay when worshipping. Like him, Myrna did not, at any point, say she would lie to people about her sexual orientation—but she would use the sacred moment of the priesthood as a way to ensemble a clear communication path with her practitioners.

This apparent negation of their sexual identity is, in actuality, a suspension of these sexuality codes, but a suspension where ultimately the identities reemerge. Myrna's powerful comments negate any kind of sexual identity status—even heterosexuality—privileging a nonsexual priest that serves as an officer of the religion. While Myrna is able to detach her sexuality from her capacity to profess as a *Santera*, her known lesbianism—of which she talks about freely—frames a lot of her activities in Santería practice and it still alerts the practitioners of her marked sexual identity.

Other ways of relating to these sexuality codes were shared with me. In the following excerpt, Bebo distinguishes between the labels gay and *maricón*:

> Para mi el maricón es, cuando uno—y eso creo que es una, es como una, es una gran correa de fuego que nos ponemos todos en ciertos momentos en nuestras vidas, las personas que se identifican como gays—Yo creo que el maricón es cuando sacamos las espadas y las lanzas, con el brillo esplendoroso, y estamos en un súper reinado, donde ahí verdaderamente estamos en un control, donde no comemos cuento, donde estamos al frente, con todas nuestras contradicciones pero estamos en un espacio donde de pronto adquirimos una fuerza, que la tildamos de necesaria en un momento X o Y, de pronto sale como esta carroza hermosa, súper fuerte, blindada, y esta ahí, y esta funcionando. . . . Y hay gente pues que somos maricones pues, mucho mas a menudo que otros, hay otros que pues, que no sabemos que somos, que son maricones hasta que llega el momento en que la situación te pide que la mariconería surja, y batalle por ti, y que te defienda, y te celebre. El gay es mas bien como una, una definición yo la encuentro un poquito mas pasiva, mas tranquilita, mas, tu sabes . . . el maricón es, "maricón" . . .

For me, a *maricón* is when one—and I think that it is like a, a big fire belt that we wear all of us at given moments of our lives, people that identify as gay—I think that a *maricón* is when we take out the swords and the spears, with the resplendent shine, and we are in a super kingdom, where there we are in control, truthfully, where we don't take nothing from nobody, where we are up front, with all our contradictions but we are in a space where suddenly we attain a strength, that we blemish as necessary in moment X or Y, and suddenly comes out like a beautiful carriage, extra strong, armored, and it's there, and it is working. . . . And there are people that, well, we are *maricones* more often than others, and then are others that, we don't know that we are, that they are maricones until the moment arrives and the situation demands that the *mariconería* emerges, and fights for you, and that it defends you, and that it celebrates you. Gay is a definition that I find a little more passive, tranquil, more, you know… a *maricón* is that, a "*maricón*" . . .

Both gay men and lesbians, then, were attempting to separate or distance themselves from a certain construct of gayness that permeates mainstream society. This type of break from identification has not been discussed at length in queer theory literature, sociology, or religious studies, except in the work of Butler (1993). In many of these cases, what is seen as homophobia by some is actually a negation of a relationship to "Americanness," a resistance to constructs of gayness, and a rejection of a culture of ethnicity-based consumerism and identification. Because the sexual identity formation literature has not given much room for anything outside of a gay identification—the alternative most often is adherence to a homophobic culture (Cantú 2000)—ruptures within sexual identities that do not belong to either of those, or to both simultaneously, are twice unintelligible.

The previous sections of the chapter have dealt with how ritual informs gay identities for its queer practitioners, but also the many ways in which identity is negotiated, always in relationship to gay constructs. The possibility for some identities to exist or be recognized more than others is what frames the final half of the chapter.

Santería's Negotiation of Identities and Participants: A Gendered, as well as Sexual, Endeavor

We have already seen that participants often self-identified in response to a gay category, either resisting it, finding alternative meanings in it, or understanding it as an "American" construct. There are, however, notions of gayness embedded within the religious structure of Santería that gender sexual orientation by ascribing femininity to homosexuality, and masculinity to lesbianism. Whenever this takes place—however biased it may sound—it opens up room for lesbians and gay men to participate and take ownership of the space of religious worship.

Another way of looking at the relationship of gender and sexuality for sexual minorities is evident in these accounts: several participants alluded to "women, men, and gays," granting "gays" a specific class status, although nobody explicitly stated that gays where like a "third gender." Besides the obvious analogy to the Hijras of India or the Berdache in Native American communities (Herdt 1994; Nanda 1999), this singling out of gay Santeros as a specific, third group brings forth the work of early scholars like McIntosh (1968), who ascribed homosexuals a social status at a time in which the medical establishment still labeled the group as mentally ill. The following sections illustrate and discuss the ways in which Santería's sense of tradition is challenged but ultimately accommodates gays into its structure.

One of the ways this happens is through stereotypes about gay male Santeros' capacities: decorating altars, adorning thrones, cooking, doing bead work, making garments, and throwing the cowry shells. All these characteristics made gay Santeros "really good" Santeros, according to some participants. At the same time, the break provided by these seemingly stereotypical aspects of labor participation in Santería forms a unique space and gives a strong sense of power to gay Santeros. It facilitates ownership of the religion, its traditions, and its history. Gay Santeros are visible, and are actively creating, Santería—and they have for several decades; reports of similar experiences with *Espiritismo* and *Candomblé* are available (Figueroa 1981; Healey 2000). Several participants estimated that no house they knew of lacked gays or lesbians. Others stated that about 30 percent or about half of the participants at *bembés* were gay, which is consistent with my own reading of the events I have observed. Ramiro also mentioned that gays were foundational in Cuba's Santería, which he learned through his involvement in the religion in Cuba back in the 1960s.

Overall, the sense is that gay Santeros have been pillars of the religion. In the words of Petra, "I don't mean to be disrespectful, but here it goes. I think that in so many ways, [gay Santeros] are foundational, because many, and I don't say all, but the ones that I am aware of don't have children don't have those kinds of responsibilities so their level of dedication can be very, it's just very central." This centrality also allows for the possibility that small changes take place from within the religion, should its gay *Santero* members want to make those changes happen.

Another way in which Santería as a religion is challenged by the participation of gays is the stereotype of the flamboyance of gay men (little was mentioned in terms of women's masculinities). This objection to visible, readable aspects of homosexuality, which are perhaps interpretations, or disruptions of essentialized gender *insignias* (West and Zimmerman 1987) understood as disrespectful, was often verbalized by various participants as "don't flaunt it." "Just as long as they do what they do, *y no se partan al frente de los otros Santeros* (and that they don't get all 'crooked' in front of the other Santeros), is okay." Petra said, based on these observations that other Santeros constantly make,

> There seems to be a sense that gay men act too . . . flamboyant. So the discretion seems to be really valued, their discretion seems to be valued as much as their contributions, so that if you are discreet and you are gay then that's very good, if you are gay and you are not discreet, then your value as an individual tends to, diminish, although, as a class of people, it doesn't [diminish].

The position taken by gays, and simultaneously given by Santería to gay practitioners to practice and advance the religion, is not in danger of being dismissed, but the individual who transgresses gender roles as expected within the religion can be rejected by other practitioners. At the same time, Santeros are often curious and supportive of same-sex relations among gay men (for example, Amaury was repeatedly asked about his partner and how he was doing, even after years of their breakup). Thus, nongay Santeros and Santeras have been supportive of same-gender relations. What really facilitates this acceptance, however, is the visual character of gendered behaviors and traditional gender roles. Within this framework, it was not surprising to hear almost every participant speak of them and their houses' members "turning their face away" from the occasional heterosexually identified man who made advances to other men for sexual encounters at Santería activities. What is punishable (for men) is the seemingly individual choice to "queen out" and to be marked as feminine. This also creates a break from sexual desire in the realm of the sacred, as some gay Santeros fear that their sexual activities might make their participation seem (more) profane. This was especially the case for Myrna, who adamantly stated this boundary as something that was necessary [to not pick up people as sexual partners while practicing and in activities], yet she said, "It happens all the time." For queer Santeros, the opportunity of sexual activity is the threat to being delegitimized; what transforms the participation of LGBTs in religious contexts is their adherence to Santería's established codes of masculinity in relationship to sexuality. But as the next section shows, some relationships between gender and sexuality, and some sexual narratives, are more welcome than others (Vidal-Ortiz 2002).

Transgenderism: Its Possibilities, Erasures, and Invisibilities

Much of the participants' understanding of transgenderism, when posed as a question, was in relationship to one of its most current narratives, that of the transsexual (Roen 2002; Broad 2002). Queer theory and transgender activism in the 1990s have challenged the dominance of such narratives (Butler 1993; Halberstam 1998; Valentine 2000)—at times by interrogating the category "trans-gender" itself (Valentine 2000). Subsequently, queer theory has been challenged overall, but specifically on these accounts, for its suspension of the everyday lived experiences of transsexuals by phenomenological advocates (Namaste 1996, 2000; Rubin 1996; see also Vidal-Ortiz 2002). The result is an ever-changing set of perceptions as to what "transgenderism" means, including differences attrib-uted to class and racial-minority experiences (Broad 2002; Valentine 2000).

Transgenderism was regulated in a number of ways in participants' views—initially, because it disrupts gendered understandings that depend on two, and only two, genders (Kessler and McKenna 1978). This regulation is connected to sexuality, as gender and sexuality are polarized constructs that value one extreme over the other. Amaury shared his understanding that the *Orishas* "did not like transgenderism," and cited a friend who was a drag queen and was told, "It's okay if you are gay, but if you are gay you are a man, you should be a man, if you are a woman, be a woman." These stories only promote a two-sex system and a rigid gendered participation, in this case, with gays as practitioners. I only heard one personal story shared with me by Julio, who used to do "drag," but who seldom identified as transgender:

I used to do drag, for a long time, and I was in the radical faeries, and then I was told that I wasn't supposed to do drag, that was taking away from me, doing drag, and that was a real thing that I went through, wondering why, and what that was about, and . . . [it was a] spirit that told me that he did not want me to do drag anymore, and that I would, had developed to a certain spiritual level, and that I was gonna lose everything if I kept doing drag. Then I talked to [my *padrino*] later about it, he felt that when you do drag that you become sort a channel for a lot of things, in sort of very open, sort of psychic ways, and that he thought that that could be very bad. . . . But I had to think [about] the fact that he had godchildren who lived transgendered as women, and that he was okay with it, I mean that he had some godchildren who were on hormones, men living as women, that he was okay, that he wasn't opposed to, so I decided that I really had to look at some-thing for me specifically, 'cuz I knew that he as a person didn't have anything against, so you are going through the levels of interpretation, his prejudices as a person, I know that he is not opposed to transgender people, he is not opposed to transgender people being involved in, dealing with them or initiate them. . . .

The opening to accept homosexuality seems to stand grounded in rigid construc-tions of gender. This particularly sacrifices cross-dressing behavior, as Julio could not "do drag anymore," yet his *padrino* had "godchildren who lived transgendered as women." But the sacrifice extends to transgenderism overall. Bebo spoke of the many transgenders he knew, who weren't initiated, but had gotten their *collares* (bead necklaces). Bebo speculates that economic priorities—to buy hormones and/or get money secured for surgery, for those interested—are competing with becoming an initiate. (Initiation rituals vary in estimates, but can cost from $3,000 to more $5,000 depending on the deity claiming one's head. There are a multitude of costs involved in the initiation of a new practitioner—from the *derecho*, or a "right" for a small sum of money for those helping in the initiation, to drummers, singers, high priests, and the initiation clothing, altar materials, food, and other items—and much of the money stays within the community of Santeros.)

Namaste (1996, 2000) has written about the erasure of transgender and transsexual people by the idea of transgenderism as solely a performative expression, as it does away with the everyday situations faced by transgender and transsexual people. This, in addition, also has had the effect of leaving "gay" untouched, and reifies it as a (legitimate) identity, with the space it necessitates, as identities often do. Most participants disclosed having heard of or having known transgenders (all stories of males to females) who had died of AIDS in the eighties and nineties, which has partially mythologized transgenderism within Santería, and perhaps continues to be the case today. Petra's quote is particularly illustrative of this,

> I know the story of someone in particular, who was a nightclub cross-dresser, and maybe more than a cross-dresser, I think he wore makeup, I don't know . . . it might be better defined by another term. . . . So anyways, and he made *Orisha*, and the *Orisha* came down, and said "I will be the only quote-unquote, woman in the house," and he in fact did change, career, like he no longer dances, because he wanted to be, live by what he considered to be his destiny. I know someone else who decided to not do that, who had the same, who decided that he was gonna go through the surgery, and he was told, the *Orisha* came down and it started hitting this young man's chest, and she kept saying, "this is not my son," because that wasn't the body that she was used to possessing, because she was used to being the only female in that house. If you think about how sort of the body is like a mode of communication. And I think that he came to a premature death, and when I heard the story, it was attributed to not following the *Orisha*.

There is a sense that the gender borders' rupture through transsexualism is punishable by this religion, as stated by some practitioners. This specific account registers a female deity in a "man," and thus is not generalizable to others, but it raises the question of the body's location on this discussion—the body is not absent, it is the mounting element that is registered by the *Orishas* as a tool to communicate with others. Initially, rigid gender constructs mediate the possession of a body, according to some of the participants' accounts. It also privileges biological understandings of self over self-identification. This quote, like the opening field note excerpt, raises another issue: whether there is an unbalanced assignment of female deities to feminine or "gay" perceived male Santeros, and whether what is being regulated is homosexuality as understood through gender in the practice of the religion. Although that is not the focus of this particular chapter, this is another area where more research is needed.

"You Be Who You Are:" On Contradictions

Most people mentioned that the desire for same-sex sexual activities was very common among practitioners related by one of the practictioners and that Santería tends to be open to all sexual orientations, but the next excerpt delineates how bisexuality is "eaten up" by the gay category—or by needing to choose.

> And then there was this story of a gay man, who was like, told, "well, be discreet. . . ." But they marry and they still have a gay lifestyle. He made *Ocha*, and he was very concerned that something would happen to him. On the contrary, his *Orisha* told him, "no, you be who you are," and in fact the name, his *Orisha* (after his initiation, he was named *Ocha*), it is a name usually given to females. He's male, and he is a gay man . . . so he took that as that he did not have to hide. . . . You are a gay man and that's how you are . . .

We don't know the sexual orientation of the man in this story, but all seems to point out to him being gay. We know nothing about his desire—even though he was married, the presumption is that he was gay. And the fact that the *Orisha* permitted him to "come out" exemplifies one account in which coming out only applies to gay and lesbian individuals; other stories discussed men's sexuality as something that needed to be questioned, either by virtue of their flamboyancy or their desire for sex with men—*irrespective of their desire for women as well*. This clearly positions men to defend their every move as a way of curtailing any same-sex desire, as in hegemonic masculinity (Connell 1995). More important to this project, it simplifies human sexuality into very discrete aspects that correlate desire with behavior and self-identification.

Mike was the only self-identified bisexual person I interviewed. He discussed with me his participation in the *Palo* religion, as well as the others' reception to bisexuality.

> The only one who knows about me is my godfather, because he asked the right question, he said to me, "Are you attracted to men?" as opposed to asking me if I was gay. . . . All these *Babalawos* are asking me whether I am gay and I've been saying to them, "no I'm not!" I've been attracted to men since first day, I never did anything about it. Before I got "scratched," my marriage had broken up, my

(ex)wife—she is also bisexual—we decided it wasn't working [between us], and so that was over, now I can look at some things, I explored it a little bit more, and I realized that "I got a lousy taste in men!" So, I thought, maybe they [the *Paleros*] are saying something to me, so [to be initiated], I have to give it up . . . . It's not something that's really gonna be a problem for me, so I can give up the act. It was a no-brainer for me. . . . I made the decision the day I got [initiated]. . .

The decision made total sense for Mike, as he felt he had tried "several times" with men. Compare this statement with Julio's decision to stop cross-dressing; even though it was a personal decision, it is informed by the constraints Santería is imposing on its practitioners. Although being a *Babalawo* was what Mike wanted, there is still a sense of giving up in his story—in this case, giving up sex with men. However, he seems to be glad that he moved forward with the decision to become a *Babalawo*. He believes that his sexual attraction is not at play—but his sexual activity is. While this resembles what some gay priests go through in the Catholic churches across the world, it does not affect his feelings toward homosexuality. And, he has pushed and asked within the religious system,

> The old rationale—and I've gotten more out of (my *padrino*) than of anybody—and he is like, the old rule is that, you are supposed to be a member of society that people can come up to, and if you are on the margins of society, then you are gonna have people that are not gonna feel comfortable for you, you got to be there for everybody. . . . The best answer I've ever heard on this. I've heard all sorts of things, "It's wrong," "God doesn't like it," you know. . . . By doing this you are stepping into a role in society, and in this society, which has very strict gender rules. . . .

Ironically, Mike is then another of those priests who have the potential to value the diversity and marginality that others would pigeonhole him to. The statement he shares is packed with several meanings: primarily, the recognition of the centrality of gender normative and heterosexually perceived men. This position, however, leaves no room for nonheterosexual attractions and behavior to be intelligible; it is not really changing perceptions of who is assigned to the center and who is perceived as marginal. Second, as a "white" man (within U.S. racial-social notions), Mike's account does not reveal him to be aware of his own racial privilege in society—quite the contrary, his claim throughout the interview was about gaining access to learning *Palo*, irrespective of the *Paleros'* reactions to his presence. He shared in several instances his feeling singled out by his whiteness in Santería and *Palo* contexts, but at no point did he express knowledge about Santeros' marginal position due primarily to a racial and ethnic minority status. Finally, these statements assume that people in the center are those with a lot of recognition of the margins—something Gloria Anzaldúa, Cherríe Moraga, and other women of color would challenge. Ultimately, even with all these critiques, Mike's perception might have a function—that perhaps it is people like Mike, "sexual minority 'insiders,'" who will also help alter some of the underpinnings that limit or do not recognize sexual-otherness. It is perhaps by occupying that central space that people like Mike will raise a certain consciousness.

LGBTs' Challenges to Santería: Innovation Emergent from their Participation?

Gay Santeros directly and indirectly—by their mere presence, as ambiguous or open as it might be—challenge some of the underpinnings of the religion, especially with regards to gender and sexuality. By embracing in full the activities of "the way of the Saints," gay Santeros open up and diversify the kind of activities all Santeros can engage in. Many practitioners mentioned the resistance of heterosexually identified men to be mounted, much less to be mounted by a female deity. Julio notes that often for women, when initiated in a male *Orisha*, they get "dressed as a man," but the opposite does not happen for men with an opposite gender-deity assignment. Petra poses the matter in one of her statements:

There are all these questions about how a dominant heterosexual culture sets up these boundaries, what men do, what women do, and that poses questions as to gays and where they fit in. . . . So it is interesting how it serves a heterosexual agenda, to maintain difference, so I think in a sense gay men push that envelope. If it doesn't make sense in terms of tradition, then it doesn't, but if it makes sense let's explore it—why wouldn't we?

These manifestations of questioning the roles given, while recognizing their functionality, are strong symbols of the critical thinking going on in Santería circles by both gay and nongay Santeros.

Race, bracketed as it is both by the challenge to essential ideas of biological differences as well as ethnically by the presence of Latinos in the United States (Rodríguez 2000), is highly evident in the accounts of the Santeros I spoke with: from the utilization of house basements for the worship of deities, the marking of darker skin *Babalawos* or *Bata* drummers, to the opening of its doors to non-Latinos. The discrimination that Latinos, as a racialized ethnic group, experience in the U.S. context is highlighted in the milieu of Santería practice, itself a marginalized religion. Moreover, a marginalized religion's opening to marginalized sexualities is taking place. Future research needs to consider the impact of transnational and migration experiences on the formation of gendered, sexual, *and* racial identities, and interrogate the relationship of race and ethnicity to the study of

Santería, given its African roots and its predominant membership by people of color. Furthermore, research that addresses the complexity of Latinos' racial, ethnic, and national identification needs to be undertaken, especially in relationship to their racial constructs by region or country of origin. Outside of the study of Santería, most studies on religion and sexual minorities in the United States focus on Euro-American, gay male identified, Judeo-Christian experiences. Further study of LGBT-identified practitioners of Santería, where Latinos and African Americans are the predominant constituencies, promises to broaden significantly the scope of scholarship on sexuality, gender, "race," and religion. It may also shed light on interracial interactions in this religious setting.

Given gay Santeros' integration into Santería, this work allows for an examination of the ways that both sexual minorities and non-LGBT-identified people negotiate and resist, as well as welcome, LGBT participation. However, it is clear that further research is needed in order to balance the higher number of gay male identified practitioners' accounts with those who are lesbian, bisexual, or transgendered-identified. Further research is also needed in order to determine if third gender constructs are operating within these understandings of sexual minorities, or whether the mechanism that allows for gay integration is gendered and rooted in a two-gendered system. In spite of the limitations of the present study, I have illustrated some of the ways in which Santería and homosexuality coexist and indeed how active and significant gay Santeros' participation is in the religion. Gay Santeros could help transform some of the seemingly hierarchical aspects of Santería, taking ownership of a space where stigma has been a significant restriction.

One significant finding of this quick assessment of Santería in relation to gender and sexuality is the sliding from tangible, rigid identity categories, to more complex, gendered and sexual identities. In most instances, participants in this study used "gay" as a referent for sexual minority status, even gender nonconformist behavior, and did not necessarily locate their experience within a gay construct. There was also a loss of certain identities—primarily, bisexuality and transgenderism—in relationship to gay (and only sometimes lesbian) constructs. Some people noted how perceived sexual identity does not follow sexual behavior or desire. Overall, these accounts are a primer to the ways in which sexual minorities are understood, and in turn take on the space of worship, in New York's Santería settings. These findings suggest that an interpretation of gender and sexual constructs within the constitution, practice, and teachings of Santería is needed. Such an interpretation requires an analysis of the ways in which these sexual identity categories are utilized, as initially suggested in this chapter, but also the ways in which these spaces provide their own understandings of sexuality and gender within their practice and celebration of the Orishas.

Note

1. An earlier version of this chapter was presented at a "Queer Visions in the Americas" conference in the Department of Religious Studies at the University of California-Santa Barbara in May 2002, and subsequently won the American Sociological Association's Sociology of Sexualities Section–Student Paper Competition in July of the same year. Many thanks to Melissa Wilcox, Rosemarie A. Roberts, and Jason Bauman, librarian with the New York Public Library, but especially to Mark Schuller and Carlos Ulises Decena for reading recommendations, research support, and critical comments on this chapter. I'd like to dedicate this chapter to the memory of Lionel Cantú, a Latino/migration and sexuality studies sociologist, friend, and mentor. Direct inquiries to svidal-ortiz@gc.cuny.edu.

Lesbian, Gay, and Bisexual Buddhist Practitioners

8

WENDY CADGE

K ELLY,[1] A WOMAN IN HER EARLY THIRTIES, graduated from an Ivy League college and went to work after graduation for a management consulting firm. After a few years, she knew something needed to change. "I was feeling really unhappy with my life," she told me, "real *dukkha* [suffering]. I didn't know what to do with myself."[2] She quit her job, began to come out as bisexual, and started to volunteer in the city where she was living. Although Kelly was born in the Philippines and was raised as a Catholic in the United States after her parents immigrated when she was an infant, she remembers being interested in Eastern philosophies even as a child. Shortly after she quit her job she remembers,

> I met this woman who was a friend of a friend and she was a bonafied dharma bum. She was my age and had just come back from travels in Asia where for two years she had been meditating and visiting ashrams. She really made a big impression on me. I was like, wow, someone I can relate to . . . she wasn't this distant figure. I don't know what I had in my mind about what people were like who meditated but she was somebody I really could relate to. She was a women of color, she was queer, and I was just coming out. . . .

On this woman's advice, Kelly visited the Cambridge Insight Meditation Center (CIMC), a Theravada Buddhist center in Cambridge, Massachusetts. When Kelly first went there she remembers, "It felt like it was coming home. . . ." When she first went to CIMC, she took meditation classes and attended silent meditation sessions with others at the center. The meditation practices, she remembers,

> were deceptively simple. They are very simple but I say it's deceptive because it is also very difficult. But I think it was exactly what I needed at the time. And

I remember this feeling of exhilaration at finding these practices and this place where I could just feel it instantly.

Kelly became very involved with CIMC over the next several years and did ten-day retreats and later a three-month silent retreat at Buddhist centers on the East and West Coasts of the United States. She continued to come out and found that the practice really supported her:

> Because of this idea that our sense of I is this fluctuating thing. From moment to moment where can you find the I that we're talking about? It really helped me to think of myself in that way and to think that that's the way it really was . . . that all aspects of our identity are fluid and are a result of circumstances and causes.

Now, many years later, Kelly practices Buddhism regularly with her partner Kim in a room in their home they turned into a meditation and yoga room. An altar, holding images of the Buddha, the Dalai Lama, several Buddhist monks, and several yoga teachers, sits in front of meditation cushions and yoga mats in this room. "It's really been important for me to be able to practice with my partner," Kelly reflects. "The mornings [when they practice] have been a really beautiful way for us to spend time together and connect on the thing that I think is at the core of our relationship." Kelly continues to attend dharma talks and classes at CIMC on occasion and to do longer retreats at other Buddhist centers in the United States.

Jon, a man in his mid-thirties, also came to Buddhism in the midst of coming out, and after he spent tens of thousands of dollars in psychoanalysis trying to learn how not to be gay. He first began to meditate, he told me, as a way to "calm my mind a little bit" when he was coming out to his parents. On Rosh Hashanah in 1999, he remembers, "I was really uninspired by services so the second day I went to a bookstore in Harvard Square and picked up Larry Rosenberg's book *Breath by Breath* and went to the beach and read the whole thing" (Rosenberg and Guy 1999).

Shortly thereafter he went to an introductory meditation class at CIMC and a second class focused around *metta* or lovingkindness meditation. Unlike the *sam_dhi* and *vipassana* meditation often taught at CIMC in which practitioners learn to follow their breath and then to become aware of all the thoughts and sensations around them, *metta* meditation is based around a series of statements practitioners repeat silently to themselves. First they send *metta* or lovingkindness to themselves with statements like "May I have mental happiness," "May I have physical happiness," "May I be free from danger," and "May I live with ease of well-being." Then they focus *metta* or lovingkindness on a friend, a person they feel neutral about, and then a difficult person. This *metta* meditation had a profound effect, Jon told me. "You really tap into the place within you that is pure, that is sort of beneath all of the crap, all of the conditioning, all of the hurts . . . you tap into the place that really is pure and unconditional love."

This experience led Jon to start seeing a Buddhist therapist and then to spend the better part of a year meditating at Buddhist centers across the country. "I wanted to sort of see what motivated me. What were these energies within me that were motivating me to do what I was doing? And that also motivated me to suppress my sexuality for such a long time." When I spoke with Jon, he had recently returned to Cambridge after his year of Buddhist practice and was involved both with CIMC and with Buddhabuddies, a nonsectarian Buddhist group for lesbian, gay, and bisexual people in Boston.

Lesbian, gay, and bisexual people are involved with a wide range of Buddhist organizations across the United States.[3] While some, like Kelly and Jon, came to Buddhism in the midst of coming out, others came to the tradition quite apart from struggles about their sexuality. Some practice Buddhism primarily with other lesbian, gay, and bisexual people in organizations like the Gay Buddhist Fellowship in San Francisco, Buddhabuddies in Boston, and the Diamond Metta group in New York City. Others practice Buddhism in organizations like the CIMC and the Los Angeles Zen Center that are composed primarily of straight people but also include a significant number of lesbians, gay men, and bisexuals.

This chapter briefly describes the history of lesbian, gay, and bisexual people's involvement in Buddhist organizations founded by non-Asians in the United States.[4] I then describe how lesbian, gay and bisexual people are involved in one organization, the CIMC. While the majority of practitioners at CIMC are straight, there is a sizeable group of gay men and particularly lesbians who are involved with the center and have been for many years.

Lesbians, gay men, and bisexuals feel comfortable at CIMC and at many other Buddhist organizations in the United States because Buddhist texts are generally read as neutral about homosexuality at these centers and because there is little anti-gay discrimination and prejudice in Buddhist organizations in the United States.[5] It is also likely that lesbian, gay, and bisexual people feel comfortable in these organizations because the people involved in them are generally upper-middle-class and well-educated, the group of people in American society who tend to be the most tolerant about homosexuality (Loftus 2001; Yang 1997). This combination of factors has led a sizeable number of lesbian, gay and bisexual people to be involved with Buddhist organizations across the United States.

Background

The Buddhist tradition is divided into three main branches or vehicles, each of which traveled to the United States from Asia in the past one hundred and fifty years. Mahayana Buddhism, the branch of Buddhism practiced in the East Asian countries of China and Japan, first arrived in the United States with Chinese immigrants to California in the 1840s and 1850s and Japanese immigrants several decades later (Fields 1981). Vajrayna or Tibetan Buddhism arrived in the 1960s after the fourteenth Dalai Lama fled from Tibet, and Theravada Buddhism, practiced in the South and Southeast Asian countries of Thailand, Sri Lanka, Laos, Burma, and Cambodia, arrived in America after 1965 (Prebish 1999; Seager 1999). While some non-Asian, American-born Buddhist practitioners trace their history to one of these three branches of Buddhism, others trace their history more generally to the transcendentalists and Theosophical Society in the mid-nineteenth century, or to the Beat poets who led Buddhism to become popular as an alternative religion in America in the 1960s (Seager 1999).

While Buddhists have been in the United States for many years, the number of people practicing Buddhism and public interest in the tradition increased significantly in the past thirty years through a combination of immigration from Buddhist countries and the interest and conversion of native-born Americans. Between 1970 and 2000 the number of books published about Buddhism more than tripled.[6] Articles have been written about Buddhism in *Time*, *Newsweek*, *Harper's*, and *Maclean's* magazines as well as *The New York Times Magazine*, *The New York Times*, and *USA Today*.[7] Buddhist-themed movies like *Kundun*, *Seven Years in Tibet*, *Little Buddha*, *The Golden Child*, *The Razor's Edge*, and *The Cup* have shown in major U.S. theatres, grossing more than $135 million from U.S. box offices.[8] Buddhist words like "karma" and "nirvana" have even begun to enter the national vocabulary.[9] The Dalai Lama became something of a household name in the 1990s, speaking to more than 30,000 people in New York's Central Park in 1997. The number of Buddhist meditation centers in the United States also more than doubled between 1987 and 1997 and whole markets devoted to meditation cushions and Buddhist art have emerged.[10] Growing interest in Buddhism, particularly in the past ten years, has led some people to describe the 1990s as something of a "Buddhism boom."

Researchers currently estimate that three to four million women and men in the United States practice Buddhism, the majority of them probably Asian.[11] Buddhists in America are a diverse group that includes Asians, Asian-Americans, and non-Asian-Americans who have lived in the United States for many generations or for only a few months. Buddhist organizations in the United States are generally divided into groups based on the branch of Buddhism in which they were founded as well as based on the ethnicity of the founders or the people who attend the organizations. Some groups are attended primarily by Asians and Asian-Americans, others are attended by non-Asian-Americans (who are mostly white), and some are attended by a combination of Asians, Asian-Americans, and non-Asian-Americans.

Lesbian, gay, and bisexual people have been particularly visible in many Buddhist organizations started by non Asian-Americans in the United States, and little research specifically examines their involvement in these groups.

An Overview

Homosexuality plays an ambivalent role in Buddhist history (Corless 1998a; Jackson 1998; Cabezón 1993; Zwilling 1985). In the United States, researchers generally argue that Buddhist doctrine is essentially neutral about homosexuality (Corless 1998a; Cabezón 1993). There is little discrimination or prejudice against lesbians, gay men, and bisexuals in Buddhist centers in the United States and no formal Buddhist policy about the topic. The Dalai Lama did discuss homosexuality publicly in 1997 with gay leaders José Ignacio Cabezón, Lourdes Arguelles of the Buddhist Peace Fellowship, and Steven Peskind, the cofounder of the Buddhist AIDS Project. As a human rights advocate, the Dalai Lama said, "It is wrong for society to reject people on the basis of their sexual orientation" and that movements to gain full human rights are "reasonable and logical" (Seager 1999).

When he spoke as the leader of a religious tradition, however, his positions were more complex. The Buddhist tradition, he explained, provides guidelines about place, time, partner, and body organ to guide people's sexual behaviors, and sex with a partner of the same sex and oral and anal intercourse are to be avoided. These guidelines are directed at all people, he explained, not at lesbians, gay men, and bisexuals specifically, and he also pointed out that the guidelines were formed in ancient India under significantly different social conditions. He encouraged delegates to build consensus in American Buddhist communities about issues related to sexuality (Seager 1999).

Lesbian, gay, and bisexual people's involvement in Buddhist organizations in the United States is generally first traced to a meeting held in the Castro District in San Francisco in April 1980. About fifty gay men, most of whom self-identified as Buddhist, gathered in the basement of a Metropolitan Community Church and began discussing what it meant to be both gay and Buddhist. They continued to meet, calling themselves the Gay Buddhist Group and later, after several name changes and a period of dormancy, the Gay Buddhist Fellowship (Corless 1998b).[12]

The Gay Buddhist Fellowship (GBF) continues to meet in the San Francisco Bay Area as an exclusively male organization that supports people from all branches of Buddhism (Corless 2000). The Fellowship "supports Buddhist practice in the gay men's community" and its mission "includes cultivating a social environment that is inclusive and caring."[13] One practitioner says the Gay GBF,

unites two of the most important components of lasting meaning and genuine hope. One is the sharing of the experiences, gifts, and challenges that come with being gay. The other is the practicing together and supporting each other in awakening and discovering our true nature. In GBF, both of these components are present (Marion 1998).

Another man says that at the Gay Buddhist Fellowship he has "found a genuine brotherhood of dedicated and intelligent practitioners" (Moon 1998). The group practices are based around meditation and mindfulness and they meet weekly in carefully timed sessions for meditation. They also publish a newsletter, the *Gay Buddhist Fellowship*, regularly. As of January 1998, the group had no permanent location, leader, or membership (Corless 2000).

About a year after the Gay Buddhist Group was formed, two Buddhist leaders had an exchange in which one, Robert Aitken Roshi, is reported to have said, "If you are not in touch with your sexuality, you are not practicing Zen." And, "You can't do zazen in the closet" (Corless 1998a). His remarks, in part, encouraged a group of men to start the Hartford Street Zen Center. Issan Dorsey, a former junkie and drag queen, became the abbot (Schneider 1993). The Hartford Street Zen Center continues to operate in the heart of the Castro District as a friendly and accepting place where people can learn about the Soto Zen tradition.[14]

In addition to organizations in the San Francisco Bay Area, there are also groups for lesbian, gay, and bisexual Buddhist practitioners on the East Coast, primarily in large metropolitan areas like New York City and Boston. In New York City, the Diamond Metta Buddhist Lesbian and Gay Society meets once a month at the New York City Lesbian, Gay, Bisexual, and Transgender Center for meditation and discussion. Since 1974, the group, formerly called Maitri Dorje, has supported gay, lesbian, and bisexual people from all Buddhist traditions in their practice. At present they host monthly speakers and in June 2002 they marched in the New York Gay and Lesbian Pride Parade.[15]

Similarly, Buddabuddies is a "Les-Bi-Gay group of women and men from many religious and non-religious backgrounds." Based in Boston, the group has satellite groups in Albany, New York; Baltimore, Maryland; Hartford, Connecticut; Minneapolis, Minnesota; and Provincetown, Massachusetts. They meet weekly for meditation practice and discussions on a range of topics based on teachings from each of the Buddhist traditions as well as experiences from their daily lives. By "practicing mindfulness and compassion in our daily lives" their web page explains, "we help stop the suffering of ourselves and of all beings."[16]

Classes and retreats for lesbian, gay, and bisexual people are also held at Buddhist centers attended by both gay and straight people. In 1994, the Zen Mountain Center, a branch of the Zen Center of Los Angeles held a retreat for gay men and lesbians led by Korean Baker and Pat Enkyo O'Hara (Corless 1998a). The San Francisco branch of Friends of the Western Buddhist Order has also held introductory meditation classes for lesbian, gay, bisexual, and transgendered people (Corless 1998a). Spirit Rock Meditation Center in the Theravada Buddhist or vipassana meditation tradition has held retreats for lesbian, gay, bisexual, and transgendered people every year since 1995, often led by Eric Kolvig and Arinna Weisman.[17] In the year 2002, they planned a retreat for people of color and lesbian, gay, bisexual, and transgendered people titled, "Working Together to Build Community: Uncovering Patterns of Racism, Homophobia, and Other Forms of Oppression." Internet mailing lists, including the Gay Buddhist Open Forum, Gaybuddhistmain, and Dharma-dykes, also facilitate communication across the country between people interested in lesbian, gay, and bisexual issues and Buddhism.

Many of these Buddhist organizations were formed in the 1980s and 1990s, in the midst of the AIDS crisis, and it is important to note that numerous AIDS organizations and hospice groups have been developed in and through Buddhist organizations in the United States. In his work with the Hartford Street Zen Center, Issan Dorsey created the Maitri Hospice for dying AIDS patients (Coleman 2001). Also in San Francisco, Steve Peskind founded the Buddhist AIDS Project, which "provides free information and referral to Buddhist resources and events and to alternative medical services for anyone living with HIV/AIDS."[18] In 1987 the Zen Hospice Project was started to "encourage and support a mutually beneficial relationship among volunteer caregivers and individuals facing death."[19] In New York, the White Plum Buddhist AIDS Network also facilitates the exchange of information and support between Buddhist groups and people with HIV/AIDS.

As this brief overview shows, gay, lesbian, and bisexual people are involved in Buddhist organizations founded and attended largely by lesbian, gay, and bisexual people and those founded and attended primarily by straight people. While it is difficult to make any generalizations about these groups, it is important to note that some of the early groups for gay, lesbian, and bisexual people were started because some people felt that groups attended largely by straight people were not completely welcoming to gay, lesbian, and bisexual people. This perception seems to have generally disappeared at this point, though groups for lesbian, gay, and bisexual people continue both as centers to support Buddhist practice and, in some cases, as social centers for gay, lesbian, and bisexual people.

The Cambridge Insight Mediation Center (CIMC)

In addition to organizations founded and attended by lesbian, gay, and bisexual Buddhist practitioners and those centers that have specific retreats for lesbian, gay, and bisexual people, a number of Buddhist organizations attended primarily by straight people across the United States have sizeable numbers of lesbian, gay, and bisexual people in their midst. The Cambridge Insight Meditation Center (CIMC) in Cambridge, Massachusetts, is one such organization. Founded in 1985 by Larry Rosenberg and a group of his students, CIMC is a Buddhist center in the Theravada tradition, where the teachings are based around meditation as taught by the Buddha and recorded in the *Anapanasati* and *Satipatthana Suttas*. Larry Rosenberg, Narayan Liebenson Grady, and Michael Liebenson Grady currently teach the four hundred members of the center through classes, dharma talks on Wednesday nights, weekend retreats, and silent meditation sessions held twice daily.[20] The majority of people who are involved with the center are white, native-born Americans, about half of whom moved to the Boston area as students or young adults. Many are baby boomers, now in their forties and fifties, and many hold graduate degrees.

Between April and June 2001, I conducted participant observation at CIMC and interviewed thirty-seven practitioners at the center as one part of dissertation research about the history and practice of Theravada Buddhism in America (Cadge 2002). These practitioners included people I met in classes, people who responded to a notice I put on the bulletin board at the center, and people who were referred to me by other practitioners and the center's director.[21] I aimed to interview a mix of women and men, people who had been involved with CIMC for longer and shorter periods of time and people who are involved in different ways. Six of these people, one man and five women, identified themselves as gay, lesbian, or bisexual in interviews without my asking any questions about sexuality or sexual orientation.

CIMC does not have a formal position about sexuality or homosexuality, and gay men and particularly lesbians are involved in the center in ways identical to how straight people are involved.[22] The teachers use gender-neutral words like "partner" when speaking about relationships in dharma talks and practitioners use similar gender neutral words in conversations with each other. No one I spoke with during this fieldwork expressed any concern publicly or privately about how lesbian, bisexual, and gay people were involved with CIMC and most people told me that all of these people are equally welcome at the center.

The stories the six people who identified as gay, lesbian, or bisexual told me about coming to Buddhism and to the CIMC were much like the stories told to me by the other people that I interviewed. While the people who went to Asia and returned to the United States to practice Buddhism in the 1960s and early 1970s, Larry Rosenberg says, were largely eccentrics and hippies, those who are involved now lead more normal lives. "They have jobs, children, or want one or both of these things," Larry explained, "And they come [to CIMC] because they are stressed out, that's the vocabulary now. But what is stress really? It's another word for *dukkha* or suffering to me."[23] Kelly and Jon, as quoted at the beginning of this chapter, came to Buddhism and to CIMC in the midst of stress and struggles about their own sexuality but none of the other four people interviewed did. Carol, a lesbian in her forties, went to a meditation retreat in another Buddhist tradition and then got involved with CIMC gradually over about five years. "I decided I needed to be around people who also practiced at least once in awhile. And my own personal friends were not participants and didn't study Buddhism. . . . . So I started going . . ." Shortly after CIMC opened, Anissa, a lesbian in her forties, attended a retreat Narayan was leading at Interface, a spiritual center in the Boston area. "I stayed there for the entire day," she remembers, "and I knew from that moment that I would work with Narayan and this would be my practice." She went to CIMC shortly thereafter and has been involved ever since. When I asked her what it was about the teaching that clicked for her, she said, "one thing is that I'm kind of a rebel at heart. So when the Buddha says, 'Don't believe me, try it out and see.' Well that's perfect for me because I'm not going to believe you anyway."

Like the straight practitioners at CIMC, the lesbian, gay, and bisexual practitioners practice Buddhism on a regular basis in their homes, largely through meditation. Carol meditates for an hour in the morning and often again in the evening in front of a statue of a goddess in her home. "According to what I understand," she told me, "the Buddha did not want any statues of himself . . . of course as soon as he died they created statues of him. I just felt if I was going to do this, I really needed to come out of that male thing." Her partner bought the goddess statue for her, "Rather than having a Buddha meditating, I have a woman meditating. That's the whole point, right? It doesn't matter. It's supposed to be a symbol of serenity and peace and she looked like serenity and peace to me." Risa, a lesbian in her thirties, also meditates in her home for about an hour and a half every day. Dawn, a lesbian in her forties, meditates wherever she happens to be sitting and Anissa meditates and does formal *metta* or lovingkindness practices while she jogs every day. In addition to the time they set aside to practice, many people at CIMC work to bring the practice into their daily lives. Anissa explained saying, "I also try to break tasks, like chores or things I have to do. So make those my practice—like making my bed . . . or brushing my teeth, or washing the dishes. . . . Or driving, I try to drive mindfully."

Like sexual identities, the religious and spiritual identities that develop for people out of their involvement in CIMC and the Buddhist tradition are complicated, and I asked people at CIMC in interviews how they identify religiously or spiritually. While some people clearly identify as Buddhist, others consider themselves followers of the Buddha's teachings, or Buddhist practitioners as well as practitioners in another religion, often Judaism. Some people do not want to identify religiously or spiritually at all, viewing these identifications as things to be let go of or taken off rather than put on through their meditation practice. Among the six lesbian, gay, and bisexual practitioners, two clearly identified as Buddhist. Dawn said, "I do call myself a Buddhist now . . . I think just that I do cue to that worldview and I have a daily meditation practice." She then told me a story about a friend who has just started practicing and really wants to be a Buddhist. "I find that really amusing," Dawn commented, "because it's like, you are a Buddhist. You know. If you say you're a Buddhist, you're a Buddhist." Kelly also clearly identifies as a Buddhist, though not to her parents, because it would likely upset them. While she has come out to her parents about her sexuality and they have met her girlfriend, she told me, "I'm Buddhist these days, but not really to my parents. . . . I'm sort of working towards that over time." Two others were ambivalent about their religious identities, saying that how they identify themselves depends in large part on who is asking the question. The other two practitioners identify in terms of Buddhist practice and another tradition. Carol says she practices Buddhism and another tradition and Jon says, "I think my religion is Judaism and I practice Buddhist meditation." When he came to CIMC, Jon told me he was not looking for a religion; rather he was "looking for real concrete stuff to make me a better person and to help me understand more what this life is all about."

Lesbian, gay, and bisexual people are involved in CIMC just as straight people are, including the marriage or commitment ceremonies some decide to have at the center. Narayan Liebenson Grady and Michael Liebenson Grady led a commitment ceremony for Dawn and her partner shortly after she started practicing about eight years ago. "My partner and I had met, we had sort of come together, we had both started practicing at the same time so it was really important to both of us and I think we just said, you want to have a ceremony, yeah, that sounds like a good idea." It was pretty low key, Dawn explains,

> I kind of feel about ceremonies of various kinds that they ought to be as painless for everyone involved as possible and still have some meaning. . . . I wanted it to be simple and nice and we invited the people who were really the closest to us, I think mostly it was family members, to the actual ceremony. It was maybe twenty people and we took the precepts [ethical guidelines] and basically used wedding vows from Cambridge City Hall, very traditional vows. It took probably twenty minutes maybe and then we had a big old party with fifty or sixty people afterwards.

The straight couples that have had weddings at CIMC describe them in much the same way.

Lesbian, gay, and bisexual practitioners also talk about using the meditation practice to improve their relationships just as many straight couples do. Carol spoke about meditating on something that was an issue in her relationship with her partner for a long time before bringing it up with her. She explained,

> With my partner, I've sat for a long time with an issue . . because I felt there's got to be a way of saying it that's not full of anger. . . . I've sat for months and months . . . And I tried to figure out where my piece was here. And as I figure out more of my piece I could figure out where the overlap was. What parts were mine? What parts were the relationship? So I could speak then without blame.

Conclusion

Lesbian, gay, and bisexual people are involved with specifically gay Buddhist organizations as well as with a range of organizations attended primarily by straight people across the United States. While some people are involved only with Gay Buddhist Fellowship or Buddhabuddies, others are involved with the San Francisco Zen Center and the Gay Buddhist Fellowship or with the Cambridge Insight Meditation Center and Buddhabuddies in Boston. People who are involved with both a primarily gay, lesbian, and bisexual organization and a mixed organization tend to describe the primarily gay, lesbian, and bisexual organization as a source of social support.

Lesbian, gay, and bisexual people are comfortable today in all kinds of Buddhist organizations founded by white people across the country because Buddhist texts are generally read in the United States as being neutral about homosexuality and there is little antigay discrimination and prejudice at Buddhist centers. While there are certainly examples of homophobic behaviors at particular centers, these examples are fewer than in centers in many other religious traditions.[24]

The vast majority of people involved with Buddhist organizations founded by non-Asians in the United States are upper middle-class and well-educated, a demographic group that is generally quite tolerant of homosexuality in the United States in general. Lesbian, gay, and bisexual people come to CIMC, practice privately in their own homes, and construct religious and spiritual identities in much the same way straight people who are involved with the center do.

While some people might expect gay, lesbian, and bisexual Buddhist practitioners to feel like outsiders based on their identification both as gay, lesbian or bisexual and as Buddhist, I did not find this to be the case at CIMC. This is probably because Cambridge, Massachusetts, is a generally progressive and diverse city. Gay, lesbian, and bisexual Buddhist practitioners' experiences in other cities may be quite different.

In future research about Buddhism and homosexuality, researchers might trace the development of gay Buddhist organizations and lesbian, gay, and bisexual people's involvement in other Buddhist organizations in more detail. There is some evidence that groups tend to be formed and attended either by men or women, but rarely both together, and the extent to which that is actually the case needs to be investigated.

Researchers should also talk directly with lesbian, gay, and bisexual Buddhist practitioners about how they understand their religious or spiritual identities and their sexual identities. While Kelly, whose story started this chapter, suggests that Buddhism really helped her develop an identity around sexual orientation, it is not clear whether this is common. Also, some researchers hypothesize that women, and perhaps also lesbian, gay, and bisexual people, come to Buddhism because there is not a male god in the tradition. None of the people described here mentioned this in interviews, and it would be interesting to investigate this further in the future.

Notes

1. The Cambridge Insight Meditation Center is a real place and the real names of teachers and staff members are used in this chapter. The names of individual practitioners, like Kelly, have been changed to protect their privacy.

2. I use quotation marks in this chapter to indicate people's exact words. Many of these phrases come from tape-recorded interviews.

3. Transgendered people are also involved in some Buddhist centers, like in the retreats held at Spirit Rock, but not at others. I am not aware of any transgendered people who have spoken publicly about their involvement in Buddhist organizations.

4. There are, of course, Asians and Asian-American Buddhists who are gay, lesbian, and bisexual, but I do not focus on them in this chapter. Lesbian, gay, and bisexual Asians who are involved with Buddhist centers are generally not very visible, based on my fieldwork at a Thai temple in the Philadelphia area.

5. There are, of course, always exceptions.

6. An electronic search of the WorldCat database, the Online Computer Library Center's (OCLC's) union database with seventy-six million entries, shows that the number of books with "Buddhism" in the subject increased from 500 in 1965, to 908 in 1975, to 1452 in 1985, to 1831 in 1995. Similar patterns are evident in other databases.

7. Jerry Adler, "800,000 Hands Clapping," Newsweek, 13 June 1994; David Van Biema, "Buddhism in America," Time Magazine, 13 October 1997; John DeMont, "Sunrise in the East," Maclean's, 19 April 1999; Kennedy Fraser, "Buddhism's Flowering in America: An Inside View," New York Times, 3 November 1997; Chris Helm, "One Tough Lama," Harper's, August 1996; Rodger Kamenetz, "Robert Thurman Doesn't Look Buddhist," New York Times Magazine, 5 May 1996; Young Bong Oh, "Buddhism in America: Can It Blend with Our Philosophy and Culture?" USA Today, July 1989.

8. http://www.adherents.com/movies/buddhist_box.html

9. The word "nirvana" is part of Pepsi's campaign to market the new drink Sobe Zen Blend.

10. Comprehensive data about changes in the number of Buddhist centers in the United States does not exist. The most systematic data that has been collected shows that the number of Buddhist meditation centers increased from 429 in 1987 to 1062 in 1997 but this data is based only on information about centers where meditation is taught or encouraged (Morreale 1998). The number of Asian temples increased during this period. For example, the number of Thai temples in the United States increased from zero to approximately eighty-two between 1965 and 2000, based on data I collected. For information about markets in Buddhist objects and art see Padgett (2000).

11. Estimates about how many Buddhists there are in the United States vary. In the 1991 City University of New York National Survey of Religious Identification (N=113,000), researchers argued that .2 percent of the U.S. population (roughly 500,000) or .4 percent (roughly one million) of the U.S. population was Buddhist. This data, however, was only collected in English (Kosmin and Lachman 1993). Martin Baumann estimated in 1997 that there were between three and four million Buddhists in the United States (Baumann 1997).

12. Issan Dorsey, a former drag queen and junkie who later became the abbot of the Hartford Street Zen Center, was present when this group was being formed and dubbed them the "Posture Queens" (Corless 1998b).

13. See http://www.gaybuddhist.org/followindex.html

14. See http://www.hartfordstreetzen.com/1maymain.asp

15. See http://home.pipeline.com/~diamondmetta

16. See http://www.buddhabuddies.org

17. Spirit Rock 2000 Annual Report: http://www.spiritrock.org/html/ann_rpt_2000_summary.html

18. See http://www.buddhistaidsproject.org

19. See http://www.zenhospice.org

20. There were 406 members as of June 2001.

21. For a detailed discussion of the methods, see Appendix A in Cadge (2002).

22. Two-thirds of the practitioners at CIMC are women. See chapter 7 in Cadge (2002).

23. Interview with Larry Rosenberg, 18 June 2001.

24. In 1996, Jeffrey Hopkins published an article about gay tantric sex in the Buddhist magazine *Tricycle* (see http://www.tricycle.com/interviews/jeffreyhopkins.html). *Tricycle* received more than fifty antigay letters in response, from its presumably Buddhist readers.

Shades of Grey or Back to Nature?   9
The Enduring Qualities of Ex-Gay Ministries

CHRISTY M. PONTICELLI

THE DAY BEFORE I WAS SCHEDULED to leave the 1992 Exodus conference I excused myself from a discussion with some women who had befriended me that week. "Maybe I'll see you two later," I said, knowing I would avoid them if possible. As I walked away, one spoke clearly and ritually, "Yes, you will." A chill spilled down my back, and it took every ounce of being to continue walking without shaking. I climbed several stairs at a time, my key poised to open the door to my second-story dorm room.

With all the windows closed and the blinds down, I huddled in the corner under the window hoping to escape further interactions. I had pecked out only a few notes on my laptop when a sensation paralyzed me. A breeze? A breeze. I inhaled the stuffy, non-air-conditioned room and checked the windows. Locked. Paranoia took hold. I stuffed everything into my suitcase and forced it closed. Shortly after 7 p.m., at a time I felt everyone had committed to an evening session or settled in their rooms, I dragged my bag downstairs. My heart raced as I completed exit forms and pushed them, with my linens and keys, into a trap door in the lobby.

Driving slowly but with a mission, I attacked my trusty recorder with every ounce of my being once outside the confines of the campus:

> All week the worship had been uplifting. Fast-paced. I mean, the place was rock-
> ing. They were singing of thanks, and rejoicing. Suddenly, two days before every-
> body was to leave the conference, the part they [Exodus] warn is so very difficult,
> the worship turns into this condemnation ritual. We are filth and dirt, according
> to the worship leader; the same man who had previously told us how much God
> loved us. I wondered why they weren't trying to be more supportive? Thanking
> God for bringing them together, thanking him for the new friendships and net-
> works fostered; giving them strength to continue the struggle. Don't lay on the
> guilt now. . . .[1]

Hours later I checked into a seedy motel under the flight path; I was only twenty miles from the conference. After scrubbing myself red in the shower, trying to remove every essence of Exodus, I counted the planes while trying to focus on the motorcycle races on ESPN. I arrived at the airport at 6 a.m. sharp, hoping to catch an early flight. On the standby list, I waited, moving from gate to gate every time another flight left its gate. I never felt out of "their" grasp. My mind somewhere else, I tried to assess each individual near me. A voice woke me . . a young couple wanted me to watch their bags while they got coffee. Finally, I worked my way onto a late-morning flight and arrived in San Jose only to collapse in my partner's arms outside the airport.

Exodus had introduced to me a set of emotions so fluid that I often felt schizophrenic that week. Initially, I was terrified that Exodus would discover that I was a researcher and throw me out. Later, I became mesmerized by the passion with which these women and men were committed to their own "healing." One minute I understood their pain; the next I became enraged at Exodus's oversimplification and reductionist understanding of the ex-lesbians "problems." Somewhere in the instability of my feelings, terror overcame me. Their philosophy on "the causes" of "lesbian tendencies" was vague enough to encompass anyone's personal history and yet specific enough to be personal. I know this; I experienced it when two women mapped those "causes" onto my seemingly normal life history. They spoke effortlessly, and worked me over like professional wrestling tag-team partners.

I had so much more to learn about this phenomenon. And more than ever before, I felt incapable of understanding why anyone chose Exodus's notion of healing; one that ultimately brings great struggle, pain, and a realization that one may only be able to modify her or his behaviors and not feelings, desires, and attractions. There were so many other options available in the larger, organized religious world. Why, I wondered, weren't these people inquiring about other denominational and nondenominational groups available to lesbians and gay men? Seventh-day Adventist Kinship is one organization, for example, that helps lesbians and gay men unify their faith and homosexuality. Though not sanctioned by the Seventh-day Adventist (SDA) denomination, the group sustains an outstanding reputation for meeting the spiritual and religious needs of Adventist lesbians and gay men. Similar groups, with varying philosophies about negotiating gay and Christian identities, exist for nearly every Christian denomination. Why choose Exodus's philosophy?

After months of silence and self-imposed isolation it became clear to me that the only way I could hope to understand the choices of these women and their experiences was to reenter the study without holding onto my personal fears of the group's impact on me. This required a blurring of my personal, spiritual, religious, and scholarly selves throughout the research process of being a participant observer, analyst, and writer. What follows is one product of that sense-making process.

The "ex-gay movement" is generally maligned by lesbian, gay, bisexual, and transsexual communities, but for many who have great difficulties accepting who they are, it is an option to which they are drawn, especially those within a conservative Christian worldview. This chapter neither argues for the correctness nor the inappropriateness of this perspective or process of attempted change, but rather tries to describe the movement in an effort to show the appeal of the approach for some persons struggling to reconcile their Christian beliefs with their sexual desires. Before continuing, however, a brief overview of Exodus International helps set the tone.

Exodus International

Exodus International is a Christian group "dedicated to equipping and uniting agencies and individuals to effectively communicate the message of liberation from homosexuality." Fundamentally, they promote heterosexuality as "God's creative intent for humanity," thereby proclaiming "homosexual expression" a sin. Unlike religions that have condemned and banished homosexuals, Exodus declares that homosexuals can be converted or healed by breaking "sin's power" (Exodus 2002a). The more "men and women mature through ongoing submission to the lordship of Christ and His Church," the more "free [they become] from homosexuality" (Exodus 2002b). Exodus's philosophy has not gone unchallenged. Groups ranging from the American Psychiatric Association and American Psychology Association to grassroots movements like ActUp have challenged the claim that homosexuals can be "healed" or changed.

Individuals, churches, and financially independent para-church ministries affiliated with Exodus International carry out this mission. Numbering approximately 150 groups worldwide[2], these ministries do not speak in terms of success rates. Rather, they argue that the more important issue is to recognize and acknowledge that there is realistic hope for those who desire change. Individual ministries vary greatly in the methods used to work toward redemption. Some offer weekly meetings that are similar to those held by Alcoholics Anonymous (Denzin 1987; 1993). Members come and go as they please; no long-term commitment is required. Still others offer a structured sequence of meetings taken over the course of several weeks or even months. New members may not join the course once it has begun. Similarly, once committed, it is expected that a person will complete the course.

Perhaps the most intense of all options are the residential programs. Love in Action (LIA), in Memphis, Tennessee, operates the longest running of these, and has programs for men and women. The program can cost an individual in excess of $6,000. These fees cover food, housing, and therapy session costs (Love in Action

2001). In addition, many members and leaders of these ministries also attend the annual weeklong international conference called "camp."

Wings[3], the ministry I attended, was open to the public and met every Friday evening from 7–10 p.m. Members strolled in anytime between 6:30 and 7:30, many appeared to be coming directly from work. On a typical night, there were six men and seven or eight women plus the two women who led the group. We sang praise songs for the first twenty to thirty minutes before gathering around several six-foot long, folding tables pushed together. Newcomers were always welcomed with smiles, shoulder pats, and reading materials.

Typically a ministry gathering began with a check-in of how the week had gone, a reporting of any special temptations members had confronted, or a discussion of how everyone felt about the previous week's discussion. The group was always receptive to any individual who requested collective reflection on a particularly troubling issue.

The group responded to individuals compassionately and helpfully, never with combative or condemning comments. For example, one Friday night I was particularly quiet and removed. After numerous attempts to draw me into the topic of relinquishing one's will to God, a member stopped the discussion and focused the group's attention on me. Eventually, she coaxed from me the fact that I had seen a fatal crash on my drive through the mountains to the meeting; that I sat in my car for what seemed like hours with evidence of one of the fatalities visible through my passenger window. Although they responded with complete and genuine acknowledgment of my experience, the group's leadership eventually shifted the discussion to moments in their "journey out of the lifestyle" when they felt numb, shocked, and helpless. The spontaneity and skill with which they transitioned from my state of shock to similar states in their own "healing" was both sensitive to my emotions and also successfully reinforcing of the reasons we were there.

Meetings were pleasant, even fun, because the group as a whole set the pace. Some weeks the group quickly jumped into very serious discussions about sexual fantasies in members' lives, and how some persons had "moved passed" this. Other weeks the group covered particular topics such as how to reveal their lesbian past to friends and intimates. Still other gatherings were a bit more social. Regardless of the apparent laxity with which meetings ran, the underlying focus was always change and "leaving the lifestyle," a topic to which I now turn.

To Change or Not To Change? What Do We Mean?

Humans and human behaviors are not static. Physiological changes, from heightened hormones in the early and latter parts of our lives, and chemical inconsistencies in the brain alter our bodies, personalities, and behaviors. We also change as we age or when we are affected by some experience (e.g., a serious accident, family death). Here lies the first premise that attracts people to ex-gay ministries: the belief in change.

Elsewhere, I have documented how women affiliated with Exodus ex-gay ministries change their sexual identities through a process requiring several social conditions (Ponticelli 1999). Women learn a new vocabulary and incorporate it into a new way of speaking. This is done within an Exodus *community* that offers unconditional love and support, while helping women *recreate their biographies* in ways that explain their lesbianism in a *detailed* and *definitive* logic. Within this logic, women come to understand and then *reveal* to their new community *precisely* what *experiences led them to leave God's chosen path* of heterosexuality and partake of "the lesbian lifestyle." Ultimately, many of these women accept their new role and work toward maintaining their ex-gay or "healed identity."

While this earlier publication helped clarify identity construction theory, it left many questions unanswered. For example, how permanent are the new identities created by these women? What attracts women to Exodus and the ceaseless struggles involved with "leaving the lifestyle?" In this chapter, I argue that it is impossible to determine any level of permanent change precisely because, although acknowledging physical sexual acts and behaviors, Exodus focuses primarily on emotional and spiritual (mind) sensibilities. Furthermore, Exodus affirms an infinite and imperfect processional that women and men employ at a point when absolute healing seems unrealistic. Within this context, I propose that Exodus's ultimate confirmation and acceptance that complete healing may not be possible not only attracts women to the group but also may help individuals maintain their commitment to change. In other words, the shift from a finite process to one marred with shades of gray may strengthen a woman's resolve to stay with Exodus. Yet, I propose that change in and of itself is not the most appealing factor of the movement. As we shall see, the concept that one can work toward change for a lifetime, faltering along the way, makes Exodus's mission more appealing to some. Initially, however, the possibility of change appeals to many who join an ex-gay ministry.

Many lesbians with whom I spoke joined Exodus believing at one time in their lives that they were a mistake, an example of God's wrath, biologically destined, or naively hopeless. Often they thought change was impossible. As a result, accepting the possibility of change can be their very first and most difficult challenge. For example, Wanda, a doctoral student in physics and an avid breeder of angelfish, offered a few words through an interview that echo comments made by most women I interviewed. Wanda confessed that at one time she blamed God, saying that He "did this to me." When her struggles heightened, she said:

W: "Yeah I wish that I had known somebody who had some success (changing). I just thought this is hopeless. Why not just, ah,"

CP: "Give up?"
W: "Yeah."
CP: "Well, I'm sure a lot of people think that."
W: "You know, why should I fight my *natural* impulses kind of thing?"

The idea that one's lesbianism is "natural" or otherwise unchangeable is not uncommon among "ex-lesbians." In her brief written testimonial, Ann Phillips, former self-proclaimed militant feminist and lesbian for twenty plus years and current program director for women at Love in Action, recalls:

> People all around me were saying things like, "I didn't ask to be gay . . ." and "I was born this way." Statements I had made all my adult life. Then a woman seated right next to me made another comment I'd said many times. "And no one can change me." Within my own mind, I heard these words crystal clear. . . .

In reality, Exodus, like the American Psychological Association (2003), discounts any possibility of biological, genetic, or hormonal cause for homosexuality. Author and former lesbian Jeannette Howard (1992) explains it this way:

> Is lesbianism inborn? There is lots of research. No conclusive evidence. The jury is out. It is true, however, that the Bible makes it perfectly clear that lesbianism is not acceptable to Him. To ask if it is inborn is totally irrelevant to me because I am responsible to my Father.

Howard offers more than clarification on Exodus's stand on the origins of homosexuality. She leads the way for women to speak about their experiences. They learn to view themselves as deviant, degenerate, or sick but as capable of being changed. They begin to see and talk about themselves as "people in process."

The Rev. John J. Smid (1992), long-time executive director of LIA, claimed in an interview that "we may never be complete in this process until Jesus returns." Personally, Smid (2002) admits on LIA's website that:

> [he is] not totally healed from homosexuality, [He] still struggle[s] at times, [He] still shut[s] down with [his] wife at times, [and] periodically [has] sexual thoughts regarding men. . . .

Thus, Exodus and its affiliate ministries like LIA and Wings advocate a progressive "healing" involving emotional, sexual, mental, physical, and spiritual components. The progression to "wholeness," however, may never end.

Despite these admissions of incomplete "healing," Exodus and its ministries present an overwhelming impression that the "journey out of homosexuality" is a complete and finite process. Christian therapists and authors Bill Consiglio and

Joe Nicolosi declare that a person can "move from exclusive homosexuality to functional (beyond just behavioral changes) heterosexuality" (27 June 1994 interview). A typical tract designed for anonymous outreach distribution makes it very clear that, '[Jesus] set me free from the lifestyle' and restored me with natural desires" (*Dear Robert* 1991). This tract carries the explicit message to a gay reader that he or she is in a form of bondage but that freedom is attainable; that homosexuality is unnatural but that one can become natural with no shades of grey.

It is precisely this dichotomous language that likely attracts gays and lesbians to Exodus. In other words, Exodus officially promotes the idea that a concrete change from homosexuality to heterosexuality is possible. Yet, entry into the ex-lesbian world quickly reveals that "grey" thinking is not only acceptable, but expected. Furthermore, scripture is used to support this notion that we can never be perfect or whole, but that we must continue to work toward wholeness. In the end, Wings's co-minister Carol summarizes the ex-gay reality in this fashion. During a discussion over coffee, she quietly stated that: "Wings believes it is okay to be gay and Christian so long as your life doesn't stop there. You must be working to overcome your sexual disjuncture."

Shades of Grey? Or Back to Nature?

Anita Worthen, wife of LIA founder and ex-gay Frank Worthen, posed several questions to the summer conference attendees: "[D]o you have the Christian façade? What do you think when you are alone?" Her questions imply answers to the issue of permanent "healing" and in doing so they suggest that it is a complex, interactional process.

This process involves what I call "front-stage thinking" and "backstage thinking." Drawing from sociologist Erving Goffman's (1956) distinction between "front stage/backstage acting," those attempting to leave the lifestyle are encouraged to present different thoughts and behaviors depending on their setting. As a migrant farm worker may "act" as though she or he is a devoted and conscientious worker in front of white supervisors (front stage), he or she may return to the fields only to "act" (backstage) wholly disrespectful of those supervisors. For Goffman, this suggests that the actor is the only one who knows which performance is authentic. We perform for an audience in a way that best promotes ourselves in a particular context. This same dynamic could be seen as applying to ex-gays. Any individual can profess, for example, a willingness and devotion to engage in a personal struggle "out of the lifestyle." Whether a person truly thinks, believes, and feels this, however, is only known by the individual lesbian or gay. An example from my own experiences at the 1992 Exodus conference demonstrates this. It was mid-week and a peer saw me with a laptop computer. Later, I wrote:

> She asked me where I got the computer. I told her a friend lent it to me; a professor so I could keep a journal. She said that my professor was very kind and thoughtful. She asked if this professor knew where I was going, and I said yes. "You are further along than you think," she declared. If she only knew....

In my mind, and at front-stage level, I performed or self-presented as a possible convert. What were really my field notes were transposed into a "journal." While I never lied, I allowed for plenty of open interpretation. Backstage, in this instance, was not located in a space away from the peer I interacted with, but was positioned in my personal thoughts while in her presence. Whether my experience is comparable to the experiences of those who seek change is not clear. It has been argued, however, that change requires not only cognitive elements but also emotional ones (Wolkomor 2001).

What I am suggesting is that an ex-lesbian might present herself, front stage, as changed. Perhaps she demonstrates mastery of Exodus's discourse, changes her physical presence to one more feminine, and even expresses physically and verbally her growing interest in men. Backstage, however, she may be thinking and acting differently. She may still desire sexual intimacy with a woman. She may act on this, or not. The combinations, ultimately, are unlimited. Still, should she divulge any portion of her backstage thoughts, acknowledging them as a slip, she may recommit to the "struggle" and be fully accepted again (see Denzin [1987; 1993] for a discussion of this in terms of Alcoholics Anonymous).

Still, a question remains: Does an "actor" really know which of any number of presentations or performances represent her or his real self (see Thumma [1994] for further discussion)? This question, like others posed in this chapter, cannot be fully answered. Perhaps it is this very ambiguity or shade of grey that ultimately keeps people wedded to Exodus and its ministries. I do not mean to suggest that "freedom from homosexuality" does not exist; only that we can never know what it is that another thinks or feels. If behavior were the only indicator of change, it would be easier for "outsiders" like myself to determine success or failure. However, Exodus and groups like it present the struggles as one of internal emotions, feelings, desires, and thoughts, involving a long process over time. This effort is highly personal and ultimately unknowable by others. Philosophical theorist Michel Foucault (1990: 26) addresses the issue eloquently, and helps bring closure:

> [One can] make the essence of fidelity consist in the mastery of desires, in the fervent combat one directs against them, in the strength with whom one is able to

resist temptations: what makes up the content of fidelity in this case is that vigilance and that struggle. In these conditions, the contradictory movements of the soul, much more than the carrying out of the acts themselves, will be the prime material of moral practice.

And this "contradictory movement of the soul" or "shades of grey" within this struggle makes the ex-gay movement an acceptable option for some lesbian and gay Christians.

Notes
Address all correspondence to Christy M. Ponticelli, Department of Sociology, University of South Florida, 4202 E. Fowler Ave. CPR107, Tampa, FL 33613. E-mail: cpontice@chuma1.cas.usf.edu.

1. I began researching Exodus in the summer of 1992 by attending their annual, international, weeklong conference ("camp"). I spent the next twelve months (my final year in graduate school) as a participant and observer with Wings (a pseudonym), an ex-gay ministry in Northern California (Ponticelli 1996). In particular, I attended and participated in their weekly meetings and interviewed (in-depth, unstructured) women from that ministry, including the two leaders. I also participated in several larger assemblies hosted by different ministries in the area. I stopped working with Wings in May 1993. I attended a second summer meeting in 1994, and conducted interviews in Florida with several more women affiliated with Exodus. The material in this chapter comes from field notes, transcribed interviews, and published documents supplied by Exodus and numerous affiliate ministries. Interviews and attendance at the summer camp were partially funded by a grant from the Graduate School at the University of California, Santa Cruz and the University of South Florida.

2. According to Exodus International figures, the United States is home to the largest number (roughly ninety) of ministries, with the most working out of the Central United States. Of those ministries not based in the United States, South Africa has the next highest number of ministries. A wide range of countries host the remaining ministries: Canada, Israel, Ecuador, Brazil, Slovakia, Sweden, Denmark, Belgium, Norway, the United Kingdom, and Australia. Locations, domestic and foreign, are added continually as Exodus International promotes its message.

3. Wings is a pseudonym, as are the names of its members.

SUBALTERN/SECTARIAN EXPRESSIONS

II

A N INTEGRAL FEATURE OF RELIGION in America is its entrepreneurial sectarian inventiveness. The free-market context of religious organizations, where no denominational or churchly entity wields monopolistic control, provides fertile soil for new niche expressions of religion (Finke and Stark 1992). If a person has a religious vision of a new or better understanding of faith and doesn't find a receptive home in an existing denomination, it has become almost a law of American religion for that person to start his or her own church. With an appealing message and time, this offshoot may develop a collection of like-minded churches into a sect. Much has been written about the character and role of sects in American religious life, often in contradistinction to the larger, more pluralistic and accommodating denominational reality (Berger 1954; Johnson 1963, 1971; Stark and Bainbridge 1979; Swatos 1981). Sectarian religions are organizations but they are often smaller and less complex than denominations. They nearly always require greater commitment from their members and are formed around a strongly held core set of beliefs or a distinctive identity.

The gay religious organizations identified in this section are sectarian communities of faith. Like the denominational groups, these have an organizational reality. They are also similar to denominational heritage groups in that they draw on and adopt many of the same traditional theological values inherent in denominations. They differ, however, in that they privilege gay identity over tradition. These groups express a spirituality that flows from the gay experience rather than from existing religious traditions or beliefs and practices. This perspective forms a distinctive identity for the group and an alternative spiritual and organizational option for LGBT persons. The gay persons described in this section have created organizations that offer a new way to understand gay religious life. Rather than attempting to work within existing structures, they have created independent, distinctly gay religious institutional forms.

As such, they are also subaltern communities.[1] These organizational forms arose in response to subordination by or exclusion from the dominant organizational realities. Out of their marginalized position, these groups created their own alternative institutions as a political act, but also to have a platform from which their voices could be heard. They not only formed their own spiritual "safe space" but also created structures that nurture and solidify a new gay religious identity out of which they could then act.

The originators of these subaltern entities often take components of the old cultural forms and rework them into innovative expressions for a new spiritual practice. The old tools are put to new uses, and in so doing a new product is created that is both contiguous with the past and also a distinctive new reality.

This impulse to create institutions that are uniquely LGBT realities is not uncommon in gay life beyond the religious sphere. One can see a parallel development in the formation of gay choruses and drama groups, LGBT sports clubs and leagues, and professional organizations such as those for gay lawyers and doctors.

Within gay religion in America, the archetypal example of the subaltern/ sectarian innovative organization is the International Fellowship of Metropolitan Community Churches, founded by Troy Perry in 1968. Perry left the Church of God of Prophecy as a disillusioned gay pastor only to found a very successful "established sect" wholly embracing the acceptance of LGBT. This quasi-denominational organization is a loose affiliation of roughly three hundred congregations in more than twenty countries. The worship and ritual life of these congregations is an eclectic mix of Anglican, Pentecostal, and mainline Protestant forms held together with its commitment to the affirmation of gay spiritual wholeness.

Bernard Lukenbill investigates the music program of one such Metropolitan Community Church (MCC) in Austin, Texas, in his essay titled "Pluralism and Diversity: Music as Discourse and Information in a Gay and Lesbian Congregation." Through its music and other means, this MCC congregation gives its members a new theological self-identity and socializes them into new group norms. Even though the MCC is a large national sectarian movement, Lukenbill's essay shows how a particular group works to establish a local sectarian identity, placing sexual orientation first but with elements from its evangelical protestant tradition, its music, close behind.

The Metropolitan Community Churches are not the only distinctively gay sectarian group in the country. Others include Reconciling Pentecostals International, the Ecumenical Catholic Church, and the Unity Fellowship Church Movement. Aryana Bates investigates a congregation within the Unity Fellowship Church in her chapter "Liberation in Truth: African American Lesbians Reflect on Spirituality and Their Church." This religious community combines innovative, liberation-oriented theology with liturgical practices consistent with the black church traditions familiar to most of its members. Bates' informants have a strong critique of religion. They prefer a more individualized and individualizable spirituality for mediating their relationship with the divine.

Drawing from a more neo-pagan tradition, the Radical Faerie community combines nature worship and spiritual practices with a gay perspective. Jay Hasbourck, in his ethnographic study of a Radical Faerie community, explores Faerie spiritual practices and what he calls "dominant social imaginaries." In this essay, entitled "Utopian Imaginaries and Faerie Practice: Mapping Routes of Relational Agency," he describes the marginal spaces where Faerie practices play out and examines the conditions under which relational forms of agency develop and transpire.

Also within a nature tradition, Mary Jo Neitz travels to the Front Range of Colorado to investigate queer pagans. She finds a transformation taking place, not within a binary gay/straight understanding, but in terms of the lesbian participants' self-understanding as marginalized and "at risk" because they violate dominant cultural norms even among pagans. This "queering of the Dragonfest" by ambiguously sexed women with horns challenges the binary understandings of sexual identity and creates a place for the women within this religious tradition.

In his chapter "'St. Gerard Teaches Him That Love Cancels That Out:' Italian American Catholic Gay Men in Newark, New Jersey," Peter Savastano describes a unique subaltern phenomenon within the dominant religion of Catholicism that has adapted the iconography, symbols, and hagiography associated with St. Gerard Maiella to make a unique place for themselves within but also as a subversion of the dominant religious tradition. Although the devotion to the saint is part of a local religious tradition quite independent of sexual identity, by adapting a standard Catholic ritual practice and taking it to certain lengths they in fact become sectarian Catholics, resisting the church's official teachings on homosexual activity and finding their own voice in the faith tradition.

Neitz's and Savastano's articles suggest a more individualistic impulse at work that has become common in American religion and has been popularized by Robert Bellah, et al. (1985) through the label of "Sheilaism." In both their works one can see a movement toward sectarian responses and subaltern expressions that are becoming more privatized.

In Melissa Wilcox's exploration of the religious themes in the life stories of lesbian, bisexual, and transgender (LBT) women in two MCCs and elsewhere in Los Angeles, this individualistic impulse is overt. In her descriptions of these women's faith in her essay "A Religion of One's Own: Gender and LBT Religiosities," there is evidence of a kind of "sectarianism at the individual level" where "I am my own sect" even within the established sect of the MCC. Wilcox suggests that women's religious belief and attendance differ in significant ways from those of gay and bisexual men. She indicates a number of reasons for this, including early responses to sexism, a preference for female leadership, and feminine divine imagery. Even given this correct insistence that women's experience of religion is radically different from men's, the individualistic emphasis seems to be a commonality across gender and religion.

These six essays draw to our attention the importance of attending to the forms of religious practice on the margins. If we focus on the traditional organizational forms and structures, or even on the diversity within them, we still miss much of the innovation that is taking place in American religious life. Even within these sectarian edge institutions of American religion, it is apparent that considerable heterogeneity of practice, diversity of forms, and a multiplicity of participants' moods and motivations exist.

Often the impetus for change comes from the prophets standing outside the city wall, bearing witness to the political oppression of the formal sanctioned institutions. These subaltern expressions not only give voice to the marginalized but as sectarian movements they may also hold the seeds of change for society.

Note

1. John Zuern offers the following definition of subaltern. "Originally a term for subordinates in military hierarchies, the term subaltern is elaborated in the work of Antonio Gramsci to refer to groups who are outside the established structures of political representation." In "Can the Subaltern Speak?" Gayatri Spivak suggests that the subaltern is denied access to both mimetic and political forms of representation—on his Criticalink web site at maven.english.hawaii.edu/criticalink/spivak/terms/subaltern.html.

Pluralism and Diversity
Music as Discourse and Information in a Gay and Lesbian Congregation

10

W. BERNARD LUKENBILL

C HIMES SOUND from the near the nave. The congregation comes to attention. The altar candles are lighted and the organ and synthesized piano
music robustly introduce the processional hymn "Our God Is Like an Eagle" and these lines are sung:

> Our God is not a woman, our God is not a man; Our God is both and neither,
> our God is I Who Am. From all the roles that bind us our God has set us free.
> What freedom does God give us? The freedom just to be.

As the hymn begins, robed celebrants and acolytes begin their march down the
center aisle toward the altar. Thus beings a worship service at Metropolitan Community Church of Austin (MCCA) at Freedom Oaks in Austin, Texas.

Music in most Christian traditions is an important form of community dialogue as it promotes communication and discourse and helps disseminate information about a church's core values regarding beliefs and behaviors. My interest is
to better understand the role of music as a form of social and cultural information and discourse within a congregation that serves a largely gay, lesbian, bisexual, and transgendered membership. In this essay I attempt to briefly assess the use
of music in the life of a local congregation, MCCA. My methodology is a natu-
ralistic investigation relying on documents found in the church archives, interviews, and conversations with church officials and members, personal
observations, and social theories about organizational life. These all help explain
the important informational role that music currently plays in the organizational
and spiritual life of MCCA at Freedom Oaks.

Information, as defined in this study, is the communication and reception of
organized knowledge or structured messages containing ideas intended to inform

or influence behaviors and attitudes (*Webster's Tenth New Collegiate Dictionary* 1999: 599). Discourse theory helps this discussion as it offers guidance to critical analysis. Discourse theory is defined as "a rational reconstructing of new concepts based on historical evidence" and those "sequences that are shaped and reshaped by political struggles" (Torfing 1999, 2002). This theory relies on documents (e.g., music) and other forms of recorded behaviors that inform reason and foster objective analysis. Discourse analysis, being political in origin, allows common values and behavior expectations found in any community to be displayed, discussed, and better understood.

For this study, I use diversity to mean accepting and recognizing differences among people and pluralism to mean accepting the legitimacy of specific traditional practices held by persons and groups within a wider, common culture. Diversity and pluralism are central to the current mission of MCCA at Freedom Oaks because much of the church's ideology about this religious community life is encased and communicated in its music. In this discussion I strongly imply that diversity and pluralism as practiced at MCCA at Freedom Oaks are not centered on gay, lesbian, bisexual, or transgendered sexual identity and expression, but embrace a much wider concept of inclusion.

Music in Christianity and Ritualistic Religious Life

Biblical references to the important role of music in Christian worship are found throughout scripture, including Colossians 3:16. This verse attests to the importance of song in worship and in dialogue among believers, advising all to sing "with psalms and hymns and spiritual songs, sing from the heart in gratitude to God" (*Revised New English Bible* 1989: 182; Ellis 2002).

Christian church music today is striving to become more inclusive and to escape from its Western, American, and European influences. Modern presentation of Christian music can range in style from medieval Latin chants to contemporary and American southern, Afro-American gospel music, and New Age music (Corbitt 1998: 27–46). The Western Christian church now seems to be more accepting of music variety in worship. Helped in this direction is the apparent decline of an ideology that promoted a future monolithic church in favor of a church that is accepting of diversity (Wilson-Dickson 1992: 245) and that explicitly embraces different musical traditions. For example, a 1990 report by the Royal Academy of Music to the archbishop of Canterbury called for more diversity in music (Wilson-Dickson 1992: 245-46).

Pluralism at its radical extremes poses significant challenges for congregational music given the importance of music's role in defining culture (Corbitt 1998). Pluralism represents change and change is often chaotic. Churches for the most part are conservative in that they have an interest in maintaining stability and certainty. On the one hand, if they protect their traditional musical boundaries and reject newer directions in music, they may risk not addressing the needs of a group of people they hope to attract. On the other hand, if they accept music of the "street," they may be presenting music as performance, and not music for the spreading of the Christian faith (Corbitt 1998: 25–32, 130–32). This is not only a problem for gay and lesbian churches where memberships often include persons often described as "young adults" (e.g., twenties to mid-thirties); but it is a problem of all churches who minister to young people who are products of contemporary youth culture and mass media music influences where music personalities and dance are prominent.

Corbitt (1998: 42) presents a model of the new church, based on Myers (1996: 8–9) that he terms, the "Kingdom Community: The Emerging Church." He argues that this new church model or form dates from around 1950. In musical terms it embraces all forms of music and uses a variety of music coming from many cultures. It accepts a variety of musical instruments, including electronic devices such as computers, amplification, synthesizers, MTV, and television. In the beginning this music was very much congregational-based; however, he feels, and I agree, that in recent years it has become less participatory in character because of the development of specialized "performance artists." He cautions that this type of church music must guard against promoting "spectator worship, commercialization, and secularization" (Corbitt 1998: 42). In many ways, I feel that this musical diversity present in this music demands a level of musicianship that the average church member may not possess. This may indeed imply that churches, including Universal Fellowship of Metropolitan Community Churches (UFMCC), must rely more on both religious and secular specialists and artists to provide the high caliber of music demanded by its congregations.

UFMCC, MCCA at Freedom Oaks and Their Music Traditions

MCCA at Freedom Oaks is a 350-member congregation, with many of its members being gay, lesbian, bisexual, and transgendered. It is a member of UFMCC. Founded in 1976 as an independent church, it gained its charter from UFMCC in 1978. An understanding of the organizational structure of MCCA at Freedom Oaks, including its musical program, requires an understanding of UFMCC and its perception of music in Christian worship.

The Rev. Troy D. Perry, who at that time was a defrocked Pentecostal minister, founded UFMCC in Los Angeles in1968. Although from the beginning the church articulated a mission of serving gay, bisexual, lesbian, and transgendered persons, it has always claimed that it is not a church only for these persons, but it is a church founded primarily to provide a safe place for all people regardless of their sexuality. Throughout its history UFMCC has rejected the idea that it is a religious cult or even a part of the gay subculture. The church has always insisted that it is a denomination within mainline Christianity. The World Council of Churches, through its credential review committee, agreed that UFMCC was Trinitarian and possessed all of qualifications for mainline church status. In its mind, it plays a role thrust upon it as a result of social, political, and cultural repression and misunderstanding. The fellowship sees itself as a haven where persons of all sexual and social persuasions can come to in safety without fear of exclusion and rejection.

UFMCC is not a local, congregational-based denomination. That is to say, each congregation must follow by-laws, directives, and organizational policies and structures as determined by UFMCC. Nevertheless, within that corporate structure, congregations are not monolithic and each congregation may define its own style and establish its own personality. Some may follow a praise and worship model of service, others may elect a more formal and ritualistic form, and still others may decide on an integrative approach.

This inclusiveness extends to membership as well where church policy embraces gay, lesbian, straight, bisexual, and transgendered persons. Both contributing to and complicating this non-monolithic structure is the tendency for both UFMCC to borrow from various Christian and non-Christian traditions. In fact, current trends indicate that cultural diversity and pluralism are becoming dominant themes within the corporate structure and organizational culture of both UFMCC and MCCA at Freedom Oaks.

Many UFMCC church Internet websites accessed during March 2002 reflect this pluralism. Numerous churches state on their websites that they attempt to meet the needs of as many persons as possible. One of the ways they attempt this is by specifically offering within their services a variety of church music traditions. Although the fellowship does not dictate liturgical or musical styles, it does hold certain theological concepts that it expects its congregations to uphold. Many of these concepts fall within the broad concept of "liberation theology," racial, cultural, social, and political diversity, gender equality, self-esteem and acceptance issues, and the gender neutrality of God.

In the early 1980s, under the leadership of the MCC San Francisco church, UFMCC published a trial hymnal titled *Hymns for the Church* as a part of the Hymnal Project (Metropolitan Community Church of Baltimore 2002). The project was created to help local UFMCC congregations understand and conform better in their music ministries to the general theological attributes of the fellowship. This hymnal was especially necessary because of the 1981 official adoption and mandated use of inclusive gender language in worship, ministry, and education programs in all UFMCC churches. UFMCC defines inclusive language as reflecting:

> an attitude of mutuality and openness toward others that recognizes everyone's right of equal access to the experiences and realization of wholeness. Inclusive language reflects a sensitivity to overcome barriers that exist between individuals and among communities in such areas as gender, race, class, age, physical differences, nationality, theological beliefs, culture and lifestyle (Universal Fellowship of Metropolitan Community Churches 1981).

Guidelines to help with the implementation of this mandate came from UFMCC headquarters, with member churches assuming the role of educating congregations at local levels. The project specifically identified existing hymns and songs that were acceptable to the inclusive mandate. Additionally, through copyright clearance, the fellowship legally modified available music to conform better to its theological concepts and inclusive language requirements. The Hymnal Project also commissioned the writing of music that reflected UFMCC's sense of Christian mission.

As stated, this hymnal writing effort was an attempt to ensure a certain level of worship conformity in musical theology. Today, some churches in the fellowship apparently find this hymnal too limited because of its lack of contemporary and praise music and have turned to other sources. For example, Living Waters MCC in Tuscaloosa, Alabama, has chosen to use alongside *Hymns for the Church* the hymnal *Songs of Faith and Praise* (1999) with its commonly used mainline mix of hymns and praise songs. Living Waters MCC justified their use of *Songs of Faith and Praise* saying that it provides for "blended worship" through its mixture of "liturgical and praise worship styles" drawn from many faith traditions (Living Waters MCC 2000). MCCA at Freedom Oaks currently does not use any formal or published hymnal and provides appropriate music for services within its church bulletins. This appears to be a trend within UFMCC churches whereby some congregations develop unique hymnal structures reflective of local needs. These may range from familiar Baptist and Roman Catholic hymns to New Age music.

Postmodernism in UFMCC and MCCA at Freedom Oaks

Postmodernism arose from the disillusionment and rejection of the ideas central to continual social progress, rationalism, and individualism expressed in modernism, and instead it embraced a variety of new views of the world including feminism, multiculturalism, and environmentalism (Edwards 2001: 11). Accordingly, only small, personal truths have any chance of really existing. All values are, therefore, subject to deconstruction, criticism, and social construction. Social construction allows individuals and individual cultures and groups to build their own identities based on needs and environmental influences (Greyling ca. 1998, citing Weeks 1998: 6, 191; Klages 2002; Corsini 1999: 742). Social construction can be influenced by older values, but these compose only one set of influences that can be considered and used in building new concepts of self and society. Discourse theory, as a part of social constructionism, maintains that social values are in constant states of change and flux and that dialogue and communication with diverse sources of information are necessary to ensure the building of adequate self and social frameworks (Greyling ca.1998, citing Reynolds 1994: 245–74). In using various sources of information and documentation, a community of dialogue is created and maintained.

UFMCC's mission of providing a safe and accepting place where people of various sexualities might worship God required it to take a postmodern, deconstructionist approach to the traditional biblical interpretations against homosexuality. To establish its legitimacy as a Christian church the denomination aligned itself strongly with modern historical-critical biblical scholarship. UFMCC has used this scholarship based on historical, sociological, and linguistic evidence and arguments to dispute the traditional values and biblical interpretations against homosexuality (Lukenbill 1998: 444). Similarly, its apologists feel strongly that their research and analyses have clearly demonstrated that UFMCC is not a religious cult or a relic of the gay subculture. According to the Rev. Kenneth Martin, Senior Pastor at MCCA at Freedom Oaks, the recent third edition of the *New Oxford Annotated Bible* (2001) reflects much of UFMCC's apologia. In fact, he sees the fellowship at the forefront of Christian religious reform largely through its reinterpretation of scriptures, its rejection of rigid roles and gender expectations, and its attention to social activism (Martin 2002).

The belief that many truths exist in the world and all of these are relative within their own contexts gives evidence of UFMCC's social constructionist tendencies. In some respects UFMCC and its congregations question the reliability of some accepted aspects of standard historical analysis, claiming that such records are not to be trusted because they present interpretations that often excluded large areas of human experiences such as the role of women and racial, class, religious, and sexual minorities in human affairs and culture (Edwards 2001: 13–18). The goal of UFMCC in questioning long-held biblical interpretations of scripture (as well as establishment history) is not to destroy traditions and scripture, but to return Christianity to its Christ-based origins. To do this, old, erroneous interpretations must be discarded and Christ must be seen as a "liberator and revolutionary whose mission was to challenge and destroy harmful ideas, beliefs, and behaviors" (Lukenbill 1998: 445). In recent years research has appeared that documents UFMCC's as well as its local churches' attempts at restructuring social conditions through social and political activism (Lybeck 1995; St. John 2001).

In building identity within UFMCC, social constructionist principles seem to have helped define UFMCC's sense of self. Social constructionist identity theory implies that no community is bound by customs, traditions, social expectations, or long-held "truths." Each community builds its own values based on its need for identity and structure. Communication of ideas and values and documents such as music that transmit such concepts are necessary within the dissemination process.

On the other hand, UFMCC appears to reject many of the attributes of postmodernism. It accepts a modernist view that society is progressively improving and that political and social actions are necessary for continued progress. It respects legitimate authority and teachers; it does not see tradition as irrelevant; and it holds to liberal but establishment interpretations of biblical truths. The influence of social constructionism on music with UFMCC is diffused because of the diverse character of its various congregations. Nevertheless, I argue that postmodernism and social constructionism have undoubtedly been influential in that the fellowship has encouraged the restructuring of music to conform better to its overall goals and mission. I must concede that the actual influence of social constructionism at the local MCC congregational level has yet to be determined.

Postmodernism in church ritual and music materialized in the 1980s within evangelical Protestantism with the goal of deconstructing traditional forms of worship that were seen as archaic and obstacles to God. I feel that in general the leadership of UFMCC well understood evangelical Protestantism, since many of them came from that tradition and were not alien to the social reconstructing of church ritual and music that the movement encouraged.

In postmodern worship, the guiding principle must be authenticity and acceptance of ambiguity. Symbols that have been subject to restructuring or rejection within Christian postmodernism have included formal liturgy and language, ornate sanctuaries, music played by organs and sung by choirs, and other symbols not readily understood by people with no or little church background. The current trend now within Protestant postmodernism seems to be to accept some of the ancient practices of Christendom, such as crosses, icons, candles, and symbolic colors as relevant, and to place these alongside new, postmodern practices. Consequently, rock music must be allowed to "[proliferate] in an atmosphere conducive to Gregorian chant" (Harrell 1999).

The MCCA at Freedom Oaks Music Paradigm

MCCA at Freedom Oaks attempts to be an inclusive church. Its music program goals seek to honor diversity and pluralism amid a theological commitment to individual Christian identity and to maintain a safe, unified politically and so-cially affirming community church structure for all persons. Historical evidence indicates that the goals of the music program at MCCA at Freedom Oaks have varied over time, but that in recent years these goals have predominated.

I have found through archival evidence and documents such as church bul-letins, hymnals, and interviews with long-standing church members that in its early period the music program was not diversified and that the church relied on tradi-tional Protestant church music. Based on interviews with MCCA at Freedom Oaks members of the time (1989–2002), laypersons who served in volunteer roles as music directors apparently had considerable influence in defining the mu-sic program and presentations. The music program emphasized congregational singing often reflective of American church hymnology. Hymns such as "Faith of Our Fathers," "I Need Thee Every Hour," "I Love to Tell the Story," and "Tis So Sweet to Trust in Jesus" frequently were used in worship. (Metropolitan Commu-nity Church of Austin 1976, *Church Bulletins*, Metropolitan Community Church Archives). This music appears to have been integrated into a formal, liturgical form of services.

The integration of both formal liturgy services and Protestant evangelicalism appears to have caused dissatisfaction among some in the congregation. In 1978 some church members requested the church's governing board to change the na-ture of the services. The board strongly defended the right of the pastor to deter-mine all forms of church worship. This board decision was based on existing UFMCC policy that gave the pastor exclusive rights to determine service formats (Metropolitan Community Church at Austin 1978 *Newsletter*, March, Metropoli-tan Community Church at Freedom Oaks Archives). The Revelation Singers, a gospel-type singing group, appeared in 1982, perhaps reflecting a need for wider musical experiences from the congregation (Metropolitan Community Church of Austin 1982, Revelation Singers, Metropolitan Community Church at Austin Archives).

Musical taste and preferences of individuals and groups often cannot be sep-arated from worship formats that emerge. As noted, within MCCA at Freedom Oaks music has ranged from Pentecostalism and evangelism to liturgical formal-ism. This variety, together with inclusive language and some theological concepts, has caused problems within this congregation. Such conflicts have sometimes re-sulted in members leaving the church to form other types of worship communi-ties. Most of these have been evangelical or Pentecostal in style, but in 1978 and 1979 a group left MCCA at Freedom Oaks and formed a short-lived church based on the Episcopal Church order of worship (Lukenbill 1998: 450). My in-terviews with church members also indicate that music that was rejected because of content has from time-to-time caused some level of resentment, especially among performers whose selections were rejected as not falling within church policy (MCCA at Freedom Oaks Membership Interviews 1989–2002).

In the early years, the director of music was an unpaid, musically trained person who was charged with managing the music program under the general direction of the pastor. In the early 1980s, a dispute arose over the role of the music director and the primary instrumentalists (i.e., organist and pianist). The dispute centered on the claim that these musicians were professionals and should be paid for their professional services. The counterargument was that their talents were gifts from God and should be shared with the congregation as Christian ministry (MCCA at Freedom Oaks Church Membership Interviews 1989–2002). In the early 1990s, church management decided to pay a music director and an organist on a part-time basis. This arrangement continued until 1998 when a full-time minister of music was appointed (Fielding lecture and interview 2002). The position reverted back to a part-time, paid position with the resignation of the minister of music in May 2002. Active recruitment for a replacement began in the spring of 2002 with church management determined to continue the current music program in style, form, philosophy, and professional leadership.

Music, Theology, and Community

Because UFMCC does not follow a prescribed order of worship, missal, or prayer book, individual congregations within UFMCC are allowed to develop their own forms of worship. The one exception to this is that the fellowship encourages communion to be offered at all major Sunday services and church feast days. This freedom has led to differences in worship styles. Some congregations may elect to follow a Christian evangelical form while a small minority may embrace a New Age or universalistic approach. Some congregations feel more comfortable with a liturgy that is formal, suggesting Roman Catholic, Lutheran, or Anglican influences. MCCA at Freedom Oaks currently follows a worship style that is formalized and that resembles churches that practice a structured, Protestant High Church order.

Music Presentations

MCCA at Freedom Oaks music presentations are carefully planned to enhance all aspects of worship. The musical prelude that introduces all formal worship services is diversified. One Sunday the prelude may include a small group of singers who sing familiar gospel music such as the recently performed "Promised Land Medley." Another Sunday's prelude may feature a keyboardist in a classical piece such as *In Thee Is Joy* by Bach. As the service develops, the sanctuary choir generally presents a formal anthem such as "Unseen, But Not Unknown" (Palmer/Curry) or the *Ave Maria* in Latin. Special music and offertory music follow the sermon. In recent years praise music has been more widely used in these portions of the liturgy. The hymn, "The Lighthouse," is an example of such praise music. It reads in part:

> There's a lighthouse on a hillside that overlooks life's sea;
>> When I'm tossed it sends out a light that I might see.
> And I thank God for the lighthouse. I owe my life to him, for Jesus is the lighthouse and from the rocks of sin. He has shone the light around me that I could clearly see. If it wasn't for the lighthouse, where would this ship be?

Nevertheless, in keeping with diversity, traditional or classical music may also be used here. For example, the "Kyrie" from *Mass for the Angels* (arr. Jalsevac) was sung in Latin by a soloist at an 14 April 2002 service.

As the "Lighthouse" example indicates, certain aspects of praise music can challenge some of the principles of UFMCC theology. Praise music is rarely inclusive in language as written and salvation and rescue themes predominate. For example, inclusive language is not used in "The Lighthouse" above and there is an emphasis on sin and rescue that has not been typical of MCCA at Freedom Oaks services in recent years. I suggest that only a few years ago, under a different pastor, this hymn would not have been allowed.

Congregational singing accompanies distribution of communion. As communicants move forward to the altar area to receive communion, they and other members of the congregation sing a variety of hymns ranging from "Holy, Holy, Holy" to "Our God Reigns." At the conclusion of communion, the congregation stands and sings the closing communion chorus "Majesty:"

> Majesty, worship God's majesty! Unto Jesus be all glory, honor, and praise!
> Majesty, royal authority flow from the throne unto God's own; this anthem raise!

A church member who also has close ties to New Age religion speaks highly of the current music program saying that he especially appreciates the caliber of performance and variety of music presented (MCCA at Freedom Oaks Church Membership Interviews 1989–2002). Nevertheless, not all members find this diversity appealing. Some members seem to have drifted away from or even left the church influenced by the use of praise music and cultural diversity in programming (MCCA at Freedom Oaks Church Membership Interviews 1989–2002).

As an ecumenical church, MCCA at Freedom Oaks is pluralistic in its observations of religious traditions, celebrating a variety of church practices and customs. Not all UFMCC churches accept this core value. Although in its past, MCCA at Freedom Oaks has been influenced by evangelical themes, it presently is not an evangelical church. Mark Fielding, the recently resigned minister of music, who came from a Roman Catholic background, was well aware of evangelical music; and during his directorship American Protestant evangelical hymnology was well integrated into its music.

Similarly music from the Roman Catholic mass is often used and is sung in Latin. Although Mariology and the music associated with Mary are present in the music of MCCA at Freedom Oaks, it is minimized so that it does not interfere with the worship of those who are not of that tradition (Fielding 2002). The *Ave Maria* is used on special occasions such as during the Christmas season and in services when faith and belief are emphasized. For example, the *Ave Maria* was used recently with the Gospel reading from Luke 24: 17–20.

As previously discussed, inclusive language is adhered to and used in the music at MCCA at Freedom Oaks as much as possible. For example, words in music associated with patriarchy are avoided—language that refers to the "kingship of Jesus" would not be sung as written. Excluded also from use would be words that have derogatory inferences such as "dark" to equate "evil" and "white" to signify "purity" and "goodness." Similarly, military connotations in music are rarely used, such as "Onward Christian Soldiers." Musical tunes that are associated with victimized repression are not used. For example, music based on the tune *"Deutschland Uber Alles"* such as "Glorious Things of Thee Are Spoken" is avoided because of the tune's frequent association with Nazism. On the other hand, "We Shall Overcome," because of its relationship with the overthrow of oppression, is widely used in services (Fielding lecture and interview 2002).

Aside from these prohibitions, inclusive language is not allowed to interfere with the selected music. This is especially true with classical music from composers such as Bach. Another language issue arises with the use of modern translations of standard hymns that use archaic language such as "thy" for "you." The use of traditional but archaic words is maintained when a modern translation might interfere with the flow and sense of the music (Fielding lecture and interview 2002).

According to former minister of music Mark Fielding, the music program at MCCA at Freedom Oaks is built around ecumenical concepts on the idea that God helps worshippers transcend boundaries in music and worship traditions. The music program is used to facilitate and develop healthy concepts in the congregation's worship of God and not to ensure conformity. Fielding suggests, and I feel this can be debated somewhat, that the selection of music is not used to educate or to provide information about dogma or theology, but rather to affirm and to offer the congregation positive avenues to the broad array of spiritual experiences available in Christianity (Fielding 2002).

One Community and One Space, Many Pluralities

Corbitt (1998: 43) raises the question that I feel needs to be revisited here: Can a church and its music program exist as one in community, while at the same time honoring diversity in practices? This question is not new to congregations within UFMCC. What appears to be unique about MCCA at Freedom's Oaks' current approach is that it sees pluralism and diversity celebrated within one community setting and in one physical space as paramount to its mission and identity. In other words, it honors diversity and pluralism, but it hopes that diversity and pluralism can be experienced by all in one community setting and in uniform community of worship. In recent times, the church leadership has resisted creating separate services for persons who prefer one worship tradition to others. Although it does offer different services based on a timed schedule, all services are practically identical in order and music.

On the whole, this arrangement differs from that taken by some other large UFMCC congregations. For example, the Cathedral of Hope MCC in Dallas offers several different services having different formats. Sunday worship includes services that are specific to several approaches, including liturgical, contemporary, Evensong, and Taizé contemplative worship formats (Cathedral of Hope 2002).

The Sunshine Cathedral, another large UFMCC congregation located in Fort Lauderdale, Florida, also offers differentiated services. Sunday morning worship services are ritualistic services based on formal "liturgy of the earliest Christian church." The Cathedral Choir and Orchestra provide music for this service. The Sunday evening service uses contemporary and praise music performed and often led by the Rainbow Praise ensemble.

On the fourth Wednesday of each month, a Taizé service of meditation is scheduled. Music for this service is ecumenical and meditative. A chamber orchestra, cantor, and singers provide music, with congregational chants in Latin, English, and sometimes Spanish and other languages. Candles and icons are used to enhance the tranquil setting and music of the service (Sunshine Cathedral 2002).

The belief in MCCA at Freedom Oaks seems to be that church identity as a Christian community regardless of members' sexual orientation or preferences must prevail over conflicting and competing traditions of music that express religious ideas. The best approach in meeting this goal is to integrate various traditions into a uniform but holistic worship environment that preserves both the physical wholeness of church community and that also celebrates diversity and pluralism found within the church community. For this reason, separate services using different styles and forms of worship and music have been avoided in recent years (Fielding 2002). For this congregation, sexual diversity and pluralism are issues that inform the church and its culture and that are addressed in appropriate ways, but they are not the prevailing issue that defines its pluralism and diversity or its music. As Pastor Martin said to me, "You can't build a church around sex."

Music and Organizational Culture

Organizational cultural theory maintains that every organization develops a culture that embraces both material and nonmaterial items. Among others, culture includes beliefs, customs, and practices. These are patterns of basic assumptions that define a core value and behavior system. Another element of organizational culture is that these core values are so central to the life and success of the organization that they must be learned and passed on to those who enter into the system (Isaac 1993: 91–110). The organization must, therefore, develop ways that will ensure that these values are maintained. Religious organizations typically do this through theological means such as creeds, education, instructional programs, and forms of worship.

Along with all aspects of church liturgy, music plays a fundamental role in informing and reinforcing religious values. As described previously, music at MCCA at Freedom Oaks does this through its goals of ecumenicalism and pluralism. Music at MCCA at Freedom Oaks is carefully selected to emphasize certain values and to de-emphasize or ignore others. For example, inclusive language in music encourages worshippers to move away from viewing God in patriarchal terms. Words that have negative connotations in relations to race, personalities, and action are avoided. Certain symbols that are offensive to some such as blood sacrifice symbolism are avoided. Music that reminds the congregation of the vulnerability and wretchedness of their souls and bodies, and "lost souls" salvation messages are not used. Although MCAA at Freedom Oaks claims to be pluralistic and many of its members come from Roman Catholic backgrounds, the Protestant origin of UFMCC lessens the use of music in which particular theological tenets of Roman Catholicism might appear. For example, music that has strong Mariology overtones and music that venerates the saints are not used. Through careful selection and presentation, music as used in this congregation attempts to offer experiences that affirm positive Christianity (Fielding lecture and interview 2002).

Music, Information, and Social Behavior

Although MCCA at Freedom Oaks takes care not to present itself as dogmatic and rigid in theological concepts, it does have a theology, and this theology is reflected in its music programs and music presentations. Music is information, and information is generally designed and presented to change behavior and attitudes.

The music program serves church objectives in that it promotes and develops in the congregation both a sense of church identity and spiritual awareness. Consequently, the music at MCCA at Freedom Oaks cannot be separated from the overall structure of the church. The music reflects a variety of issues and concerns, and historically it has changed and evolved to meet varying circumstances. Recent emphasis has been placed on music of social liberation and pride, music of diversity and pluralism and music that meets and affirms what is seen as the positive spiritual aspects of Christian worship. The presentation of music is likewise educational and informational in that it must help persons who come to the church with or without a church tradition to understand the role of MCCA at Freedom Oaks, and it helps integrate and socialize all into the church community (Fielding 2002). Although the music may not contain strong elements of Christian dogma, it nevertheless presents an educational and informational message of acceptance and affirmation that is planned with care to be heard, internalized, and acted on by the congregation.

Conclusion

The music at MCCA at Freedom Oaks gives evidence of promoting social, political, psychological, and spiritual development, based on a perceived value system of diversity, pluralism, positive spirituality, social justice, and acceptance of one's sexuality. Through its various programs, including its music ministry, the church offers a structured approach whereby individuals are encouraged to listen, observe, participate, question, and debate ideas of what it means to be Christian within a diverse and pluralistic community. The uniting factor and the music that supports this are Christian identity, spiritual development, and growth, and acceptance for those who have experienced rejection and condemnation because of sexual orientation or even those who have been rejected because of their support or acceptance of diversity in sexual orientation. The challenge to this congregation is to protect its vision of Christian plurality and diversity within its present uniform, worshiping community.

"St. Gerard Teaches Him That Love Cancels That Out"
Devotion to St. Gerard Maiella among Italian American Catholic Gay Men in Newark, New Jersey[1]

11

PETER SAVASTANO

THIS ESSAY EXPLORES THE DIFFERENT WAYS that Italian American Catholic gay men who are devoted to St. Gerard Maiella in the greater Newark, New Jersey, area use the iconography, symbols, and hagiography associated with the saint to make a place for themselves in a church that both marginalizes and disenfranchises them unless they comply with its teachings on homosexuality. In most cases, though not all, they use their devotion to the saint to resist the Roman Catholic Church's teachings that homosexual activity is "intrinsically disordered."[2] These findings are based upon approximately five years of ethnographic research among devotees of St. Gerard Maiella of varying stripes, in and around the city of Newark, New Jersey. Devotion to St. Gerard was the subject of my doctoral dissertation entitled "'Will the Real St. Gerard Please Stand Up?' An Ethnographic Study of Symbolic Polysemy, Devotional Practices, Material Culture, Marginality and Difference in the Cult of St. Gerard Maiella" (Savastano 2002).

The National Shrine of St. Gerard Maiella is located at St. Lucy's Roman Catholic Church in Newark. Devotion to St. Gerard Maiella in and around Newark is more than one hundred years old. Although the National Shrine of St. Gerard is located at St. Lucy's Church, I did not restrict my ethnographic research to the National Shrine. Along with conducting life history interviews and holding personal conversations with devotees of the saint who do attend St. Lucy's Roman Catholic Church on a regular basis, I did the same with devotees of the saint who only go to the National Shrine of St. Gerard once a year for the October procession and *festa* that honors the saint, as well as among those devotees who very rarely or never go to the National Shrine at St. Lucy's.

A Brief History of the Devotion

Among the waves of southern Italian immigrants who came to the United States during the great migration of 1880 to 1924 (Churchill 1975: 18–27) were those from the small villages and towns of *Regione di Avellino* (Avellino province) that lie in close proximity to the city of Naples, the largest city in the province. Upon arrival in the United States, a large number of these *Avellinese* settled in what was to quickly become the Little Italy section of Newark, New Jersey, a section later to be known as the old First Ward. These southern Italian immigrants brought with them their devotion to the various Madonnas and saints who were the patrons of their native villages and towns. Among them was one holy personage, Gerardo Maiella. While not himself born in Avellino province, Gerardo Maiella (born 1726 in the town of Muro Lucano in the *Regione di Potenza*) lived most of his earthly life in and around the cities, towns, and villages of Avellino, most especially in the small town of Caposele, where this Redemptorist lay brother died at the monastery of *Materdomini* from tuberculosis in 1755 at the age of twenty-nine.

Brother Gerard was not yet canonized a saint of the Roman Catholic Church at the time when these first southern Italian immigrants began to arrive in Newark to settle in the old First Ward, nevertheless in the minds and hearts of many of them, Brother Gerard already enjoyed the reputation as a great wonderworker and holy person. Eventually, Brother Gerard Maiella was beatified by Pope Leo XIII on 29 January 1893, and subsequently canonized a saint on 11 December 1904 by Pope Pius X (Savastano 2002: 8).

Devotion to St. Gerard Maiella was first observed in a formal way in Newark in 1899, although there is evidence suggesting that devotion to him was informally observed as early as 1887 (Immerso 1997: 88). Since that time an annual procession and *festa* honoring St. Gerard Maiella, surrounding his feast day of October 16, has been observed at his National Shrine at St. Lucy's Church in Newark by generations of southern Italians whose ancestors emigrated to Newark's Little Italy during the great migration of 1880 to 1924. My own family is among these immigrants, as it is among the devotees of St. Gerard. Because of my maternal great-grandmother's successful appeal to St. Gerard Maiella's wonder-working powers on behalf of my mother, who was born in Newark in 1924 with a life-threatening illness, my family has kept a vow to St. Gerard in some form for four generations.

As is inevitably the case in most ethnic communities and religious traditions, albeit vehemently denied by some, among the succeeding generations of southern Italian Catholic immigrants who settled in the old First Ward of Newark, some of their descendants are homosexual or, in contemporary parlance, "gay," even though the label "gay" is an uncomfortable fit with how some of these men understand the nature and expression of their sexual desire.[3] What I recount below is the various ways that the gay male devotees of St. Gerard have performed a "queer" reading of the saint's iconography and life, changing both their own lives and the saint's by what I have termed "processual hagiography." Thus, these Italian American Catholic gay men write themselves into the script of the saint's life and locate themselves in the devotional economy of the cult[4] of St. Gerard Maiella in such a way that both resists the Catholic Church's teachings that homosexual practice is "intrinsically disordered" and uses their devotion to the saint to transcend the limits of the institutional church. In this regard they make the distinction between "church" and "religion" that Robert A. Orsi notes in *The Madonna of 115th Street* (Orsi 1985: xvii, 57).[5]

Who is St. Gerard Maiella?

For the official Roman Catholic Church, St. Gerard Maiella is the eighteenth-century Redemptorist lay brother born on 6 April 1726 in the town of Muro Lucano, in the region of Campania, province of Potenza, in southern Italy. According to the church, St. Gerard lived an exemplary life of holiness and asceticism. He performed countless works of Christian charity. As the hagiographies written about him attest, the Redemptorist lay brother Gerard Maiella embodied the orthodox teachings of the church. He strictly adhered to all the tenets formulated in the Nicene Creed. He defended, lived by, and sought to promulgate the church's authority as the representative of Christ on earth. He lived in total obedience to the official church's authority in Rome and in the same total obedience to his immediate religious superiors in the Congregation of the Most Holy Redeemer (the Redemptorists).

Gerard Maiella met all of the requirements for sainthood: heroic virtue, orthodoxy, and the necessary postmortem miracles that prove that he is in Heaven with God and could be heard by the faithful who called upon him for assistance. As if this was not enough, all the hagiographies recount the many supernatural signs he exhibited and the miracles he performed during his earthly life. These include visions and mystical raptures, the ability to levitate and bilocate, the capacity to read people's hearts and minds, clairaudience and clairvoyance, the multiplication of substances, and the ability to control the natural elements. Gerard also performed countless miraculous healings.

The institutional church claims St. Gerard, even if unofficially, as the patron saint of mothers and childbirth, with a particular focus on the difficulties of conception, infertility, and now, more than ever, as the patron saint against the forces of antilife (abortion). My hypothesis is that these are very recent assignations. If the hagiographical (sacred biographies) and historical literature I have consulted are correct, then not all of his devotees have called upon him for these reasons nor was this his domain until the mid-twentieth century (Tannoia 1849; Priest 1893; Saint-Omer 1907; Carr 1946; Cevetello 1979; Massa 1999). My research suggests that for divorced Catholics, for those who use birth control, for gay and lesbian Catholics, he is a sympathetic friend. For the many of these latter, St. Gerard is an illuminated being who, like St. Francis of Assisi, no longer belongs to the institutional church alone but to whomever appeals to him regardless of doctrinal orthodoxy, religious tradition, ethnicity, or sexual orientation. Additionally, whereas St. Gerard is associated with the fertility of biological reproduction and the traditional patriarchal family for his heterosexual devotees, for some of his gay male devotees St. Gerard is associated with fecundity—the fecundity of romantic and sexual relationships with all of the emotional, spiritual, and physical fulfillment such relationships can bring—and with a new and creative configuration of family that extends beyond the traditional patriarchal family structure that is so much a part of Italian/Mediterranean culture.

Images of St. Gerard in the Lives of Catholic Gay Men

In what ways have Catholic gay men created points of confluence between their own lives and that of St. Gerard, the latter being drawn from hagiographies, oral tradition, and images of the saint? To what degree have these gay men speculated about St. Gerard's sexuality? When it comes to the saint's sexual practices we will never know for certain whether he was heterosexual or homosexual. We can only speculate. Yet, what McGuire states for Aelred of Rievaulx in *Brother and Lover: Aelred of Rievaulx* is also true for St. Gerard: "It is not so easy to transfer Aelred from his own day directly into the questions of our time" (1994: 150). Yet, I am interested in the use of the creative imagination and desire by St. Gerard's gay male devotees, as a way to create a place for themselves in a script that, according to the institutional church, has no role for them to play. I am interested in how, based on their lives as Catholic gay men, they have developed a theology that reflects their own experiences (Gramick 1992b: 190).

Given the conservative atmosphere at St. Lucy's, whatever theologizing has been done by St. Gerard's gay male devotees there has been done despite the local clergy and the wider community of devotees. In fact, gay men themselves have not always communicated with or supported each other in this process. Some of the gay men I have spoken with find it offensive that other gay men speculate on St. Gerard's sexuality. Emilio, a forty-three-year-old devotee of the saint, and Gerard, an eighty-four-year-old devotee, both feel this way.[6]

I asked Emilio about other gay men speculating that St. Gerard was himself gay. "I never heard that!" he said. Later he confessed that perhaps he had. He recounted that his friend Madonna, a heterosexual devotee of the saint, had a picture of the statue of St. Gerard in the shrine at St. Lucy's. When she showed the picture to a gay male friend he responded that the statue "looked like a mannequin or that he was dressed in drag." This offended Emilio greatly, who retorted, "He is not a mannequin, he is our saint!" Yet he did this only after he had put his own imagination in check. He remembers thinking, "Does he?" But then, he told himself to "dispel that thought from your mind!"[7]

Gerard gave me his opinion without my having to ask for it. "And by the way, don't think that St. Gerard was gay, because he wasn't!" He noted that some of "these queens who are real nasty" will say of the saint, "Oh he was a queen," but Gerard insists that regardless of what they may say, "He wasn't." Gerard thinks that the blame for this speculation about St. Gerard's sexuality lies with the images of the saint and not with any events in the saint's life. Referring to the picture of the saint he himself owns, he said that people might think St. Gerard was gay from looking at that picture, because the saint has "red lips."[8] This line of thinking plays upon stereotypes of the male homosexual as gender-bending and effeminate.

Another gay male devotee, Giorgio, who is thirty-years-old, speculates about St. Gerard's homoeroticism. Yet his speculations also emerge from stereotypes that gay men are feminine, exotic, and emotionally effusive. When Giorgio first saw the statue of St. Gerard at St. Lucy's he claims that "to me he looked very gay. So I was struck by that. I was interested in that." Pressing him for a fuller explanation all he could say was that he "looked very gay." It's "the pose that he's struck in. It's interesting, like a gay saint."[9] These comments can be easily misconstrued as the blasphemous utterances of "nasty queens," as Gerard defines it. It's possible, however, that there is another process at work here.

The Roman Catholic Church cultivates silence on the presence of homosexuality in the church, while it simultaneously utilizes certain categories for talking about homosexuality such as "unnatural," "objectively disordered," or "a threat to the family" (Jordan 2000: 50). Yet, Catholic gay men find ways to give meaning to their faith. Some do so by fixing on an idea or an image with which they can identify in order to navigate their way within the church's borders, however close to its margins they may be positioned. The media pundit Andrew Sullivan, a gay Catholic himself, writes of his own experience of groping in the dark to find ways to connect his homosexuality to his Catholicism.

With regard to homosexuality, I inherited no moral or religious teaching that could guide me to success or failure. In my adolescence and young adulthood, the teaching of the Church was merely silence, an increasingly hollow denial even of the existence of homosexuals (quoted in Jordan 2000: 51).

In this essay I have mapped some of the ways that St. Gerard's gay male devotees have used the saint as a symbol with which to navigate the rough waters of being both gay and Catholic. Images have the power to stimulate the creative imagination, arouse the emotions, and inflame sexual desire. Along with the hagiographical narratives of saints, images play a very important role in the creative process by which Catholics make contact with Jesus, the Madonna, and the saints.

Even though there are events in St. Gerard's life with which gay men can easily identify, for many of them an encounter with a picture or the statue of the saint is a primary means by which they forge an emotional bond with him. Through this connection they set out upon uncharted waters in search of a meaningful relationship between their homosexuality and their religious faith. They enlist the saint as an ally in this process. In *Material Christianity*, Colleen McDannell notes that devotional pictures and sculptures connect the human and the divine because they evoke a range of powerful emotions in the viewer (1995: 25).

The style in which the statue of St. Gerard located in St. Lucy's Church is sculpted and painted is well suited to the process McDannell describes. The statue is ornate and warm, exotic and erotic, romantic and sentimental. St. Gerard has a certain androgynous quality, too, which suggests a masculinity touched by a femininity that is incongruent with the hyperbolized masculinity of Italian culture.

When I asked Giorgio to try and put his finger on what he thought attracted gay men to St. Gerard, he told me "it's the connection to femininity," a quality he attributed to the saint as a result of his encounters with the statue at St. Lucy's and the painting of St. Gerard he saw at Gerard's house.[10] Hearing once again in Giorgio's remark the invocation of the stereotype that gay men are effeminate, I challenged him to explain what he means. "Yeah, but um, well gay men are more in touch with femininity. I don't mean like a flamboyant femininity, just a femininity in general," was what he offered in response.[11] Giorgio and I went together to see Gerard's private altar to the saint. Seeing the painting of the saint with the "red lips" already mentioned by Gerard, Giorgio exclaimed, "God, he looks so gay." A similar comment was offered without solicitation by Giorgio's lover Pat, who, when he saw the photographs Giorgio had taken of the statue of the saint for the first time said, "Wow, he really looks gay, doesn't he?"

The saint's image is a ready visual source for an imagination sensitive to the issues of sexual orientation. In short, it is an object for the projection of gay men's desires and affections. Here I take my cue from McGuire who suggests the possibility for a reading of Aelred of Rievaulx as transforming his homoerotic desires into "agapetic love" by transferring his homosexual desires to the body of Jesus (1994: 142, 148).

In 1996, when I first interviewed Donato about gay male devotion to St. Gerard, we talked about the image of the saint and what he thinks it arouses in gay men. Here the stereotype of the gay man as youth-obsessed and in hot pursuit of young men came into play, as did the notion that homosexual desire is sado-masochistic and that gay men are self-hating and tortured about their sexual desires.

> First of all . . . if anyone has done any reading or has just explored the life of St. Gerard, they'll see that it's very possible that the homoerotic imagery that one sees in St. Sebastian is also quite stunning and vivid and real in St. Gerard's life. The other reason that I feel that St. Gerard is very popular to gay Italian men is the idolization of youth. St. Gerard died at a very young age. And [he] appears in all of his imagery as an unspoiled, virginal young man, whose only life's desire was his own suffering and agony for Christ, to emulate Christ's suffering and dying on the cross.

There are, in fact, historical reasons based on his image for reading femininity or homosexuality into the life of St. Gerard. These have more to do with the particular style in which the images were created than whether or not St. Gerard was actually effeminate or homosexual. McDannell writes that "Catholic images have an exotic and erotic quality" (1995: 61), and she suggests that when they have been "freed from their ideological context" (p. 63) they become the source for creative imagination and emotional expression. The church, she tells her readers, is very much aware of this. McDannell traces a movement in the Catholic Church, which, as early as 1958, sought to counter this potential by "defeminizing" Catholic art, art that had become too realistic and thus aroused the body and the emotions, all of which were associated with women (1995: 178). According to church reformers good art assists in the masculine drive toward transcendence whereas bad art distracts the devotee from focusing on what was most important in the churches, "the sacrifice of the mass" (1995: 174, 178). Likewise, David Freedberg in *The Power of Images* notes the power of saintly images to arouse devotees sexually (1989: 332).

Another point needs to be stressed. At the local level, gay male devotion to saints is not limited to St. Gerard. Gerard is quick to point out that devotion to the saints among Italian Catholic gay men is evident in other areas of New Jersey where *feste* and processions in other saints' honor are also observed. In July, there is the Feast of Our Lady of Mt. Carmel in Jersey City. "There's a lot of gay people there who are devoted to Our Lady of Mt. Carmel," Gerard claims. In August, he adds, "there's a lot of gay people that go to Mt. Carmel [Church] in

Montclair [for] St. Sebastian. There's a lot of queens there. . . . It's with all the saints," he said. "It's with all the saints."[12] Likewise, Emilio recently reported to me that there were a large number of gay men present at the Feast of St. Anthony of Padua held each year in June, in the nearby town of Belleville, New Jersey.

Giorgio made a similar point. In July 2001 he attended the *Giglio Festa*[13] in honor of St. Paulinus of Nola and Our Lady of Mt. Carmel at the Shrine Church of Our Lady of Mt. Carmel in the Williamsburg section of Brooklyn. Giorgio reported that it was only a matter of minutes before he met groups of gay men, many of whom were devoted to St. Paulinus of Nola and the Madonna del Carmine. He also met a number of priests who, according to him, were fully cognizant of the gay presence at the *Giglio Festa* and were quite open and accepting. One of the priests even invited him to come back next year. He offered to let Giorgio go up to the roof of the church in order to take wide-angle pictures of the *festa*.[14]

Given what the teachings of the Roman Catholic Church are about homosexuality, each of these gay men must inevitably find ways to deal with their homosexuality in relation to their religious, ethnic, and gender identities, as well as their devotion to the saints. More often than not, they do so creatively in spite of the church's adverse teachings. What Gramick writes in relation to other gay and lesbian Catholics applies to some of these men as well. They have come to understand that they can be fully Catholic and still dissent from "non-infallible teaching," and that because of their marginalization and disenfranchisement from the institutional church they have matured to a point where they can make their own decisions, take responsibility for them, and also accept accountability for the moral decisions in their lives (1995b: 171).

The Hagiographies of St. Gerard and Gay Men's Lives

Some of St. Gerard's gay male devotees place the hagiographical accounts of St. Gerard's life within the context of their own lives.[15] Idiosyncratic versions of St. Gerard's life must be interpreted from the marginalized social position of his Catholic gay male devotees. I do not mean the life of St. Gerard should be rewritten, casting him as homosexual in the way that Derek Jarman did in *Sebastiane*, his gay porno rendition of the life and martyrdom of St. Sebastian. Rather I point to a contextual reading based upon "specific cultural competencies as a result of their particular social location," as Janice Radway describes it (cited in Sinfield [1998: 99]). Bearing Radway in mind, what I want to explore is how some of St. Gerard's gay male devotees "read" the events of the saint's life as if they were events in their own lives and thus find in St. Gerard a being to whom they can relate as gay men.

In some instances the idiosyncratic version of the saint's life incorporates elements that go against the grain of orthodox teachings of the church. Such is the case for one man, Carlo, a forty-nine-year-old devotee, who describes himself as a Tibetan Buddhist by choice, but a Roman Catholic by birth. For him St. Gerard is purely an historical higher being, a bodhisattva. He relates to St. Gerard in the same way he does to the tantric deities of Tibetan Buddhism. For him St. Gerard is a symbol of his own Buddha or Christ nature and meditation upon the image and prayer to St. Gerard is a way of accessing the energy the symbol signifies. Carlo explained his relationship to the Roman Catholic saints: "Being brought up an Italian Roman Catholic, the first images I can remember are saints. And for some reason in my childhood I was really attracted to them. . . . So, just the look on a saint's face is worth a thousand words, let's say."

Carlo describes his religious practice as one that "shape-shifts, for my needs . . . at times." He understands his relationship to Catholicism and to St. Gerard as fundamental to his identity and way of life, but he does not describe the saints as historical personages. Rather he refers to them as energies by which he can access memories or arouse different spiritual states of being.

> I still have that once-an-Italian-Catholic boy, always-an-Italian-Catholic boy in my head. So I use the images for myself. And because of that childhood attraction, I guess it brings me back to that feeling of being in a warm safe space. I just remember church being a warm safe place as a child. Kind of awe inspiring.

Yet, Carlo's relationship to St. Gerard, and to all the saints, is quite personal. It is not mediated by the institutional church. For him saints have transcended the control and limits of any institution, and the constraints of orthodoxy. As he describes it, "it's kind of almost extremely personal, because they are saints and they can be extremely personal for everybody. And at the same time they're beyond extremely personal and they're somewhere in this like large universal kind of energy realm. . . ."

I interviewed Carlo in November 1999. At the time he described himself as "doing a lot with St. Gerard." It was shortly after the centennial celebration of the devotion to St. Gerard in October 1999. I had been with Carlo at the annual procession where I spent some time walking and talking with him. Later, during our interview, he elaborated upon what he means by "doing a lot" with St. Gerard. He made use of printed prayers and novenas to the saint to learn about the saint's life and function.

> Lately I've been doing a lot with St. Gerard, as you know. Only because I'm looking for a new vocation in my life. And for some reason in his prayers and in the litany of St. Gerard there's a thing where it says . . . in his history [that] he would

help people find their right vocation. And since that's what I'm looking for, I fig-
ured well, maybe this energy will help me find it.

In Carlo's idiosyncratic version of the myth of St. Gerard, the saint has been transformed into a Tibetan Buddhist meditational deity or bodhisattva who is the per-
sonification of a particular kind of universal energy. This means Carlo chooses to
make sense out of the diverse religious symbols he employs in his devotional practices, practices drawn from various religious traditions, rooted in his sense that he
is disenfranchised as a gay man in most of the world's religious traditions. This is
the motivation for creating his own religion.

> This is something I've been doing since childhood. And it always used to freak my
> parents out too. I mean I always used to have different religious symbols around.
> For me it makes sense because somewhere I have this feeling that everybody
> [thinks] there is the one path. I don't believe that. There's numerous paths to the
> same source. And maybe it's because, in certain ways I feel disenfranchised from
> orthodox religious traditions. I mean there are certain religious traditions that
> have no standing in my life. . . . But for me, I guess . . . instead of following any
> religion I've kind of created my own, I think. To fit my life, and maybe that's not
> right in other peoples' eyes, but for me it's perfectly okay.

For Carlo there is a direct link between his homosexuality and the spirituality he
has tried to foster in his devotional life.

> I really connect with sex as a connection with the infinite and the finite at the same
> time. I mean none of the sex I have is procreative. But that procreative sex just
> leads to death. It begins life, but it also ends in death. And so it kind of brings in
> the transitory nature of all things. I mean sex is a transitory thing. Like death is a
> transitory thing. And all of life. So I guess it can be used because of the ecstasy
> one experiences in sex and orgasm and I feel it can be used in my spiritual growth.

In Carlo's shrine to St. Gerard the images of the saint are surrounded by skulls,
one of the elements of the saint's iconography, a feature of the saint's ascetic practices, and a reminder of the transitory nature of earthly life. Meditation on skulls
was also an important element of Catholic devotion until Vatican II; it has since
gone out of fashion.[16] Carlo's understanding of St. Gerard is an example of an
idiosyncratic myth in which the saint is made to fit with a Tibetan Buddhist
worldview. Even more to the point, Carlo's devotion to St. Gerard and his interpretation of the saint's life is a radical departure from the other readings by his
gay male devotees.

Only four gay males—Dominic, Giorgio, Donato, and Carlo—have been
willing to share their thoughts with me on the saint's life and sexuality. Others

either avoided answering or denied having ever given any thought to the matter. I asked Emilio about his thoughts on how, as a gay man, he related to the life of St. Gerard and what he thought about the saint's sexuality. His response was, "It never entered my mind. I never looked at him that way period,"[17] even though, at the 2000 changing of St. Gerard's clothes, he entered a public debate on the matter with Mario, recounted in chapter 2 of my dissertation (Savastano 2002: 87–111).

Similarly, when I asked the same of Gerard he quickly went from the specific person of St. Gerard to the category of saints in the abstract. For him the saints' lives are what he called "exemplary lives." Gerard's reason for why there is gay interest in saint's lives is because "they want to live the same way" as the saints, or at least "they are going to try." What is it, I pressed further, about the saints that they want to imitate? His response: "Their sanctity."[18]

Growing up, I exercised my own creative imagination a fair bit in relation to my sexuality and St. Gerard.[19] My thoughts were tamed by my fear that to imagine too much would bring down the saint's wrath upon me. In this respect I probably was not very different from Emilio. I exercised this creative imagination in my late teens and early twenties, as I was exposed more and more to gay culture and to the gay liberation movement. My own point of entry into the imaginative exercise was not unlike Dominic's, a sixty-two-year-old devotee of the saint. Reading the events of the saint's life through the lens of our sexuality, we both latched onto the fact that as a young man St. Gerard exhibited a desire to enter religious life[20] and eventually did.

This was an important point of identification for many Catholic gay men in a way that does not carry the same meaning for our straight counterparts. It is certainly true that at one point or another most young Catholic men express desire to become a priest or a monk, yet with the onset of puberty heterosexual males replace that desire more easily with a desire to marry. This is a legitimate alternative for them to live out good Catholic lives. It is, however, an alternative not available to Catholic gay men, unless they deceive themselves and the women they marry. For gay men who are Catholic, the priesthood or religious life is a viable alternative to conspicuous bachelorhood. This is especially true for those gay men who were adolescents prior to Vatican II or during the first years of reform that it brought and, thus, before the rise of the gay liberation movement in 1969.

Even now in 2001, the priesthood or religious life offers a legitimate alternative to marriage for Catholic gay men. Priesthood or religious life deflects the unwanted inquiries by family members as to "when are you going to meet a woman and get married?" an already suspicious question. Yet, in all fairness, I remember too that the decision to enter the priesthood or religious life was no absolute protection against the same kind of suspicion. In the Italian community there is still the folk belief that if you become a priest it is because you are homosexual and you are doing it primarily to save face.[21]

While reading about the zeal with which St. Gerard as a young man sought to enter religious life, I can clearly remember seeing myself in him. Dominic also found himself in St. Gerard for similar reasons. Describing his own process in considering the priesthood and religious life, he recalls "I think we go into it . . . because we don't know what else to do with our lives. Especially in our time, we weren't as accepted as we are today. So you look for a lifestyle . . . [where] questions won't be asked." Dominic easily makes the transition from his own experience to the life of St. Gerard.

> So I think many of us tend to go into that lifestyle because of that [homosexuality]. Now let's go to St. Gerard. . . . Was he? Reading some of the things about him, very possible. . . . I think he realized that was his only way to live, to become a religious. There's no way I think he could have survived life as a tailor. And again, we have no proof.

Continuing to exercise his creative imagination and using St. Gerard's life as the means to do so, Dominic reads his own life's path through that of St. Gerard's rather than actually making claims about St. Gerard's sexuality. Dominic uses important decisions in the saint's life to frame the important decisions in his own, even if in the long run the decisions St. Gerard made were different from those Dominic would eventually make. This is especially true when it comes to the issue of celibacy.

Dominic made it very clear to me that he has a problem with priests and religious, straight or gay, who do not live according to the vow of celibacy the church requires of them. McGuire (1994; 1994a) and Russell (1982) claim for Aelred of Rievaulx that, "if a certain erotic preference rather than performance of specific acts makes a person gay then, despite the chaste life he led as a monk, Aelred was assuredly gay" (Russell 1982: 51). And, Dominic makes a similar claim for St. Gerard.

> It's like, you know, he lived the rule of the order. . . . I always get the feeling that homosexuality and the gay lifestyle of those days wasn't lived [except] maybe in the big cities. What about just in a farm town, in Italy? What kind of life . . . if he did have attractions to men; what kind of life could he have had? He couldn't!

Dominic speculates about the saint's homosexuality, remembering how difficult it was to make sense out of his own emerging sexual feelings as a young man, feelings and desires for which he at first had no label. Musing about the saint's sexual desires, Dominic suggests that perhaps similarly "he didn't even know what his feelings were."

In my late twenties I was equally fascinated with the homoerotic elements of Catholic imagery and with how the saints were represented visually in sculpture and paintings. My attempt to reconcile what I knew of gay male culture with my Catholic heritage was worked out to some degree in my creative imaginings about St. Gerard. In *Decadence and Catholicism* (1997) Hanson discusses a similar process at work in the lives of many of the "decadent," romantic poets of the nineteenth century.

Inspired by the image of St. Sebastian, "the pincushion of homoerotic art," as Hanson names the Roman soldier saint, he includes in his discussion of the homoerotic in Catholic art and hagiography verses from a poem written by the Catholic homosexual poet Frederick Rolfe. Rolfe sought to make sense out of his own homoerotic desires by directing them toward the semi-naked figure of St. Sebastian (Hanson 1997: 339).

Similarly, somewhere around 1979 I can remember going to St. Lucy's during the annual *festa* and procession of St. Gerard, after many years of not attending. It was early in the morning and I was alone. Standing before the statue of St. Gerard, I exercised my own creative response to the homoerotic elements of Catholic art that I saw in the image of the saint. Dressed in blue jeans, flannel shirt, and work boots—the standard uniform of the gay men of my generation—I remember looking at the short hair on the statue of St. Gerard, which looked very much like mine, and thinking to myself that if he had on the same clothes that I did, he would look like many of my gay contemporaries, in fact he would look like me. In retrospect, I realize that what I was trying to do was to read my own life through St. Gerard's to create an idiosyncratic version of the myth of St. Gerard, to recast him as a gay clone. It was a transparent attempt to bring together my newly acquired enculturation as a gay man and my older Roman Catholic heritage.

I remember many points of identification in the hagiographies. They made it possible for me to feel that St. Gerard is empathetic and sympathetic to my life circumstances as a gay man. And yes, I too wondered if he might have had homosexual feelings, even though I know that if he did he might not have identified them as such. The languages of late twentieth-century psychology and gay and lesbian liberation would not have been used to put a name on his desires.

I identified most strongly with the childhood events of the saint's life. I saw myself through him. I particularly identified with the saint's religiosity, recalling that it was my own unexplained religiosity that aroused my parent's suspicion that something was "wrong" with me. Oddly, it was my religiosity that also became my refuge in moments of great fear and anxiety as I struggled to accept what it meant to be a sexual outcast. That is what I felt like and what troubled me most about being gay. I feared what others would think of me, and more important, what they would do.

Writing of the saint's early childhood years the Rev. Joseph Cevetello notes that:

> In reading of the saints we find their early years often enough not unlike those of most people. This cannot be written of Gerard. He was spiritually precocious from his earliest years; even the ordinary games and toys of children held no allurement for him. His mind and heart gravitated toward God and the supernatural. . . . He would set up a miniature altar and decorate it with statues and flowers (1979: 3).

The few times that, as a child, my parents brought me to mass, I remember being fascinated by the images of the saints and the Madonnas. As a young child who was very much aware of his homosexual feelings, although I did not yet have a label to put on them, I remember seeing the rituals, the vestments, and the paraphernalia of the church, and being transfixed by their power and their beauty. As I watched the priest and glanced around at all the images of the saints, particularly the male saints, I saw without the words to describe it, that they represented for me an alternative model of masculinity. Here was another way of being a man, one in which I might be able to conform, a model in sharp contrast to the harsh masculinity I experienced on the streets of the predominantly Italian neighborhoods of Newark.

What St. Gerard and I had in common, it seemed to me, even if it was not a homosexual orientation, was our differentness, our marginality, our profound sense of the sacred and our total absorption in it. In later years I compared my story with other Italian Catholic gay men, who recounted their own childhood stories of a heart that gravitated toward God and the supernatural. Cevetello uses these same words to describe St. Gerard's childhood. Like so many of us gay men who grew up Catholic, we paid dearly for our difference and our marginality. Later, I was to discover that St. Gerard did too, in his own childhood and young adult years.

Saint-Omer tells us that around the age of ten (1907: 15) (while Carr says it was at twelve [1946: 35]) St. Gerard's father died and financial difficulties forced his mother Benedetta to place the young Gerard as an apprentice to a tailor named Panutto (Saint-Omer 1907: 15). It was at this point that the young Gerard began to suffer abuse at the hands of the foreman who hated him for his gentleness and spirituality. The foreman beat the young saint many times, and mocked him continuously. The young saint would also suffer at the hands of the local toughs who made a target of him because of his sensitivity. As an Italian Catholic gay man I, too, had my stories to tell of having to contend with the neighborhood bullies. The other gay men with whom I exchanged stories over the years also recognized the bullies.

Having lost my father—who died when I was seven—we quickly went from being a middle class family to being a poor one. At the same time, I became the target of violence for the older and tougher boys in the neighborhood. They beat me up and ridiculed me. There is no way of knowing whether St. Gerard was called a "sissy" or a "girl," but the verbal and physical abuse he experienced in his late teens in the streets of Muro Lucano was more than enough for me to read into the saint's life experiences of my own.

> Many . . . set Gerard down as a fool. Some of these were unthinking youths, oth-ers were such as read into a tailor's holy life a condemnation of their own . . . And so jeers and stinging names followed him freely in the street. Some went further and drove home their abuse with blows. The bludgeoning again! The poor lad should be used to it by now (Carr 1946: 61).

St. Gerard's ascetic practices and his attempts to subdue his desires have also pro-vided the means through which some of his gay male devotees see their own strug-gles with their desires, religious and social. All of the hagiographies in print devote considerable time to the saint's ascetic regimen. A glance at any of the pictures of him reveals a young man made frail from fasting. Usually, placed on the table be-fore him, next to the skull and the lilies upon which he meditated is a flagellum, a whip. He used it to mortify his flesh on a regular basis.[22] This was a practice the saint engaged in from early childhood. "His sisters have told us," writes Tannoia, "that from the time he was nine years of age he used to discipline himself several times a day, especially after Holy Communion, with knotted cords, which he had tied together. Such was the childhood of Gerard Majella" (1849: 244).[23]

The hagiographies actually allude to the saint's heterosexuality. Specifically, they mention the paternity case in 1754, when St. Gerard was falsely accused by Neria Caggiano of Lacedonia of fathering a child with Nicoletta Cappucci, the young daughter of a family the saint had befriended (Carr 1946; 193). When questioned by his superiors, in particular St. Alphonsus Liguori, the founder of the Redemptorists, the saint offered no defense against the charges. To do other-wise would have violated the vow the saint had taken to neither deny any charges brought against him nor challenge his superiors in any way. His heterosexuality is also alluded to in the story of Dona Emmanuelle's daughters. In the story the saint thanks the woman for being mindful of his "great weakness" for women (Tannoia 1849: 328).[24]

Dominic's thinking on these incidents in the saint's life puts a different spin on them. "He was accused of being with a girl, and he was silenced and sent to Nocera for so many months, [that] makes you say, 'Well, gee, he was undoubtedly straight, but what did he think of himself...? Maybe because he had homosexual tendencies he felt he wasn't worthy even to become a priest, [or to] become a brother."

What function could meditating upon St. Gerard's ascetic practices hold for a Catholic gay man? Along what lines might his creative imagination travel, and how far must it go until he can locate himself in the saint's life? Here, Dominic's imagination travels not too far from the institutional church's view. He suggested that homosexuality is something that can be overcome or that must be sublimated through mortification of the flesh. Yet Dominic goes too far when it comes to suggesting that this might be one reason why St. Gerard practiced the mortifications that he did. "Maybe that's why he whipped himself. Because he was trying to drive this demon from his body. I mean they talk about him whipping himself. Let's go into that." Elaborating more upon the possible meaning of the saint's ascetic practices, Dominic reinscribes them along homoerotic lines.

> Now throughout history, with the saints and with the disciplines, the main reason for that was because of impure thoughts. It wasn't because you have doubted your faith in the Trinity, or in the Eucharist. That was not a religious temptation. It was done because of impure thoughts. What impure thoughts [did] he have? It could have been something so minor. We don't know. But he did it to the point where he bled . . . He hired people to do this to him, because of these impure thoughts. . . . I think that the only thing in his life that I can really say to make you really think about it [is] "Gee, what was it all about?" What was his problems? And unfortunately, I wish I knew.

More than Dominic, Donato allows his imagination to travel to places where few others have dared to go in thinking about the meaning of the saint's life in the context of some contemporary gay men's lives. Donato meditates upon St. Gerard's life, placing his ascetic practices within the context of tensions between spirituality and sexuality, pleasure and pain, personal pathology and redemption. He does not do this to recreate St. Gerard as the patron saint of sadomasochism, as Emilio does with St. Sebastian. Rather, Donato's point is that for him religion and sexuality, pain and pleasure, pathology and spiritual growth are not so easily separated out, nor is anyone exempt from having to battle with the shadow aspect of themselves, not even St. Gerard. Hagiography is often a site where such battles can be glimpsed. Hanson notes that the lives of the saints have long been fertile ground for Catholic homosexual men, ground for staging the battle between personal pathology and redemption and sexuality and spirituality (1997: 336).

Traveling along a similar route, Donato interrogates St. Gerard's practice of enlisting the service of young men to assist him in his mortifications, suggesting as Mark D. Jordan does in *The Silence of Sodom* that perhaps there is in this particular ascetic practice of the saint something to be learned about the pleasure of submission (2000: 216-17).

Cevetello gives an account of one such instance in his life of St. Gerard:

> He intensified the scourges he had been giving himself over the years. He even went further; he enlisted the services of a young man—Farenga who tells us how he bound the body of Gerard to a stage (sic) and beat him unmercifully with wet and knotted cords, causing blood to flow from his bare shoulders (1979: 15).

In his hagiography of the saint, Tannoia describes another such scenario:

> His ardent desires were seconded by a man whom he had converted and in whom he placed great confidence, and by a youth of Lacedogna, named Andrew Longarello, who was anxious to become a lay-brother; for while Gerard acted the part of a victim, they served as his executioners. As he wanted to imitate the flagellation of Jesus Christ, as he had done at Muro, he caused them to tie his hands together, and was fastened to a beam; after which he made them strike his shoulders with knotted ropes, until blood gushed forth in all directions and his body was a mass of wounds. As he also wished to imitate the crowning of thorns, he placed a crown of sharp thorns on his head, after flagellation had ended, and persuaded them to beat them into his head by the blow of a hammer (1849: 265–66).

Like Dominic, Donato wonders about the psychosexual dimensions of these severe ascetic practices in which the saint enlisted the services of other men. He cannot help but imagine what might have been going on in the psyche of the saint and what it might reveal about the nature of St. Gerard's sexual desires.[25]

These musings, however, say more about the effects of gay male sexual culture on Donato's imagination than about St. Gerard. Nevertheless, unorthodox and almost blasphemous as it must appear to ask such questions, the spirit in which Donato asks them is one of sincerity and deep soul-searching. He uses the saint's life as the lens by which he tries to makes sense of the complexities of human sexuality, its pleasures and dangers.

For so many Catholic gay men who live in the greater Newark area, it is fair to say that the formation of their identities as gay men has been influenced by their proximity to New York City, one of the most visible gay meccas in the world. After all, Newark is just 11.5 miles away. A simple walk in Greenwich Village or Chelsea provides the most naive of gay men with some exposure to the various sexual subcultures associated with big city gay male life. It is, therefore, inevitable that what Dominic, or Donato, or Emilio, or I may witness in New York City, will travel back to Newark with us and have some bearing on our local life, and certainly upon our imaginations.

Both Dominic's and Donato's musings about St. Gerard's ascetic practices raise an important point to be considered. Gay male sexual culture and its various practices, whether indulged in or not, play as much a role in their attempts to locate themselves in the church via the life of St. Gerard as the church and the life of St. Gerard do in their attempts to locate themselves within gay male culture. These realms are not hermetically sealed off from each other.

Fertility or Fecundity?

In his essay "Theological Contributions to the U.S. Church," Robert Nugent plays on an important distinction in contemporary theological thinking about human relationality, issues of fertility and fecundity. Speaking specifically about Catholic moral theologians, Fr. Nugent notes that "these theologians are willing to expand the meaning of sexuality to include relatedness, self-disclosure in sexual acts, and even fecundity beyond strictly biological life" (1992c: 152). In chapter 1 of my dissertation I suggest that in the same way that St. Gerard is a symbol of reproductive fertility for heterosexual couples who appeal to him when they are unable to conceive, for some of his Catholic gay male devotees he is a symbol of the fecundity of intimate relationships. Although I have not found it to be a widespread practice, some gay men I have talked with about their devotion to St. Gerard have indicated to me that they have turned to the saint for assistance in finding a meaningful relationship with another man that is based upon love and commitment, which also includes sexual activity.

During my conversation with Gerard, I was interested to learn if he had ever approached St. Gerard about matters of the heart. "Nope. Nope," he replied, indicating further that he "wasn't interested." He suggested that a romantic homosexual relationship is more trouble than it's worth. I attribute Gerard's response to generational differences. Gerard grew up at a time, both in the church and in Italian American culture, when homosexuality was seen as an illness. Even though Gerard has managed to incorporate some elements of gay culture into his life, mostly in the form of language and humor, the idea of living openly in a committed relationship with another man is just not part of his reality. This I think is made obvious in the comment he made that he prays to St. Gerard to make him go in a "straighter line."

Emilio on the other hand prays to St. Gerard about matters of the heart regularly. "Yes, I have asked him for help in finding a mate," he said, as he recounted that he was without a partner for seven years. Emilio said that he had friends and sexual partners, but when he needed an "arm to put around me" or someone to "lie with and confide," to have companionship with and "intimacy that I didn't have," then he prayed to St. Gerard. "I prayed," he explained, "for whatever he thought was best for me." And then he met his current boyfriend, right on "St. Gerard's weekend." He said, "It was time." For Emilio that was "a sign" that St. Gerard "approved," both of his sexuality and of his entering into relationship. The saint sent this guy along "just at the right time."

Emilio explained to me that prior to meeting his current partner he was not free to have a relationship because his mother had been very ill and he had to care for her. When she got better he was "free again," as he put it, "and just at that point, on the weekend of St. Gerard's feast and procession, I met my current lover."[26] For Emilio the saint had worked a miracle of fecundity in his life, which he considers to be the gay equivalent of the miracles of fertility that St. Gerard has worked in the lives of Emilio's heterosexual counterparts.

Tom, twenty-five, is also a devotee of St. Gerard. His partner's name is John. He describes himself as coming to devotion for St. Gerard "through marriage. I have a significant other and he is an Italian Catholic and very heart-drawn to St. Gerard." Tom explained to me that he has prayed to St. Gerard for many things, one of them being for his niece when she was pregnant. There had been complications. "I did pray to him that everything would work out, and then we'd fast once everything went well, and things like that. Now this year will come, and the baby will be a year old, when they [will] have the blessing of the newborn."

Tom told me how he thinks the congregation of other devotees feel about the relationship he and John have, and also how St. Gerard may feel about it.

I've gone through the bit, as I want to say, that no you aren't gay, no you aren't a homosexual. . . . I've been engaged, the whole thing. And it just really wasn't my cup of tea. I couldn't live a lie for myself . . . I understand where the church is coming from, and I'd love to change for them, but I can't. This is who I am. And I think as time goes on they're a lot more willing and understanding of where you're coming from. A lot of times I think, now they look at your heart rather than where your sexual preference is. . . . They know what the situation is. It is not open. . . . But they know we are friends, we're a so-called couple. And when we are invited one place, we've been to the priest's house for dinner. We were not invited as one, we went as a couple. And I think St. Gerard does understand . . . I think he would . . . it wouldn't be maybe his choosing of where [we] are. But I think he understands where [we] are and as long as we are happy in the relationship [we] have, I think [that] is a lot more important. And I think the entire Catholic religion is understanding that a lot more.

During my interview with Tom I asked him, "If someone were gay and prayed to St. Gerard for a life partner, how do you think St. Gerard would respond?"

I don't know, I think he would try to find you something. There's always a lid to every pot, as they say. Sometimes the pot's all cracked, or the lid may be. But I think St. Gerard would try to find you somebody that would make you happy. I have prayed to St. Gerard and thanked him for bringing John [his lover] into my life. The same with Jesus . . . I've prayed to Him to thank Him for bringing John into my life. And the church has also brought us together a lot more. We have a good group of friends within the church. We go out together socially, as well as being in church together.

In my dissertation I entitled the chapter upon which this essay is a based "St. Gerard: 'Is he really the saint all the gay boys follow?'" The question is rhetorical. Certainly, from the institutional church's point of view St. Gerard is not a saint that gay men should follow unless they are praying to him, as Gerard does, to help them go in a straighter line. And I do not doubt that there are other gay men doing just that at St. Lucy's, along with Gerard.

Yet from an ethnographic point of view, what St. Gerard's gay male devotees have to say about their relationship with the saint, their understanding of his life in the context of their own, and the devotion they have for the saint are important elements of the cult of the saint. I present them here in order to give a more thorough understanding of how the cults of the saints function in general, and how that of St. Gerard functions in particular, in contemporary Italian American Catholicism and in a pluralistic environment such as Newark, New Jersey. Obviously there is no definitive answer to the question I ask in the title of this chapter of my dissertation.

Ironically, I think it is Gerard who sums up best what the gay men I have spoken to feel about their sexuality, their ethnicity, their Catholic faith, and their patron saint, Gerard Maiella. While talking with Gerard he explained to me that despite the church's position that active homosexuality is a sin, his relationship with St. Gerard teaches him that love cancels that out. According to Gerard, what matters most to St. Gerard is that "you show genuine love to him." St. Gerard, he further explains, could not care less whether you are actively homosexual or not. "If the gay person has faith in St. Gerard then St. Gerard will stick by him." "Even though he's gay?" I asked. "Even though he's gay," Gerard replied.[27]

Notes

1. Research for this essay was conducted under the auspices of the Newark Project at Drew University in Madison, New Jersey, and was generously funded by the Ford Foundation.

2. Unfortunately, there is no time or space to explore it here, but there are also some Italian American Catholic gay men in the cult of St. Gerard Maiella who use their devotion to the saint as a way of conforming themselves to the Catholic Church's official teachings on homosexuality and sexual behavior. For a further discussion of this see Savastano (2002: 152–65)

3. During the course of my research among men with same-sex desire I have encountered, on the part of some of these men, a discomfort with putting labels on their sexuality. For some this has to do with generational differences, for others it has to do with

both the fragmentary and fluid nature of the postmodern self, such as Jeffery Weeks discusses in *Invented Moralities: Sexual Values in an Age of Uncertainty* (1995: 28–34).

4. My use of the word *cult* to refer to the devotion to St. Gerard is used in the sense that sociologist Michael P. Carroll defines it. "A cult is a group of people who all engage, individually or collectively, in some particular pious practice" (1989: 7). I do not use the word with any of the derogatory meanings it has acquired during the past thirty years.

5. "Italians often make a rather clear distinction between religion and church, and they often view the latter with critical cynicism" (Orsi 1985: 57).

6. While none of my gay male informants, with the exception of one, requested that I change their names, ages, or life circumstances, I have, nevertheless, done so in order to protect their anonymity and privacy.

7. Personal conversation, 11 June 2001.

8. Personal conversation, 13 June 2001.

9. Personal conversation, 15 June 2001.

10. Personal conversation, 15 June 2001.

11. Ibid.

12. Personal conversation, 13 June 2001.

13. There is a detailed description of the *Giglio Festa* in Salvatore Primeggia's essay "The Social Contexts of Religious Devotion: How Saint Worship Expresses Popular Religiosity" in Varacalli et al. (1999, 68–90).

14. Dr. Joseph Sciorra, assistant director of academic and cultural programs at the City University of New York's John D. Calandra Italian American Institute, conducted ten years of research on the *Giglio Festa*. He also reported to me that during his research in Brooklyn he met many Italian Catholic gay men who kept home altars to the Madonna del Carmine and to the saints. Personal conversation, 23 October 2001.

15. "A text does not exist by itself," Obeyesekere writes, "it is embodied in a context" (1990: 130).

16. For a fascinating discussion of the use of skulls in popular Italian Catholic practice and on the cult of the dead in Italian Catholicism, see Carroll (1996).

17. Personal conversation, 11 June 2001.

18. Personal conversation, 13 June 2001.

19. While I understand myself to be Catholic by sensibility and culture, I am no longer a practicing Catholic. To be Catholic by sensibility and culture means that I fully acknowledge and greatly value from whence I come by heritage and tradition, neither am I bound by it nor shut down to other possibilities, at least not consciously.

20. In Catholic culture a person, man or woman, who enters a monastic religious order such as the Benedictines or Trappists, or a religious congregation such as the Jesuits or Redemptorists, for example, is said to have entered "religious life." The monk or nun or member of a religious congregation is referred to as a "religious."

21. Obviously, since 2001, when the original material from which this essay is derived was written, much has changed in the Roman Catholic Church in America. Given the widespread child sex abuse scandal of 2002 involving Catholic priests and bishops, and the subsequent attempts on the part of the Catholic Church hierarchy to suggest

that homosexual men in the priesthood and religious life may be part of the problem, the priesthood and religious life may no longer be a viable option for Catholic gay men who are so inclined to a career in the ordained ministry or consecrated life. For those gay men who choose to remain in the Roman Catholic Church, they will have to find other ways to carve out a niche for themselves in order to express their spirituality and religiosity while at the same time providing a way for them to save face, especially if they come from Catholic communities where ethnicity still plays a central role in the construction of identity.

22. Carroll makes mention of St. Gerard's ascetic practices, too, describing them as "flamboyant." He writes: "Maiella was (and is) strongly associated in the popular mind with some fairly flamboyant mortification, not the least of which was violent and bloody self-flagellation" (1992: 57).

23. In Italian St. Gerard's family name is Maiella, however, in many of the hagiographies and in popular devotional literature, especially in English-speaking countries, his family name has been anglicized as Majella.

24. "Now it so happened that one day while D. Emmanuelle, the wife of D. Constantine, was on the ground floor, Gerard was talking to her two daughters and her servant on the first floor. The lady grew inpatient at this, as she was in want of her daughters, and said within herself, 'Saints have always trembled when they were in dangerous positions, but this man is conversing with my daughters and maid without any fear or restraint whatsoever'" (Tannoia 1849: 238).

25. Personal conversation, 7 August 2001.

26. Personal conversation, 11 June 2001.

27. Personal conversation, 13 June 2001.

A Religion of One's Own
Gender and LGBT Religiosities

12

MELISSA M. WILCOX

VIRGINIA WOOLF IS PERHAPS BEST KNOWN for her assertion that every woman should have "a room of one's own." To objections that the entire house belonged to women, she replied that also inhabiting that house were men, children, and their needs. Whereas a (middle class white) man could sit in his study undisturbed to contemplate literature, philosophy, and the like, a woman's meditative moments were constantly at risk of being shattered by a screaming child, a burning roast, or laundry that needed folding before sunset. For a woman to develop her full intellectual ability, Woolf argued, she needed among other things a space that she alone defined and controlled.

The same argument could be made—indeed, has been made—for religion. In a number of the world's religions the official texts, doctrines, and practices have been shaped mainly by men. Women have certainly participated as fully as they could in these religious structures, but they have also created woman-centered spaces. Such communities, in turn, have produced alternative forms of belief and practice—often in combination with official forms—that speak directly to women's experiences of life and of the world. Some examples of this sort of "lived religion" include Catholic women's devotion to the Virgin Mary, Jewish feminists' Rosh Hodesh celebrations, and African women's religious sodalities.

Studies that focus solely on "official" religion often miss these "non-official" forms, and in the process they frequently ignore central parts of women's religiosity, as well as the religiosity of other disempowered groups. To understand a religion fully, then, we need to take gender into account. We need to ask whether women act, think, believe, or practice differently from men, whether they inhabit or value different spaces, and whether, like men, they also differ among themselves. The complexity of women's lives is an integral part of the complexity of religion.

This essay explores the ways in which understanding the complexity of lesbian, bisexual, and transgender (LBT) women's lives might broaden or even change how we understand the roles of religion among lesbian, gay, bisexual, and transgender (LGBT) people.[1] Based on two separate research projects—a study of two Metropolitan Community Church (MCC) congregations and a community-based study of LBT women in Los Angeles—I offer a glimpse of the ways in which LBT women create "a religion of one's own." These patterns are as diverse as the women who wield them, but for the sake of analysis they can be grouped into six categories, from which one woman may draw several different strategies. The categories include: *leaving* one's religious tradition before coming out; *staying in* through the coming-out process; *switching* to another denomination or congregation; *struggling* with a homophobic, bi-phobic, or transphobic tradition; *seeking* new forms of religiosity among alternative or new religious movements; and relying on *divine assistance*.

Absent Women

"When I first began observing CBST [Congregation Beth Simchat Torah in New York City]," reports anthropologist Moshe Shokeid, "women accounted for a third of the synagogue membership...That underrepresentation of women characterized most CBST activities, committees, and leadership positions" (1995: 174). E. Michael Gorman (1980), one of the first scholars to study gay and lesbian congregations, found similar gender differences in the gay and lesbian Protestant (MCC), Catholic (Dignity), and Jewish congregations he studied. And Leonard Norman Primiano (1993) found that Dignity/Philadelphia attracted roughly 10 women and 225 men to its masses in 1986 and 1987. Though gender is not a central analytical category for Gorman, he does mention its importance to the three congregations he studied: each had made a concerted effort to include women and to address their needs within the limits of the institution. Shokeid and Primiano find the topic to be of enough concern that each devotes significant space to explaining the absence of women—an absence that is especially notable given repeated sociological findings that women in the United States tend to be more active than men in religious attendance and practice.

Primiano's and Shokeid's answers to this question of why there is an absence of women cover a number of variables, but for the most part they remain within an approach sometimes termed "supply-side": explanations based on the congregation itself rather than on the women who are choosing not to attend. Both authors point out that these congregations are unwelcoming to women because they express a predominantly gay male culture. This state of affairs came about, they suggest, over the course of several years. First, both congregations seem to have been founded by men and initially attended by more men than women. This resulted in the creation of a male-focused culture and a male-centered power structure. Furthermore, some of the men in the congregation were unsympathetic to feminist concerns such as gender-inclusive language and liturgy or, in the Catholic case, women's ordination. As a result, when interested women visited these congregations seeking to join, they found a group led mostly by men, expressing male interests and sometimes antifeminist or sexist sentiments, and populated mostly by men. No matter how warm the welcome or how interested the leadership was in bringing more women to the group, Primiano and Shokeid argue that to become more welcoming to women these congregations would have to undergo deeper, more radical changes than they seemed willing to make at the time.[2]

Congregation Beth Simchat Torah, Dignity/Philadelphia, and the groups studied by Gorman are not alone, nor are these phenomena specific to the 1980s and early 1990s. In March of 2002, for instance, I visited St. Thomas the Apostle Episcopal Church in Hollywood, California, and found myself one of about fifty women in a predominantly gay congregation of roughly two hundred people. The church's new rector is concerned with increasing his parish's diversity by reaching out not only to lesbians but also to heterosexuals. Other mainline Protestant churches in the vicinity of West Hollywood who are open to LGBT people seem to have similar problems, as do some of the Metropolitan Community Church congregations I have visited. These churches find it relatively easy to bring gay men through their doors, but lesbians simply are not attending in large numbers.

The Consequences

What does this mean for the ethnographic study of LGBT religiosities? Though the essays in this book indicate that the field is becoming broader, for the past three decades scholars have often studied LGBT religiosities by studying LGBT congregations. This has been so because LGBT people are notoriously difficult to identify and "measure" using other sociological methods. We cannot simply choose telephone numbers at random, say, "Hello, is there anyone gay in this household?" and expect an easy or accurate study. Many people do not wish to reveal their sexual orientation or transgender identity to a stranger over the telephone or during a mail-in survey.[3] In LGBT congregations, on the other hand, one has a ready-made sample of LGBT people who are religious, and one can often rely on the trust of the religious leader to inspire trust among the congregation.

There are still a few problems here, though. First, congregations are often made up mostly of gay men, which means that ethnographers have been studying not LGBT religiosities but gay religiosities. What if, as in many other communities, women's experiences are different? What if bisexuals go through different struggles or find different rewards in religion? What if religious teachings affect transgender identities differently from the identities of orthodox-gendered gay men, lesbians, and bisexuals? Furthermore, the studies undertaken so far focus predominantly on white, Christian congregations. What can we learn from the experiences of African-Americans, Native Americans, Latinas, Asian Americans, Arab Americans, and recent immigrants? Are there differences between coming out among Jews, Buddhists, Hindus, Sikhs, or Muslims? What are women, bisexuals, transgender people, people of color, and non-Christian people doing and believing that might deepen our understanding of religion among LGBT people? A number of the essays in this book address such issues.

By asking these questions, moreover, we also shift the analytical focus. Shokeid, Primiano, and numerous religious leaders across the country have asked: What are these congregations doing that prevents women (people of color, transgender people) from attending? This question assumes that they are still *interested* in attending and would come if only the congregations managed to "get it right." Perhaps it is time to ask questions that sociologists of religion would call "demand-side": What do those people believe who are *not* attending the congregations studied so far? If they do attend religious services, where are they going, and why? In short, what is taking place outside of MCC, Dignity, and the LGBT synagogues, and how much must we broaden our definition of religiosity to obtain an accurate understanding of religion in the lives of LGBT people?

The Los Angeles Women and Spirituality Project

I began thinking about such questions when I was conducting my own congregational study: an ethnographic exploration of two MCC congregations (Wilcox 2003). Given my strong interest in women's studies and gender studies, I was watching for noticeably gendered differences in my findings. There were a few: overall, men seemed to struggle more than women did with the tension between traditional Christian teachings and their sexual or transgender identities; and women seemed more likely to identify as non-Christian or eclectically Christian (Christian with a bit of Buddhist and pagan mixed in, for instance). But there were women who were devoutly Christian, especially among the charismatic congregation I studied, and there were men who no longer identified strictly as Christian. Could it be that LGBT identities affect religious beliefs and practices so strongly that they drown out gender differences, or (as a few have unfortunately persisted in arguing) that being lesbian or gay alters one's own gendered behavior to such an extent that gender differences found in studies of the general population fail to apply to lesbians and gay men? Given the apparent tendency of these congregations to be mostly male, and given my own knowledge of lesbian, bisexual, and transgender women, these answers seemed insufficient.

The Los Angeles Women and Spirituality (LAWS) Project was designed to provide case studies that address some of these questions. Rather than using a congregation-based method, the project began with a community: greater Los Angeles, or specifically anyone living within roughly twenty miles of the heavily LGBT city of West Hollywood. Los Angeles was not only a convenient choice (as the closest metropolitan area to my home), but a strategic one as well, since I could have selected any number of smaller communities in Central or Southern California. Los Angeles, however, offered immense diversity in terms of religion, race, ethnicity, nationality, sexual, and transgender orientation, immigration status, and so on—all of which were necessary to a project that sought to explore religious beliefs and practices across a wide spectrum of LBT women.

In order to recruit participants without focusing specifically on religious congregations, I advertised in secular locations: through a booth at the annual Los Angeles Dyke March and Pride Parade, through a lesbian-focused magazine, and through flyers mailed to the LGBT community center, to bookstores, and to various LGBT-focused organizations. Nearly sixty people volunteered initially to take part in the project; these volunteers were contacted by telephone a few weeks later for a brief screening interview. After confirming that each person was in fact eligible for the project (by virtue of identifying or having formerly identified as female; identifying as lesbian, bisexual, transgender, transsexual, queer, or questioning; being a legal adult; and living within the target area), I asked several basic, demographic questions and then arranged an in-depth interview for a later date. Almost thirty of the initial volunteers were not included in the final set of interviews, because they could not be contacted, because they were in some way ineligible, or because they chose not to continue with the project.

In the end, twenty-nine women were included in the in-depth interviews, which averaged roughly ninety minutes in length but sometimes lasted as much as five hours. Fourteen of the twenty-nine participants—almost exactly half—currently attend one or more religious groups with some regularity; the final phase of the project involved conducting limited fieldwork at these congregations in order to explore the range of religious resources and communities available to lesbian, bisexual, and transgender women in the greater Los Angeles area.

The Participants

The LAWS Project participants range in age from twenty-four to sixty-six, with a mean age of forty-four. Eighteen of the twenty-nine identify as white, Caucasian, or European American; four identify as multiethnic; three as black or African-American; three as Chicana, Mexican, Latina, or Hispanic; and one as Native American (Laguna Pueblo). Most are orthodox-gendered, with two being

male-to-female transgender and one female-to-male transgender.[4] Most are also
lesbian; two identify as bisexual and two simply as questioning.

It is in the area of religion, however, that the diversity of this group of women
becomes most vividly apparent. Of the twenty-nine, thirteen were raised in Protestant churches ranging from fundamentalist and Southern Baptist to Episcopalian.
Ten were raised Catholic, two Jewish (one Orthodox), two Mormon, one Christian Scientist, and one New Age. Whereas twenty-six of the twenty-nine women in
the study were raised Christian, only seven of them still identify with that religion:
two Protestants, one Catholic, one Mormon, and three who identify simply as
"Christian." Two women attend Unitarian Universalist churches and three are involved with metaphysical groups such as Religious Science. Two follow New Age
or shamanic practices, one is atheist, one is Jewish, and one is involved in Santería.
Twelve—almost half of the group—identify their current spiritual beliefs and
practices as "eclectic," "agnostic," "searching," or simply "spiritual" (see table 12.1).

**Table 12.1.   Childhood Religious Background of LAWS Participants Compared to Their
Current Beliefs**

Catholic	→	seeking
Presbyterian	→	Unitarian Universalist
Catholic	→	Unitarian Universalist
Catholic	→	seeking
Baptist	→	eclectic
Catholic	→	agnostic
Southern Baptist	→	Christian
Baptist	→	Religious Science
Presbyterian	→	Presbyterian
Christian Science	→	eclectic
Baptist	→	Christian
Mormon	→	Mormon
Catholic	→	atheist
Mormon	→	shamanic
Baptist	→	Religious Science
Catholic	→	Catholic
Catholic	→	metaphysical
Orthodox Jewish	→	agnostic
Catholic	→	spiritual
Church of God in Christ (COGIC)	→	Christian
Jewish	→	Jewish
Disciples of Christ	→	eclectic
Presbyterian	→	New Age
Fundamentalist Protestant	→	eclectic
Mixed Protestant	→	eclectic
Catholic	→	spiritual
New Age	→	eclectic
Episcopalian	→	Episcopalian
Catholic	→	Laguna Pueblo/Santería

The diversity does not stop with religious beliefs. Indeed, a confession may be in order here: I began this project expecting that relatively few of the women involved in the study would be attending any sort of religious group, and that there would be some overlap among them—resulting in a total of eight to ten groups to cover during the fieldwork phase of the project. While it is true that only half of these women attend regularly, each attends a different group and some attend more than one. Furthermore, many of the "seekers" include religious services from time to time in their search for spiritual fulfillment. All told, the women in the LAWS Project attended twenty-one different organizations as part of their spiritual practice during the course of the study. These ranged from a Buddhist meditation center to Affirmation (a Mormon LGBT organization), from a Religious Science mega-church to a small Wiccan circle, and from the Gay and Lesbian Sierrans (a branch of the Sierra Club) to the flamboyant and usually gay male Sisters of Perpetual Indulgence. Also included were a Siddha yoga center, a Catholic church, the above-mentioned Unitarian Universalist churches, a largely gay Presbyterian church, a Dianic Wiccan circle, an LGBT synagogue, three Episcopalian churches (one largely gay, the others mixed), two Metropolitan Community churches, Unity Fellowship Christian Church (see Bates, this volume), and Santería (see table 12.2).

Where Have All the Women Gone?

The life stories of the women in the LAWS Project include several key themes involving religion, any number of which may appear, simultaneously or in succession, in an individual woman's life. What makes this remarkable is not the themes themselves, but the range of possibilities. There is an assumption in many

Table 12.2. Organizational Religious or Spiritual Resources Utilized by Women in the LAWS Project

Buddhist Meditation Center
Siddha Yoga Meditation Center
Catholic Church
2 Unitarian Universalist churches
Presbyterian Church
Affirmation Reclaiming-based Wiccan circle
Dianic Wiccan circle
Religious Science Church
LGBT synagogue
3 Episcopalian churches
2 Metropolitan Community churches
Christ Chapel
Unity Fellowship Church
Sisters of Perpetual Indulgence
Gay and Lesbian Sierrans
Santería

U.S. subcultures, from secular LGBT communities to religious heterosexual ones, that devout believers in a traditional form of religion have only two choices when they come out: they must either reject their religion or reject their LGBT identity, because the two cannot go together. Over the past thirty years, an increasing number of stories have emerged of LGBT people—especially gay men—who struggle with these two identities and eventually find a way of bringing them together (see, for example, Thumma, Gray and Thumma, and Shokeid in this volume, as well as the work by Gorman, Primiano, and Shokeid discussed previously).

Many of the LAWS Project participants come from traditional religious backgrounds, yet their stories are far more complex than these three scripts—rejecting religion, rejecting LGBT identity, or integrating the two—would suggest. Indeed, it is important to note that simply by organizing these women's stories into themes I have significantly reduced their complexity. These diverse tales can neither be classified easily nor be separated strictly into categories; many of those that I include as examples of one theme include other themes as well. These examples highlight the important differences as well as the similarities between these women's religious and spiritual journeys.

1. Leaving Early

The standard narrative of LGBT people's religious struggles revolves around the severe identity clash that arises when someone "religious" begins to acknowledge an identification with the opposite gender or an attraction to people of the same sex. The standardization of this particular narrative may be one outcome of the focus on men's experiences, and also one explanation for the relative invisibility of LBT women in traditional religions: women have more reasons to leave. Mark Jordan made this point recently when considering why gay men are more likely than lesbians to remain in the Roman Catholic Church: "they are held in place more tightly by the systems [and, one might add, the rewards] of male obedience" (2000: 238). But Gorman noted a similar issue nearly twenty years earlier: many of the gay men in MCC, Dignity, and Congregation Kol Emeth wished to see their religion stay exactly the same aside from the inclusion of homosexuals. Dignity was split in its early years over the question of whether to support women's ordination (it is now a strong advocate of that cause); MCC struggled at the denominational level with inclusive language liturgy during the 1970s; and both Kol Emeth and Congregation Beth Simchat Torah grappled with similar issues of women's inclusion during their formative years. If even the LGBT congregations had trouble with these issues, traditional religiosity might not seem as attractive to women as it might to men.

But what if this never becomes an issue? In my study of MCC, I found that a number of women, whether or not they were currently Christian, had left their churches in their teens or early twenties—*before* they came out. By the time they began to explore their identities as lesbians or bisexuals, organized religion was not an important force in their lives. Leaving traditional religion "early," whether for nontraditional groups or for no religion at all, thus becomes a sort of bypass that avoids entirely the clash between religion and sexual or transgender identity.

Ronni Sanlo's experiences are one example of this theme. Raised in an Orthodox Jewish home during the mid-twentieth century, Ronni determined as a small child that she wanted to be a rabbi, and recalls being devastatingly disillusioned when she finally discovered that she could not be ordained. She left Judaism in her late teens, and when she came out as a lesbian later in her life, religion was simply not an issue. Society was, however: Ronni lost custody of her children because of her sexual orientation. Though she has renewed contact with them as adults, she was deprived of any role in the late childhood and teenage years of their lives.

Ronni attended Christian services with a partner for a while, but only since moving to Los Angeles a few years ago has she become interested in returning to Judaism. She currently attends Beth Chayim Chadashim (BCC), a congregation that holds the distinction of being the world's first LGBT synagogue. Perhaps significantly, BCC has a woman rabbi.

Adesina, on the other hand, was raised in the Baptist church "which I really didn't take to," she told me. In high school, she began learning about European history and was appalled by Christian involvement in the African slave trade, the Inquisition, and the oppression of women. She stopped going to church. Soon thereafter, however, she became interested in Yoruba religion, and it was a Yoruba priest who gave her the name she uses now. Still identifying as heterosexual, Adesina moved from Philadelphia to California and began to work as a chef for an alternative-style restaurant in San Diego. Groups representing various Asian religions were invited to the restaurant frequently to educate both employees and customers, and as a result Adesina branched out even further in her religious search. Still rooted in "African spirituality," she also studied several different forms of meditation, read a wide variety of books, and eventually became involved in a metaphysical mega-church known as the Agape International Spiritual Center. Both traditional Christianity and Adesina's version of Yoruba religion did not create much room for homosexuality.[5] However, she had already left parts of her Yoruba practice behind—and had rejected Christianity entirely—by the time she came out as a lesbian. Like Ronni, Adesina felt far greater negative pressure from society than she felt from religion. As an African-American, she has had to struggle with both homophobia in the black community and racism in the LGBT community. However, she stressed, "I didn't feel that God would condemn me or punish me because I was gay—I didn't feel that at all."

2. Staying In

When I first spoke with Danielle over the phone, she told me she had been raised Mormon. "How would you describe your spiritual beliefs and practices now?" I asked. "Still Mormon," she replied wryly, "but with some disagreements." Danielle is a male-to-female transgender lesbian. Unlike other Mormons (such as Christie Tuttle, an orthodox-gendered lesbian who left the church well before she came out), Danielle has chosen to continue identifying with the church. Also unlike other Mormons, she has not retained her Mormon identity in order to fight her sexuality or gender; she feels that the church should accept her as she is. Her main involvement right now is with Affirmation, a "denomination heritage" organization for LGBT Latter-day Saints (see Crapo, this volume).

Like Danielle, Coco Gallegos has remained within the religion of her childhood: the Roman Catholic Church. She describes herself as "very active;" indeed, on the day I attended Mass with her, she arrived early to speak with a priest, greeted at least ten different people before Mass began, and left early to open the church's bookstore. She recently received an award for her volunteer efforts, and she is co-coordinator of the parish's gay and lesbian outreach program. Unlike many Catholics, Coco never felt that God would condemn her for loving another woman, and God has always remained central in both her life and her partner's life.

Some Catholics negotiate a gay or lesbian identity through celibacy, but Coco does not feel that is necessary, either. In fact, in her parish the approach to gay and lesbian members (of which there is a sizeable number) seems to be "don't ask, don't tell"—at least not explicitly. Yet people speak openly of their partners and come to church as couples; one lesbian couple will soon be bringing a baby to Mass as well, and the members of the outreach group were busily planning a baby shower when I joined Coco for Mass that evening.

Many different factors lead people to stay within their religions, just as a range of factors induce them to leave. First among the reasons for staying, in fact, is simply that despite dissatisfaction with attitudes toward women, historical misdeeds, or contemporary hypocrisy, one chooses to try to reform the religion from within rather than leaving it behind. How did Coco and Danielle avoid the agonizing coming-out process experienced by other Mormons and Catholics? The answer to this critical question unfortunately remains elusive, but it seems to be related to an individual relationship with God and a sense of independence.

Also important, however, are religious identity and community. Some of those involved in my study of two Metropolitan Community Churches enjoyed the inclusiveness of the MCC congregations, but yearned for the familiar hymns and rituals of their childhood years. Tradition and identity run deep; rejection by one's community may bury both aspects of one's faith, but rarely does it eradicate them entirely.

3. Switching

Some women stay within their religions of birth, but switch denominations or traditions in an attempt to find a more welcoming religious atmosphere. Their stories overlap quite a bit with Coco's and Danielle's, since the latter two found congregations rather than denominations that were more to their taste. Leavers, stayers, and switchers all undergo change in their religious practices. The leavers change most radically and the stayers least radically; the switchers are somewhere between these two extremes.

Betty Walker, like Adesina, was raised in an African-American Baptist church, and struggled with social sanctions when she came out as a lesbian later in her life. Unlike Adesina, however, she did not become disillusioned with Christianity. Rather, she switched from the Baptist church to Unity Fellowship Christian Church—a "subaltern" organization founded in 1985 to minister to African-American gays and lesbians. At its powerfully energetic services, gays, lesbians, and bisexuals create music that flows like waterfalls and rapids into the clapping crowd; LGB people speak from the pulpit; lesbian couples bring their children and teach them to worship, free from the censure they encounter in some African-American churches;[6] people with AIDS receive spiritual sustenance and support; transgender people are welcomed and valued; and all this takes place in the name of God. Betty's religious beliefs and practices are becoming more eclectic over time; she left Unity Fellowship a few years ago, and has recently become involved with Agape International Spiritual Center, the metaphysical mega-church that Adesina attends as well.

Emile was also raised Christian, but in the Church of God in Christ—a Pentecostal denomination that is predominantly African-American. Like Coco and Danielle, she was raised in a religion that strictly condemns homosexuality; unlike them, she was unable to find a congregation of other COGIC people that would accept and support her. Emile struggled for many years with her sexuality, and she is one of surprisingly few women in this study who struggled for religious reasons. Despite being aware of her attraction to women at a young age, Emile buried that attraction and tried harder to match her own image of a "good Christian." She married a man and had children, but remained unhappy. Finally, she left religion behind and began to frequent gay clubs, where "I felt my soul was set free." Gradually, she returned to studying the Bible and realized that Jesus "taught about love and compassion" and "never said anything about sexual orientation."

As she made her way back into the church, Emile tried attending Unity Fellowship Church, but found it to be too political. Eventually she found MCC-Long Beach and Christ Chapel Long Beach, both charismatic churches with predominantly LGBT congregations. As she wrote in a recent online article:

> I live today happy, content and a believer in Christ. I am in a committed relationship with Christ at the center. We had our union ceremony and our covenant was blessed by our heavenly Father. Even though we are not recognized by man's law, we are by God's. It is well with my soul and I have faith in Jesus Christ because I am a whosoever.

4. Struggling

Emile was not the only woman in this study to experience some sort of religious struggle. But while this theme is perhaps the least surprising according to common stereotypes, it, too, has its own complexity. While some women, like Emile, do grapple internally with religious teachings, others grapple externally with religious communities while at the same time remaining fairly certain of themselves internally. Still others appear to do a bit of both—indeed, it is unlikely that either internal or external struggle could exist without at least a hint of the other being present as well.

For Christine, most of the religious struggle was external. Raised a Christian Scientist, Christine remained within that church when she married a man and started a family. She was also an alcoholic, however, and eventually she joined an Alcoholics Anonymous (AA) group in West Hollywood that included a number of gay men. Christine learned new approaches to spirituality from AA ("I went from religion to spirituality," she told me), and eleven months after becoming sober, she fell in love with another woman. During this period of time she wrote to the Christian Science Mother Church annually, asking about the religion's position toward homosexuality, but she never received an answer. This fact, along with her new experiences in AA, made it clear to Christine that Christian Science was no longer the place for her. She explored several other churches, including a Metropolitan Community Church, but she continued to believe firmly in the healing power of prayer. Recently, she discovered in the Agape International Spiritual Center the combination that she had been seeking: Mary Baker Eddy's teachings, spirituality, and acceptance of her sexual orientation.

Vanessa, on the other hand, is currently in the midst of a powerful internal struggle. Having recently begun to acknowledge and act upon her attraction to women, she currently identifies her sexual orientation as "open": bisexual but leaning toward lesbian. Like Ronni, Vanessa was raised as an Orthodox Jew—but she was still involved in the religion when she began to come out. Sounding in turn angry, defensive, and desperately lost, she told me that she is probably agnostic right now, Jewish still by culture but no longer by belief.

Part of Vanessa's struggle is external. She has attended one of the local LGBT synagogues but found it "too Reform"—the richness of ritual with which she had been raised was missing. Yet she also is painfully aware that she could not bring her girlfriend with her to *shul* at the Orthodox synagogues of her childhood or even the Conservative synagogues she has considered more recently.

There is also a strong internal factor in the struggle—when we spoke early one morning, Vanessa appeared to be grappling as well with her understanding of God. She had been taught that God condemns homosexuality, yet she had begun to perceive herself as undeniably, irreversibly attracted to women. What did that make her—an unwilling abomination? Sounding exasperated, confused, and hurt, Vanessa belligerently declared that she no longer cares what God thinks.

5. Seeking

The theme of seeking is especially powerful among the women in the LAWS Project: thirteen of them describe their current spiritual beliefs and practices as "eclectic," "mixed," "agnostic," "searching," or "spiritual." Some, like Vanessa, became agnostic after experiencing severe religious doubts when they came out. Others, like Adesina, were "early leavers": they became seekers long before they came out. One of the most interesting examples of seekers among the participants in this study, however, is Dean Bramlett.

Dean was raised attending "whatever church was open"—she called her upbringing "Heinz 57 Christianity." This seems to have prepared her for an even more eclectic religious practice as an adult. She appreciates the ritual of Christianity and attended services at an Episcopalian church near her apartment until shortly after the September 11 attacks. When the church failed to provide the atmosphere she needed in the aftermath of the attacks, she began practicing meditation at the local Siddha yoga center. She also maintains an interest in Wicca. The most central part of her spiritual practice, however, is her alternate existence as Sister Vibrata Electric of the Flaming Labia, in the Los Angeles house of the Sisters of Perpetual Indulgence.

The Sisters of Perpetual Indulgence have their roots, quite improbably, in Cedar Rapids, Iowa, where in 1976 a drag show version of the *Sound of Music* managed to borrow permanently a set of retired habits from a convent. By Easter of 1979 the habits were in the streets of San Francisco's Castro district, draping the bodies of three men in an early version of performance-art protest. After a few more appearances, the "Sisters" developed a following and began to recruit new members. The money they earned from their performances soon became a source of charitable donations, and the three-man protest began to evolve into the international organization it is today. "Houses" of Sisters now exist in many major metropolitan areas, and their members make public appearances at everything from Pride parades to charity dinners. Dressed in their distinctive black and white headdresses and white makeup (originally used for anonymity and continued today out of a sense of tradition), they wear full habits when in their formal dress. When appearing informally, they are still drag queens, and below the white face anything goes. Sister Vibrata often takes full advantage of being the only anatomical female in the Los Angeles house: her real breasts can support outfits that would never work with the other sisters' "falsies."

But as sacrilegious as the Sisters often seem (the fact that the organization's anniversary is on Easter has sparked numerous Catholic protests over the years), they are also a very serious charity organization dedicated to safe-sex education and to support of their local LGBT communities through the funds they raise. While their early efforts in 1980 and 1981 were dedicated to such causes as gay Cuban refugees, the Sisters were also on the scene and already in action when AIDS hit the gay community. They immediately became involved in the safe-sex movement and began to dedicate large amounts of their funds to AIDS causes. This remains a central focus for the organization today.

New applicants go through a period of observance, a postulancy, and a novitiate before becoming fully professed Sisters, and every Sister takes vows upon taking the veil. Dean feels very strongly that she is a nun, even though her order is very different from the Catholic orders. The work she does as a Sister may be "campy" and often outrageous, but in a community recently devastated by AIDS and still suffering the internal and external ravages of prejudice—a community rarely served by Catholic nuns—that work is also deeply spiritual.

6. Divine Assistance

A theme I heard occasionally during my research in the Metropolitan Community Church has returned in the LAWS project: sometimes, people feel that the divine not only accepts them as they are, but actually helped them to come out. Such is the case with Corrine Garcia, a transgender person who was raised as a Latina Catholic only to discover later in hir life that ze is Laguna Pueblo (hir grandmother moved to Los Angeles and changed the family's identity to Latino in order to escape the bitter oppression experienced by Native Americans).[7] From an early age, Corrine believed very firmly that ze was a boy. There was a problem, though: hir mother insisted on dressing hir incorrectly—in girls' clothes. Ze tried to be fairly polite about the situation, ze recalls, but whenever possible ze simply stripped the dresses off and played naked (much to hir mother's distress).

One day, though, Corrine met another little boy whose backyard adjoined hirs. He wore a dress, too. Ze saw him repeatedly, each time in a red-and-white-checked dress. Hir brother was extremely uncomfortable with the boy, and asked him insistently why he wore a dress. The boy answered: "Because I like to." Hir brother was unsatisfied, but Corrine was pleased—if this boy could wear a dress, then it was all right for hir to wear one, too.

Today, initiated in Santería as a child of Changó, Corrine has a deeper understanding of that childhood event. Ze sees Changó as a saint who crosses genders as ze does, identified as both a male warrior and as the Catholic Saint Barbara.[8] Furthermore, his colors are red and white. Corrine believes it was not by chance that ze met a boy wearing a red and white dress: perhaps, ze thinks, it was Changó himself who appeared on the other side of the fence, trying to help hir through a transgender childhood.

Congregations

One question remains from my introductory section: if nearly half of these women are in some sort of religious congregation, where are they, and why are so many LGBT congregations dominated by gay men?

The women in this study—I would suspect like many gay men and bisexuals, if not transgender people as well—attend a wide variety of congregations. Some are involved in nonreligious groups, alternative religions, or new religious movements, such as the Gay and Lesbian Sierrans, Santería, and Wicca. Some are in heterosexual or mixed congregations that are welcoming to LGBT people: the Unitarian Universalist, Episcopal, and Catholic churches, for example. Six attend LGBT-focused congregations such as the Metropolitan Community Church, Unity Fellowship Church, Beth Chayim Chadashim, Affirmation, and St. Thomas the Apostle Episcopal Church.

The phenomenon of male-dominated churches is complex, but several factors appear to be influential in creating such a situation. The first issue is the relationship between leadership and congregational demographics. It is worth noting in this context there are female-dominated churches as well as male-dominated ones: for instance, the congregation of one MCC I studied was predominantly lesbian. Interestingly, among the two churches in my MCC study, the one with 60 percent to 70 percent men in the pews on any given Sunday had three male pastors and a transgender female pastoral candidate, while the church with about 90 percent women had a female pastor. Given the ongoing tendency for LGBT communities to fracture along gender lines, it is likely that the presence of a female leader will bring women into a congregation, while the presence of a male leader may keep them out.

A case in point is MCC Los Angeles, which lost long-time senior pastor and well-known queer theologian Nancy Wilson in 2001. During a visit to MCC-LA early in 2002, I spoke with a woman who has been closely involved with the church for more than a decade. She told me that when a male interim pastor took over upon Wilson's departure, many of the women left the congregation—despite the ongoing presence of two female associate pastors. While she estimated that the congregation had been fairly evenly divided between men and women during Wilson's tenure, on the Sunday following the installation of the new (also male) senior pastor women composed between 25 percent and 30 percent of the congregation during the English-language services.[9] The woman with whom I spoke suggested that the new pastor will need to "prove his feminism" before women will again attend MCC-LA in large numbers. In contrast, Unity Fellowship Church has a mixed-gender pastorate with a woman as senior pastor, a man as associate pastor, and both men and women as "ministers"; the congregation is fairly evenly divided between men and women. Glory Tabernacle MCC in Long Beach and Los Angeles LGBT synagogue Beth Chayim Chadashim follow this pattern as well. In these four congregations, at least, and in the two MCC churches I studied earlier, having a woman as senior religious leader seems to attract women but generally not to drive men away (Glory Tabernacle may be an exception to this). On the other hand, it appears that having women either in the lower levels of leadership or absent altogether can adversely affect the number of women attending services.

A second, purely sociological factor is also at work here. In congregations dominated by heterosexuals, one can count on a relative gender balance when people leave or join. If a heterosexual woman becomes interested in a particular religious group, for instance, and eventually decides to join, and if she brings another person in with her, it is likely to be her husband or partner—a man. The reverse also holds true. So although not all husbands join or leave a group when wives do, and not all wives join or leave when husbands do, one can expect a relative amount of gender balance when people arrive or leave: one woman leaving generally does not take several other women with her, nor one man several other men, unless there is a split in the congregation.

In LGBT communities, dominated as they are by gay men and lesbians, if a member leaves and that person's spouse leaves too, the congregation loses two men or two women. Given, again, the tendency for LGBT communities to fracture along gender lines, there may be a critical percentage of women or men below which the sex that is under-represented begins to leave in large numbers, taking their same-sex partners with them and prompting a snowball of change. Some will always remain, because they enjoy that community or the religion it represents, because they get along better with gay men than lesbians, or because they are not particularly interested in the gender of the rest of the congregation. Clearly, though, gender is a critical factor to which we need to attend in elucidating the institutional dynamics of LGBT congregations.[10]

Conclusions: Gender and Lived Religion

More than anything else, this essay shows the importance of taking diversity—of gender, sexuality, religion, and race at the very least—into account in the study of LGBT religiosities. Being homosexual, bisexual, and transgender are all different experiences, and they affect one's religious life history differently. Being female makes a difference, too: Ronni might not have left Judaism so early, or at all, if she had been a man. In fact, she might be a rabbi now. Race is also critical: Adesina left Christianity in part because of its complicity in the slave trade, and Corrine finds her religion in a combination of Laguna Pueblo practices (her birth heritage) and Santería (her cultural heritage). Religious upbringing, as well as race, made Emile's coming-out experience different from Dean's, and affected each woman's current religious practices—the one a charismatic Christian, the other a Sister. And finally, individual values and priorities have shaped each of these women religiously: they influenced Danielle's decision to remain a Mormon while Christie left, and brought Betty to Unity Fellowship Church while Emile turned to MCC-Long Beach and Christ Chapel.

Is this variety among women's religious practices the result of gender or of the study's methods? Although congregational studies have found traditional congregations populated mostly by men, this in no way suggests that men are not also leavers, switchers, and seekers. Further research is necessary to fully clarify the effects of gender on LGBT religious practices.

Finally, it is worth pointing out the critical importance of "lived religion" in these women's lives. While official religious statements continue to delimit a narrow range of choices for them, LGBT people seem fairly often to refuse such choices. Instead, they create new options by living them into existence: each of the women described here has created "a religion of one's own."

Notes

Funding for the broader project out of which this article stems was generously provided by the Association for the Sociology of Religion, the American Academy of Religion, and the Interdisciplinary Humanities Center and the Faculty Senate at the University of California at Santa Barbara. Thanks are due also to UC Santa Barbara for the postdoctoral fellowship that enabled this research, and to Scott Thumma and Edward Gray for their insightful comments on earlier drafts of this article.

1. In discussions of transgender men and women, gendered pronouns sometimes become difficult. Many transgender and transsexual people identify with a single gender; thus a "male-to-female" transgender or transsexual person is a woman, and someone who is "female-to-male" is a man. Others prefer a certain gender ambiguity; one person in the Los Angeles Women and Spirituality Project identifies as transgender, and terms hirself (this is a gender-neutral pronoun) "a woman who lives as a man." Hir body is genetically and anatomically female, but hir gender is male, and ze feels no need to make the two coincide. The practical result of this fluidity is that the category of "transgender women" includes both male-to-female and female-to-male transgender people, but not all people of either identity.

2. Shokeid also notes that the synagogue hired a woman rabbi in 1992 (Shokeid, 1995: 61–62); as discussed later in this chapter, this seems to be a critical change for congregations wishing to attract more women.

3. For the same reason, nationwide surveys such as the General Social Survey (GSS) provide incomplete and unreliable data on LGBT people.

4. I refer to all of the LAWS Project participants as women because the female-to-male transgender person in the study identifies as a transgender woman (as do both of the male-to-female transgender participants)—see note 1. Interestingly, the English language has no word for non-transgender people—this category is so normative that it is nameless. I use the term "orthodox-gendered" to refer to those who do not identify as transgender.

5. Homoeroticism and gender-crossing do exist in a number of African indigenous traditions, though often in very different forms from those composing Western LGBT identities (see, for instance, Conner 2003). However, Adesina believed that Yoruba teachings conflicted with her self-identification as a lesbian.

6. Though it should be noted that several prominent African-American church leaders have been staunch supporters of LGBT people.

7. I use the pronouns ze and hir to refer to Corrine, who identifies as "a woman who lives as a man." Female by sex and male by gender—and satisfied with that state of affairs—ze does not fit the binary system imposed by gender pronouns; to use either "she" or "he" would be inaccurate (see note 1).

8. In some African traditions, Changó is both male and female; however, Corrine understands Changó's African aspect to be male. Thanks to Robert Baum for pointing out this discrepancy.

9. MCC-LA also has a Spanish-language ministry that is headed by a female pastor; I have not yet been able to determine whether Wilson's departure affected the number of women at these services as well.

10. It is worth noting that this phenomenon may parallel the dynamics of race in many congregations (both LGBT and straight)—thanks to Edward Gray and Scott Thumma for bringing this to my attention.

Liberation in Truth
African American Lesbians Reflect on Religion, Spirituality, and Their Church[1]

ARYANA BATES

> *We believe that all people have access to the love of God. Creating a safe space for people of color, LITUFC has become a support base of love for everyone within the community, regardless of race, gender or sexual orientation.*
> Liberation in Truth, Mission Statement, an excerpt:

THIS EXPLORATION of the participants and leaders at Liberation in Truth Church (LIT), Newark, New Jersey, grows out of observations and interviews that I conducted with fourteen African American lesbians who attend there. This church was founded in 1995 by the Reverend Elder Jacquelyn Holland, and is one of twelve member congregations in the Unity Fellowship Church (UFC) movement. The UFC movement itself first emerged in Los Angeles in 1985 to address the particular spiritual and social needs of lesbian, gay, transgender, and bisexual people of color. Founded by Archbishop Carl Bean, D.M., the movement has congregations located across the country, from Seattle to Detroit to Washington, D.C. The Unity movement claims to be "rooted in spirituality, not in religion," and identifies itself as a church that "celebrates all of God's diverse creation."

My focus is on the ideas of religion, spirituality, and sexuality as expressed by the individual women. Their perspectives do, however, develop within the LIT community, and it is within this context that I posed my questions. This church and the people who create it represent a subaltern community on several levels— as lesbian and gay people practicing religion, as black people in a racist society, as people creating innovative religion that both challenges traditional black church ideology—and draws upon the liturgical practices of that same heritage. These women and their church demonstrate how people can claim all aspects of their identity and work to create a liberative community in the face of multiple forms of oppression.

Liberation in Truth

African American lesbians and gays are, like the wider African American community, generally very religious. Reverend Elder Jacquelyn Holland maintains that church, as a place to socialize, sing, and energize, is in fact part of African American women's heritage. Her vision for Liberation in Truth is to create a space that demystifies church so that individuals are able to develop a critical evaluation of their denominational heritage and embrace religious practices without denying their own identities. Holland intends to provide a safer environment than church communities usually provide for black lesbians to embrace their religious heritage as "churched" black women. Further, she believes that since lesbian and gay people have been harmed within the church, they must also be healed there.

Liberation in Truth encourages people to practice religion as a form of spirituality. Participants create community through intentional affirmation and fellowship. Critical of the power dynamics in traditional church doctrines and institutions, Liberation in Truth's participants contribute to an open religious environment. Attracted to and reassured by the ritual, congregants are able to embrace "church" as manifest through Liberation in Truth. Services offer a familiar religious structure free of the typical forms of condemnation; a belief system that is revitalized through a theological philosophy that speaks to their experience; and a vision that charges them to further growth. Liberation in Truth provides community space where people can experience and express themselves as whole beings. Here the women I interviewed feel they can express their sexual, spiritual, and religious identities, along with all the other aspects of self. This is a community where, to varying degrees, they feel they belong as whole persons.

Services reflect Pentecostal and Baptist worship style, and a theology of liberation that is interwoven with twelve-step recovery language as well as references to African ancestors. Some congregants continue to use traditional gender biased language in their praise, but most employ a wider lexicon, including references to God as She, Mother, and Spirit. The Yoruba word *Ashe* (sacred power) is repeated throughout the service. The liturgy defines God as love, and love as being everybody's birthright. The intention is to create an environment where all people, replete with religious, economic, racial, religious, and sexual differences, are welcome to participate in self-reflection and community building.

The congregation rents meeting space at Trinity and St. Philip's Episcopal Cathedral, a spacious building with a rich interior and tall stained-glass windows. The rhythm of the service is consistent from week to week. Ushers direct people toward the front to seats directly behind the section reserved for the choir, church elders, and trustees. Attendance at service varies. Some days no more than ten or fifteen come to worship. During holidays, church anniversaries, and other special occasions, such as a visit from Archbishop Bean or a pastor from a sister church, the cathedral overflows with celebrants. On some occasions people are encouraged to dress along theme lines: all in African attire, or entirely in white or lavender. Usually, however, the message encourages people to "come as they are."

Once people are settled into the wooden pews with bulletins, tithing envelopes, and sometimes a Bible in hand, service begins with silent meditation. A deacon invites congregants to reflect and center themselves. Deacon Leslie, the choir director, plays soft music on an electronic keyboard, sometimes accompanied by a drummer. Deacons then lead a period of song and devotions, during which time people stand and speak about Spirit (God) in their lives. Members testify to troubles and give praise to God for bringing them through. The problems and praise people bring are not so different from those brought into other black churches, particularly those serving the poor and disenfranchised: poor health, incarceration, drug addiction, employment issues, communication with family, and gratitude to God. But at Liberation in Truth these issues are specific to lesbian and gay experience, and are compounded by the struggle to negotiate society, church, and family, as such. The church has taken an activist stance in addressing HIV/AIDS, an especially critical issue in the community, both by speaking openly on the subject during service and by developing Loving in Truth, a ministry and outreach center dedicated to safer sex and HIV/AIDS education and advocacy.

After the testimonial time the congregation stands to welcome clergy and choir as they process the center aisle, singing and clapping, to their places at the head of the church. A deacon leads the way. Reverend Elder Holland precedes the retinue in full robes; usually purple, black, or white, with an embroidered stole across her shoulders and hair hanging down her back in long locks. She is followed by fifteen or so church staff dressed in robes or color-matched street attire. Most, but not all, are women of varying ages, statures, skin tones, hairstyles, and timber of voice.

After Reverend Holland takes a seat on the altar and the rest are arranged in the front pews, a clergy member calls the congregation to worship with a welcome invocation. Another pours libations from a chalice into a wide bowl, addressing the ancestors, the spirits, and various leaders in African American history ranging from Sojourner Truth to Malcolm X. Liberation in Truth expands on the African tradition of calling on the ancestors by including contemporary sociopolitical and spiritual leaders in the pantheon. Clergy next offer the affirmation and healing, which tell every person in the room that regardless of the negative messages imposed by society, family, and even self-perception, God loves each person unequivocally. This healing message emphasizes that sexual orientation, hair texture, facial features, skin color, choice of clothing, and even patterns of behavior are all according to God's intention and are a part of God's love. The affirmation points to the problem of social stereotypes that circumscribe people's sense of self and encourages pursuit of wholeness despite these factors.[2]

After the affirmation members are invited together to the altar for a communal prayer. The congregation then moves throughout the room smiling and embracing. A deacon welcomes first-time visitors, assuring them that they are part of the "church family." The theme of family is central at Liberation in Truth. Part of the church's purpose is to create a spiritual family where, in the case of many congregants, a physical family does not exist. The conflation of church and family and the employment of familial symbolism are in keeping with Black church tradition.[3] Of course, the idea of family at Liberation in Truth is different from the traditional hetero-patriarchal family typical of, for instance, Elder Holland's original Pentecostal church. The emphasis at Liberation in Truth is on creating an intimate, supportive network, but one not modeled on a hierarchical and heterosexist nuclear family. This is one example of how people in this community claim, incorporate, and transform a part of their tradition so that it affirms rather than condemns them.

After visitors have been welcomed, the service moves on with a trustee, a person responsible for the church's financial and administrative affairs, announcing the church events for the week. Events range from spiritual (Wednesday prayer circle, women's and men's support groups), to social (Fierce Fridays poetry night, bowling night), to seasonal (summer seafood fest, annual formal ball). Voices of Liberation, the church choir, take to the stage singing several selections from a repertoire ranging between refigured traditional gospel pieces and new compositions. These songs include "This Morning When I Woke, Lord," "I'm Blessed Because God Says I'm Blessed," "More than a Conqueror," and "I Still Have Joy."[4] Music transitions into the day's sermon, which a deacon introduces with a scriptural reading. This is the sole point in the service when the Bible is formally brought into play. Elder Holland refers to the selected passage during the sermon, but only insofar as it supports her overall message. Neither she nor her clergy rely on the Bible as the sole or inerrant purveyor of holy truth. For them it is one of many sources of spiritual wisdom.

The sermons, whether given by Elder Holland, a deacon, or a guest pastor, draw connections between a chosen theme—of love, of liberation, of faith, of trouble and understanding—and the daily experiences of the congregants. Holland describes herself as a teacher-preacher. Her sermons are heady and thought provoking. Others at the pulpit vary in style, some keeping with the teacher mode, others opting for a more charismatic, emotion-oriented approach. Regardless of style, the sermons generally focus on urging people to accept and love themselves, to strengthen their spirituality in relation to whatever understanding of God they believe. An example of one sermon, given by Deacon Kimberly[5], and reflective of Reverend Holland's philosophy, describes the power of focus:

> We make our own reality. Even with society's influence and the oppression that we have experienced, ultimately we decide what our lives are going to look like. The experiences that we have growing up definitely influence our ideas of what's real and what's possible for us. If our ideas of what we can have in life are not giving us what we want, then we need to change our concept of what's real and what's possible. . . .
>
> In the area of our emotions, what does this power of focus look like? What's going to give me the miracle breakthrough that I'm looking for? If you usually hold your emotions at a distance, ignoring your feelings when you're uncomfortable, or swallowing them and pushing them down when you're upset, then you're focusing on fear. Instead, focus on having faith in Spirit, and in yourself. Trust that you won't be overwhelmed by whatever comes up. Because God does not give us more than we can handle! Focus on how blessed you are, and name those blessings one by one in your mind. Remind yourself that those blessings are proof of God's love for you. Undeniable and concrete evidence that God's promise to protect you and provide for your needs is real. . . .

Holland's pastoral emphasis is on individual spirituality. The message she and her deacons mean to get across is that the truth, God, is within each individual, and that it is up to each person to manifest that divinity. Holland assures people of their intrinsic value. She advocates the importance of every person to the Liberation in Truth community. The church and the community, Holland maintains, will grow as the individual needs of each person are met.

After the sermon, Voices of Liberation sings again. On first Sundays the congregation takes communion together, to honor "the blood of Jesus and of every last ancestor that struggled for freedom." On these days members who wish to participate proceed to the front to take a piece of salt cracker and a thimbleful of grape juice back to their pew. Wine is intentionally avoided in recognition of congregation members who are in recovery. The pastor and deacons eat and drink, and then the whole congregation partakes simultaneously, in a gesture of spiritual solidarity. People then flow together from the pews to the altar and back, giving offering. Service closes with a communal prayer and silent reflection. On some days a potluck community gathering follows church.

The service means different things for different people. For some it represents a more or less comfortable and familiar space within which to practice religion. For others it is a way of embodying their spirituality. Most definitively, Liberation in Truth is a safe place to be lesbian, gay, bisexual, and transgender and to explore the religious and spiritual dimensions of one's identity as such.

The Women's Voices

The fact that Liberation in Truth functions as a safe haven for sexual and spiritual identity exploration is seen most clearly in the interviews that formed the heart of my research. The women I interviewed for this study come from a variety of religious traditions including Pentecostal, Baptist, Southern Baptist, Methodist, African Methodist, Reformed Episcopalian, Muslim, Catholic, and the United Church of Jamaica. Almost all were raised in a church atmosphere, and each has, at some point, left or come into conflict with her church due to theological disagreements, sociopolitical critiques, or the church's condemnation of her lesbian identity. Each woman has also returned to church, to varying degrees, through her involvement at Liberation in Truth. My purpose here is to introduce these women's perspectives on religion and spirituality and on their involvement with this particular church community.[6]

The women self-selected for interviews. With the help of Elder Holland I proposed my project during a service, and they met with me afterwards for appointments. Responses to my presence and request were mixed. Overall the congregation welcomed me, as they do all people who attend services. Some individuals were, as I thought they might be, somewhat suspicious of my motivations. In the end, I worked with the perspectives of those women who showed interest in my project, and who saw it as potentially valuable enough to chance the encounter. The result is a cameo: a few thoughts expressed by some but not all of the women at Liberation in Truth, interpreted through my nonreligious, white, academic lesbian perspective. This is a partial, condensed, but nonetheless telling representation of many intense hours of conversation between people who are simultaneously contextually determined and self-determining, mutable subjects.

I build the discussion around excerpts from my interview with one of these fourteen women. Alicia Heath-Toby is an entrepreneurial hairstylist, a self-described butch, and a deacon at Liberation in Truth church. She is also a staff member of the church's HIV/AIDS education and outreach program office, Loving in Truth. By emphasizing one woman's observations I do not mean to imply that her perspective sufficiently represents the other women in the study. Rather, Alicia's moment in the spotlight provides a beginning.

The excerpts suggest several themes that emerge from all of the women's reflections on my interview questions about religion and spirituality. Generally speaking, the women stage a strong critique of religion. They nevertheless consider religion to be important and most invest concerted effort into creating a fulfilling practice at Liberation in Truth. Such practice is for them a matter of exploring and cultivating their conceptions of spirituality. This practice involves a dynamic understanding of sexual identity.

Religion

> *Deacon Alicia*: I don't consider myself a religious person. Religion is manmade, it's an institution designed to oppress people, and to control people. Jesus Christ was not about religion, as opposed to a way of life . . . living right, and being just, being fair, being compassionate and being honest. All of those things. Religion is not that for me.

Several of the women I interviewed describe coming to Liberation in Truth as the discovery of a safe haven. Whether they participate fully or only on an occasional basis all the women characterize Liberation in Truth as unique from and qualitatively superior to their past experiences of religious institutions. Liberation in Truth offers the opportunity to practice spirituality without the restrictions typically associated with religion.

The women consistently set religion and spirituality in contrast to one another as, respectively, social construct and personal experience.[7] Deacon Leslie Oliver, chanteuse and choir director at Liberation in Truth describes, "religion as man's understanding of what God is supposed to be and feel like. [And] spirituality as that one-on-one with you and the God of your understanding." Religion is the framework built by humans to explain and make comprehensible the spiritual experience. It is a social institution, a structure and practice grounded in tradition and ritual. According to these women religion, like experience, is mutable and subject to context. Religion can provide necessary comfort to those who need guidelines for worship. On the other hand, it can become a thoughtless, rote reinforcement of behavioral patterns.

> *Deacon Alicia*: I was raised a Pentecostal child. Went to church at least five times a week. Stayed in church from morning until night on Sunday. Sang in the choir. My mother was an Evangelist, a preaching woman. I left the church. At the time it wasn't about being a lesbian as much as it was the politics. They were politicking instead of serving the community. . . . And I left the church because I didn't like the way they treated women. There were a lot of women who could teach, and preach, and give something to the other women . . . but there was no room for us in the pulpit. . . .
>
> It wasn't until I was maybe nineteen that I started to feel that because I was a lesbian, I was going to be damned to hell. I had heard the whole abomination thing in the church. But it wasn't until I became a young adult that I started to have a problem with God, and what God meant, and what the Bible meant. And

with who I was. And was I going to go to hell, because I was someone that I could not help being.

As these women see it, the problem with contemporary religion in general and Christianity in particular is that conservative and even mainline interpretations dictate a narrow evaluation of the traditions. Or as Deacon Shonda, who leads Bible study classes and is also a staff member at the Loving in Truth office puts it, "they're holding Christianity hostage." Overall, the women criticize religion for its complicity in different forms of oppression. The primary faults they identify are religion's tendency toward unwarranted control over people, its considerable internal hypocrisy, and the fact that it sometimes and paradoxically causes people to turn away from God. As Alicia points out, religion in her experience was a locus for politicking, condemnation, and sexist hierarchy. She found the authoritarianism of her early church experience to be incompatible with what she understands to be the spiritual lesson exemplified in Jesus Christ, that is, justice, compassion, and honesty in everyday life. Like Alicia, Deacon Leslie grew up in the Pentecostal church, daughter to a preaching woman. She, too, expresses vehement disgust with religion. "I've experienced religion to the extreme, and know it's full of crap. I'm over religion now. I have no use for it." Church for Leslie was a prison, a community isolated from the outside world that dictated strict rules to its members. She felt watched, paranoid, and constrained in her Pentecostal community.

According to the women I interviewed, no religion is all encompassing or all affirming, and so none fully represents Spirit (God). Within each religion there are also troublesome doctrines that undermine its integrity, such as the claim that those not within the particular tradition will "burn in hell." Religious traditions, in fact, often function as one of many control systems used to keep people subservient to a given ideology. Some of the women note that a lot of religions "yell" at people, frightening them into uncritical submission to externally imposed codes of conduct. Religion can be and often is dictated to people who are unable or ill equipped to understand it.

Several of the women identified bad faith among the leadership and the lay population as another of religion's faults. Ministers, out of fear and internal oppression, are often resistant to difference. Too often they are hypocritical, preaching condemnation and hatred when they should have a better message for the people in their pews. The women point out that many people in our country's congregations are substance abusers, homeless, gay, or people who just need support as they go through transitions in their lives. Instead of receiving spiritual and material succor from churches they are further marginalized by religiously sanctioned bigotry. Kim, a mother of three, whose own mother moved her as a child from the

Baptist church to an Islamic school to a Catholic school in search of an acceptable education, reflects the anguish shared, to varying degrees, by many of these women. "Religion" states Kim, "can fill a person with uncertainty about her status in the eyes of God, which causes misery."

At some point in each woman's experience religion has driven a wedge between her own self and God. Nevertheless, all but four of them are deeply involved with church at Liberation in Truth. Recognizing the pervasive presence of religion and its influence on their lives, they express a need for and appreciation of the religious setting and ritual. While a few are content to commune with Spirit (God) in solitude, most seek community context. Kim reflects this sentiment. "I know that I'm just me, trying to have this constant contact with God. . . . And sometimes I really have the desire to be in church. I would like to be able to go and to learn, because I do get a very overwhelming feeling when I'm there."

The value of religion as a general concept, these women say, is that, ideally, it can provide connection with one's traditions and with other people. Participation in church can potentially also help a person find and deepen her own sense of spirituality. The opportunity for religious community, these women point out, is especially important for people who are marginalized by their natal churches. For Sandy L., who has explored a number of churches in her spiritual quest, "religion is a form of spiritual discipline. . . . Church, when it enables contentment with self and God, provides a sense of completion, a sense of feeling at home, like [the feeling] I have when I'm involved with a woman." Sandy values the company of people who have similar beliefs and spiritual goals. She appreciates being around people who believe in God, because that shared conviction helps them to understand and help one another in their spiritual pursuits.

Sandy appreciates the church community of Liberation in Truth in particular, because she likes being with people who understand and accept that people can be both gay and spiritual. In fact, the characteristic she and other interviewees value most about Liberation in Truth is the church's affirmation of their whole being, its acceptance of them beyond mere tolerance. At Liberation in Truth the women are learning to embrace religious practice through a process of reinterpretation and reformulation on their own terms. These terms include celebration of one's sexual identity as inherent to whole self. The women describe the reinterpretation and reformulation as being a matter of spirituality rather than religion.

Spirituality

Reclaiming religion is simultaneously a process of spiritual introspection and the building of a liberative community. Through spiritual introspection the women recognize their intrinsic connection with Spirit (God). They insist on the divine, multidimensional, and fluid nature of their identity, one aspect of which is sexuality in all its complexity. Conviction of divine connection inspires a sense of belonging and yields a fundamental resource for negotiating dynamics of oppression, including the shortsightedness of their religious traditions. Deacon Alicia speaks of her spirituality as reflecting a sense of divine purpose.

> I have always been very connected with Spirit. The Spirit that is within me. Even when I was doing drugs, I was always connected. It was just a little connection then, something that kept me aware that there was something about my being created that was special, and that the Creator wouldn't have kept me even through all of that if I wasn't special. So, I'm real clear that there is a purpose, and that everyday that purpose is manifesting itself. . . . And I am grateful to be able to see that for what it is, and know that who I am is not a mistake, not something to be condemned. I realize I am just who I am supposed to be.

Alicia's favorite saying, "where I am, God is," reflects her belief that who she is— a butch woman who practices her spirituality through her hair styling business, her work with Liberation in Truth, and her day-to-day interactions—is fundamentally in keeping with the path chosen for her by Spirit (God). This conviction comes through long struggle with religious teachings that dictate otherwise. Alicia and the other women work to exorcise such "religious" condemnation from their self-perception and to affirm their inherent connection to Spirit. They seek a personal sense of peace and harmony within the self and with God despite the various impositions of social context. As such, spirituality is for them a practice of self-affirmation, as Spirit and through Spirit, a practice of inner growth and greater effectiveness in changing the world. For Alicia this means that living a righteous life, fulfilling her purpose on earth, involves both giving God pride of place and recognizing her lesbian self as part of that pride. "And if a person can't accept me as a lesbian God, then we can't connect. God is first in my life. And if we can't connect on the idea that God is love and love is for everyone, then I can't work with you. . . ."

Que, an artist and a woman determined to heal herself of "the virus" (HIV/AIDS) maintains that spirituality, unlike religion, "requires focus, and clear, specific intentions on connecting with the universe, which is greater than us all." For Que this focus involves reflecting on her life experiences, both negative and positive, as being lessons in deepening her humanity. Her statement also reflects a sense of relationship with the divine as being both universal and uniquely intimate. She and the other women intentionally cultivate a consciousness of the love and compassion of God, and of a universe that is simultaneously greater than the individual and inherently interconnected. They hold dear the premise advocated at Liberation in Truth that "God is love and love is for everyone."

Several of the interviewees also assert that participation at Liberation in Truth engenders attitude adjustment, expanding their capacity for insight, reflection, and action. Cynthia, a proud grandmother and "sports widow" to her athletically inclined wife of nearly twenty years, has been challenged to deal with her impatience and fiery temper. She now finds herself considering the circumstances of other people's lives more thoroughly before passing judgment on their actions. Similarly, involvement with the church has helped Monica, a mental health professional and deacon at Liberation in Truth, understand, in a more comprehensive way, the beauty of diversity and how to employ her own spiritual tools, her compassion and willingness. She appreciates more and more that "not everybody has to be clones from the same experience. I can be exactly who I am at LIT, even though I don't know anything about shouting or speaking in tongues. . . . I can appreciate that my brothers and sisters are feeling that sense of praise even if I don't understand it. . . ." Liberation in Truth has, for Monica, been a reality check, a reminder of her own good fortune, and a challenge to take up her charge in life to help better the world around her. As she puts it, "I'm here for a reason; there are things I am supposed to do."

Sexuality

Racism, sexism, classist attitudes, and homophobia all have an impact on these women's lives. As Monica describes it, "the African-American female community [is] just always under siege." To variously intentional degrees, the women I interviewed counteract oppression, at least partially, by subverting notions of fixed identity. They are critically aware of the fact that their whole selves, their interior sensibility, and their external representation do not fit into any tidy categories.[8] As Deacon Alicia states,

> I identify as butch. Now, like pastor [Reverend Holland] says, somebody wouldn't look at me and say I'm a real butch. I've found over the years when I have said to people, I'm a butch, they get all tight. And I'm like, why are you getting all anxious? That's how I identify! But I'm probably one of a dying breed of butches who address the feminine side of them. My feet are always done. And I do my nails. The way my hair looks is real important. I just appreciate that part of me. My friends tease me. They call me a faggot. Because . . . looking at me you would think, "Oh, she's a femme." But once you start to know me, you know definitely I am not a femme.

The women are skeptical of predefined roles and rules of conduct, whether imposed by racist and heterosexist norms in the wider society or by the lesbian community itself. They experience their own selves as mutable, complex, and hardly consistent with the reifying categorizations, such as race and gender, that stratifies our society. Insisting on this complexity of self is indeed part and parcel of their presence in and through Spirit. Since I asked in particular about sexual identity, the women's understanding of identity is most thoroughly illustrated through their thoughts on sexual orientation. As Deacon Alicia said,

> I have learned to appreciate that my sexuality is a gift from Spirit, and in that, is one and the same. I identify Spirit as both male and female. And depending on what I'm feeling that particular day, it may be She or She may be He. And that's because I identify myself as He and She. Spirit and my sexuality are definitely one and the same, because who I am is a manifestation of Spirit. One does not exist without the other.
>
> I think for lesbians, gays, transgenders, bisexuals, we have to be real clear about our sexuality being a gift from Spirit. Because if we don't, we get hoodwinked and bamboozled. A lot of us become suicide attempts; a lot of us become abusers of self and others. Because we're not identifying that Spirit has given us our sexuality and has created us as we are. God makes no mistakes. We are born lesbian, gay, transgender. It's just a manifestation of Spirit, [who] is infinite and encompasses all and everything.

Alicia points to the infinite power of God as evidence for the rightful existence of sexual diversity. She complicates sexual dimorphism by identifying both God and herself as sometimes He and sometimes She, depending on her own epistemic experience of the moment. Identifying their sexual identity is, for these women, a process of dissembling categories (Lewin in Behar and Gordon 1995). They take exception to "deep seated cultural assumptions, including the notion that the world is made up of two fixed genders and that individuals display a consistent set of gender 'traits'" (Weston 1996: 8). Their employment of the terms lesbian, butch, and femme further illustrates what they think of their own sexual identity and by extension, identity in general.

The women primarily define themselves as lesbian, but the term is polymorphous, a relatively incidental description of a multidimensional experience of being. As with all labels, they adopt it cautiously, well aware that people tend to assume a label reflects one's whole identity and so pass judgment accordingly.[9] As Robin, who likes to wear baggy clothes and walks with "just a little baby bop" strut, puts it, "I don't need more titles other than I already have. I mean, I'm already . . . I'm a black woman. And then that's like, and then, you're a lesbian too?! And then it's like, you're a butch too?! No titles. Just call me Robin. That's my name." Indeed, being imposed upon by other people's preconceived notions of identity is detrimental to one's own agency and well-being. Audrey Skeete, a founding member of Liberation in Truth and self-described "proud Jamaican," has suffered job loss on several occasions because supervisors interpreted her as being too hard-edged and overbearing to be a good nurse. Audrey suspects that they saw her solid, crew cut, black butch appearance as something other than the deeply caring and compassionate person she considers herself to be.

To be lesbian is first of all to be a woman, the individual self that each of these women is. The characteristic that they all identify as particularly lesbian is a focused but not exclusionary love of, commitment to, and desire for other women. "Lesbianism is a recognition, an awakening, a reawakening of our passion for each (woman) other (woman) and for same (woman)" (Guy-Sheftall 1995: 242). The women understand other terms, like butch and femme, to be mutable feelings that one experiences and expresses, rather than fundamental states of being or constant "roles" to which one might subscribe. Like Alicia, some acknowledge feeling consistently more one than the other, even as they practice signifiers of that other. And some employ the terms as stereotypes, even as they challenge such reifying moves by other people. For instance, in the same breath with which she criticizes friends for defining her as "hard" or "butchy" based on how she dresses, Robin claims to dislike "femmes, because they're all gold-diggers." As a rule however, the women are careful to distinguish between having a predominantly butch or femme sense of self, and subscribing to fundamentally gendered identities. As Sandy states, "gender and sexuality are fluid. The barriers [of fixed identity] are because of society and whatever psychological reasons people have for fitting into them."

The only element that these women explicitly claim as being essential to their sense of identity is the divinely intended and fluid nature of their sexuality. For some this claim is still tenuous, and some have only just begun to understand sexuality and spirituality as being in relationship to one another. Rikky, a seamstress and in recovery from drug addiction, articulates sexuality as being just a part of her overall identity and spirituality as being thoroughly pervasive. Sexuality and spirituality are therefore both related and not related. Sandy, on the other hand, suggests that sexuality is a form of spirituality, a deep way of touching. Physical contact can be a conduit for touching in a way that allows people to "almost know each other in a deep spiritual way; [to] start to really see the heart." And for Alicia, sexuality and spirituality are one and the same, interdependent manifestations of the Divine. For her, recognizing one's sexuality as a gift from Spirit is requisite to lesbian survival.

Whether they consider sexuality and spirituality as one and the same or as distinct aspects of self, the women describe them in terms of wholeness. They advocate understanding and practicing sexuality and spirituality as vital parts of whole being. Sexual being encompasses heart, mind, soul, and physical experience. While the physical self is not everything, it can be spiritual insofar as one conducts her body as an instrument for God's purposes. In some cases, as for Rikky, sexuality can be a catalyst for spirituality. In struggling to "accept and love" her sexuality in the face of hostile religious tradition and to reconcile that sexuality with her affection for church, she has had to engage in critical spiritual reflection. However they define the connection, the interviewees generally recognize sexuality as being, at least potentially, one avenue for spiritual development, and spirituality itself as underlying every aspect of identity.

Indeed, the openness around sexual orientation that is advocated at Liberation in Truth seems to be the main attraction for those women who are only occasionally involved with this church community. Kim, for one, hopes this church environment can help her to work through some of the confusion in her life about her sexuality, her uncertainty over God's acceptance of it, and the challenge of guiding her three children through a morass of mixed social messages about their mother's moral validity. And for those women who are fully involved with Liberation in Truth, the affirmation of their sexuality as divinely intended is crucial even though they may get tired of hearing the message repeated every Sunday. Deacon Victoria, an usher in the church, notes that "sometimes it's just that, a hug or a kind word, that keeps a person from committing suicide. This affirmation is especially important in the lesbian and gay community where there's a lot of pain."

Conclusion

The church, and the broader Unity Fellowship movement, is not without tension. Criticisms certainly exist. Even as Liberation in Truth's uncompromising openness about homosexuality provides respite for people rejected by other churches on that account, some participants find the emphasis on gay-affirmation uncomfortable. Some continue to wrestle with reconciling their sexual orientation with religious integrity. Some women also harbor doubts over differences in worship style and find the ecumenism challenging. Building community together across class differences, working out deeply engrained attitudes about physical characteristics and other indicators of social worth, is a laborious process. Participation levels in the church wax and wane. There are ongoing tensions over leadership, including some strain between the women and the men of the community.

Nevertheless, the women I spoke with identify Liberation in Truth as a place where they can remember and celebrate their ties to religion, foster their spiritual identities, and explore the connections and contours of whole self. Encouraged through religious community, they reclaim religious practice in their private lives as well. For example, Cynthia now swaggers her Southern Baptist upbringing by intentionally reclaiming prayer from "wacko far right Christians." She asserts herself in public as being a person touched by Spirit by giving praise and thanks often, every day, and out loud. Shirley Spriggs, an elder in the church, is discovering after years of uncertainty a kinder relationship with God. "I've learned a lot about praying, how to bow down and be humble. I used to pray angry, with an attitude. I'm not a religious fanatic, but now I just want to give thanks to Her (God). If it wasn't for knowledge from prayer, I wouldn't be alive today."

The women also speak of ways in which Liberation in Truth addresses other forms of alienation. For Monica coming to Liberation in Truth has been a turning point in her relationship with the black community. Educated in predominantly white Catholic schools and disassociated throughout her youth from black church experience she had for a long while lacked a group of black friends. At Liberation in Truth she feels "able to finally find . . . a circle of brothers and sisters that [she] can even just talk about this to." Still other congregation members testify during service to their experiences of alienation, depression, and familial rejection. As Victoria points out, "Heavy souls walk into LIT. People who feel they are outcast from society. . . ." Whatever their sense of difference, interviewees' prevalent attitude is that at Liberation in Truth everyone is welcome, and that in this community socially marginalized people in particular have space for spiritual self-discovery and expression.

All of us, myself and the women of this community included, are pushed and shaped by dynamics of power into contextually specific locations. Liberation in Truth Church, and the women I interviewed who are a part of that community, are subaltern agents on several fronts, as lesbians, as lesbians practicing religion, and as black women in a racist society. I believe that these women's reflections on their church, spirituality, religion, and sexuality offer profound insight into the nature of living at the nexus of our contemporary, neo-colonial reality and of transforming the dynamics of oppression inherent to that reality. I am politically and spiritually compelled by the way in which these women negotiate their particular context. Each one grows her subjectivity up through oppressive impositions, and does so as a form of spiritual practice. I have tried in this anthropological study to illustrate some of the ways in which the women play this process out by highlighting their perspectives on identity, especially sexual and spiritual identity, as being multiple and mutable. In so doing, I play my own part in negotiating oppression and subjectivity. I hope for nothing short of epistemological and social transformation. Here, I have taken my cues from these women of Liberation in Truth, whose spirituality is a process of "love in action."[10]

Notes

1. The research for this study was partially funded by the Newark Project through a program grant from the Ford Foundation.

2. Garth Kasimu Baker-Fletcher defines wholeness in relation to the black community as "a complex set of behaviors developed against the ongoing existential psycho-spiritual

state of fragmentation, ontological sense of incompleteness, biological disease, and the sociopolitical and economic realities of rupture whereby selves seek to complete, heal, mend, and become reintegrated" (Baker-Fletcher, ed. 1998: 156).

3. See Lincoln and Mamiya (1990, especially p. 402). See Williams (1974) on the topic of nuclear family imagery in Pentecostalism (13).

4. Several other favorite songs are "Praise God's Holy Name," "I'm So Glad that Love Lifted Me," "I'm Looking for a Miracle," "Oh Magnify the Lord (for She Is Worthy to Be Praised)." Along with their annual church concert, the choir is releasing a record and has recently begun singing at invited events outside of the church.

5. As of the Los Angeles Convocation of Unity Fellowship Churches, October 1997, Deacon Kimberly was ordained Reverend K. Bell-Greene. This excerpt comes from her sermon titled "The Miracle of Focus," given at Liberation in Truth, 8 March 1997.

6. Because of my reservations about being a white person entering into a black community in order to conduct an anthropological study, I attended service for two years before feeling justified in requesting interviews. See Margery Wolf (1992); Ellen Lewin, ed. (1996) Lewin and Leap, eds. (1996); and Spickard, et. al., eds. (2002). Gayatri Chakravorty Spivak points out that "Much so-called cross-cultural disciplinary practice, even when 'feminist,' reproduces and forecloses colonialist structures: sanctioned ignorance, and a refusal of subject-status and therefore human-ness [for the subaltern]" (Spivak 1999: 167 in Donaldson and Kwok 2002: 44). It is my own ethical imperative and spiritual hope to subvert such objectification. My key concern has been to conduct and write this study in a way that fractures such ignorance and recognizes the subjects speaking for themselves. With this intention, I foreground the women's diverse perspectives and draw the overall discussion directly from the nexus of our conversations. In so doing, I mean to participate in the "epistemological shift" called for by anticolonialist, antiracist, antisexist, and liberation-oriented scholars. Laura E. Donaldson describes this epistemological shift in "The Breasts of Columbus: A Political Anatomy of Postcolonialism and Feminist Religious Discourse," *Postcolonialism, Feminism and Religious Discourse* (2002: 45). See also Kwok Pui-Lan's essay in the introduction to this book (p. 29) for the emerging descriptive language of this epistemological process.

7. Unless otherwise noted, the ideas outlined throughout this document are drawn, in a condensed format, from interviews with: Deacon Alicia Heath-Toby, 27 October 1998; Deacon Victoria Castillo and Audrey Skeete, joint interview, 12 November 1998; Cynthia, 3 November 1998; Kim, 19 December 1998; Monica, 28 October 1998; Deacons Leslie Oliver and Shonda Nicholas, joint interview, 2 January 1999; Que, 20 December 1998; Rikky, 22 October 1998; Robin, 4 December 1998; Sandy L., 30 October 1998; Shirly Spriggs, 29 October 1998; Reverend Elder Jacquelyn Holland, 19 March 1997; and private discussions, including one during the Newark Project Methods in the Study of Urban Religion graduate seminar, Drew University, 28 March 2000.

8. Speaking of sexual identity, queer theorists argue that gender is a cultural construct, something that we "do" as part of our cultural enactment, not something we inherently "are." Most lesbians, or heterosexuals for that matter, do not fit neatly into gendered categories. See, for example, Kathy Rudy, "Queer Theory and Feminism," in *A Rainbow of Re-*

ligious Studies (1996), and Deborah P. Amory, "Club Q: Dancing with (a) Difference," in Lewin (1996: 150).

9. Patricia Hill Collins points out, for example, that "portraying African American women as stereotypical mammies, matriarchs, welfare recipients, and hot mommas has been essential to the political economy of domination fostering black women's oppression." (1990: 67).

10. bell hooks calls for precisely this kind of "loving justice" in *Salvation: Black People and Love* (2001: 224).

Utopian Imaginaries and Faerie Practice   14
Mapping Routes of Relational Agency

JAY HASBROUCK

A Sanctuary and Its Stewards

ZUNI MOUNTAIN SANCTUARY lies at the far north end of a sweeping valley of cacti and juniper trees in rural New Mexico. Situated in the middle of a 315-acre tract are a dozen or so buildings and tents scattered around two ponds, collectively evoking the feel of something like a summer camp or retreat with Southwestern, New Age influences. The community's main structure, an adobe and glass building designed for maximum solar gain, faces south over an expansive plain contrasted at its far end by a grand mesa with sides of towering red and orange rock formations. At 7,000 feet in elevation, winter brings subzero temperatures and plenty of snow. Spring and summer are highlighted by vast fields of wildflowers that bloom in waves of color across the valley floor. Late summer is punctuated by powerful lightning strikes amid clusters of thunderstorms that churn through otherwise clear afternoon skies.

The sanctuary was established in early 1996 and is one of a handful of permanently settled Radical Faerie collectives in the United States. Although difficult to define as a cohesive group or movement, Faeries generally agree that they are people who seek an anarchistic departure from what they see as the inevitable products of Western capitalist society: bureaucracy, competition, consumerism, alienated work, careerism, pollution, suburban sprawl, oppressive hierarchies, corporate control, isolation and dissolution of a sense of community, sexual oppression and possessiveness, and heterosexism. While the Radical Faerie phenomenon shares a common ancestry with today's gay rights movement[1], most Faeries break from the gay liberationist focus on lesbian and gay identity as a means of effecting social change. In fact, many Faeries view gay identity as a false Western construct that is at least partially based in, and dependent on, a Western dichotomy of sexuality: nonconforming versus "normal." These false constructs, they argue, label and ghettoize lesbians and gay men, thereby forcing those who assume "gay" or "lesbian" as their primary identity to interpret their life experiences under the watchful gaze of dominant "normalcy."

The result, many Faeries posit, is an inescapable integration with an oppressive "mainstream"—an alternative imitation of the very social system that devalues their nonconforming sexualities. Some Faeries point to the development of an urban-centered "gay establishment" (whose efforts they see as concentrated on tolerance by the Euro-American "mainstream" rather than challenging its understandings of sexuality) as one of the unfortunate results of contemporary sexual identity politics. From their perspective, the battle for same-gender marriage is a good example of how this "gay establishment" often strives toward conformity rather than creatively resisting dominant paradigms of sexuality and gender.

The response of Faerie members has been to create and explore their own interpretations of sexuality and identity, often through self-marginalization and explorations of "alternative" spiritualities. Some early Faeries fled urban gay ghettos and settled in rural areas in the early 1970s. Many others now organize and attend gatherings that focus on individual and cultural "healing." These usually involve neo-pagan and Native American inspired celebrations, rituals, and performances in which participants focus on interpreting the relationship between their spirituality, sexuality, and "the earth" (Thompson 1987; Timmons 1990). Faerie spirituality, however, is a complex mix of often conflicting imaginaries and practices. One Faerie offers the following:

> The Radical Faerie Fellowship is a diverse and unorganized group of gay men who center their spiritual lives around various and sundry pagan doctrines. While no particular doctrine predominates, the movement is deeply rooted in the precepts of Native American spirituality. Nonetheless, there are druids, wiccans, taoists, shamans, Hindus, and any number of other recognized or unrecognized beliefs present among Radical Faeries. We embrace life in its entirety, yin and yang, drag and mufti. We create rituals meaningful to us in our lives, pagan rituals that validate and celebrate our lives as Gay men (Elfstone 1996).

Much of the Faerie critique of the North American "mainstream" is closely aligned with Roszak's (1969) early description of the counterculture position that took shape in the 1960s. To this, many Faeries add a feminist-inspired critique of dominant Western culture, its implicit enforcement of gender and sexual dichotomies (Rubin 1993), and the concurrent history of oppression of women and sexual minorities. These positions are often linked directly to a set of Faerie practices that enable them to embody an "alternative" consciousness as well as engage in an interplay with Faerie utopian imaginaries that reflect that consciousness. In its most obvious manifestations, this frequently involves changing birth names to Faerie names (which are assumed to be more accurate reflections of Faerie "selfhood"), and wearing clothing and accessories that have Native American, Asian, counterculture, or drag influences.

Zuni Mountain Sanctuary in particular began to take shape in Taos, New Mexico, when a small group of men first recognized their common interest in forming a permanent Faerie-centered collective. With the financial support of one member, they eventually purchased the land on which they now live. A number of members of this founding group had already been conducting their own research into "off-the-grid" living (solar and wind energy, environmentally sound housing, waste management, and agriculture, etc.), which allowed them to more easily begin their efforts to make the former ranch land habitable. In addition, most residents (or, stewards, as they refer to themselves) contribute approximately $100 a month from their own resources for food and supplies. Their income sources vary from inheritances, disability payments, and off-site jobs in nearby communities. Donations from supporters also supplement their income and stock of supplies. In its present state, the beginnings of sustainable farming have begun to take shape at the sanctuary and, in addition to the main building, the number of permanent structures now includes two residences, a phone "hut," shower facilities, pit toilet, and a firing kiln (the community also operates a pottery business called Oso Notch Pottery, from which it derives a small income). The stewards with whom I worked most during my fieldwork (Arcturus, Buffy, Dipper, Eden, Granite, Maqui, and Owl) were primarily middle-class, Anglo-American gay men in their thirties or forties who were raised as Protestants. Most were either from, or had recently resided in, the southwestern United States and had worked in a wide range of jobs including computer programming, aromatherapy, sex work, pottery and craft production, and nursing.

Today, the number of people residing permanently on the land fluctuates between five and fifteen. This is actually quite common for a Faerie community, each of which is part of a larger dispersed and inter-evolving network of Faerie culture. A particularly telling example of how I originally began to conceptualize this network (which includes the sanctuary) comes from one of my early struggles during my fieldwork there. In my first (and, in retrospect, rather naive) attempts to grasp Faerie culture and to understand the community at the sanctuary, I would inquire about the status of various people who were residing there. I suppose my unspoken goal was to make some sort of distinction between those holding steward status and those who were "just visiting." After a number of stewards responded to my inquiries with somewhat quizzical expressions or repeatedly described people's status within the community in equivocal and conditioned terms, it became apparent that the sanctuary was, and is, a community in a continual state of flux, with permeable borders and many transfused boundaries. Of course, this could be said of many communities (i.e., Anderson's *Imagined Communities*, 1991), but the physically isolated location of the sanctuary initially led me to assume that there would be some sort of marked distinction between insiders and others. What I found is that there is often a different configuration of people at the sanctuary each day. Stewards come and go, take extended trips to other communities and cities, and change their status with the community often. Some move away and then return months later. In addition, there are often visitors making extended stays on the land who participate fully in all functions of the community, further blurring the distinction between what I tried to define as "permanent" stewards and others. Phone and e-mail contact with other Faeries is frequent at the sanctuary, and messages, gossip, and other interpersonal information are passed on regularly via these routes as well as word of mouth.

Bringing Sanctuary into View

Stewards and other Faeries create a collective sense of sanctuary through practices that engage utopian imaginaries unique to the Faerie community network. For most of the stewards, this includes constructing and maintaining an environment where people can eschew what they see as the limitations of the North American "mainstream," while integrating nonconforming conceptions of community, spirituality, gender, and environment. Eden, a steward in his mid-forties from Albuquerque, describes it as:

> a tract of land in New Mexico where the people living there are living an alternative lifestyle based on spiritual growth, environmental awareness, and self-sustaining farming and agriculture. It's a sanctuary for people to come to with comfort and support . . . and a solid base.

Similarly, Buffy states:

> Everybody's vision is unique and yet there's something common about it and I think it's . . . probably something to do with a connection to the earth, and maintaining that, and building that, um, and providing a place for others to come and do the same . . .

When I first arrived at the Sanctuary, I was given a tour of the property by Granite, during which I was taken to a charred patch of earth at a high elevation on the land and told that some of the original stewards performed the first Faerie ritual there (they lit a fire, meditated, held hands, and spoke aloud to each of the four directions), in which they asked the spirits of the land for their permission to settle there. Many similar practices occurred repeatedly in various forms during my visits, each reflecting spiritual beliefs and practices patterned after those of Native Americans (Allen 1986, Brown 1982, Grim 2001, Redington 2000, Swan 1990) and other indigenous groups (Smith 1999, Gonzalo 1999, and especially Arango and Andoque 1999).[2] Regardless of specific origin, what guides most of these practices is a holistic spirituality that conceives of humans as part of a dialogic and interdependent network of cosmic harmony that includes the earth and all of its elements. And, unlike their prior experiences with private property and Western land development, the stewards could now integrate their spiritual practices with a particular place, thereby creating both a home and a sanctuary at the same time.

Another Faerie practice in which an interplay with Faerie utopian imaginaries of spirituality fosters a sense of sanctuary is the convening of heart circles, a practice with neo-pagan references. These meetings, in which a talisman is passed and participants take turns articulating feelings they might not have expressed in other circumstances, are meant to build bonds among participants. Such bonds are assumed to be obstructed in the North American "mainstream," due to dominant cultural imperatives that privilege individualism and competition in the interest of maintaining and defending one's ego or masculinity. Typical topics addressed at heart circles include interpersonal relationships, conflicts, and emotional responses. Their effect is to demonstrate the strong commitment participants have for each other's emotional, psychological, and spiritual well-being. It is, in many ways, a structured kinship-building process that engages utopian imaginaries of assumed mutual care, respect, and interest among those who are not consanguineous kin, but are expected to take on similar characteristics and roles.

Heart circles have also been described as "healing" practices that facilitate a process of recovery from presumed emotional and psychological damage inflicted upon Faeries by the oppressive "mainstream." The shared experience of the heart circle, then, becomes an act in which participants engage in utopian imaginaries of unity, rooted in assumptions that participants share a history and relationship with the "mainstream" in which oppression has played a large role in the formation of their identity. Referring to the weekly heart circles held at the Sanctuary, Arcturus states:

> As I understand it, heart circle has evolved to where people are just talking about their feelings rather than the person. They're talking about what the effect the person had rather than, say, you know, oh you're an awful person because you did this. I can come to a heart circle and say, what you did the other day really made me feel bad and its been burning in me and I just need to release it . . . and it really is [sic] started to heal now.

Perhaps the most visible set of Faerie practices that engage utopian imaginaries of spirituality and facilitate a sense of sanctuary are references to, and appropriations of, the dual-gendered berdache role (see Williams 1986; Jacobs, Thomas, and Lang, eds. 1997). Most Faeries at the Sanctuary cross-dress (often partially) on a regular basis and participate in "gendered" craft production and activities such as crocheting and weaving. Maqui states:

> All my life I knew I was different . . . and . . . going through all of the expression of the sexual Self and the emergence of gay people standing up and saying "here we are." And . . . seeing . . . that most of my friends and myself were all drawn to some kind of expression of the arts . . . I, I had noticed that. And then reading . . . reading like . . . *Zuni Man-Woman*,[3] um, and seeing that we're two-spirited, that we possess the masculine and the feminine Self, and, not being able to express that in this society, um . . . I believe drove a lot of people to another lifetime. With the vex of alcoholism and drugs, we all went out looking for that . . . ways to make an effect, and couldn't, and wasn't being heard. So, I believe that giving a place for that, a person to come and discover that, to try doing something else, is . . . is important.

Maqui sees practices that reflect identification with the berdache role as acts of psychological healing that engage utopian imaginaries of Native American spirituality as a form of refuge from gender oppression in the "mainstream." This is also a practice through which Faerie utopian imaginaries of otherworldly idealism are engaged, where "being" two-spirited (through frame of mind, style of dress, etc.) also means creating a world in which stewards and others have the freedom to "discover" their (presumably inherent?) two-spirited nature and reposition it within positive cultural contexts (Roscoe 1998, Sell 2001).

Blurring Boundaries, Transgressing "Norms"

Beyond developing and maintaining a sense of sanctuary, a large number of Faerie practices engage utopian imaginaries that transgress "mainstream norms" and challenge dominant imaginaries by blurring boundaries between categories that have been well-established throughout Western history. Of particular note are those practices that challenge traditional Western dichotomies such as self vs. other, man vs. nature, us vs. them, and public vs. private (Sedgwick 1993).

One of the most basic of Faerie practices that transgress the first of these is how kinship is defined at the sanctuary. Interpersonal relationships among stewards reflect a set of practices that are indicative of an interplay with Faerie utopian imaginaries that privilege a flexible, "fictive" kinship that transgresses the fixed and consanguineous-centered kinship structure of dominant North American culture and its assumptions regarding the essential nature of blood ties. For example, the stewards often refer to each other as "brothers":

Owl: They're my brothers . . . yeah, definitely more, as it goes along, they're more and more like a family, brothers, type, without a doubt.

At other times, their relationship is described as a kind of group marriage:

Granite: Creating a relationship with nine or twelve people at one time . . . is . . . you know, they're intimate relationships, it's the same amount of work as having a boyfriend. And so, so to have twelve boyfriends and working on them all at one time is . . . is a difficult thing. I've been in a relationship with two other people in the community . . . um, Mike, and Ajita, and now Eden . . . and somewhat, Brandon. So, I think we're learning about what relationships are, in community. And that's, that's really great. Its very different than having a relationship in an apartment in the city, or two guys living alone on a farm. It's, it's really about the relationship of all of the people in the community living together. Um, just because we're sleeping together, in the same bed, I don't see our relationship as any different as, as Dipper, who I've never slept in the same bed with.

Or, even a single organism:

Arcturus: There were times during this winter when we got down to two or three people and it's a completely different dynamic than when there are ten, twelve, twenty people here. And you would think it would become more chaotic, but it becomes more self-organizing, almost as if we're becoming an organism ourselves.

All three statements reflect an interplay with Faerie utopian imaginaries that render their interpersonal relationships intimate, multifaceted, flexible, and inextricably connected. For example, rather than a "mainstream"-style divorce, a "boyfriend" can return to the status of "brother" (or even an occasional sexual partner) all without ever having left the "family." What in other contexts might be seen as contradictions or conflicts becomes a set of practices that interact with imaginaries of a nearly taboo-free set of interpersonal configurations. Berger (1981), Popenoe (1984), and Kanter (1972) might position Faerie sexual kinship within the longer tradition of "responsible sexual freedom" that was central to the practices and principles of many intentional communities in the West, beginning in the late nineteenth century with religious collectives, reemerging in 1960s' counterculture communes, and continuing to a lesser extant today in neo-Marxist opposition to the bourgeois family.

In a manner similar to this blurring of self and other in interpersonal relationships, a number of stewards have developed practices that actively engage imaginaries that blur boundaries between self and the earth or environment. Dipper calls it a form of "engagement":

I'm looking for a certain state of being, a certain way of using my mind and my body, that, um, that feels right, that works well. It's sort of, it's a kind of, it's a way

of engagement. Um . . . the basic quality of it, is uh, I call it this relaxed atten-
tiveness, where ah, if I'm relaxed and paying attention to things around me, I can
often accomplish things that are incredible.

I have dreams, I constantly dream about building these terraces. I just dream
and dream and dream about it. I mean, especially in the spring. And I dreamt
about when the rains would come and what it would look like and how the water
would flow. And in the dream, it was like, I was constantly processing all this information, and . . . when your dream life and your waking life become that intertwined . . . have you ever read the book *Birdie*? . . . the beauty of the book is that
he describes this boy's dream life and his relationship with these birds that he's
keeping, and um . . . it's astounding. And the moment I read the book, it smacked
of truth to me. I mean it was so real to me . . . I knew that that was an imminent
possibility. And I, and I, kind of, I've always sort of felt like, that there's something in me that cries out for that kind of life, that kind of engagement.

The terraces to which Dipper refers are a series of flat stones lining a creek that
runs near the showers. They are one set of a variety of constructions at the sanctuary that are designed to reflect and complement the surrounding landscape,
which include adobe buildings, garden enclosures, mazes, and countless shrines
and altars of various natural materials, shapes, and sizes. Some of these works are
dedicated to special features in the landscape like a rock outcropping, while others are small and simple areas that designate spots for reflection or meditation.

A particularly large and unique set of four altars were constructed at the sanctuary to commemorate each of the four directions. Their inspiration came from a
series of communications that a few of the stewards had with "earth-spirits," in
which the stewards were told to enlist the efforts of all stewards to build altars to
the land to help it "heal." These conversations were actually referred to often during my latter visits at the sanctuary. Buffy references them here:

I don't know if you talked to Owl about his experiences with the earth-spirits here,
recently, since you were here last year I think this happened. When the spring came
along, we were all here . . . and I felt their presence too . . . saying that they are here
to help us, and you know, just do what you're doing. And, um, that's what these
four altars are about, they said to build an altar and visit it and we will, um, help
you do what you're doing here because we're behind it. And then the day that the
trees arrived I felt was the day that they were arriving and everyone else knew that
too, that the spirits were coming here, and we welcomed them along with the trees.
And, um, that was when we sort of called in the rainstorm, and this huge cloud
just came over, and we were all out by where the fire circle is now, and circled there
banging on drums and shaking rattles and this rain came over and this thunder-
storm . . . it was amazing. And we needed it too, we just planted trees, you know,
it was like water for the trees.

The practice of altar building and other land works engages an interplay with Faerie utopian imaginaries that blur boundaries between body and environment and appropriate a blend of Native American and other animistic landscape interpretations (cf. Redington 2000, Roe and Taki 1999). These include assumptions about achieving a "natural balance" between human use and the earth (which, according to many of the stewards with whom I spoke, precludes the existence of cities and appears to depend more on spiritual guidance and appropriated spiritual beliefs than interpretations such as ecosystem paradigms or biodiversity). It also includes assumptions that the stewards are close to achieving this balance, and that their land use and interpretations of the landscape reflect some form of "truth," or even manifest destiny (due, at least in part, to directions from, and conversations with, earth-spirits).

On numerous occasions, both Dipper and Owl referred to gardening, treeplanting, and other earthwork such as altar building as "healing the land." Owl states:

> I see that a lot of people come here, after they're here a while, they do get really attached to the land here. And so, I think a lot of stuff is going to come out of that. We'll see a lot more attention to healing the land.

Similarly, Buffy comments:

> I really feel like we are on some verge of an evolutionary change, and that um, this is really one of the keys to it, is reconnecting with the earth. And that's what this whole project is about, it's about people inhabiting a land that needs recovery . . .

While, on the one hand, these efforts represent attempts to revive the parched earth that was poorly managed for years (heavily logged and then overgrazed by cattle), they also function as a set of healing rituals that revive and sustain the lives of the stewards. The healing process occurs within imaginaries of spirituality where the earth and the stewards are one, and where healing rituals provide a therapeutic effect for both material and emotional and spiritual resuscitation. It is seen as the spirit of the land as transfused with the spirituality of the stewards; the recovery of the life on the land as transfused with the recovery of the lives of the stewards who are being addressed through these healing rituals.

In these practices that tap an imaginary of a land/steward "biome," the goals for the healing process are multiple, overlaid, integrated, and interactive. On the physical and material level, these healing rituals focus on reclaiming the land and the sustenance the land provides through gardening, permaculture, and an environment free of urban pollutants for the stewards themselves (many of whom are living with compromised immune systems due to HIV or AIDS). On the emotional and spiritual level, these healing rituals target the recovery of a respect for a human relationship with the land, as well as the recuperation of the stewards from stress and other negative associations they have with urban life.

Another set of Faerie practices that blur self and other are behaviors that reflect imaginaries of an interconnected—yet often physically dispersed—Faerie community, in which each person is somehow linked to all other Faeries through an assumed sense of unity, cohesion, and kinship. For example, during gatherings I attended at the sanctuary, many visitors—some of whom were complete strangers to the stewards—were greeted by Arcturus and others with the phrase "welcome home" and were immediately treated as if they belonged to the community. This practice is indicative of an interplay with Faerie utopian imaginaries that transgress common boundaries found among "strangers" in the "mainstream." It would seem that part of this imaginary is likely to include the assumption that anyone who has taken the effort to find and attend geographically remote sanctuary gatherings already shares at least some common perspectives and interests, making them "family" almost by default. The effect, in any case, is to reconfigure interpersonal difference in a new context, deflate the potential for conflict or alienation, and foster altruistic behaviors.

This conception of an interconnected Faerie community is not, however, entirely insular. Arcturus comments:

> We're [the Sanctuary] like a separate little world of our own, but there are other worlds that will be coming, each person I see as a world, will be coming and bringing their own subtleties with them, or personalities and whatever. And it's wonderful to see how the dynamics change as people start coming in.

By seeing each visitor "as a world," Arcturus is incorporating the broader cultural influences and sense of community of visitors into those of the stewards at the sanctuary. The sanctuary community, then, *is* the visitor's community and vice versa. This move expands outwardly from perspectives of blurred body boundaries to one that integrates representations of culture and cultural realms through embodied representations. From this perspective, a visitor's "body" at the sanctuary brings with it not only the basic needs for food and water, and the potential to interact interpersonally with others (emotionally, physically, etc.), but also those cultural elements that are attached to, or part of, that body. This is often most evident when considered in light of how Faerie culture is imbued in common practices such as eating (meals are always collective, with visitors often participating fully in planning, preparation, and clean-up), and sex (open relations with visitors and stewards alike, sometimes involving multiple partners, and spiritual practices such as tantra or other techniques).

The view of the Faerie community as an ever-adapting organism is also evident during many ritual practices at Faerie gatherings. The following excerpt is from a collective poem (one line per person) written at the Sanctuary during the 1996 winter solstice gathering.

> VISION POEM, Zuni Mountain Sanctuary, Winter 1996
> Believe in the space between solitude and commonality
> Suspended between the right now and forever,
> Celestial-earthly miraculous home and sanctuary
> Dancing out into spirals across the land
> Queers dancing now and forever
> As one being

Other practices at gatherings that reflect this perspective include drumming circles, sweat lodges, "ohming" workshops, feasts, heart circles, birthday parties (for both the land and people), and other rituals and activities. During the summer solstice gathering in 1997, I attended an initiation ritual that reflects both the interplay between practice and utopian imaginaries of Faerie community-as-organism and a sense of spirituality that conflates notions of self, other, and earth. The ritual—which seems to be specific to the Sanctuary in some ways—is described as both an initiation for visitors who have not yet attended a Faerie gathering as well as a way for everyone in attendance to "celebrate the land." It is usually held near the beginning of the solstice gathering as a sort of kick-off event. Although it varies from year to year, I was told that there is usually a rough "script" that is agreed upon in advance by the stewards leading it and any other interested participants. The following is an abbreviated version of my observations during fieldwork:

> The ritual began at mid-morning with the ringing of the community iron signaling everyone on the land to dress (or undress) in preparation for the ceremonies and convene at a hilltop near the main building. Most chose to dress in various combinations of Faerie "drag" (skirts, dresses, and other articles of Western women's clothing . . . found in the "drag tent" near the point where everyone convenes), counterculture wear (tie dye, bandannas, jewelry, etc.), South Asian-styled clothing (primarily sarongs and saris), and Native American-styled accessories (headbands, feathers, jewelry), mixed with t-shirts, shorts, jeans, and other casual Western clothing. A significant minority chose to attend the event nude and covered completely in a clayish mud prepared from on-site soil and water. A majority of participants also applied some form of decorative mud markings on their body, even if they remained clothed.
>
> Once everyone was almost ready, Owl blew a conch shell to signal everyone to gather, and Granite (both stewards) made the following statement to the group of

approximately fifty to seventy participants: "This parade is about celebrating the land we live on, and play on, and love on . . . [describes route] . . . enjoy the walk, enjoy the land, enjoy your music."

The group was then lead in a procession by Granite around the perimeter of the property. A majority of the participants carried musical instruments (especially drums) and played them throughout. A number of participants also carried handfuls of earth with them. After completing the procession, they gathered in a circle in a large cleared area to the continual beat of increasingly synchronized drumming. A series of ceremonies were then performed, beginning with the passing of a kiss around the circle (and then back again), and impromptu commemorations to each of the four directions by those standing at the points associated with north, south, east, and west. Then, all those who had not attended a Faerie gathering before (approximately ten) were asked to move to the center of the circle, and form an outward-facing circle by joining arms at the elbows. Jude then read aloud a poem he'd written, while skipping around the inner circle of new initiates to the beat of drumming.

When he finished, there was a period of loud applause and the Faeries in the outer circle (still holding hands) began to run in an ever-tightening ring around the initiates. A few Faeries from the outer circle broke from the circling ring and moved inward to smudge the initiates' foreheads with mud, kiss them, and sprinkle their heads with glitter. When the outer circle finally converged on the inner, they forced the entire group together in a tightly compacted clump. Once everyone stopped moving and all empty spaces were completely filled with their bodies, the drumming stopped and the group began to "ohm" for about two or three minutes. A short period of silence followed, and Jude read a few final lines from his poem while circling the entire group. Then the drumming recommenced, and the circle broke.[4]

The practices described both in this ritual, as well as others in this section, bring into focus Faerie utopian imaginaries of spirituality that transgress many dominant Western beliefs and assumptions regarding the boundaries between individuals, their bodies, their "spirits," their community, and the environment. They illustrate the ways in which sanctuary stewards appropriate Native American and neo-pagan spiritual practices as means to engage imaginaries that cast all forms of life within an interdependent, interconnected, and continually evolving biome (Grim, ed. 2001; Grim and Tucker, eds. 1994). These ideas stand counter to those in the West that have shaped most recent relationships between people (where competition and individuality have historically predominated) and between people and the environment (where manifest destiny, development or, in some cases, a science-based culture and nature dichotomy have reigned).

Imaginaries and Practice

While Faerie practices manifest themselves in specific forms, the collective imaginaries they engage, like the community itself, are continually changing and often never entirely determined. One of my objectives here is to identify the role that Faerie imaginaries might have within a larger process of social change. This includes an attempt to integrate the ever-changing cultural contexts of imagining through the concept of shared, or social, imaginaries. In *Lectures on Ideology and Utopia*, Ricoeur calls the social imaginary a set of collective stories and histories that do not necessarily bear the signature of any one person, and that exercise a formative influence on social actions and behaviors (1986). Kearney contextualizes the social imaginary in a summary of Merleau-Ponty's interpretation:

> The world is full with the imaginary. Not, as Sartre maintained, because the imaginary is its negation, but because it is its expression. Even society itself is, in a fundamental sense, an incarnation of human imagining. Each institution, Merleau-Ponty affirms, is a symbolic system that human subjects incorporate into their behaviour as a certain style of conduct. And every individual imagination is charged accordingly by the symbols of society which surround it—as it in turn recharges these symbols with its own creativity. . . (Kearney 1991: 128).

Cornelius Castoriadis contributes similarly through his concept of the radical imaginary. He argues that one of the primary characteristics of imaginings (both individual and shared) is that they are never fully defined, and that social institutions are the products of shared (or sociohistorical) imaginaries. He states:

> The imaginary of which I am speaking is not an image *of*. It is the unceasing and essentially *undetermined* (sociohistorical and psychical) creation of figures/forms/images, on the basis of which alone there can ever be a question *of* "something." What we call "reality" and "rationality" are its works.
>
> Beyond the conscious activity of institutionalization, institutions have drawn their source from the *social imaginary* (Castoriadis 1987: 3, 131).

Utopian imaginaries can clarify this process. It has always been clear that the specifics of attempting to live in "utopia" are often radically different amongst those advancing the concept. This is especially the case when considering the histories of the many different North American intentional communities (cf. Popenoe 1984). However, as Spann (1989) argues, many of these communities have shared a collective set of imaginaries that are less clearly defined than their living practices or purported doctrines. For example, as different as the sanctuary may be from religious intentional communities of the late eighteenth and early nineteenth centuries, the stewards do share a collective set of utopian imaginaries that are similar to these groups. These imaginaries include idealistic associations with living in a close-knit community, a frontier mentality, forms of environmentalism, and survivalism. Most of these communities also formed in order to commit themselves to new systems of faith that combined both traditional religion and the emerging principles of social science. Spann positions these two systems in terms of millenarianism and rationalism, and argues that this combination of social critique and collective community served as a means for personal and collective transformation through an active engagement with utopian imaginaries of spirituality (Spann 1989: 279). These imaginaries in particular, while often not entirely determined, have been, and continue to be, instrumental in shaping the organization and function of most North American intentional communities.

However, it is not imaginaries per se on which I intend to focus here, but the role they can play within the process of social change. Many political activists and cultural analysts have cast intentional communities, including Radical Faerie communities, as isolationist, separatist, and escapist, thereby rendering their actions ineffectual in the larger scheme of liberationist agendas (e.g., gay rights and second-wave feminism). I argue, however, that such a perspective is short-sighted, and fails to recognize how cultures of queerness such as Radical Faeries can develop vehicles for broader social change that go beyond traditionally recognized paths of action. Buffy, a long-time activist and sanctuary steward, offers the following interpretation of his own sense of agency:

> When I came out, I considered myself gay, and not very long after that I got connected with Queer Nation and started using the political term queer more often than gay. And so, and then that sort of progressed to Faerie. While I still consider myself political, in a completely different way, I've chosen a less, you know, overt way of being political. When people look at something like this . . . it's such a . . . it's such a strange thing, and it, and to connect being gay with the earth, with, with some sort of connection with the earth is such a, you know, it's a different kind of thing totally than being in the city and going to Act Up demonstrations.

Similarly, Maqui states, "I think that what we're saying is a statement, like my life is a political statement without having to demonstrate."

As a framework for an analysis of the kind of Faerie agency Buffy and Maqui describe, Wolfgang Iser offers a useful rubric that establishes an interrelated triad between imaginaries, the fictive, and what he calls "reality." He argues that fictionalizing is a guided act that ". . . aims at something that in turn endows the imaginary with an articulate gestalt—a gestalt that differs from the fantasies, projections, daydreams, and other reveries that ordinarily give the imaginary expression in our day-to-day experience" (1993: 3). In this context, ". . . the act of fictionalizing is a crossing of boundaries . . . an act of transgression" (p. 3). He continues:

> Just as the fictionalizing act outstrips the determinacy of the real, so it provides the imaginary with the determinacy that it would not otherwise possess. . . . We can now see two distinct processes, which are set in motion by the act of fictionalizing. Reproduced reality is made to point to a "reality" beyond itself, while the imaginary is lured into form. In each case there is a crossing of boundaries: the determinacy of reality is exceeded at the same time that the diffuseness of the imaginary is controlled and called into form. . . . The text, then, functions to bring into view the interplay among the fictive, the real, and the imaginary. Although each component of the triad fulfills a significant function, the act of fictionalizing is of paramount importance: it crosses the boundaries both of what it organizes (external reality) and of what it converts into a gestalt (the diffuseness of the imaginary). It leads the real to the imaginary and the imaginary to the real, and it thus conditions the extent to which a given world is to be transcoded, a nongiven world is to be conceived, and the reshuffled worlds are made accessible to the reader's experience (Iser 1993: 3–4).

Iser is operating in the realm of literary criticism here, and his functionalist triad leaves little room for considerations of the extent to which his neatly categorized triad might collapse, or the possibility for fictionalizing acts to reinforce rather than transgress social imaginaries (cf. Eagleton's critique of reception theory [1983]). However, I would assert that with some modifications, the triad he constructs can offer some insight into an ethnographic analysis of Faerie practices. In particular, the practices on which I chose to focus during my fieldwork can be interpreted as fictionalizing acts. In Iser's terms they are the means through which Faerie imaginaries attain determinacy, or are factualized (although this process varies due to fluctuating subjectivities, is destabilized by continually changing Faerie texts, and may not necessarily be interpreted as transgressive for the reader, as Iser assumes). Their texts are spoken word, body language, the construction of objects such as shrines, and other expressions that are presented in order to outstrip everyday experience (that which may not be commonly associated with links to imaginaries, or what Iser calls "reality") and to tap Faerie imaginaries. Iser refers to these texts as activators and proposes that imaginaries reveal themselves to the "reader" through an interplay between the imaginaries and the various activators that reference them. He states: ". . . play may be seen as a product of activation as well as a condition for the productivity brought about by the interaction it stimulates. It is this dual process that gives the imaginary its presence" (1993: 223).

Within Iser's construct, both the act of fictionalizing and the act of "reading" are crucial in the function of his triad. They are both active sites of agency within the interplay he describes; points at which "new worlds" are constructed, and then interpreted, within a continual interplay between imaginaries and everyday experience. For the Faerie practices I examine in this work, their execution (as fictionalizing acts) brings a set of ever-changing imaginaries into view, resulting in texts that are "read" by those present in an interplay with the referenced imaginaries. Those who "read" these acts in turn engage in their own processes of fictionalizing. In my reconfiguration of Iser, the entire cycle (fictionalizing and reading and again fictionalizing, etc.) is in continual flux; where individuals (constituted as multiple and fluctuating subjectivities) are influenced by shared imaginaries while they also reshape them through their practices, thereby influencing the interpretation others take away, who, in turn, construct more practices within this ongoing interplay. Ritual practices at Faerie gatherings are perhaps the most obvious demonstration of this, where visitors and stewards alike engage and co-modify collective Faerie imaginaries.

Mapping Routes of Agency

In the previous analysis, Faerie practices are interpreted as boundary-crossing acts that challenge dominant "norms" while also providing determinacy to Faerie imaginaries. However, in order to locate possible routes of agency related to these practices, we need to understand how the relationship between imagination and imaginaries plays out in terms of Faerie transgressions, as well as some of the range of possible relationships between the Faerie community and dominant North American culture.

Faerie imaginaries are influenced differently each time they are engaged by those who reference them, and the participants' practice, in turn, is shaped by these ever-changing shared imaginaries. It is through practice, then, that individuals witness manifestations of each other's imaginaries, and through practice as well that they collectively and individually modify them. If we assume that identity can be characterized as multiple and continually fluctuating (Butler 1993), and we couple this with the fact that many Faeries are "nomadic" and often move from one community to another, it would seem that their forms of practice, when referenced or enacted outside of exclusively Faerie contexts, have a great deal of potential to influence dominant social imaginaries and eventually effect broader change (cf. Deleuze and Guattari 1986, 1991).

For example, many people continually arrive and depart from the sanctuary in stays that range between a day to several months to years. Some live for a while in cities to earn money (where they take on other identities through their interactions there), and then reside at the sanctuary or other counterculture communities until they feel the need for change. By physically relocating, and interacting with dominant culture via traditional kinship networks and other non-Faerie contexts and identities, these "nomads" carry with them the Faerie imaginaries they helped to shape. And when they carry them into the broader North American culture, they can, in turn, engage in the same interplay with, and modification of, those dominant imaginaries as well.

It could be argued that Faerie gatherings are an important venue for this strategy, given the fact that they are often attended by many people who have never been to one before, and that the practices and events have the potential to open new possibilities within the attendees' interplay with imaginaries of community, spirituality, sexuality, and other concepts Arcturus once offered:

> A lot of people coming to the gatherings are coming from other communities themselves like Wolf Creek or Short Mountain in Tennessee. But some people will be coming along who've only tasted just gatherings. They don't realize that this is a way of life. They usually go for two weeks, live in a tent, and then go back to the city. They don't realize that some people do this all the time. And that it's, it's just like the gathering. The intensity doesn't fade. Like, every morning I get up, it's like being at rainbow again, rainbow festival. You know, you're in loving surroundings, you feel love toward the naturalness for things . . . I feel whole out here. I feel like we need to share that with other people . . .

Owl has commented similarly:

> We're here to share what we have . . . I'm here to show people that there is an alternative to the corporate world. I mean the best way to counter that corporate mentality is just showing people that there is a viable option . . . I'm here for everyone else. To me, I feel like I'm doing a service to people by being here. I'm not in this for me, I'm in this for everyone.

However, this approach has a distinct history associated with it that limits its ability to reach large segments of dominant culture (e.g., the "failure" of hippie communes, an association with drug use, cults, dangerous charismatic leaders). Some of the work created by Couillard, a Faerie from Toronto, seems to respond to this challenge. In addition to the rituals he has organized at many Faerie gatherings, Couillard has also created an installation and performance piece for urban settings that attempts to use Faerie practice, and its references to imaginaries, to reconfigure the range of imaginaries that shape dominant institutions. He states:

> For me, it took a lot of courage to create this playhouse atmosphere and call it "art"—but so far the reaction has been unexpectedly positive. . . . Everyone is completely charmed by the focus around food—where else do you get tea and fresh-baked goods when you come into a show? And all the while I'm in a subtle performance mode, shaping their experience just enough to push them

a little bit, interjecting bits of Faeriedom, getting them to do simple things like play with the costumes, or sit down and quilt with Jules, or leave something in the altar room. It's been great to have a place to come to every day and just be creative, and have people come by to play. It's also been fun to slowly take over, first the initial rush of having something ready for the opening, but then living in the space (I don't sleep here most nights, but Jules is actually resident here, since he normally lives on the farm where we do our gatherings) and making little adjustments, adding our touch, taking it over inch by inch and transforming it . . . (Couillard 1996).

A reference to Iser's work is helpful. He argues that social institutions are actually "fictional texts" of a sort, which are drawn from social imaginaries. He states that because "change is an integral element of society, the imaginary replaces myth as the foundation, not only in order to emphasize the fact that society is a product but also in order to make the actual stage of this production available to analysis" (1993: 208). He continues:

> Social life has no original content of its own that is independent of imaginary significations and their resultant institutions. . . . Imaginary social significations—at any rate, those that are truly primary—denote nothing at all, and they connote just about everything . . . And precisely because they do not denote an existing world of objects, the things they connote lack determinacy, and such a lack cannot ultimately disguise the fact that their "being" is a mere positing which can be undone or replaced by something else (p. 217).

This position, when considered in light of the potential influence that practice can have over social imaginaries as described above, suggests that the interplay between some practices and social imaginaries also has the potential to restructure or "undo" social institutions as well. This is because, as Iser argues, social change actually takes place at the level of social imaginaries, which are continually reshaped by individual practices (fictionalized acts) and the subsequent "readings" of their "texts." This interplay to which Iser refers is in line with Kenneth Gergen's idea of "relational engagement":

> . . . let us consider individual action as always already embedded within patterns of relationship. One acquires impetus (indexed as a sense of motive, consciousness of value, or desire) by virtue of the manner in which one is enmeshed in relationship. . . . We possess telos or direction in life not because of some inner possession of motive, calling, or biological proclivity, but by virtue of the forms of relationship of which we are a part. Agency, then, may be more usefully conceptualized as a form of relational engagement. (To want is to "want with," to "chose" is to reflect the condition of one's relatedness) (1999: 9).

Gergen's view of agency integrates cultural contexts in a way that broadens not only the influence of imaginaries on individual acts, but also the potential for individual acts to shape imaginaries without presuming that agency necessitates reconstructions of new forms of order (Dirks 1994, Ortner 1994). Agency, then, is the fabric that conducts Iser's conception of interplay, not simply resistance as a counterpart to domination.[5]

This mode of influencing the dominant from the margins is different from the traditional battles we've seen in identity politics wars, where social change is often conceived of as a process of conflict, enforcement, or censorship. Instead, this process seeks out points or areas of relation between subjects and creates opportunities for the marginalized to consciously use the co-opting nature of the dominant culture as a vehicle for persuasion. Practice, as fictionalizing act and narrative-generating process, becomes crucial here. It is a process where transgressions of dominant norms can be introduced in the context of narratives and acts that reference dominant imaginaries.

While the practices described in the previous section transgress many North American "norms" of kinship, gender, divisions of labor, and Western hierarchic social structures, the Faerie utopian imaginaries share a number of significant commonalities with dominant utopian imaginaries in the United States. For example, the Faerie critique of the "mainstream" engages utopian imaginaries of otherworldly idealism long associated with the founding of the United States as a nation of immigrants fleeing various forms of oppression from cultural "establishment," starting over, and creating new identities. Similar utopian imaginaries common to both the United States' dominant culture and Faeries include those associated with an allegiance to often idealized imagined communities (Anderson 1991), where ties between individuals are generated through culturally-constructed affiliations (e.g., nationality, ethnicity, and neo-paganism) via various media.

In addition to the ability utopian imaginaries have to offer alternatives to dominant social imaginaries, and to provide engagement with a larger process of continual "improvement," they often have romantic associations, which are frequently aligned with notions of progression, optimism, idealism, hopefulness, enthusiasm, transcendentalism, and a state of well-being. This can be seen in dominant imaginaries in the United States, in which "The Promised Land" was, and remains to many, a place where abundant opportunity, ease of mobility, relative wealth, and, perhaps most importantly, the notion of freedom dominate (McCord 1989, Vance 1990). Jean Baudrillard (1989) comments: America is "utopia achieved . . . utopia made reality . . . [a society] built on the idea that is the realization of everything that others have dreamt of—justice, plenty, rule of law, wealth, freedom: it knows this, it believes in it, and in the end, the others have come to believe in it too." It is perhaps for these reasons that the United States has also been unique in its openness to social experimentation for utopianists of all persuasions and beliefs. Kumar (1991: 82) states: "If America as a nation was not itself utopia, if it remained shackled by the structures of private property and cut-throat competition, America was nevertheless the place where utopias of the most diverse kind could be realized." This is the area where the "mainstream" and Faeries may find common ground, since they share a history and set of imaginar-ies (and related practices and narratives) that are associated with seeking a better life through active self-marginalization (the frontier), "otherworldly" idealism, hopefulness, progression, well-being, and concepts like justice, freedom, and abundance.

Notes
Paper presented originally at American Anthropological Association Ninety-ninth Annual Meeting, San Francisco, CA. November 2000.

1. See Timmons (1990).

2. Some Faeries have questioned these practices, arguing that such appropriations are uncritical, decontextualized, and romanticized replications that don't properly integrate re-spect for the history and culture of Native Americans. This has been a topic of debate and concern among Faeries (as I have witnessed both in the field and on the Faerie Internet listserv), and many academics (cf. Aldred 2000, Haly 2000, Hernandez-Avila 2000, and Jocks 2000).

3. Roscoe (1991, 1995, 1998) as well as Thompson, ed. (1987) and Connor (1993) are among works that have had an influence on Faerie spiritual and political ideas.

4. I was later told by one of the stewards that last year's ritual was similar, but ended in a different location and that after the final "ohming," a large number of participants engaged in sexual activity at the site. This year's ceremonies may have differed due to a larger number of participants, the presence of my video camera, and the fact that there was one woman in attendance.

5. It is important to recognize that this mapping of Faerie practice does not imply the use of a static or fixed model of the "mainstream." There are, of course, numerous and often conflicting sets of imaginaries and related practices that are not considered resistant or counter to North American "norms." In fact, it is essential to my argument that this multiplicity of, and interplay between, dominant or nonresistant imaginaries and cultur-ally sanctioned practices exists so that new possibilities for change might be introduced from the margins as they "play out" and evolve within a blend of practices that are refer-encing a range of imaginaries. The fact that some of these nonresistant imaginaries actu-ally conflict with one another while remaining dominant is actually indicative of an evolving and potentially receptive social system.

Queering the Dragonfest
Changing Sexualities in a
Post-Patriarchal Religion

MARY JO NEITZ

N *INVITATION TO SOCIOLOGY*, Peter Berger described the sociological consciousness as characterized by debunking, unrespectability, relativizing, and cosmo-
politan qualities (1963: 52). Berger influenced generations of sociologists with
his view that the goal of sociology was to look beneath taken-for-granted assumptions, to debunk them, and lay bare the processes of social construction (p. 38).
He portrayed sociology as a tool for this debunking, and told us how difficult the
work can be. "How can I be sure, say, of sociological analysis of American middle-
class mores in view of the fact that the categories I use for this analysis are conditioned by historically relative forms of thought . . . ?" Although Berger and
Luckmann described this epistemological problem with a wonderful metaphor—
they say that studying one's own culture is like "trying to push the bus in which one
is riding"—at the same time, they argued for the separation of epistemology from
"the empirical discipline of sociology" (1967: 13). They wanted to build a sociology of knowledge that concerns itself with commonsense knowledge, that is, what
everyday people know as "reality" in their daily lives (p. 15).

One of the things that has happened to me in my career as a sociologist is that
I have become ever more aware of how complex the task is that we have taken on.
Even the idea that sociology is the tool for unmasking the taken-for-granteds of
everyday life seems too simple. I am ever more aware of the extent to which our
theories themselves are profoundly implicated in what Dorothy Smith calls the
"relations of ruling." The theories themselves are not "clean," not objective tools
for analyzing the "messiness" of daily life. The theories themselves and the understandings they produce must be called into question. The assumptions that
undergird our own theories must also be debunked. [1]

It was my encounter with feminism that provoked a radical questioning of not
only the way things were in the world, but also of sociology. Under the influence

of feminist standpoint theory, I looked for "gendered analyses" that went beyond asking "where are the women," or "add women and stir" approaches.[2] Feminist analysts such as Dorothy Smith called for a sociology for women. Feminist theorists asked what would happen to the theories themselves if we were to put women at the center of the analysis? Would that process suggest new categories and relations? Would there be a change in the ways that we understand the world?

Putting women at the center of our analysis did indeed provoke new understandings of many of the things sociologists study. Results of this process also suggested looking at different sorts of things. For example, the history department at my university hired as their American Civil War historian a woman who studies what the women did during the Civil War—African-American women, white women without property, as well as planter class women. As you might imagine, there were complaints from those who expected her courses to focus on military battles, but studying the experience of women during the war revealed how their lives were also profoundly altered by the changes that occurred during and after the war, changes that had enduring effects on southern life, even though the changes did not occur on the battlefield (Whites 1995). For feminist scholars of my generation, putting women at the center of analysis also produced— sometimes implicitly, sometimes explicitly—a vision of the world as gendered, a world experienced differently by men and women. And how were we to understand the world of sociology? Too often we experienced that defined by men for men. Who were we as sociologists? Dorothy Smith wrote about what she called "the line of fault" to describe the bifurcation of her experiences in the world of sociology, on the one hand, and her experiences in the world of women (1987). It was a description that resonated for many feminist women in the 1970s as we tried to build professional identities in what often felt like "the world of men," and at the same time to maintain relational worlds as friends, daughters, mothers, partners, and wives.

As feminist sociologists we sought to create a new angle of vision. We sought to "de-center" the very notion of objective science; we experienced the science of our discipline as masculinist science (Harding 1986). We saw it as socially and culturally dominant, but not as "objective truth." The project of decentering however was not about putting a sociology of women in place of masculinist thought. Some of us came to understand that we were embarking on a different sort of project. We were not working on a "successor science" to take the place of what had gone before. And we came to understand we could not talk about "the standpoint of women" as if women were a single group. We listened to voices of the women of color talking about their understanding of knowledge as "partial." Patricia Hill Collins's influential book, *Black Feminist Thought* (1990) powerfully articulated a vision of a black feminist standpoint that reflected the thinking of those in the academy and the experiences and forms of expression—novels, journals, poems—of those outside of it. Voices from the postcolonial writers splashed over from anthropology (Behar and Gordon 1995; Trinh 1989; Spivak 1988). We began to think in terms of the intersectionality of race, class, and gender. We began to think of our understandings as local, particular, and contextual (Geertz 1973, 1983). Some of us found ourselves moving from being "social constructionists" to being deconstructionists.

One of the problems—or maybe it is an opportunity—of doing a long-term project is that the world doesn't stand still while one conducts one's study. And one's frameworks for thinking can change as well. Poststructuralist thought challenges me; queer theory has become one of the tools I use to problematize the standard sociological understanding that "gender" is socially constructed, whereas sexuality is biologically given. Queer theory also pushes me to ask what it means to think of identity as performative, and what it means to define "queer" as transgressive of categories and boundaries (Butler 1990; Sedgewick 1990; Seidman 1996; Warner 1993).

In this chapter I present two moments in my study of contemporary witchcraft, one in 1987 and the second in 1996. These two moments provide a frame for examining some of the changes in the embodiment of gender and sexuality at the Dragonfest, illustrated by the appearance of women with horns, which I first observed in 1996. I also show how feminist theory and queer theory help in analyzing the cultural changes we can see here. Finally, I suggest some questions that arise out of the application of these theories to the sociology of religion.

From a Gender Frame to a Queer Frame

I began my research on witches working out of a gender analysis frame. When I started this work on Wicca in the 1980s, I was interested in women and spiritual power. The question of the relation between women's social power and women's access to spiritual power came out of my research on Catholic Charismatics (Neitz 1987). Catholic Charismatics subscribed to the normative position that women should submit to the authority of men, yet the women whom I interviewed claimed that they found the spiritual practices—including direct access to God—to be very liberating for them as women. But social theory suggested that traditions that allowed women access to spiritual power were always accompanied by restrictive social norms because of the need to keep subordinates under control and maintain order (Durkheim 1954; Lewis 1971). I started studying witches in a search for other "effervescent spiritual traditions," defined as those that take as of central importance beliefs and practices regarding the existence of spiritual powers and the use of them to get benefits in the here and now. I specifically sought out traditions in which women as well as men had access to those powers. In contemporary witchcraft, people practice magic defined as "bending and shaping reality." What I soon discovered rendered my original question moot: while the witches did not have restrictive social norms, they didn't have much order either.[3] However, for a sociologist of gender and religion, Wicca presented an interesting case, for a number of reasons.

In the first place, Wiccan theology and cosmology are goddess centered. That led me to ask whether women could have more power in traditions that imagined deity as female. I questioned how the goddess symbolism might constitute a cultural resource for religious women wanting to reimagine gender relations. Secondly, unlike some cultures with powerful goddesses in their pantheons, Wiccans espouse norms of gender equality. Equality between men and women is one dimension in which they seek "balance." Although equality and balance are always constructed through practices, everyone at least endorses balance between the men and women. Thirdly, it is a pro-sex culture, but, as I discussed in some detail later in this chapter, it is not "patriarchal," that is, heterosexuality is not tied to an ideology of male ownership of women and children or to a more diffuse idea of the legitimacy of male dominance in the sexual, or any other, realm. These factors make it a good place to try to examine the intertwining of sexuality and gender. Early second-wave feminists pointed to patriarchal religion as a key institution for the social control of women, and one way that has been accomplished is through the controlling of women's sexuality (Young 1989; Rich 1980; Daly 1967, 1978). The example of Wicca helps us think about the possibilities of "nonpatriarchal religion" and "queer heterosexuality."

A Note about Words and Places

I use the words "Wicca" and "witchcraft" interchangeably. Both words describe a set of beliefs and practices embraced by networks of individuals, loosely organized, without a hierarchical structure. Witches' networks overlap with many others in a cultural milieu that includes women's spirituality, alternative healing, Native American, and other New Age movements (Neitz 1994). In many cases, the boundaries are shifting, the definitions changing. This is even more true today than when I began my research. I studied Dianic, or feminist, witches and the Neogardnerian, or Neopagan, witches.[4] Both follow a yearly cycle, based on the movement of the sun, and see themselves as resurrecting the pre-Christian nature religions of western Europe. Not surprisingly, membership in both networks is primarily, but not exclusively, Euro-American. Neither tradition worships nor even believes in Satan, a figure whom they associate with Christianity. They argue that the pre-Christian (pagan) nature religions were also prepatriarchal and precapitalistic, and that the

Wiccan revival offers models for more egalitarian and ecologically sound ways of living today.

Initially I sought to explore several dimensions of Wiccan groups. These dimensions attempted to capture key elements of cultural critique present in the work of some of the prominent Wiccan writers: a feminist critique, a political critique, and an economic critique. I was interested in finding witches who identified as feminists and who practiced in women-only groups, as well as mixed groups (with both men and women). I also sought out some groups that explicitly combined their religious practice with political activism. Finally, I looked for groups whose members had regular nine-to-five jobs and were relatively integrated into the dominant culture of consumer capitalism, and groups whose religious practice was part of a broader countercultural stance, often characterized by a rural, subsistence lifestyle and a marginal relation to capitalism. The first dimension became a central factor in my analysis, reflecting what amounted to two significantly different witchcraft cultures, with different associational networks.

In the summer of 1986 I attended a national women's music festival with the intention of making initial contacts for doing fieldwork among witches. Although I knew of witches in the university town where I lived, for both personal and ethical reasons I decided against doing fieldwork there.[5] At the music festival I met two women who had just founded the Reformed Congregation of the Goddess. I made arrangements to go to Wisconsin to learn more about their plans. My identification as a feminist researching questions about women and religion gave us an immediate common bond, although I came to learn that being a feminist was not the same as being a witch.

Also in the late 1980s I met witches in the Denver area. The Denver Area Wiccan Network (DAWN) included witches who lived along the Front Range of the Rocky Mountains in Colorado, ranging from Colorado Springs to Denver to Boulder to Fort Collins. At that time DAWN sponsored a neo-pagan festival, the Dragonfest, around the time of the August full moon. When I first attended the Dragonfest and began interviewing Denver area witches, most described themselves as adherents of Neogardnerian traditions.[6]

My difficulty with describing these two cultures indicates the intertwining of gender and sexuality. The Reformed Congregation of the Goddess defines itself as "explicitly feminist." I describe the Front Range pagans, however, as "not explicitly feminist" given that they believe in equality, but are reluctant to label themselves feminist. More to the point, while the two groups are distinctive in terms of being composed of only women, or of men and women, the groups could also be defined in terms of different sexual cultures. Although women who slept with men were tolerated, the culture at Reformed Congregation of the Goddess, especially in its early years, derived from the lesbian feminist culture of the 1980s. The culture of the Front Range pagans, in contrast, was explicitly heterosexual, stemming in part from their Neogardnerian interpretation that the practice of ritual magic necessitates sexual polarity. It is a heterosexuality, however, modeled on some pre-patriarchal imagining, and looking at it may help us imagine a post-patriarchal heterosexuality.

This chapter reflects a movement in my work on this project: It started out being about gender, about women and spiritual power, but I have come to believe that we cannot understand religion and gender without examining issues of sexuality. The comparison of gendered differences leads to a discussion of sexual norms and practices, and social control and alleged deviance. I believe that this movement in my work also reflects a dialectical relation between changes in the world and changes in our ways of understanding the world. At the end of the twentieth century, gender norms appear relaxed, and a wider range of practices is in evidence. In many contexts, however, there is a limit on allowed practices, and that limit occurs at the place where heterosexuality itself is called into question.[7] In most cases, however, that limit is never reached. The "heterosexual imaginary" prevails.[8] Despite changes in gender practices, we live in a culture in which institutionalized heterosexuality, or what Chrys Ingraham has called heteronormitivity, "the view that institutionalized heterosexuality constitutes the standard for legitimate and prescriptive social sexual arrangements," remains in place (1994: 204). The story of the "queering of the Dragonfest" is the story of the disruption of those assumptions.

Approaching the Dragonfest

To get to the Dragonfest I drive southwest out of Denver into Pike National Forest. When I first attended, the festival was held on Pikes Peak. I missed the earliest years, when it was held on private land. Through a witch who worked at a New Age bookstore, I first learned about a Front Range Pagan Festival, thus named because it was organized by a coalition of witches who lived just east of the continental divide, from Colorado Springs to Fort Collins. This woman facilitated my registration, and in August of 1987, my sister and I found ourselves driving south to Colorado Springs, and then west. As we bumped along gravel roads, we attended carefully to the photocopies map we had been sent along with a list of items for camping, rituals, the community "stone soup" supper, and confirmation of our registration. That year attendance at the four-day festival neared two hundred, and the organizers began to look for a bigger site. Now I drive through the towns of the foothills—Evergreen, Conifer, Pine—and turning off onto the inevitable gravel roads and into the mountains. The road follows the creek. My eyes light on the willows that border it, the meadows, the ponderosa pine forests, the face of the mountain. A born-and-bred westerner, this landscape is sacred and holds magic for me on any occasion.

In 1996, the drive was familiar. Although the festival had moved to yet another site, one that could accommodate seven hundred people, I felt that I knew this part of the national forest. I turned into the spectacularly sited campground, almost automatically looking for familiar faces and structures, and checking also for what might be different. I stop my vehicle at the gate, and trade my paper registration for a button. I enter the campground observing the people with small backpacking tents like mine, beat up pickups with campers, and the not so temporary compounds, whole covens camping together with large car-camping tents, screened gazebos, flies erected over tables for cooking and eating, their areas festooned with all sorts of banners making political statements and claiming the space. In a central area is a space marked off for rituals, a large community area, with seating for several hundred people covered by rain flies, kiosks for posting work shifts and announcements, a notice board. Another fly covers the community kitchen, where juice and hot water and coffee are available. Tents are set up for the medical staff; "Grandma's Place" for the little kids; Kids' Fest with activities for the older kids. Further down the road, the endlessly fascinating tents of the merchants, selling handmade soaps, crystals, knives and swords and chain mail, drums, leather goods, ceramics, clothing, jewelry, singing bowls, and massage, among other things. Close to the center, and the line of toilets, is a camping area set aside for people with disabilities. Deeper into the camp I see more ritual sites, the "clothing optional" camping area, and a gathering place for late-night drummers.

People of all ages throng the road. A goodly number in their forties and fifties, the men with long hair and beards, the women with long hair. A younger group in their twenties. Lots of children. Most people look "White" (Caucasian). Dress varies, but I can't easily visualize this group transported to the mall on Saturday afternoon. With their bodies and dress they offer a visible resistance to fashions in the dominant culture. Some, although fewer than in the eighties, look like escapees from a Renaissance fair. Among the over thirty crowd, hair is not cut with concern for current styles, nor do they appear to subscribe to dominant culture norms mandating thin and muscular bodies. Conventional makeup on women is uncommon. Among the younger adults, other body decorations such as piercings, tattoos, or face paintings are common. Men wear shorts or jeans and t-shirts, but with capes and odd hats. Leather costumes, either of a Native American or European medieval style, are popular. Many men carry sheathed knives or swords at their waists. Some people walk the mountain road with heavy wooden staffs. Many women wear flowing clothes with long skirts. Weather can be extreme at 8,000 feet. (I usually pack my down vest, rain poncho, long underwear, plenty of sunscreen, and a sundress.) In the heat of midday, women wear tops that reveal lots of skin. Men appear in leather loincloths. When it is colder, men and women wrap themselves in woolen capes, long cloaks. People wear lots of jewelry: large chunks of amber, semiprecious stones, headpieces with bead work and feathers, large ornate silver ornaments shaped into Celtic knots. People carry musical instruments. (I look like a visitor from the L. L. Bean catalog with my bandanna, camping shorts, mosquito-proof canvas shirt, and hiking boots.) People are friendly, happy to be gathered in this place with people like themselves: what makes them marginal in the outside world is the norm here.

In 1996, one of the things that was new in this mix was a significant gay presence. Not that gays and lesbians had not been present before. But during the last decade, the gay and lesbian presence has emerged here slowly and in marked contrast to the striking lesbian influence among the Dianic witches I have been studying in Wisconsin.[9] There was an organized, although still somewhat marginal, gay male presence. Along with workshops on "herbs for women," "mask making," and the "history of the Tarot," an adults-only workshop sponsored by two gay leather men titled "The Sundance and the Scourge: The Ceremonial Uses of Pain" (described as being about doing magic through sadomasochistic sexual rituals) made it onto the official Dragonfest program. Other activities were announced publicly but occurred in the spaces for more spontaneous workshops and rituals organized at the festival itself. Another workshop organized by gay males appeared on the program under the title "HIV and Transformation: On Working with People Dying of AIDS." A late night ritual, a memorial for people who had died of AIDS, did not appear on the official program, but was announced at the kiosk. Also at the communications kiosk were posters for the Rainbow Network and information about the rainbow pavilion with directions on how to find it in the camping area. It was not located in the more public market area, but rather in the clothing optional camping area. It was clearly marked not only with rainbow flags, which were common throughout the camp, but also with pink triangles. A number of the merchants offered merchandise featuring gay and lesbian symbols from interlocked male symbols and interlocked female symbols, to pink triangles and labryses.[10] One woman had stained glass pieces inspired by feminist theologian Mary Daly's book, *OuterCourse*, featuring a large naked woman leaping over a moon. The few openly gay and lesbian couples appeared comfortable expressing affection with each other in ways comparable to those of heterosexual couples at the festival. There was little evidence that anyone objected. One exception was a graffitied exchange at the kiosk: someone wrote an objection to the presence of the Rainbow Network poster on the kiosk, eliciting a response of "we are here, get used to it."

As discussed in the following section, these things in themselves represent a change. In 1996, however, there was more than an emerging gay presence. There was gender-bending. There were men wearing skirts—not just men with bagpipes and kilts of earlier years, but bare-chested young men wearing brightly colored, batiked sarongs. There were highly visible male-to-female transsexuals in key organizational positions. Then there were, as discussed in greater detail in the following section, the women wearing horns. Dragonfest was "queer" in a way that it had not been before.

Gender and Sexuality at the Dragonfest

Yearly festivals draw together many segments of the pagan community: groups that come as covens, solitaries (individuals who practice on their own), the pagan party crowd, and the professional pagans who make their living within the craft doing body work, doing tarot readings, performing healing arts, or making and selling merchandise that reflects pagan sensibilities. People camp out in a remote location, which both makes it cheaper to attend and reduces the risk of harassment from nonpagan society. Those who attend have the opportunity to participate in large group rituals, as well as workshops on topics that range from magical practices to discussions of the history of various traditions to discussions of issues facing the community. People who attend this festival from outside Colorado tell me that it has a reputation for being "serious about ritual."

The Dragonfest has a local and homegrown character. The people who come prefer it that way, and they want to keep it that way. In 1987, they invited a witch of some renown from the San Francisco Bay area to do a workshop and lead a ritual. The Dragonfest community was not happy with how that went, and they have not done it since. In this it differs from many other pagan festivals. It is not like Starwood, which brings in the pagan elite, or like Pagan Spirit Gathering, perhaps the largest pagan gathering, or Heartland, which, despite it smaller size, brings in people with national reputations (in recent years musicians in particular) to draw participants. The Dragonfest started out small and local, held on some land one of the active couples owned, and it grew to its present size of around seven hundred. Stars of the neo-pagan world may come into the region for talks, workshops, and book signings, but they are not paid to do workshops or rituals at the festival, nor, for the most part, do they come on their own. Perhaps related to that, my perception is that things changed more slowly here than in other parts of the United States: the Neogardnerian roots of much of contemporary neo-paganism persisted longer here than it did in other places.[11] Local practices resisted feminist/Dianic Wicca and Native American influences longer. Sweat lodges, women-only circles, and body decorations piercing, for example, showed up later than at festivals on the West Coast.

The year I first attended, 1987, was the year the outsider had been invited. Despite that anomaly, however, the festival displayed the strong influence of neo-paganism of Gerald Gardner and his followers. The core leaders of the festival had trained in covens that used books of shadows written by Gerald Gardner and others in the Neogardnerian tradition. Several rituals I attended, for example, were taken out of the *Grimoire of Lady Sheba*.[12] Coven leaders addressed each other by their craft names, often with the title "Lord" or "Lady." (These titles are also used to refer to the god and the goddess.) Newcomers like myself were expected to attend an orientation workshop on circle etiquette, where various rules about dress (including what one could wear to a skyclad ritual—women need to wear a necklace symbolizing the eternal return), appropriate jewelry (according to rank and gender), and what to do and not do in a ritual circle were discussed. They also taught us a simple grapevine dance step to do in the ritual circle. (More than a year's participation at Dianic rituals had not exposed me to any of these rules!)

In the 1970s and 1980s women-only rituals, often sponsored by Dianic witches, were extremely controversial at pagan festivals (Adler 1986). The first year I attended the Dragonfest there were no rituals only for women. A tradition has since evolved of doing rite of passage rituals, initiations into adulthood. There are separate rituals for males and females, but those began with a ritual for men.[13] While none of the witches I have met actually practice in the "ideal coven" (described in Sheba 1972) composed of six couples and a priestess and her high priest, when I first encountered them, most of the Front Range pagans adhered to the idea that ritual magic required a group of initiated men and women for "the balancing of energies."

While lesbians, feminists, and gay men in fact practice in single-sex groups, the public stance of the Front Range pagans was that such practices simply were not valid. The conceptualization of "balance" between male and female energies, a conceptualization based on a particular idea of what constitutes gender equality, cemented specific arrangements of sex, gender, and sexuality, in which people who identified as male, had bodies that were recognized as male, and slept with women, were expected to engage in specific relations in rituals with other people who identified as female, had bodies that were recognized as female, and who slept with men. In the late 1980s, however, there was some tension between the implicit feminism, on the one hand, and the maintenance of heteronormitivity.

It is worth looking more closely at the implicit feminism and the practices of femininity and masculinity, as revealed in interviews with community leaders and teachers.[14]

Implicitly Feminist

The Front Range pagans I interviewed had little sympathy for the anger they saw in women of second-wave feminism, and none of those I interviewed embraced the label of feminist.[15] Yet, they advocated a form of magical practice that emphasized the equal participation of men and women.

The following woman's response to a question from me about feminist witches was typical. "Those early women were very angry. Some of them are still very hostile, very angry. I think it is sad. They came in from the feminist movement and they were very, very angry with men."

Another commented: "I feel that this is one of the greatest flaws in feminist Wicca, is that they tend to project some of their own personal misgivings about the masculine side of the human race, and apply that to magic and I think this creates an imbalance. I can understand somebody's getting into not having anything to do with men. . . . But have a son, just have one son and you realize you cannot hate men. . . ."

Another woman also talked about balance.

> [Balance between male and female aspects] has to be achieved internally first, but then once you achieve it internally, or at least are trying to achieve it internally, then you can work at manifesting that balance externally between yourself and other people, and even there—in groups of women—they must find their male/female balance within themselves and then express that male/female balance externally amongst themselves, even in just a group of women. And certainly to have that in a mixed sex group, the people involved as individuals must first find out who their animus or anima is, come to terms with that other half, embrace that other half, and then the two of them, ah—within the one being—they have to proceed to make connections with the rest of a universe in a balanced way. It's a tough job.

These witches, while not feeling comfortable with what they saw as the "pro-woman" position of contemporary feminism, engage in practices designed to express the equality of men and women. For example, one woman described her holiday practices. I asked, "Does Santa Claus come to your house?" And she replied.

> My kids believe he is a god of Christmas, you know, him and his wife. And I have things—I have an altar in my front room which I rearrange with the seasons, and at that point we have a Santa Claus and a Mrs. Santa Claus there, and we put all the bows and ribbons and things around them. They are surrounded by it to imitate the spirit of Jupiterianism, you know, which is really what Santa Claus is, a Jupiter type god.

Although these women do not explicitly identify as feminists, they do talk about a clear connection between their paganism and their support for women's equality. Several said that women relate to paganism because it affirms them as women. For some, being a pagan is consistent with practices that promote gender equality. As one woman said, "It is so important for me to stand up for women. I try to do it in my life, also where I work and when I vote."[16]

These woman also see neo-paganism as affirming to them as women and supportive of their seeking out expressions of their femininity that are outside those provided by the mainstream culture.[17] This sense of having a feminine or masculine identity but not conforming to conventional gender norms is evident in the following woman's talk about her understandings of masculinity and femininity and how it is embodied by pagan men and women.

> Pagan women are essentially trying to be the goddess. They all look—well they are expressing their view of the goddess and likewise, pagan men should be expressing their view of the god, who's not this white haired, old [guy] who lives on top of a mountain, nor the [emasculated] version that the Christians are coping with; he is more multifaceted than that, just as the goddess is more multifaceted than the Virgin Mary, although she's the only goddess we've got left in mainstream religion. And so, once you find an internal balance, you don't have to play stupid games, you can BE. And for many women, not all, but many, that means taking that feminine expression and creating something that feels comfortable to them: . . . There are too many women in this lifetime who have an artificial view of what feminine is, as what the patriarchy has told them feminine is, and they are doing this Tammy Faye Bakker number. And, that doesn't work, and then they think the answer to that is like, "if this isn't working, if this is an uncomfortable mode, then my answer is to wear business suits and carry a briefcase." And that probably isn't real comfortable either, Reeboks aside (laughs). So, perhaps what the pagan woman is trying to do for women, and for men, is to help them find an expression of the masculine or the feminine, on the surface—externally—that they can present that they're comfortable with.

When I asked her explicitly about men in the Craft, she replied as follows.

> I know a fair number of men in the Craft, because I've always been involved in mixed sex Craft, and most of them, with very few exceptions, are not the standard, traditional, currently available, street model men. They are generally more open, more willing to change. Patriarchy is just as crippling for men as it is for women. It's just that most men don't understand that. They're in a gilded cage, so they think it's a nice cage. The men who are in the Craft are aware that it's a cage— (laughs). Gilded or not, it's still a cage. And they are trying to find a way out. They are much more willing, most of them, to be flexible and to change. . . . There are men now who are trying, for their own reasons—for their own healing, for their own sense of wholeness. I know men who feel that they have been robbed of having a feminine half, and being told culturally that any kind of female behavior was wrong for them, and they are reclaiming their right to have a feminine side. But they are also now freer to find an expression for their masculine energy that makes them feel comfortable and find an expression for their female energy that is more balanced and more true to themselves.

In these interviews pagan men and women see themselves resisting conventional gender norms, but there is still an essentialism in the way that they think about gender itself. And that essentialism is verbalized most clearly in defining sexual relations, as we can see in the following interview segment.

> You need to have a balance. It is not that one is better than the other. But we believe the feminine is a little bit more important than the masculine. That is because women give birth. And you have to have birth before you can have death. Birth comes first. You have to have birth and then the rest follows. So that gives her a very slight edge. We know that a long time ago people worshiped the goddess. This was before any one knew anything about the male role in procreation. All we knew was of the female role. And so when we worshiped a divinity it was female after the female part in creating new life. What the feminists have done is to go back to that tradition. That's okay. It is a perfectly legitimate tradition, but for me it is incomplete. We learned about the male role in procreation. And so the people who worshiped the goddess began to add a male figure to that. They included the horned god. At first the horned god was the consort of the goddess. . . . But women can relate to it [pagan tradition] because they can identify with the goddess. And men can relate to it to because they can identify with the horned god. They can relate to it as the lover of the goddess.

In her discussion there is the unquestioned assumption of heteronormitivity. The defining characteristic of what it is to be defined as men and women is their (hetero-) sexuality.

Sexuality in the Central Myth

For witches part of observing nature is observing the changes of seasons. One version of the Neogardnerian story recites this circle of birth, death, and rebirth. In the cycle of the year the goddess gives birth to her son the god, in the dark of winter, at the winter solstice. The god grows in power through Candlemas (2 February) to the spring. At the vernal equinox the god and goddess are in balance. Beltane (May eve) is a celebration of god and goddess mating, of fertility. At the summer solstice (21 June) god and goddess unite "in the love that is death." Lammas (1 August) is a harvest festival—first fruits, yet first fears of winter, the god is leaving. Mabon (fall equinox) is harvest—acknowledgment of the god's presence in the underworld. Hallowmas, end of the year, is a visit to the king of darkness, but it is also the time of conception of the sun child (Starhawk 1989: 169–84).

Divine union is critical to this story. In abstract terms, it is union with the life force, symbolized as union with the goddess. In the mythologies that have come down to us, many cultures express this as a sexual union. Sexual union between the god and the goddess can be reproduced in ritual by a priest and priestess with varying degrees of approximation. But the act of sex between any two people (not the god and the goddess) is also seen as a way of "raising power" or achieving the divine ecstasy that is basic to the religious practice.

While Wiccan discourse is full of references to "the Great Rite," actual sexual intercourse rarely—if ever—occurs in public rituals. Symbolic sex, on the other hand, is frequently present. For example, in ritual, swords, knives, wands, or candles are often symbolically plunged into chalices. The rituals sometimes feature the passing of a symbolic kiss around the circle, and may be conducted "skyclad" (in the nude). Furthermore, they are performed in the context of a belief system that affirms sexuality and uses sexual symbolism to achieve a state of ecstasy. Goddess is life and birth; the God is death, but death seen as necessary and leading to re-birth. In spring the god is a pan figure, young and playful, but sexual. In summer the god is often visualized as the stag, magnificent and powerful. Yet, he never possesses the goddess—it is he who dies in the fall, to be reborn of the eternal goddess.

Witches who are not so attached to the Gardnerian version offer formulations that are less rooted in hetero-gendered assumptions than this one. For example, Starhawk, a noted witch, also sees divine ecstasy at the heart of creation, and creation is an orgasmic process: "Ecstasy is at the heart of witchcraft—in ritual we turn the paradox inside out and become the goddess, sharing in the primal throbbing joy of union" (1989: 25). But rather than returning to an imagined heterosexual pre-Christian rite she expands the scope of the metaphor: "Witchcraft is a shamanistic religion, and the spiritual value that is placed on ecstasy is a high one. It is the source of union, healing, creative inspiration, and communion with divine—whether it is found in the center of a coven circle, in bed with one's beloved, or in the midst of a forest, in awe and wonder at the beauty of the natural world" (p. 26). These stories and symbols provide a positive evaluation of both men's and women's sexual expressions. Although often heterosexual, they reflect Gardner's nostalgic envisioning of a prepatriarchal, precapitalist utopia. They form the basis for imagining post-patriarchal sexualities.

Women with Horns

The significance of women with horns derives from the significance of men with horns. The cover of the program for the festival in 1996 is embellished with an intricate black and white drawing illustrating that year's festival theme of "Mirth and Reverence." A huge dragon wearing ritual robes holds a chalice in one hand and a ritual sword in the other. His widespread wings form a circle and within the circle ten men and women dance and drum in what appears to be carnivalesque revelry.

None of the women but three of the five men in the drawing have horns on their head; the elaborate branched antlers of the stag,[18] curling horns of rams, and the pronged horns of the antelope. In addition, two of the other men in the drawing wear costumes that include caps adorned with cloth "horns." At the festival itself, some of the men wear small goat horns attached to their heads, giving them a rather satyr-like appearance. The horns are a symbol of these men's identification with the god, a god to whom they often refer as "the horned one." Within neo-paganism a common name for the god in chants and songs is the "Horned One."[19] In rituals he is invoked and honored with a stance in which participants stretch out their arms, make a fist, and extend index and little finger. This god is not primarily a ruler or a protector. Rather, he is the consort of the goddess. He gives the goddess pleasure, and his sperm brings fruition to her fertility. A widely used pagan encyclopedia tells us that "perhaps the most distinguishing feature of a divine being used to be a horned head. Masks and crowns of incarnate deities were often those of horned animals—bulls, goats, stags" (Walker 1983: 409). Many images of pagan gods, shamans, or warriors convey "male vitality" by showing them wearing horns of animals on their heads. Pagan men wear their horns as a symbol of their virility.

In Western society, the horns of the pagans came to have other meanings. The "horned one" came to be identified with the Christians' devil. Of course, there is another meaning in Western cultures of men "wearing horns," that of being a cuckold. Under patriarchy that has a particular meaning: it indicates the deeply shameful, and even ridiculous, state of a man who cannot control his women. But it can only have that meaning under a particular construction of sexuality, one in which men are expected, by themselves and other men, to control the sexuality of their women, their wives and daughters.[20]

The horns of the men are an assertion of sexuality, which at the Dragonfest has been normative heterosexuality. In reaching into the past, however, into an imagined prepatriarchal era, they have created a culture of sexuality that is suggestive of a possible move into post-patriarchy. I am not saying that these witches do not have committed relationships or that they never establish monogamous unions. But a "consort" is not quite the same kind of role model as a patriarch. Pushing it further, the image especially of the goat horned gods—Pan, Dionysus—calls to mind a celebration of ecstatic sexuality, of the body as a route to rapture, as opposed to seeing the body as something that must be controlled or denied to achieve spiritual states.

For women at Dragonfest to wear horns, then, is to claim for themselves this virility, this sexuality, in an act of conscious gender-bending. Both in their wearing of the horns, and in an apparently spontaneous revision of some of the chorus to songs, changing lines about "men with horns" into lines about "women with horns," the women "queered" the Dragonfest. Previously at Dragonfest, women had rights to sexual expression. Yet, at the same time, a heterosexual imaginary prevailed: sexuality was understood as gendered male and female. The gender-bending act of women wearing horns crossed a barrier that defined and separated sexuality as male and female. In wearing horns, the women transgressed the male/female binary: women with horns are not the same as men with horns, nor are they the same as women without horns.

This outcome was not inherent in the original Gardnerian formulations. As I encountered it among the Front Range Pagans in 1987, Neogardnerian witchcraft was a highly gendered practice, reflecting particular notions about gender—the need to balance distinct male and female energies. But, at the same time, those ideas about gender were not used to sustain male privilege. Over time more individuals reinterpreted the ideas about balancing male and female energies to stress the need for internal balancing of the male and female energies people carry within themselves. Feminists who wanted to have all women circles and gay and lesbian witches who believed that male and female energies were manifest in their single-sex circles challenged the Gardnerian and Neogardnerian practices. In the current cultural context, the explicitly post-patriarchal beliefs allowed practices to open up between 1987 and 1996.

Queering the Dragonfest

How did it change? Gays, lesbians, and feminists—those who identified with Neogardnerian forms of Wicca or the Front Range community—pushed for inclusion. But that inclusion did not come easily. The tensions in the community can be seen through discussion of a workshop I attended in 1990. The Dragonfest program listed the workshop as "Gay and Lesbian Outreach." On the morning of the workshop, at the community meeting (these occur at the end of the community breakfast sponsored by the festival each morning) the facilitator of the workshop got up to explain that, although the workshop had been sponsored by the Gay and Lesbian Task Force of DAWN, the title did not convey how they thought about the workshop.[21] The speaker explained that a better name would be "Letting Go of Your Fears of the Other."

Ten people were present when I got to the site of the workshop. The conversation was at an impasse. On one side were two women who identified as lesbian. They were saying "Why do you care what we do in our circle, and whether it is the same as what you do?" Another person disagreed, asking "but why do you have to call it by the same name?" One of the lesbian women spoke out. She said when she first met the pagan community she had been struck by all the love, symbolized for her in the witches' custom of saying "we enter the circle in perfect love and perfect trust." She had felt that witches were a gentle, joyous people and was drawn to that. It felt especially welcome because, in her life, she had many experiences of exclusion, of people telling her what she was not, what she could not do. She broke into tears, then she said with anger in her voice: "How dare you tell me that I am not a witch, or that I cannot do what you do in my own way?"

The facilitator of the group led an exercise, and then wanted to talk about individuals changing. She said that everyone had to learn to be more tolerant of each other. There was some talk about the need for opening the third chakra, the heart chakra, that would allow us to embrace differences. My field notes read, "I left not feeling like 'fears of the other' were much lower after the workshop, even among the few who had attended. Still to have it on the program was notable."

In 1992 there was a discernable gay and lesbian presence at the Dragonfest. I attribute the shift in part to the conjunction of two very different events. In 1992 in Colorado, Amendment Two, an initiative to prevent communities from enacting antidiscrimination rulings that would include discrimination against gays and lesbians, was coming up on the November ballot. Ironically, 1992 also marked the 350th anniversary of the Salem Witch Trials. While rituals at Dragonfest commemorated the Salem Witch Trials, the talk at the festival was about Amendment Two. Many people wore buttons against the initiative; these were distributed from a booth in the central community area. At the booth the witches networked with others who were campaigning against the initiative. At the community meetings people gave speeches supporting gays and lesbians.[22]

Witches at the Dragonfest expressed a sense of identification with the gays and lesbians who were marked by the ballot initiative. There was a sense of linked fates that was based on a shared marginality, not on the basis of a shared sexual orientation but on the basis of a sense of shared resistance to the dominant culture.

I started this research with questions about gender. One of the things I wanted to know was in what ways the goddess symbolism, and access to spiritual power, could serve as a cultural resource for the social empowerment of women. I asked this question with some hopefulness, but also with skepticism, having knowledge of cultures where goddess symbolism coexisted with extremely repressive conditions for women. In this chapter I argue what the witches are doing that is most radical is not captured by talking only about gender, although it does have to do with gender. What is most radical is the challenge to heteronormitivity, a challenge initiated, but not fulfilled, by the evocation of imagined prepatriarchal heterosexuality, where sexual relations are not defined in terms of the ownership of women and children by powerful males. The conceptualization of prepatriarchal heterosexuality allows them to imagine what I am calling post-patriarchal heterosexuality. It is a sexuality that evades the hetero-homo binary.

Lessons from the Dragonfest

In our culture it has been easy to think that it is people of color who belong to a race, it is women who carry gender, and it is gays and lesbians who have sexual orientations or sexual preferences. White, middle-class, heterosexual men are "just people." They define themselves as the norm. Their race, gender, class, and sexuality usually go without comment. Yet we live in a world in which the boundaries delimiting marked identities from those that are unmarked are increasingly ambiguous.

Queer theory is one of several poststructuralist theories that challenges the "binaries." Observations of the Dragonfest in 1996 provide an example that disrupts binary assumptions that there are two genders, male and female, and that people are either homosexual or straight and that these terms have fixed meanings. The men in skirts and the women in horns suggest a fluidity of identifications, of practices. The use of the word "sexualities" in my title is significant.

What exactly does it mean, sexualities? The plurality of the term may be unsettling to some who recognize three (or two or one) forms of sexual identity: gay, straight, bisexual. But there are those who identify as straight, but who regularly indulge in homoeroticism, and of course, there are those who claim the identity of gay or lesbian, but engage with heterosexual sex. In addition, some people identify themselves sexually but don't actually have sex, and there are those who claim celibacy as a sexual practice (Takagi 1996: 245).

I have argued here that during the last ten years the Dragonfest has gone from a Neogardnerian and heterosexual gathering to a surprisingly diverse gathering. I have called this a "queering" of the Dragonfest and have argued that it illustrates the potential for change opened up by an openly sexual but nonpatriarchal culture in the current climate, and in a particular and local social and political context.

This chapter is not about the pagans getting it right. I am not advocating that everyone immediately don horns. Yet through such actions, these neo-pagans are opening up new possibilities for conceptualizing and enacting sexualities.

The language of "queer theory" helps us talk about those possibilities. There is a sense in which the idea of heteronormativity is not new. Certainly Mary Daly's works (1967, 1978) offer trenchant critiques—indictments—of how institutional religion contributes to the social control of sexuality and the oppression of women. Adrienne Rich's essay, "Compulsory Heterosexuality and Lesbian Existence," published in 1976, also argued that the control of women's sexuality under patriarchy is accomplished through normative heterosexuality. In her analysis, heterosexuality is not a biological given, but is rather imposed on women by patriarchy.

Yet to say this again, to say it now, as the queer theorists do, is not merely repeating what was said earlier. In the first place, we still live in a culture in which heterosexuality is taken for granted. Some things have changed: there are fewer rules defining gender appropriate practices. Whatever unconventional practices a woman may engage in, it is still true that having a boyfriend legitimates her "femininity." In the context of conscious social and political challenges to conventional gender norms, normative heterosexuality continues to define gender, although the heterosexual imaginary prevents us from recognizing it. This needs to be reasserted to challenge the notion that "post feminism" is the result of the end of patriarchy, rather than an expanding and deepening of the critique of intersecting structures of oppression. Second, the formulations of queer theorists move us beyond the binary notions of previous generations of critics. For queer theorists, the alternative to normative heterosexuality is not gay or lesbian sexuality, but rather a fluid and shifting performance of sexual practices, where the enactment of a particular sexual practice does not lock one into a particular sex or gender identity.

The story I tell, a local and particular story, allows us to see gender and sexuality from a perhaps distant vantage point—that of the Front Range pagans. Their understandings of their own beliefs and history changed when they saw themselves as "queer," when they saw themselves as marginal like the gays and lesbians. The witches themselves did not necessarily change their sexual orientations. The transformation was not within a binary gay or straight understanding. But they saw themselves as marginalized, and at risk, because of their transgression of the dominant cultural norms. They saw themselves as witches and nonheterosexuals—on the shifting margins of the dominant culture. In this is the queering of the Dragonfest. The transgressive performance of gender by the ambiguously sexed women with horns continues the challenge to binary understandings.

It is my hope that what we can see from this vantage point helps us to question what we thought we saw from other, perhaps nearer, vantage points. The challenge of queer theory to us as sociologists of religion is a challenge to our own assumptions about the naturalness of male/female and hetero/homo binaries, and how these assumptions remained unquestioned in our own analyses. It is a call to develop gender analysis in the sociology of religion that looks much more closely at the construction of sexuality, and the ramifications of the social construction of sexuality for gender structures and practices.

Notes

Reprinted with permission from *Sociology of Religion* 61 no. 4 (Winter 2000): 369–92.

1. In their enormously important and influential work, Berger and Luckmann (1967) argued that sociologists of knowledge had attended overmuch to "ideas" and not enough

to commonsense knowledge. Their attempt to redefine the sociology of knowledge was predicated on the assumption that epistemological questions referred to theory and their desire to move the sociology of knowledge away from being primarily concerned with "intellectual history." However, at the end of the twentieth century, the question of "how do we know what we know" has in fact been defused, and the distinction that Berger and Luckmann made between ideas of intellectuals on the one hand and commonsense knowledge of everyday reality is no longer so clearly defined: popular culture has absorbed social science theories; social science now draws on popular cultural understandings and expressions. In neither case can we assume any longer a shared and taken-for-granted knowledge without regard for location. This shift is the basis for the movement from social constructionism to deconstructionism.

2. A more formal name for the latter is "feminist empiricism." Advocates, for example, argue that including women in samples provides better tests of sociological theories. They believe that feminist sociologists can create a more objective science by including women. See Harding (1986) for discussion.

3. See Douglas (1973) for a discussion of the relations between restrictive social norms and social cohesion.

4. The current witchcraft revival can be traced to Gerald Gardner, in England in the 1940s. Gardner said he was initiated into one of the few covens that had lasted through the centuries, and he claimed to be reviving the ancient religion of the British Isles. Gardner's origin account has fallen into disrepute, but most give him credit for putting together a set of stories and practices that were reasonably attractive and coherent enough to be transmitted. After the repeal of anti-witchcraft laws in England in 1951, Gardner published a series of books that made his ideas more widely available on both sides of the Atlantic. Kelly (1981) and Adler (1986: 80–86) argue that most of neo-paganism comes, directly or indirectly, out of Gardner. I use the term Neogardnerian to describe those witches who trace their practices to Gardner or one of his followers. Neo-pagan is a broader term, and encompasses those groups who use mythologies with fewer or no Celtic elements. For a description of the differences between Dianics and Neogardnerians and a discussion of the relations between them see Neitz (1990).

5. I had already had a student complaining to the dean that I was a man-hating, lesbian, feminist witch, on the basis of my having assigned Mary Daly's book *GynEcology* in a women studies class, and I wondered about possible repercussions from conservative state legislators. I also worried about possible ethical dilemmas arising from getting to know people in a fieldwork setting and then being in a position of having to grade them in the classroom—fairly likely given the overlap between the women studies student body and the women's spirituality community.

6. Denver Area Wiccan Network no longer exists as an organization, although the Dragonfest continues to be sponsored by a new organization that exists specifically for that purpose. In this chapter I refer to the ongoing Wiccan community I have been studying as the Front Range pagans, although there is no specific organization by this name.

7. For an interesting example of exactly this process in the area of sport see Downing (1999).

8. Ingraham draws here on the work of Althusser (1984) for whom ideology represents the imaginary relationship of individuals to material conditions. Ingraham applies this to the structures of gender in a way that emphasizes the crucial importance of heterosexuality: "Althusser argues that the imaginary is that image or representation of reality which masks the historical and material conditions of life. The heterosexual imaginary is that way of thinking which conceals the operation of heterosexuality in structuring gender and closes off any critical analysis of heterosexuality as an organizing institution. The effect of this depiction of reality is that heterosexuality circulates as taken for granted, naturally occurring, and unquestioned, while gender is understood as socially constructed, and central to the organization of everyday life" (1984: 203–4).

9. Also in contrast with groups affiliated with Covenant of the Goddess (COG). Beginning in the Bay Area in the mid-1970s, COG is the largest and longest-running pagan umbrella organization. In the 1980s it developed regional councils across the country, and has, from its founding, been inclusive of diverse sexualities.

10. A labrys is a double-headed ax, found in the iconography of early Mediterranean civilizations. Within the women's spirituality and lesbian feminist cultures it is a symbol of the power of the women leaders of prepatriarchial societies. For some, but not all, women a labrys represents the power of the Amazons in particular. Although there is no historical basis for this association with Amazons, the wearing of such jewelry—small gold labrys earrings, for example—is a subtle signal of one's identity.

11. See for example Berger (1998), Bloch (1998), and Griffin (1999).

12. According to witch's lore, a "grimoire" or Book of Shadows was a witch's personal notebook, recording the magical practices as they were learned. It was supposed to be handwritten and destroyed upon the death of its owner. Lady Sheba was born in the United States and then initiated into a Neogardnerian coven in London in the 1960s. The Grimoire of Lady Sheba was the first "how to" book published in the United States, and it reflects the Neogardnerian tradition in which Lady Sheba was initiated, as well as a bit of Kentucky folklore. See Kelly (1981) for an interesting discussion of the publication history of Books of Shadows in the United States.

13. These are different from the traditional initiations into the craft, which would occur within a coven. Some feminist witches believe that one is a witch by virtue of being born a woman and being aware. See my discussion of initiation practices in Neitz (1994).

14. In 1987 and 1988 I conducted interviews with community leaders and public pagans—people who were known as teachers and or had healing arts practices or practiced divination in the Denver and Boulder area. I located these people through bookstores, advertisements in alternative publications, as well as pagan directories.

15. This differs from what Berger (1998) reports from her observations of pagans in the Northeast over a similar time period.

16. Concerns about gender balance were also addressed in more public ways. In the late 1980s there was discussion among pagans nationwide about the need to have a public presence as religious organizations in their local communities if they wanted to gain respect for their spiritual tradition. In various places, individual pagan clergy joined ministerial alliances, visited schools with informational programs, and volunteered as chaplains

in prisons and hospitals. DAWN decided that they needed, as an organization, to raise money to contribute to a community-based charity. The charity they chose was a local battered women's shelter, because they felt that in that location their money would help "restore balance" in nature by helping to restore the balance between men and women.

17. Eller (1993) has suggested that women involved in the women's spirituality movement are looking for alternative understandings of femininity because they are unsuccessful at the conventional ones. My data does not let me assess how successful the women were at conventional femininity, but their presentation of self was of women who violated the conventional definitions while maintaining a sense of being women in a gendered universe.

18. As Rhys Williams pointed out to me, technically these are antlers. The iconography of contemporary neo-paganism, following its custom of freely borrowing from many cultural sources, does not, to my knowledge, distinguish between antlers (which are shed yearly) and horns, which are not. They invoke the god as "The Horned One" and have images of stags. The association of horns of bulls, goats, and rams with divinity was common in ancient civilizations of the Mediterranean and Middle East. Images of the stag may be more common among the Celts of Northern Europe.

19. For example, one chorus goes "Hoof and horn, hoof and horn, all that dies shall be reborn."

20. Barbara Walker offers the following etymology that makes connections between the pagan practices of wearing horns, nonexclusive sexual practices, and the bird. She says, cuckold is "derived from 'cuckoo' bird of May, anciently sacred to the promiscuous May-games that medieval Europe inherited from the man who became a cuckoo, or cuckold, was one who didn't care if his wife was faithful or not, for them attended the May time festivities when the ritual promiscuity was the rule—or the fertility charm—late as the 16th century" (1983: 196–97.) Her sources—nineteenth-century folklorists—say that the pagan who participated in the rites wore horned masks and headdresses in the god's honor, thus the wearing of horns was associated with the cuckold.

21. She seemed to fear that the title might be interpreted as an attempt to recruit gay and lesbian pagans.

22. Several times I heard spontaneous recitations of the speech of the Nazi resister, Pastor Niemoller: "They came for the Communists, and I didn't speak up because I wasn't a Communist. Then they came for the Jews, and I didn't speak up because I wasn't a Jew. Then they came for the trade unionists, and I didn't speak up because I wasn't a trade unionist. They came for the Catholics, and I didn't speak up because I wasn't a Catholic. Then they came for me, and by that time there was no one else to speak up."

POPULAR EXPRESSIONS III

J UST WHEN WE HAVE ARRIVED at highly sectarian, indeed almost mystical experiences available individually and personally, such as Faerie practice and the
Dragonfest, our essayists move further into undiscovered religious territory to
trace in the next chapters how forms of gay popular culture are used for spiritual
ends. This third and final section offers half a dozen essays examining how gay,
lesbian, and bisexual persons have found and developed innovative media for new
spiritual practices in and through popular culture. Here the authors examine gay
religion as popular culture. Popular culture, of course, is not religion at all. The
events, performances, and practices reported are available outside religious institutions and other settings normally understood as religious. Gay religion as popular culture does not privilege religious traditions or organizations. Nor does it
address them explicitly. Nonetheless, our researchers demonstrate how certain
forms of popular culture provide gay persons with new media for individual and
also shared spiritual expression.

Modern religious life, Robert Bellah has pointed out, operates without the
formal direction of religious organizations (1970). The cultural commodification
of religion in the modern period means that religious symbolization, including
ritual, is available widely and no longer only exclusively from or through religious
institutions or organizations alone. The essays in this section contribute significantly to an understanding of gay and lesbian religious practice and expression
that are outside religious institutions and organizations. Therefore, they are in
many ways different from the previous essays. Readers will find no churches or
synagogues, no priests, no formal sacraments. Nonetheless, these essays—like the
ones before them dealing with denominations and subaltern groups and
practices—provide a careful examination of gay religion by examining what gays

and lesbians are doing spiritually in and through popular culture. The stories here can be understood as reports of new spiritual practices, others as slices of gay popular culture not explicitly spiritual or religious but well illumined by categories and methods from the study of religion.

Gay religion as popular culture completes the three-part heuristic typology offered for understanding innovation and tradition in gay spiritual practice. The essays do not examine denominational heritage groups or those that follow a more sectarian religious impulse to create new subaltern communities of faith as those in earlier sections did. Here the authors move outside the precincts of more easily recognized religious structures to examine ad hoc, shifting, diffuse, and nascent forms of spiritual practice in popular culture. Gay religion as described in this final section takes forms that identify with nonreligious culture. These cultural forms include gospel music, gender identity and roles, drug use, theater, leather bars, and cruising for casual sex.

Gray and Thumma examine what is the most explicit religious event of the several reported here, Atlanta's Gospel Hour. They argue that the Gospel Hour is both a gay cabaret and a Southern evangelical revival hour. The largely gay male audience reconciles different identities, one focused on Southern evangelical religion and the other on urban male homosexuality by participation in this colorful slice of popular culture in Atlanta.

Next, Edward Gray examines another specimen of gay popular culture. Although it is a performance like the Gospel Hour (and was also performed in Atlanta), it is of a very different kind. *The Harvey Milk Show* is an imaginative hagiographic account of the life and death of the first openly gay elected official in the United States. It is also, Gray argues, a specimen of an emerging gay spiritual orientation, which is very comfortable and adept at using popular cultural forms, especially the performing arts. This spiritual orientation is detached from religious organizations, although not completely independent of religious tradition. The essay argues that gay spiritual sensibility as expressed in popular culture is erotic rather than logical, extemporized rather than textual, physically mediated rather than meditative.

An example of this eroticism may be found in Paul J. Gorrell's examination of the gay male circuit party as a spiritual phenomenon, "Rite to Party." This essay continues the movement in this section further and further outside of traditional religious experiences to investigate the nontraditional spiritual awakenings or encounters with the "other" in the lives of gay men. Gorrell explores the symbols, rituals, and ecstasy of these liminal experiences of spectacle, music, drug use, and gay solidarity to show how a circuit party can be a spiritual experience.

Ingrid Sell's qualitative study of "third-gendered" individuals, "Intermediaries," shows how a group, raised in mainstream religious traditions, understands its new sexual and spiritual niche. She suggests how members' spirituality has been carved out in a manner similar to how they identify as neither male nor female. She shows how binary sexual categories can be ad hoc rather than "natural" for those who experience themselves as neither male nor female. The accepted binary public categories of gender don't hold in every case of individual human sexuality, showing the danger of using categories (or typologies) to do all of our thinking. Yet, with few cultural resources to access, these intermediaries are creating new spiritual opportunities for self-expression through popular culture.

Tom Peterson takes us into the world of leathermen. "Gay Men's Spiritual Experience in the Leather Community" reports how some seek in the leather community spiritual experiences through rites of domination and subordination. They do so even while acknowledging their sadomasochistic nature. Leathermen engage in rites of initiation and transformation through carefully orchestrated play. This play finds its spiritual expression through the exploration of creative and destructive urges and ritual annihilation of ego. This leads, Peterson argues, to ritual transformation in many practitioners and an integration of gay masculinity into the lives of leathermen.

In "The Spirit Within," Donald Boisvert attempts to show that certain dimensions of gay male cultural life are indeed religious in Durkheim's sense of the term, that is, as being integral to social life. Boisvert examines three specific "sites" of urban gay male culture: the strip joint, the public cruising space, and the public celebration of gay pride. He frames them as "manifestations of a distinctively gay spiritual impulse."

Spirituality is clearly now detached from organized religions not only descriptively but also, for many, normatively. The ethnographers and essayists in this section begin with this presupposition. They explore an undiscovered country. Moving to areas of popular culture not much visited by scholars of religion, they inquire about new spiritual practices, about the religious intentionality of what they observe, how these phenomena help the individuals and groups investigated to be religious, what balance of continuity and innovation they have struck, and for what ends.

Nearly all of the essays examine cultural phenomena that are without question ritualized activities. According to Malinowski, ritual makes what was essentially biological activity socially meaningful. Ritualization gives meaning by making the newly developing biological capacity of an individual public, and thus socially meaningful (1984). These chapters suggest that gays and lesbians may be developing rites of passage not tied to biological change but to psychological transformations that mark the coming-out experiences. These allow gay men to identify more publicly and perhaps more spiritually as gay or lesbian. Developing rituals around sexual and psychological (instead of biological) change may be tied to the impulse to make such deep transformations meaningful by sharing them publicly as Malinowsky first showed.

There are many vendors of the religious today. In the urban gay milieu, such vendors include the gay bar, gay-themed theater, circuit parties, drag performance, and more. These forms of popular culture and the roles they provide for participants may erase symbolically in their particular subcultural settings the gender rankings and expectations created and maintained symbolically as well as socially in the dominant heterosexual world. Urban gay men and lesbians must rehearse these categories daily in some segments of their lives. They are increasingly free, however, to ignore dominant gender and religious forms in other precincts of modernity.

The essays in this section explore very specialized, narrow segments of the gay and lesbian community. These accounts rely on sustained observable activities and events that themselves are dependent on both the dominant heterosexual culture and a vibrant urban gay subculture. In each case, the urban surround is critical. Gay life is not limited to—but certainly reaches its fullest expression in—the big city. Iris Marion Young's normative ideal of social life based on modern urban realities is directly relevant here. In this ideal vision of the city "persons and groups interact within spaces and institutions they all experience themselves as belonging to, but without those interactions dissolving into unity or commonness" (1990). The city holds the promise of compatibility among strangers, of an eventual working out of respect among radically different parties. In this city, the difference of strangers is not frightening, but erotic.[1]

The essays in this section demonstrate how gay men and lesbians are finding their ideal city. It is urban but it is not secular. In these cities, gays have not dissolved entirely the distinctions, indeed, the contradictions, between gay and traditional religious identities. Instead, they have learned to live with, accept, and embrace the contradiction, the inconsistency, and the tentativeness of life in the urban gay ghetto where religion is a small but important part of the scene. The equanimity of gay persons before the ambiguity and tentativeness of cultural innovation bringing sexuality and spiritual practice closer together allows them to move, sometimes fitfully but often with grace, from one social setting to another, from precinct to precinct of the modern big city on angels wings.

Note

1. Strangers, to customers in a gay bar, of course, are candidates for cruising, potential sexual partners. To Christians, the stranger is not a stranger at all, but the neighbor, a brother. Participants at the Gospel Hour must negotiate this distinction, too.

The Gospel Hour 16
Liminality, Identity, and Religion in a Gay Bar[1]

EDWARD R. GRAY AND SCOTT THUMMA

E SQUEEZE THROUGH A CROWD thick with gay men. Some ignore us; others greet us with smiles. Everyone is animated. Bartenders race back and forth opening bottles of beer and mixing gin tonics for the hot and thirsty assembly. Dance music is playing loudly. Suddenly, the music changes incongruously to a stirring orchestral version of the "Hallelujah" chorus. This is Morticia Deville's cue. Unnoticed in the rear of the darkened room, Morticia starts to navigate her large figure through the audience slowly toward the dance floor. The crowd begins to applaud. A spotlight—after what seems a long moment—strikes her sequined gown, perfectly made-up face, and blond wig. She looks the perfect Southern Gospel singer on a televised revival hour as she takes the stage. With all eyes on her, Morticia begins to sing, "Living in the Presence of the King." The song is a popular contemporary Christian hymn. The Gospel Hour at this midtown Atlanta gay bar has begun.

Morticia is a gay man in drag in her early thirties. She sings as a member of "The Gospel Girls" with a popular black drag queen and a straight black woman. Each week they and their audience use Christian symbols and song to create a unique gay gospel cabaret, The Gospel Hour. It is a two-hour-long gospel performance and sing-along. Performers sing or lip-sync traditional gospel hymns and contemporary numbers. Morticia and other Gospel Girls perform in drag for a mostly white gay male audience. Many in this audience are from Evangelical backgrounds and many are Christian still.

Morticia DeVille is the founder and star of the Gospel Hour. She is also a make-believe character; an identity created by a man we call Paul.[2] As Morticia, Paul combines religious sensibilities and songs learned as a child in the mountains of north Georgia with the art of high drag learned as a gay man in the bars of Atlanta.

Even as a child, Paul was drawn to both drag and religion. He told us how he would sneak into his grandmother's bedroom to steal her lipstick. Afterwards he retreated to the loneliness and safety of an empty mountain hollow. Robed in a bedsheet, he preached to the winds, pretending he was Billy Graham. Paul has exchanged bed-sheets for sequined frocks and covert wearing of lipstick in rural Georgia for a pub-lic identity as a drag queen in Atlanta.

The Gospel Hour is a fascinating institution on the Atlanta gay scene. It is also an event well suited to ethnographic study. It is open to repeated participant observation to determine regular and deep patterns. Regular participants—in ad-dition to the principals—can be identified, approached, and interviewed. Others can be talked to more casually—or their conversations overheard. As well as being accessible to observation, the Gospel Hour is a multilayered symbolic event. This ethnographic investigation uncovers these levels of symbolic meaning. Is it a reli-gious event or mere spectacle? Is Paul continuing to pretend to be someone else at the Gospel Hour, presiding over a group of gay men likewise pretending to have church? Or is the Gospel Hour a ritual generative of new and not make-believe identities and models for being both gay and Christian?

Evangelical gospel music blends with drag not for parody but for purpose at the Gospel Hour. The performance challenges everyday categories of experience by absorbing these categories and transforming them. The Gospel Hour merges gospel performance models with high drag. It also blends southern Evangelical Christian sensibilities and cultural norms with urban gay ones. Its audience of gays, straights, blacks, and whites has multiple experiences of the Gospel Hour. Participants have differential encounters to the Gospel Hour based on individual and shared experiences. We acknowledge this as an opportunity for further study. Nonetheless, for the segment of the audience we observed—and for the per-formers themselves—the Gospel Hour is a ritual of identity negotiation. South-ern gay men reconcile their newly achieved modern urban gay identity with their childhood and young adult Evangelical Christian formation. The Gospel Hour—a drag show—is the setting for this identity work. Its product is a model that de-fies dominant cultural norms and establishes new ways to organize social relations.

The Gospel Hour generates what Victor Turner (1969) has called "templates or models" that reclassify social relationships. They provide motives and guides to action. We examine how the model or template of gay drag gospel performance allows participants to reclassify ordinary, taken-for-granted social relationships and cultural categories framing Christianity and gay sexuality. Turner described modern "social life as a type of dialectical process involving successive experience of high and low, *communitas* and structure, homogeneity and differentiation, equal-ity and inequality" (Turner 1969: 96). Our investigation employs Turner's insight to show how culturally marginal groups create new cultural forms and practices through ritual. His theory illumines how our informants use the ritual template generated by the Gospel Hour to negotiate their identity as southern gay Christian men. The performance is a liminal time and space set apart from the everyday. It is betwixt and between dominant cultural and subcultural norms. Being gay and Christian, within this liminal moment, is not exceptional or odd. It is normal.

Singing gospel songs in a gay bar led by men in drag defies most norms and experiences of both urban gay culture and Evangelical Christianity. Because it is a drag show in a gay bar, the Gospel Hour is alien to the Evangelical world. Because it is a Christian gospel music performance, it falls outside the expected parameters of gay drag. Yet the Gospel Hour is a gay drag show and a gospel music performance. Morticia DeVille *is* a gospel singer *and* a drag queen. Singing gospel hymns in drag is a ritual act redefining everyday classifications of experience and creating a new model for identity. This model or template has a normative function. It reconciles being gay and Christian. "All rituals have this exemplary, model displaying character," according to Turner. Rituals create society "in much the same way as Oscar Wilde held life to be 'an imitation of art'" (1969: 117). A young man, a former Christian charismatic, may have said it best to us one night after the Gospel Hour.

> It's hard [to get used to at first] because you grow up and you believe that these are praises to God and you see this big drag queen camping it up, and you are thinking "Oh no, something is really wrong here and we can't let this go on. . . ." It clashes with all the preconceived ideas you have. . . . Later on, you realize that it can be this way, too.[3]

Ethnography beyond the Local Congregation

The Gospel Hour is the longest running drag show in Atlanta. Our first exposure was in 1992, its seventh year. Sporadic but enthusiastic attendance by one of us led to this formal investigation in the spring and summer of 1994. The Gospel Hour had just moved from the bar that had been its home for more than four years. During our study, the Gospel Girls increased the frequency of new numbers, rehearsed more often, and wore the occasional coordinated costume. Our regular presence as identified researchers may have helped prod these changes. We cannot determine, however, if our observation had any direct effect. Nevertheless, the Gospel Hour remained basically unchanged during the course of our study.

Using participant observation, we collected our data over twelve evenings, or twenty-four services. We interviewed informally, chatted with, and eavesdropped on participants. These included the owner and several bartenders. We also formally interviewed Morticia DeVille, Ramona Dugger, and thirteen participants, including several who were regular guest performers. The audience members volunteered to talk with us after a general announcement by Morticia. She encouraged "her flock" to help us in our research. Of those we formally interviewed, all but one was male. Seven interviewees reported that they were born and raised in the South. Two others hailed from the northeast and central regions of the country. Four interviewees did not provide this data. They were all white, middle class, in their twenties and thirties, and the majority had at least some college education. They gave us a less than fully representative picture. We spoke informally, however, with many African Americans and older participants. Our informants (although not a randomly selected sample) are part of an important segment of the participants—those who identify as gay and Christian. These sons of the church have creatively reappropriated cultural forms they once thought off-limits. They—like other members of modern fragmented urban society—create ritually generated forms to negotiate religious and social identity in a multiplicity of settings, many of them contested. In addition, they *choose* from among these ritually created and sustained forms.

The Gospel Hour as Ritual: Fully Gay and Altogether Southern Evangelical

Twice each Sunday the Gospel Girls conduct what they call "services" for their "congregation." During the first half of the nearly two-hour performance, they sing solo numbers. Some of these are signature pieces. Special guests often sing during this time from a repertoire of classic and contemporary gospel music. The songs differ at each service, but they are selected from a circumscribed range of a few dozen pieces. The quality of performance, nonetheless, is uniformly high week-to-week. "That's the good thing about us," Morticia told us one day in a slow drawl. "The music is so powerful. It's so good. And Southern."

Morticia is sweet and warm—grandmotherly in a Sunday school teacher sort of way. She can stir the audience with her singing. For some songs, like "Standing in the Presence of the King," she lip-syncs to another performer. Most often, however, she sings well-known hymns in her own strong and beautiful voice. Audience members place dollar bills in her hands and kiss her on the cheek.

Morticia introduces Ramona Dugger after her opening segment. Ramona is the number two Gospel Girl. She has a remarkable vocal range. When she sings "Amazing Grace"—a signature number for her—you begin to fear for the glassware in the bar. Her songs are emotional and passionate. Ramona is straight, young, and African American. She favors contemporary gospel music. Her background is Episcopalian. Many songs in the Gospel Hour repertoire, therefore, were unfamiliar. When she does sing traditional Evangelical hymns, she favors the classics like "Amazing Grace" and "How Great Thou Art." Sometimes she sings,

THE GOSPEL HOUR   289

"If You're Happy and You Know it, Clap your Hands" changing the words to "If you're happy and gay, clap your hands!"

Ramona became a Gospel Girl in 1994. She had been a regular guest performer for five years—most of the ensemble's career. When Morticia announced that Ramona would become "official," one owner of the bar objected. He said that bartenders were getting complaints about the explicitly religious nature of Ramona's onstage comments. The barkeep's description of the usual thrust of Ramona's remarks—explicitly Christian—struck us as accurate. Soon after, the Gospel Hour moved. We asked Ramona about proselytizing during her performance. She said,

> We're treading a fine line as it is. You know, it's a very fine line. And I quite frankly identify with it probably most strongly more than anyone else in the show on a higher spiritual level. And because of that I probably step over that line. Tish never says "God." She never says "Jesus." I will. I don't do it on a regular basis because I don't want people to feel like "I'm coming into a bar and I'm just getting preached at" because I'm not preaching to anybody. But I do think there are so many people who are so hungry to know that God does love them, you know, and that they're under so much stress and so much trouble in their lives that they need to be reminded that it's just not all here and now. There's more to that. You got to look up and know you are not alone in all this . . . And try to give them some comfort. So I do, I admit I do cross that line a bit.

After her initial song—usually "Friends Are Friends Forever" sung powerfully and warmly with Morticia—Ramona invites an American sign language interpreter to the stage. He reported to us that deaf people come regularly. As he signs, Ramona moves to the rear. Under the spotlight, his hands sing gracefully and energetically for the unhearing. The beauty and grace of the signing captures the audience.

Alicia Kelly is the most recent Gospel Girl. She is a young muscular black man. Ramona and others report she does an amazingly realistic Patti LaBelle. We believe it. She lip-syncs her numbers but everything else about her performance is authentic. She pours a fantastic amount of energy into her dancing, or "shouting." Kelly imitates a Pentecostal devotee possessed by the Holy Spirit. The congregation watches her transport herself acrobatically across the stage and they respond with loud applause. Many toss crumbled bills onto the stage and shout "Amen, Sister!" Alicia dramatically concludes by throwing her wig into the crowd and dousing herself with a bottle of beer or mineral water grabbed from a startled member of the audience. They roar.

Alicia, Ramona told us, "is doing the style she grew up with. They're the women that she saw in church. Often she will say, 'Well, this is Sister so-and-so,' and she'll become Sister so-and-so." The manager of the group—echoing an assessment that could have come from anyone in the audience—said, "If [Alicia Kelly] doesn't light your fire, your wood's wet!" Her electrifying performance concludes the first half of the hour.

Immediately, Morticia introduces the "Greeting Portion" of the service, a time, she says, for the congregation to meet and greet one another. She invites strangers to introduce themselves. Morticia leads the way and begins to mingle with the crowd. Most people do not follow her example, but some do. Romances have started at the Gospel Hour, including some lasting ones. Morticia takes this portion of the service seriously.

> I really want them to meet each other. The greeting portion . . . I mean, it's very difficult for them to talk to each other. Nobody will go up and speak to a stranger. And at Drakes I'd make a point to go all the way around the entire room. I don't do that so much anymore. I really do try to push. . . .

Gospel music continues to play during the quarter-of-an-hour break. The service resumes with the crowd eagerly anticipating the "High Church Sing-Along"—the highlight of the performance. Morticia, Ramona, Alicia, and guest singers sit on bar stools. They lead the crowd in favorite hymns like "When the Roll Is Called Up Yonder," "Because He Lives, I Can Face Tomorrow," and "There Is Power in the Blood of the Lamb." The volume, quality, and passion of the singing would be the envy of any church. During these hymns, participants occasionally close their eyes, some bow their heads. A few others raise their hands. "I really missed gospel music," Gary, a tall, handsome son of a famous Pentecostal minister told us. "There is a part of me that likes to sing," Gary continued, "so now I sing gospel music in a gay bar." Like so many at the Gospel Hour, Gary loves to sing, and he loves to sing *these* songs.

The Gospel Girls then invite individual members of the audience to sing a verse of "Amazing Grace." The ability of the audience participants covers a wide range. On Easter Sunday, 1995, a young man in a wheelchair sang. He chose the verse including the line "I once was lost but now I'm found, was blind but now I see." The bar fell silent straining to hear his weak voice. Later, Morticia DeVille confided that she wanted to cry because she found the young man's singing so sweet.

Although weeping is not *supposed* to happen in a gay bar, tears are no strangers at these services. We have seen men cry during the Gospel Hour, caught up in the music and the emotion of the evening. One Sunday, a young man began to sob after the mention of the many who have died of AIDS, sometimes abandoned by family at their deaths but often surrounded by

friends. The man—who we assumed was mourning the loss of a loved one—
was embraced and comforted by his circle of friends. He did not hide his tears.
No one made any move to the door. The emotion was very public—like at a
revival meeting.

Participants have reacted emotionally since Morticia began to sing gospel
songs in the gay bars of Atlanta. She recalled how her first audience responded in
1984.

> I did a show at Doug's. And it was just me and this piano player. And it just went
> so well. All those leather men like, had tears, they were all singing, they were cry-
> ing. It was, it was really moving. . . .

Each Gospel Hour concludes in the same fashion. Perched on a row of bar
stools, the Gospel Girls lip-sync a rousing version of "Looking for a City." Members of the audience grab cocktail napkins to wave them as hankies back-and-
forth, to-and-fro, round and round, in time with the music. The Gospel Girls
mirror back the movements of the enthusiastic crowd. "See You in the Rapture,"
a contemporary song, follows immediately and is the grand finale. A dozen or
more men take the stage with no prompting to form a chorus line. Among them
are some who join every week. New people also join making the line several deep.
The dancing—like the napkin routine—is campy. The theology behind the lyrics
of "See You in the Rapture" and "Looking for a City" is explicitly eschatological.
The heavenly city is a place where residents will never die, where they "will be with
Jesus and their loved ones too. Where the Holy Spirit all [their] hopes renew."
Both songs promise an imminent new order marked by what Turner called "communitas" (Turner 169: 94–129). The eternal home "Looking for a City" envisions and the bliss "See You in the Rapture" eagerly awaits—like Turner's
communitas—stand against all human works and ways. The songs describe an
eternity of acceptance. Despite "all we have been through," participants await the
day they will see Jesus and each other—including those taken by age, accident, and
disease—"in the air some sweet day." Contrary to current social structure, these
hymns anticipate a time and space based on spontaneous relations among equal
human beings.

We do not know the choreographic origins or theological referents of the han-
kie waving during "Looking for a City" or the line dancing during "See You in the
Rapture." Neither was planned by the performers. When asked about them, Morticia admitted,

> I don't understand the napkins. The napkins were way before our time. They were
> other queens who did "Looking for a City" [in their drag shows] and they always
> waved napkins. I don't know where that came from.

She shed no more light on the line dancing but did volunteer that she was "just a little offended by the dance." Recalling the enthusiastic participation of the audience that previous Sunday, however, she began to soften. "But it is okay." Then, coming further around, admitted to perhaps a guilty pleasure in the enthusiastic participation of her audience. "I mean . . . Sunday, there was just an incredible amount of people up there!" Morticia and the Gospel Girls are not the only creators of the rituals of the Gospel Hour.

Morticia and Ramona explicitly address the crowd as they might in a church service. One often hears, "Say Amen, congregation!" and "Hang around for the next service." Morticia carries on a relaxed banter with insider references. She jokes about where she has eaten that day or how hard it is to find clothes. (She is a large woman.) They tell an ongoing joke about their old gospel bus. Sadly, it was lost in a fire. They plan a fund-raiser in order to replace it. One of the original Gospel Girls started the unfortunate blaze while she was frying chicken in the rear of the bus during a tour.

The bus never existed. Yet some "churchly" accouterments do. These have included faux stained glass windows, choir robes, bulletins, and guest choirs. The Gospel Girls regularly recognize ministers in the crowd. Some Metropolitan Community Church (MCC) pastors are regulars. The choir of a local MCC church sings once each month. They "pass the plate" to collect for their church building fund. On Palm Sunday the bar was decorated with fronds. Finally, of course, there are the hymns. The Gospel Girls go right up to the line of creating an explicitly religious environment. On occasion they call the bar a "cathedral." "If I had my way," Morticia told us, "when we moved to Prism from Drake's we would have had furniture, you know, church furniture. I thought I could make it myself. Spray paint it white."

The Gospel Girls and participants behave themselves during the hour. They sometimes openly enforce a standard of conduct on the audience. Morticia once chastised some rowdy participants with the rebuke, "As my Mamma used to say to me, 'Girl, you can give one hour a week back (to God)!'" They avoid the kind of bawdy sexual remarks typical of drag performances. Morticia, however, can be sexually suggestive but subtly. The hour never seems so sexually charged as when Alicia Kelly dances her ecstatic black Pentecostal shouts. Yet none of this sexuality is overt. Like church, there may be undertones of sexuality, but the worship service is not the place to act on these feelings.

One Sunday, a male stripper danced between services. The bar scene before, between, and after each performance is indistinguishable from any other drag show. In that regard, a male stripper was not out of place. Morticia said that while there is nothing wrong with strippers, they are inappropriate as part of the Gospel Hour or in proximity with it. She explained this to the crowd. The stripper never returned.

Restrained sexual expression is just one of the several informal rules at the Gospel Hour. The Gospel Girls never charge a cover. They never make fun of religious personalities. When the audience chooses to, however, they do not object. One recording popular with the audience captures Jimmy Swaggert giving a warm welcome to some unidentified religious group. He encourages them to hug, embrace, and show how they love each other. Participants enjoy the irony (or perhaps the ambiguity) of the liminal setting. Although they perform almost exclusively in bars, the Gospel Girls are careful not to drink in public. Seeing anyone drunk during the performance, for that matter, is rare although the bar does a brisk business. Almost no one cruises overtly. Audience members, however, get picked-up on occasion.

The two other bars in the immediate area attract their own crowds. One fills when the Gospel Hour ends. Many participants go there afterwards rather than stay at Prism after singing "See You in the Rapture." The transition from its concluding notes to dance music is abrupt but most people seem to prefer to go elsewhere to dance. They maintain the distinction between sacred time and secular entertainment. One comment summarized the attitude of many participants. "I don't normally do here what I do in a bar. I just feel funny about doing it . . . I don't chase men when I come to the Gospel Girls. That's not the purpose of coming here." Participants separate from the straight world by coming to the gay bar. They actively set themselves apart from norms of the gay world, too. They do this by making the choice to listen to and sing gospel music.

The "ritual subject," according to Turner (1969: 95) has an "ambiguous" social role as he negotiates a new identity. We found no one with a more ambiguous identity than Morticia DeVille, the presider at the Gospel Hour. Our interview was the first time we had seen Morticia/Paul away from the Gospel Hour, out of role, as a man. It was a startling sight. It was only dimly, however, that we could see him. One small kitchen light illumined our way through Paul's darkened home. We talked out on the enclosed porch. We sat on the floor among potted plants, exercise equipment, and shadows. Gone were the sequined gowns, blond wigs and makeup, faux stained glass windows, and stage lights. During our interview, Morticia/Paul described Paul as a bitch, Morticia as sweet and grandmotherly. Paul— not in drag, away from the bright lights of the stage—struck us as shy, almost withdrawn. Where, we wondered, was the bitchy queen? Part of our confusion may have stemmed from Morticia Deville's sexual ambiguity and Paul's ambivalence about the religious nature of the event. (We discuss this below.) This ambiguity shapes the liminal nature of the entire Gospel Hour.

In addition to multiple and ambiguous meanings, the phases of liminal ritual at the Gospel Hour leading to identity negotiation are more generalized than in Turner's model. Plenty of nonreligious activity goes on. People come and go constantly. Many participants are out with their friends, having a good time. The performance dominates, but it does not monopolize. Participants and the singers alike combine behaviors learned in church and in bars. They have created a new model or template of identity mixing Evangelical and gay forms seamlessly.

The Participants: Identity Negotiation in a Modern Fragmented World

The first time visitor to the Gospel Hour immediately notices the predominantly young white crowd. A second glance, however, uncovers the approximately 10 percent who are African Americans, along with a few Hispanics and Asians. On any given night ten to fifteen women attend. Perhaps 20 percent are older than fifty-five years of age. Several of those interviewed attested to this unique diversity. One person claimed that Gospel Hour participants were "not your normal S and M gays . . . you know 'Stand and Model' gays." One fourth of our informants insisted they were not "bar people." Not only was this an older and more mature group, most did not have gym-perfected bodies. Many, in fact, were overweight, short, bald, or unattractive. The youngest, most handsome participants whom you might see in any popular gay bar often gather in small groups hugging the railing around the large stage. Directly in front, a group of regulars, many of them members of the MCC, enthusiastically sing along. Most of the audience crams into the space behind these clusters. A middle-aged mother of a gay man or a sympathetic minister may sit at the few small tables to one side of the bar. Morticia is careful to greet and introduce them and other special guests each week. When she does, the audience receives the newcomers warmly.

Many in the crowd are regulars. Some come, we suspect, because they want to be in a bar full of gay men. Some are visitors from out-of-town. (Variety in participants' familiarity, interest, and motives, of course, is common to most groups.) More unusual are those attracted by the beehive of activity who enter and become confused. A few of the uninitiated are further drawn in by the spectacle and stay. Others remain because of the familiarity of the music or fascination at the setting. Some participate to reconcile Christian belief and practice with modern urban gay identity in the safety of the gay bar (a sort of cultural womb of the urban gay community).

Donald, a former Southern Baptist and middle-aged man with no current church affiliation, reported that "at the Gospel Hour we can feel safe, like we won't be condemned." Regular participation allows him and others to identify more openly as Christian to gay friends. "We can say, 'Come go to the Gospel Hour.' We could never say 'Come go to church,'" he explained. "The Gospel Hour is fine because it's in a bar." "Going here I now can realize that I can be gay and still be with God," Mark, another regular participant, said. "God can reach out and say, 'I love you!'" For him, a man in his twenties from South Carolina, this was a significant realization. Mark was raised, like many we spoke with, as a Southern Baptist. He grew up knowing that he couldn't be both gay and Christian at the same time. By the time he came out he had been an ordained minister for five years. Since then, Mark has left institutional religion. "I was very fearful of incorporating the two concepts together," he confided. "I was told by most organized religion that I was wrong and damned to hell."

Mark was not the only one to believe and fear the message of nonacceptance and condemnation from American religious institutions. Nearly three-quarters of the respondents to the 1984 General Social Survey considered same-sex relations to be always or almost always wrong (Roof and McKinney 1987: 213). Likewise, most Gospel Hour participants know all too well the historic incompatibility of Christianity and homosexuality. Their childhood and adult experiences of the church, its ministers, and indirectly of the Christian God are ample proof. What takes place at the Gospel Hour is not important for participants alone. Nonetheless, the Gospel Hour provides a model for the place of gay people in the church contrary to dominant Christian practices and beliefs.

For gays and lesbians of Evangelical Christian heritage, religious support and advocacy have been nearly nonexistent. A few tolerant churches and support groups exist. For the most part, however, gay Evangelical and Pentecostal Christians face hard choices. They must remain closeted in their conservative churches, switch into a liberal denomination, or leave organized Christianity all together (Thumma 1987: 125). With the two latter options, the gay Evangelical Southern man must leave behind the symbols, rituals, hymns, and religious culture in which he was raised. The Gospel Hour is another option. It offers a setting in which participants can be both gay and Christian openly. High drag (an art form to which urban gay men become acculturated) combines with the familiar and cherished worship style of participants' early religious formation.

Our informants report considerable early religious formation as Evangelical Christians. Six were raised Southern Baptist, two Methodist, three Pentecostal or charismatic, and one Presbyterian (one person did not answer). Evangelical churches and institutions educated and employed these men. Three attended Christian colleges, three attended seminaries or Bible schools. Four spoke of being "called" to the ministry. One person sang at Jerry Falwell's Liberty University. Gary sang at Church of God congregations throughout the South. One person was currently a minister. Mark and another man were former clergy; a third was a former Southern Baptist missionary. The remainder reported their earliest religious formation in moderate and liberal Protestant Christian churches. We encountered few who were Catholics, Jews, non-Christians, or not religiously identified at all.

The MCC dominated informants' current church affiliation. The Universal Fellowship of the Metropolitan Community Churches is an independent denomination of approximately 290 churches and 30,000 members. Gay Christians created the denomination to fill a religious void for gay (and heterosexual) believers. MCC's founder, Troy Perry, was raised and served as a minister in a conservative Pentecostal church. The MCC as a whole reflects some of Perry's theological heritage and early religious formation. Of the three MCC congregations in Atlanta, one borrows predominantly from Baptist worship, one from Methodist, and the eclectic third congregation from high Episcopal to low Methodist (Cotton 1996: 295). Unfamiliar or high church rituals or even the overt gay emphasis of MCC worship can deter gays from Evangelical backgrounds from participation and membership (Perry 1972; Warner 1994; Bauer 1976).

Six of those interviewed claimed the MCC to be "their church" (including an MCC associate pastor). Three others had attended an MCC congregation but no longer. Two of these said they "didn't connect" with the church, and one complained that it was "too ritualistic." Two other informants attended Presbyterian and Episcopal churches where they were organists. (One of these persons pointed out that many gay church organists and choir directors attend the Gospel Hour regularly.) Except the six active MCC members, all informants reported little current involvement in churches.

Almost every person spoke of nonacceptance of gays and lesbians by religious groups. Many said they had experienced animosity from religious persons. Hostility is the normal, everyday posture of Christianity toward gays and lesbians. Our informants believe that gays have been, as one said, "shut off from Christianity." "If you are gay, you are going to hell!" said another, summarizing the prevailing message of the church of his youth. This older message sharply contrasts with what gay men see, hear, and do at the Gospel Hour.

"I realized that the God that the Baptists preached hated me," Shannon, the former missionary, said one Sunday between services. "I was told for so long that [as a gay man] I was hated by God." Many told us of their personal negative experiences. "I always thought that God completely hated me. I was told, 'You are gay and you are going to hell.'" Another informant told of his church friends' reactions after he shared his sexual orientation with them. "My best friends in the world turned their backs on me," he remembered. In the face of overt rejection by the Christian community, many gays decide to have nothing further to do with religion. Gary described his response plainly but with some of the cadence of an Evangelical preacher. "I jumped out of the closet and slammed the door right behind me. I left in the closet my family, my religion, and my God."

Surveys of Christians from every denomination, from the most liberal to the most conservative, confirm these recollections of intolerance and hurt. One denominational study found that 81 percent of the lay members and 68 percent of clergy thought the "homosexual lifestyle" was always or almost always wrong (Edion 1993; 174). George Gallup, Jr. and Jim Castelli found only 19 percent of Evangelicals and 42 percent of mainline Protestants favor legalization of homosexual acts (Gallup and Castelli 1989: 190). Likewise, Roof and McKinney reported that an average of 64 percent of those surveyed from liberal denominations, 77 percent of those from moderate denominations, 79 percent from historically African American denominations, and 89 percent from conservative denominations thought homosexuality was always or almost always wrong. Sixty-nine percent of the Catholics surveyed agreed (Roof and McKinney 1989: 211–12). In a 1990 study of Southern Baptists, only 2 percent of respondents thought homosexuality was a "viable" Christian lifestyle (Ammerman 1990: 109). It is not surprising that nearly every study of gays and lesbians shows very low levels of participation in organized religion. In one study more than 50 percent responded that they were not religious in the conventional sense at all (Bell and Weinberg 1978). Various studies, on the other hand, report powerful childhood religious influences and a desire for spiritual meaning among gays and lesbians (Thumma 1987, 1991; Greenberg 1988, Boswell 1980; McNeill 1976).

In spite of almost always negative, frequently hostile, and occasionally violent responses to homosexuality in and outside the church, many at the Gospel Hour are still Christian—when construed in broad, cultural terms—although not active church members. For many Southern gay men, Evangelical churches provided important models of identity. Many at the Gospel Hour are still the choirboys, testifying and witnessing lay members, and even clerical leaders that they were in the Evangelical churches of their youth and young adult lives. As children and youths, these churches taught them their religious identity and helped prepare them to be (white) Christian men in the South. In the more diverse and tolerant cultural spaces of the city where they have learned to be gay, they are mastering how to be Christian again too—on their own terms.

Some Gospel Hour participants attending for the first time are hostile, ambiguous, or conflicted about Christianity. Others still respect the church or cherish a childhood memory of it. For six of the thirteen interviewed, the Gospel Girls' performance initially seemed wrong, even disgusting. Ben, a former fundamentalist Southern Baptist who attended Jerry Falwell's University, recalled his first impression. "I thought it was hypocritical and blasphemous." Guy, deeply involved in the charismatic movement, left after his initial visit and did not return for six years. "The first time I came, I was just totally disgusted. I thought, 'How could they be doing this in a gay place—singing gospel music and trying to be religious?'" Gregory recalled for us his first visceral reaction. "At first I was appalled.

I just knew the ground was going to open up and we'd be sucked straight into hell
. . . *but* after a while I began to notice the look of joy on people's faces."

These participants no longer find the Gospel Hour appalling or hypocritical.
To the contrary, they spoke of feeling the presence of God. "I do, many times,
sense the presence of the Spirit," one said. Another commented, "I never feel like
I leave here without getting something out of this." The Gospel Hour stands in
stark contrast to the message that gay life and Christianity are irreconcilable. The
Gospel Hour does more than send a countervailing message. It enacts in a specific
time and space a new model of gay Christian identity and a new template for cultural and social relations between Evangelicalism and gay life.

Half of those we interviewed attended the drag show regularly for several
years. One person missed only four times in three years. We think our informants
reflect the audience on any given Sunday. We estimate almost half are very committed, constituting the core participants. Another 20 to 30 percent attend occasionally, about once each month. In addition, a fifth to a third are marginal. This
group attends infrequently, only once, or to cruise the crowd. A marginal group,
these men likely view the Gospel Hour as pure entertainment, an oddity, or even
disturbing. One of us overheard the conversation of three first-timers who walked
in during the middle of the performance unknowingly. After looking confused
and uncomfortable, one fellow turned to his friends and implored them, "Let's get
out of here!"

For our informants, the drag show is a moving spiritual experience. "Everybody gets something out of (the Gospel Hour)," Gregory said in his subtle southern accent, "even if it is just that God doesn't hate them. It is a good and positive
outlet." "It is a form of ministry," another maintained. Paul, however, is reluctant
to talk about his work as Morticia DeVille as anything approximating a religious
calling. In fact, he explicitly denies it. Paul, who earns his living as Morticia, speaks
of her as a different person, someone apart and different from himself. Morticia
is "jovial and funny and loving and trying to be grandmotherish" in Paul's description. He acknowledges that the *character* of Morticia DeVille might be ministerial, but not the person we call Paul. Other Gospel Girls and regular participants,
however, are not hesitant to claim that Paul is following his calling. One Sunday,
Morticia read a card from a MCC minister, a regular at the services. "You wear
makeup and a wig," he wrote to her. "I wear a robe. But we both serve the same
person."

That Morticia does wear a dress, however, is essential to the ritual. Drag is an
ambiguous art. The drag performer embodies a picture of the gay man—as the
feminine—rejected by many gays. Drag erases symbolically in a particular subcultural setting the gender lines created and maintained symbolically and socially in
the dominant culture. Urban gay men must rehearse these daily in some segments

of their lives. They are increasingly free in the American urban milieu, however, to ignore dominant gender lines in others.

The Gospel Hour functions differently for each person, and sometimes on multiple levels. For core participants it was their church. One said, "I always call it 'coming to church'... my friends and I call it 'coming to services.'" Another participant stated, "It is just an extension of church." Some participants have attended the Gospel Hour regularly for years, but have not stepped foot in a church.

For others the Gospel Hour gave them an opportunity for spiritual reconnection and restoration. Shannon (the former missionary) said, "Many (gays) are scared to go back to church because [it] turned them away. This is their one touch with God." James, a Presbyterian from New Jersey who is an Episcopal church organist, stated, "Gay anger against God is dealt with here." Hurt, too. A gay man visiting from Minnesota broke down during the singing. Regaining some composure, he confessed, "I can still identify with God, there is hope for me, a backslidden Christian. . . . I really want to get involved in church again," he tearily told Ramona. The comments of other participants echoed this sentiment.

> The Gospel Hour has helped me find an outlet to develop my spirituality.
> It showed me a void. A need in my life...it created a hunger for (church) again.
> The Gospel Hour made me aware of the longing I had for a relationship with God that I had turned away from.

For these and other informants the Gospel Hour offers fellowship and a sense of community. James, the organist, stated plainly, "It's a time of fellowship, that is what it is all about." Ben, the former fundamentalist, added, "I look forward to this as much as I do Sunday morning. . . . This is the fellowship portion." Finally, Mark, the former Southern Baptist preacher, found intimacy and an acceptance of his spirituality. "I could talk to others about what I feel and it was at the deepest, most intimate spiritual level." At the Gospel Hour new norms and new classifications of social relations take hold.

The Gospel Hour is most overtly a structured time for singing the old gospel songs. The act of singing these hymns has its own power, fulfilling a deep need created during early years of church life for our informants (Clark 1993: 105–6). One reported that part of him likes to sing, another attested that "music communicates in a way that words cannot." Some missed gospel music because singing it reminded them of home and family. Singing gospel music, Shannon said, is "my way of showing my religion, my relationship to God." Singing these songs, he continued, "is when I feel closest to God." Guy, the former charismatic, told us that "the music makes you feel real good about yourself."

Above all, almost every informant found the combination of gay and Christian cultural templates the most compelling feature of the Gospel Hour. It is a time and space they can be fully gay and altogether evangelical—on their own terms. Informants saw it as "our own place," a place of security and divine acceptance. Mark exclaimed, "I am able to be myself . . . I can do both [be gay and Christian] and be happy!" Shannon, his friend, explained,

> Here were people who knew "the songs" . . . knew what I had been raised with. I could identify all of a sudden. I was in a bar and it was not a sexual thing, not a social thing, it was a spiritual thing. . . . I could talk to others about what I feel and it was at the deepest and most intimate spiritual level.

Conclusion: Gay Liminality and Christian Identity

This ethnography has described how an urban gay bar becomes each week a religious space. The Gospel Hour transforms the bar into a liminal setting. High drag blends with southern Evangelical Christian music and song to create a new model or template for the relationship between being Christian and gay. Some embrace the exemplary template enacted ritually at this gay drag gospel cabaret to negotiate their identity as Christian and gay.

The strength of ethnographic work is not to discover the single answer to a research question. It is to uncover the multiple levels of meaning in an event. Ethnography provides a thick enough description of a phenomenon to make it available for others and their interpretations. There are different experiences being had and multiple levels of meaning engaged at the Gospel Hour. That is what makes the event so compelling. The reality of multiple experiences makes the ethnographic method ideal for the Gospel Hour.

The Gospel Hour provides a model of identity and a template for social relations. But the liminal space it creates is not a simple egalitarian communitas. It is a structured social setting, an institution with its own norms. Its ritual enactments of liminal identities and social roles are contingent on a wider social and institutional surround. In modern cities like Atlanta residents have the opportunity to create and sustain liminal rituals—and to choose from among them. Liminality may comprise an entire ritual event. It may involve an entire segment of an audience. The models and templates created may be more durable than fleeting communitas. Such durability makes ritual a richer source for normative, exemplary behaviors and practices. It also demonstrates that liminality, although ritually generated, is institutionally sustained in wider settings. The Gospel Hour ritually creates a "make believe" picture of gay and Christian social relations and turns the make believe into reality by replacing dominant norms with its own and institutionalizing them.

The Gospel Hour provides a safe haven for gays coming from Evangelical and other Christian traditions. The songs remind them of the comfort they once found in their faith. The drag performance marks the space and time as uniquely gay. Our informants used cultural models extant in gay and Evangelical subcultures as tools to negotiate a new identity and a new set of relationships with Christianity, gay culture, and even God. The Gospel Hour fuses both gay and Evangelical realities. It is gay and Christian, cabaret and revival.

At the Gospel Hour life imitates art.

Notes

Reprinted with permission from Penny Edgell Becker and Nancy L. Eisland, eds., 1997, *Contemporary American Religion: An Ethnographic Reader*, Walnut Creek, CA: Altamira.

1. An earlier version of this study, "Amazing, Grace! How Sweet the Sound! Southern Evangelical Religion and Gay Drag in Atlanta," appears in *Gay Men's Issues in Religious Studies*, vol. 7, *A Rainbow of Religious Studies* edited by J. Michael Clark and Robert E. Goss (1996: 33–53). In addition, we thank our colleagues at Emory University for numerous discussions of some of the ideas in this study.

2. The stage names of all performers, unless otherwise noted, are accurate. Personal names and the names of the taverns and clubs have been changed.

3. All quotations of informants' comments are from our transcribed interviews, 1995, Atlanta.

Intermediaries   17
Spirit and Transcendence in a Sample of
"Third-Gendered" North Americans

INGRID SELL

MANY IN THE LESBIAN AND GAY COMMUNITIES are uncomfortable with those who blur gender lines "a little too much": transgendered people who have argued for inclusion in the community as well as those gay men who embody the limp-wristed effeminacy stereotype or lesbians butch enough to be mistaken for male on a regular basis. Yet in a number of other cultures, these characteristics would mark one as specially gifted, chosen for what is often a spiritual calling. In these other cultures, those who live "between the worlds" of men and women are thought to also be able to walk "between the worlds" of heaven and earth and are groomed for spiritual guidance and shamanic roles.[1]

A sample of thirty LGBT North Americans who identify as "neither man nor woman but more like a third gender" were interviewed to explore whether there might be any parallels with their non-Euro-American counterparts. In fact, the results of this study showed a surprising number of correspondences, despite the fact that those in non-Western cultures are acknowledged and groomed for their "third-gendered" roles while their American counterparts meet primarily active (even violent) resistance for simply being themselves.

American cultural gender norms are strictly enforced. As those whose gender expression varies (to a greater or lesser degree) from what is expected know only too well, both the inner sense of difference and the cultural policing and enforcement of these unwritten "gender rules" begins when they are very young. Most participants (90 percent) in this study reported feeling very different from their peers in terms of their gender from a very early age—on average, by age five. This is but one small parallel to the appearance of cross-gendered tendencies in their non-Euro-American counterparts. There is, however, a vast difference in how this evidence is treated by their respective cultures.

In American society (and most of the Western world), biology is believed to be the sole legitimate determining factor in whether someone is a man or a woman, guided by the belief that there are only two actual options, based on the male and female sexes. When biology defies these notions, as in the birth of an intersexed child, the typical response is medical intervention, treating anomalies as abnormalities calling for surgical or hormonal "corrections" that have lasting devastating consequences for the individuals involved (Burke 1996; Chase 1998; Fausto-Sterling 1993).

Western cultures, built upon a foundation of duality, recognize only two real options. Postmodern theories aside, in a vernacular sense, the entrenched dualistic view becomes clear when we see how commonly sex, gender, and sexual orientation are confounded—even within the LGBT community! Those who do not fit expectations in one way are often confused with those who don't in another (and things become really complex for those who differ in multiple ways!). Although confusing sexual orientation with gender identity is not normally an issue within the LGBT community, in the mainstream it is still not uncommon to see gay men as not quite "real men" or to question the femaleness of lesbians. On the other hand, men exhibiting a degree of effeminacy and strong women are presumed to be gay, both by the mainstream and within the LGBT community ("Why doesn't she/he just come out now already?") regardless of whether they have any desire for someone of the same sex or not. And those whose gender identity is at odds, to a greater or lesser degree, with their birth sex—transgendered and transsexual people—are often also assumed to be gay, although this is often not the case. The reverse—the stereotype of gay men and lesbians "really" wanting to be the opposite sex—continues to hold in much of the mainstream as well.

Despite much recent work on transgender (Cromwell 1999; Feinberg 1996; Israel and Tarver 1997; Jacobs and Cromwell 1992) and a growing acceptance of gender diversity within the LGBT community, conclusions based on binary assumptions die hard, so that, for instance, the term "transgender," originally coined to describe those who found their most authentic sense of self in the space between "man" and "woman" and often used to designate the entire community of gender-difference, is still commonly viewed as a synonym for "transsexual" (i.e., crossing over, from one to the other). For those who live in the intersections between men and women, this is similar to the experiences of bisexuals, whose desires are questioned not only by the larger, more ignorant mainstream, but even within the lesbian and gay communities, where the disbelief in the possibility of multiple or intermediate desires continues to hold sway (Fox 1996; Klein 1978; Rust 1995).

Yet in many non-Western cultures, gender is conceptualized differently. Where dualism is not the norm, intermediate variants not only fit within cultural schemas, they often are celebrated. Of course biological males and females, with corresponding culturally constructed roles, are recognized everywhere. But in many non-Western cultures, *gender*, as opposed to sex, may be seen as a function of social, spiritual, or occupational roles, rather than biology (Kessler and McKenna 1978; Roscoe 1993, 1998).

Many of these non-Western cultures have socially established roles that allow for holding both "man" and "woman" as genders at the same time. In numerous African tribes, women may become men through the institution of "female husbands," an economically based kinship arrangement in which they are recognized as men, with all the attendant privileges that men enjoy. Although the fact of their femaleness is not openly acknowledged, it is not forgotten (Carrier and Murray 1998; O'Brien 1977; Oboler 1980). In some instances, they may simultaneously still be married to men, in which case they are seen as wives (women) with their husbands and as husbands (men) with their wives. Likewise, in the Balkan highlands of the former Yugoslavia and Albania, some women also step outside the strictures of a highly gender-polarized society by becoming "sworn virgins," where they dress, work, and live as men, although they are understood to be "not-men" as well (Gremaux 1993; Young 2000).

Many other cultures recognize a third entity as neither male nor female. Most of these correspond to culturally established roles that involve some form of mediation between the divine and the mundane (and often other sorts of mediations, such as between locals and outsiders), based on the belief that those who have the capacity to move between the worlds of men and women can also balance other opposites.

In northern India, the *hijra* (Nanda 1986, 1993) and, in southern India, the *jogappas* (Bradford 1983) are sacred "female men," biological males who wear women's clothing and are seen as mostly female, although clearly an intermediately gendered variant. In the case of the *hijras*, many undergo ritual castration. Both *hijras* and *jogappas* are "called" to their positions by mother goddess figures, in whose service they perform at weddings, births, and festivals, bestowing blessings upon the celebrants. As such they serve in a recognized and mostly respected cultural and religious capacity.

In Myanmar (formerly Burma), boys who show cross-sex inclinations at an early age are thought to be called by the Goddess Manguedon. As adults, they are known as *acault*, wearing feminine dress and taking on feminine behaviors. They act as shamans and seers, and their intermediate gender status is thought to bring with it considerable powers (Coleman, Colgan, and Gooren 1992).

In the South Pacific, variations on a third-gendered "half-man, half-woman" include the *mahu* of French Polynesia (Elliston 1999), Tahiti, and Hawaii, as well as the Samoan *fa'afafine*, Tongan *fakaleiti* and *fakafafine*, and Tuvaluuan *pinapinaaine*

(Besnier 1993), who typically are artists and carriers of cultural traditions and who often act as mediators between island societies and outsiders. In particular, the *mahu* have been linked with shamanistic powers.

Closer to home, in native North America alternative gendered "berdache"[2] roles have been documented in more than 150 different tribes (Roscoe 1998; Tafoya 1992) in which either males or females who usually evidenced cross-sex inclinations at an early age assumed cross-gendered occupations and wore either opposite-sex clothing or a modified third alternative. Known by a third (or in some cases, also a fourth [Roscoe 1998]) gendered term, they were understood to be intermediate beings between men and women, and appreciated as part of tribal life (Wilson 1996) and where "if a person is different from the average individual, this means the spirits must have taken particular care in creating this person" (Williams 1992: 32).

This study explored the lives of thirty contemporary North American people who identify as neither male nor female but "more like a third gender." The study involved completion of a brief, primarily demographically oriented survey and in-depth interviews with a qualitative analysis based on grounded theory. Participants ranged in age from twenty-nine to seventy-seven, and hailed from across the United States, with major concentrations in California and New England. Sixty percent of interviews were conducted in person, 40 percent via telephone. Responses using either method showed no qualitative or substantive differences.

The defining criteria for inclusion in the study were a sense of self that included either significant amounts of both male and female characteristics, or a sense of falling into some "gray area" in between, as well as some kind of recognition by others (whether positive or negative) of falling in between or outside of "acceptable" gender norms. Participants identified variously as butch lesbians, "queens," "androgynous," "two spirit" as well as many other terms to describe themselves (e.g., "boy dyke," "bi-gendered"). Most of the male-born respondents to the call were associated with the Radical Faeries. Roughly half of participants identified with the term "transgender," although some quite loosely so. Eight out of the thirty were exploring surgical and/or hormonal bodily alterations, although all were clear that their intent was not to replace one sex or gender with the other, but rather to foreground characteristics that better reflected their sense of themselves. Several others were adamantly opposed to bodily alterations, feeling that it rendered people like them even more invisible.

In terms of religious backgrounds, nearly all were raised in conventional, mainstream religions, yet none currently follow an exclusively traditional religious path now. Half (50 percent) were raised in Protestant denominations: four (13 percent) Episcopalian, two (7 percent) Methodist, three (10 percent) Baptist, two (7 percent) Presbyterian, and one Congregationalist. Thirteen (43 percent) were raised Catholic, five (17 percent) Jewish, two (7 percent) Buddhist, one without any spiritual tradition, and two in other faiths (Rosicrucian and Native American). Several mentioned that they were raised in more than one tradition.

All participants spoke of the importance of spirit in their lives. Nine stated that they were "spiritual but not religious" and followed a practice of their own, often connected to nature or an informal, personal sense of connection with something bigger than themselves. Many listed multiple, eclectic spiritual practices, such as one who combines Creation Spirituality with elements of Buddhism and Sufism, while another mixes Christian, Buddhist, Taoist, and New Age practices. Others wrote that their practices involved meditation, yoga, hospice work, music, and twelve-step programs.

Of the thirty, only two still maintain connection to the religions they were raised in. One, a Latina woman[3] with close ties to her family, maintains a loose connection to Catholicism. The other, raised in a combination of Catholicism, Rosicrucianism, Buddhism, and Judaism, maintains a deep Buddhist practice and feels that her martial arts practice (Baghwan karate and Tai Chi) is an integral part of her spiritual practice. She also continues be a member of a Reform Judaism congregation.

One participant described personal struggles with her spirituality. She was raised Jewish and Episcopalian and finds that she has a hard time separating out what is meaningful from her less than satisfying religious background. Another, who was raised without any religious tradition, has found inspiration through Tibetan Buddhism. A participant who was raised nominally Jewish but with an agnostic, highly political focus has developed a fusion of Judaism with Buddhist, Hindu, Sufi, and Native American practices that guides the work he does as a psychospiritual leader of others.

A Native American woman was raised Catholic but now practices Native religion. A Native American man who was raised partly in his tradition and partly Catholic practices his own form of spirituality that is informed by his past. Two (Caucasians) follow a shamanic path, while a third, who called his practice "pagan," has been instrumental in establishing a shamanic-type tradition together with Native American elders.

Two are currently Unitarian, and four listed "pagan" or "neo-pagan" under their spiritual practice. Six of the (born) male participants are or have been involved with the Radical Faeries. Two participants belong to an existentialist congregation.

Guided by the literature on other cultures, a number of the interview questions explored whether traits and abilities ascribed to non-Western third gender people and seen as part of their cultural roles might be present in this sample as well. In fact, results showed a much greater than expected incidence of parallel interests and attributes.

Nearly half were healers: thirteen work in the health and helping professions. Most were highly creative and artistic. Seven were writers, four musicians, three performing artists (one drag queen, another an actor, the third a performance poet). Of these, five earned all or a substantial portion of their incomes from their art. Three others were employed in other creative fields, including a landscape architect, a fashion designer, and a graphic artist. Nearly all felt that some form of artistic expression was important in their lives.

Most found that they naturally served in mediating functions. Twenty-three of the thirty reported being called upon to mediate between men and women, being seen by both as carrying a wider perspective that could encompass both sides. Many also mediated between other groups, such as between racial groups, different age groups, different cultures or subcultures, and found that they were called upon to navigate the contested area of the "border wars" between lesbian, gay, bisexual, and transgender (LGBT) subgroups such as between butch dykes and transmen or gay and transgendered groups.

Most significantly, twenty-eight out of the thirty, or 93 percent, reported having experienced transcendent spiritual events and/or having unusual "paranormal"-type abilities, both of which have been associated with non-Western spiritual third gender roles. This compares with general population surveys in the United States and Europe that show 40 percent to 50 percent reporting "spiritual experiences of *any* intensity" (Haraldson and Houtkooper 1991; Palmer 1979; Thomas and Cooper 1980). It is particularly notable that in the Thomas and Cooper (1980) study, which involved a more detailed investigation than the survey tabulations of the other studies, only 9 percent of the respondents experienced the sorts of profound or repeated "psychic" or "mystical" experiences reported by 57 percent of the sample in this study, with another 16 percent in the Thomas and Cooper study reporting "moving incidents of faith," which compares with the remaining 36 percent of this sample who reported milder or single transcendent experiences.

Note that while such experiences are expected and cultivated in non-Western cultures with established third-gendered roles, they arise here spontaneously, with no apparent connection to gender difference. However, they are no less powerful. One participant spoke about her early propensity for transcendent experiences. With no means of integrating them into her life, she turned to drugs and alcohol to numb herself to them. Now sober, she finds that she continues to have these experiences, and has embarked on a career in ministry as a result. She describes one experience:

> It was the first Jewish service that I had ever been to, and I had a transcendental experience. I mean, I could speak Hebrew, I sung Hebrew songs, the woman next to me didn't believe me that I had never sung Hebrew before. I sung one we didn't

have the words to. I felt like I met God in that group. . . . I had never had that in a group experience before. . . . [That is a] dramatic one, but it happens a lot.

Another, with monastic experience notes that he experienced signs of spontaneous spiritual connection in his youth:

> I've had that sort of thing, but I can't describe it. St. Theresa goes into that in some detail, but there are some things you just cannot describe. The best language is the language we also use for sex. . . . I know that in my teens I had some experiences like that, but I attribute them partly to glandular changes that go on in your early teens. . . . And I tend to discount them because that's a fleeting time of change. . . . But when . . . you're in a monastery, which is a quiet setting, and something happens, then I think you get closer to something you take seriously.

A Native American participant said:

> I know that I see things beyond what's apparent. . . . I know that . . . I can see into the future and things have come true. I have connections with ancestors. . . . I've definitely been told that I've got some kind of gift or something.

While another, who is white and grew up in conventional suburbia noted:

> I always had totem animals. I didn't know what they were when I was a kid, but I had what were to me, what I thought of as, imaginary friends who were animals, who guided me a lot. . . . I felt very much a secret life that at my core I was someone that I couldn't talk to other people about.

Whereas paranormal types of abilities are seen as part and parcel of shamanic roles elsewhere, here they are at best seen as parlor game fun. Yet one participant noted hir uncanny abilities in this regard as a child:

> They had the five-card game, with five black images, and the sender sends one and the receiver gets one, and it was like, ok, if you get this right five times out of twenty, it's just chance. And if it's more, the more you get, it's progressively stronger ESP. . . . And I got twenty right in a row.

Although not groomed for these abilities, three participants noted familial lineages where other relatives shared their abilities:

> Yes, I have seen things. And . . . looking back over my mother's life and my grandmother's life, I think that they were gifted also. . . . I have told women when they were going to go into labor, I have walked into situations unknowingly and sort of knew . . . how things were going to fall out, without a lot of information.

For some, transcendent experiences were deeply spiritual, life-changing moments:

> The first thing I could say was really a clear spiritual experience happened when I was eighteen or nineteen. I wasn't doing anything to get it. I happened to be standing outside . . . and this energy came into me, for about three seconds . . . and utterly, in that time, transforming, because in that time I knew everything. If you had come up to me at that moment and said, "Joshua, how many grains of sand are there on the planet?" I could have told you. And then it was gone, absolutely gone. But that experience really moved me. Because coming from a very political family, I was involved in SDS and it was . . . student riots and antiwar movement, it was the 1960s and all that. It's like I made this incredibly sharp left turn on my journey. . . . I mean, I watched my parents and grandparents and great-grandparents be various kinds of revolutionaries and . . . it was like, uh-uh, I'm going *this* way.

Part of a shamanic "calling" and initiation often involves suffering life-threatening illness and healing oneself. Four of the study participants had suffered life-threatening events, including two who suffered viral meningitis-type infections at age four and two who had experienced clinical death and revival, one as a result of illness, the other as a result of being shot. Nine suffered from chronic conditions, including asthma and allergies, chronic fatigue syndrome (two participants), hearing difficulties, eye problems (for which this participant underwent multiple surgeries as a child), lupus, HIV, a blood clotting disorder, and diverticulitis.

In addition, one third of the sample had suffered from drug or alcohol addictions, although in and of itself this is similar to earlier studies placing addiction rates at around 25 percent for gay men and 35 percent among lesbians (Nardi 1982). (All but one reported being in recovery at the time of this study.) A third had also suffered from significant clinical depression (half of whom overlapped with the group suffering from addictions). Yet when the incidence of addictions and depression are included among illnesses suffered by this group, twenty-five of twenty-eight participants who responded to questions about illness reported experiencing significant forms of illness, in a group with a median age of thirty-nine!

For some, the encounter with life-threatening events touched off some soul-searching:

> I almost drowned. . . . That was around twenty. And I realized I hadn't done anything. And I was in touch for a while, there, realizing what was important was how much we helped others, love others.

One participant who lives with chronic fatigue syndrome (CFIDS) describes how facing death provided a doorway into a deeper, more spiritual outlook on hir life:

I feel that the summer that I got really sick was the summer I died. . . . I felt
like I died in a way, and I sort of had to pull myself up from that to come back
into the world. And I confronted my death so much because I was so, so sick,
and I really felt like I was dying. And I didn't know, and I was afraid. I was really, really scared; it was horrible. But in a way it helped—it made me not fear
death. . . . Getting sick was a very spiritual thing for me. I think, I really felt
like I had a certain responsibility in it and that my body was demanding that I
get more in touch spiritually.

These findings suggest that there may be elements of third-gender identity that
are transcultural and inherent to gender intermediacy. In addition, they suggest
that there may be an element of "calling" to falling between the cracks of
gender—and perhaps, in a wider sense, in our being men, women (regardless
of the bodies we are born with), both, or something in between. At a minimum,
the lives of the participants of this study show that to live a life of authenticity,
to be true to one's own inner inclinations regardless of social disapproval and punishment, brings with it significant gifts that have potential to contribute a great
deal to the greater society, if only they were to be acknowledged and appreciated
as they are elsewhere.

Notes

1. Refer to Bradford 1983; Coleman, Colgan, and Gooren 1992; Eliade 1964; Herdt
1994; Jacobs and Cromwell 1992; Kessler and McKenna 1978; Murray and Roscoe 1998;
Nanda 1986, 1993; Piedmont 1996; Roscoe 1988, 1991, 1993, 1998; Tafoya 1992;
Williams 1992; and Wilson 1996).

2. The term "berdache" has been criticized in recent years (Jacobs, Thomas and Lang,
1997; Roscoe, 1998; Tafoya, 1992), as it derives from a Persian term meaning "slave-boy"
and was applied by the European colonists, who approached the phenomenon of alternatively gendered Native Americans with alarm and disgust (Williams 1992). However,
"two-spirit," which is used currently by Native American LGBT people to describe themselves, is a contemporary term with twentieth- and twenty-first-century meanings.
"Berdache" is used here as it is in most anthropological writing, as an umbrella term to encompass the hundreds of different tribal manifestations of third- and fourth-gendered
roles (each of which have their own discrete tribal names).

3. Gendered terms including "man," "woman," "his," and "hers" are used here following the preferences of individual study participants. In cases where participants felt that
both or a hybrid were more appropriate, terms such as "s/he" and "hir" are used.

Rite to Party
Circuit Parties and Religious Experience

18

PAUL J. GORRELL

WHERE'S THE PARTY? Madonna's 1986 song is a perfect reference point to begin writing on the topic of gay subculture and religion: Madonna is an unreal character made real by pop culture, self-promotion, and disco dancing. She often steals religious symbols and personas to define and redefine herself. She has also become a symbol to gay men of the defiant queen. A very different diva for us than the campy and fabulous Judy Garland was to pre-Stonewall gays, Madonna connotes transgression and continual self-creation. And, she loves and celebrates pleasure.

Just after the release of *Evita*, her long-version music video, called a film, based on a musical about the life of Eva Peron, wife of Argentina's dictator, I stood on a dance floor filled with hundreds of shirtless gay men dancing to the disco version of "Don't Cry for Me Argentina." They moved to the music together as if the whole dance was badly choreographed, but rehearsed nonetheless. And the troop was performing well. Why? Because the power of this performance rested on their own beauty. The beauty of the men was, in fact, arresting. It sought to take prisoners. But, I sensed that it did not intend to capture hearts. No, the beauty was more about an erotic charge than a search for endless love. Romance was not in the air. Eroticism was. This eroticism was a subcultural defiance to erotophobia calling upon ancient rituals that celebrated communal oneness.

Welcome to a circuit party. In gay urban centers, when someone asks, "Where's the party?" they want to know where the circuit pilgrims are about to stop, strip, and adore. The circuit is a contemporary subculture in which gay men strive to be transformed by ritual experience. Their rites are intimately wrapped around the erotic, pleasure, and a certain degree of narcissism.

The circuit is made up of party events that occur in cities around the country and internationally. Mostly made up of urban gay men, the circuit crowd travels from city to city to join the weekend parties. Whether it's the Black and Blue Party in Montreal, Miami's famous White Party, or the Cherry Party in Washington, D.C., these events include famous club DJs like Junior Vasquez, Victor Calderone, and Susan Morabito and corporate sponsorships from liquor companies like Tanqueray and Seagram's and hotel chains like Ramada or Embassy Suites. They are often run by professional party companies like Jeffrey Sanker Productions at elaborate settings like MGM Studios in Orlando and are promoted by the likes of *Out* and *Genre*, two leading gay magazines. Charities often benefit from donations related to the events or the parties are directly linked to nonprofits who host them as major fund-raising opportunities. The circuit revelers remain in circuit mode from Friday night to Sunday night, often taking over public buildings for the "main event" or key party of their weekend. Many of these men engage in drugs to both enter into the party and have the staying power for partying all night long. These circuit boys or queens have their own rituals, language, and ideals that are directly related to these events. For instance, recalling tribal expressions of mourning and loss, some individuals participate in fan dancing at the events. Creating their own flags, large semicircular strips of fabric made to perform acrobatic feats powered by gym-defined shoulder muscles, these men fan dance in order to release the spirits of those who have died into the life of the party. Fan dancing was a popular expression of dance in gay clubs in the 1980s. Circuit parties have revived interest in fan dancing and help connect it to the struggle with AIDS. Individuals with this interest have formed clubs like Lloyd Pease's in Akron, Ohio, the place where circuit parties were born.

The circuit is site of popular gay religious expression and, as such, gay religious thinkers should analyze this kind of subcultural movement. Certainly, some have raised ethical issues associated with these events. Do they promote unsafe sex while raising money for AIDS organizations? Do they foster a worship of masculinity and beauty that is exclusive and damaging to the gay and lesbian movement? Do they promote drug use and other health problems related to addiction and disease? Are they unfairly representing gay male culture while the majority of gay men never participate in them?

While these issues are very important for further reflection, I would like to move away from ethical considerations and, instead, discern whether this is a religious phenomenon in our midst. When we consider the spiritual and religious dimension, we are moved to a different set of questions than the ones listed previously. First, and most difficult to answer, is this a religious movement? Related to this we need to ask if this is a form of spirituality? Moreover, what does this movement say to gay men who study religion? While these questions may not represent and deal with the life and death questions listed above, they may get to the heart of the core issues relative to the enterprise of gay religious scholars.

Circuit events communicate and provide insight into the religious sensibilities of gay men. Because of this, they require attention when theologians do gay theology or sociologists or others document gay religious movements and beliefs. I would argue that circuit parties are a more transgressive approach to worship, human desire for the divine, and religious ritual, than the current "gay take" on theology and the admirable search for a place at the table that many gays and lesbians are fighting for in traditional religious communities. Clearly, the circuit experience is not about reforming society in order to assimilate like the groups described in the denominational heritage section of this volume. Moreover, it is even more transgressive than the so-called subaltern groups in the previous section. Queers acting up like Jesus to set up "our own" safe communities that speak against oppression while still standing around the Book and rituals that the oppressors use may not go far enough. Pushing the envelope, participation in a circuit event, an all-night, drug-infused, multimedia experience, gives gay men the opportunity to make the erotic and the desire for male beauty the god that demands worship.

The dance floor at a typical circuit event includes thousands of shirtless gay men who gather to demonstrate beauty and witness beauty at the very same time. In fact, the Black and Blue Party has been known to include as many as twenty thousand participants who come from all over the world to join together. When you walk in the midst of a circuit party dance floor, you are prone to bump up against bare muscular chests and backs as dramatic lights flash around you and music driven by rhythm more than words or key changes carries you to a trance-like space. You might feel compelled to experience the heat and energy of the bodies. This very heat can bring you to remove your own clothing, to want to be one with what is happening around you, and to gaze at the beauty of the male body as it appears before you over and over and over again. Greg, a forty-year-old Chicagoan who for the past ten years has traveled the circuit, discusses his first event this way: "I remember a rush came over me. I was in the middle of incredibly attractive guys who were friendly, half-naked, dancing, and producing an amount of energy that I had never experienced before. I felt gay and alive. There was a sense of abandon, a sense that people lose their inhibitions."

Philadelphia's 1997 Blue Ball event was held in an atrium of a large gothic-like office building in downtown. Fountains that sent streams and jets of water down marble stairs surrounded one end of the large room. A pool at the bottom of the steps collected the water and provided a separation from the main part of the room that was typically well-traveled by business people during the day. The top step above the water fountain provided the Blue Ball with a stage where carefully selected dancers were permitted to stand before the crowd to demonstrate their beauty and dance. The streams of water appeared to flow from their feet and, along with the steps that lifted them above the crowd, created a distance between them and the dance floor. Their beauty was performative and worthy of the participants' gaze. Other events have even more elaborate scenes: The first Cherry Party, in Washington, D.C., in 1996, had an elaborate mock up of the Emerald City from the Wizard of Oz that provided the stage for live performances from pop singers. The main event party of Gay Disney often winds up outside with a huge fireworks display over the crowd of dancers.

While it is hard to develop an argument that circuit parties advance political quests, we need to remember how our pleasure is at stake when our lives are at stake. Politically, circuit queens reignite the homosexual desire that the writer Guy Hocquenghem sees as revolutionary in the fight against sexual repression in society[1] (1982: 137). Sexuality, even in the face of disease and death, is not left for the private but is celebrated and revolutionized within public settings and rituals. Worshiping homosex, the sex that gay men share, and responding to the beauty of other males is what a circuit party has as its core function.[2] Greg's most profound memory of beautiful men at a party included a collusion with another avenue toward erotic fantasy: At the White Party in Palm Springs in 1999, he stared across the crowd to see many famous gay porno stars in attendance. Like other rituals, the worship of male beauty conceivably leads to a sacrifice of the individual self so that the ritual can create intimate communion. While participation in a circuit event mirrors the ritual search of religion, it's not your father or mother's religion. But, then again, tribal music and drug-induced ritual are not without precedent. One can argue that circuit parties are closer to the rituals of the Radical Faeries than the Metropolitan Community Church will ever be or want to be.

Circuit parties are a contemporary aspect of queer culture, which owns rituals and beliefs that mirror and, possibly, replace religious rituals and beliefs in the lives of its participants. These rites of pleasure are constructed around notions of gay sex, male beauty, the power of eroticism, muscle, transformation through paradoxical experience, and the desire for an oasis of freedom and authenticity in an oppressive world. At the same time, this culture can present images, practices, and ideals, which potentially challenge the real progress we seek for the gay and lesbian political movement.

For the record, I am not a circuit queen and have little interest in being an apologist for it. My own story leads me to integrate religion and circuit parties: I went from the priesthood of the Roman Catholic Church to a role as an employee of one of the parties on the circuit. My major exposure to these events was as a paid coordinator of a party held annually in Philadelphia to raise tens of thousands of dollars for an AIDS charity.

Fresh out of the priesthood, I was able to get very close to this culture without being a part of it. I worked side by side with the planners of the event and communicated with members of the culture on a national basis for about six months. At the party, I was a worker who received a certain amount of welcome without being a baptized member of the congregation. In anthropology, they call this ironic distance. I was part of the experience without having to lose my perspective as an outsider.

You can imagine what I was experiencing personally and psychologically and why I may easily align the event with religious experience. I am not the only one who struggles with this notion. There is an ongoing academic debate regarding how we should discuss religious imagination and experience outside of their traditional structure or ideas of the sacred. Some devote their academic study to examining religion as it appears outside of religion. Sometimes, these scholars debate the reality and dimensions of religious experience in and through rock music, movies, and cultural events. I do not suspect that I can add much insight into this position and do not choose to spend time here developing the arguments. While my academic field is religious ethics, I have been exploring the notion that we often find sources outside of religion to provide us with ethical wisdom and knowledge. In fact, the more we are marginalized by the churches, I argue, the more we utilize these sources. Quite possibly, if this idea is accurate, we also seek out experiences that have as their goal and purpose similar intentional changes in moods and motivations found in church ritual. We find rituals that provide a certain degree of transcendence, contact with the other, and profound experiences of community.

Is the circuit party a religious ritual? To answer this question, I rely on my Roman Catholic past. Liturgist Joseph Martos defines ritual as an "expression of values and attitudes in the form of symbolic action (1966: 26)."[3] He claims that society acts out meanings through ritual expression. Each time the individual participates in the rite, he or she is reintroduced to that sacred meaning as it is communicated. Clifford Geertz understands ritual as "the main context in which religious symbols work to create and sustain belief" (1968: 100).[4] Individuals, he claims, participate for psychological, sociological, and cultural reasons. The latter involves the search for meaning in light of the complexities of lived experience.

Meanwhile, like many religious experiences, a paradox looms over the entire rite. Circuit queens celebrate muscle at a moment in history when gay men have had to reflect on the meaning of death and the drama of being unhealthy, uncertain, and, at some moments, hopeless. This hopelessness has shifted in the gay community since the arrival of new drug therapies that have to an extent effectively battled AIDS. As death appears to have less of a grip on the gay community, circuit parties have become an even stronger magnet. Andrew Sullivan's famous semiautobiographical *New York Times* piece on life after AIDS included the telling of his experience of The Black Party in New York City. Possibly, these parties are no longer a way to escape reality but are a way to celebrate a changing reality?

We can also gain invaluable perspective from the work of Victor Turner.[5] Turner focuses on the idea of liminality as key to religious ritual. He means that there is a transitional aspect of ritual in which the participant is moved over the edge of their boundaries to enter into the boundaries of another or the other. The ritual is a threshold to a new space. He talks about three aspects of this transformation. First, there is the experience of separation. He argues that our societal roles are stripped away as we enter into the ritual. Liturgist Michael Cowen further elaborates on this when he claims that we enter into a separate enclave of meaning that requires us to either leave everyday life outside the door or set it against the ultimate meaning found in ritual (Cowen 1987: 42).[6] Second, the participant experiences marginality. The person dies to himself or herself in order to embrace the process of becoming an ambiguous person in this transitional experience. This is the moment of passage where the participant discovers a new self, which is defined by connection with others. Third, the individual becomes reincorporated into the social structures but only does so changed by the experience. Turner argues that ritual provides individuals with an experience of communitas, which is the colluding of structure and anti-structure. This play involves the discovery of new possibilities. This occurs for the participant as his or her world is overturned. Ritual is anti-structural in that it dismantles the structures of our world and initiates the participant into a threshold of new discovery. The person enters into the ritual separation via a call and, in turn, sacralizes its elements. As liturgist Regis Duffy notes, rites of passage that lead to communitas are meant to "revitalize the group's purpose and vision and invite its renewed commitments."[7] However, much of the effect on our lives can be subtle and even subconscious.

At the party event, the person transitions from the place they are in into an elaborately decorated and theatrically lighted space of fantasy where emotions are further transformed by the power of state-of-the art sound systems managed by world-class DJs. Circuit participants feel called to enter into this pilgrimage together. Many speak of their first party in a similar way to gay men who discuss their first time entering a gay bar. They feel free to be who they are and love the idea of being erotically charged through the experience. While this event is most accessible for men with money, participants tend to divorce themselves from their "nine to five" careers. Most with whom I worked never discussed what they did for a living or any progress relative to career. They pulled out of their world to experience euphoria and ecstasy. However, it is not simply career that they leave at the door.

As they strip off shirts and gather closer to others, physically touching strangers and friends, the margins of their world are dramatically adjusted. Circuit queens have done what many marginalized people do with their religious rituals. They gather together to experience a different world. Often, oppressed groups do this by focusing on the saving God who can provide an exodus out of their bondage. Here, these men leave the world that hates gays by focusing on the very thing they are hated for: their sexuality. Ritualizing the love of men is a way to find a kind of oasis in a straight world where there is no need to translate language and "explain ourselves." Greg described his experience as follows: "This is a gay world, a big gay world. The world inside the party feels like one world. I am not normally outgoing, but here I meet strangers and spend a good part of the evening connecting with others. I feel connected to something different in my own life."

Can we speak of a circuit party as a liminal experience? Participants do tend to separate from their world in such a way as to redefine themselves. This definition is thoroughly wrapped up in the event itself. From here, through the excitement of the experience, individuality is somehow lost. Alan Brown, who is called the shaman of the circuit parties by Michelangelo Signorile, told me about the experience that makes a circuit party a success. He says that it is a euphoric instance of unity among the revelers. This ecstatic moment is a selective reality; it does not happen at each and every event. Which of us in religion haven't experienced the selectivity of this spirit in ritual? When I was a priest or participant in Catholic ritual, I had moments when I questioned in my mind if some liturgies were a moment of "real presence," while other times I had a keen sense of marginality and boundary redefinition through shared ritual prayer. Often this was a shared experience with other members of the assembly. Circuit reveler Greg said that parties are not successful when participants lack friendliness because it interferes with forming community.

What is the euphoric moment that Brown describes like at a circuit party? He claims that it is a moment of thrill and awe when the music and dance drive the participants to an apex that is intense and inescapable. The entire room mysteriously becomes one organism at this moment. Communal oneness is the climax of a successful circuit event. Participants can refer to the unifying moment days later. All of them know exactly what precise experience is being talked about when someone refers to it. Brown says that the communitas moment is always connected to the music, typically driven by a familiar or classic record that takes the room to another place. "It's like corks pop around the room," he said. Many rituals within traditional religion are brought to an apex through music and have a long tradition of using music as a central path toward religious experience. While Brown is not inclined to develop the understanding of circuit parties as a form of religion, he does allude to this. For instance, in *Genre*, he has defined the parties as tribal rites that are instinctual: "People have been gathering around fires, dancing and beating drums for years. We've just refined the art" (DeCaro 1998).

This subculture involves a network of people who become a band of brothers that gathers together in a homoerotic manner. They travel throughout the country on pilgrimage to be together and hope that their ritual encounter will make corks pop around the room. They mark the times of the year creating a hierarchy of dates whereby some holy days take on more importance than others. They correspond between parties. They share intimacy when together. Greg's best memories related to parties are about reconnecting with old friends and enjoying the people who gather together. And, if you will, on holy days of lesser importance, large gay nightclubs such as the former Twilo in New York City and Blu in Atlanta provide regular opportunities for this experience closer to home, especially when a big name DJ comes to town.

Most circuit party relationships stay at the party: these men seldom visit each other's homes or see the other's day-to-day life. This is about the party and the experience of becoming deeply and profoundly lost inside a community at an extreme, almost unreal, moment of pleasure and self-gratification. This is the very community that often feels lost and forced to negotiate their personhood within a homophobic world. In their daily lives, the community members find their form of sexual pleasure attacked, chastised, and worthy of murder. Because of this, they may experience a self-image that is fragile or a profound sense of difference. Circuit queens, like members of the gay ghetto, seem to desire a space where they are allowed to desire what they desire: the company of men. Interestingly, while their relationships are about the party, they do not tend to go to these events alone. Circuit boys gather at private settings or hotel rooms and travel to the party as smaller groups hoping to connect with the awaiting community.

Kathy Rudy has argued that community and unitivity are the goal of men who choose multiple partners instead of monogamous relationships.[8] Using Catholic moral theology, she notes how a sexual encounter involves a giving of the self to the other. When this is shared with multiple partners, she argues, it is about entering into the organism of the community, the Body of Christ if you would. More sexual encounters further entrench an individual in the community that they desire to join. She claims it goes beyond sex; it is about belonging to the community in a relational way. This is a new notion of family and oneness. In this reasoning, homosex becomes procreative and the driving force toward intimate communion.

The erotic dimension of the circuit party takes this experience of sexual community to the next level. The party celebrates sexual communion through ritual praxis, it honors and sacralizes the male body as the way to this unitivity, and it creates an environment of eroticism that forms community for its members while not depending upon sexual acts to get there. Greg describes the men at a circuit party as consistently head-turning because of their beauty and muscle; this inspiration is a key reason why he keeps going back for more and aligns the event with what it means to be gay. If we agree with Rudy's definition of homosex's goal, we can say that a circuit party is the queer liturgical rite that tries to do what homosex does. It's erotic power and symbols of male beauty draw men together in a ritual form the way that Rudy claims the multipartnered practice of gay men creates communitas, or communal relationality.

If the circuit party is a kind of liturgical rite, we need to be attentive to its symbols and the liturgical space to understand the sacred meaning communicated and celebrated. In *God's Gym*,[9] Stephen Moore writes about Venice Beach's Gold's Gym, the first and most famous Gold's gym, as a postmodern Herodian temple. His detailed explanation of the different rooms of the gym show how each relate to disciplined and ritualized avenues toward the worship of the muscular God.

When I worked with the Philadelphia circuit party known as the Blue Ball in 1997, I was struck by a similar notion. The space utilized was the atrium of a large office building. The shape and structure of the building and the queer use of its narthex reimagined the form of the temple. The separation of groups, which we might criticize for its hierarchical structure, mirrors the stratification of the Herodian Temple. The temple's Court of Women, the outer space that made room for women while still preventing them from access to the holy, was found at the Blue Ball in its volunteer lounge. Volunteers who took their breaks together went off to a separate place, which was not linked to the dance floor or key to the life of the party. The volunteers managed the event in a conscientious and charitable way. While they may have enjoyed the music and experience, they never entered into the event like the circuit queens.

Sadly, at a circuit party, a hierarchy does exist across gender lines. You did not find any circuit queens, stars of the event, at the volunteer lounge. In a similar way to the Roman Catholic Church, women were able to work at the event without having the honor and privilege of presiding or serving at the altar. Why did the circuit boys have lesbians there? Because, the group of gay men who ran the coat check a year earlier were disorganized and bad workers. So, the priests brought in the sisters. After all, they are more organized than the queens and this allows the sacred priests to perform the sacrament more effectively. When asked why some parties fail, Greg shared that poor logistics and organization are often the things that hamper a party from being euphoric. Thus, while the volunteers are not at the core of the event, they prove invaluable to the path toward communitas in the event.

The Herodian Temple's Court of Israel included men who were not priests and were involved only at significant spatial distance from the holy of holies. At the Blue Ball, this area was found on the outskirts of the dance floor. Here, gay men who are not part of the circuit pilgrimage aim to be part of an event while it is being held in their local city. These individuals have a hard time breaking into the core of the party at the center of the dance floor. Many of them experience participation through voyeurism. They are part of the party but not key members for creating the ritual.

Circuit boys make up the court of priests. Shirts off, muscled bodies fill the center of the dance floor. The elite participants move through this sea of flesh continually rubbing against one another. In my experience of these parties, this is where many of the drugs are used. In small circles, men turn toward each other to take ecstasy, GHB, and coke. This seems to add to the charge of eroticism in the air. Ecstasy makes men more outwardly physical and intimate with each other. I remember leaving the Blue Ball and having a beautiful man that I had known in a surface way grab me, hold me tenderly, and kiss me sensuously on the lips. This caught me by surprise. As I walked away, a bit flush, I noticed many men expressing the eroticism of their drugged up, seminude state. Does this lead to sex and unsafe sex? One of the jokes about circuit parties is that they involve thousands of the most beautiful men in the world who cannot sustain an erection. Of course, my involvement with this phenomenon was pre-Viagra. At the time I was involved, the beauty and eroticism found in the court of priests provided a communal experience of pleasure that was not simply about the thrill of orgasm. It was sexuality celebrated and adored in itself, a sexuality that was beyond and larger than the act of sex. While we may talk of sexual performance and sexuality as an integral aspect of our lives, that is always at play, we may tend to limit this power as a covert part of our relating to each other. The circuit party is an overt expression of what makes us tick sexually. While it does not necessarily lead to sex, the court of priests worships all that leads to homosex and all that is homosex.

Where is the holy of holies at a circuit party? While I struggled to identify this place, and it should be a somewhat elusive place for the unconverted to find, Alan Brown did not take a second to respond to my question about where it was at a circuit party when I asked him. "It's the DJ booth!" he exclaimed. In Moore's analysis of the gym, the most sacred spot is a private flexing room for bodybuilders who make up a holy elite. In our analysis, the DJ booth is even more like the Herodian holy of holies, which was restricted to only one high priest whose prayer and intercession were to make a difference in the lives of the others. The DJ enters the chamber of his or her booth alone to encounter the power, which captivates the participants.[10] Moreover, this is done to bring the rest to the boundaries of their very selves. While the booth is often very separate from the party— at the Blue Ball it was three floors higher than the dance floor available only through an elevator that required a special key—the booth is decorated with flowers and fabrics that mirror the theme of the circuit event.

The DJ is the high priest who stands alone to meet, invoke, and instruct the divine presence about showering the erotic power upon the court of priests and the others who come to dance. DJs are celebrities in this subculture. Known by all in the court of priesthood, they are the charismatic leaders of this religion who require believers to shift their lives in order to be participatory members. Their fame has not stayed limited to the circuit scene; many are highly sought out by current pop music stars who choose them to remix their records as crossover dance hits. Many times, the DJ's name appears in the title of the remix, one of the fastest growing trends in pop music today.

To quote another Madonna-as-Evita song: "Where do we go from here?" When I interviewed Brown, I noticed a sadness about these events that was strangely balanced with comments about how fabulous they are. Brown cannot help but struggle with the ethical problem of drug use, exclusiveness, and the negative role modeling that circuit queens provide to younger gay men. Greg was also continually apologetic about drug use when describing his experience of circuit events. Despite these kinds of reservations, Brown still wants these celebrations to play a key role in the lives of the community and in his own life. In essence, he may want the subculture to weed out its extremism or, you might say, its fundamentalist wing. Signorile, who enjoys calling the parties a cult, might suggest that Brown is on the verge of being deprogrammed onto a more righteous and secular path. I prefer to find in Brown a healthy struggle to embrace the good while struggling with the bad. He even started a nonprofit group, which monitors party drug use, provides medical assistance on-site for partygoers, and documents the history of the movement.

In his commentaries on contemporary gay life, Signorile, the man who started the early nineties agenda of outing celebrities and politicians, provides sharp criticism of the circuit phenomena likening it to cults. He believes that participants become addicted to escape, euphoria, and masculinity through narcissistic and self-destructive means. He links this to an obsession with masculinity. In his popular book *Life Outside*, Signorile devotes a chapter on this topic entitled, "The Evangelical Church of the Circuit." In recognizing the cult-like devotion of circuit followers, Signorile is able to explain a "church theology" linked to these phenomena. He writes that this unfairly represents the majority of gay men who would never attend, creates "Stepford homos" and an unhealthy separation from society, and glorifies sex, drugs, muscles, and youth. While Signorile's spends time challenging the circuit's ethical issues, he at the same time recognizes and calls it a religious movement.

Before I respond to Signorile, it helps to return to my experience of circuit parties. A year after my work at the Blue Ball, I had a new business job far away from this gay subculture. But, when the next Blue Ball was to be held a year later,

I returned to the main event of the weekend as a volunteer. There I was back in the midst of the temple once again. In looking out across the dance floor, while I did see many beautiful men, I did not feel very connected to anyone and was not personally moved by the event. However, I do not want to demean this community because I failed to get it. Personally, I was troubled by the drug use and the exclusiveness related to age, race, gender, and beauty. That year, the mainstream news media had been heavily reporting drug overdoses that were happening at many circuit events that year. This was on my mind and filled me with some concern and wonder about why anyone would want to devote themselves to this way of being.

The year before, when I worked with the lead committee who volunteered to manage the planning stages of the event, I became more connected to the committee. They were highly passionate about creating a very special and successful event. They worked long hours; networked to obtain volunteers, promotional opportunities and sponsors; and responded to the drug problem of that year with a very carefully written and enforced drug policy. From the outside, I did see a real sense of belonging that grew as the party met dawn. The night of the main event, I could see them huddled together, arm in arm, staring in each other's eyes, sharing a special kind of euphoric intimacy. Occasionally, out of respect for my accomplishments as the paid coordinator, they would bring me into their inner circle and I would, for a moment, feel the connection that was part of their religious rite.

Four hours after we would shut the doors of the main event of this weekend, these men would gather again for a "brunch" party and start all over. And, when the brunch ended, they were off to private parties held at homes and hotel rooms throughout Philadelphia. They did not want the party or the intimacy to end. The intimacy they longed for was powerfully found in the moment. While I could sense it at times and feel connected to it, the intensity of the ritual eluded me and I could not join them. Then, I felt as if I was losing my religion all over again not engaging in the acts, not embracing the symbols that could bring me to a sacramental oneness with others. This was not my party, and its holy of holies did not call to me. Yes, there was a "real presence" in the air that these men were creating. While I was not initiated into their world, I left with some level of understanding, maybe even appreciation. For, because of my experience of Catholicism and priesthood, I know the power of ritual and community. There was even a time I would stop everything in order to experience it. Maybe this reminded me too much of the religion that I had walked away from. Or, at least, it was too soon. Actually, my first logistical meeting with the Blue Ball committee was the evening of the same day I told my bishop that I was leaving the priesthood.

One mistake we can make when analyzing the ritual of a group of believers is to assign an all-inclusive meaning to the event. This is what Signorile does when he develops his view that this is a cult of masculinity.[11] Signorile's analysis of the circuit party as a religion stays with this singular notion covering its meaning in a surface manner. He fails to interpret the meaning of the subculture because he only speaks of one meaning. Rituals and their symbolic content are multivalent by their nature. At the very same time, they mean different things to different people. To discuss an assigned meaning for other people's rituals without wrestling with the complexity of these rituals is to take the first step toward moralism—a moralism that wears the mask of prophetic ethics. Eric Rofes challenged Signorile on this very issue claiming that he utilizes sound-bite solutions when discussing complex social problems.[12] Rofes attempts to take social commentary on contemporary gay culture back from the many popular thinkers who are condemning its elements.

When I reflected on my experience with the circuit world, Madonna was in the process of discovering the power of Jewish mysticism, which she incorporated into her music and image. She released her 1998 album *Ray of Light* on religious themes with a heavily electronic sound that was meant to stimulate tribal dance through its drumbeat. If Madonna can become, at least for an instant, a popular voice in religion, we probably should ask questions about the state of religion and religious expression today among gay men. If circuit parties have become a popular expression of the religious for many gay men, should we not ask questions about the state of religion and religious expression for gay men today?

It is time for gay theologians to delve more deeply into these kinds of movements within the gay community in order to be in touch with the religious beliefs and expressions that are in our midst. For, when we look to traditional church symbols, rites, and books to identify the religious sensibilities of the gay community, we miss how the sacrament of male beauty is a core belief of gay men that not only inspires them to devotion but also, like any sacrament, instructs them about how to live their lives. When we ignore these kinds of religious experiences, we miss that which calls gay men to gather to experience communitas: eroticism and male beauty. Since the erotic is often what gay men identify as sacred, it has earned a place within our religious, ethical, and theological discussions. These events found outside of religion can help gay theologians to answer the problem of erotophobia within religions, something they often identify as problematic and deeply damaging for gay men. When we study gay theology, we need to be in the sacred spaces that gay men create and understand what it is they worship, how they reach communitas through ritual, and what beliefs their religious experiences communicate.

Notes

1. Guy HocQuenghem, *Homosexual Desire* (Durham: Duke, 1983), 137.

2. Ron Long has focused on the idea that gay men's desires lead them to worship male beauty. See his "The Sacrality of Male Beauty and Homosex," *Que(e)rying Religion: A Critical Anthology* (New York: Continuum, 1997), 266–86.

3. Joseph Martos, *Doors to the Sacred* (Garden City, NY: Image, 1966), 26.

4. Clifford Geertz, *Islam Observed* (Chicago: University of Chicago, 1968), 100.

5. See Victor Turner, *The Ritual Process* (Chicago: Albine Publishing Co., 1969).

6. Michael Cowen, "Sacramental Moments," *Alternative Futures for Worship*, vol. I (Collegeville: Liturgical Press, 1987), 42.

7. Regis Duffy, *Real Presence* (San Francisco: Harper & Row, 1982), 112.

8. Kathy Rudy, "'Where Two or More Are Gathered': Using Gay Communities as a Model for Christian Sexual Ethics," *Theology and Sexuality* 4 (1996): 81–99.

9. Stephen Moore, *God's Gym* (New York: Routledge, 1996).

10. We should note that there are several successful female DJs on the circuit. This is a challenge to the male hierarchy found in the Herodian structure. At the event with which I was involved, the DJ's booth was unseen by the party participants and, therefore, the DJ's gender would not have made a difference to those who celebrated the party rituals.

11. Michalangelo Signorile, *Life Outside* (San Francisco: Harper, 1997), 75.

12. Eric Rofes, *Dry Bones Breath* (New York: Harrington, 1998), 142.

The Harvey Milk Show
Violence, Desire, and Gay Popular Culture

19

EDWARD R. GRAY

ARVEY MILK (1930–1978) was the first openly gay elected official in the nation. His election to the San Francisco Board of Supervisors alone makes the life of Milk historic. A Jew from New York, Milk came to San Francisco in 1972, part of a large gay migration into the city, a mass social movement that began after World War II and intensified throughout the 1960s. San Francisco, like so many of the nation's major urban centers, was experiencing great change in the 1970s: near endless construction of new downtown skyscrapers and highways; gentrification of old neighborhoods along with the deterioration of others; rising real estate prices; and significant generational, racial, and ethnic change in municipal politics. While most participated in local San Francisco politics by casting ballots, a very few cast bombs. In addition to the brazen attempt on the life of President Ford during a 1975 visit, San Franciscans witnessed two other near assassinations. The San Francisco district attorney and then Supervisor Dianne Feinstein were the intended victims of two foiled bombings. Against the background of this political violence were two unrelated but simultaneous local political mobilizations: that of San Francisco gays and lesbians led by Milk and that of an interracial group of the poor led by the Rev. Jim Jones of the People's Temple. Both movements would end days apart in deadly fashion.

By many measures, the 1970s were the best of times for gay men and lesbians. AIDS was unknown, sexual expression flowered. Milk, who had opened a camera shop in the newly gay Castro Street neighborhood, won election in 1977 to the board of supervisors, San Francisco's version of a city council, on his second attempt. Before his shocking, violent end at the hands of a political rival, he was hailed as the "Mayor of Castro Street," presiding as the nation's first and only openly gay elected official from the nation's most famously gay neighborhood in one of its most sexually open and liberal cities.

His tenure was brief. On 27 November 1978, another supervisor, newly-elected from an Irish Catholic district, shot and killed Milk and Mayor George Moscone separately in their city hall offices. Some forty thousand predominantly gay San Franciscans marched by candlelight from the Castro district, down Market Street, to city hall in a spontaneous memorial. The march is repeated each year.

Somehow, a composer saw in the life of Harvey Milk the makings of a musical. The resulting *Harvey Milk Show* ran not in San Francisco, or New York, but in Atlanta. It premiered and ran to full houses in 1991 at Atlanta's Actor's Express. It was later reprised as part of the Cultural Olympiad that accompanied the 1996 athletic competition. The geography of Milk's hagiography may be as striking as his biography. *The Harvey Milk Show* has a strong regional sensibility. One of the Atlanta producers proudly noted that their musical reading of the life of the New York Jew murdered by a devout Roman Catholic in one of the most secular cities in America was a "completely homegrown production." The religious sensibilities of the Evangelical South are present in covert and overt ways in *The Harvey Milk Show*. Several leading characters are, in fact, southerners. They include an unmistakable fundamentalist preacher and a young man from Texas. Desire and sacrifice, defeat and resurrection are also among the uncredited dramatis personae in *The Harvey Milk Show*. Given this rich material, this essay frames the play as an exhibit from an emerging, but still indeterminate, movement creating alternative spiritual practice in and through gay popular culture. It shares this with experiences like the Gospel Hour and other phenomena described in this section. *The Harvey Milk Show* articulates an evangelically inspired religious sensibility that skillfully uses popular cultural forms such as the spectacle to describe an alternative gay religious sensibility. Like the other subjects in this section, *The Harvey Milk Show* is not a denomination or subaltern group. It is instead an example of gay popular culture. *The Harvey Milk Show* combines Christian theology and symbolism with modern gay experience. I read *The Harvey Milk Show* as a religious text in gay popular culture.

The play bears the marks of the religious heritage of its creators in both explicit and implicit ways. *The Harvey Milk Show* is a hagiography. The play reconstructs Milk as a Christlike martyr while portraying Christianity as the very seat of gay oppression. Casting Milk as a gay Messiah and his movement as a prophetic ministry with millennialist aspirations is not to read too much into it. Nor is it to read too deeply. But this alone does not make the play religious in any way. Yet, *The Harvey Milk Show* uses Christian symbols and templates to make Milk's life and death meaningful to its audience of southern gay men and lesbians. Other essays in this section use ethnographic methods to illumine how popular culture is being used to express an imaginative gay religious sensibility. Milk's life is transformed to become a moral lesson steeped in Christian evangelical symbols and expressed in popular culture.

During *The Harvey Milk Show*, its audiences are compelled to identify with the spiritual, emotional, and sexual journey of Jamey, Milk's young lover. Jamey represents both the Prodigal Son and Mary Magdalene. Milk, on the other hand, is the scapegoat—an object and eventual fatality of what Rene Girard has called "mimetic desire." *The Harvey Milk Show* explores the fundamental roles of desire, violence, and religion. It is an artifact of a desire-filled, fully embodied, material gay spirituality that relies on popular culture for expression. As other essays in part three of this volume suggest, this gay spirituality operates in and through popular culture, often in gay bars and clubs. Here, as in the case of the Gospel Hour, this gay spirituality is gently evangelical as well.

While the play explicitly portrays conservative evangelical Christianity negatively, it relies on Christianity to support much of its dramatic structure. *Harvey Milk* relies on Christian themes and symbols to interpret the life of Milk and make his sacrificial violent death meaningful. In short, it is a story about personal and collective conversion, redemption, forgiveness, and resurrection. It shows how Christian symbols and categories continue to resonate with the experience of gay folk, particularly southern gay men. I use an extended interview with the librettist, an analysis of the text, and participation as an audience member on two occasions to demonstrate how *The Harvey Milk Show*, relying on Christian symbols, creates its own mimetic desire on the part of the audience. It offers its audience an overt caricature of a darling diva of the religious Right. This provides a comic trope to be sure. But it does not exhaust the religious sensibilities of the work. More disguised—or in Girard's terms "concealed"—themes of redemption and resurrection are also present in *Harvey Milk*. It mocks Christianity on one level and appropriates it on another by modeling its principal characters on Jesus, Mary Magdalene, the Prodigal Son, and others. I analyze the play's covert and explicit treatments of Christianity and explore how violence knits them together in a way that makes *Milk* a compelling example of a gay religious sensibility found in and expressed through popular cultural forms.

There is much explicit material in *The Harvey Milk Show* concerning religion. Christianity is portrayed as intolerant, a school for hatred, and a camp for terrorism against gays. *Milk* creates a Bible-thumping version of conservative evangelical Christianity and holds it up for ridicule to a knowing Southern audience, ready to ridicule. Anita Bryant, not especially identified with either Milk or San Francisco, but well known for her antigay campaigns in Florida, is used as a comic trope. As a thinly disguised character, "Miss Anita" (played by a man in Carmen Miranda-like tropic drag—this is pure camp but also a modeling of the famously cosmetically over-painted, intentionally hyper-feminine television evangelists well known in the South) represents some of the worst of the good-old-time Southern evangelical religion of Dan Pruitt, the musical's librettist. This is a religion, I suspect, better known to Pruitt and Atlanta gay audiences than to the Jewish Milk or the residents of San Francisco.

Curtain up: *The Harvey Milk Show* opens by introducing Jamey, a young Texan new to San Francisco. In the prologue, Jamey's father, encouraged by his local fundamentalist minister, casts his son out of his home when he comes out to them. Jamey then travels to the gay promised land of San Francisco. Young, cute, unattached, and without prospects, he soon makes his affections available for a price. Jamey turns his religiously motivated moral condemnation into a temporary asset by fully embracing his intense sexual desire and youthful beauty in pre-AIDS San Francisco.

Scene one. Early morning on Castro Street, at the time an Irish, working-class neighborhood. Heather and John are posting flyers for "Mr. Milk." He is the local, small businessman running a community-based campaign for municipal office. Next, the police officer Dan White, who will later murder Milk and Moscone, comes upon a small street scuffle. He intervenes with a heavy hand. Milk as well happens by the scuffle and deploys his charisma to defuse the situation. Just when coincidence seems unable to go any further, Jamey, too, comes by the group. He and Milk have a heated exchange sparked by Milk's high-principled activism and Jamey's studied political apathy. They meet soon for a second time immediately after Jamey is attacked in a gay-bashing incident. Milk takes the wounded, friendless Jamey home to nurse him back to health and enlists him as a lieutenant in his next political campaign.

Next come scenes of domestic bliss as Harvey and Jamey make a home for each other. We get a peek back at Tyler, Texas, to see the confusion and hurt of Jamey's sister. We see Dan White's entry into local politics, motivated by a growing disgust with the increasing moral liberalism of San Francisco. This disgust is tinged with a more than a bit of jealousy for the success of gay men and their open sexual practices. We see Milk ostracized by much of the local gay establishment. He is too new, too loud, and too Jewish. Nonetheless, the portrayal is one of an appealing hero, without weaknesses or foibles, uncomplicated, morally clear, and powerfully charismatic. In one scene, a San Francisco queen says of Milk, "I'd agree we really need a new Messiah, but I always rather thought it would be me."

Messiahs as well as prophets are not immediately welcomed at home. Milk loses his first campaign but he is undeterred, excitedly encouraged, in fact. At the end of act one, Milk is poised for his first political victory. On the eve of Election Day, 16 November 1977, he delivers a stirring, beautiful speech. These are Dan Pruitt's words, not Milk's but the speech resonates with Milk's oratory and popular legacy.

> Tomorrow is Election Day. Tomorrow the people of San Francisco have the opportunity to give the rest of the world a great gift. That gift is hope. San Fran-

cisco has a long history of welcoming the refugee. And tomorrow San Francisco is going to walk into the voting booth and deliver a resounding message to the rest of the world—and particularly to these—these American refugees: come in. We're glad you're here. Welcome home.

Act one concludes with the stirring "We the People." This song is a combination of the Declaration of Independence and the Beatitudes of Jesus. In the play's only full-blown campaign scene, Harvey appeals on behalf of "the refugees in their own land"—the disenfranchised, the disillusioned, the forgotten. These are his constituents.

We the people/stand united/ For the rights of everyone. Let the slightest/ not be slighted/ No one's due/ must go undone. /These the smaller/ these the younger/ These who crave a gentle breast. / These whose hearts and bellies hunger/ these who strive and find no rest. These the slighted, mocked and taunted. These outside the rightful feast.

Act two. Scene one. Supervisor Milk announces his first piece of municipal legislation. It is not a proposal for greater civil rights for gays. Instead, it is a "pooper scooper" law mandating cleaning up after one's dog. The lightheartedness of this scene is followed by the receipt of death threats, which Milk and staff—led by Jamey—take in stride. The real Supervisor Milk was soon preoccupied fighting the Briggs Initiative, an attempt to ban gays and lesbians from serving in public schools in California. *The Harvey Milk Show* offers up a different opponent, Anita Bryant, the has-been singer and actress, who led an antigay campaign in Dade County, Florida, in the early 1970s.

As Milk and the increasingly hostile Dan White—now also a city supervisor—debate gay rights, the audience sees an antigay backlash in full force:

Wichita's Gay Rights Ordinance: Repealed!
St. Paul's Gay Rights Ordinance: Repealed!
Seattle's Gay Rights Ordinance: Repealed!
Eugene, Oregon's Gay Rights Ordinance: Repealed!

In a subsequent scene, Dan White unexpectedly resigns as a supervisor. He cites financial reasons for leaving the board but quickly relents. White makes repeated calls to Mayor Moscone first asking to rescind his resignation and then asking for reappointment to the board as his own replacement. He even appeals to Milk, his bitter political rival, to intervene with Moscone on his behalf.

Back at the Milk household, Jamey calls home to speak with his parents. The call goes badly. His hurt reopened, the relationship with Harvey on a rough patch, Jamey gets drunk. White becomes crazed by bitterness at the mayor and Milk, seeing Milk as the obstacle to his reappointment. White confronts Milk. Darkness. Shots. The figure of a blood-stained Diane Feinstein announces that White has murdered Moscone and Milk. This horrific double homicide in city hall comes only days after the tragic events in Jonestown, Guyana. The mass suicide and murder at the commune of the San Francisco religious leader Rev. Jim Jones had just taken the lives of nine hundred San Franciscans, including Congressman Leo Ryan.

The play continues with news of the verdict in White's (offstage) trail. White is found guilty of the much lesser crime of voluntary manslaughter. His maximum sentence: seven years and eight months. The infamous "Twinkee defense," clouded judgment stemming from a surfeit of sugar, carries the day in court but enrages San Francisco's gay community. Thousands march on city hall and attack the building; more than one hundred are injured, including police. They respond by clubbing gays outside Castro Street bars, some miles away.

Religion was not a significant factor in Milk's life but becomes an important actor in *The Harvey Milk Show*. The Christianity present in *The Harvey Milk Show* is not the mainstream Protestantism or ethnic Roman Catholicism of San Francisco. It is instead the conservative, evangelical Christianity of the South. Fundamentalist Christians are enemies. They are found everywhere, in churches, on street corners, and across the family kitchen table.

In the prologue, we know that Jamey's family has rejected him because of their religious beliefs about homosexuality. Later, Jamey recounts the story of his coming out to Milk. The play moves to Tyler, Texas, to give the audience a glimpse of its local religious ecology. In this scene, the family minister, a fundamentalist preacher, stands in for Jamey's father and casts him out of town in the name of the father. Dogmatic religion figuratively replaces familial love. The preacher explicitly holds up Jamey as another Prodigal Son. (However, in the biblical story, it is the son who chooses to leave.) In Tyler, the preacher informs Jamey that no one, not even the first-born son, can ask his father to "embrace the unholy. And so you must leave. You no longer have a home."

When it is not bitter, small, and intolerant, Christianity in *The Harvey Milk Show* is an object of parody and ridicule. Christianity is collapsed into the Religious Right. The Religious Right is portrayed, in turn, as continually in the act of constructing homosexuality as sinful, deviant, and dangerous.

In the scene, "Dressing of the Gladiator," the conspirator Mr. Jones prepares Dan White for his political career. Mr. Jones feeds White's growing resentment, his straight white male discontent, and frustration with changing social and sexual mores. White sings, "I believe in my God, who is the One True God . . . I believe in Duty, in the Lord and the Mission, in protecting the Glory, Order, Pride, and Tradition." Milk, in contrast, is the opposite of the traditional, religious, patriotic American and becomes his scapegoat.

White grows into a murderous rage. He is, he tells us, a good family man, someone who "has played by the rules. Church. Little League." Mr. Jones, who complains that no one will do anything about the vermin who "disdain what God hath wrought," eggs on White to be the one to save society.

Milk himself is a cynic when it comes to religion. He says: "Catholics don't like me because I'm a Jew. Protestants don't like me because I'm a Jew. Protestants, Catholics, and Jews don't like me because I'm gay."

When Milk is praised in the press, he notes wryly, "Next month they will have me walking on water." He charges middle-class morality with making poverty the "original sin." He condemns the Religious Right for preaching a gospel of contempt. Where, he asks, are gay children exempt from the American dream?

Southern fundamentalism is represented in the figure of the pious Anita Bryant, who led a crusade to push gay people out of public life. As the character, Miss Anita, Bryant and others of her religious ilk become an easy foil for anti-Religious Right sentiment. Miss Anita is a cartoonish caricature—played by the actor who portrays Mr. Jones. Dressed in camp drag to resemble Carmen Miranda in a ridiculous headdress of tropical fruit and bad makeup, Miss Anita sings:

She's peddled cosmetics and real estate. Orange juice and Avon and pills for losing weight. And when our gal's career seemed to have lost its fizz, it seems she found the Jesus biz!

The Harvey Milk Show's explicit construction of Christianity is of a Religious Right obsessed with gays. This obsession leads it to construct a picture of gay life to suit its own purposes and will inevitably lead to violence. Gays and fundamentalists are perfect Girardian rivals. For Girard, cultural distinctions preserve, rather than detract from, social order. The loss of distinctions—and in this case it is the disestablishment of heterosexual normativity—can lead quickly to fierce rivalries and violence. If Girard is correct that groups renew their common life through the regular imputation of the cause of social problems to scapegoats, then the obsession with homosexuals by White and the Religious Right in the play is a strategy for maintaining the social order. To maintain its status, the Religious Right must seek the ritual sacrifice of its chosen scapegoat and this is dramatically accomplished on stage.

There is an implicit construction of Christianity present throughout *Milk* as well. The lyrics are filled to overflowing with Christian imagery, if not Christian theology. The play opens with a millennial moment. It is the first day of spring, 1973. The day is pregnant with the promise of a better future to be ushered in by a salvific agent of change, Harvey Milk. A couple sings:

> Makes no diff'rence what we'd wish. We won't hold back the dawn. / Lovely, the memories. Lovely as lullabies. Sweet refrains that linger still. /But still another Sun must rise.

Harvey's campaign workers pick up the theme from the local residents.

> Tides are turning. Time to take advantage of a wave that's cresting. / Time to break the ties with yesterday. We make our way. Mad and gay and here to stay./ Some tomorrow comes a better day.

The millennial theme continues. On the eve of his election, supporters sing:

> Time to lend the world a wider scope—a brighter hope. Time to open up the closet.
> Some tomorrow history's gonna be rewritten. Some tomorrow we'll demand a brand new page; / Some tomorrow we won't have to try to fit in. /Some tomorrow when we welcome a grand new age.

Harvey's slogan, "San Francisco is at the crossroads of its history!" is heard again and again. He uses it to rally his campaign—and the audience. At the conclusion of act one, a musical Pruitt had planned to subtitle "A Passion Play," Harvey becomes an agent of personal salvation. He sings:

> When you're lost/ When it's cold / Take my hand/Here's a shoulder /Never mind, come inside, there's a fire. Come inside where it's warm/ There's a balm for the soul/ There's a calm from the storm/ When it's out of control, when you're lost, scared to death /We'll get thru it together.

Later, Harvey explains the campaign and the meaningfulness of his life to Jamey. He is on a mission to rescue the emotionally, physically, and spiritually homeless.

> I'd like to get a whole fleet of those great big yellow school buses and drive up into the front yard of every kid in the world who's ever been called "sissy" or "tomboy" and say: "Hey, come on, kid, you're going with me. And we're all gonna go to some place we can all be together, where none of us will ever again have to explain anything to anybody."

If the Harvey Milk of the play wanted to change the lives of gay children by ending any requirement for them to explain themselves, Milk the activist expected an affirmative and bold act from adults. Milk's message was to come out of the closet. It might be described as an act of conversion. Come out and the world around you will change, he promised. Milk asked his followers to be publicly gay. He recognized that such public witness required an internal change of heart. Come out, come out, Milk preached, and you will be saved if you do. The number of gay men and lesbians would stun the nation. And the nation would be saved from its bigotry.

Milk recognized that coming out could have a price. This cost makes coming out a sacrificial act. For Girard, sacrifice is at the heart of religion. A group founds religion and all of culture on the murder of an individual. What Girard calls "mimetic desire" motivates the urge to such violence. This is an imitative desire for the material and social status of others. For Girard, the human impetus toward communal violence only finds its release when directed to surrogate victims. Violent acts are ritually committed against scapegoats and mythically explained. The role of religions is to deflect our violent tendencies toward one another and, in fact, to conceal the violent impulse that is the founding act of human culture. Religious cloaking conceals the violent sacrifice of the scapegoat and its generative relationship to the social order.

Mimetic rivalry is simply, for Girard, a basic human need or drive to possess or replicate what another person has. It therefore "inevitably threatens to tear apart a society by fomenting unchecked rivalry between individuals and groups." Societies eventually find a way to contain this threat of violence by inventing a scapegoat. The scapegoat is construed as the cause of all social problems and therefore becomes a proper object of violence.

There are violent acts throughout *The Harvey Milk Show.* Harvey and Jamey meet due to an act of violence. They are separated by violence. Jamey is a victim of violence and its agent when he, in the play, helps to incite the riot after the conviction of Dan White on lesser charges of voluntary manslaughter. Harvey's former colleagues are concerned that "things could turn ugly fast" as gay men and lesbians gather to protest. Jamey responds, "Good! Let them feel *our* violence for once."

Jamey's sister pleads with him to intercede to stop the riot. He rejects her pleas with fury, explaining,

> Right now all I have is this rage. . . . I thought it began the day Harvey died, but I was wrong. I think it's been there my whole life. The world has always drawn a line between us—those of us like me and those of you like you. And we've never been allowed to cross that line, not really. Now you can't cross over either. Not unless you know what it feels like to be despised for this—the things here (points to his heart)—to be despised for your very heart. And you will never know what that feels like, thank God. BURN IT DOWN, GODDAMMIT!"

Tumult follows. This is the stage direction:

> [Jamie] runs off. All hell breaks loose. A few rioters come on, throwing rocks, bricks, battles, then more. Jangling music, sirens, patrol car calls, angry chanting

mob sound, radio announcements of the riots of City Hall, newsreel footage of burning cars projected onto the actual smoke that fills the stage, other violent effects underline the confrontation of an outraged community against a heavily armored riot squad. When the smoke clears, the stage has been left in a shambles.

In this scene, mimetic rivalry is turned on its head. The scapegoat gets a measure of revenge.

To call Milk a Jesus-like figure in the play is not too deep an analysis. He delivers a Sermon on the Mount. He is killed, like Jesus, as a scapegoat. And he is resurrected, too. In the epilogue, Milk reappears to Jamey. What Jamey is experiencing is not described as a vision, but a real experience of the living Harvey. In terms of the play, Milk is resurrected. "Young man," Harvey says, "don't believe in the used-to-be. Dare and believe in what we've begun. Still there's so much, Jamey, left undone." Harvey commissions Jamey (and thus the audience) to pursue this mission. Jamey the Prodigal Son—become Mary Magdalene—now becomes St. Peter.

The Harvey Milk Show constructs Milk as a Christ-like figure and as a scapegoat victimized by heterosexual intolerance. A New Yorker and a secular Jew, Milk becomes Jesus at the hands of a gay Southern man who knows how to make new use of Christian symbols. Despite this, Milk is not the central character of the play. That character is Jamey. Jamey who embodies mimetic desire, his own and that of the audience as well. It is Jamey with whom audiences, and particularly Southern gay male audiences, identify; Jamey, the victim of fundamentalist religion made homeless.

This essay has attempted to establish a starting point for understanding a generalized religious sensibility among gay men, recognizably Christian and Girardian in its emphasis on desire. It, along with others in part three of this volume, points to the unusual energy and creativity given to carving out areas of spiritual endeavor in gay popular culture.

The evangelical Christianity, which explicitly cast Jamey out of his home, also provides the set of symbols that promise a better future. This millennium is delayed but not deterred by the sacrifice of Milk. Evangelical Christian intolerance is represented as the enemy of the gay community, most pointedly in the figure of Anita Bryant and Dan White's shadowy supporters. This same religious heritage, however, provides the symbolic resources needed to create this hagiography of Milk in the first place. *The Harvey Milk Show* is a rite in a desire-filled, fully physical, material spirituality of gays and lesbians. It takes evangelical Christian symbols and fashions them into an expression of gay spirituality and popular culture. *The Harvey Milk Show* is like a trip on that big yellow school bus filled with gay children as it travels to that expected brand new day. It leaves behind religiously motivated intolerance and finds a new spiritual home right in the middle of popular culture.

Gay Men's Spiritual Experience in the Leather Community

20

THOMAS V. PETERSON

IN THIS ESSAY I ARGUE that gay men in the leather community frequently seek spiritual release through rites of bondage, domination, and sadomasochism (SM). Suggesting that many leathermen seek and find spiritual liberation through such rites will seem odd to most people, blasphemous to others, and perverse to some. Gay men who enter the leather world find it difficult to share their experiences openly with friends, both gay and straight alike, because of deeply held suspicions and prejudices. Mark Thompson, a prominent journalist who has held several editorial positions at *The Advocate*, a national gay and lesbian newsmagazine, writes that "announcing my homosexuality was child's play compared to the struggle I'd had in admitting my interest in leather sex" (1997: 185). Eric Rofes, an AIDS activist, details the problems he has had leading and working in "organizations in the gay and lesbian community" because of his openness about his identity as a leatherman (1991: 179–84).

The rituals of leathersex are, of course, not limited to gay men. There are lesbians and straight folks who find bondage and SM play deeply meaningful. While acknowledging more similarities than differences in the spiritual experiences of all these leather groups, gay men do share one unique experience: we have frequently been alienated from our masculinity because our heterosexual male counterparts have so frequently cast us as "sissies." For many gay men, the rituals of leathersex are a means for finding and reclaiming masculinity by undertaking an initiation rite. In any case, my conversations about leathersex have largely taken place within the gay male community, which I focus on in this essay. Some of these conversations have taken place in leather bars in Toronto; Rochester, NY; Cleveland; New York City; Atlanta; Minneapolis; and Pittsburgh. Others have been initiated in leather chat rooms on the Internet. I have had extended e-mail conversations with eight leathermen (six bottoms and two tops) about the spirituality of leathersex.

Many of their insights and a few quotations are included in this essay. I also include reflections that have been published by others who have reflected on the spiritual context of the gay leather world.

Where do leathermen meet and where do they enact their rites of bondage, domination, and SM? Traditionally, the most common meeting place has been in bars that are more or less exclusively frequented by leathermen. There are leather bars in most major cities in North America and probably elsewhere in the world. Especially on Friday and Saturday nights, leathermen start gathering in the late evening, usually after 10 p.m. Many men who frequent these bars are simply enjoying a hypermasculine gay environment, where they play pool, get their boots shined by bootblacks, and have conversations with friends. Others are looking to find a partner to take home and play with. Not only are verbal negotiations in these bars very specific about desires and limits, but also there are all sorts of visual clues. These clues include the color of handkerchiefs, whether the keys or armbands are hanging from the left or right side of the body, and bodily posture. These clues help match those who would dominate with those who would submit and sometimes indicate the types of play that the leathermen prefer.

Some of the most serious leathermen are members of clubs and these clubs often meet in the most traditional leather bars—for example the New York City Renegades who hang out at the Lure and the Rochester Rams who frequent the Bachelor's Forum. These clubs sometimes have a play night in their bar and engage in public rituals of SM, domination, and bondage that are not overtly sexual—for example, a public flogging or a master holding a leash attached to his slave's collar. Many of the leather clubs also have "runs." While these used to be organized motorcycle trips that ended in an encampment, most nowadays are simply leather encampments. To join a run, one has to be sponsored or invited by someone in the leather club or "recommended" by someone who has gone on the "run" before. At these encampments, the rituals of SM, bondage, and domination are very public. What often goes unreported is the degree of caring, hugging, and gentle affection that is manifested by the couples who are engaged in these rituals.

There are many other contexts for public rituals in the leather world—gay campgrounds frequently have leather weekends where they "crown" the camp's "leatherboy" and "leatherman" for the year. And there are public celebrations of leather such as the annual Folsom Street Fair in San Francisco that draws thousands of leathermen from all over the United States.

In sum, the rituals of the leathermen take place both in private bedrooms and in more public arenas. Leathermen meet each other in cyberspace and in leather bars. A big, unanswerable question is how important the leather scene is in the gay community. I have encountered anecdotal evidence, at least, that suggests the leather scene is growing larger within the gay community. One AIDS outreach worker, who has been working in the gay community for more than twenty years, told me that he found many young men who were just coming out who seemed more interested in the leather community than had previously been the case. When I asked him why, he suggested that many of these guys wanted to affirm both their "gayness" and their "masculinity." He suggested that many of these guys would have remained in the closet in the past, letting the queens, nellies, and twinks define being gay. Because of social stereotypes, it is easier for men who fit the cultural norms of masculinity to be closeted than it is for those who more openly celebrate cultural norms of the feminine. Michael Bronski also argues that the realization of leather fantasies in the lives of gay men represents an acceptance of masculinity—that gay men have as much right to images of masculinity as anyone else in our culture. Even more, he argues, it is a statement of political power in our culture: "The blatant, public image of the leather man (or woman) is an outright threat to the existing, although increasingly dysfunctional, system of gender arrangements and sexual repression under which we have all lived" (1991: 64).

In any event, it is certainly true that the symbols of the leather world are hypermasculine—pirates' earrings, gladiators cuffs, policemen's uniforms and handcuffs, cowboy hankies, military boots, bikers' tattoos—merged into a peculiar ritualistic garb. Interestingly, these hypermasculine symbols, often used for oppression, even against the gay men who are displaying them, have been subverted and transformed into the erotic realm of pleasure (see Mohr 1992: 162–73).

How many leathermen find spiritual meaning through sexual rites of bondage and SM? The answer to this question is complicated because many leathermen are uncomfortable using any religious discourse. They, like many gay men in our culture, have frequently suffered from religious intolerance. Or, they may find nothing attractive about any analogies with mainstream religion. Sam, a fifty-year-old leatherman and English professor who has shared many of his personal experiences with me, expressed disapproval of my use of the term "spiritual" to describe bondage and SM experiences, even though he was adamant that the "rituals" of leathersex were "psychologically profound and liberating."

Anyone associated with the leather scene knows that there is a disproportionate number of men with religious backgrounds. Sam, himself, had attended a Catholic seminary. Many, like Sam, had worked hard to discard all explicit vestiges of their religious backgrounds and wanted nothing to do with any religious discourse. On the other hand, I have found several clergy in the leather world who found it to be a relief to make connections between their leather experiences and their religious backgrounds. One man told me that he avoided identifying himself as a Catholic priest partly because it so frequently became a barrier to sharing the deep experiences he was seeking in the leather world.

Although I deeply respect those leathermen who prefer to discuss their experiences in psychological terms, most frequently in Jungian language, there is an important reason to use spiritual language as well. Whether or not one assents to specific religious beliefs, there is significant continuity between the experiences of leathermen and people who have described their experiences in religious terms. For example, Lakota men who have hung in the hot sun from hooks that pierce the pectoral muscles have said that they were sacrificing themselves to Wakan Tanka (the Great Spirit or the Great Holiness). In this heroic quest they have had visions and discovered a deeper spiritual meaning to their existence. Examples of Catholic Penitentes and Hindu Sadhus who have engaged in extreme forms of bodily mortification are certainly known among religious scholars and others. Using religious discourse, then, to think about the experiences of leathermen helps bridge a gap between the experiences of many people across cultures and historical periods.

In *Urban Aboriginals*, published in 1984, Geoff Mains broke new ground within the leather community by openly proclaiming that spirituality is central to the leatherman's experience. For the religious leatherman, "this spirituality is a natural complement of both the symbolism of play and of deep emotions and trust that move it." However, even for those who totally distrust organized religion, "this spirituality is an important element of the scene that conventional religions have seemed unable to provide." Interestingly, Mains believed this "spirituality" was based on physiological processes. He detailed how endorphins flood the mind when the body is pushed to its limits of endurance (1987: 112).

But Mains also thought that religious discourse best described the process: "The spiritual leanings of leather space are not surprising; many of its elements are shared in common with religious experience." He even suggested that leathermen were on the cutting edge of introducing a new religious sensibility into American culture: "There is something holy in a leather scene. . . . like the words and acts of shamans, the spiritual utterances of leather men can take on special importance to the fellow members of their tribe" (1987: 113).

In the two decades since Mains wrote his watershed work, many others have written about the leather world as the locus for spiritual activity. Reverend Troy Perry is a pastor in the Metropolitan Community Church who opened himself to leathermen who shared their experiences with him. He was asked to be part of a panel at the National Leather Association in Portland, Oregon. He later wrote about his experience: "A real eye-opener for me . . . was the depth of spirituality I witnessed in many attendees. . . . I was amazed at the depth of maturity and spirituality exhibited" (1987: 250).

Two other highly respected men in the leather world have written about the centrality of spirituality in leathersex rituals. Mark Thompson writes about the spiritual liberation that he had from the standpoint of a bottom in his extraordinarily thoughtful autobiography, *Gay Body* (1997). And Guy Baldwin, a psychotherapist and contributor to *Drummer* magazine, has described his spiritual experiences as both a top and bottom in *Ties That Bind* (1993).

In the leather world men are almost always paired as either tops or bottoms in their ritual play, though men may "switch" these roles at different stages in their lives or even from one scene to another. These pairings have many other names— masters/slaves, dominants/submissives, sadist/masochist to name those used in this essay. All of these terms are loaded within the leather world and are frequently misunderstood outside of it. Although tops/bottoms is the most all-encompassing term, some leathermen find it too general to capture the power and vulnerability that is at the heart of their experience with bondage, domination, and SM. Master/slave refers to the roles the two men are playing; often, though not necessarily, this refers to an ongoing relationship. Dominant/submissive most usually refers to the mental attitude that is cultivated in the scene, while sadist/masochist refers to the bodily experiences of pain and pleasure that are at the heart of the power exchange that takes place in the ritual activities of leathermen.

Leathermen who are comfortable with spiritual discourse frequently speak of bondage and SM as rites of initiation that are somehow transformative. Sam, who usually plays as a bottom, said that something deep inside him impels him to seek leather masters who will push him to his limits of endurance. Although he works out regularly in a gym and seems to exude masculinity, he told me that he did not engage in sports as a child and had been picked on by bullies. Although he only began experiencing bondage and SM rites after he turned forty-five, he feels he has gained confidence by facing some of his deepest fears. Although he doesn't set many limits, he asks that his doms refer to him as a "manslave" rather than "slaveboy" (the more usual term even for older subs), because he feels he is "man enough" to accept "whatever punishment the top wants to give me." Brad, a sub in his thirties, expressed a similar sentiment when he admitted to me that he feels he can "take a lot more pain" than all those guys in his high school who had once picked on him.

Robert Hopcke, a Jungian-oriented psychotherapist who also holds an MA in theology and pastoral counseling from Pacific Lutheran Seminary in Berkeley, writes that while the lack of effective male initiation rituals is a general problem in American culture, it is particularly acute among gay men, some of whom have internalized homophobic attitudes of guilt and shame that alienate them from their bodies. Although Hopcke admits that some gay men engage in SM activities for frivolous or unhealthy reasons, he insists that there is a very serious side to these rites that can be profoundly transformational. They can and do transform gay men by helping them accept their masculinity and their bodies (72–75).

For the most part, leathermen refer to their rituals as "scenes." These scenes are so varied that it is difficult to describe any one scene as *the* typical ritual activity. In fact, subs prize a dom's inventiveness greatly, because new activities keep the scene fresh. One sub told me that he was able to stay most focused when he was never quite sure what would happen next. Nevertheless, leather play follows a pattern that is remarkably similar to initiation rituals in established religious traditions, as Robert Hopcke has noted (1991: 65–70).

In the first place, both subs and doms have already entered a world that is apart from their everyday life when they enter a bar dressed in leather to negotiate the terms of the ritual play. But when a scene begins, perhaps in the master's "dungeon," there are further activities that emphasize one man's total submission to another. Often it includes a master stripping a slave, having him kneel before him with his head bowed, having him kiss his boots. Sometimes the activity is as simple as a dom and sub hugging each other with the slave inclining his head and putting it on the master's chest. The activities that emphasize a slave's willingness to submit to a master can include many other possibilities, such as water sports (pissing on a slave in a bathtub), a master putting his fingers in his slave's mouth, or squeezing his balls or tits. The list is endless. But at the beginning of a scene, there is some physical activity where one man submits to another. Like all ritual activity, the acts convey a large range of meanings. When I talked to one sub about why he wanted his master to piss on him, the sub corrected my terminology, calling it a "golden shower." This activity was not degrading for him, but made him feel more owned by his master than anything else.

These activities that emphasize dominance and submission gradually flow into the main activity of the scene. Sometimes the initial activity is itself the whole activity of a scene. There are, for example, masters and slaves who are totally into the foot scene with a slave licking his master's feet and massaging them, and then allowing his whole body to become his master's footstool. But the main scene could also be different from the initial actions that emphasize domination and submission. Here the list of activities is endless—flogging, bondage, mummification, tickling, spanking, interrogation, tit torture, sucking, fucking, and more. Most important, whatever the activity, the sub experiences his loss of control and even his loss of ego. The rest of the essay fleshes out how and why transformation sometimes occurs through these activities.

Before examining this question in detail, it is important to note that there is frequently some ritual activity that signals a return to a more ordinary community. At the end of some scenes, for example, it is most usual for the two men to hug each other with the sub thanking the dom for the trip. If the scene is in a private apartment or house, the two men might share a beer or a meal. If the players are intimate, they might sleep together and engage in loving, sexual activities. Some leather communities (leather clubs or bars) even have organized activities where men, subs and doms alike, simply enjoy each other's company. Every Sunday at the Tool Box in Toronto, for example, leathermen gather for brunch with much animated conversation, joking, and camaraderie. Again, the list of activities could be quite extensive and include everything from campouts to contests to select a leatherman or leatherboy to mudwrestling events.

But how do all these leathermen's rituals work? How do they help promote transformation? Most basically, all rituals promote understanding through body-knowing. Perhaps the basic reason for our de-emphasizing rituals in Western culture is that we have separated mind and body, locating knowledge (and often spirituality) in the mind and appetites in the body. The rituals of the leather world work on both the mind and body simultaneously. It is not enough for a master to be skilled at binding and flogging a slave; he must convey a total attitude of dominance. It is not enough for a slave to endure pain; the discipline must convey a total response of submission.

But how does being bound and flogged, gagged and spanked, promote a sub's initiation into masculinity. Bottoms suggest many answers. Mark Thompson writes about his submission in leathersex play as a way to face his deepest fears, to face his childhood pain of being called a sissy: "In the curious way that elements are reversed and become their opposite thing in psyche's dungeons, my humiliation became powerful food for my soul" (1997: 189). For Thompson the "soul" seems to be the metaphorical construct where body and mind are united in a truthful relationship to the world. Since that truthfulness seems to rest on facing "one's indispensable condition" in Thompson's words, it requires shattering the ego by "fearless treading into the inflamed location of one's suffering and shame" (p. 192).

Philosopher Richard Mohr has explained how gay culture in general and the leather world in particular has directly confronted the dominant culture's oppressive symbols and then subverted and transformed them. He writes, "One is liberated, not (simply) by coming to see that the constituents of oppression are artifices, but in the making of something new out of the old evil ways in a manner that defuses what was evil about the old ways" (1992: 172). He gives many examples of this transformation, the most powerful examples from the leather world. For example he discusses Robert Mapplethorpe's 1979 photograph, *Elliot and Dominic*, which portrays a master standing behind his bound slave who is hanging upside down in a cruciform position. The master's hand is squeezing his slave's balls. Mohr writes,

> the iconographic allusion to Roman martyrdom of Saint Peter ceases to be an eroticizing of death and the pictograph of the expression "having someone by the balls" ceases to portray a cool act of violent coercion. Rather, both actions—inverted

crucifixion and clutched balls—are taken up into what I take to be a kindly, caring, uniquely gay, classic marriage portrait" (1992: 185).

Thus the rituals of the leather world often subvert the violent, fearful acts of exploitation, not by denying them, but by changing them and making them part of gay eros.

Exploring one's vulnerability, then, seems to be at the heart of the sub's quest. Baldwin writes that by making himself vulnerable, "my 'self' becomes stripped of all its external trappings. . . . What I am left with is an ecstatic contact with Self. There are no words passing through my mind; there are no cerebral events taking place" (1990: 186–87). As most religious scholars know, this last statement could have been written by mystics in many religious traditions who claim to have experienced the true self through annihilation of the ego.

What is frequently obscured, however, is how pain may become the means to finding the self. Perhaps religious scholars have focused too much on the mental states of Zen practitioners, for example, and too little on the physical pain and endurance in explaining experiences of satori. Ironically, Zen masters all insist that the bodily posture is an integral part of the experience. From a ritual perspective, the body must physically experience its vulnerability if there is to be transformation and growth through the shattering of ego. From this ritual perspective, body-knowing is essential for transformation. Geoff Mains clearly recognized the importance of body-knowing and physicality in leathersex rituals. Leather play is "a form of human interaction requiring total absorption. This interaction is ritualistic and is full of overtones of the socially forbidden. It might involve bootlicking, restraint or greasing of a butthole" (1987: 104).

An adept master understands that there are no set routines in leathersex play. Master Dan, a sociology professor in his early fifties who was more willing than most tops to discuss the spirituality of his activities, said that his sexual arousal was especially heightened by trying to find the "key" to making "a slave totally submit to him." He said that bondage was essential to some who could only lose themselves when physically restrained and forced to do what he wanted. He said that there were others who could only lose themselves if they felt they were submitting freely to a master's personality.

Quite simply, in the words of Baldwin, a leather master must give his sub "a real experience of his vulnerability." Correspondingly "the top must experience as real the fact that his bottom's life is in his hands and feel his own urges to push the bottom's vulnerability" (1990: 188). In an e-mail answer to my question about what was most central to him in a dom/sub relationship, Rob, a forty-eight–year-old lawyer from Pittsburgh, discussed how his spiritual needs were met as a bottom:

What's at the core—are you sitting down?—is "kenosis" [humbling or emptying]. I don't believe I've yet, in my shyness, written to you of this. Or does it seem not shy, but arrogant (even blasphemous) to perceive a parallel in the dynamic celebrated in Philippians 2:5 as the core of Christian soteriology? Whichever it may be, this is something one can't broach lightly, or even hint at with most. . . . When the bottom (in collaboration—wonderous work indeed—with the top) thoroughly empties himself of all illusions and pretentions, indeed of virtually all connections to the world in which he conventionally participates, the resultant vacuum in his mind and soul readily fills with a rush of thoughts and feelings that well up from the ground of his being, and his true self becomes known in its natural glory.

Rob's reticence to speak about the spiritual dimensions of leather play is typical, although one French Canadian college professor from Montreal said to me without hesitation, "Leather is my religion and leather masters are my gods." More usual is the comment made by a man from Texas to Guy Baldwin: "My buddies would laugh at me if I told them what happens in my mind sometimes when I play." Baldwin clarifies, "He was referring to the spiritual—transcendental? mystical?—experiences he has when he plays" (1993: 237).

One doesn't have to scratch too deeply to get subs to talk about the serious nature of their quest to explore their vulnerability. Mark Thompson describes it as "the work of the hero" and "a new kind of vision quest: a spiritual search involving reconciliation with the past, catharsis in the present moment, and, with any luck, birth of clarity for future life" (1997: 192, 187). Brad told me that his work with his master helped give him a new sense of masculinity. Other subs talk about the "zone" to refer to their feeling of clarity and oneness with all life. One forty-two-year-old sub, Frank, who had lived in a Benedictine monastery for several years, echoed Hindu tantrists when he told me that it was very important for him that his master "makes him do acts" that transgressed cultural norms because that allowed him "to give up social expectations and realize my true nature."

The parallels in all of these examples between the rituals of the leather world and those of the major world religions are obvious. The Zen adept attempts to glimpse satori by emptying his mind of all thoughts. Interestingly the process of "just sitting" includes episodes of significant pain that may be a more essential aspect of the meditational process than usually emphasized. Hindu Tantra insists that adepts find ways of freeing themselves from cultural norms and taboos, reportedly through such "disgusting" activities as watching a corpse decompose or eating the flesh of animals. And Christianity certainly has a long tradition of insisting that exaltation will come through humiliation, to paraphrase Paul's famous hymn in Philippians 2.

It is far more difficult to suggest the spiritual path of doms, tops, or masters in the leather world. Interestingly, the spiritual path of gurus, priests, and roshis is equally hidden in the study of world religions. I have always wondered what's in it for the guru who surrounds himself with disciples who are often so self-centered that they will self-righteously abandon and decry their leaders at the first sign of real or perceived weakness. The established religious traditions seem to avoid this question by claiming that *their* religious leaders are operating on altruism or enlightenment. Or in the Christian traditions, the priest or minister has an interior "calling" or "vocation." Although "altruism" and "vocation" might certainly be true, these facile answers do obscure the spiritual path of the religious leader. At times these explanations fail in sexual and financial scandals that rock the foundations of established religions. When that happens cynics gloat in the exposure of hypocrisy and believers are scandalized.

In the leather world, however, power relationships are very much in the open and are almost always "negotiated" by tops and bottoms. The right of the top to demand sex and power within agreed upon limits is built into the relationship from the beginning—the top has the "right" to demand that the bottom serve him completely. As a matter of fact, the relationship wouldn't work for the bottom if the top weren't greedy and aggressive. But how can the top also be on a spiritual path? Within the context of Christianity or Buddhism, we might be able to accept the bottom's experience of "emptying" himself of his ego and thereby finding his larger "self," but how can the top be on a spiritual path by exercising his will to dominate and by shamelessly making the sub serve his needs, oftentimes, but not always, including raw sexuality and lust? Humility, sacrifice, and giving are part of our religious vocabulary, but how is exercising ritual power part of the religious quest?

Although there seems to be a reluctance (or a lack of conceptual language) in the leather world for tops to discuss their needs, desires, hopes, and fulfillments, there is a clear acknowledgment that bottom and top are involved in a symbiotic dance that either succeeds or fails by both together. Mark Thompson is very clear about this: "The point in exploring dark eros, I found, was not to formulate an identity as either masochist or sadist—they are, after all, opposite sides of the same construct—but rather to ask what our relationship to suffering is" (1997: 190). Guy Baldwin writes that both "the top and the bottom" together "walk along the razor's edge of good and evil and are able to glance indifferently from one side to the other, reveling in our ability to find a peaceful serene unity within those two polar opposites" (1990: 193). In a conversation, Master Dan told me that when everything was really working he felt that his bottom took him to a place beyond pleasure and pain where the opposition between dom and sub evaporated.

But why is it so difficult to get masters to discuss their deep meaningful experiences during leather play, whether or not one wants to call them "spiritual?" I suspect that part of the answer lies in the mythology of the leather play itself. The sub must be convinced that the dom knows what he's doing. In our culture, at least, a dom cannot, therefore, discuss his "needs" without implying weakness. So, like the religious guru, the dom insists on his "rights" to make the demands that he does, and usually ends by saying something about it being his "nature" to be dominant. This is very similar to the people in established religious traditions talking about their "calling," though the priest's and guru's "rights" are more clearly buried in some kind of authority—scriptural, educational, or even experiential with the old guru designating his successor. Compared to the bottom's claim of "humility," "loss of ego," "sacrifice," "kenosis," among others, the top's religious vocabulary to express his spiritual experience seems quite meager.

To my knowledge, Guy Baldwin is the only leather top who has written explicitly about the spiritual experience of tops. He believes that tops are as numerous in "nature" as bottoms—even though far fewer choose to travel the path of the leathersex master. From his experience as a psychotherapist, he thinks that tops are actually more vulnerable than are bottoms. Not only have the tops struggled with the question of their rights to dominate other human beings, but they have a great deal of "fear and guilt" when "they come face to face with the magnitude of their needs to be sadistic, their urges to control, and to dominate" (1993: 229). Baldwin believes that the more that tops and bottoms are involved in a spiritual quest, the more fear there is. "The top is afraid of his own impulses to destroy, of destroying another person and thereby himself—his mortality, his self-respect. The bottom is afraid of being destroyed, of nonexistence" (1990: 198).

Master Jerome, a large muscular man in his early fifties, agreed with Baldwin's position when I sent him an earlier draft of this essay, but thought it was much deeper. He felt that his "spiritual" satisfaction came from "giving bottoms what they truly need." He felt most at peace when he knew he was taking a sub to a forbidden place where few others have dared to go. His intense feeling of fulfillment came when he could feel the sub lose himself in his will. He said that the most intense, personal moment for him was often at the end of the scene when he would "embrace the slave in a hug" and know for sure that he had taken his sub "to a place where he needed to go."

A master's experiences might parallel those of religious gurus in eastern religious traditions. These men claim that they have experienced their godlike natures. While the guru continually reiterates that there is no difference between himself and his disciples—all are equally godlike—he does claim that he has experienced his godlike nature directly. Westerners frequently misunderstand the guru's claim. The guru cannot do *anything* that he wants, because he knows he is god; if the guru misuses his power, then followers will know that he is a fake. Actually it is even clearer in leathersex rituals when a master exceeds his authority, because master and slave have together negotiated the limits.

When I sent an early draft of this essay to Frank, the forty-two-year-old ex-Benedictine monk, he said that he thought everything I said was accurate, but that I didn't emphasize enough the love that flowed between a master and his slave. He said that his "master understood his needs and desires" better than he did himself. So maybe the master does potentially experience the power, responsibility, and humility of becoming divine, as blasphemous as that may sound to Western ears. But both Master Dan and Master Jerome emphasize that if one is to talk about "spirituality" at all, it rests somewhere in the careful way that the master orchestrates the scene and gives the slave the experience he is seeking.

How many gay men are irresistibly drawn to the leather world to explore what Thompson called the "dark eros?" In my experience, many gay men occasionally hang out on the periphery, but hesitate getting deeply involved. If Baldwin is right, this hesitation is greater in tops than bottoms. He writes that fear paralyzes many of these men. He acknowledges that he was paralyzed by that fear for two years and unsuccessfully tried to dismiss the leather world from his life. It is scary for tops and bottoms alike to engage in serious rites that are played out on the "platform of vulnerability." While some men become paralyzed by their fear, others engage in the rites for sexual reasons. Baldwin is scathingly critical of these men who "risk being reduced to male impersonators or, at best, sport fuckers. . . . To undertake the rite without making the passage simply reduces us to being ritualists or liturgists—empty and meaningless—the jewel box without the jewel" (1993: 233–34). Baldwin understands that some fear is healthy so that tops stay within the boundaries of "safe, sane, and consensual" and bottoms make sure they are playing with "a responsible top." But he insists that both top and bottom, if they are engaged in rites of the leather world, must take "the transformational journey" and "move toward the Black Hole of experience" (1993: 235).

Master Dan told me that he sees himself as participating in Shiva's dance of destruction and creation when he is with a sub who is truly willing to travel the spiritual path. He feels himself at the center of an incredible spiritual energy when he seriously goes into the rituals of the leather world. Baldwin doesn't refer directly to the dance of Shiva, but he seems to be saying the same thing when he talks about bottoms being the "necessary witnesses to, and participants in this drama. They watch us play with holy fire, and accompany us as each scene reconfirms us in a rite of passage." Interestingly he talks about the top's "transformation" as a transformation of the childish "impulses to destroy . . . spontaneously for pleasure" into a dynamic creative energy (1993: 231). The spiritual excitement, he claims, comes precisely from the top's inner war "between the need to destroy versus the need not to destroy." Although Baldwin doesn't explicitly use the "dance of Shiva" paradigm, he seems to be saying the same thing when he talks about "the war between the id and the superego" (1990: 197).

So in a sense both bottom and top together are involved in Shiva's dance of creation and destruction. The top pushes to destroy the bottom's ego by symbolically becoming part of cosmic energy. The bottom witnesses these acts by the top who is an equal witness to the annihilation of the bottom's ego. Since all ego is partially created by cultural mores and moralities, this process can be extremely liberating to gay men who have been trapped by feelings of guilt and fear in a homophobic culture. Both top and bottom are together transgressing those cultural norms. And while the ritual work centers on smashing the sub's ego, the dom, too, must get beyond his own fears and get beyond social and cultural restraints to make absolute ritual demands on the bottom.

In the final analysis there is an incredible balancing act that is taking place in the ritual dance of domination and submission among leathermen. The balancing can be seen as a dance between two guys, one of whom is exploring his feelings of vulnerability and another who is experiencing power in its rawest form. But there is also a balancing that takes place within each individual. Although there are many different character types in this ritual dance of dark eros, I hazard a tentative conclusion about a major type of balancing act that takes place in both dom and sub. Master Dan gave me the clue to this interior balancing act when he told me that he was essentially an other-directed extrovert who had a long history of finding his meaning in other people's approval. He told me that as a child he had felt responsible for keeping a fairly dysfunctional family operating, and had rarely considered his own desires and needs. For him, becoming a master meant that he had to own these needs and desires. For him that was both the hardest part and the most liberating. Since he made this comment to me, I have noticed a significant, but not all-encompassing pattern: masters in everyday life are often very attuned to the needs of others; slaves are frequently more self-centered. Master Dan told me that the subs he most frequently played with were men who were in charge of others in their daily lives—doctors, lawyers, police officers. He thought that their need to relinquish control in leather play was partly a balancing act for these men.

For some gay men, then, the play of the leather world seems to promote wholeness and acceptance. Leather rites provide a ritual balance in these men's lives. But even more, the play seems to be about facing the deep truths about our human condition and our spiritual lives. A half-decade ago, theatre critic and artist Antonin Artaud chastised Western theatre for its obfuscation of the deepest parts of our nature and called for the establishment of a "Theatre of Cruelty," which would deal with "metaphysical reality" rather than those social, psychological, and cultural inventions that obscure our true natures: "Renouncing psychological man, with his well-dissected character and feelings, and social man, submissive to laws and mis-shapen by religions and precepts, the Theatre of Cruelty will address itself only to total man" (1938: 123).

The lure of the leathersex world for gay men should be obvious. Those of us who are trying to cast out homophobic social and psychological demons that have been imposed on our lives and our natures are drawn to rituals where we can experientially face our destructive urges, our vulnerabilities, and our fears. Even though Artaud was scathing toward Western religion's doctrines and dogmas, he wanted to establish his Theatre of Cruelty on the models of ancient and oriental religious traditions, such as those in Bali and Haiti. Our lives lack "brimstone, i.e., a constant magic" because we have turned ourselves into observers who avoid our deepest reality by inventing conceptual and psychological systems of belief. "Far from believing," Artaud writes, "that man invented the supernatural and the divine, I think it is man's age-old intervention which has ultimately corrupted the divine within him" (1938: 8). It is in this Artaudian sense that I have been willing to use the language of spirituality to refer to the rites of the leathersex world.

The Spirit Within
Gay Male Culture as a Spiritual Venue

21

DONALD L. BOISVERT

CENE ONE. Walking up the short, steep flight of stairs, Jason, a fifty-year-old professor in a large university, enters the dark strip bar from the harsh light of a summer afternoon. Squinting, he surveys the interior of the place. A few dancers mill around in their underwear, talking among themselves or with scattered middle-aged clients sipping beers. Jason always takes a table to the side, near the dance floor. He doesn't really like to be the center of attention. Some of the newer dancers approach him, but Jason limits himself to a few conversational banalities, and they walk away slightly miffed. Out of the corner of his eye, he sees Marco, his favorite, striding toward him. Marco has been dancing for a long time, and Jason met him when Marco was going through his cowboy phase. Jason likes the kid (though Marco's now more than thirty), and he has always been unduly generous with him. They order beers and shooters from a former dancer-turned-waiter that Jason also liked. Strippers follow each other on stage, dancing in various stages of undress to their particular choice of songs. Each does two dances: the first, a fast one meant to begin the stripping process and entice potential one-on-one customers; the second fully unclothed, preferably erect. Jason watches each with mixed interest: some are definitely better and more attractive than others. The hours pass. Jason and Marco drink a fair amount. At one point, they decide to move to the more secluded area in the back reserved for lap dancing. It is here that Jason and Marco begin their real interaction, here that Jason thinks he has glimpsed something special.

Scene two. After leaving the bars at three in the morning, Michel, a twenty-seven-year-old local food store manager, walks home. He lives not very far from the city's gay neighborhood, right next to a major park. The air is sharply cool and crisp, one of those delightful autumn nights with a faint smell of firewood on the breeze. Michel feels good. Though slightly drunk, he remains alert enough to see

351

the shadows moving slowly in the darkness as he approaches the park. He was looking for them. There always hangs a slight tinge of danger about this place. Michel has heard stories of people being beaten by roving groups of teenage boys, or of slow police cars with glaring headlights telling people to move on. It doesn't happen all that often, he tells himself gratefully. He's already come here a few times when he was feeling particularly bold or adventuresome, and he likes it. The cover of darkness, the company of other men like him looking for fast sex, the potential for peril at any point: all of this entices him. He feels as though he were acutely alive, standing outside himself, transcendent in a surreal sort of way. Leaning against a tree, he sees two men not far away engaging in oral sex. Shapes gather around, watching them with outstretched hands. An attractive, hairy man walks by, and Michel's eyes follow him carefully. He starts moving toward him to an isolated area of dense bushes and overhanging trees. The sound of footsteps crushing fallen leaves tears the overwhelming silence. The other man stops and turns, and Michel pauses in mid-stride. Full of unspoken desire, each converges slowly on the other.

Scene three. Every year during early-August gay pride week, known officially as Divers/Cité, in Montreal, Gaston, a forty-three–year-old provincial civil servant, goes through a transformation. Usually quite critical of what he sees as the sad emptiness and commercialism of the so-called gay lifestyle, he becomes quite proud of who and what he is at around this time. Seeing all those other gay men in their sexual prime camping it up for the straight world, he realizes that he stands as part of something bigger and far more significant than his isolated self. This year was no different. In fact, it was perhaps more striking in its intensity. The highlight was the parade, as it usually is. The day was incredibly hot and muggy. After brunch with a few close friends, he walks to the major street downtown where the parade will pass. There's loads of excitement in the air, and a lot of puzzled-looking straight people have come to watch the queers make fools of themselves. Gaston always resents that. It makes him feel like a wild animal in a zoo. There's energy in the air. Gaston can almost touch its electrifying force. He has his rainbow pin on his T-shirt and his flag in his back pocket. He feels good today, happy to be part of this celebration marking his place in the world. The music blares from one of the floats as it goes by. Semi-naked men standing on it grind to the wild, loud rhythm. Gaston screams and dances to the beat. Later, after the parade has passed, he and hundreds of other men will follow its trail down to the Gay Village, walking hand-in-hand, celebrating and carousing far into the hot summer night.

Contrary to popular misconception, some of which comes from members of the gay community itself, gay male culture is quite varied and multidimensional. While it is diversified, I want to concentrate on how it is also an intensely eroti-

cized culture. Most importantly, and despite its increasing mainstream commercialization, it remains, in many unexpected ways, a marginalized phenomenon.
Heterosexism still assumes its dominant normative role in this regard, and its values and assumptions still define the unspoken and unwritten rules of cultural homogeneity. As much as gay men may acquire rights and straight allies, their culture,
particularly in its more blatant public or erotic aspects, continues to raise doubts,
suspicions, fears, and anxieties. At times, moral panic ensues. Gay male culture still
disturbs the norm. Some of this reaction is without doubt religiously conditioned.
Some of it, however, comes from the hope for sameness, from the unconscious
wish we all have not to be too different from everyone else.

It is this very difference, this uniquely charged male desire, that can reveal itself
as the special carrier of "a spirit within," of a certain spiritual impulse within gay
male culture. Some gay writers (Boisvert 2000; Johnson 2000; Long 1997, 2001)
make the point that it is from the material elements of gay culture, notably same-
sex male eroticism, that one can discern the roots of a uniquely gay way of appre-
hending the sacred, the transcendent, or the religious. I want to argue, in fact, that
gay male spirituality is both a reappropriation and a reaffirmation of the notion of
religion: first, because it is a deliberate strategy used to counter long-standing religious or moral condemnation and ostracism of what we do and are; second, because it is an engaging discourse spoken from a position of self-acceptance and
pride. In *Out on Holy Ground*, I argue that gay spirituality, or a gay experience of the
religious, consists of three interrelated elements: critical religious discourse, political analysis and engagement, and affirmation of the erotic (Boisvert 2000: 14).
These three components make gay men different from the norm. They speak to
their spirit, their community, and their sexuality. They also address important issues of social positioning and marginality. Where one stands necessarily determines
how one relates to the center. If one hovers near the margins, the center always appears a bit distant and off-kilter.

I agree that for the sociologist or anthropologist of religion, religion is above
all a social and cultural construct. Revelation and faith, as critical as these may be
to the theologian or apologist of religion, do not normally enter into the equation, except as pieces of the picture to be studied or the puzzle to be solved. One
major theoretical stream argues that religion and society are coextensive, and that
the power of the latter is founded on, and located in, the former. More precisely,
it is at moments of social extremity, of intense and collective effervescence, that
certain euphoric states are produced in the participating individuals, and these
states then give rise to the religious impulse. This impulse is really only the concentrated power of society, or of the group, itself (Durkheim 1915: 22). Social
or collective effervescence best occurs in group ritual settings, when persons isolated from the mainstream re-create euphoric states of excitement that reinforce

group solidarity and cohesion (Bird 1980), much like a gay pride festival. These "social rites," apart from producing states of agitation or frenzy, serve to solidify and "sacralize" group identities, the very foundation of social or cultural unity (Mol 1976). In addition to classic queer theory (see Annamarie Jagose [1996]), more recent work by Björn Krondorfer (1996) on male bodies and religion, by Karmen MacKendrick (1999) on pleasure, and by Robert Goss and Mona West (2000) and Ken Stone (2001) on queer scriptural studies have opened up new vistas with respect to the theological and social construction of male homoerotic desire—or queer desire more generally—as sites for the emergence and acting out of a religious and spiritual impulse.

I focus on three specific forms or "sites" of gay male culture in this essay: the first, the gay strip bar where we meet Jason; second, Michel's gay public cruising space; and third, Gaston's annual religious highlight, the public celebration of gay pride and identity. I have chosen these three sites because (a) they speak to issues of erotic sensibility and marginality, and how the two are interconnected, (b) they raise questions with respect to contested notions of public space and its occupation by the nonnormative, and (c) they touch upon issues of identity, both cultural and political. I propose an understanding of these three cultural forms as unique and dynamic manifestations of a distinctively gay male spiritual sensibility. Not only can they give rise to a sense of the religious, but, for some gay men, they can be in and of themselves intensely spiritual experiences.

My urban setting is Montreal, certainly one of North America's premier gay destinations, known for its active and open gay lifestyle and such well-attended mega-events as the Black and Blue circuit party. As well, Montreal boasts some of the best and most openly permissive strip clubs on the continent, in addition to having the largest number of saunas. Much that is noted, however, can be applied to any similar gay urban environment. One of the distinguishing marks of contemporary gay life, at least in the North American urban context, is its relative homogeneity, despite the differences that help account for the rich and intricate tapestry of a given locale.

A Touch of the Sublime

Montreal is a city where male strip joints occupy a vital place in the ecology of gay life. At any given time, some six or seven such clubs are in operation. They remain one of the city's main drawing cards for gay tourists, particularly American. What distinguishes them from most other clubs found in similar large North American cities are the facts that the dancers dance naked and erect and that lap dancing is not considered illegal in Canada. Patrons can therefore delight in the visual benefits of an aroused dancer, while enjoying their charms one-on-one in a more secluded area if they feel so inclined. The posted rate for a lap dance is six dollars but the actual cost is ten dollars, more if intimate touching or some form of sexual activity is involved (though this remains rare). The names of the clubs evoke masculine, exotic images: Campus, Adonis, Stock, Taboo, and Nirvana. On weekends, particularly holidays, they are packed. For those clubs that are open from 3 p.m. to 3 a.m. (the closing time for bars in Montreal), there are two distinct shifts of dancers: the 3 p.m. to 9 p.m., who tend to be considerably younger, into drugs, and at times into hustling; and the 9 p.m. to 3 a.m., who are older, muscular, and occasionally professionals. Each group appears equally disdainful of the other (see DeMarco 2002).

Jason's preferred club is Campus, the oldest in the city, and his choice time is the afternoon. He has been coming here for several years, more regularly at certain periods. He has his favorites: dancers he has known for a long time, or with whom he gets on especially well. Jason is a fifty-year-old professional, highly educated, with a disposable income. He treats the dancers, particularly his usual coterie of three or four, very well, and often pays handsomely for private dances. This "buys" him their loyalty and time when he is present. In the highly demanding environment that is his professional life, Jason finds the strip bar therapeutic. It permits him to transcend many of the constraints and demands, whether self-imposed or enforced by others, that constitute his daily existence. He occasionally goes on binges of excess, spending and drinking quite heavily with some of the dancers. He sees these times as positively beneficial. They allow him to escape temporarily from the normal tedium of everyday life, while making it possible for him to glimpse, if only fleetingly, something beyond the smug facade of the routinely habitual and perhaps to enter into communion with it.

Jason believes that the strip bar constitutes a place of insight. He comes here "to play," as he is fond of asserting when asked about why he frequents such places. In fact, he despises those hungry and desperate men who naively assume that the strip club will bring them love eternal, or that one of its boys will suddenly transform himself into the gracious and perfect life companion. Apart from playing, Jason also comes to think. "I like going to the dancer clubs," he states, "because they are so much outside, so unlike my daily life. They allow me to indulge in a certain form of hedonism which is neither threatening nor dangerous, like playing a game. In a way, strip bars are safe: sexually, emotionally, and even physically. I can make believe, and I have a great deal of power." As well, they reaffirm his fondness for the enticements found beyond the limits of his conventional existence. "Being there really takes me outside and beyond myself, almost as though I were finally tapping into my true nature as a pleasure-loving gay man. I don't sleep around, but I like playing these sexual games with the strippers."

When he goes in the back with Marco or some other favorite for a lap dance, Jason enters a highly ritualized space that is circumscribed by the dual forces of money and eroticism. At its core, this remains a financial transaction, one obviously marked by the fluid exchange of power: monetary for Jason, the client; sexual for Marco, the service provider. This dynamic is well understood by both parties, though it is rarely alluded to in any overt or blatant way. Jason pays handsomely, so he is allowed a fair measure of latitude with respect to physical touching. Intimate touching is often invited by Marco. There appears to be an unusual emotional bond between the two, no doubt due to their long-standing client–dancer relationship. "I've known this kid for almost ten years, and I've spent a lot of money on him. Of course I have feelings for him," claims Jason. Yet the potent combination of alcohol, music, sex, and power sets the stage for something that goes well beyond a simple pecuniary exchange. "The place of insight" alluded to by Jason is also a site of transcendence, of the sublime.

Gay writer Frank Browning (1995: 99–100) speaks perceptively of this uncommon experience:

> . . . many of these men only find it possible to explore the unity of the flesh and the spirit in the shrouds of night. They sit, gazing on the star-boys. They reach up to touch forbidden flesh, and they gratefully deposit their offering—a single, a five, a ten, occasionally a twenty—into the gym sox that ride above the boys' leather boots. In that moment—sad surely, undeniably objectified, and utterly ritualized—there is often, if not always or even usually, a sublime unity of spirit and flesh, a touch of continuity in a cold, greedy, brutal, and discontinuous city. . . . To be in a state of contemplative solitude is not to withdraw and sever the spiritual from the physical, but to order and contain the physical in sublime celebration of the continuity between spirit and flesh.

Browning's notions of sublimity and contemplation are key to understanding the gay male strip joint as a place of potential spiritual insight.

For Jason, the gay male strip joint offers a radically sensual hiatus from ordinary existence and from its mundane and occasionally impossible demands. In this sense, it is a venue that makes extraordinary things possible. It is a place "set apart," a uniquely gay space wherein the most uninhibited forms of erotic play and power can be safely and confidently indulged. In this environment, a number of things happen to Jason. First, he enters a make-believe, almost surreal world that breaks with that of the majority. In that instant, he sets himself on the margins of the everyday. In and of itself, this can be a powerfully liberating experience, allowing him to glimpse, with keen critical insight, the limitations and contradictions of what is too often taken for granted. As such, the bar becomes a site of contemplation and special, almost esoteric, knowledge. The physical "journey" from the job at the office to the threshold of this dark and engaging homoerotic site becomes a pilgrimage, full of promise and adventure. The setting of the club itself, with its constant alternation of light and obscurity, and the slippage between the open display on stage and the intimate seclusion of the back cubicles, blurs the too often unassailable lines separating fact from fiction, public from private, the erotic from the rational.

Second, the bar puts on display a spectrum of erotic options and possibilities and, most importantly, it heavily ritualizes them. The monetary transactions, for example, while remaining at the very center of the client–dancer dynamic, assume the qualities of offerings to unattainable gods. A sense of worship permeates the place: from the dancers seductively grinding on their pedestals, tumescent and cocky in their nakedness, grabbing and enticing supplicants in bold, controlling ways, to the clients in the back lifting their unworthy hands to touch and adore naked torsos and rounded backsides or offer total and boundless praise to the phallic deities. The interchange between god and devotee is all embracing, signifying not only a necessary though discrete pecuniary relationship, but also one heavily overlaid with theological and spiritual intent.

Third, the heady mixture of sex, alcohol, music, and money as a power medium sets the stage for the emergence of a very special form of intimacy. Though transactional in nature, as all such human interactions are, it is also conditioned by play, by a type of suspended animation that can only exist in the land of make-believe. As play, it is excessive, creative, and artificial, yet pregnant with moments of awe and wonder. This strip bar becomes the visionary foci of genuine religious feeling and of potential spiritual enlightenment. In religious ceremonies, various liturgical and ritualized forms of expression play a similar role: they intensify and codify feeling, thus giving rise to a sense of suspended, though intensely meaningful, time. Ritual sharpens feeling and radically transforms normal, everyday time. Here in the strip club, the regular yet constantly changing parade of dancers, clothed and unclothed, the intensely charged visual and aural environment focused on the male body and its tumescent member, the slow passing away of the hours, the erotic play and arousal of both client and dancer, the flirting with sexual and financial power dynamics all help fashion a unique world functioning by its own laws and rituals, and by its own sense of unmitigated time. Pleasure remains the cardinal rule.

Finally, Jason experiences a sense of wholeness and integrity, whether between the erotic and the spiritual, the body and the mind, the mundane and the extraordinary, or the transitory and the eternal. Not only is the strip bar a physical and mental space "set apart," but the time spent there is also of a different nature: more flowing, less punctured. The bar provides a glimpse, even if only transitory, of the transcendent. It allows Jason to feel whole, as though the different parts of his life were finally synchronized. "When I go to the strip club, especially if my favorite boys are there, I always leave feeling that something special and out-of-the-ordinary has happened. I remind myself that excess is a good and necessary thing. It really sharpens my appreciation for the other parts of my life. I like that I can experience this sudden shift between what is mundane and boring and what is more extraordinary."

In his use of the term "sublime" to describe the experiences of men who frequent such places as gay strip bars, Browning (1995: 101) does not speak of fixed, changeless moments, but rather of constant transposition:

> By the sublime I don't mean the merely beautiful, although, of course, only the most conventionally beautiful men are chosen to dance atop the bar. Unlike the figures on a Grecian urn, these men are not preserved in timeless eternity. They are momentary. They will be replaced. The hardness of their bodies and of their market strength will soften and sag. They may, in only a few years, compete with their current customers for space on the bar stools. That is the key to the rapture.

The sublime, then, moves beyond the surface intensity of the here-and-now. It taps into some eternal core verities: the cyclical and ever-changing reality of the natural world, and the artificial line separating matter from spirit. When Jason admires his dancing boys, it is as though he were worshipping the eternal spirit, for he knows instinctively that they are part and parcel of the cycle of life and that they are able to take him outside and beyond himself onto a different plane. "Some of my friends say that I exaggerate the meaning of what is really only a strip bar with hustler dancers. But I'm not convinced. There's a real pleasure in taking the time to indulge in this. I see things differently. It charges me."

Gods of the Night

As with any other urban environment, Montreal has its public spaces for gay sex, though these invariably shift over time as the gay population itself undergoes social and cultural mutation. Man-on-man sex can occur anywhere, subject only to the imaginations of its participants and the tolerance of inhabitants and the local police. Streets and alleyways still remain popular sites of sexual activity. In years past, two of the more well-frequented spaces were a park in the eastern part of the downtown core, known as Parc La Fontaine, located on the margins of the gay neighborhood, and "the mountain," a large wooded area and park that dominates the city skyline. These two locales have assumed almost mythological stature in Montreal gay folklore. Activity has shifted away from these places more recently, however, due in no small measure to recurring and periodic waves of police crackdown. Parc La Fontaine, for example, is located next to a police station. Cruising there late at night is still considered risky business. Though Montreal may have a reputation as a more open and tolerant environment for gays than is perhaps the case in similar North American urban settings, this does not mean that public sex, as everywhere, does not remain stigmatized, suspicious, and highly problematic.

Public sex plays upon, and ultimately undermines, the very familiar distinction between the public and private domains. With the emergence of a postmodern view of sexuality that understands human sexual behavior to be unstable and diffused, this distinction has come under strong and persistent attack (see Leap 1999). "Public" and "private" are best understood as fluid categories, heavily contingent upon social hierarchy and cultural notions of propriety. In the same way, they are tied to sexual identity. Men, for example, tend to engage in public sexual activity far more frequently than women, largely because their sexuality is considerably less tied to fixed forms of conventionality. Gay men share these masculine privileges, even while their sexual marginality frees them to experiment with the contingency and risk of the anonymous sexual exchange. In this sense, gay men are doubly "privileged."

In his classic study of sex in washrooms, Laud Humphreys (1970) underscores the highly structured nature of gay male public sex, and the particular role that silence plays in these interactions, arguing that ". . . there exists a sort of democracy that is endemic to impersonal sex" (Leap 1999: 34). Finally, some activists and scholars have challenged, from the perspective of queer politics, the culturally contingent nature of queer sexualities and their public construction (Warner, ed. 1993). From this viewpoint, public, impersonal sex between men partakes of the process of gay world construction in that, on the one hand, it creates alternate gay public spaces while, on the other, it subverts traditionally heterosexual definitions and usage of these sites.

As Michel leans uncertainly into the bulky body of his anonymous companion, he engages himself with those hidden faces and hands, down through the centuries, that have stroked and kissed each other under the silent cover of night. Just as desire begets religion, so ostracism begets subversion. The secret Dionysian ritual of excess and mad fervor is recreated under the contemporary guise of anonymous strangers groping each other feverishly and silently. Michel reflects on the experience:

> I feel so alert and sexy when I cruise the park late at night. It's like a hunt. The one thing that keeps me going is my need for sex. I feel like an animal driven only by his instincts. Of course it's risky, but that's a big part of the thrill. I never know who I'll meet or end up having sex with.

Many years ago, a close friend, now dead from AIDS, brought me to the secluded spot on "the mountain" where men would have sex. I was quite struck by it, and wrote the following description of the experience as something primitively religious:

> The sacred rite begins as the worshipers gather around the most beautiful of their number, the young god leaning seductively against a tree. Men in T-shirts with their jeans open, caressing themselves invitingly. He stares in awe and wonder, still unsure of why he is here. Groups form in circles and then disperse, naked shapes moving libidinously across the damp forest floor. Kneeling men raise their arms to naked chests, touching the chiseled bodies of the gods, eating the flesh and drinking the holy liquids. The dampness of the leaves mingles with the exciting mustiness and scent of males. Off in the distance, faintly, he hears the clatter of hooves. He fears these guardians of law and order, their heavy beasts bearing down sacrilegiously on this liturgy of desire and transgression. But he need not fear. It is only the mad god crossing the centuries, come to be with his own. (2000: 95)

Michel's participation in anonymous sex in a public park after curfew parallels this scene of men engaging in an orgy on "the mountain" in the very early hours of a spring dawn. The vivid intensity and transcendence of the moment, aided by the erotic charge of equally desirable and desiring men, are what give it the aura of a spiritual experience. Michel explains:

> I wouldn't necessarily call my experience of public sex a religious experience, basically because I'm not a religious person. But there's no doubt that something mysterious and almost primitive happens. I feel so open and alive; my senses are on maximum alert. Maybe that's what having an experience of God is all about.

Here again, the artificial line between the erotic and the religious collapses. As Georges Bataille (Rambuss 1998: 1) wrote: "The underlying affinity between sanctity and transgression has never ceased to be felt. Even in the eyes of believers, the libertine is nearer to the saint than the man without desire."

In considering gay public sex as a form of spiritual exercise or enlightenment, several elements need to be examined. The most significant has to do with the collapse of the private–public dichotomy, thereby making possible a reappropriation of everyday heterosexual spaces as sites of potential same-sex erotic encounters. This is obviously a subversive activity. It calls into question, at a profound level, the cultural construction of heteronormativity and its claims on who does and does not belong in its public spaces. In many respects, this is a necessary process of liberation, not only politically but also spiritually. The circumstances and mood are also important: "the cover of night allows for the emergence of a sense of mythical time and space where everything and anything can be created anew through the simple yet disturbing touch of the unknown" (Boisvert 2000: 83). This shift in perception, which opens up the participants to any number of extraordinary experiences, parallels, in some fundamental ways, the process of religious illumination wherein spiritual awakening is a function of the acuity of the senses. By no means negligible is the ritual edifice that structures and conditions these public sexual encounters. Everything involved—from the expected and necessary silence to the rules governing sexual role taking—is marked by a fluid choreographic flavor. The sexual exchanges themselves, as spontaneous as they may appear at first glance, remain strongly conditioned by an atmosphere of illegality and risk-taking. Such dangerous excitement no doubt plays into the exceptional intensity of the experience.

Michel's forays into this land of public sexual contacts in the dead of night make him feel not only alive, but also in solidarity and communion with others like him. Even within the gay community itself, those who engage in such activities stand in a minority. Despite this, the bonds created by the electrifying charge of anonymous erotic attraction, by the unspoken pull between "the hunted" and "the hunter" and between "dark, handsome strangers," impart to Michel a precious and tangible sense of belonging and desire. The fact that such desire can be acted out secretly yet boldly in a public venue, under the cover of darkness and supposed wrongdoing, only serves to heighten the intensity of the experience for him. When he returns to the solitude of his home, he feels grateful for this glimpse of life's uncertain, transcendental urges. As with Jason, he has gone beyond himself: "I love the fact that I can do these things outside in the dark. The greatest part is just as dawn is breaking. Everything is covered in this soft light. It's like another world. Listen, I lead a pretty boring life. Sex in the park brings excitement into it. When I crawl into bed, it's like I've touched another dimension of life, something I don't get to feel everyday."

A Call to Remembrance

Montreal's 2001 lesbian, gay, bisexual, and transgendered pride celebration, also known as Divers/Cité, was a ten-day public extravaganza consisting of some forty events, culminating in a huge pride parade and street celebration. With close to one million participants and spectators, the attendance reached its highest level ever. As with most similar activities marking the anniversary of Stonewall, it attracted its usual mixture of curious onlookers and flamboyant, extravagant partygoers. The most striking element of the extensive schedule of activities was its remarkable diversity. Attempts were made to appeal to all segments of the divergent sexual communities: drag shows, Latino nights, academic conferences, and lesbian cinema. In a city known for its never-ending cycle of festivals, whether jazz, comedy, or film, throughout the warm summer months, Divers/Cité stands in a class by itself. It is certainly one of the best attended, and its open events are among the most widely sought after. Though it remains very much a confident, loud, and celebratory affirmation of sexual difference, Divers/Cité still manages to appeal to the more mainstream heterosexual population, as witnessed by the large number of families who are seen cheering the parade. Its spirit is exuberant and festive, but it is also a time of remembrance and defiant assertion for the gay, lesbian, and transvestite communities (transsexuals and bisexuals are, in fact, considerably less visible). History is once again reclaimed through the act of the feast.

Gaston has attended several pride celebrations over the years. His response to them tends to vary depending on the current political context and his own state of mind. Generally, they elicit a two-tiered response from him: at the level of his identity and self-acceptance as a gay man and in terms of his sense of belonging to, and identification with, the wider gay community. The two can also be synonymous; they can, in fact, hardly be separated. Gaston told me, "I'm a rather shy person, and public shows of gay pride tend to make me nervous. But I like Divers/Cité. There are so many of us. It's great. It makes me really feel that I'm not alone. For once, the world belongs to us. We're on the stage." By publicly affirming his desires, Divers/Cité brings a sense of common brotherhood and solidarity to Gaston's identity as a gay man, thereby creating a firm bond between the social and the personal. A sense of wholeness emerges from the festivities. It is this integration of too often dimorphic identities that characterizes the impact of gay pride celebrations on both the individual and the broader culture. By positioning himself as an out, proud gay man with others who are like him and in being able to declare this publicly at the very heart of a heterosexist world, Gaston can attain a state of integrity and wholeness, one not unlike what the person of faith may experience.

Durkheim's (1915) concept of "effervescent social environments" is synonymous with human festivity and celebration. A feast is a collective ritual whose purpose is to recreate euphoric states of mind in its participants. It evokes a strong sense of something transcendent and far more important and meaningful than the disparate identities of those persons who may be involved. Though collective in structure and content, it remains intensely psychological in its impact on the participants. A feast is also representational: it mediates, via mixed symbolic categories and images, that which it is meant to recall or remember. As with all forms of ritual expression, it wavers between spontaneity and ossification. Feasts are in a state of permanent flux. Most importantly, the feast recalls time and transcends it. It is an extraordinary moment wherein the past, present, and future become merged as one. Eternity is in the here-and-now, and vice versa. In this sense, a feast is a paradigmatic event. It is a memorial, a return to the original times. Though deliberately transgressive of everyday cultural norms and boundaries, a feast's apparent anarchism is really meant to reassert social cohesion, either within the group itself or between the group and the broader social network. A feast thus "sacralizes" identity, while at the same time "fixing it" within conventional cultural categories.

Gay pride celebrations recall the birth of the modern gay liberation movement at New York City's Stonewall Inn in June 1969. This one historical event has become a universal symbol of gay and lesbian resistance and affirmation. Wherever and whenever pride celebrations are held around the world, the emblematic continuity with Stonewall is reclaimed and reaffirmed.

> Stonewall functions in a symbolic register as a convenient if somewhat spurious marker of an important cultural shift away from assimilationist policies and quietist tactics, a significant if mythological date for the origin of the gay liberation movement. (Jagose 1996: 30)

Pride festivities therefore integrate personal identity with transcendent and transnational historical identity. In addition, the loud and brash celebrations not only underscore a visible and self-confident public gay presence, they claim individual gay men for that same gay community. The personal, by virtue of the highly conspicuous fact of being "out" and "in your face," becomes the defiantly and jovially political. Marching down the center of main street in drag or leather, as commonplace and as much of a spectator sport as it may have become, still challenges and subverts the hegemonic claims of heterosexuality. Gay pride celebrations retain a subversive streak. As any dynamic feast must, they question, if only temporarily, the seemingly normal.

The effervescence of the pride celebrations taps into a variety of issues and feelings operating at different levels: psychological, sociological, political, and, by no means least, religious. At its most basic, the intensity of the festivities, whether visually or audibly, marks both participants and onlookers with a sense of excess. This is its convivial, intensely social dimension. The endless parties that distinguish the celebrations—and the consequent use and overuse of alcohol and other mood-altering substances—induce a state of revelry and carousal. Almost everything becomes possible under these unusual conditions, from the mildly amusing to the intensely sexual. Psychologically, people feel as though they can transcend any limit. At the social level, the cohesion and camaraderie of those who, on this one day, choose to affirm themselves publicly as gay, lesbian, and particularly transvestite or transsexual, create a temporarily safe space for the display and modeling of alternative gender roles in society. For gays and lesbians, this presents a perfect occasion for them to live fully out in the open; for the curious onlookers, it serves to remind them of the presence and continuous deployment of difference in their midst.

Of course, these celebrations are an intensely political affair, if for no other reason than that they remind the politicians of the influence and clout of this particular segment of the voting public. The political aspect is a matter of personal statement. At the tail end of the pride parade, for example, thousands of people—straight, gay, lesbian, or bi—march and dance, de facto "outing" themselves in a very public way to friends, acquaintances, and strangers alike. This has been my own experience. I have seen colleagues from work as well as familiar faces marching. Some I suspected were gay or lesbian, others I knew were straight and just there out of a sense of solidarity. But one is always kept guessing, because one is never completely sure. This deployment of sexual and erotic ambiguities is a typically postmodern phenomenon.

To say that Montreal's annual pride celebrations are a source of religious insight for Gaston means that they contain within them the possibility of spiritual awakening and transcendence. If spirituality is really about wholeness and integrity, then gay pride can do these things. When he attends and participates in the festivities, Gaston is making a statement both to himself and to others about who and what he is. More importantly, he chooses to reaffirm publicly that he is not alone, but rather part of a much larger vibrant community, one that celebrates and remembers with pride its birth at the revolutionary moment that was Stonewall. The act of remembering is a spiritual one. When Gaston marches in the parade or dances the night away, he remembers not only himself but all those who have walked in silence, and he claims them as constituent of his own gay life:

> I like that I can march in the parade and feel part of something big and powerful, almost as if I was walking through history. I know we've been hated and killed and all that, and I guess that bothers me. But I'm proud that we're still here. We're real survivors.

Desiring and Celebrating "The Sprit Within"

Spirituality deals with questions of transcendence and ultimate meaning: Why am I here? What is the purpose of my life? How can I best live a moral existence? When the same or similar questions are asked of a community, the focus shifts slightly: Why do we exist as a distinctive group? What role do we play in the world? How can we best embody and live out our collective values? These sets of questions are, of course, interrelated. The individual does not stand apart from the group, and vice versa. Meaning, though it can be an intensely personal construct, ultimately draws its grounding and force from a shared perception of certain common values. In the case of individuals or communities "at the edges," however, the equation is not so simple or clear-cut. A sharp disjunction can and often does exist between the expectations of the broader culture on the one hand and those of the marginalized individuals on the other. Compelling existential questions of meaning are thus often asked in a context of opposition and counter-definition.

Ultimately, spiritual questions are forged from the material "stuff" of culture. In this sense, gay male culture is no different. What differentiates it, however, is that the "stuff" of gay male culture does retain a distinctively erotic coloring. The norms, values, aspirations, and worldviews of gay men, though no doubt similar in many respects to those of the heterosexual majority, manage to contain and exhibit their own uniquely bold standards. Foremost among these, and by no means to be neglected, dismissed, or underestimated, is homoerotic desire. Not only does it separate gay men from other men, it also embodies the quality that makes them atypical and distinctive. This desire and need for other men, because it is so central to the experience of what it means to be gay, is the only legitimate grounds upon which a distinctively gay male spiritual sensibility can be constructed, and the most fitting outlet for its expression. When Jason touches his dancing boy, or Michel his twilight stranger, or Gaston his partying friends, they all embody, in a very real and tangible sense, the special transcendence found and celebrated in and through homoerotic desire. Sexual marginality and the erotic can serve as the gateway to a form of spiritual awakening, just as desire can be the spark that opens up unspoken and untapped sources of insight.

For gay men, our bodies and same-sex erotic cravings condition our approach to what is holy or sacred in our lives, including our life cycles. In a recent article on the spirituality of aging within the gay community, Ron Long writes:

> Indeed, we are the stuff such dreams are made of. And such dreams fire our moral imagination. In the radical religion which I sketch here, that religion in which piety towards the sources and conditions of our lives, and a worshipful regard for the compellingness of the wholly desirable, replaces faith in god—in such a religiosity, a person must content him or herself with so negotiating with necessity that we might nevertheless witness to the authoritativeness of the morally compelling impossible dream of heaven. Indeed, therein lies the religious art of life. (2001: 105)

Long touches upon the core of what a gay spiritual vision might look and feel like, and of what Jason, Michel, and Gaston might, in their various homoerotic peregrinations, aspire to. Long speaks of a world—and of a religion—in which desire replaces the notion of the divine. He argues that this is a moral way of living, compelling individuals to create sites of worship and contemplation from the very fabric of their lives. In the manner in which Jason, Michel, and Gaston choose to live their gay lives, and in the language that they use to describe their encounters, there emerges an overwhelming sense of gay culture as potentially spiritually powerful. Whether this be in terms of the sublime, the excessive, or the commemorative, the tableau of gay male culture as spiritual venue is a varied and shifting one, for, in the words of Long, "therein lies the religious art of life." For gay men, celebrating "the spirit within" is a deliberately subversive attempt at reclaiming institutionalized religious discourse—mythic, symbolic, and ritualistic—for themselves. It is, at heart, the best and boldest kind of religion. It is also a rich and salutary engagement with desire as a form of spiritual discipline, a practice of the heart and of the soul that tempers as much as it liberates, and which ultimately can be the source and the path of our spiritual journey.

Gay religion remains rooted in desire. It represents a form of spiritual practice that draws its inspiration and sustenance from the erotic and emotional needs that men have for other men. The culture that gay men fabricate for themselves, as fast-changing as it may appear at times, necessarily conditions and illuminates their modes of religious expression. Too often, this culture is neglected or ignored as a legitimate and enriching source of spiritual engagement, generally because it is dismissed as superficial and transitory. On the contrary, it needs to be understood and valued as a fertile source of potential illumination. Homoerotic desire, as with any other form of human exigency, taps into the wholly and unalterably transcendent. The strip club, the cruising park, the pride celebration, or any other site of gay male affirmation all contain within themselves endless and luxuriant possibilities. The spirit moves within, the better to express itself without.

Conclusion: Gay Religion as a Cultural Production

R. MARIE GRIFFITH

NOT SO LONG AGO, the title *Gay Religion* would have seemed absurdly discrepant. How could religion—popularly coded as institutional, hierarchical, conservative, and fixed—pair smoothly with what many traditionalist sectors still deem an unorthodox if not aberrant or even heretical sexual orientation? Even as separate categories, "gay" and "religion" have lengthy histories of debate, spiced with the fury of groups dueling over cultural thresholds reckoned to separate normal from deviant, masculine from feminine, good from evil. Conjoined, the phrase starkly evokes these lasting moral conflicts, obscuring commonplace sexual (and spiritual) caprice while fabricating a kind of ersatz clarity. However familiar in contemporary parlance, "gay" and "religion" each splinter apart under scrutiny, and their union sounds a jangled note.

Stoking this unease is the pivotal role each rubric has played in rendering the other alien. Particularly since the mid-twentieth century, religious persons and institutions have, often via repudiation, helped forge the American history of homosexuality. The best known instance is fundamentalist Baptist Jerry Falwell's long campaign against gays as the apotheosis of America's supposed devolution into wickedness, even blaming them (along with so-called pagans, abortionists, and feminists) for the terrorist attacks of 11 September 2001. Religious settings that professedly shun such histrionics have nonetheless waged choleric battles over ordaining gay men and lesbians to pastoral ministry, spawning new forms of sectarianism while aligning estimable institutions such as Princeton Theological Seminary more closely with Falwellian ultraism than recent generations had cause to foretell. Pedophilia scandals involving Catholic priests and bishops have spurred still more frothy condemnations of homosexuality—decried in some circles as the alleged root of child molestation—and so further complicated hopes for reasoned reflection. Even the brutal murder of gay Wyoming college student Matthew Shepard suited religious antigay activism: a Primitive Baptist church in Topeka, Kansas, for instance, manufactured a gruesome online image in which an actual photograph of Shepard is shown "burning in hell" and screaming in pain while paying for his sexual sins (http://www.godhatesfags.com). These and kindred instances advise onlookers that self-identifying as gay amid this bloated American religious hostility entails some shocking hazards. This reality has, in turn, dramatically politicized the issue of homosexuality by motivating gay persons and their allies to conduct fresh assaults on religiously evinced contempt.

Viewed from the reverse angle, gay persons and organizations have played a proportionately dynamic role in remolding American religious attitudes and networks, forcing institutions to clarify their views on sexuality and in some cases to advertise their inclusiveness so as to dissociate themselves from their religious confreres. Assailing homophobic establishments such as Topeka's crusading church, many religious persons have sought to create alternatives and new alliances, some abandoning cherished creedal loyalties in favor of seemingly more flexible structures of spiritual practice and communal worship. In the varied cycles of mutual influence, this revisionist impulse has thrust sundry factions toward increased leniency while others preach more sternly against so-called sexual perversion. Conservative religious folk offer a personally credible, even if legally untenable, defense of their own pure intentions when they assert that their heightened antagonism has evolved not from hatred—"hate the sin, love the sinner" is their motto—but from their resistance to militant demands for sexual license that, they believe, God simply forbids. Whatever private convictions abide behind the wrath spewing from all sides, we well know that religious neutrality on gay issues has become nearly impossible to sustain. If this volume's attempt to collate a disparate bundle of studies under the singular designation "gay religion" jolts some readers' sensibilities, it is partly because we grasp this fact of widely variant responses to ever escalating conditions.

Paradoxically, however, amid the more recent explosion of scholarly interest in gay history, transsexualism, intersexuality, and queer theory, the title *Gay Religion* may already feel familiar. By now books abound at this very crossroads: readers have for some time made use of memoirs such as Mel White's *Stranger at the Gate: To Be Gay and Christian in America* (1995) or life story compilations such as Leyland's *Queer Dharma: Voices of Gay Buddhists* (1998); as well as numerous case studies of homosexuality within particular denominations and broader traditions, from John Boswell's *Christianity, Social Tolerance, and Homosexuality* (1980) to Mark Jordan's *The Silence of Sodom: Homosexuality in Modern Catholicism* (2000), among others. Beyond these genres, witness a range of prescriptive and descriptive treatments such as Toby Johnson's *Gay Spirituality* (2000); Christian de la Huerta's *Coming Out Spiritu-*

ally (1999); Peter Sweasey's *From Queer to Eternity: Spirituality in the Lives of Lesbian, Gay and Bisexual People* (1997); Arlene Swidler's *Homosexuality and World Religions* (1993) ; and, above all, Gary David Comstock and Susan E. Henking's sizeable essay collection, *Que(e)rying Religion: A Critical Anthology* (1997), which assembles a broad spectrum of previously published work on gay religion by historians, anthropologists, theologians, and biblical scholars.

One is obliged to acknowledge the impressive range of scholarly reflection establishing a vital foundation for Scott Thumma and Edward R. Gray's current contribution to this oeuvre. What these other volumes do not do is effectively scrutinize the distinct multiplicity of contemporary gay religious experience in the United States, and for that reason alone the current text is an essential addition to the literature. The fine-grained descriptions of the individual essays argue still further for the book's distinction.

As with any edited collection—any book, for that matter—this one is inevitably finite, and contributors would doubtless acknowledge that there is far more multiplicity within both gay life and lived religion than a single volume can convey. Comprehensiveness is impossible, everyone knows, and I do not wish to raise trifling quibbles about editorial selectivity, particularly in a volume as rich as this one.

To a historian's eye, though, a more pressing taxonomical issue buzzes too insistently to blink away. Recent studies of identity and culture have raised suspicions of overarching models that reify loaded descriptors such as gay (among others), so that it is by now impossible to avoid grappling with the limits of this kind of representationality. Here, then, we need to ask: what counts as gay religion and what valuations are implied by that classifying scheme? How is this categorically different from other identifications—say, those surrounding women and gender, including feminist religion—that have increasingly come under fire for being conceptually naive or even politically ineffectual? Is the typology offered here—institutional units, subaltern expressions, and manifestations within popular culture—adequate and does it help us learn something new, or does it simplify, even if inadvertently, the profoundly pluralistic nature of both religious experience and gay experience in America? At a time when many critics have labored to refine, or even depose, social contrivances that once assigned persons to discrete social types corresponding to distinct bodies—woman/man, lesbian/straight, black/white, and even Protestant/Catholic/Jew/Muslim/or the like—it is worth asking whether workaday categories of sexuality and religion remain sufficient.

In my assignment to comment broadly upon this collection and to contextualize gay religion within the broad span of American religious history, I want to exert some pressure on these framing devices, for as heuristic tools they are not wholly straightforward. Proceeding in this way allows me to review some entrenched assumptions of our historical moment, from those pertaining to the development of religion in the United States to others relating to current theoretical models of subjectivity. Let me clarify that I am not in any way singling out Thumma and Gray or their contributors for criticism, as if they somehow lag behind the rest of their field: to the contrary, addressing the question of categories at this relatively advanced stage of gay/lesbian/queer studies requires first recognizing (and regretting) how belatedly we American religionists are entering much longer scholarly conversations and debates.

As the editors note, the best-known conversations about sexuality in religious studies have been limited to normative and ethical concerns. Considering the wealth of sexuality studies in classical scholarship, medieval studies, and the history of early modern Europe—not to mention the many parallel investigations within U.S. social history circles—the neglect of American religionists across the humanities and social science disciplines is conspicuous. My task, as I see it and as the editors have generously allowed, is to wrestle with this field-wide reticence, using the current volume as a convenient starting point into broader questions of interpretive significance. These comments aim, in short, to query the premises beneath the morphology of "gay religion," to note how paradigms shift in order to make room for this sphere of inquiry, and above all to suggest further contributions that a compilation of this and related kinds may make to our broader understanding of religion in America.

In their introduction, Thumma and Gray describe American religious history as being composed of two competing yet deeply interconnected impulses: an attachment to tradition, on the one hand, and an inclination toward innovation and experimentation, on the other. As they rightly point out, these impulses have not resulted in distinct or separate trajectories but have, instead, mutually influenced and abetted one another. Within the historiography of American religion, scholars have long credited two historical phenomena as the root for these interlaced impulses: on the side of tradition, there is the long trajectory of Protestant ascendancy and influence upon the American nation and society; while on the side of experimentation, there weighs the inheritance of "disestablishment," free competition, voluntarism, and church-state separation through which religion stands independent from government control. Historical treatments from the Swiss-born American church historian Philip Schaff's *America* (first published in English in 1855 and later republished by Perry Miller in 1961) to Sydney Ahlstrom's monumental tome, *A Religious History of the American People* (1972), have sought to interpret this mix of Protestant dominance and religious autonomy.[1] By being freed from state interference, Schaff and many others have argued, religion in America was saved from falling into the irrelevance that was the fate of established religion in much of Europe. The voluntarism of American forms of faith proved to be a source of both vitality and proliferation, opening the way for a dazzling array of inventive rival fellowships. Nevertheless, whether the offshoots were Protestant in origin or non-Protestant immigrant religions, many religions sought survival and expansion by claiming allegiance to tradition, often looking back to their primitive origins in a supposed Golden Age that had ostensibly been lost.

Numerous variations have been offered on these cardinal themes, not only by historians but also increasingly by social scientists interested in applying market models to patterns of religious participation. This is not the place to review in detail the vast scope of these efforts, but certainly in their most general sense, the themes of tradition and experimentation have rarely encountered wholesale opposition. Academic and popular commentators have so tirelessly invoked this dance between custom and innovation, in fact, that one could argue that it has become a kind of catchall explanation for every new topic of interest.

Here is where things get interesting, however, for it is precisely the prosaic quality of this model that has long allowed representatives of "new" religious movements, along with their supporters, to show that they practice religion like other Americans and hence deserve recognition. New immigrant religions have recurrently worked for both social and sometimes legal acceptance in the United States in part by adopting a kind of established church model that normalizes tradition while also celebrating a limited degree of experimentation and innovation. Examples from early Mormonism to early-twentieth-century Hindu and Buddhist movements to much later legal battles over Santería come to mind. New or shifting religious expressions birthed at home may follow similar patterns of seeking legitimacy—one can even think of paganism or Wicca in this regard, characterized by insistence both upon historical continuity with pre-Christian traditions and upon presumably boundless freedom of spiritual play. Relying upon truisms about historical continuity and change, establishment and experimentation, normalizes both the phenomena under consideration and the scholarly attention paid to such phenomena. Scholars of American religion are trained to think this way: here, we say, are legitimate topics of investigation because they follow long-established patterns of adaptation and accommodation to American structural norms of religious propagation. Following this logic, as the editors have, the study of gay religion is as legitimate a field of scholarly religious study as any other.

One can be, as I am, in complete accord with this final conclusion while feeling some discomfort with this way of establishing authenticity. Asserting that gay religion fits into existing interpretive frameworks, these being broad enough to accommodate historical unfolding of many kinds, may ultimately prove less resourceful than permitting new interpretations to burst forth from the material worlds of gay religion. Others have also noted that the urge to dovetail with established explanatory models rings contrary to creative reassessment of the changing role of religion in American society. Theologian Ronald Long, to name an example from gay theological circles, has persuasively argued against the conservative impulse to normalize (or perhaps heterosexualize) homosexuality by disavowing the promiscuous gay ghetto as an embarrassing or immoral aberration. For Long, as for some of the contributors in the third section of this volume, notably Paul J. Gorrell, Thomas V. Peterson, and Donald L. Boisvert, this world of cruising and anonymous sex may itself be interpreted as religious.[2] While such religiousness may beg for fuller evidential grounding (and I return to this point), these and other authors rightly note the inadequacy of overlooking extravagant sexual practices—whether of so-called gays, straights, or anyone else—in hopes of portraying compliance with wider behavioral norms. One could likewise argue against domesticating gay religious history by making it conform to other spiritual castings, as if conservative ire would thence abate before the airy spectacle of a wholesome religious orientation.

As most who study lived religion have come to realize, religion is not a particularly chaste or predictable venue once surface pieties give way to daily experience, including sexual experience. Priests, it turns out, have bodies, and many—not just Catholics either—use their bodies sexually in ways that may or may not be officially sanctioned. Some feel badly about behavior they believe to be sinful, while others surely think the church's definition of sin is narrow and moralistic. Deeply religious people of all sexes and from all traditions engage in sexual activity, in ways both permitted and forbidden by religious authorities. Surely religion's power stems to some substantial degree from its animating passion and volatile excess, as testified in the lives of untold saints, prophets, mystics, and perennial seekers, those often seen as heretics in their own time only to be tamed afterward into models of impossible virtue. The study of religion and religious history already suppresses far too much of this affective extravagance, including the linkages among some forms of religious experience and explicit eroticism. Were the study of gay religion to evade or conceal the sexiness of its subject, it would outwardly capitulate to deep cultural fears about religion's rapturous power. Fortunately, the content of this volume proves that such is not the intent here.

Consider the wealth and diversity of LGBT manifestations that emerge in these pages: how many observers have thought about gay life in Buddhist, Mormon, or Santería settings? Wendy Cadge, Richley Crapo, and Salvador Vidal-Ortiz give us rich ethnographic depictions of identity reformation that help us rethink these religions much more generally. The attention to religious practice and devotion by Peter Savastano, Bernard Lukenbill, Jay Hasbrouck, Mary Jo Neitz, Ingrid Sell, and Edward Gray and Scott Thumma in their piece on the Gospel Hour is riveting and unforgettable, illuminating yet again the pluriformity of gay religion. And the painful ambivalence evoked by themes of community and memory in Catholic, Seventh-day Adventist, Jewish, African American, and, perhaps most chillingly, ex-gay communities is wondrously evoked by Leonard Primiano, René Drumm, Moshe Shokeid, Aryana Bates, and Christy Ponticelli. Here, yes, we see persistent collisions between tradition and experimentation, but we see far more as well. The material cannot be bound by or to these two ideas; it spills over into new arenas for which fresh vocabulary is called for and this leakage at the level of everyday life, of lived religion, is part of what it means to call the emergent category of gay religion a "cultural production."

If the variety of these essays alone teaches us anything, it ought to be once again that "gay" is a more polymorphic than stable category, so much so that it is perhaps as inconvenient and limited a classification as "woman" or "primitive" or "Black" have often shown themselves to be. Likewise the astonishing diversity of what stands for religion in this collection either empties the term of coherent significance or, depending on one's point of view, wondrously opens the way to much more expansive conceptualizations. From either angle, this can be seen as a positive outcome, since it forces us to confront substantive questions within both the study of religion and the study of sexuality; engaging this collection, that is, invites reconsideration what it is we are studying when we say we are studying religious or sexual practice. It is fascinating to see how little the essays treat the substance of belief, which seems to be a concern mostly of those groups described today as religious conservatives: belief arises strongest as a theme among Thumma's evangelicals, for instance, or Crapo's Mormons.

It is further revealing to note how the essays invoke distinctive presumptions for delimiting religion or spirituality, from self-identification to the farthest extent of imposing the vocabulary of spirituality upon gay subjects who seem to find its jargon foreign to their pursuits. Is it wishful thinking to describe as "spiritual" practices of cruising or party circuits, or does this analytic move promise to uncover deep impulses toward religious sex? At some points in the volume, as in the broader field of religious studies, the categories used to describe religion almost seem counterproductive, as though to suggest that human beings have inherent religious impulses that cry out for expression, rather than recognize the social and cultural production of these kinds of needs.

There may be both revelations and dead-ends, then, in trying to make "gay religion" fit into prefabricated structures of meaning or confirm older paradigms, whether those relating to religion or to sex. That is not to say, however, that this field of study is, in either its mainstream or outermost incarnations, superfluous or irrelevant. To the contrary, the rigorous and enthusiastic study of gay religion embodied in this collection is an arresting medium for achieving discernment into many pertinent lines of inquiry. One of the most exciting reasons for this is that gay studies has evolved outside of the older institutional models governing the conventions of American religious history (which not so long ago was still narrowly conceived as "church history") as well as those of sociology.

Gay studies comes from cultural studies, which means that a constitutive element from the very start has been the study of everyday life, and it is here where the study of gay religion can likewise make its most distinguished contributions. Certainly the study of sexuality is an arena ripe for fresh apprehensions, particularly when religion is so often either ignored or reviled in cultural and social studies devoted to this topic. The study of religion is another, and since this volume seeks to make its chief mark in that field, my remaining comments focus prospectively on the gains ahead. I speculate upon only three interrelated cultural areas where analysis of gay religion should be of special use to American religionists, broadly construed: the study of religion and the body; the impact of socialized self-definitions of "badness" upon later religious associations; and the import of relationality to religious practice.

The association between religion and the body, readers know, is always a concrete rather than abstract one, one that exists between particular forms of religion and particular bodies. Scholars working in a variety of contexts have rendered the interlaced effects of religious discipline upon the bodies of historical subjects, disclosing multiple ways in which intense forms of religious practice often correspond with extreme attempts at physical self-mastery or asceticism. The vast majority of studies in this area, however, take a historical rather than sociological view, so that we know far more about the embodiment practiced by monks in late antiquity or mystical women in late medieval Europe than about contemporary American religious practitioners. Yet for American religionists, studying a society replete with escalating bodily fixations seemingly like no other, this association turns out to be a rich one indeed.

As several studies in the current volume suggest, implicitly and explicitly, children growing up in religious households who grow aware of their feelings for their own sex may strive vigorously to control or even punish their bodies for these perceived sins. Whether gay children from religious homes in the United States develop more of a self-castigating pattern of identity than their counterparts who don't identify as gay, we do not know; plainly, children's narratives, whether told in the present or as retrospective memoirs, can provide urgent information about the effects of particular religious settings upon sexual, religious, and embodied development. More concentrated studies of the role played by religious teachings in the body obsessions endured by some gay men and lesbians would be of crucial import not only for specialists in gay religion but also for many other scholars intent on understanding this complex dynamic and its linkage to preoccupations from eating disorders to sexual dysfunction to patterns of erotic desire.

If we shift our gaze to the impact of exclusion and learned feelings of "bad-ness" upon later religious participation, we might locate other ways in which the study of gay religion may unveil fresh truths about American religious experience. Psychoanalytic theories have long contended that religion serves to fulfill deep hu-man needs while also forbidding their full and authentic expression—sublimating mundane desires into a desire for a divine beloved who cares deeply for those he (or she) adores, better than any mother or lover possibly could. This holy figure could conceivably appear as a god of complete mercy and acceptance, but ob-servers have more often envisaged its appearance in diverse cultures as a wrathful god in need of propitiation and repentance. According to this perception, most gods in the human pantheon have alternated between love and anger, threatening abandonment of those who do not manifest utter servility and obedience. For their adherents, the presumed meaning and end of human life becomes the search for approval and the recovery of one's own sense of personal goodness to replace the self-loathing cultivated by such a belief system. Historians and social scientists may rightly contest some of the universalism and flawed anthropology undergird-ing such theories, particularly as they were promoted a century ago, but even dis-passionate inspections of some American popular religions—notably, evangelicalism—have highlighted the overriding dynamics of an authoritative parent–child relationship between God and worshiper so central to devotional life.

Studies of women and men raised in these disciplinary environments have oc-casionally focused on their embodied effects—the clinical literature, unfortu-nately, tends to avoid religious upbringing as if it were irrelevant or embarrassing—but we have heretofore done far less investigation of gay persons in and from these settings than of their ostensibly straight counterparts. Even such personal narratives as that of queer literary theorist Michael Warner, raised in a strict Pentecostal environment, sheds little light on the impact of that upbringing upon other aspects of his life (1997: 223–31). Often enough, now as ever, chil-dren learn to fear and hate the desires that, according to their religion, make them bad—even though they may see those hungers mobilizing the adults around them. The intervention of gay religion—perhaps of any category of religion marked in pivotal ways by a mix of sexuality and of social persecution—into the psycho-logical dynamic of these stricter religious forms ought surely to tell us something new about the cultural workings of appetite and desire. That is, through work in this area we may begin to see religious practices as repositories of hunger, a kind of cultivated need for both authority and freedom in select portions, and hence we may begin to fathom more creatively the highly influential nexus tying together eroticism with devotionalism.

This last point leads to the import of relational desire and experience upon religious preferences. As these concluding speculative comments suggest, the

significance of divinely beloved figures to the experience of many ordinary
worshippers appears inestimable. "What a friend we have in Jesus," sing evangelicals young and old, who from the earliest Sunday School lessons learn that
the relationship between them and God is the pivot of their faith. Christian
wives who feel despondent at the state of their marriage can look to God as
the perfect lover or husband, one who will never strike them or their children;
God, in such instances, is truly a savior on earth as in heaven. Catholics have
their own forms of intense relationships with divine saints, also seen in profoundly human and corrective terms. The social impact of varied forms of devotionalism throughout American history has only been spottily investigated,
yet those studies that we have unanimously affirm the long-term effects of this
form of faith upon other cultural spheres. Contributions to this volume such
as Savastano's richly suggest how studying the interconnections among gay life
and devotionalism may develop our understanding of personal compromises
with tradition of the sort that gay persons have long been called to make.

The study of gay religion cannot address or solve all the many puzzles that
continue to bedevil observers of American religion, but it offers up innumerable
ways both to invigorate shopworn interpretive schemas and to unfold nascent or
tentative theoretical paradigms. Gay people, it seems, do live their religion in ways
that sometimes comport with and other times wrestle against the norms of their
equally diverse religious counterparts who do not self-identify as gay. Like these
others, gay persons seek the religion that fits them, whatever its mix of traditional
or experimental elements and whatever its dramatic shiftings over time. More importantly, however, the study of gay religion is advancing at a historical moment
when the field of American religion is ripe for fresh studies of everyday practice
at all levels to extend and correct the institutional assumptions yet binding us. The
terminology of lived religion, influenced multiply by sociology, anthropology, and
cultural history, first struck many observers as promising yet has not always fulfilled the exhilaration that greeted its early arrival. With the illuminating and insightful potential embodied in this volume, observers can find the makings of new
breakthroughs in the social and cultural investigation of American religion, including some that may have been wholly unexpected.

Notes

1. A recent very helpful survey of the tradition of critical historiography is John F.
Wilson, *Religion and the American Nation: Historiography and History* (Athens: University of
Georgia Press, 2003).

2. Ronald E. Long, "The Sacrality of Male Beauty and Homosex: A Neglected Factor
in the Understanding of Contemporary Gay Life," in *Que(e)rying Religion: A Critical Anthology* (Comstock and Henking 1997: 266–81).

LGBT Religious Support
and Advocacy Group Information

A Common Bond

Affiliation/tradition/religious family: Jehovah's Witnesses

Contact information: www.gayxjw.org
E-mail: webmaster@gayxjw.org

Statement of Purpose/Vision: "*A Common Bond* is an international support network of gay, lesbian, bisexual, and transgendered individuals whose common bond is that we are now, or have been, associated with Jehovah's Witnesses. Our purpose is to share our experiences with one another, giving and receiving encouragement, hope, and recovery, to others whose lives have been impacted by their sexual orientation and association with the Watchtower. As a group, we are not associated in any way with any organized religion. Our members are free to choose their own spiritual path, or none at all without condemnation. We do not charge membership dues, nor are there any attendance requirements. We are not governed by any leadership; each chapter operates independently, with the primary purpose of support and recovery in mind." Quoted from *A Common Bond*'s website

Date began: San Francisco group began in 1994
Size: 19 independent chapters worldwide, most meet once a month.

Relationship to organized tradition: Not recognized by the Jehovah's Witnesses. The website also supports two listserves and a chat room. Additionally, national conferences are held each year.

Affirmation

Affiliation/tradition/religious family: Mormon, Church of Jesus Christ of Latter-day Saints

Contact information: www.affirmation.org
Mailing address: AFFIRMATION: Gay & Lesbian Mormons, PO Box 46022, Los Angeles, CA 90046-0022
Phone: 323-255-7251
E-mail: executive_committee@affirmation.org

Statement of Purpose/Vision: "Affirmation is a fellowship of gays, lesbians, bisexuals, their family and friends who share the common bond of the Mormon experience. Its purpose is to provide a supportive environment for relieving the needless fear, guilt, self-oppression and isolation that LDS gays and lesbians can experience in an era where willful ignorance about human sexuality is too often a reality. We believe that a same-gender orientation and same-gender relationships can be consistent with and supported by the Gospel of Jesus Christ. We affirm that we are children of Heavenly Parents who love us the way they created us and will judge us, as they do all, based on what we make of our lives here and how we have treated our sisters and brothers."

Date began: Mid-1977 informal group met at BYU, 1979 became a national organization.
Size: 40 chapters worldwide. Affirmation also maintains an "at-large" web-based chapter on its website.

Relationship to organized tradition: Not recognized by the Church of Jesus Christ of Latter-day Saints.

Al-Fatiha Foundation

Affiliation/tradition/religious family: Islam

Contact information: www.al-fatiha.net
Mailing address: Al-Fatiha Foundation, USA, PO Box 33532, Washington, DC 20033
E-mail: gaymuslims@yahoo.com

Statement of Purpose/Vision: "The Al-Fatiha Foundation is an international organization dedicated to Muslims who are lesbian, gay, bisexual, and trasngendered, those questioning their sexual orientation or gender identity, and their friends. Al-Fatiha's goal is to provide a safe space and a forum for LGBTQ Muslims to address issues of common concern, share individual experiences, and institutional resources. The Al-Fatiha Foundation aims to support LGBTQ Muslims in reconciling their sexual orientation or gender identity with Islam. Al-Fatiha promotes the Islamic notions of social justice, peace, and tolerance through its work, to bring all closer to a world that is free from injustice, prejudice, and discrimination." Quoted from the Al-Fatiha website December 2002.

Date began: 1997
Size: Membership—listserve has more than 275 subscribers
Affiliated groups or chapters—11 worldwide

History: Al-Fatiha began as an e-mail discussion group then developed into several face-to-face chapters and now also hosts annual international conferences for its members.

Relationship to organized tradition: Not recognized as a legitimate Muslim organization.

Association of Welcoming & Affirming Baptists

Affiliation/tradition/religious family: American Baptist

Contact information: www.WABaptists.org
Mailing address: The Association of Welcoming & Affirming Baptists, PO Box 2596, Attleboro Falls, MA 02763-0894
Phone: 508-226-1945
Fax: 508-226-1991
E-mail: Mail@WABaptists.org

Statement of Purpose/Vision: "The mission of the Association of Welcoming & Affirming Baptists (AWAB) is to create and support a community of churches, organizations and individuals committed to the inclusion of gay, lesbian, bisexual and transgendered persons in the full life and mission of American Baptist churches." Quoted from the Association of Welcoming & Affirming Baptists' website December 2002.

Date began: 1991
Size: 55 affiliated groups and member congregations.

Relationship to organized tradition: "As cooperating churches within the ABCUSA, W&A churches seek to abide by the Common Criteria for Cooperating Churches as listed in the Covenant of Relationships. Nothing in this Covenant requires individual churches to abide by the majority opinion, whether expressed regionally or nationally, on matters of mission, theological understanding, or biblical interpretation. In fact, many W&A congregations feel a deep sense of calling to be a prophetic voice for justice, calling the church to accountability and action wherever there is exclusion and oppression of any of God's children." Quoted from the Association of Welcoming & Affirming Baptists' website December 2002. In September of 2002, American Baptists Concerned (see below) and AWAB decided to unify under one governing body.

Axios: Eastern and Orthodox Gay and Lesbian Christians

Affiliation/tradition/religious family: Eastern Orthodox Christian

Contact information: www.qrd.org/qrd/www/orgs/axios/

Statement of Purpose/Vision: This site was last updated in 1997 and was originally intended to be a support for gay and lesbian Orthodox Christians. Much of the content is no longer available.

Beyond Inclusion

Affiliation/tradition/religious family: Episcopal Church

Contact information: www.beyondinclusion.org

Mailing address: Beyond Inclusion, All Saints Church, 132 N. Euclid Avenue, Pasadena, CA 91101
Phone: 626-583-2740
E-mail: info@beyondinclusion.org

Statement of Purpose/Vision: "Beyond Inclusion, an organization of gay and straight people together, wants to convince the mainstream parishioner, and help the mainstream parish, move toward blessing same-sex relationships. Beyond Inclusion testifies that same-sex relationships are holy and beautiful in the sight of God, are theologically and liturgically justifiable, are compatible with Scripture, and should be blessed and recognized by the church. Additionally, the ordination of lesbians and gays represents an asset to the church community. Beyond Inclusion also recognizes all justice issues are inter-related; homophobia, racism, sexism, and xenophobia all come from the same source. Where you find one, you are likely to find the others." Quoted from the Beyond Inclusion website December 2002.

Date began: 1995

History: Advocacy group that organized out of All Saints Episcopal Church Pasadena, California, around the defense of Bishop Walter Righter who was charged 1995 with heresy for ordaining an openly gay man in a committed relationship. The organization has continued to promote its cause at conferences and at the national gatherings (General Convention) of the Episcopal Church.

Relationship to organized tradition: *Beyond Inclusion* is not an official organization of the Episcopal Church. There are a number of other similar organizations providing support within the Episcopal and Anglican tradition sponsored by local congregations or dioceses. These groups include The Oasis site by the Diocese of Newark, New Jersey, www.dioceseofnewark.org/theoasis; the Alliance of Lesbian and Gay Anglicans, www.alga.org; and The Oasis site of the Diocese of California, www.oasiscalifornia.org.

Dignity, USA

Affiliation/tradition/religious family: Roman Catholic

Contact information: www.dignityusa.org
Mailing address: DIGNITY/USA 1500 Mass. Ave. NW, Suite #11, Washington, DC 20005
Phone: 800-877-8797 or 202-861-0017
Fax: 202-429-9808
E-mail: dignity@aol.com

Statement of Purpose/Vision:
"Dignity/USA envisions and works for a time when Gay, Lesbian, Bisexual and Transgender Catholics are affirmed and experience dignity through the integration of their spirituality with their sexuality, and as beloved persons of God participate fully in all aspects of life within the Church and Society." Quoted from Dignity's website. For the full text of Dignity's statement see www.dignityusa.org/purpose.html

Date began: 1969, official organization 1973
Size: Membership—3000
Affiliated groups or chapters—65

History: "Dignity/USA is the oldest and largest national lay movement of lesbian, gay, bisexual and transgender (GLBT) Catholics, our families, and our friends. Begun in 1969 in San Diego under the leadership of Fr. Patrick Nidorf, OSA, first as a counseling group and then a support group in Los Angeles, Dignity/USA has been a national organization since 1973. An independent nonprofit group, our national office is in Washington, DC, with chapters located throughout the United States. In local chapters, we worship openly with other GLBT and supportive Catholics, socialize, share personal and spiritual concerns, and work together on educational and justice issues. Members gather at periodic regional meetings and biennial national conventions." Quoted from the Dignity website.

Relationship to organized tradition: Both Dignity and the gay and lesbian rights movement in the Roman Catholic Church have had a checkered history. Traditionally, the Catholic Church taught that homosexual acts are immoral and sinful, but homosexual persons have inherent worth if they remain celibate. In 1976 the U.S. Catholic Bishops reasserted this position, highlighting the difference between being homosexual and engaging in same-sex acts. Additionally they stressed that the orientation itself is not chosen and is not inherently wrong or sinful. However, like heterosexual sex outside of marriage, homosexual acts are sinful and are not permitted in the church's teaching. Twenty years later the bishops again stressed this position and the need for compassion, love, and respect of the gay community within the church. In a 1986 letter and in a subsequent 1992 letter, however, the Vatican took a more hard-line position against homosexuality and instructed all bishops to remove their support of same-sex groups within the Catholic Church, namely Dignity. Many of Dignity's chapters were expelled from Catholic churches as a result, although a few still meet on church property.

Throughout its history Dignity has had to wrestle with the tension between remaining a marginalized participant within the Catholic community, especially worldwide, and working to establish its own independent religious institution. With the recent actions of the Vatican, this tension remains.

Affirmation: United Methodists for Lesbian, Gay, Bisexual and Transgendered Concerns

Affiliation/tradition/religious family: United Methodist

Contact information: www.umaffirm.org
Mailing address: Affirmation, PO Box 1021, Evanston, IL 60204
Phone: 847-733-9590
E-mail: umaffirmation@yahoo.com

Statement of Purpose/Vision: "Affirmation is an activist caucus of lesbian, gay, bisexual and transgendered people organized to speak for ourselves. Together we: proclaim a gospel of respect, love and justice; relentlessly pursue policies and processes that support full participation of lesbian, gay, bisexual and transgendered people in all areas and levels of The United Methodist Church; overcome the barriers that diminish our common humanity by excluding or judging people because of their race, gender, class, or physical abilities; empower people to undertake works of inclusion and justice where they are." Quoted from the Affirmation website December 2002.

Date began: 1976

Relationship to organized tradition: Affirmation is an independent, not-for-profit organization with no official ties to the United Methodist Church. Affirmation is entirely supported by contributions from interested individuals and receives no support from any official body of the United Methodist Church. It attempts to promote its agenda at the national meetings of the UMC (General Conference meeting every four years). The organization has an e-mail newsletter and organized "Covenant Relationships Network" (CORNET), www.umaffirm.org/cornet/, an Internet-based organization that provides information and strategies for those engaged in the issue of same-sex commitment ceremonies. The group was also instrumental in creating the Reconciling Ministries Network, www.rmnetwork.org (see below), which is a large organization of hundreds of congregations and other groups and thousands of individual Reconciling United Methodists.

Reconciling Ministries Network

Affiliation/tradition/religious family: United Methodist Church

Contact information: www.rmnetwork.org
Mailing address: 3801 N. Keeler Avenue, Chicago, IL 60641
Phone: 773-736-5526
Fax: 773-736-5475
E-mail: marilyn@rmnetwork.org

Statement of Purpose/Vision: "Reconciling Ministries Network is a national grassroots organization that exists to enable full participation of people of all sexual orientations and gender identities in the life of the United Methodist Church, both in policy and practice."

Date began: 1982
Size: Membership—As of May 2003 the Reconciling Ministries Network encompasses 192 Reconciling Congregations, 26 Reconciling Campus Ministries, 19 other "reconciling" groups, and a total of more than 17,000 Reconciling United Methodists.

Relationship to organized tradition: The Reconciling Ministries Network is an independent, not-for-profit organization with no official ties to the United Methodist Church.

Brethren Mennonite Council for Lesbian and Gay Concerns

Affiliation/tradition/religious family: Brethren/Mennonite

Contact information: www.bmclgbt.org
Mailing address: Brethren/Mennonite Council for Lesbian and Gay Concerns, PO Box 6300, Minneapolis, MN 55406
Phone: 612-343-2060
E-mail: bmc@bmclgbt.org

Statement of Purpose/Vision: "Our objectives are: To provide support for Mennonite and Church of the Brethren gay, lesbian, transgender, and bisexual people, their friends and families; To foster dialogue between gay and non-gay people in churches; To provide accurate information about homosexuality from the social sciences, biblical studies, and theology. BMC supports all people as they seek to know God's will for their lives, including those open to same-sex relationships, those seeking a life of celibacy, and those exploring questions of sexual orientation. We also believe that God does celebrate the love shared in same-sex relationships." Quoted from the Brethren Mennonite Council website December 2002.

Date began: 1976
Size: Membership—more than 30 supportive congregations and many individuals.
Affiliated groups or chapters—seven local groups

Relationship to organized tradition: The Brethren Mennonite Council is not affiliated with the Brethren or Mennonite Church denominations. The group maintains a magazine, a newsletter, an electronic newsletter, a discussion forum listserve, a biennial convention, and networks for parents, college age adults and supportive congregations.

Lutherans Concerned

Affiliation/tradition/religious family: Evangelical Lutheran Church of America

Contact information: www.lcna.org
Mailing address: PO Box 10461 Chicago, IL 60610
E-mail: cochairs@lcna.org

Statement of Purpose/Vision: "Lutherans Concerned/North America stands as a community of faith, modeling the gospel with the church and within the gay, lesbian, bisexual, and transgendered communities. We seek to employ the Gospel's principles of inclusiveness and justice, celebrating God's gifts of sexuality and diversity. Lutherans Concerned helps people reconcile their spirituality and sexuality in an uplifting way. We seek to minister to people who the institutional church often shuns. We also seek to lead the church to live the Gospel to the fullest, affirming sexual diversity, as we all grow in faith and understanding of God's grace." Quoted from the Lutherans Concerned website December 2002.

Date began: 1974
Size: 45 chapters in North America
More than 250 congregations are members of the Reconciling in Christ program.

Relationship to organized tradition: Although Lutherans Concerned is an independent membership organization that is supported entirely by donations and member contributions, in the fall of 2002 the Board of Directors of the Division for Outreach passed a resolution which establishes a formal relationship between Lutherans Concerned and the Evangelical Lutheran Church in America. Lutherans Concerned also host several listserves on the website and in 1984 started the Reconciling in Christ program to recognize Lutheran congregations which welcome lesbian and gay believers. Another resource group for Lutherans called Lutheran Lesbian and Gay Ministries has recently formed and can be found at www.llgm.org.

More Light Presbyterians

Affiliation/tradition/religious family: Presbyterian Church, USA

Contact information: www.mlp.org
Mailing address: More Light Presbyterians, PMB 246 4737 County Road 101, Minnetonka, MN 55345-2634

Phone: 505-820-7082
Fax: 505-820-2540
E-mail: michaeladee@aol.com

Statement of Purpose/Vision: "Following the risen Christ, and seeking to make the Church a true community of hospitality, the mission of More Light Presbyterians is to work for the full participation of lesbian, gay, bisexual and transgender people of faith in the life, ministry and witness of the Presbyterian Church (USA)." Quoted from the More Light Presbyterians website December 2002.

Date began: 1974
Size: Affiliated groups or chapters—More than 9 Seminary or Campus chapters, 24 Presbytery or regional chapters, and 110 "More Light" congregations nationwide.

History: "Since 1974, More Light Presbyterians and its predecessor organizations have been working to transform the church into a true community of hospitality. As we engage in bible study, dialogue, personal sharing and debate, MLP keeps before congregations, presbyteries and General Assembly, the vision of a truly inclusive church." Quoted from the More Light Presbyterians website December 2002.

Relationship to organized tradition: The More Light Presbyterians organization is an independent, not-for-profit organization with no official ties to the Presbyterian Church (USA). A listing of additional Presybterian groups working for greater inclusivity in the Presbyterian Church (USA) can be found at the website at www.mlp.org/resources/other.html. Additional resources can be found at Presbyterian Parents of Gays and Lesbians at www.presbyterianparents.org .

Integrity

Affiliation/tradition/religious family: Episcopal Church

Contact information: www.integrityusa.org
Mailing address: Integrity, 1718 M Street NW, PM Box 148, Washington, DC 20036
Phone: 800-462-9498
E-mail: info@integrityusa.org

Statement of Purpose/Vision: "Integrity is a nonprofit organization of lesbian, gay, bisexual, and trangender [LGBT] Episcopalians and our straight friends.

Since our founding by Dr. Louie Crew in rural Georgia in 1974, Integrity has been the leading grassroots voice for the full inclusion of LGBT persons in the Episcopal Church and our equal access to its rites. However, advocacy is only one facet of our ministry. At the national level and in local chapters and diocesan networks throughout the country, the primary activities are: worship, fellowship, education, communication, outreach, and service to the church. Through Integrity's evangelism, thousands of LGBT people, estranged from the Episcopal Church and other denominations, have returned to parish life." Quoted from the Integrity website December 2002.

Date began: 1974
Size: Affiliated groups or chapters—52 local chapters, 3 congregational circles, 27 diocesan networks, and 46 official Integrity partners

Relationship to organized tradition: Integrity is a nonprofit organization with no official tie to the Episcopal Church. Other groups within the Episcopal and Anglican tradition include The Oasis site by the Diocese of Newark, New Jersey, www.dioceseofnewark.org/theoasis; the Alliance of Lesbian and Gay Anglicans, www.alga.org; and The Oasis site of the Diocese of California www.oasiscalifornia.org.

Friends for Lesbian, Gay, Bisexual, Transgender, and Queer Concerns

Affiliation/tradition/religious family: Quakers/Religious Society of Friends

Contact information: www.quaker.org/flgbtqc
Mailing address: refer to the website

Statement of Purpose/Vision: "FLGC is a Quaker faith community within the Religious Society of Friends. FLGC deeply honors, affirms, and upholds that of God in all people—lesbian, gay, bisexual, heterosexual, transgender, and transsexual. It is our hope to offer an oasis to those who have been spurned by the world at large. . . . We are learning that radical inclusion and radical love bring further light to Quaker testimony and life. Our experience with oppression in our own lives leads us to seek ways to bring our witness to bear in the struggles of other oppressed peoples." Quoted from the FLGC website December 2002.

History: "FLGC (historically "Friends for Lesbian and Gay Concerns") is a North American Quaker faith community that affirms that of God in all people—lesbian, gay, bisexual, heterosexual, transgendered, and transsexual. Gathering twice yearly for worship and play, we draw sustenance from each other and from the Spirit for our work and life in the world. We are learning that radical inclusion and radical love bring further light to Quaker testimony and life." Quoted from the FLGC website December 2002.

Relationship to organized tradition: The Friends for Lesbian and Gay Concerns is an affiliated organization with the Society of Friends. The organization hosts several gatherings throughout the year and individual meetings around the country. They also publish a newsletter and a listserve.

Q-Light

Affiliation/tradition/religious family: Quakers/Religious Society of Friends

Contact information: groups.yahoo.com/group/Q-Light
E-mail: q-light-owner@yahoogroups.com

Statement of Purpose/Vision: Q-Light is a discussion group list for queer (lesbian, gay male, bisexual, transgendered, transsexual, or questioning) Quakers and interested guests to discuss issues relating to being queer, being a Friend (Quaker), and the intersection thereof. Discussion will be respectful and non-homo-/bi-/transphobic. Q-Light is for all Friends, and thus we endeavor to respect all those who call themselves Friends, without regard to their beliefs or branch of the Society of Friends. 263 members in the discussion list.
The American Friends Service Committee has worked for decades for gay, lesbian, bisexual, and transgendered human and civil rights and recognition. ww.afsc.org/glbt.htm

American Baptists Concerned/Rainbow Baptists

Affiliation/tradition/religious family: American Baptists

Contact information: www.rainbowbaptists.org
Mailing address: American Baptists Concerned, PO Box 3183, Walnut Creek, CA 94598
E-mail: ambaptists@aol.com; abc@rainbowbaptists.org

Statement of Purpose/Vision: "The purpose of American Baptists Concerned is to unite sexual minority people and their families and friends within the ABC/USA for mutual assistance, education, support and communication. To this end we cooperate with other ABC groups, as well as groups affiliated with other denominations, in tasks of mutual interest. American Baptists Concerned for Sexual Minorities is a support, education and advocacy group for lesbian, gay, bisexual and transgender Baptists. We are an affirming and inclusive organization that also provide support and resources to families and friends of sexual minority Baptists, churches and clergy." Quoted from the American Baptists Concerned website December 2002.

Date began: 1972

Size: Affiliated groups or chapters—5 chapters

History: "American Baptists Concerned has been a voice for justice on behalf of sexual minority American Baptists since 1972. Although our primarily outreach is to American Baptists, our support, fellowship and membership is offered to ALL. We invite you to learn more about American Baptists Concerned and Rainbow Baptists." Quoted from the American Baptists Concerned website December 2002.

Relationship to organized tradition: The American Baptists Concerned and the Rainbow Baptist's website have no official relationship to the American Baptist Church.

Emergence International

Affiliation/tradition/religious family: Christian Science

Contact information: www.emergence-international.org
Mailing address: PO Box 26237, Phoenix, AZ 85068-6237
Phone: (800) 280-6653
E-mail: info@emergence-international.org

Statement of Purpose/Vision: "Emergence International (EI) is a world-wide community of Christian Scientists, their families and friends, that provides spiritual and educational support for lesbians, gay men, and bisexual and transgendered people, as they deal with homophobia and hetrosexism. EI honors the integrity of individual growth through the leadership of Mary Baker Eddy in her writings, and by fellowship with similarly-minded Christian Scientists." Quoted from the Emergence International website December 2002.

Date began: 1979

Size: Membership—Emergence International has members in many cities and towns in most states in the United States, as well as in Canada, Mexico, South

America, Australia, Germany, England, Spain, and the Middle East. They also have a listing of gay-friendly Christian Science practitioners, teachers, and nurses from which they make referrals.

Relationship to organized tradition: Emergence International is not affiliated with and is not recognized by the Christian Science. EI provides both an electronic newsletter and a print journal. It hosts an annual conference and has a listserve that can be subscribed to at its website.

Evangelicals Concerned

Affiliation/tradition/religious family: Evangelical Christian

Contact information: www.ecinc.org www.ecwr.org
Mailing address: Evangelicals Concerned, 311 E. 72nd Street, New York, NY 10021
Mailing address: Evangelicals Concerned—Western Region, PO Box 19734, Seattle, WA 98109
Phone: (206)621-8960
E-mail: rblair@ecinc.org, ecwr@ecwr.org

Statement of Purpose/Vision: "Evangelicals Concerned, founded as a grass roots volunteer organization, is a non-denominational evangelical resource providing a community of fellowship that is a safe place for gay and lesbian Christians to reconcile and integrate their faith and sexuality, and to grow toward Christian maturity. E.C. is highly visible, easily accessible, financially stable, geographically diverse, and open and affirming to all who embrace the Christian faith regardless of sexual orientation, age, ethnicity, or church membership. Through conferences, retreats, local groups, bible studies, resource materials, education, leadership training, and personal support, E.C. serves as a role model to all evangelicals (gay or straight), to foster an integrated and healthy gay/lesbian Christian life. In realizing its mission, E.C. provides organizational outreach so that no gay or lesbian Christian will disown their faith or suffer unnecessarily because of who they are." Quoted from the Evangelicals Concerned website December 2002.

Date began: 1975
Size: Affiliated groups or chapters—more than 15 groups

Relationship to organized tradition: Evangelicals Concerned is an independent organization with no affiliation ties to any Evangelical Christian denomination.

The Evangelical Network

Affiliation/tradition/religious family: Evangelical Christian

Contact information: t-e-n.org
Mailing address: 1029 E. Turney, Phoenix, AZ 85014
E-mail: ten_mail2001@yahoo.com

Statement of Purpose/Vision: "The Evangelical Network (T-E-N) is a network of Bible believing churches, ministries, Christian workers and individuals bound together by a common shared faith, united in purpose and witness and established as a positive resource and support for Christian gays and lesbians." Quoted from the Evangelical Network website December 2002.

Date began:
Size: 12 affiliated groups or churches

Relationship to organized tradition: The Evangelicals Network is an independent organization with no affiliation ties to any Evangelical Christian denomination.

GLAD Alliance

Affiliation/tradition/religious family: The Christian Church (Disciples of Christ)

Contact information: www.gladalliance.org
Mailing address: GLAD Alliance Inc., P.O. Box 44400, Indianapolis, IN 46244-0400
E-mail: glad@gladalliance.org

Statement of Purpose/Vision: "The Gay, Lesbian and Affirming Disciples Alliance, Inc., is a presence working for the full dignity and integrity of gay, lesbian, bisexual and affirming people within the Christian Church (Disciples of Christ). GLAD Alliance welcomes all who make common cause with us and conducts its activities through the congregations, regions and general agencies and bodies of the Disciples of Christ. Communications with members and friends are carried on through two quarterly publications, *Crossbeams* and *Crosscurrents*, and periodic mailings." Quoted from the GLAD Alliance website December 2002.

Size: Affiliated groups or chapters—8 area chapters, 17 regional contacts, and 53 listed "open and affirming" congregations

Relationship to organized tradition: GLAD Alliance has no official relationship to the Christian Church, Disciples of Christ Denomination.

GALA (Gay and Lesbian Acceptance)

Affiliation/tradition/religious family: Community of Christ (formerly Reorganized Church of Jesus Christ of Latter-day Saints)

Contact information: www.galaweb.org
Mailing address: Gay and Lesbian Acceptance, PO Box 2173, Independence, MO 64055
E-mail: GALA@galaweb.org

Statement of Purpose/Vision: "GALA is a safe place for homosexual, bisexual and transgendered persons, and their loved ones to join together and experience spiritual growth as they share sorrow and joy. We publish a quarterly newsletter; support regional retreats and workshops; send representatives to speak at RLDS jurisdictional and World Church gatherings; and sponsor an annual international retreat. We feel we are on a journey of spiritual growth that has brought us to the point of confronting issues of acceptance, prejudice, and justice for all persons alienated by society and organized religions, particularly people of different sexual (affectionate) orientations. Together, we continue to learn, share, and expand our understanding of the world and Christ's love for each one of us." Quoted from the GALA website December 2002.

Date began: 1987
Size: GALA has more than 500 supporters.

History: "In the mid 1980s a group of gay members of the Community of Christ began meeting together in the Kansas City, MO, area for fellowship, support, and worship. In 1987, a retreat was held at Camp Manitou in Michigan where GALA was formally organized with the adoption of bylaws and the election of officers. GALA established a safe place for homosexual people and their loved ones to join together and experience spiritual growth as they shared sorrow and joy. GALA has grown to over 500 supporters in the United States, Canada, Australia, and Europe. We publish a quarterly newsletter; support regional retreats and workshops; send representatives to speak at Community of Christ jurisdictional and World Church gatherings; and sponsor an annual International Retreat." Quoted from the GALA website December 2002.

Relationship to organized tradition: GALA is not officially recognized by the Community of Christ denomination.

Seventh-day Adventist Kinship International

Affiliation/tradition/religious family: Seventh-day Adventist

Contact information: www.sdakinship.org
Mailing address: SDA Kinship International, PO Box 7320, Laguna Niguel, CA 92607-7320
Phone: (866) 732-5677
E-mail: office@sdakinship.org

Statement of Purpose/Vision: "Seventh-day Adventist Kinship International is a support organization devoted to the spiritual, emotional, social and physical well-being of current and former Seventh-day Adventists who are lesbian, gay, bisexual or transgendered (LGBT). We believe all are created in the image of God and that no one should be mistreated or discriminated against because of their sexual orientation differences. Kinship is a volunteer organization that champions human rights for all people." Quoted from the Kinship website December 2002.

Date began: 1976
Size: Many regional and international groups and more than 1,000 members worldwide.

Relationship to organized tradition: Kinship has no official relationship to the Seventh Day Adventist Church. Kinship sponsors an annual meeting, regional gatherings, a newsletter and a discussion board and chat at www.sdakinship .org/discus/index.html.

OrthoGays

Affiliation/tradition/religious family: Orthodox Judaism

Contact information: members.tripod.com/~orthogays/
E-mail: OrthoGays@newmail.net

Statement of Purpose/Vision: "The purpose of this site is to provide a home on the Internet for Orthodox Gay Jewish Men. At present, there are only a few groups around the world for gay, lesbian, bisexual, and transgendered [GLBT] Orthodox Jews, and only one, of which we are aware, for men only." Quoted from the OrthoGays website December 2002.

Relationship to organized tradition: The OrthoGays website is an independent web-based reality. Additional resources can be found on the website Frum Gay Jews at members.aol.com/gayjews/index.html and at the Internet Directory of Twice Blessed: The Jewish GLBT Archives Online at www.usc.edu/isd/archives/oneigla/tb/Online.html .

OrthoDykes

Affiliation/tradition/religious family: Orthodox Judaism

Contact information: www.orthodykes.org
E-mail: info@orthodykes.org

Statement of Purpose/Vision: "The purpose of this site is to provide a home on the Internet for Orthodox Gay Jewish Women." The group also supports a listserve.

Relationship to organized tradition: The OrthoDykes website is an independent web-based reality.

United Church of Christ Coalition for Lesbian, Gay, Bisexual, and Transgender Concerns

Affiliation/tradition/religious family: United Church of Christ

Contact information: www.ucccoalition.org
Mailing address: The Coalition, PBM 230, 800 Village Walk, Guilford, CT 06437
Phone: (800) 653-0799
Fax (203)789-6356
E-mail: officemngr@UCCcoalition.org

Statement of Purpose/Vision: "The Coalition provides support and sanctuary to all our lesbian, gay, bisexual and transgendered sisters and brothers, their families and friends, advocates for their full inclusion in church and society; brings Christ's affirming message of love and justice for all people." Quoted from the Coalition website December 2002.

Size: More than 425 open and affirming congregations in the United States.

Relationship to organized tradition: The United Church of Christ Coalition for Lesbian, Gay, Bisexual, and Transgender Concerns is officially recognized by the UCC as a related, self-created organization.

Interweave, Unitarian Universalists for Lesbian, Gay, Bisexual and Transgender Concerns

Affiliation/tradition/religious family: Unitarian Universalist Association

Contact information: www.qrd.org/qrd/www/orgs/uua/uu-interweave.html
Mailing address: 167 Milk St. #406 Boston, MA 02109-4339
E-mail: postmaster@interweave.uua.org

Statement of Purpose/Vision: "Interweave is a membership organization affili-ated with the Unitarian Universalist Association, dedicated to the spiritual, polit-ical, and social well-being of Unitarian Universalists who are confronting oppression as lesbians, gay men, bisexuals, transgender persons, and their hetero-sexual allies; and facilitates the celebration of the culture and lives of its mem-bers." Quoted from the Interweave website December 2002.

Size: Affiliated groups or chapters—26 Interweave chapters. There are also 359 "welcoming congregations" within the Unitarian Universalist Association.

Relationship to organized tradition: Interweave is a membership organization af-filiated with the Unitarian Universalist Association (UUA). The UUA "has been on record as supporting the rights of bisexual, gay, and lesbian people since 1970. The Office [of Bisexual, Gay, Lesbian and Transgender Concerns] was formed in 1973. We have advocated against sodomy laws and job and housing discrimina-tion. We have advocated for ceremonies of union and same-gender marriage, the right to serve in the military, the right to lead congregations as ministers and reli-gious professionals, and the right to be parents. We are now on record as sup-porting the rights of transgender people." Quoted from the Office of Bisexual, Gay, Lesbian and Transgender Concerns website December 2002. The office has a website full of excellent resources at www.uua.org/obgltc/index.html.

Q-Spirit

Affiliation/tradition/religious family: General Spirituality

Contact information: www.qspirit.org
Mailing address: Q-SPIRIT, 3739 Balboa Street, #211, San Francisco, CA
94121
Phone: 415.281.9377
E-mail: info@qspirit.org

Statement of Purpose/Vision: "Q-Spirit is a strategic organization catalyzing the
necessary conditions for queer people to fully claim our spiritual roles of service,
leadership and community enrichment in the world." Quoted from the Q-Spirit
website December 2002.

Date began: 1995
Size: More than 2,500 receive Q-Spirit's newsletter.

History: "Originally founded by as Berdache, a spirituality group for gay men, it
evolved from longings deep within the gay community for a forum to facilitate their
spiritual evolution. In June 1995 the first meeting attracted 40 men. . . . The group
continued to evolve. In January 1997, the name was formally changed to Q-Spirit,
a name which reflects a commitment to the inclusion of women and to honoring
all spiritual traditions." Quoted from the Q-Sprit website December 2002.

Relationship to organized tradition: Q-Spirit is an independent organization. The
efforts of Q-Spirit includes a newsletter, techno-rituals (drug- and alcohol-free
dance celebrations involving music, dance, rituals, guided meditative and interactive process, chanting, drumming, and artistic performances), discussion groups,
retreats, and spiritually-based events, programs, and activities.

Rainbow Wind

Affiliation/tradition/religious family: Pagan Spirituality

Contact information: hometown.aol.com/RainboWind/rbwintr.htm
E-mail: SarahG@qx.net or rainbowind@aol.com

Statement of Purpose/Vision: "Rainbow Wind is an Internet resource for Lesbi-
gay Pagans and their friends. It was formed in the summer of 1995 as a response
to three needs: (1) the need of Pagans to develop a greater sense of connectedness
with the Pagans community, (2) the need to define the frequently undefined role
of Lesbigays and trangendered people in Paganism, and (3) the need to respond
to the wave of attacks on Lesbigays, TGs, and Pagans by the radical Christian fun-

damentalists who have gained great influence over both the Republican and Democrat parties." Quoted from the Rainbow Wind website December 2002.

Date began: 1995

Relationship to organized tradition: The Rainbow Wind website is an independent web-based reality. It supports an online discussion group and provide links to other LGBT pagan sites.

ChristianLesbians

Affiliation/tradition/religious family: Christian

Contact information: www.christianlesbians.com
E-mail: anita@christianlesbians.com

Statement of Purpose/Vision: "The purpose of christianlesbians.com is three-fold: To proclaim the Good News of Jesus and God's unconditional and abiding love for all people. To offer information and resources for those women who are presently struggling to reconcile their faith and sexuality and to let them know that God need not be forsaken simply because of their sexual orientation. God has definitely not forsaken you! To create a circle of fellowship and support for Christian Lesbians, many of whom feel isolated by living in 'the closet' or from having experienced rejection from family, friends and their own church community." Quoted from the ChristianLesbians website December 2002.

Date began: 1994

Relationship to organized tradition: The ChristianLesbians website is an independent web-based reality. The site offers a chat room, a discussion board, a listserve, a guest book, and numerous links.

TransFaith On-line

Affiliation/tradition/religious family: Spiritual/Christian

Contact information: www.angelfire.com/on/otherwise/transfaith.html
Mailing address:
Phone:
E-mail: cpaige@juno.com

Statement of Purpose/Vision: "TransFolk carry a sacred wisdom within—it is OtherWise and invites each of us to be transformed. This OtherWise knows the Both-And and also the In-Between. It speaks prophetically and powerfully to a world which is divided against itself.

TransFaith on-line is dedicated to educating churchfolk about TransFaith, Trans-Folk, and OtherWisdom supporting Transfolk in our sacred role as OtherWise nurturing the expression of the sacred OtherWise. TransFaith on-line seeks to be inclusive of Transexuals, Intersexuals, Crossdressers, Transvestites, and all other Transgendered individuals however they may be defined. TransFaith on-line seeks to be inclusive of all spiritual traditions and orientation—while placing a particular emphasis on support and education within the Christian tradition and Christian communities." Quoted from the TransFaith website December 2002.

Relationship to organized tradition: The TransFaith website is an independent web-based reality. The site offers many resources including numerous online writings and links to additional information.

Lesbian Messianics

Affiliation/tradition/religious family: Messianic Jewish Christians

Contact information: lesmess.2itb.com
E-mail: miryam@lesmess.2itb.com

Statement of Purpose/Vision: "What is a lesbian Messianic? 'Messianic' is short for Messianic Jew (MJ), a denomination of Protestant Christianity . . . Though I talk about lesbians, really this is a place of worship, fellowship, and prayer for anyone who is gay, lesbian, bisexual, transgendered, straight, or questioning." Quoted from the Lesbian Messianics website December 2002.

Relationship to organized tradition: The Lesbian Messianics website is an independent web-based reality with no ties to any Messianic Denomination. The site offers a discussion board, a guest book, numerous links, and extensive information.

Gay Lesbian Arabic Society

Affiliation/tradition/religious family: Muslim

Contact information: http://www.glas.org/
E-mail: lazeeza@glas.org or ramzinyc@hotmail.com

Statement of Purpose/Vision: "We are the Gay and Lesbian Arabic Society (GLAS), an international organization established in 1988 in the USA with worldwide chapters. We serve as a networking organization for Gays and Lesbians of Arab descent or those living in Arab countries. We aim to promote positive images of Gays and Lesbians in Arab communities worldwide, in addition to combating negative portrayals of Arabs within the Gay and Lesbian community. We also provide a support network for our members while fighting for our human rights wherever they are oppressed. We are part of the global Gay and Lesbian movement seeking an end to injustice and discrimination based on sexual orientation." Quoted from the Gay and Lesbian Arabic Society website December 2002.

Date began: 1988
Size: Affiliated groups or chapters—4 chapters worldwide

Relationship to organized tradition: The Gay and Lesbian Arabic Society is an independent entity. Several other organizations are hosted on the same website, including Lazeeza, the Arab Lesbian Group at www.glas.org/lazeeza.html and Ahbab, the online community for Queer Arabs worldwide, glas.org/ahbab/. There are a number of other LGBT Islamic sites offering support to Muslims from different parts of the world such as the Queer Muslims, www. angelfire.com/ca2/queermuslims/;,Assyrian Gay and Lesbian Forum, pw2. netcom.com/~out/index.html, and South Asian Gay, Lesbian, Bi, and Transgender Organization and Support Group, hometown.aol.com/youngal/sangat. html.

GayJews.Org

Affiliation/tradition/religious family: Judaism

Contact information: http://members.tripod.com/~djs28/
E-mail: info@gayjews.org

Statement of Purpose/Vision: "GayJews.Org is committed to providing up to date, accurate information for Orthodox Jews who are gay, lesbian, bisexual or transgendered. We have links to all other *frum* GLBT content here on the web as well as a number of features of our own. We hope you enjoy visiting our site and will come again soon. Also, please remember, you are not alone. You are not the only one who feels this way and we're here for you." Quoted from the GayJews website December 2002.

Relationship to organized tradition: The GayJews website is an independent web-based reality. The site offers many resources, including a discussion board, listserve and chat room, online writings, and links to additional information.
The Reform branch of Judaism has had a long history of openness to and acceptance of gays and lesbians. See the website of the Committee on Gay and Lesbian Inclusion of the Union of American Hebrew Congregations at http://uahc.org/jfc/inclusion.shtml for more information.

The World Congress of Gay, Lesbian, Bisexual, and Transgender Jews: Keshet Ga'avah

Affiliation/tradition/religious family: Judaism

Contact information: www.glbtjews.org
Mailing address: PO Box 23379, Washington, DC 20026-3379 USA
Phone: (202) 452-7424
E-mail: info@glbtjews.org

Statement of Purpose/Vision: "Our vision is an environment where Lesbian, Gay, Bisexual, and Transgender (LGBT) Jews worldwide can enjoy free and fulfilling lives. In support of our vision, our goals are: To be the worldwide voice of LGBT Jews; To support, inspire, and strengthen local groups; To foster a sense of community among diverse individuals and organizations; To achieve equality and security for LGBT Jews worldwide. To achieve our goals, we value: Diversity among groups and individuals; Self-determination and respect for the autonomy of local organizations and individuals; Transparent organizational structure; and Close ties between LGBT Israelis and LGBT Jews around the world." Quoted from the World Congress website December 2002.

Date began: 1980
Size: There are more than 65 member groups worldwide.

Relationship to organized tradition: The World Congress is an independent entity but is applying for full membership in the World Jewish Congress.

Gay Buddhist Fellowship

Contact information: www.gaybuddhist.org/index.html
Mailing address: 2215-R Market Street PMB 456, San Francisco, CA 94114
Phone: 415-974-9878

Statement of Purpose/Vision: The group has a strong local face-to-face presence as well as an online presence. They offer a newsletter six times a year, hold retreats, sponsor lectures, have a vital prison ministry, and have a discussion group on Yahoo groups. Many of the public lectures are available on the web.

Date began: Newsletter since 1999

Relationship to organized tradition: The Gay Buddhist Fellowship is an independent entity with ties to local Buddhist groups and is part of a Buddhist webring.

Lesbian Buddhist eSangha

Contact information: www.geocities.com/candacevan/lesbianbuddhistesangha.html
E-mail: Lesbian-Buddhist-eSangha-owner@yahoogroups.com

Statement of Purpose/Vision: "This group is an on-line Sangha for lesbian, bisexual, and transgender Buddhists. . . . This eSangha is especially intended for those who, due to health, location, or other reasons, are not able to participate in a face-to-face Sangha. This is an active, participatory attempt to build a real community in cyberspace. Lurkers are discouraged. Please do not join unless you have a sincere desire to become part of a Buddhist cyberSangha." The group hosts a discussion board and an e-mail listserv.

Relationship to organized tradition: The Lesbian Buddhists eSangha is an independent web-based entity.

Diamond Metta Lesbian and Gay Buddhist Society

Contact information: home.pipeline.com/~diamondmetta/
Mailing address: The New York City Lesbian, Gay, Bi-sexual and Transgender Center, 208 West 13th Street, Greenwich Village, New York
Phone: 212-803-5192
E-mail: diamondmetta@pipeline.com

Statement of Purpose/Vision: "Diamond Metta Lesbian and Gay Buddhist Society is an organization for Lesbian and Gay Men committed to or interested in following the path of Buddhism or related meditation-based organizations. Society participants come together to share their understanding and experiences as mediators of various traditions, practice meditation together, come to know and provide support for like minded individuals interested in learning more about Buddhism and meditation. The Society also endeavors, as resources allow, to address issues of social justice and illness, especially in the areas of homophobia and HIV." The group, located in New York City, offers meditation, talks and discussions about Buddhist teachings designed especially for the New York City area LGBT communities.

Date began: 1992

Relationship to organized tradition: The Diamond Metta Lesbian and Gay Buddhist Socidety is an independent entity with ties to local Buddhist groups.

RadFae.org

Contact information: www.radfae.org
E-mail: websters@radfae.org

Statement of Purpose/Vision: "The RadFae.org website exists to pull together Radical Faerie information links to resources and web pages, news, information, and pointers to other faerie lists. Our site is also available to host various faerie projects."

Relationship to organized tradition: "We are not official—nobody is. Nobody speaks for Radical Faeries as a whole; certainly not us! We're keeping our process as open as possible, so this site can reflect the community as a whole. But our main goal is to provide a neutral clearing-house, which can point to (or host) faerie sites with a variety of perspectives."

The Defenders

Contact information: www.dignityusa.org/defenders/index.html
Mailing address: Defenders USA, c/o Dignity USA, 1500 Massachusetts Avenue, NW, Washington, DC 20005
E-mail: lthrbuddy2@aol.com

Statement of Purpose/Vision: "The Defenders is a club for individuals who value and wish to celebrate both their leather 'lifestyle' and their Christian spirituality. Contrary to common belief, the two are not mutually exclusive. The Defenders believe that the leather experience can, when integrated and spiritually informed, actually produce a richer spirituality for us, and for the Church. We strive to provide a space that leathermen and leatherwomen will find welcoming and familiar, yet unique in its spiritual dimension."

Relationship to recognized tradition: "The Defenders was established in 1981 in New York City as an affiliate of Dignity New York. By 1987, we had become a national organization. . . . The Defenders has been affiliated with Dignity USA from the beginning and maintains close ties to this very day. Each Defenders club [nine clubs] is associated with a local Dignity Chapter. . . . We are a bridge between the Leather Community and the Christian Community."

Independent LGBT Religious Denominations
Unity Fellowship Church Movement

Contact information: www.ufc-usa.org
Phone: 323-938-8322
E-mail: info@ufc-usa.org

Statement of Purpose/Vision: "The inspiration or vision to establish Unity Fellowship Church was given to its Founder, Reverend Carl Bean. After many years of study and seeking spiritual truth, it was revealed to Rev. Bean that the spiritual path is eternal and traveled by all. 'We all partake of spirit for without spirit there is no life.'
The one fact that was consistently revealed to Rev. Carl Bean in dreams, visions and other heightened spiritual experiences is nothing compares with, equals or surpasses 'LOVE' and 'GOD is LOVE' and 'LOVE HAS NO RESPECT OF PERSON'.
We are the very essence of Love as is all creation regardless of race, creed, color, religious affiliation, sex, sexual orientation, class, whether animal, fish, plant life, planets, galaxies known or unknown. There is no place in creation where Love is not present.
If we, the world over, would learn to say yes to Love, regardless of what spiritual path we take, there would be no need to fear anyone and thereby we would embrace everyone."

History: The Unity Fellowship Church Movement was founded, incorporated and chartered (as a 501(C)(3) nonprofit religious organization) in Los Angeles, California, in 1985. The "Mother Church," also known as Unity Fellowship of Christ Church, is located at 5818 West Jefferson Blvd., Los Angeles, CA.

Reconciling Pentecostals International

Contact information: http://www.reconcilingpentecostals.com/
Mailing address: Reconciling Pentecostal Assembly, 34522 N. Scottsdale Rd. D-8, Suite 238, Scottsdale, AZ 85262
Phone: 480-595-6517
E-mail: RPIFellowship@aol.com

Statement of Purpose/Vision: "We have a diverse fellowship, which rallies around some similar beliefs and shares some similar experiences. We are all Pentecostal and love the full gospel of Christ! The fellowship is led by Apostolics and is organized as an outreach to Apostolics. However, our ministry extends beyond just them.
We are a gay affirming organization with an old fashioned message that transcends time! The power of God's affirming love and His inclusive gospel will meet the needs of anyone who is seeking to serve the Lord transparently. The Holy Ghost stands ready to flood your soul with a revelation of His amazing grace that embraces everyone who calls upon His Name.
Until we all come into the unity of the faith, we have elected to recognize, love, and fellowship all Pentecostals who are pursuing godliness and who have credible, anointed ministries."

Size: 25 ministers/congregations are associated with this denomination.

History: RPI was founded in the hearts of five ministers in 1999 but not formally established until June of 2000. RPI is under the leadership of three of its ordained ministers, Rev. Douglas E. Clanton, Rev. Lonnie Parks, and Rev. Robert L. Morgan, who serves as Chief Presiding Presbyter.

Ecumenical Catholic Church

Contact information: ecchurch.org/
Mailing address: 20 Lincoln St., Irvine, CA 92604
Phone: 949-451-1531
Fax: 949-654-3703
E-mail: Archbishop@ecchurch.org

Statement of Purpose/Vision: "The Ecumenical Catholic Church is a separate denomination within the universal Christian Church. We share with all Christians the belief that Jesus is the Son of God and Redeemer of humanity. We are united with others through the rebirth of Baptism and the fellowship of the Eucharist. We are like other churches in most ways, but there are some important differences, too. Everyone is Welcome!
The ECC and its people love you as you are—as God made you and loves you—unconditionally, without regard to your race, gender, sexual orientation, marital status, education, social background, financial status, or any other standard used to divide people. Who you are will not be measured against the standards of an ancient moral code or against the demands of modern materialism. Your individuality will be celebrated rather than judged for nonconformity to what some hold as the ideals of society. You will be encouraged to integrate your faith with your intellect and feelings, not set them at opposition to each other. We will do our best to encourage you to grow into the potential that God has lovingly created within you. Above all, we will clearly present God's unconditional love to you and everyone else." Quoted from the Ecumenical Catholic Church website December 2002.

International Fellowship of the Metropolitan Community Church

Contact information: www.mccchruch.org
Mailing address: Metropolitan Community Churches Headquarters, 8704 Santa Monica Blvd., 2nd Floor, West Hollywood, CA 90069-4548
Phone: 310-360-8640
Fax: 310-360-8680
E-mail: info@MCCchurch.org

Statement of Purpose/Vision: "The Universal Fellowship of Metropolitan Community Churches is a Christian Church founded in and reaching beyond the Gay and Lesbian communities. We embody and proclaim Christian salvation and liberation, Christian inclusivity and community, and Christian social action and justice. We serve among those seeking and celebrating the integration of their spirituality and sexuality."

History: The first Metropolitan Community Churches (MCC) was founded by Rev. Troy D. Perry in 1968 in Los Angeles, California. This Fellowship of Churches plays a vital role in addressing the spiritual needs of the lesbian, gay, bisexual, and transgendered community around the world.

Size: Since its founding in 1968, MCC has grown into a denomination of approximately 300 churches in 18 countries throughout the world. Worldwide membership surpassed 40,000 in early 2000

Additional Web-based Resources for LGBT Religion

www.iwgonline.org/links/—The Interfaith Working Group has a superb list of links to LGBT religion websites. This site also contains online magazines and many articles that have been written on the subject.

www.whosoever.org —Whosoever is an online magazine dedicated to the spiritual growth of gay, lesbian, bisexual, and transgendered Christians. This site also contains an excellent resource of links to LGBT religion sites www.whosoever.org/resources.html

www.lgbtran.org—The website of the LGBT Religious Archives Network (LGB-TRAN) is "an innovative venture in developing archives and encouraging historical study of lesbian, gay, bisexual and transgender (LGBT) religious movements." It is an excellent information clearinghouse and central electronic directory of the many archival collections of LGBT religious leaders and organizations.

www.religioustolerance.org/homosexu.htm—This website contains a very fine collection of basic information about homosexuality and religion, from a perspective of tolerance and openness. The site has a listing of the official positions on homosexuality of most denominational religious groups and how these positions have developed over time.

Bibliography

Adler, M. 1986. *Drawing Down the Moon.* Rev. edition. Boston, MA: Beacon Press.

Ahlstrom, Sydney E. 1972. *A Religious History of the American People.* New Haven, CT: Yale University Press.

Aldred, Lisa. 2000. "Plastic Shamans and Astroturf Sun Dances: New Age Commercialization of Native American Spirituality." *American Indian Quarterly* 24 (3): 329–52.

Allen, Paula Gunn. 1986. *The Sacred Hoop.* Boston: Beacon Press.

Althusser, L. 1984. *Essays on Ideology.* London: New Left Books.

American Psychological Association. 2003. "Resolution on Appropriate Therapeutic Responses to Sexual Orientation." www/apa.org/ pi/sexual.htm.

Ammerman, Nancy. 1985. Data from an unpublished study done by the Center for Religious Research, Emory University, Atlanta, GA.

———. 1987. *Bible Believers: Fundamentalists in the Modern World.* New Brunswick, NJ: Rutgers University Press.

———. 1990. *Baptist Battles: Social Change and Religious Conflict in the Southern Baptist Convention.* New Brunswick, NJ: Rutgers University Press.

———. 2000. "New Life for Denominationalism." *Christian Century,* 15 March.

Anderson, Benedict. 1991. *Imagined Communities: Reflections on the Origin and Spread of Nationalism.* London and New York: Verso.

Arango, Monica Espinoza, and Fisi Andoque. 1999. "Managing the World: Territorial Negotiations Among the Andoque People of the Colombian Amazon." In *The Archaeology and Anthropology of Landscape: Shaping Your Landscape,* edited by P. Ucko and R. Layton, 240–53. London: Routledge.

Artaud, Antonin. [1938] 1958. *Theatre and Its Double,* translated by Mary Caroline Richards. New York: Grove Press.

Bailey, Derrick Sherwin. [1955] 1975. *Homosexuality and the Western Christian Tradition.* Hamden, CT: Archon Books.

Baker-Fletcher, Garth Kasimu, ed. 1998. *Black Religion after the Million-Man March.* Maryknoll, NY: Orbis Books.

Baldwin, Guy. 1990. "Reclaiming the Exiled Self." In *Gay Soul: Finding the Heart of Gay Spirit and Nature*, edited by Mark Thompson, 183–95. San Francisco: Harper.

———. 1991. "A Second Coming Out." In *Leather-Folk: Radical Sex, People, Politics, and Practice*, edited by Mark Thompson, 169–78. Boston: Alyson Publications.

———. 1993. *Ties That Bind: The SM/Leather/Fetish Erotic Style, Issues, Commentaries and Advice*. Los Angeles: Daedalus Publishing Company.

Barnet, Miguel. 1997. "La Regla de Ocha: The Religious System of Santería." In *Sacred Possessions: Vodou, Santería, Obeah, and the Caribbean*, edited by Margarite Fernandez Olmos and Lizabeth Paravisini-Gebert, 79–100. New Brunswick, NJ: Rutgers University Press.

Batchelor, Edward, ed. 1980. *Homosexuality and Ethics*. New York: Pilgrim Press.

Baudrillard, Jean. 1989. *America*, translated by C. Turner. London: Verso.

Bauer, Paul. 1976. "The Homosexual Subculture at Worship: A Participant Observation Study." *Pastoral Psychology* 25:115–27.

Baumann, Martin. 1997. "The Dharma Has Come West: A Survey of Recent Studies and Sources." *Journal of Buddhist Ethics* 4, jbe.la.psu.edu.

Becker, Howard. 1963. *Outsiders: Studies in the Sociology of Deviance*. New York: Free Press.

Behar, Ruth, and Deborah Gordon. 1995a. *Women on Culture*. Berkeley: University of California Press.

———. 1995b. *Women Writing Culture*. Berkeley: University of California Press.

Bell, Alan, and Martin S. Weinberg. 1978. *Homosexualities: A Study of Diversity Among Men and Women*. New York: Simon & Schuster.

Bellah, Robert N. 1970. *Beyond Belief: Essays on Religion in a Post-Traditional World*. New York: Harper and Row.

Bellah, Robert, Richard Madsen, William M. Sullivan, Ann Swidler, and Steven M. Tipton. 1985. *Habits of the Heart: Individualism and Commitment in American Life*. Berkeley, CA: University of California Press.

Benson, Brad. 2001. "Perceived Family Relationships Associated with Coming Out of Mormon Male Homosexuals." Doctoral dissertation, Utah State University, Logan, Utah.

Berger, Bennett M. 1981. *The Survival of a Counterculture: Ideological Work and Everyday Life Among Rural Communards*. Berkeley, Los Angeles, and London: University of California Press.

Berger, H. 1998. *A Community of Witches: Contemporary Neopaganism and Witchcraft in the United States*. Columbia: University of South Carolina Press.

Berger, Peter. 1954. "The Sociological Study of Sectarianism." *Social Research* 21:467–85.

———. 1963. *Invitation to Sociology: A Humanistic Perspective*. Garden City, NY: Anchor Books, Doubleday.

Berger, Peter, and Thomas Luckmann. 1967. *The Social Construction of Reality: A Treatise in the Sociology of Knowledge*. Garden City, NY: Doubleday.

Bernier, Laurence. [ca. 1982]. "Our God Is Like an Eagle." [Composed in 1974, based on a tune by George J. Webb]. Universal Fellowship of Metropolitan Community Churches. *Trial Hymnal*, 88. MCCA at Freedom Oaks Archives, Historical Resource File, Music and Musician Folder Set.

Besnier, N. 1993. "Polynesian Gender Liminality Through Time and Space." In *Third Sex, Third Gender: Beyond Sexual Dimorphism in Culture and History*, edited by G. Herdt, 285–328. New York: Zone Books.

Bird, F. 1980. "The Nature and Function of Ritual Forms: A Sociological Discussion." *Studies in Religion/Sciences Religieuses* 9 (Fall): 387–402.

Blair, Ralph. 1977. *An Evangelical Look at Homosexuality.* New York: Homosexual Community Counseling Center.

Bloch, J. 1998. "Individualism and Community in Alternative Spiritual Magic." *Journal for the Scientific Study of Religion* 37:286–302.

Boisvert, D. L. 2000. *Out on Holy Ground: Meditations on Gay Men's Spirituality.* Cleveland: Pilgrim Press.

Boswell, John. 1980. *Christianity, Social Tolerance and Homosexuality: Gay People in Western Europe from the Beginning of the Christian Era to the 14th Century.* Chicago: University of Chicago Press.

———. 1994. *Same-Sex Unions in Premodern Europe.* New York: Villard Books.

Boyer, Pascal. 2001. *Religion Explained: The Evolutionary Origins of Religious Thought.* New York: Basic Books.

Bradford, N. 1983. "Transgenderism and the Cult of Yellama: Heat, Sex and Sickness in South Indian Ritual." *Journal of Anthropological Research* 39 (3): 307–22.

Brandon, George. 1983. "The Dead Sell Memories: An Anthropological Study of Santería in New York City." Doctoral dissertation, Rutgers University, New Brunswick, NJ.

Brasher, Brenda E. 2001. *Give Me That Online Religion.* San Francisco: Jossey-Bass.

Broad, Kendal L. 2002. "Fracturing Transgender: Intersectional Constructions and Identization." In *Gendered Sexualities (Advances in Gender Research, Vol. 6)*, edited by Patricia Gagné and Richard Tewksbury, 235–66. New York: JAI Press.

Bronski, Michael. 1991. "A Dream Is a Wish Your Heart Makes: Notes on the Materialization of Sexual Fantasy." In *Leather-Folk: Radical Sex, People, Politics, and Practice*, edited by Mark Thompson, 56–64. Boston: Alyson Publications.

Brophy, Don. 2001. "The Parish of Choice." *America*, 185 (16): 12–14.

Brown, David H. 1999. "Afro-Cuban Religions and the Urban Landscape in Cuba and the United States." In *Gods of the City: Religion and the American Landscape*, edited by Robert A. Orsi, 155–230. Bloomington, IN: Indiana University Press.

Brown, Joseph Epes. 1982. *The Spiritual Legacy of the American Indian.* New York: Crossroad.

Brown, Karen McCarthy. 1991. *Mama Lola: A Vodou Priestess in Brooklyn.* Berkeley: University of California Press.

———. 2001. "Telling a Life Through Haitian Vodou: An Essay Concerning Race, Gender, Memory, and Historical Consciousness." In *Religion and Cultural Studies*, edited by Susan L. Mizruchi, 22–37. Princeton, NJ: Princeton University Press.

Browning, F. 1995. "The Way of Some Flesh." In *Wrestling with the Angel: Faith and Religion in the Lives of Gay Men*, edited by B. Bouldrey, 97–115. New York: Riverhead Books.

Burke, P. 1996. *Gender Shock: Exploding the Myths of Male and Female.* New York: Doubleday.

Butler, J. 1990. *Gender Trouble.* New York: Routledge.

Butler, Judith. 1993a. "Imitation and Gender Insubordination." In *The Lesbian and Gay Studies Reader*, edited by H. Abelove, M. Barale, and D. Halper, 307–20. New York and London: Routledge.

———. 1993b. *Bodies That Matter: On the Discursive Limits of "Sex."* New York: Routledge.

Cabezón, José I. 1993. "Homosexuality and Buddhism." In *Homosexuality and World Religions*, edited by Arlene Swidler. Valley Forge: Trinity Press International.

Cadge, Gwendolyn A. 2002. "Seeking the Heart: The First Generation Practices Theravada Buddhism in America." Dissertation, Princeton University.

Cadge, Wendy. 2002. "Vital Conflicts: The Mainline Denominations Debate Homosexuality." In *The Quiet Hand of God: Faith-Based Activism and the Public Role of Mainline Protestantism*, edited by Robert Wuthnow and John H. Evans, 265–86. Berkeley: University of California Press.

Campbell, Debra. 1990. "The Struggle To Serve: From the Lay Apostolate to the Ministry Explosion." In *Transforming Parish Ministry: The Changing Roles of Catholic Clergy, Laity, and Women Religious*, edited by Jay P. Dolan, R. Scott Appleby, Patricia Byrne, and Debra Campbell, 201–80. New York: Crossroad.

Cantú, Lionel. 2000. "Entre Hombres/Between Men: Latino Masculinities and Homosexualities." In *Gay Masculinities*, edited by Peter Nardi, 224–46. Thousand Oaks, CA: Sage Publications.

Carr, John, C.S.S.R. 1946. *To Heaven Through a Window: St. Gerard Majella*. London: Sands & Co., Ltd.

Carrier, J., and S. O. Murray. 1998. "Woman-Woman Marriage in Africa." In *Boy-Wives and Female Husbands: Studies of African Homosexualities*, edited by S. O. Murray and W. Roscoe, 255–66. New York: St. Martin's.

Carroll, Michael, P. 1989. *Catholic Cults and Devotions: A Psychological Inquiry*. Kingston, Montreal, London: McGill-Queens University Press.

———. 1992. *Madonnas That Maim: Popular Catholicism in Italy since the Fifteenth Century*. Baltimore and London: Johns Hopkins University Press.

———. 1996. *Veiled Threats: The Logic of Popular Catholicism in Italy*. Baltimore: Johns Hopkins University Press.

Casino, Joseph J. 1987. "From Sanctuary to Involvement: A History of the Catholic Parish in the Northeast." In Vol. 1, *The American Catholic Parish: A History from 1850 to the Present*, edited by Jay P. Dolan, 7–116. New York: Paulist Press.

Castoriadis, Cornelius. 1987. *The Imaginary Institution of Society*, translated by Kathleen Blamey. Oxford: Oxford University Press.

Cathedral of Hope. 2002. "Worship Services." Available at www.cathedralofhope.com/worship. Accessed 4 March.

Cevetello, Rev. Joseph F.X. 1979. *Crucified with Christ: The Life of St. Gerard Majella, The Mothers' Saint*. Privately published.

Chase, C. 1998. "Hermaphrodites with Attitude: Mapping the Emergence of Intersex Political Activism." In *The Transgender Issue [Special issue]. GLQ: A Journal of Lesbian and Gay Studies*, 4 (2): 189–211.

Churchill, Charles Wesley. 1975 [1942]. *The Italians of Newark: A Community Study.* New York: Arno Press.

Ciesluk, Joseph E. 1944. *National Parishes in the United States.* Washington, DC: Catholic University of America Press.

Clark, J. Michael, and Robert E. Goss, eds. 1996. *A Rainbow of Religious Studies.* Las Colinas: Monument Press.

Clark, Linda J. 1993. "Songs My Mother Taught Me: Hymns as Transmitters of Faith." In *Beyond Establishment,* edited by Jackson Carroll and Wade Clark Roof. Louisville, KY: Westminister John Knox Press.

Clough, P. 1994. *Feminist Thought.* Cambridge, MA: Blackwell Press.

Coleman, E., P. Colgan, and L. Gooren. 1992. "Male Cross-Gender Behavior in Myanmar (Burma): A Description of the Acault." *Archives of Sexual Behavior,* 21 (3): 313–21.

Coleman, James W. 2001. *The New Buddhism: The Western Transformation of an Ancient Tradition.* New York: Oxford University Press.

Coleman, S. S., and D. Gerald. 1995. *Homosexuality: Catholic Teaching and Pastoral Practice.* New York: Paulist Press.

Collins, Patricia Hill. 1990. *Black Feminist Thought: Knowledge, Consciousness, and the Politics of Empowerment.* Boston: Unwin Hyman.

Comstock, Gary David. 1996. *Unrepentant, Self-Affirming, Practicing: Lesbian/Bisexual/Gay People within Organized Religion.* New York: Continuum.

Comstock, Gary David, and Susan E. Henking, eds. 1997. *Que(e)rying Religion: A Critical Anthology.* New York: Continuum.

Connell, R. W. 1995. *Masculinities.* Berkeley: University of California Press.

Conner, Randy. 1993. *Blossom of Bone: Reclaiming the Connections between Homoeroticism and the Sacred.* New York: HarperCollins.

———. 2003. "Sex and Gender in African Spiritual Traditions." In *Sexuality in the World's Religions,* edited by David W. Machacek and Melissa M. Wilcox. Goleta, CA: ABC-CLIO.

Coogan, Michael D., et al., eds. 2001. *The New Oxford Annotated Bible.* 3rd ed. New York: Oxford University Press.

Corbitt, J. Nathan. 1998. *The Sound of the Harvest: Music's Mission in Church and Culture.* Grand Rapid, MI: Baker Books.

Corless, Roger. 1998a. "Coming Out in the Sangha: Queer Community in American Buddhism." In *The Faces of Buddhism in America,* edited by Charles Prebish and Kenneth Tanaka. Berkeley: University of California Press.

———. 1998b. "Grassroots Gay Buddhism: The Gay Buddhist Fellowship of San Francisco." Paper presented at the second annual New York Conference on the History and Philosophy of Religion, Hunter College.

———. 2000. "Gay Buddhist Fellowship." In *Engaged Buddhism in the West,* edited by Christopher S. Queen, 269–79. Boston: Wisdom.

Cornelius, Steven Harry. 1991. "Drumming for the Oris Has: Reconstruction of Tradition in New York City." In *Essays on Cuban Music: North American and Cuban Perspectives,* edited by Peter L. Manuel, 137–55. Lanham, MD: University Press of America.

Corsini, Raymond, J. 1999. "Postmodernism." In *The Dictionary of Psychology*, 742. Ann Arbor, MI: Taylor and Francis.

Cotton Angela. 1996. "Religion in Atlanta's Queer Community." In *Religions in Atlanta: Religious Diversity in the Centennial Olympic City*, edited by Gary Laderman, 291–310. Atlanta: Scholars Press.

Couillard, Paul. 1996. *Askance Thoughts.* [Listserv] majordomo@queernet.org, 19 December.

Cowen, Michael. 1987. "Sacramental Moments." In *Alternative Futures for Worship*. Collegeville, MN: Liturgical Press.

Crapo, Richley H. 1997a. "LDS Doctrinal Rhetoric and the Politics of Same-Sex Marriage." Invited paper presented at the annual meeting of the Society for the Scientific Study of Religion, San Diego, CA.

———. 1997b. "The LDS Church and the Politics of Same-Sex Marriage." Paper presented at the annual meeting of the Sunstone Theological Symposium, Salt Lake City, Utah.

———. 1998. "Ministering Angels and Eunuchs for Christ: Being Mormon in the Sexual Margins." Paper presented at the annual meeting of the Society for the Scientific Study of Religion, Montreal.

Cromwell, J. 1999. *Transmen and FTMs: Identities, Bodies, Genders and Sexualities.* Urbana: University of Illinois Press.

Curb, Rosemary, and Nancy Manahan, eds. 1985. *Lesbian Nuns: Breaking Silence.* Tallahassee, FL: Naiad Press.

Curran, Charles E. 1998. "Sexual Orientation and Human Rights in American Religious Discourse: A Roman Catholic Perspective." In *Sexual Orientation and Human Rights in American Religious Discourse*, edited by Saul M. Olyan and Martha C. Nussbaum, 85–100. New York: Oxford University Press.

Daly, M. 1967. *The Church and the Second Sex.* New York: Harper and Row.

———. 1978. *Gyn/Ecology: The Metaethics of Radical Feminism.* Boston: Beacon Press.

———. 1992. *OuterCourse: The Be-dazzling Voyage.* San Francisco: HarperCollins.

Dear Robert. 1991. American Tract Society. Garland, TX: 75046.

DeCaro, Frank. 1998. "Report on the White Party." *Genre Magazine.* Alan Brown quote can be found at www. geocities.com/SouthBeach/5857/white_party_3.html.

Deleuze, Gilles, and Felix Guattari, 1986. *Nomadology*, translated by B. Massumi. New York: Semiotexte.

———. 1987. *A Thousand Plateaus: Capitalism and Schizophrenia*, translated by B. Massumi. Minneapolis: University of Minnesota Press.

DeMarco, J. R. G. 2002. "The World of Gay Strippers." *The Gay & Lesbian Review Worldwide* IX (March-April): 12–14.

Denzin, Norman K. 1993. *The Alcoholic Society: Addiction and Recovery of the Self.* New Brunswick, NJ: Transaction Publishers.

Denzin, Norman K. 1987. *The Alcoholic Self.* Newbury Park, CA: Sage Publications.

Dignity/Philadelphia Information Sheet. 1987.

Dignity/USA. 1989. *Sexual Ethics: Experience, Growth, Challenge.* Dignity/USA. XXI (December): 2–16.

Dirks, Nicholas B. 1994. "Ritual and Resistance: Subversion as a Social Fact." In *Culture/Power/History*, edited by N. Dirks, G. Eley, and S. Ortner, 483–503. Princeton: Princeton University Press.

Dolan, Jay P. 1985. *The American Catholic Experience: A History from Colonial Times to the Present.* Garden City, NY: Doubleday.

Donaldson, Laura E., and Kwok Pui-Lan, eds. 2002. *Postcolonialism, Feminism & Religious Discourse.* New York: Routledge.

Douglas, M. 1973. *Natural Symbols: Explorations in Cosmology.* New York: Vintage Books.

Downing, J. 1999. "Welcome to the Ball Cinderella: Investigating Gender, Race, and Class Through a Study of the Lived Experience of Women Athletes." Doctoral dissertation, Department of Sociology, University of Missouri, Columbia, MO.

Drumm, René D. 1998. "Becoming Gay and Lesbian: Identity Development Among Seventh-day Adventist Homosexuals." Dissertation, Texas Woman's University, Denton, TX.

Duffy, Regis. 1982. *Real Presence.* San Francisco: Harper & Row.

Durkheim, E. 1954 [1915]. *The Elementary Forms of Religious Life.* Glencoe, IL: Free Press.

Eagleton, Terry. 1983. *Literary Theory: An Introduction.* Minneapolis: University of Minnesota Press.

Edion, Marvin M. 1993. "Homosexuality and Protestantism." In *Homosexuality and World Religions*, edited by Ann Swidler. Valley Forge, PA: Trinity Press International.

Edwards, Linda. 2001. *A Brief Guide to Beliefs: Ideas, Theologies, Mysteries, and Movements.* Louisville, KY: Westminster John Knox Press.

Elfstone. 1996. *An Annotated FQA.* Available online at www.eskimo.com/~davidk/Faeries/FQA.htm.

Eliade, M. 1964. *Shamanism: Archaic Techniques of Ecstasy.* New York: Bollingen.

Ellis, Larry D. 2002. "Philosophy of Ministry of Music." Available at www.worshipandchurchmusic.com/philosophymusic.html. Accessed 18 February.

Elliston, D.A. 1999. "Negotiating Transnational Sexual Economies: Female Mahu and Same-Sex Sexuality in Tahiti and Her Islands." In *Same-Sex Relations and Female Desires: Transgender Practices Across Cultures*, edited by E. Blackwood and S. E. Wieringa. New York: Columbia University Press.

Epstein, Steven. 1987. "Gay Politics, Ethnic Identity: The Limits of Social Constructionism." *Socialist Review* 93-94 (May-August): 9–54.

Eller, Cynthia. 1993. *Living in the Lap of the Goddess: The Feminist Spirituality Movement in America.* New York: Crossroad.

Exodus International. 2002a. "Policy on Homosexuality." Available online at www.exodusnorthamerica.org.

———. 2002b. "Q&A." Available online at www.exodusnorthamerica.org.

Farley, Margaret A. 1998. "Response to James Hanigan and Charles Curran." In *Sexual Orientation and Human Rights in American Religious Discourse*, edited by Saul M. Olyan and Martha C. Nussbaum, 101–9. New York: Oxford University Press.

Fausto-Sterling, A. 1993. "The Five Sexes: Why Male and Female Are Not Enough." *Sciences* 33 (2): 20–26.

Feinberg, L. 1996. *Transgender Warriors: Making History from Joan of Arc to Dennis Rodman.* Boston: Beacon Press.

Ferguson, R., and M. Gever, 1990. *Out There: Marginalization and Contemporary Cultures,* edited by T. Minh-ha and C. West. New York: New Museum of Contemporary Art.

Festinger, Leon. 1957. *A Theory of Cognitive Dissonance.* Palo Alto, CA: Stanford University Press.

Fields, Rick. 1981. *How the Swans Came to the Lake: A Narrative History of Buddhism in America.* Boston: Shambala Press.

Figueroa, Jose. 1981. "The Cultural Dynamic of Puerto Rican Spiritism: Class, Nationality, and Religion in a Brooklyn Ghetto." Dissertation, Sociology Department, City University of New York (CUNY).

Finke, Roger, and Rodney Stark. 1992. *The Churching of America, 1776–1990: Winners and Losers in Our Religious Economy.* New Brunswick, NJ: Rutgers University Press.

The First Presidency and the Council of the Twelve. 1995. *Proclamation on the Family.* Salt Lake City: The Church of Jesus Christ of Latter-day Saints.

Fish, Lydia. 1982. "Ethnicity and Catholicism." *New York Folklore* 8:83–92.

Fisher, Sethard. 1982. *From Margin to Mainstream: The Social Progress of Black Americans.* New York: Praeger.

Flores, Ysamur M. 1990. "'Fit for a Queen: Analysis of a Consecration Outfit in the Cult of Yemayá." *Folklore Forum* 23 (1–2): 47–56.

Foltz, T. 1999. "Thriving, Not Simply Surviving: Goddess Spirituality and Women's Recovery from Alcoholism." In *Daughters of the Goddess: Studies in Healing, Identity, and Empowerment,* edited by W. Griffin. Thousand Oaks, CA: AltaMira Press.

Foucault, Michel. 1990. *Use of Pleasure: The History of Sexuality, Vol. 2.* New York: Random House.

Fox, R. 1996. "Bisexuality in Perspective: A Review of Theory and Research." In *Bisexuality: The Psychology and Politics of an Invisible Minority,* edited by B. Firestein. Thousand Oaks, CA: Sage.

Freedberg, David. 1989. *The Power of Images: Studies in the History and Theory of Response.* Chicago and London: University of Chicago Press.

Friedman, Richard C., and Jennifer I. Downey. 1994. "Homosexuality." *The New England Journal of Medicine,* 6 October. 331 (14): 923–31.

Gallup, Jr., George, and Jim Castelli. 1987. *The American Catholic People: Their Beliefs, Practices, and Values.* Garden City, NY: Doubleday.

———. 1989. *The People's Religion: American Faith in the 90s.* New York: Macmillan.

Gardner, G. 1974. *Witchcraft Today.* Secaucus, NJ: Citadel Press.

Garfinkel, Harold. 1967. *Studies in Ethnomethodology.* Englewood Cliffs, NJ: Prentice-Hall.

Gecas, Victor. 1981. "Contexts of Socialization." In *Social Psychology: Sociological Perspectives,* edited by M. Rosenberg and R. H. Turner, 165–99. New York: Basic Books.

Gecas, Victor. 1982. "The Self-Concept." *Annual Review of Sociology,* edited by R. Turner and J. Short. Palo Alto, CA: Annual Reviews.

Gecas, Victor. 1986. "The Motivational Significance of Self-concept for Socialization Theory." In *Advances in Group Process 3,* edited by Edward Lawler, 131–56. Greenwich, CT: JAI Press.

Geertz, Clifford. 1968. *Islam Observed*. Chicago: University of Chicago Press.
———. 1973. *Interpretation of Cultures*. New York: Basic Books.
———. 1983. *Local Knowledge*. New York: Basic Books.
Genovesi, S.J., Vincent J. 1994. "Social Implications of Homosexuality." In *The New Dictionary of Catholic Social Thought*, edited by Judith A. Dwyer, 447–53. Collegeville, MN: Liturgical Press.
Gergen, Kenneth. 1999. *Social Theory in Context: Relational Humanism*. Taylor and Francis.
Goffman, Erving. 1956. *The Presentation of Self in Everyday Life*. New York: Doubleday.
———. 1959. *The Presentation of Self in Everyday Life*. Garden City, NY: Doubleday.
———. 1963. *Stigma: Notes on the Management of Spoiled Identity*. Englewood Cliffs, NJ: Prentice-Hall.
Golphin, Vincent F. A. 1986. "Black Catholics Angry About Closing of Parish." *National Catholic Reporter*. 9 May: 24.
Gonzalo, Almudena Hernando. 1999. "The Perception of Landscape Amongst the Q'eqchi', a Group of Slash-and-Burn Farmers in the Alta Verapaz (Guatemala)." In *The Archaeology and Anthropology of Landscape: Shaping Your Landscape*, edited by P. Ucko and R. Layton, 254–63. London: Routledge.
Gorman, E. Michael. 1980. "A New Light on Zion: A Study of Three Homosexual Religious Congregations in Urban America." Dissertation, University of Chicago.
Goss, Robert. 1993. *Jesus Acted Up: A Gay and Lesbian Manifesto*. San Francisco: HarperSan Francisco.
Goss, R. E., and M. West, eds. 2000. *Take Back the Word: A Queer Reading of the Bible*. Cleveland: Pilgrim Press.
Gramick, Jeannine, ed. 1983. *Homosexuality and the Catholic Church*. Chicago: Thomas More Press.
———. 1985. "Lesbian Nuns' Book: Ignored, Rapped, Sexploited." *National Catholic Reporter*. 6 September:14.
———. 1992. "Surfacing the Issues." In *Building Bridges: Gay & Lesbian Reality and the Catholic Church*, edited by Robert Nugent and Jeannine Gramick, 91–104. Mystic, CT: Twenty-Third Publications.
———. 1992a. "The U.S. Church and Global Significance." In *Building Bridges: Gay & Lesbian Reality and the Catholic Church*, edited by Robert Nugent and Jeannine Gramick, 157–71. Mystic, CT: Twenty-Third Publications.
———. 1992b. "Lesbian/Gay Theology and Spirituality: The New Frontier." In *Building Bridges: Gay & Lesbian Reality and the Catholic Church*, edited by Robert Nugent and Jeannine Gramick, 184–94. Mystic, CT: Twenty-Third Publications.
Gramick, Jeannine, and Pat Furey, eds. 1988. *The Vatican and Homosexuality: Reactions to the "Letter to the Bishops of the Catholic Church on the Pastoral Care of Homosexual Persons."* New York: Crossroad.
Gramick, Jeannine, and Robert Nugent, eds. 1995. *Voices of Hope: A Collection of Positive Catholic Writings on Gay and Lesbian Issues*. New York: Center for Homophobia Education.
Greeley, Andrew. 1981. "Religious Musical Chairs." In *In Gods We Trust: New Patterns of Religious Pluralism in America*, edited by T. Robbins and D. Anthony, 101–26. New Brunswick, NJ: Transaction.

Greenberg, David F. 1988. *The Construction of Homosexuality*. Chicago: University of Chicago Press.

Greil, Arthur, and David Rudy. 1984a. "Social Cocoons: Encapsulation and Identity Transformation Organizations." *Sociological Inquiry* 54:260–78.

———. 1984b. "What Have We Learned from Process Models of Conversion? An Examination of Ten Case Studies." *Sociological Focus* 17:305–23.

Grémaux, R. 1993. "Woman Becomes Man in the Balkans." In *Third Sex, Third Gender: Beyond Sexual Dimorphism in Culture and History*, edited by G. Herdt, 241–81. New York: Zone Books.

Greyling, Marc. ca. 1998. "Inventing Queer Place: Social Space and the Urban Environment as Factors in the Writing of Gay, Lesbian and Transgender Histories." BA thesis, University of Sydney. Available at www.maya.eagles.bbs.net.au/~marcq/queer-pl.html. Accessed December 2000.

Griffin, W., ed. 1999. *Daughters of the Goddess: Studies in Healing, Identity, and Empowerment*. Thousand Oaks, CA: AltaMira Press.

Grim, John A., ed. 2001. *Indigenous Traditions and Ecology: The Interbeing of Cosmology and Community*. Cambridge, MA: Harvard University Press.

Grim, John A., and Mary Evelyn Tucker, eds. 1994. *Worldviews and Ecology: Religion, Philosophy, and the Environment*. Maryknoll, NY: Orbis Books.

Guy-Sheftall, Beverly, ed. 1995. *Words of Fire: An Anthology of African-American Feminist Thought*. New York: The New Press.

Guzmán, Manuel. 1997. "'Pa' La Escuelita con Mucho Cuida'o y por la Orillita': A Journey through the Contested Terrains of the Nation and Sexual Orientation." In *Puerto Rican Jam: Rethinking Colonialism and Nationalism*, edited by Ramón Grosfonquel and Frances Negrón-Muntaner, 209–28. Minnesota: University of Minnesota Press.

Halberstam, Judith. 1998. "Transgender Butch: Butch/FTM Border Wars and the Masculine Continuum." *GLQ: A Journal of Lesbian and Gay Studies: The Transgender Issue* 4 (2): 287–310.

Haly, Richard. 2000. "Nahuas and National Culture: A Contest of Appropriations." In *Native American Spirituality: A Critical Reader*, edited by L. Irwin. Lincoln: University of Nebraska Press.

Hanigan, James P. 1998. "Sexual Orientation and Human Rights: A Roman Catholic View." In *Sexual Orientation and Human Rights in American Religious Discourse*, edited by Saul M. Olyan and Martha C. Nussbaum, 63–84. New York: Oxford University Press.

Hanson, Ellis. 1997. *Decadence and Catholicism*. Cambridge, MA, and London: Harvard University Press.

Haraldson, E., and J. M. Houtkooper. 1991. "Psychic Experiences in the Multinational Human Values Study: Who Reports Them?" *Journal of the American Society for Psychical Research* 85:145–65.

Harding, S. 1986. *The Science Question in Feminism*. Ithaca, NY: Cornell University Press.

Harper, James. "No Santería Ties Are Seen in Shootings." *St. Petersburg Times*, 2000.

Harrell, Daniel M. 1999. "Post-Contemporary Worship: What? Ambiguity and Antiquity? Candles and Icons? A Glimpse at What Might Be Next." *Leadership Journal* (Spring).

Available online at www.christianitytoday.com/le/912/912037.html. Accessed 13 March 2002.

Harris, Joseph. 1999. "The Church and Its Choices If the Priest Shortage Continues." *National Catholic Reporter*. 3 September 1999:18.

Hart, John, and Diane Richardson. 1981. *The Theory and Practice of Homosexuality*. London: Routledge and Kegan Paul.

Hartman, Keith. 1996. *Congregations in Conflict: The Battle over Homosexuality*. New Brunswick, NJ: Rutgers University Press.

Hartmann, Susan M. 1989. *From Margin to Mainstream: American Women and Politics since 1960*. New York: Temple University Press.

Harvey, John F. 1967. "Homosexuality." Vol.VII, *The New Catholic Encyclopedia*, edited by William J. McDonald, 116–19. New York: McGraw-Hill.

———. 1979. "Homosexuality." *The New Catholic Encyclopedia*, edited by Berard Marthaler, OFM, 17 (Supplement): 271–73. New York: McGraw-Hill.

———. 1987. *The Homosexual Person: New Thinking in Pastoral Care*. San Francisco: Ignatius Press.

Healey, Mark Alan. 2000. "The Sweet Matriarchy of Bahia: Ruth Landes' Ethnography of Race and Gender." *Disposition* 23 (50): 87–116.

Helminiak, Daniel A. 1996. "Catholicism, Homosexuality, and Dignity: Questions and Answers." Dignity/USA Pamphlet.

———. 1998. "Homosexuality in Catholic Teaching and Practice." *Culturefront* 7 (3): 65–68.

Herbst, Susan. 1994. *Politics at the Margin: Historical Studies of Public Expression Outside the Mainstream*. New York: Cambridge University Press.

Herdt, Gilbert H. 1994. "Introduction: Third Sexes and Third Genders." In *Third Sex, Third Gender: Beyond Sexual Dimorphism in Culture and History*, edited by G. Herdt, 21–81. New York: Zone Books.

Herman, D. 1997. *The Anti-Gay Agenda: Orthodox Vision and the Christian Right*. Chicago: University of Chicago Press.

Hernandez-Avila, Inez. 2000. "Mediations of the Spirits." In *Native American Spirituality: A Critical Reader*. edited by L. Irwin. Lincoln: University of Nebraska Press.

Heyward, Carter. 1984. *Our Passion for Justice: Images of Power, Sexuality, and Liberation*. New York: Pilgrim Press.

Hinson, Glenn. 2000. *Fire in My Bones: Transcendence and the Holy Spirit in African American Gospel*. Philadelphia: University of Pennsylvania Press.

Hocquenghem, Guy. 1983. *Homosexual Desire*. Durham: Duke University Press.

Holtz, Raymond C. 1991. *Listen to the Stories: Gay and Lesbian Catholics Talk About Their Lives and the Church*. New York: Garland Publishing.

hooks, bell. 1990. *Yearning: Race, Gender, and Cultural Politics*. Boston: Southend Press.

Hopcke, Robert H. 1991. "S/M and the Psychology of Gay Male Initiation: An Archetypal Perspective." In *Leather-Folk: Radical Sex, People, Politics, and Practice*, edited by Mark Thompson, 65–76. Boston: Alyson Publications.

Hout, Michael, and Claude S. Fisher. 2002. "Why More Americans Have No Religious Preference: Politics and Generations." *American Sociological Review* 67 (April): 165–90.

Howard, Alton H., ed. 1999. *Songs of Faith and Praise.* West Monroe, LA: Howard.

Howard, Jeannette. 1992. Roots of Lesbianism. San Diego, CA.

Humphreys, L. 1970. *Tearoom Trade: Impersonal Sex in Public Places.* Chicago: Aldine Publishing Co.

Hunt, Mary. 1991. *Fierce Tenderness: A Feminist Theology of Friendship.* New York: Crossroad.

Hunter, James Davison. 1983. *American Evangelism: Conservative Religion and the Quandary of Modernity.* New Brunswick, NJ: Rutgers University Press.

de la Huerta, Christain. *Coming Out Spiritually: The Next Step.* New York: J. P. Tarcher/Putnam.

Immerso, Michael. 1997. *Newark's Little Italy: The Vanished First Ward.* New Brunswick and Newark, NJ: Rutgers University Press and Newark Public Library.

Ingraham, C. 1994. "The Heterosexual Imaginary: Feminist Sociology and Theories of Gender." *Sociological Theory* 12:203–19.

Intellectual Reserve. 1998. *Church Handbook of Instructions.* Salt Lake City: The Church of Jesus Christ of Latter-day Saints.

Isaac, Robert. G. 1993. "Organizational Culture: Some New Perspectives." In *Handbook of Organizational Behavior*, edited by Robert T. Golembiewski, 91–110. New York: Marcel Dekker.

Iser, Wolfgang. 1993. *The Fictive and the Imaginary: Charting Literary Anthropology.* Baltimore: Johns Hopkins University Press.

Israel, G., and D. Tarver. 1997. *Transgender Care: Recommended Guidelines, Practical Information and Personal Accounts.* Philadelphia: Temple University.

Jackson, Peter A. 1998. "Male Homosexuality and Transgenderism in the Thai Buddhist Tradition." In *Queer Dharma: Voices of Gay Buddhists*, edited by Winston Leyland, 55–90. San Francisco: Gay Sunshine Press.

Jacobs, S. E., and J. Cromwell. 1992. "Visions and Revisions of Reality: Reflections on Sex, Sexuality, Gender and Gender Variance." *Journal of Homosexuality* 23 (4): 43–69.

Jacobs, Sue-Ellen, Wesley Thomas, and Sabine Lang, eds. 1997. *Native American Gender Identity, Sexuality, and Spirituality.* Chicago: University of Illinois Press.

Jagose, A. 1996. *Queer Theory: An Introduction.* New York: NYU Press.

Jocks, Christopher Rowaniente. 2000. "Spirituality for Sale: Sacred Knowledge in the Consumer Age." In *Native American Spirituality: A Critical Reader*, edited by L. Irwin. Lincoln: University of Nebraska Press.

Johnson, Benton. 1963. "On Church and Sect." *American Sociological Review* 28: 539–49.

———. 1971. "Church and Sect Revisited." *Journal for the Scientific Study of Religion* 10:124–37.

Johnson, T. 2000. *Gay Spirituality: The Role of Gay Identity in the Transformation of Human Consciousness.* Los Angeles: Alyson Books.

Jordan, Mark D. 1997. *The Invention of Sodomy in Christian Theology.* Chicago: University of Chicago Press.

———. 2000. *The Silence of Sodom: Homosexuality in Modern Catholicism.* Chicago: University of Chicago Press.

Kanter, Rosabeth. 1972. *Commitment and Community: Communes and Utopias in Sociological Perspective.* Cambridge, MA: Harvard University Press.

Kearney, Richard. 1991. *Poetics of Imagining: From Husserl to Lyotard: Problems of Modern European Thought*. London: HarperCollinsAcademic.

Kelly, A. 1981. "Inventing Witchcraft." Unpublished manuscript in the American Religion Collection, Davidson Library, University of California, Santa Barbara.

Kennedy, Morris. 2000. "Santería Faith Much-practiced in Tampa," *The Tampa Tribune*. Nation/World Section, 1 January 2000.

Kessler, Suzanne, and Wendy McKenna. 1978. "Gender Construction in Everyday Life: Transexualism." In *Gender: An Ethnomethodological Approach*. New York: John Wiley and Sons.

Kilbourne, Brock, and James Richardson. 1989. "Paradigm Conflict, Types of Conversion, and Conversion Theories." *Sociological Analysis* 50:1–21.

Klages, Mary. 2002. "Postmoderism." Available at www.colorado.edu/English/ENGL2012Klages/pomo.html. Accessed 4 March.

Klein, F. 1978. *The Bisexual Option: A Concept of One Hundred Percent Intimacy*. New York: Arbor House.

Kosmin, Barry A., and Seymour P. Lachman. 1993. *One Nation Under God: Religion in Contemporary American Society*. New York: Harmony Books.

Krondorfer, B., ed. 1996. *Men's Bodies, Men's Gods: Male Identities in a (Post-) Christian Culture*. New York: NYU Press.

Kumar, Krishan. 1991. *Utopianism*. Minneapolis: University of Minnesota Press.

Lach, A. D. 1989. *Homosexuality and Scripture*. Los Angeles: Affirmation.

Lassiter, Luke Eric. 2000. "Authoritative Texts, Collaborative Ethnography, and Native American Studies." *American Indian Quarterly* 24 (4): 601–14.

———. 2001. "From 'Reading Over the Shoulders of Natives' To 'Reading Alongside Natives,' Literally: Toward a Collaborative and Reciprocal Ethnography." *Journal of Anthropological Research* 57:137–49.

Lawless, Elaine. 1988. *Handmaidens of the Lord*. Philadelphia: University of Pennsylvania Press.

———. 1992. "'I Was Afraid Someone Like You...an Outsider...Would Misunderstand': Negotiating Interpretive Difference Between Ethnographers and Subjects." *Journal of American Folklore* 105:301–14.

———. 1993. *Holy Women, Wholly Women: Sharing Ministries Through Life Stories and Reciprocal Ethnography*. Philadelphia: University of Pennsylvania Press.

Lawson, Ronald. 1987. "Trouble in an 'Ex-gay Ministry': Quest Learning Center/Homosexuals Anonymous." Paper read at the meeting of the American Sociological Association, August, Chicago.

———. 1992. "The Caring Church?: The Seventh-day Adventist Church and its Homosexual Members." Paper read at the meeting of The Andrews Society for Religious Studies, November, San Francisco.

LDS Social Services. 1995. *Understanding and Helping Those Who Have Homosexual Problems: Suggestions for Ecclesiastical Leaders*. The Church of Jesus Christ of Latter-day Saints.

Leap, William L., ed. 1999. *Public Sex/Gay Space*. New York: Columbia University Press.

Lewin, Ellen, and William L. Leap, eds. 1996. *Out in the Field: Reflections of Lesbian and Gay Anthropologists*. Urbana and Chicago: University of Illinois Press.

Lewin, Ellen, ed. 1996. *Inventing Lesbian Cultures in America*. Boston: Beacon Press.

Lewis, L. M. 1971. *Ecstatic Religion: An Anthropological Study of Spirit Possession.* Harmondsworth, England: Penguin Books.

Leyland, Winston, ed. 1998. *Queer Dharma: Voices of Gay Buddhists.* San Francisco: Gay Sunshine Press.

Lincoln, C. Eric, and Lawrence H. Mamiya. 1990. *The Black Church in African American Experience.* Durham and London: Duke University Press.

Living Waters MCC. 2000. "New Hymnals." *Spirit of Living Waters,* December. Available at home.talkcity.com/SpiritSt/dcbell7/newsletterdec2000.html. Accessed 13 March.

Loftand, John. 1969. *Deviance and Identity.* Englewood Cliffs, NJ: Prentice-Hall.

Loftus, Jeni. 2001. "America's Liberalization in Attitudes Toward Homosexuality, 1973 to 1998." *American Sociological Review* 66 (October): 762–82.

Long, Ronald E. 1997. "The Sacrality of Male Beauty and Homosex: A Neglected Factor in the Understanding of Contemporary Gay Reality." In *Que(e)rying Religion: A Critical Anthology,* edited by Gary David Comstock and Susan E. Henking, 266–81. New York: Continuum.

———. 2001. "Becoming the Men We're Ceasing to Be: A Gay Agenda for Aging in a Youth Culture." *Theology & Sexuality* 15 (September): 94–113.

Long, Theodore, and Jeffery Hadden. 1983. "Religious Conversion and the Concept of Socialization: Integrating the Brainwashing and Drift Models." *Journal for the Scientific Study of Religion* 22:1–14.

The Los Angeles Times. 1988. "Detroit Prelate Backs Plan to Close 43 Churches." 15 October.

Love in Action. 2001. www.loveinaction.org.

Lozada, Angel. 1998. *La Patografía.* Colección: Autores Latinoamericanos. Mexico, D.F.: Editorial Planeta Mexicana.

Lukenbill, W. Bernard. 1998. "Observations on the Corporate Culture of a Gay and Lesbian Congregation." *Journal for the Scientific Study of Religion* 37:440–52.

Lybeck, Eric Scott. 1995. "The Social Expression of Religiousness: The Case of the Metropolitan Community Church." MA thesis, Arizona State University.

Machalek, R., and D. A. Snow. 1985. "Neglected Issues in the Study of Conversion." In *Scientific Research and New Religions: Divergent Perspectives,* edited by B. Kilbourne, 123–29. San Francisco: American Association for the Advancement of Science.

MacKendrick, K. (1999). *Counterpleasures.* New York: State University of New York Press.

Mains, Geoff. 1984. *Urban Aboriginals: A Celebration of Leathersexuality.* San Francisco: Gay Sunshine Press.

———. 1987. "Urban Aboriginals and the Celebration of Leather Magic." In *Gay Spirit: Myth and Meaning,* edited by Mark Thompson, 99–117. New York: St. Martin's Press.

Malcolm, Teresa. 1988. "Parish Closings Predicted." *National Catholic Reporter.* 3 April: 7.

Malinowski, Bronislaw. 1984. *Magic, Science and Religion and Other Essays.* Westport, CT: Greenwood Press.

Marion, Mark. 1998. "Grief and the Path to Awakening: Appreciating What a Gay Sangha Offers." In *Queer Dharma: Voices of Gay Buddhists,* edited by Winston Leyland, 163–70. San Francisco: Gay Sunshine Press.

Martin, David. 1962. "The Denomination," *British Journal of Sociology* 13:1–14.

Martin, Emily. 1994. *Flexible Bodies: The Role of Immunity in American Culture—From the Days of Polio to the Age of AIDS.* Boston: Beacon Press.

Martin, Kenneth. 2002. Lecture on gender within a biblical context,

Martos, Joseph. 1966. *Doors to the Sacred.* Garden City, NY: Image.

Massa, Mark, A. 1999. *Catholics and American Culture: Fulton Sheen, Dorothy Day, and the Notre Dame Football Team.* New York: Crossroad.

McBrien, Richard P. 1995. *The HarperCollins Encyclopedia of Catholicism.* San Francisco: HarperSan Francisco.

McCord, William. 1989. *Voyages to Utopia: From Monastery to Commune: The Search for the Perfect Society in Modern Times.* New York: W. W. Norton and Company.

McDannell, Colleen. 1995. *Material Christianity: Religion and Popular Culture in America.* New Haven and London: Yale University Press.

McGreevy, John T. 1996. *Parish Boundaries: The Catholic Encounter with Race in the Twentieth-Century Urban North.* Chicago: University of Chicago Press.

McGuire, Brian Patrick. 1994a. *Brother and Love: Aelred of Rievaulx.* New York: Crossroad.

———. 1994b. "Sexual Awareness and Identity in Aelred of Rievaulx (1110–67)." *American Benedictine Review* 45 (2): 184–226.

McIntosh, Mary. 1968. "The Homosexual Role," *Social Problems* 16 (Fall): 182–92.

McNeill, John J. 1976. *The Church and the Homosexual.* 4th rev. ed. Kansas City: Sheed Andrews and McMeel; [1993] Boston: Beacon Press.

———. 1988. *Taking a Chance On God: Liberating Theology for Gays, Lesbians, and Their Lovers, Families, and Friends.* Boston: Beacon Press.

———. 1995. *Freedom, Glorious Freedom: The Spiritual Journey to the Fullness of Life for Gays, Lesbians, and Everybody Else.* Boston: Beacon Press.

———. 1998. *Both Feet Firmly Planted in Midair: My Spiritual Journey.* Louisville, KY: Westminster John Knox.

Mead, George Herbert. 1934. *Mind, Self, and Society.* Chicago: University of Chicago Press.

Metropolitan Community Church of Austin. 1976. *Church Bulletin,* 1 February, 18 July. MCCA at Freedom Oaks Archives, Historical Resources File, "Newsletters and Bulletins" File Set.

———. 1978. *Newsletter* (March). MCCA at Freedom Oaks Archives, Historical Resource File, "Newsletters and Bulletins" Folder Set.

———. 1982. "Revelation Singers." MCCA at Freedom Oaks Archives, Historical Resource File, "Music and Musicians" Folder Set.

Metropolitan Community Church of Baltimore. 2002. "MCC Baltimore History." Available at www.mccbaltimore.org/history.html. Accessed 13 March.

Mickells, Rev. Anthony Bernard. 1950. *The Constitutive Elements of Parishes.* Washington DC: Catholic University of America Press.

Mills, C. Wright. 1940. "Situated Actions and Vocabularies of Motives." *American Sociological Review* 5:905–29.

Mizruchi, Suzan L., ed. 2001. *Religion and Cultural Studies.* Princeton, NJ: Princeton University Press.

Mohr, Richard D. 1992. *Gay Ideas: Outing and Other Controversies.* Boston: Beacon Press.

Mol, H. 1976. *Identity and the Sacred: A Sketch for a New Social-Scientific Theory of Religion.* Agincourt, Ontario: Book Society of Canada.

Moon, Dawne. 2001. "The Limits of Christian Love: Homosexuality and the Politics of Church." Dissertation, Department of Sociology, University of Chicago.

Moon, Tom. 1998. "My First Year in Buddhist Practice (September 1995-September 1996)." In *Queer Dharma: Voices of Gay Buddhists,* edited by Winston Leyland, 184–94. San Francisco: Gay Sunshine Press.

Moore, Stephen. 1996. *God's Gym.* New York: Routledge.

Moreno Vega, Marta. 2000. *The Altar of My Soul: The Living Traditions of Santería.* New York: Ballantine Books.

Morreale, Don, ed. 1998. *The Complete Guide to Buddhist America.* Boston: Shambhala Press.

Morris, Charles R. 1997. *American Catholic: The Saints and Sinners Who Built America's Most Powerful Church.* New York: Times Books.

Murray, Stephen O., and Will Roscoe. 1998. *Boy-wives and Female Husbands: Studies in African Homosexualities.* New York: St. Martin's Press.

Myers, Bryant L. 1996. *The New Context of World Mission.* Manrovia, CA: Mission Advanced Research and Communication Center: 8–9.

Namaste, Ki. 1996. "Tragic Misreadings: Queer Theory's Erasure of Transgender Subjectivity." In *Queer Studies: A Lesbian, Gay, Bisexual, and Transgender Anthology,* edited by Brett Beemyn and Mickey Eliason, 183–203. New York: New York University Press.

Namaste, Viviane K. 2000. *Invisible Lives: The Erasure of Transsexual and Transgendered People.* Chicago: University of Chicago Press.

Nanda, Serena. 1986. "The Hijras of India: Cultural and Individual Dimensions of an Institutionalized Third Gender Role." *Journal of Homosexuality* 11:35–54.

———. 1993. "Hijras: An Alternative Sex and Gender Role in India." In *Third Sex, Third Gender: Beyond Sexual Dimorphism in Culture and History,* edited by G. Herdt. New York: Zone Books.

———. 1999. *Neither Man nor Woman: The Hijras of India.* 2nd ed. Belmont, CA: Wadsworth Publishing Company.

Nardi, Peter M. 1981. "Children of Alcholics: A Role-theoritcal Perspective." *Journal of Social Psychology.* 115 (2): 237–46.

National Catholic Reporter. 1998. "Talk of More Church Closings Provokes Ire in Philadelphia." 3 July: 2.

Naughton, Jim. 1996. *Catholics in Crisis: The Rift Between American Catholics and Their Church.* New York: Penguin Books.

Neitz, M. J. 1987. *Charisma and Community.* New Brunswick, NJ: Transaction Press.

———. 1990. "In Goddess We Trust." In *In Gods We Trust,* edited by T. Robbins and D. Anthony, 354–72. New Brunswick, NJ: Transaction Press.

———. 1994. "Quasi Religions and Cultural Movements: Contemporary Witchcraft as a Churchless Religion." In Vol. 4 *Religion and the Social Order,* edited by A. Greil and T. Robbins, 127–49. Greenwich, CT: JAI Press.

Nugent, Robert, ed. 1983. *A Challenge to Love: Gay and Lesbian Catholics in the Church.* New York: Crossroad.

———. 1992. "Seminary and Religious Candidates." In Robert Nugent and Jeannine Gramick. *Building Bridges: Gay & Lesbian Reality and the Catholic Church*, 105–120. Mystic, CT: Twenty-Third Publications.

———. 1992a. "U.S. Bishops and Current Thinking." In Robert Nugent and Jeannine Gramick. *Building Bridges: Gay & Lesbian Reality and the Catholic Church*, 137–45. Mystic, CT: Twenty-Third Publications.

———. 1992b. "Theological Contributions of the U.S. Church." In Robert Nugent and Jeannine Gramick. *Building Bridges: Gay & Lesbian Reality and the Catholic Church*, 146–56. Mystic, CT: Twenty-Third Publications.

Nugent, Robert, and Jeannine Gramick, eds. 1982. *A Time to Speak: A Collection of Contemporary Statements from U.S. Catholic Sources on Homosexuality, Gay Ministry and Social Justice*. Mt. Rainier, MD: New Ways Ministry.

———. 1992. *Building Bridges: Gay and Lesbian Reality and the Catholic Church*. Mystic, CT: Twenty-Third Publications.

Núñez, Luis Manuel. 1992. *Santería: A Practical Guide to Afro-Caribbean Magic*. Woodstock, CN: Spring Publications, Inc.

Oaks, Dallin H. 1995. "Same-Gender Attraction." *Ensign* (October): 6–14.

Obeyesekere, Gananath. 1990. *The Work of Culture: Symbolic Transformation in Psychoanalysis and Anthropology*. Chicago and London: University of Chicago Press.

Oboler, R. 1980. "Is the Female Husband a Man? Woman/Woman Marriage among the Nandi of Kenya." *Ethnology* 19 (1): 69–88.

O'Brien, D. 1977. "Female Husbands in Southern Bantu Societies." In *Sexual Stratification: A Cross-cultural View*, edited by A. Schlegel, 109–26. New York: Columbia University Press.

Olson, Mark. 1984. "Where to Turn: A Guide for Gay and Lesbian Christians." *The Other Side* 151 (April): 16–31.

Omi, Michael, and Howard Winant. 1986. *Racial Formation in the United States: From the 1960s to the 1980s*. New York: Routledge.

Orsi, Robert, A. 1985. *The Madonna of 115th Street, Faith and Community in Italian Harlem, 1880–1950*. New Haven and London: Yale University Press.

———, ed. 1999. *Gods of the City*. Bloomington, IN: Indiana University Press.

Ortner, Sherry B. 1994. "Theory in Anthropology Since the Sixties." In *Culture/Power/History*, edited by N. Dirks, G. Eley, and S. Ortner, 372–411. Princeton, NJ: Princeton University Press.

Padgett, Douglas. 2000. "Americans Need Something to Sit On or Zen Meditation Materials and Buddhist Diversity in North America." *Journal of Global Buddhism* 1:61–81.

Palmer, J. 1979. "A Community Mail Survey of Psychic Experiences." *Journal of the American Society for Psychical Research* 73:221–51.

Pattison, E. Mansell, and Myrna Pattison. 1980. "Ex-gays: Religiously Mediated Changed in Homosexuals." *The American Journal of Psychiatry* 137:1553–1562.

Peddicord, Richard O.P. 1996. *Gay and Lesbian Rights. A Question: Sexual Ethics or Social Justice?* Kansas City: Sheed & Ward.

Perry, Rev. Troy D. 1972. *The Lord Is My Shepherd and He Knows I'm Gay*. Los Angeles: Nash.

———. "A Meditation on Religion and Leatherspace." In *Leather Folk: Radical Sex, People, Politics, and Practice*, edited by Mark Thompson, 247–51. Boston: Alyson Publications.

Perry, Rev. Troy, with Thomas L. P. Swicegood. 1990. *Don't Be Afraid Anymore: The Story of Reverend Troy Perry and the Metropolitan Community Churches*. New York: St. Martin's Press.

Peshkin, Alan. 1986. *God's Choice: The Social World of a Fundamentalist Christian School*. Chicago: University of Chicago Press.

Phillips, Ann McNeill. 2002. "In Him Alone I Found Mercy." Love in Action website, www.loveinaction.org/Annphillipstest.html.

Phillips, R. D. 1993. "Prophets and Preference: Constructing and Maintaining a Homosexual Identity in the Mormon Church." Master's thesis, Utah State University, Logan, UT.

Piedmont, O. 1996. "The Veils of Arjuna: Androgyny in Gay Spirituality East and West." Doctoral dissertation, Department of East-West Psychology, California Institute of Integral Studies, San Francisco.

Ponticelli, Christy M. 1996. "The Spiritual Warfare of Exodus: A Postpositivist Research Adventure." *Qualitative Inquiry* 2 (2): 198–219.

———. "Crafting Stories of Sexual Identity Reconstruction." *Social Psychology Quarterly* 62 (2): 157–72.

Popenoe, Cris, and Oliver. 1984. *Seeds of Tomorrow: New Age Communities That Work*. San Francisco: Harper & Row, Publishers.

Prebish, Charles. 1999. *Luminous Passage: The Practice and Study of Buddhism in America*. Berkeley: University of California Press.

Prell, Riv-Ellen. 1989. *Prayer and Community: The Havurah in American Judaism*. Detroit: Wayne State University Press.

Priest of the Same Congregation. 1893. *Blessed Gerard Majella, Lay-Brother of The Congregation of the Most Holy Redeemer, A Sketch of His Life and the Many Wonderful Favors Obtained Through His Intercession*. Translated from the Italian. New York and Cincinnati: Fr. Pustet & Co.

Primiano, Leonard Norman. 1993. "'I Would Rather Be Fixated on the Lord': Women's Religion, Men's Power, and the 'Dignity' Problem." *New York Folklore* 19 (1–2): 89–99.

———. 1993a. "Intrinsically Catholic: Vernacular Religion and Philadelphia's" *Dignity*. Doctoral dissertation, Departments of Folklore and Folklife and Religious Studies, University of Pennsylvania, Philadelphia, PA.

———. 1993b. "'I Would Rather Be Fixated on the Lord': Women's Religion, Men's Power, and the 'Dignity' Problem." *New York Folklore* 19 (1–2): 89–103.

———. 1995. "Vernacular Religion and the Search for Method in Religious Folklife." *Western Folklore* 54: 37–56.

———. 1999. "Post-Modern Sites of Catholic Sacred Materiality." In *Perspectives on American Religion and Culture*, edited by Peter W. Williams, 187–202. Malden, MA: Basil Blackwell.

———. 2001. "What Is Vernacular Catholicism? The 'Dignity' Example." *Acta Ethnographica Hungarica* 46 (1–2): 51–58.

Prus, Robert. 1984. "Religious Recruitment and the Management of Dissonance: A Sociological Perspective." *Sociological Inquiry* 46:127–34.

Rambuss, R. 1998. *Closet Devotions.* Durham: Duke University Press.

Redington, Robin. 2000. "Voice, Representation, and Dialogue: The Poetics of Native American Spiritual Traditions." In *Native American Spirituality: A Critical Reader,* edited by L. Irwin. Lincoln: University of Nebraska Press.

Revised New English Bible. 1989. Oxford: Oxford University Press; New York: Cambridge University Press.

Reynolds, E. 1994. "Post Modernism and Gay/Queer Identities." In *Gay Perspectives II: More Essays in Australian Gay Culture,* edited by R. Aldrich, 245–74. Sydney: Australian Centre for Gay and Lesbian Research.

Rich, A. 1980. "Compulsory Heterosexuality and Lesbian Existence." *Signs* 5:631–60.

Richardson, Diane. 1984. "The Dilemma of Essentiality in Homosexual Theory." *Journal of Homosexuality* 9:77–90.

Richardson, James, Mary White Stewart, and Robert Simmonds. 1981. "Conversion to Fundamentalism." In *In Gods We Trust: New Patterns of Religious Pluralism in America,* edited by T. Robbins and D. Anthony, 127–39. New Brunswick, NJ: Transaction.

Ricoeur, Paul. 1986. *Lectures on Ideology and Utopia.* New York: Columbia University Press.

Risen, James. 1988. "Day Bittersweet for Detroit's Aging Parishes." *The Los Angeles Times.* 25 December.

Roberts, Rosemarie A. 1999. "Metal, Fire, Stone and Water: Sustaining Community Through Difference and Conflict—The Orisha Community in New York City." Master's thesis, Psychology Program, Graduate School and University Center, City University of New York.

Roche, Pat, ed. 1995. *Dignity/USA 25: A Chronology, 1969–1994.* Washington, DC: Dignity/USA.

Rodriguez, Clara E. 2000. *Changing Race: Latinos, the Census, and the History of Ethnicity in the United States.* New York: New York University Press.

Roe, David, and Jerry Taki. 1999. "Living with Stones: People and the Landscape in Erromango, Vanuatu." In *The Archaeology and Anthropology of Landscape: Shaping Your Landscape,* edited by P. Ucko and R. Layton, 411–22. London: Routledge.

Roen, Katrina. 2002. "'Either/Or' and 'Both/Neither': Discursive Tensions in Transgender Politics." *Signs: Journal of Women in Society* 27 (2): 501–22.

Rofes, Eric E. 1991. "Snapshots of Desire: Surviving as a Queer among Queers." In *Leather-Folk: Radical Sex, People, Politics, and Practice,* edited by Mark Thompson, 179–84. Boston: Alyson Publications.

———. 1998. *Dry Bones Breath.* New York: Harrington. 1998.

Roof, Wade Clark, and William McKinney. 1987. *American Mainline Religion: Its Changing Shape and Future.* New Brunswick, NJ: Rutgers University Press.

———. 1993. *A Generation of Seekers: The Spiritual Journeys of the Baby Boom Generation.* San Francisco: HarperSanFrancisco.

Roscoe, Will. ed. 1988. *Living the Spirit: A Gay American Indian Anthology.* New York: St. Martin's Press.

———. 1991. *The Zuni Man-Woman.* Albuquerque, NM: University of New Mexico Press.

———. 1993. "How to Become a Berdache: Toward a Unified Analysis of Gender Diversity." In *Third Sex, Third Gender: Beyond Sexual Dimorphism in Culture and History*, edited by G. Herdt. New York: Zone Books.

———. 1995. *Queer Spirits: A Gay Men's Myth Book*. Boston: Beacon Press.

———. 1998. *Changing Ones: Third and Fourth Genders in Native North America*. New York: St. Martin's Press.

Rosenberg, Larry, with David Guy. 1999. *Breath by Breath: the Liberating Practice of Insight Meditation*. Boston: Shambala.

Roszak, Theodore. 1969. *The Making of a Counter Culture: Reflections on the Technocratic Society and Its Youthful Opposition*. Garden City, NY: Doubleday.

Rubin, Gayle S. 1993. "Thinking Sex: Notes for a Radical Theory of Politics of Sexuality." In *The Lesbian and Gay Studies Reader*, edited by H. Abelove, M. Barale, and D. Halperin, 3–44. New York: Routledge.

Rubin, Henry S. 1996. "Transformations: Emerging Female to Male Transsexual Identities." Dissertation, Sociology Department, Brandies University, Waltham, MA.

Rudy, Kathy. 1996 "Where Two or More Are Gathered: Using Gay Communities as a Model for Christian Sexual Ethic." *Theology and Sexuality* 4:81–99.

Russell, Kenneth, C. 1982. "Aelred, The Gay Abbot of Rievaulx." *Studia Mystica* 5 (4): 51–64.

Russell, Stephen T., and Kara Joyner. 2001. "Adolescent Sexual Orientation and Suicide Risk: Evidence from a National Study." *The American Journal of Public Health*. August. 91 (8): 1276.

Rust, P. 1995. *Bisexuality and the Challenge to Lesbian Politics: Sex, Loyalty, and Revolution*. New York: NYU Press.

Saghir, Marcel, and Eli Robins. 1973. *Male and Female Homosexuality: A Comprehensive Investigation*. Baltimore: Williams and Wilkins.

Saint-Omer, C.S.S.R., Rev. Edward. 1907. *The Wonder-Worker of Our Days: Life, Virtues, and Miracles of St. Gerard Majella*. Boston: Mission Church Press.

Santino, Jack. 1982. "Catholic Folklore and Folk Catholicism." *New York Folklore* 8:93–106.

Savastano, Peter. 2002. "Will the Real St. Gerard Please Stand Up?: An Ethnographic Study of Symbolic Polysemy, Devotional Practices, Material Culture, Marginality and Difference in the Cult of St. Gerard Maiella." Ph.D. dissertation, Drew University, Madison, NJ.

Scanzoni, Letha, and Virginia Mollenkott. 1978. *Is the Homosexual My Neighbor?: Another Christian View*. San Francisco: Harper & Row.

Schaller, L. E. 1984. *Looking in the Mirror: Self-Appraisal in the Local Church*. Nashville: Abingdon Press.

Schneider, David. 1993. *Street Zen: The Life and Work of Issan Dorsey*. Boston: Shambhala.

Scott, Marvin, and Stanford Lyman. 1968. "Accounts." *American Sociological Review* 33:46–62.

Seager, Richard H. 1999. *Buddhism in America*. New York: Columbia University Press.

Secter, Bob. 1990. "Chicago Archdiocese to Shut 31 Parishes, Many Schools in Sweeping Cost-Cutting." *The Los Angeles Times*. 22 January.

Sedgwick, Eve Kosofsky. 1990. *Epistemology of the Closet.* Berkeley: University of California Press.

———. 1993. "Epistemology of the Closet." In *The Lesbian and Gay Studies Reader,* edited by H. Abelove, M. Barale, and D. Halperin, 45–61. New York: Routledge.

Seidman, S., ed. 1996. *Queer Theory/Sociology.* Cambridge, MA: Blackwell Publishers.

Sell, Ingrid. 2001. "Not Man, Not Woman: Psychospiritual Characteristics of a Western Third Gender." *Journal of Transpersonal Psychology,* 33 (1): 16–36.

Sheba. 1974. *The Grimoire of Lady Sheba.* Minneapolis: Llewellyn Publications.

Shils, Edward. 1975. *Center and Periphery: Essays on Macrosociology.* Chicago: University of Chicago Press.

Shokeid, Moshe. 1995. *A Gay Synagogue in New York.* New York: Columbia University Press.

Signorile, Michelangelo. 1997. *Life Outside.* San Francisco: Harper.

Sinfield, Alan. 1998. *Gay and After.* London and New York: Serpent's Tail.

Smid, John J. 1992. *Overcoming Homosexuality.* San Diego, CA.

———. 2002. Available at loveinaction.org/Resources.

Smith, Clare. 1999. "Ancestors, Place, and People: Social Landscapes in Aboriginal Australia." In *The Archaeology and Anthropology of Landscape: Shaping Your Landscape,* edited by P. Ucko and R. Layton, 189–205. London: Routledge.

Smith, D. 1987. *The Everyday World as Problematic.* Boston: Northeastern University Press.

Smith, Herbert F., and Joseph A. Dilenno. 1979. *Sexual Inversion: The Questions with Catholic Answers.* Boston: St. Paul Editions.

Smith, Richard L. 1994. *AIDS, Gays, and the American Catholic Church.* Cleveland: Pilgrim Press.

Snow, David, and Cynthia Phillips. 1980. "The Lofland-Stark Conversion Model: A Critical Reassessment." *Social Problems* 27:430–47.

Solitano, Nora. 1994. "The Alternative Mainstream: Gay Catholics Practicing the Faith." *The Critic: A Journal of American Catholic Culture* 49 (2): 2–12.

Spann, Edward K. 1989. *Brotherly Tomorrows: Movements for a Cooperative Society in America 1820–1920.* New York: Columbia University Press.

Spickard, James V., J. Shawn Landres, and Meredith B. McGuire, eds. 2002. *Personal Knowledge and Beyond: Reshaping the Ethnography of Religion.* New York: NYU Press.

Spivak, Gayatri Chakravorty. 1988. *In Other Worlds: Essays in Cultural Politics.* New York: Routledge.

———. 1999. *A Critique of Postcolonial Reason: Toward a History of the Vanishing Present.* Cambridge, MA: Harvard University Press.

St. John, Debra Dee. 2001. 'Unexpected Participants in Democracy': Refuge, Community, and Activism in a Congregation of the Metropolitan Community Church." Dissertation, University of Oklahoma.

Staples, Clifford, and Armand Mauss. 1987. "Conversion or Commitment? A Reassessment of the Snow and Machalek Approach to the Study of Conversion." *Journal for the Scientific Study of Religion* 26:133–47.

Starhawk. 1989. *The Spiral Dance: A Rebirth of the Ancient Religion of the Great Goddess*, 10th ed. San Francisco: Harper and Row.

Stark, Rodney. 1985. *Sociology*. Belmont, CA: Wadsworth.

Stark, Rodney, and W. S. Bainbridge. 1979. "Of Churches, Sects, and Cults." *Journal for the Scientific Study of Religion* 18:117–131.

———. 1985. *The Future of Religion: Secularization, Revival, and Cult Formation*. Berkeley: University of California Press.

Stoltz, Eric. 1998. "Notes from a Community—Catholic and Gay." *America*. 178 (10): 10–13.

Stone, Jeff. 1998. "The Truth Shall Make You Free: Dignity and the Gay Catholic Movement." *Culturefront* 7 (Fall): 69–72.

Stone, K., ed. 2001. *Queer Commentary and the Hebrew Bible*. Cleveland: Pilgrim Press.

Straus, Roger. 1976. "Changing Oneself: Seekers and the Creative Transformation of Life Experience." In *Doing Social Life*, edited by John Lolland, 252–73. New York: Wiley.

Sullivan, Andrew. 1996. *Virtually Normal: An Argument about Homosexuality*. New York: Vintage.

Sullivan, Patricia Ann, and Lynn H. Turner, eds. 1996. *From the Margins to the Center: Contemporary Women and Political Communication*. Westport, CT: Praeger.

Sunshine Cathedral. 2002. "When We Worship at the Sunshine Cathedral." Available at www.sunshinecathedral.org/extra/extra_index.html. Accessed 5 March.

Swan, James A. 1990. *Sacred Places: How the Living Earth Seeks Our Friendship*. Santa Fe, NM: Bear Publishing.

Swatos, William H., Jr. 1981. "Church-Sect and Cult." *Sociological Analysis* 42:17–26.

Sweasey, Peter. 1997. *From Queer to Eternity: Spirituality in the Lives of Lesbian, Gay, and Bisexual People.* London and Washington, DC: Cassell.

———. 1998. "Denomination." In *Encyclopedia of Religion and Society*, edited by William H. Swatos, Jr. Walnut Creek, CA: AltaMira Press.

Swidler, Alrene, ed. 1993. *Homosexuality and World Religions.* Valley Forge, PA: Trinity Press International.

Tafoya, T. 1992. "Native Gay and Lesbian Issues: The Two-spirited." In *Positively Gay*, edited by B. Berzon, 253–59. Berkeley: Celestial Arts.

Takagi, K. 1996. "Maiden Voyage: Excursion into Sexuality and Identity Politics in Asian America." In *Queer Theory/Sociology*, edited by S. Seidman, 243–58. Cambridge, MA: Blackwell Publishers.

Tannoia [Tannoja], Antonio Maria. 1849. "The Life of Brother Gerard Majella." In *The Lives of the Companions of St. Alphonso Liguori*, edited by Tannoia [Tannoja], et al. The Modern Saint Series. London: Richardson & Son.

Task Force on Gay/Lesbian Issues, San Francisco. 1986. *Homosexuality and Social Justice*. San Francisco: The Consultation on Homosexuality, Social Justice, and Roman Catholic Theology.

Thomas, L. E., and P. E. Cooper. 1980. "Incidence and Psychological Correlates of Intense Spiritual Experiences." *Journal of Transpersonal Psychology*, 12:75–85.

Thompson, Mark. 1997. *Gay Body: A Journey through Shadow to Self*. New York: St. Martin's Press.

———, ed. 1987. *Gay Spirit: Myth and Meaning*. New York: St. Martin's Press.

———. 1987. "This Gay Tribe: A Brief History of Faeries." In *Gay Spirit: Myth and Meaning*, edited by M. Thompson, 260–78. New York: St. Martin's Press.

Thumma, Scott. 1987. "Straightening Identities: Evangelical Approaches to Homosexuality." Master's thesis. Emory University, Atlanta, GA.

———. 1991. "Negotiating a Religious Identity: The Case of the Gay Evangelical." *Sociological Analysis* 52 (Winter 4): 333–47.

———. 1994. "Negotiating a Religious Identity: The Case of the Gay Evangelical." In *Symbolic Interaction: An Introduction to Social Psychology*, edited by Herman and Reynolds, 224–38. Bayside, NY: General Hall.

Timmons, Stuart. 1990. *The Trouble with Harry Hay: Founder of the Modern Gay Movement*. Boston: Alyson Publications.

Torfing, Jacob. 1999. *New Theories Discourse: Laclau, Mauffe and Zizek*. Oxford: Blackwell.

———. 2002. "Introduction to Discourse Theory: Meaning and Politics." Available online at www.essex.ac.uk/methods/courses2002/2Q.htm. Accessed 13 March.

Travisano, Richard. 1970. "Alternation and Conversion as Qualitatively Different Transformations." In *Social Psychology Through Symbolic Interaction*, edited by G. P. Stone and H. A. Faberman, 594–606. Waltham, MA: Ginn-Blaiedell.

Trinh, T. 1989. *Woman, Native, Other: Writing Postcoloniality and Feminism*. Bloomington: Indiana University Press.

Troiden, Richard. 1984. "Self, Self-concept, Identity, and Homosexual Identity: Constructs in Need of Definition and Differentiation." *Journal of Homosexuality* 10:97–107.

Turner, Victor. 1969. *The Ritual Process: Structure and Anti-structure*. Ithaca, NY: Cornell University Press.

Twiss, Susan B. 1998. "Introduction to Roman Catholic Perspectives on Sexual Orientation, Human Rights, and Public Policy." In *Sexual Orientation and Human Rights in American Religious Discourse*, edited by Saul M. Olyan and Martha C. Nussbaum, 57–62. New York: Oxford University Press.

Udis-Kessler, Amanda. 2002. "Lines in the Sand: The Struggle Over Lesbian/Gay/Bisexual/Transgender Inclusion in the United Methodist Church." Dissertation, Department of Sociology, Boston College.

Universal Fellowship of Metropolitan Community Churches. n.d. "Statement of Faith." Available online at www.ufmcc.com/state.htm. Accessed 14 March 2002.

———. 1981. "[Statement:] Inclusive Language." Available online at www.ualberta.ca/~cbidwell/UFMCC/uf-inclu.htm. Accessed 13 March 2002.

Valentine, David. 2000. "'I Know What I am:' The Category 'Transgender' in the Construction of U.S. American Conceptions of Gender and Sexuality." Dissertation, Anthropology Department, New York University.

Vance, Jr., James E. 1990. "Democratic Utopia and the American Landscape." In *The Making of the American Landscape*, edited by M. Conzen, 204–20. London: HarperCollinsAcademic.

Varacalli, Joseph A., Salvatore Primeggia, Salvatore J. LaGumina, and Donald, J. D'Elia, eds. 1999. *The Saints in the Lives of Italian-Americans: An Interdisciplinary Investigation*. Stony Brook, NY: Forum Italicum, Inc.

Vidal-Ortiz, Salvador. 2002. "Queering Sexuality and Doing Gender: Transgender Men's Identification with Gender and Sexuality." In *Gendered Sexualities*. Vol. 6, *Advances in Gender Research*, edited by Patricia Gagné and Richard Tewksbury, 181–233. New York: JAI Press.

Wagner, Glenn, James Serafini, Judith Rabkin, Robert Remien, and Janet Williams. 1994. "Integration of One's Religion and Homosexuality: A Weapon Against Internalized Homophobia?" *Journal of Homosexuality* 26 (4): 91–110.

Walker, B. 1983. *Encyclopedia of Women's Myths and Secrets*. New York: Harper.

Warner, M., ed. 1993. *Fear of a Queer Planet: Queer Politics and Social Theory*. Minneapolis: University of Minnesota Press.

Warner, Michael. 1997. "Tongues Untied: Memoirs of a Pentecostal Boyhood." In *Que(e)rying Religion: A Critical Anthology*, edited by Gary David Comstock and Susan E. Henking, 223–31. New York: Continuum.

Warner, R. Stephen. 1995. "The Metropolitan Community Churches and the Gay Agenda: The Power of Pentecostalism and Essentialism." In *Religion and the Social Order: Sex, Lies, and Sanctity: Religion and Deviance in Contemporary North America*, edited by D. G. Bromley, M. J. Neitz, and M. S. Goldman, 81–108. Greenwich, CT: JAI Press.

Warner, Stephen. 1994. "The Place of the Congregation in the Contemporary American Religious Configuration." In *American Congregations: New Perspectives in the Study of Congregations*, edited by J. P. Wind & J.W. Lewis. Chicago: University of Chicago Press.

The Washington Post. 1987. "Landmark Catholic Churches Closing: Changing Populations, Economics Hurting Chicago Archdiocese." 27 December.

Webster's Tenth Collegiate Dictionary. 1999. Springfield, MA.: Merriam-Webster.

Weeks, Jeffrey. 1995. *Invented Moralities: Sexual Values in an Age of Uncertainty*. New York: Columbia University Press.

———. 1998. *Sexuality and Its Discontents: Meanings, Myths, and Modern Sexualities*. London: Routledge and Kegan Paul.

Weinberg, Martin, and Colin Williams. 1974. *Male Homosexuals: Their Problems and Adaptations*. New York: Oxford University Press.

West, C., and D. H. Zimmerman. 1987. "Doing Gender." *Gender & Society* 1(2): 125–51.

Weston, Kath. 1991. *Families We Choose: Lesbians, Gays, Kinship*. New York: Columbia University Press.

———. 1996. *Render Me, Gender Me: Lesbians Talk Sex, Class, Color, Nation, Studmuffins . . .* New York: Columbia University Press.

White, Mel. 1995. *Stranger at the Gate: To Be Gay and Christian in America*. New York: Plume.

Whites, L. 1995. *The Civil War as a Crisis in Gender*. Athens: University of Georgia Press.

Wilcox, Melissa M. 2000. "Two Roads Converged: Religion and Identity among Lesbian, Gay, Bisexual, and Transgender Christians." Ph.D. dissertation, Department of Religious Studies, University of California, Santa Barbara, CA.

———. 2003. *Coming Out in Christianity: Religion, Identity, and Community*. Bloomington: Indiana University Press.

Wilkes, Paul. 2001. *Excellent Catholic Parishes: The Guide to Best Places and Practices*. Mahwah, NJ: Paulist Press.

Williams, Melvin D. 1974. *Community in a Black Pentecostal Church: An Anthropological Study.* Pittsburgh: University of Pittsburgh Press.

Williams, Walter. 1986. *The Spirit and the Flesh: Sexual Diversity in American Indian Culture.* Boston: Beacon Press.

Williams, W. 1992. *The Spirit and the Flesh: Sexual Diversity in American Indian Culture,* reissue ed. Boston: Beacon Press.

Wilson, A. 1996. "How We Find Ourselves: Identity Development and Two-spirit People," *Harvard Educational Review.* 66 (2):3–17.

Wilson, Bryan. 1959. "An Analysis of Sect Development." *American Sociological Review* 24:3–15.

Wilson, Nancy. 1995. *Our Tribe: Queer Folks, God, Jesus, and the Bible.* San Francisco: HarperSanFrancisco.

Wilson-Dickson, Andrew. 1992. *Story of Christian Music: From Gregorian Chant to Black Gospel: An Authoritarian Illustrated Guide to All the Major Traditions of Music for Worship.* Oxford: Lion Publishing.

Wilson, John F. 2003. *Religion and the American Nation: Historiography and History.* Athens, GA: Unversity of Georgia Press.

Wolf, Margery. 1992. *A Thrice Told Tale: Feminism, Postmodernism, and Ethnographic Responsibility.* Stanford, CA: Stanford University Press.

Wolkomor, Michelle. 2001. "Emotion Work, Commitment, and the Authentification of the Self." *Journal of Contemporary Ethnography* 30:3, 305–34.

Wood, James R. 2000. *Where the Spirit Leads: The Evolving Views of United Methodists on Homosexuality.* Nashville: Abington Press.

Wood, James, and Jon Bloch. 1995. "The Role of Church Assemblies: The Case of the United Methodist General Conference's Debate on Homosexuality." *Sociology of Religion* 56 (2): 121–36.

Worthen, Anita. 1992. *Conquering Impure Thoughts.* San Diego, CA.

Wuthnow, Robert, and John E. Evans. 2002. *The Quiet Hand of God: Faith Based Activism and the Public Role of Mainline Protestantism.* Berkeley: University of California Press.

Xavier, Emanuel. 1999. *Christ-Like.* New York: Painted Leaf Press.

Yang, Alan. 1997. "Trends: Attitudes Toward Homosexuality." *Public Opinion Quarterly* 61 (3): 477–507.

Yoder, Don. 1990. "Toward a Definition of Folk Religion." In *Discovering American Folklife: Studies in Ethnic, Religious, and Regional Culture,* edited by Don Yoder, 271–81. Ann Arbor, MI: UMI Research Press. Previously published in *Western Folklore* 33 (1): 1–15.

Young, A. 2000. *Women Who Become Men: Albanian Sworn Virgins.* New York: Berg.

Young, K. 1989. "The Imperishable Virginity of Maria Goretti." *Gender and Society* 3:474–82.

Young, Iris Marion. 1990. *Justice and the Politics of Difference.* Princeton, NJ: Princeton University Press.

Zanotti, Barbara, ed. 1986. *A Faith of One's Own: Explorations by Catholic Lesbians.* Trumansburg, NY: The Crossing Press.

Zuern, John. 2003. CriticaLink website definition, maven.english.hawaii.edu/criticalink/spivak/terms/subaltern.html. Accessed November.

Zwilling, Leonard. 1985. "Homosexuality as Seen in Indian Buddhist Texts." In *Buddhism, Sexuality, and Gender*, edited by José Ignacio Cabezón, 203–14. New York: State University of New York Press.

Index

About the Authors

Edward R. Gray is visiting assistant professor of religion at Emory University and the executive director of YouthPride, a community-based youth service and advocacy organization in Atlanta. His teaching interests extend to religion, media, and U.S. religious history. He is working on a monograph on religion and disaster.

Scott Thumma is professor of sociology of religion and of web and distance education at Hartford Institute for Religion Research, Hartford Seminary. His research interests include the study of mega-churches, Evangelicalism, religion on the Internet, and homosexuality within conservative Protestantism. He is the author of several articles and chapters including "Goliaths in the Midst" in *Lutherans Today*, and "Methods for Congregational Study" in *Studying Congregations*, and he is the webmaster and administrator for numerous websites and web-based resources.

William McKinney, president and professor of American Religion at Pacific School of Religion (PSR), is a teacher, administrator, writer, and consultant whose work focuses on helping faith communities play an active role in public life. McKinney's research interests include religious leadership, congregational studies, the future of historic old-line churches, and emerging faith communities. He is coauthor of several books including *American Mainline Religion: Its Changing Shape and Future* (Rutgers, 1987), *Handbook for Congregational Studies* (Abingdon, 1986), and *Varieties of Religious Presence* (Pilgrim, 1985). *The Responsibility People* (Eerdmans, 1994) focuses on Protestant leaders in the postwar period. His coedited volume, *Studying Congregations*, was published by Abingdon Press in 1998.

Mary Ann Tolbert is the George H. Atkinson Professor of Biblical Studies at Pacific School of Religion (PSR) in Berkeley, California. Since the fall of 2000, she is also the executive director of PSR's Center for Lesbian and Gay Studies in Religion and Ministry. Her first book was published under the title *Perspectives on the Parables* (Fortress, 1979). Professor Tolbert has published many articles on feminism and the Bible and was editor of *Semeia 28*, "The Bible and Feminist Hermeneutics." Her writings on the gospel of Mark, including *Sowing the Gospel: Mark's World in Literary-Historical Perspective* (Fortress, 1989), have established her as an expert on the literary, rhetorical, and historical dimensions of the gospel of Mark. The author of numerous articles and book chapters, she is currently teaching and writing on the pressing issues of lesbian and gay liberation and of queer theory and the Bible.

Wendy Cadge received her PhD in sociology from Princeton University. She is currently assistant professor of sociology at Bowdoin College. In addition to research about religion and homosexuality, she conducts research about religious pluralism in America. Her first book, *Heartwood: Theravada Buddhism in America*, will be published by the University of Chicago Press.

Mary Jo Neitz was born and raised in Montana. She received her BA degree from New College in Sarasota, Florida, and an MA and PhD from the University of Chicago. She is interested in gender and sexualities, qualitative methods, and feminist theories. Her research takes American religions as sites for studying cultural change, and she has studied Pentecostal Catholics, contemporary witches, and Missouri rural churches. She teaches sociology and women studies at the University of Missouri in Columbia.

Moshe Shokeid, professor of anthropology at Tel Aviv University, was born in Israel. He studied sociology for his BA and MA in Jerusalem (Hebrew University) and gained a PhD in anthropology from Manchester University, England. Among his publications are *The Dual Heritage: Immigrants from the Atlas Mountains in an Israeli Village* (Manchester University Press, 1971; Transaction, 1985); *Children of Circumstances: Israeli Emigrants in New York* (Cornell University Press, 1988); *A Gay Synagogue in New York* (Columbia University Press, 1995; University of Pennsylvania Press, 2002).

Thomas V. Peterson, professor of religious studies at Alfred University, specializes in ritual studies, American religion, and religion and art. He is author of *Ham and Japheth: The Mythic World of Whites in the Antebellum South* (Scarecrow Press, 1977) and *Linked Arms: A Rural County Resists Nuclear Waste* (SUNY Press, 2002). He was chair of the AAR Teaching and Learning Committee and member of the AAR Board of Directors (1997–2002).

Donald L. Boisvert is a lecturer in the department of religion at Concordia University in Montreal and also involved with its sexuality studies program. He is the author of *Out on Holy Ground: Meditations on Gay Men's Spirituality* (Pilgrim, 2000), and currently serves as co-chair of the Gay Men's Issues in Religion Group of the American Academy of Religion.

W. Bernard (Bill) Lukenbill is a professor in the School of Information at the University of Texas at Austin. He has lectured and published widely in several areas of information organization and use, including youth literature, popular culture, gay and lesbian studies, and HIV-AIDS information delivery within library environments.

Melissa M. Wilcox is the Visiting Johnston Professor of Religion at Whitman College. Author of *Coming Out in Christianity: Religion, Identity, and Community* and coeditor of *Sexuality and the World's Religions*, she has also written articles on various aspects of LGBT religiosity and on religious responses to violence.

Paul Gorrell is doctoral candidate in social ethics at Drew University, writing his dissertation on the concept of erotic conversion. A former Roman Catholic priest, Paul now works as an executive in a human resource consulting company that specializes in talent management.

Salvador Vidal-Ortiz is a PhD candidate in the sociology program at the Graduate Center of the City University of New York. He received a bachelor's degree from the University of Puerto Rico, Río Piedras, and a master's degree from California State University, Humboldt. His areas of research interest are queer theory, the sociology of sexuality, gender, "race," ethnicity, and the sociology and anthropology of religion. Salvador is a 2003–2004 Social Science Research Council–Sexuality Research Fellow, working on his dissertation on Santería's reception and resistance to the participation of lesbian-, gay-, bisexual-, and transgender-identified practitioners, as well as gender and sexuality constructs within the religion.

Peter Savastano earned his PhD in religion and society from Drew University in Madison, New Jersey. His scholarly interests include peoples' devotional practices within the Roman Catholic, Anglo-Catholic, and Eastern Orthodox traditions and people who hold multiple religious allegiances. His scholarship engages the intersection of religion with sexuality, gender, race, and ethnicity.

René Drumm is an associate professor of social work and coordinates the Advanced Interpersonal Practice track of the Master of Social Work program at

Andrews University. Dr. Drumm holds a master's degree in social work from Michigan State University and a PhD in sociology and family studies from Texas Women's University. Dr. Drumm's practice and research interests include mental health and family issues, feminist perspectives, substance abuse, and sexual orientation.

Aryana Freya Bates studies and teaches ethics and anthropology of religion and women's studies. She is especially interested in elements of identity and the ways in which people negotiate their context. She tries not to take any situation so seriously as to preclude its inherent humor.

Richley H. Crapo is a professor of anthropology at Utah State University. His areas of specialization are the anthropology of gender, the anthropology of religion, and psychological anthropology.

Leonard Norman Primiano is associate professor of religious studies at Cabrini College, Radnor, Pennsylvania. His book length study of Dignity/Philadelphia is forthcoming as is his documentary film on Father Divine's Peace Mission Movement. He was a consultant on folk and popular religion for the touring exhibition "Angels from the Vatican: The Invisible Made Visible."

Ingrid Sell, PhD, is a psychotherapist currently working with a rural population in a community mental health center in Vermont. Her prior clinical experience includes hospice care and working with LGBT clients. She teaches in the global division of the Institute of Transpersonal Psychology in Palo Alto, California. Her doctoral dissertation, from which this article is derived, received the Sidney Jourard Award of Division 32 of the American Psychological Association. She shares her life on twenty peaceful acres with her spouse Sharon, who was the chief inspiration for this work.

Christy M. Ponticelli is an associate professor of sociology at the University of South Florida where she also teaches in the Honors College and the College of Medicine. She is currently engaged in field research at the College of Medicine, hoping to assess the possibility that medical education may contribute to the health disparities experienced by lesbians. If warranted, she hopes to contribute to changes in medical education that could lessen these disparities. She lives in Tampa with her partner of twenty years and their family of two dogs and three cats.